Contents

Contents

THIRD EDITION

WRITING
MATTERS

A **Handbook** for Writing and Research

Rebecca Moore Howard

Syracuse University

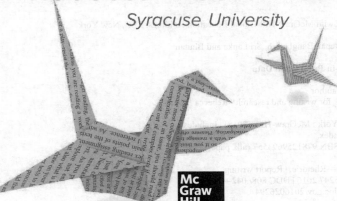

Mc
Graw
Hill
Education

McGraw Hill Education (India) Private Limited
CHENNAI

McGraw Hill Education Offices

Chennai New York St Louis San Francisco Auckland Bogotá Caracas
Kuala Lumpur Lisbon London Madrid Mexico City Milan Montreal
San Juan Santiago Singapore Sydney Tokyo Toronto

McGraw Hill Education (India) Private Limited

McGraw Hill Education (India) Edition 2018

RXAQCRQELDRRD

Reprinted in India by arrangement with McGraw-Hill Global Education Holdings, LLC, New York

Sales territories: India, Pakistan, Nepal, Bangladesh, Sri Lanka and Bhutan

Library of Congress Cataloging-in-Publication Data

Names: Howard, Rebecca Moore, author.
Title: Writing matters : a handbook for writing and research / Rebecca Moore
     Howard.
Description: Third Edition. | New York : McGraw-Hill, [2018] | Includes
     bibliographical references and index.
Identifiers: LCCN 2016026294 | ISBN 9781259693557 (alk. paper) | ISBN
     1259693554 (alk. paper)
Subjects: LCSH: English language—Rhetoric. | Report writing.
Classification: LCC PE1408 .H685247 2016 | DDC 808/.042—dc23
LC record available at https://lccn.loc.gov/2016026294

ISBN-13: 978-93-5316-214-6
ISBN-10: 93-5316-214-9

01 02 03 04 05 MAG 22 21 20 19 18

Published by McGraw Hill Education (India) Private Limited
444/1, Sri Ekambara Naicker Industrial Estate, Alapakkam, Porur, Chennai 600 116, Tamil Nadu, India
Printed and bound in India at Magic International Private Limited, Greater Noida 201 306

Visit us at: www.mheducation.co.in; Phone (Toll free in India): **1800 103 5875**
Write to us at: info.india@mheducation.com

CIN: U22200TN1970PTC111531

Writing Matters is dedicated
to the memory of my sister, Sandy

Dear Colleagues:

Thank you for taking the time to consider *Writing Matters*! I started this project as a way of giving back to the composition community and helping students with their development as writers. Working on this handbook has also been a source of my own development: My life and teaching have been immeasurably enriched by the students and instructors I have met during my travels to discuss *Writing Matters* and my responsibilities-focused approach to writing.

The third edition of *Writing Matters* includes more than a dozen new student papers on current topics. Found in the text or in Connect Composition, these provide a rich resource for instructors who want students to analyze and understand how writers build an effective, fulfilling text. This edition also includes a heightened attention to types of argument, especially explorative (Rogerian) argument, and it offers fresh attention to questions of audience accessibility, so that students can craft and present projects for a diversely abled audience. Instructors will also find updated guidance on MLA-style citations, reflecting the streamlined approach described in the eighth edition of the *MLA Handbook*.

Rebecca Moore Howard is Professor of Writing and Rhetoric at Syracuse University. Her recent work on the Citation Project is part of a collaborative endeavor to study how students really use resources.

While developing all the editions of *Writing Matters*, I have also been working on the Citation Project, a study of the researched writing that 174 students (from 16 colleges and universities nationwide) produced in their composition classes. Some of the results of that research are available on the Citation Project website: citationproject.net. There you will see a variety of evidence that students may not be reading their sources carefully and completely and that their research projects suffer accordingly. Drawing on the findings of the Citation Project, *Writing Matters* includes an array of materials that help students think dialogically as they work from sources. These include best practices in concrete techniques, such as marking where the source material ends and the student writer's own voice begins. These materials provide coaching to guide students as they fulfill their **writer's responsibilities to other writers, to their readers, to their topics,** and most especially, **to themselves.**

The result is a teaching and learning framework that unites research, rhetoric, documentation, grammar, and style into a cohesive whole, helping students to find consistency in rules that might otherwise confound them. Students experience responsible writing not only by citing the work of other writers accurately but also by treating those writers' ideas fairly. They practice responsible writing by providing reliable information about a topic at a depth that does the topic justice. Most importantly, they embrace responsible writing by taking their writing seriously and approaching writing assignments as opportunities to learn about new topics and to expand their scope as writers.

Students are more likely to write well when they think of themselves as writers rather than as error-makers. By explaining rules in the context of responsibility, I address composition students respectfully as mature and capable fellow participants in the research and writing process.

Sincerely,

Rebecca Moore Howard

Make It Your Own! McGraw Hill Education **connect**

Change the Conversation about Writing . . .

Writing Matters offers instructors and students an accessible four-part framework that focuses the rules and conventions of writing through a lens of responsibility, ultimately empowering students to own their ideas and to view their writing as consequential.

Writing Matters helps students see the conventions of writing as a network of **responsibilities . . .**

to other writers by treating information fairly and accurately, and crafting writing that is fresh and original

to the audience by writing clearly, and providing readers with the information and interpretation they need to make sense of a topic

to the topic by exploring an issue thoroughly and creatively, assessing sources carefully, and providing reliable information at a depth that does the topic justice

to themselves by taking writing seriously, and approaching the process as an opportunity to learn about a topic and to expand research and writing skills

Writing
Responsibly | Establishing Yourself as a Responsible Writer

As a writer, you can establish your ethos not only by offering your credentials, but also by providing readers with sound and sufficient evidence drawn from recognized authorities on the topic, thereby demonstrating your grasp of the material. By adopting a reasonable tone and treating alternative views fairly, you demonstrate that you are a sensible person. By editing your prose carefully, you establish your respect for your readers.

to SELF

© *Photodisc/Getty Images RF*

Revision Highlights of the Third Edition

Writing Matters includes hundreds of new or revised examples showing college students how good writing can serve as their greatest asset. Exploring the features of both professional and student models, *Rebecca Moore Howard's unique framework of responsibilities—how writers' choices best serve their audience, the topic, other writers, and themselves—will lead to a lifetime of powerful, targeted, and elegant communication:* as a college student, as a citizen, and as a professional.

Sample student projects. Five student projects are new to this edition, and a number of papers were heavily revised. Topics include "Alternative Energy," a research report whose first and final drafts are found in Chapter 3 ("Organizing and Drafting Your Project") and Chapter 6 ("Revising, Editing, Proofreading, and Formatting"); a *Chicago*-style research paper, "Foot Binding in China," in Chapter 20 ("Documenting Sources: *Chicago* Style"); a critical analysis of a long-lost Shelley poem, in Chapter 22 ("Writing in Literature and the Other Humanities"); and "Ride the Wave," a business news article on marketing outdoor adventure to women, which appears in Chapter 25 ("Professional and Civic Writing").

Professional models. A diverse selection of professional writings appear throughout the third edition, including a speech by then president-elect John F. Kennedy (Chapter 4: "Crafting and Connecting Paragraphs"), an opinion piece from an academic journal (Chapter 7: "Thinking and Reading Critically"); and a newspaper's review of a Chekhov play (in Chapter 25: "Writing in Literature and the Other Humanities").

Coverage of current databases and technology. Academic databases and their functionality and scope change over time. The third edition explores best practices for using the Internet and technology responsibly to enhance communication.

Current MLA citations. All in-text citations, bibliography notes, and Works Cited pages were revised to reflect the rules of the Eighth edition of the *MLA Handbook*, the Modern Language Association's 2016 update on citation formats.

ADA guidance. Additional suggestions on document design and presentation strategies were added to Part Three, *Media Matters,* to aid students with visual and listening challenges.

Student project library. More than a dozen new student projects were added to Connect Composition's library of readings. Topics include research pieces on the stigma of depression, the popular media's depictions of dwarfism, and social media's effects on family communication; an appraisal on food culture in the US; an essay on the debate over paying college athletes; and two literary analyses, on Chaucer's *Canterbury Tales* and Woolf's *Mrs. Dalloway*.

Writing Responsibly citation tutorials. Five mini-lessons, at the end of Chapter 17 ("Citing Expertly"), model best practices when working with Sources: "Explaining Your Choice of Sources"; "Understanding and Representing the Entire Source"; "Choosing and Unpacking Complex Sources"; "Blending Voices in Your Text"; and "Acknowledging Indirect Sources."

Special Features of *Writing Matters*

Writing Responsibly tutorials. Five 2-page tutorials in Chapter 17 ("Citing Expertly") draw from Rebecca Moore Howard's published Citation Project, a research study which used empirical methods to explore the top challenges experienced by composition students when they work with sources. These five tutorials offer best practices for researched composing, and include practical insights, relatable "before and after" examples, and a targeted self-assessment checklist.

Writing **Responsibly**

Understanding and Representing the Entire Source

Make It Your Own! For a research project to be worthwhile, it should represent the overall arguments of its sources—more than just a few sentences—so that readers can understand what the sources were saying and how they fit together.

Each time you write from sources, push yourself to work with them in more substantial ways. Take the time to read each source—the entire source—carefully. Next, **summarize** it, as a way of processing the information: Restate, concisely and in fresh language, the main claims (and the most important supporting evidence) of an entire source. Then when you draft your research project, blend in summaries of your important sources, so that your readers understand how they, too, contribute to your discussion.

You can also draw from sources by quoting or paraphrasing brief passages. But if you simply paste a quotation into your draft, how much do you or your audience actually understand the source or even the passage you are quoting? **Paraphrasing** is a better alternative, because it pushes you to think about the passage: to know the material well enough to restate it in your own words. Changing just a few words in the passage, however, is not paraphrasing; it is **patchwriting**: a mixture of your words and the source's. This is an error interpreted by many readers as plagiarism.

Because quoting and patchwriting do not require much comprehension and are easy to do, inexperienced college writers rely on them too heavily. Frequently, too, the quotations come from the first few pages of the source—which some students feel is all they have to read. Researchers with the Citation Project found that the majority of college writers' citations came from the first two pages of the source (see chart) and felt the quality of these projects suffered. That is because, in most sources, the first few pages discuss only general findings, while the insightful, detailed examples and evidence that are important to a good analysis or argument are deeper in the text.

When a writer provides only isolated quotations from sources ("dropped quotations"), the result may be uninformative, like this passage from a project about social media and individual identity:

Page Cited
DATA FROM **The Citation Project**

Percent of citations (n = 1,911)

Page of source cited	
Pages 5 or higher	18
Pages 3-4	13
Page 2	23
Page 1	47

Researchers found that although most college writers quote from the first pages of a source, the best research projects drew from the entire source.

First draft

Student's voice — People value their personal lives and try to separate their private and public selves. Many are aware of being different people in the workplace, in school, on a date. All this may be changing, though. "The fact that the Internet never seems to forget is threatening, at an almost existential level, our ability to control our identities; to preserve the option of reinventing ourselves and starting anew; to overcome our checkered pasts" (Rosen). — Quotation / Parenthetical citation

viii

1. EXPLAINING YOUR CHOICE OF SOURCES
2. UNDERSTANDING AND REPRESENTING THE ENTIRE SOURCE
3. CHOOSING AND UNPACKING COMPLEX SOURCES
4. BLENDING VOICES IN YOUR TEXT
5. ACKNOWLEDGING INDIRECT SOURCES

The example presented across these two pages, "Understanding and Representing the Entire Source," encourages students to avoid pasting an isolated "killer quote" from the first couple of pages of the source, and to instead read through their sources in order to incorporate their insights purposefully and responsibly.

Notice how, in this draft, readers are given no information about the source; they are presented only with one sentence from it. This causes the reader to wonder: Does the writer understand the source, or has she simply found a "killer quote" that supports her argument? Because the writer provides only the isolated quotation, it is not even clear what her purpose is in including it.

Now consider how this passage is transformed by adding a summary and contextualized quotations:

Revised draft

> People value their personal lives, and many deliberately work to keep their private and public selves separate. Many of us are aware, too, of being different people in the workplace, in school, on the athletic field, on a date. Some value these differences, happy to switch from dedicated intellectual in the classroom to enthusiastic player on the soccer field. 〈Student's voice〉
>
> All this may be changing, though. 〈Signal phrase providing information about the author〉 Writing in *The New York Times*, journalist Jeffrey Rosen points out that we may no longer be in control of the multiple identities that were previously taken for granted. In our online lives, what we post on Facebook and Twitter can easily merge with what we post on a school blog, in our comments on a news story, or in our pictures on Flickr. Rosen explains that even in untagged pictures, our faces can be identified through facial-recognition technology. 〈Summary of the source / Summary of the parts of the source relevant to the student's argument〉 He also describes the privacy-protecting laws that are in development and the companies that offer services to clean up our online reputations. 〈Student's voice〉 Most central to my research, though, is his explanation for this claim: "The fact that the Internet never seems to forget is threatening, at an almost existential level, our ability to control our identities; to preserve the option of reinventing ourselves and starting anew; to overcome our checkered pasts." 〈Quotation (no page reference because source is unpaginated)〉

Source: Rosen, Jeffrey. "The Web Means the End of Forgetting." *The New York Times*, 21 July 2010, www.nytimes.com/2010/07/25/magazine/25privacy-t2.html?pagewanted=all&_r=0.

The writer has shown responsibility to her source, her topic, and her audience. Because she has taken the time to read and understand the source, she is able to summarize it to show what its main claims are. Her audience now knows how the quotation was used in the source and how it supports her argument. With this brief summary, the writer has also explained her ideas clearly and established a "conversation" between herself, her source, and her audience—that is, rather than just "using" sources, she is thinking about them, interacting with them, and giving her audience enough information that they can do the same.

Assessment

Review and revise your work with each source. Have you done the following?

☐ Read, understand, and accurately represent the whole source. Did you look for the details deeper in the source?

☐ Summarize the main ideas of the source. Did you put the source's ideas in your own words, fairly and accurately? ▶ *Paraphrasing*, 253–57

☐ Incorporate your summary into your source analysis. Did you use the best examples and evidence?

☐ Locate the most relevant passages. Did you cite from *throughout* the source?
  ▶ *Critical reading*, 111–35

Focused exercises. More than 170 exercises help students explore the most important chapter concepts. Exercises gauge individual students' grasp of key skills, and group projects promote teamwork, peer-to-peer feedback, and collaboration.

➡ **EXERCISE 12.1** Writing with your audience in mind

For each of the assignments listed below, determine whether the purpose is informative, persuasive, or inquiry-based. Then choose one assignment and write a paragraph about how you would approach it if you were writing for an academic audience, for the readers of your college newspaper, and for a website appealing to readers already interested in the topic.

1. Analyze the effect that monitoring Internet searches at the library would have on patrons.
2. Argue for or against the monitoring of Internet searches at libraries.
3. Evaluate the treatment options for gambling addictions—which option seems most effective, and why?
4. Describe the symptoms of a gambling addiction.
5. Explain how genetic engineering is currently used to diagnose and control disease in humans.

Make It **Your Own**

From a source for a research project (or from another college-level text), choose three sentences you consider important. Then paraphrase them following the guidelines in *section 15d*. Attach a copy of the source to your paraphrase.

Work **Together**

In groups of two or three, compare the original source with the paraphrases that each group member wrote for the Make It Your Own exercise above. Did group members paraphrase accurately? Did they avoid patchwriting? Discuss any sentences that may lean too heavily on the language or sentence structure of the original source. What might the writer do to avoid patchwriting? If the paraphrase avoids patchwriting, identify the paraphrasing strategies each writer used.

Writing Responsibly guidance. Suggestions throughout the text frame writing skills in terms of a writer's responsibilities—to their audience, topic, other writers, and themselves. Contextualized best practices encourage the writer-as-citizen. In this tip from Chapter 14 ("Evaluating Information"), students are encouraged to see how keeping an open mind helps prevent bias, resulting in a stronger argument.

Writing Responsibly · Keeping an Open, Inquiring Mind

Read sources with an open mind, use reliable sources, avoid exaggerated claims and logical fallacies, and criticize unreasonable or poorly supported conclusions but not the people who hold them. As a researcher, you have a responsibility to avoid bias. Consider all sides of an argument, especially those that challenge the positions you hold. Use difficult sources, too: Do not reject a source because it is written for a more expert audience than you. Find the time to study it carefully and gain at least a provisional understanding of it.

to TOPIC

Quick Reference toolboxes. Major concepts are summarized to focus students on the important skills, strategies, and issues to keep in mind when writing. In this reference box from Chapter 14 ("Evaluating Information"), the characteristics of a source are listed, to help students assess the quality and reliability of the texts they discover during the research process.

Quick Reference · Judging Reliability

Scholarly work. Was the source published in a scholarly journal or book, or in a popular magazine, newspaper, or book?

Expertise. Is the author an authority on the subject?

Objectivity. Do tone, logic, quality of the evidence, and coverage of the opposition suggest that the source is unbiased?

Scope. Does the author attempt to test his or her own assumptions and explore alternatives?

Citations. Does the text cite sources, and is it cited in other texts?

Scrutiny. Was the text subjected to scrutiny by someone else before you saw it? For example, was it selected by the library, reviewed by another scholar, or fact-checked for accuracy?

Presentation. Is the text clearly written, well organized, and carefully edited and proofread?

Domain. Does the main portion of the URL end in .edu or .org, suggesting a noncommercial purpose, or does it end with .com, suggesting a commercial purpose?

Site sponsor or host. Is the site's host identified? Does the host promote a viewpoint or position that might bias the content?

Self-Assessment checklists. Helpful checklists guide students to review their work at every step of the writing process, from drafting to revising to proofreading a piece before publication. In Chapter 17 ("Citing Expertly"), this checklist reminds students to emphasize their own insights when working with sources, and to provide contextual information that shows why a source is authoritative.

Self Assessment

As you revise projects that use sources, review your draft, revising as necessary, to be sure you:

- ☐ Cite your sources. Did you name any from which you are paraphrasing, summarizing, or quoting?
- ☐ Use signal verbs. Did you convey the attitude of your source?
- ☐ Use signal phrases and parenthetical references. Did you show where each source use begins and ends, even when it is unpaginated?
- ☐ Emphasize your own insights. Did you comment on or analyze the source, rather than just repeat it?
- ☐ Provide relevant contextual information. Did you identify the type of source, its date of publication, and its publisher?
- ☐ Reveal your reasoning. Did you explain why you chose and trusted your sources?

EFL tips. Targeted advice on grammar, usage, and culture provide additional support for students for whom English is a foreign language. This EFL tip in Chapter 37 ("Using Verbs") reminds students that, in English, modals do not have an impact on tense or number.

Modal Verbs English modal verbs have a range of meanings and unusual grammatical characteristics that you may find challenging. For example, they do not change form to indicate number or tense:

- ▶ In a close election, one or two votes ~~cans~~ *can* make a difference.

Tech tips. While today's students are tech savvy, *Writing Matters* draws their attention to potential complications that may occur when using even the most familiar technology. Chapter 37 ("Using Verbs") includes a warning that grammar checkers are not foolproof, explaining why proofreading is an important step in the writing process.

Tech — Grammar Checkers and Verb Problems

Grammar checkers in word processing programs will spot some errors that involve irregular or missing verbs, verb endings, and the subjunctive mood, but they will miss other errors and may suggest incorrect solutions. You must look for verb errors yourself and carefully evaluate any suggestions from a grammar checker.

Annotated student and professional models. More than one dozen student projects and professional articles—including literary analyses, reviews, press releases, outlines, and cover letters—are explored in detail, with callouts identifying the unique features of each and analyses of the components of compelling writing. Annotations in the student project in Chapter 22 ("Writing in Literature and the Other Humanities"), for example, call attention to the important elements of a literary analysis, such as the thesis statement, citations, and supporting evidence in a student project on Zora Neale Hurston's *Their Eyes Were Watching God*.

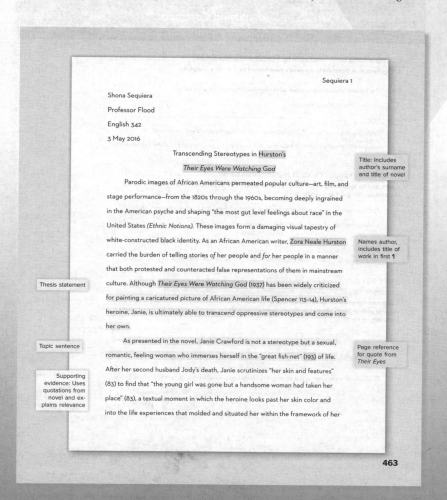

Sequiera 1

Shona Sequiera

Professor Flood

English 342

3 May 2016

Transcending Stereotypes in Hurston's

Their Eyes Were Watching God

> Title: Includes author's surname and title of novel

Parodic images of African Americans permeated popular culture—art, film, and stage performance—from the 1820s through the 1960s, becoming deeply ingrained in the American psyche and shaping "the most gut level feelings about race" in the United States (*Ethnic Notions*). These images form a damaging visual tapestry of white-constructed black identity. As an African American writer, Zora Neale Hurston carried the burden of telling stories of her people and for her people in a manner that both protested and counteracted false representations of them in mainstream culture. Although *Their Eyes Were Watching God* (1937) has been widely criticized for painting a caricatured picture of African American life (Spencer 113–14), Hurston's heroine, Janie, is ultimately able to transcend oppressive stereotypes and come into her own.

> Names author, includes title of work in first ¶

> Thesis statement

As presented in the novel, Janie Crawford is not a stereotype but a sexual, romantic, feeling woman who immerses herself in the "great fish-net" (193) of life. After her second husband Jody's death, Janie scrutinizes "her skin and features" (83) to find that "the young girl was gone but a handsome woman had taken her place" (83), a textual moment in which the heroine looks past her skin color and into the life experiences that molded and situated her within the framework of her

> Topic sentence

> Supporting evidence: Uses quotations from novel and explains relevance

> Page reference for quote from *Their Eyes*

Grammar tutorial. Part Eight, *Grammar Matters*, begins with a six-page reference section that explores common grammar challenges such as subject-verb agreement, comma splices, and shifting tenses. On the page below, two sentence fragments and four agreement conflicts are modeled, each with edits showing how to correct the problem. Cross-references point students to the chapters that discuss the concept.

Grammar Matters | Identifying Common
Sentence Problems

Recognizing and Correcting Fragments (628–38)

A fragment is an incomplete sentence punctuated as if it were complete.

education is
frag   The system of American higher education. It is founded on principles of

honesty and academic integrity.

Reducing the incidence of plagiarism among college students will be difficult,
however, without
however. Without an understanding of its causes that goes beyond simplistic explanations.

Maintaining Subject-Verb Agreement (648–58)

A verb and its subject agree when they match each other in person (first, second, or third) and number (singular or plural).

sv agr For this reason, nearly everyone invested in this system—students, instructors, and
recognizes
administrators—recognize that plagiarism cannot be tolerated.

have
That plagiarism and related misconduct has become all too common is beyond dispute.

Maintaining Pronoun-Antecedent Agreement (658–63)

A pronoun agrees with its antecedent (the word the pronoun replaces) when they match each other in person (first, second, or third), number (singular or plural), and gender (masculine, feminine, or neuter).

students are
pn ag In this myth, the student is too apathetic and slothful to finish their assignments on their

own; instead, they cheat.

Such students may treat the attainment of impressive marks as a necessity and will betray
they revere   *their*
the very academic system he or she reveres in order to sustain his or her average.

596

MLA Style and APA Style citation tutorial. Part Five, *Documentation Matters*, begins with a special four-page reference section modeling citation styles. Pages from books, journals, websites, and databases present the features of popular and academic sources. On the page below, citations for a printed book are shown in both MLA and APA style. All MLA citations follow the current guidelines of the 2016 *MLA Handbook*.

Documentation Matters | Documenting a Source: MLA Style and APA Style

Book (Printed)

MLA style:

author   title   publication information
King, Laura A. *Experience Psychology*. McGraw-Hill Education, 2016.
                             imprint-publisher   publication date

APA style:

author   title   publication information
King, L.A. (2016). *Experience psychology*. New York, NY: McGraw-Hill Education.
   publication   place of   imprint-publisher
      date   publication

Look for the information you need to document a printed book on the book's title page and copyright page. In APA style, if more than one location for the publisher is listed on the title page, use the first. (For more about documenting a book, see pp. 321–30 for MLA style, pp. 374–81 for APA style.)

300

Connect Composition

Connect Composition helps instructors use class time to focus on the highest course expectations, by offering their students meaningful, independent, and personalized learning, and an easy, efficient way to track and document student performance and engagement.

Feature	Description	Instructional Value
Simple LMS Integration	• Seamlessly integrates with every learning management system.	• Students have automatic single sign-on. • *Connect* assignment results sync to LMS's gradebook.
LearnSmart Achieve	• Continuously adapts to a student's strengths and weaknesses, to create a personalized learning environment. • Covers *The Writing Process, Critical Reading, The Research Process, Reasoning and Argument, Multilingual Writers, Grammar and Common Sentence Problems, Punctuation and Mechanics,* and *Style and Word Choice.* • Provides instructors with reports that include data on student and class performance.	• Students independently study the fundamental topics across composition in an adaptive environment. • Metacognitive component supports knowledge transfer. • Students track their own understanding and mastery and discover where their gaps are.
***Writing Matters* eBook**	• Provides comprehensive course content, exceeding what is offered in print. • Supports annotation and bookmarking.	• The *Writing Matters* eBook allows instructors and students to access their course materials anytime and anywhere, including four years of handbook access.
Connect eReader	• Provides access to more than 60 readings that are assignable via *Connect Composition.*	• Sample essays provide models for students as well as interesting topics to consider for discussion and writing. Can replace a costly standalone reader.
Power of Process	• Guides students through the critical reading and writing processes step-by-step.	• Students demonstrate understanding and develop critical thinking skills for reading, writing, and evaluating sources by responding to short-answer and annotation questions. Students are also prompted to reflect on their own processes. • Instructors or students can choose from a preloaded set of readings or upload their own. • Students can use the guidelines to consider a potential source critically.
Writing Assignments with *Peer Review*	• Allows instructors to assign and grade writing assignments online. • Gives instructors the option of easily and efficiently setting up and managing online peer review assignments for the entire class.	• This online tool makes grading writing assignments more efficient, saving time for instructors. • Students import their Word document(s), and instructors can comment and annotate submissions. • Frequently used comments are automatically saved so instructors do not have to type the same feedback over and over.

Feature	Description	Instructional Value
Writing Assignments with *Outcomes Based-Assessment*	• Allows instructors or course administrators to assess student writing around specific learning outcomes. • Generates easy-to-read reports around program-specific learning outcomes. • Includes the most up-to-date Writing Program Administrators learning outcomes, but also gives instructors the option of creating their own.	• This tool provides assessment transparency to students. They can see why a "B" is a "B" and what it will take to improve to an "A." • Reports allow a program or instructor to demonstrate progress in attaining section, course, or program goals.
Insight	• Provides a quick view of student and class performance and engagement with a series of visual data displays that answer the following questions: 1. How are my students doing? 2. How is this student doing? 3. How is my section doing? 4. How is this assignment working? 5. How are my assignments working?	• Instructors can quickly check on and analyze student and class performance and engagement.
Instructor Reports	• Allow instructors to review the performance of an individual student or an entire section. • Allow instructors or course administrators to review multiple sections to gauge progress in attaining course, department, or institutional goals.	• Instructors can identify struggling students early and intervene to ensure retention. • Instructors can identify challenging topics and/or assignments and adjust instruction accordingly. • Reports can be generated for an accreditation process or a program evaluation.
Student Reports	• Allow students to review their performance for specific assignments or the course.	• Students can keep track of their performance and identify areas they are struggling with.
Pre- & Post-Tests	• Precreated non-adaptive assessments for pre- and post-testing.	• Pre-test provides a static benchmark for student knowledge at the beginning of the program. Post-test offers a concluding assessment of student progress.
Tegrity	• Allows instructors to capture course material or lectures on video. • Allows students to watch videos recorded by their instructor and learn course material at their own pace.	• Instructors can keep track of which students have watched the videos they post. • Students can watch and review lectures from their instructor. • Students can search each lecture for specific bits of information.

Spotlight on Three Tools in *Connect*

LearnSmart Achieve

LearnSmart Achieve helps learners establish a baseline understanding of the language and concepts that make up the critical processes of composition—writing, critical reading, research, reasoning and argument, grammar, mechanics, and style—as well as guidance for writers whose first language is not English. Across 8 broad units, *LearnSmart Achieve* focuses learners on proficiency in more than 60 topics and 385 learning outcomes.

UNIT	TOPIC	
THE WRITING PROCESS	The Writing Process Generating Ideas Planning and Organizing	Drafting Revising Proofreading, Formatting, and Producing Texts
CRITICAL READING	Reading to Understand Literal Meaning Evaluating Truth and Accuracy in a Text	Evaluating the Effectiveness and Appropriateness of a Text
THE RESEARCH PROCESS	Developing and Implementing a Research Plan Evaluating Information and Sources	Integrating Source Material into a Text Using Information Ethically and Legally
REASONING AND ARGUMENT	Developing an Effective Thesis or Claim Using Evidence and Reasoning to Support a Thesis or Claim	Using Ethos (Ethics) to Persuade Readers Using Pathos (Emotion) to Persuade Readers Using Logos (Logic) to Persuade Readers
GRAMMAR AND COMMON SENTENCE PROBLEMS	Parts of Speech Phrases, Clauses, and Fragments Sentence Types Fused (Run-on) Sentences and Comma Splices Pronouns Pronoun-Antecedent Agreement	Pronoun Reference Subject-Verb Agreement Verbs and Verbals Adjectives and Adverbs Dangling and Misplaced Modifiers Mixed Constructions Verb Tense and Voice Shifts
PUNCTUATION AND MECHANICS	Commas Semicolons Colons End Punctuation Apostrophes Quotation Marks Dashes	Parentheses Hyphens Abbreviations Capitalization Italics Numbers Spelling
STYLE AND WORD CHOICE	Wordiness Eliminating Redundancies and Sentence Variety Coordination and Subordination	Faulty Comparisons Word Choice Clichés, Slang, and Jargon Parallelism
MULTILINGUAL WRITERS	Helping Verbs, Gerunds and Infinitives, and Phrasal Verbs Nouns, Verbs, and Objects Articles	Count and Noncount Nouns Sentence Structure and Word Order Verb Agreement Participles and Adverb Placement

Outcomes-Based Assessment of Writing

The *Outcomes-Based Assessment* assignment tool in *Connect Composition* is a way for any instructor to grade a writing assignment simply, using a rubric of outcomes and proficiency levels. A pre-loaded rubric is available that uses the current Writing Program Administrators (WPA) outcomes for composition courses; however, instructors may adapt any of these outcomes or use their own. Instructors work through a student's piece of writing and assign a score for each outcome, indicating how well the student did on that specific aspect of the writing process. These scores can be useful in assigning an overall grade for the specific assignment and may also be combined with other assignments to get a sense of a student's overall progress. The *Outcomes-Based Assessment* tool offers a range of clear, simple reports that allow instructors to view progress and achievement in a variety of ways. These reports may also satisfy department or college-level requests for data relating to program goals or for accreditation purposes.

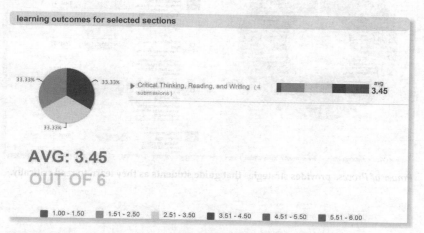

The *Outcomes-Based Assessment* tool offers a range of clear, simple reports that allow instructors to view progress and achievement in a variety of ways.

Connect's *Power of Process*

Power of Process helps students engage with texts closely and critically so that they develop awareness of their process decisions, and ultimately begin to make those decisions consciously on their own—a hallmark of strategic, self-regulating readers and writers. *Power of Process* provides strategies that guide students learning how to critically read a piece of writing or consider a text as a possible source for incorporation into their own work. After they progress through the strategies, responding to prompts by annotating and highlighting, students are encouraged to reflect on their processes and interaction with the text.

Power of Process provides strategies that guide students as they learn to read critically.

Connect Composition Reports

Connect Composition generates a number of powerful reports and charts that allow instructors to quickly review the performance of a specific student or an entire section. Students have their own set of reports (limited to include only their individual performance) that can demonstrate at a glance where they are doing well and where they are struggling. Here are a few of the reports that are available:

- *Assignment Results Report*: shows an entire section's performance across all assignments.
- *Assignment Statistics Report*: provides quick data on each assignment, including mean score as well as high/low scores.
- *Student Performance Report*: focuses on a specific student's progress across all assignments.
- *Learning Outcomes Assessment Report*: provides data, for instructors who use the *Outcomes-Based Assessment* tool to grade a writing assignment, on student performance for specific outcomes.
- *At-Risk Report*: provides instructors a dashboard of information, based on low engagement levels, that can help identify at-risk students.
- *LearnSmart Reports*: focuses on student usage, progress, and mastery of the modules contained within *LearnSmart Achieve*, *Connect*'s highly personalized, adaptive learning resource.

LMS and Grade Book Synching

The raw data from the *Assignment Results Report* synchronizes directly with Learning Management Systems so that scores automatically flow from *Connect Composition* into school-specific grade book centers.

	Blackboard	Canvas	Angel, D2L, Moodle, Sakai, Pearson Learning Solutions (eCollege)
Single sign-on	X	X	X
Gradebook sync	X (auto-sync)	X (auto-sync)	X (manual sync)
Deep linking to assignments	X	X	

Easy Access to a *Connect* Account

Request access to *Connect* from your local McGraw-Hill Education representative at **www.mhhe.com/rep** or write to **english@mheducation.com** and we will be happy to help!

If you have an account already, log in at **http://connect.mheducation.com**.

Students will have their course materials on the first day of class thanks to a 14-day courtesy access period for *Connect Composition*.

How to Find the Help You Need in *Writing Matters*

Writing Matters is a reference for all writers and researchers. Whether you are writing a research project for class, giving a multimedia presentation for a meeting, or preparing a résumé for a job interview, you are bound to come across questions about writing and research. *Writing Matters* provides you with answers to your questions.

Check the table of contents. If you know the topic you are looking for, try scanning the brief contents on the inside front cover, which includes the part and chapter titles as well as each section number and topic in the chapter. If you are looking for specific information within a general topic (how to evaluate a source for relevance and reliability, for example), scanning the detailed table of contents xxvii–xxxix will help you find the section you need.

Look up your topic in the index. The comprehensive index at the end of *Writing Matters* (I1-I38) includes cross-references to all of the topics covered in the book. If you are not sure how to use commas in compound sentences, for example, you can look up *"commas"* or *"compound sentences"* in the index.

Access the documentation resources for citation models. By looking at the examples of different types of sources and the documentation models displayed in Part Five, you can determine where to find the information on MLA, APA, *Chicago*, and CSE style that you need to document a source.

Look in the Grammar Matters pages for guidance on errors similar to the ones you sometimes make. Part Eight explores the most-common errors students make. Each chapter gives examples of grammar challenges, models how to correct them, and gives cross-references to pages where the concept is discussed.

Look up a word in the Glossary of Usage. If you are unfamiliar with a grammatical term or are not sure if you are using a particular word (such as *who* or *whom*, *less* or *fewer*, *can* or *may*) correctly, try looking it up in the Glossary of Key Terms (G1–G13) or Glossary of Usage (G15–G20).

Refer to Part Nine if you are a multilingual writer. Chapters 43–47 provide tips on the use of articles, helping verbs, prepositions, and other problem areas for writers for whom English is a foreign language.

Check the Quick Reference menu of resources. On the pages preceding the inside back cover you will find comprehensive lists of student and professional writing models, self-assessment checklists, EFL and tech tips, Quick Reference toolboxes, and guidance on writing responsibly.

Go to *Connect Composition* for online help with your writing. *Connect Composition* provides individualized instruction and practice with all aspects of writing and research, with immediate feedback on every activity. In addition, a digital version of the handbook gives you the ability to build your own personalized online writing resource.

Running heads and **section numbers** give the topic covered on that page as well as the number of the chapter and section letter in which the topic is discussed.

Main headings include the chapter number and section letter (for example, 33d) as well as the title of the section.

Examples, many of them with hand corrections, illustrate typical errors and how to correct them.

EFL boxes provide useful tips and helpful information for writers whose first language is not English.

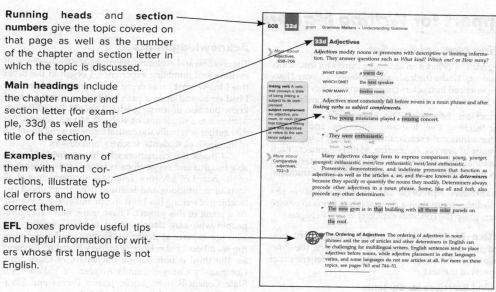

Chapter table of contents identifies the topics covered in the text.

Chapter introductions contextualize concepts explored in the upcoming lesson.

Annotations show how to edit or correct a sentence to make writing more effective.

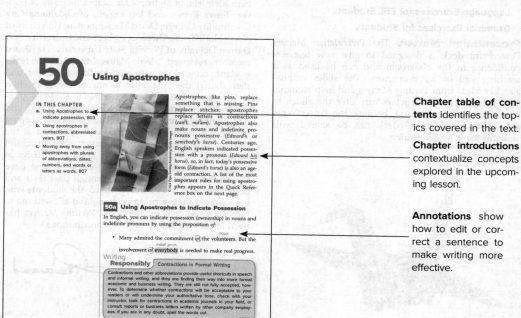

Support for *Writing Matters*

Writing Matters Tool Set

Writing Matters includes an array of resources for instructors and students. Under the leadership of Rebecca Moore Howard, experienced instructors created supplements that help instructors and students fulfill their course responsibilities.

Instruction Matters The instructor's manual includes teaching tips, learning outcomes, and suggestions for additional exercises using *Connect Composition* and *Power of Process. Instruction Matters* connects each instructor and student resource to the core material and makes the exercises relevant to instructors and students.

Assessment Matters The *Assessment Matters* test bank includes more than a thousand test items to ensure students grasp the concepts explored in every chapter.

Practice Matters Corresponding to content presented step-by-step throughout the chapters, the *Practice Matters* collection gauges student comprehension of all aspects of the text.

> **Writing Exercises for Students**
>
> **Language Exercises for EFL Students**
>
> **Grammar Exercises for Students**

Presentation Matters The *Presentation Matters* PowerPoint deck is designed to give new teachers confidence in the classroom and can be used as a teaching tool by all instructors. The slides emphasize key ideas from *Writing Matters* and help students take useful notes. Instructors can alter the slides to meet their own needs and, because the PowerPoints are ADA-accessible, the deck can be shared with students using screen readers.

Acknowledgments

The creation and evolution of *Writing Matters* has been an exciting and humbling experience. I began in the belief that I knew what I was doing, but I quickly realized that I had embarked upon a path not only of sharing what I know but also of learning what I should know. *Writing Matters* lists a single author, Rebecca Moore Howard, but that author is actually the central figure in a collaboration of hundreds of students, teachers, and editors.

I thank the instructors who have provided invaluable insights and suggestions as reviewers and members of the board of advisors. Talking with instructors at all sorts of institutions and learning from them about the teaching of writing has been an unparalleled experience. As a result of this project, I have many new colleagues, people who care deeply about teaching writing and who are experts at doing so. Particularly helpful were the members of the *Writing Matters* Board of Advisors for the third edtion: Laurie Buchanan, of Clark State Community College; Camila Alvarez, of Indian River State College-Port St. Lucie; Jessica Parker and Elizabeth Kleinfeld, of Metropolitan State University of Denver; Tonya Kymes and Jon Inglett, of Oklahoma City Community College; David MacKinnon, of University of North Florida; Jose Otero, of Weber State University; and Darren DeFrain, of Wichita State University. The Board members reviewed "Media Matters" to ensure the text's guidance on working with multimedia was current; and they shared their expertise to ensure the instruction in "Research Matters" was accessible to students grappling with the concepts at play when engaging with and documenting sources. I appreciate the Board keeping in mind accessibility challenges as they looked at the sections on design and presentation; their insightful suggestions will help all students to be as inclusive as possible. I also thank the many students who have shared their thoughts with us through class tests and design reviews. I particularly thank the students who have shared their writing with me and allowed me to publish some of it in this book. *Writing Matters* has been improved greatly by their contributions.

Manuscript Reviewers

Abraham Baldwin Agricultural College: Jeff Newberry

Allen County Community College: Tracy R. Lee (*Board of Advisors*), Bruce Symes

Baton Rouge Community College: Rosemary Mack, Jaimie Stallone (*Board of Advisors*)

Boise State University: Gail Shuck

Bowie State University: Stephanie Johnson, Sidney Walker

Brigham Young University: Brian Jackson, Jennifer Lindsey, Brett McInelly

Butler Community College: John Buaas, Sheryl LeSage, Troy Nordman (*Board of Advisors*)

Butte College: Molly Emmons, John Osbourne

Caldwell Community College: Paula Rush

Cameron University: William Carney, John Hodgson, Carolyn Lindsey Kinslow

Catawba Valley Community College: Polly Watson

Central Piedmont Community College: Amy Bagwell, Brad Bostian, Patricia Bostian (*Board of Advisors*), Jack Summers, Barbara Urban

Clark State Community College: Laurie Buchanan (*Board of Advisors*), Cecilia Kennedy, Kathryn Ward

Clayton State University: Mary Lamb, Dan Mills

Community College of Allegheny County: Pamela Jean Turley

Delaware Technical and Community College Dover: Bonnie Ceban, Nicholas David, Theodore A. Legates

Eastern Arizona College: Ida Nunley, Margaret Simonton

Florence-Darlington Technical College: Marjory Hall, Mark Rooze, Alan M. Trusky

Florida International University: Andrew Golden, Kimberly Harrison, Ben Lauren, Robert Saba, Andrew Strycharski

Frederick Community College: Kenneth P. Kerr, Kelly Trigger

Georgia College and State University: Craig Callender, Robert Viau

Georgia Gwinnett College: A. Keith Kelly, Scott Reed

Georgia State University: Lynee Lewis Gaillet, Marti Singer

Greenville Technical College: Julie Gibson

Harding University: Nicholas Boone, Terry Engel (*Board of Advisors*)

Howard University: David Green

Hutchinson Community College: Bonnie Feeser, Trudy Zimmerman

Indian River State College: Camila Alvarez (*Board of Advisors*), Ray Considine, Roderick Hofer, Tammy Powley (*Board of Advisors*), Donald Skinner, April Van Camp

Indiana University-Northwest-Gary: Pat Buckler, William K. Buckley, Lou Ann Karabel, Doug Swartz

Indiana University-Purdue University Indianapolis: Steve Fox

John Jay College: Tim McCormack

Jones County Junior College: David Lowery, Patti Smith, Tammy Townsend, Cheryl Windham

KCTCS Western Kentucky Community and Technical College: Kimberly Russell

Kent State University: Andrea Adolph, Charles Douglas Baker, Robert Miltner, Stephen E. Neaderhiser, Beverly Neiderman, Lindsay Steiner

Kent State University-Stark: Brooke Horvath

Lamar State College: Andrew Preslar, Arlene Turkel, Gwen Whitehead

Loyola University of Chicago: Victoria Anderson, Margaret Loweth, Sherrie Weller

Luzerne County Community College: Stephen Housenick, Mary Stchur

Marist College: Joseph Zeppetello

Marquette University: Virginia Chappell

Marshalltown Community College: Connie Adair, Carolyn Briggs

Metropolitan State College of Denver: Elizabeth Kleinfeld (*Board of Advisors*), Mikkilynn Olmstead, Jessica Parker (*Board of Advisors*), Jim Sundeen, Jane Chapman Vigil

Miami University of Ohio: Heidi McKee, Jason Palmeri, James E. Porter (*Board of Advisors*)

Morehouse College: Consuella Bennett, Corey Stayton, Albert Turner

Mount Hood Community College: Jonathan Morrow

New England College: Susan Nagelsen

New Jersey Institute of Technology: Mark Arnowitz, Norbert Elliot

Northern Virginia Community College-Alexandria: Shonette H. Grant (*Board of Advisors*)

Northwest Florida State College: Vickie Hunt, Julie Nichols

Norwalk Community College: Cindy Casper (*Board of Advisors*), Lisa Dresdner

Oklahoma City Community College: Jon Inglett (*Board of Advisors*), Tonya Kymes (*Board of Advisors*)

Olympic College: Sonia Begert, Ian Sherman

Palo Alto College: Ruth Ann Gambino, Caroline Mains, Diana Nystedt

Purdue University-Calumet-Hammond: Karen Bishop-Morris, Susan Roach`

Robert Morris University: Diane Todd Bucci, Tracy Gorrell, Edward Karshner, Sylvia Pamboukian, Connie Ruzich, Scott Wyatt

Rutgers University-Camden: William FitzGerald

Saint Johns River State College: Paul Robert Andrews, Melody Hargraves, Jeannine Morgan, Roger Vaccaro

Salisbury University: Elizabeth Curtin, Loren Loving Marquez (*Board of Advisors*), Nicole Munday

San Diego State University: Candace Boeck (*Board of Advisors*), Chris Werry

Seton Hall University: Gita Dasbender, Edmund H. Jones, Judith Pike

Shawnee Community College: Susan Woolridge

Snow College: Melanie Jenkins

Southwestern Oklahoma State College: Jill T. Jones, Kelly S. Moor, Valerie A. Reimers

Syracuse University: Krista Kennedy, Patrick Williams

University of Arkansas at Little Rock: Paul Yoder

University of Cincinnati-Blue Ash College: Sonja Andrus

University of Illinois-Urbana-Champaign: Courtney Caudle, Cara Finnegan, Grace Giorgio, Greg Webb, Jessica Wong

University of Miami: Andrew Green, Gina Maranto

University of North Florida: David MacKinnon (*Board of Advisors*)

University of Utah: Jay Jordan

University of Wisconsin-River Falls: Kathleen Hunzer

US Air Force Academy: Andrea Van Nort

Waynesburg University: Jill Moyer Sunday

Wayne State University: Jeff Pruchnic

Weatherford College: Sarah Lock

Weber State University: Sylvia Newman, José Otero (*Board of Advisors*), Scott Rogers

Wichita State University: Darren DeFrain (*Board of Advisors*),

York College of Pennsylvania: Julie S. Amberg

Personal Acknowledgments

Writing Matters is the result of rich collaboration with a creative, supportive, knowledgeable team who have a deep understanding of both teaching and publishing:

Tom Howard, senior lecturer in University Studies at Colgate University, has worked with me from the beginning to the end, and his intelligence and ingenuity are evident everywhere in this project. Colleagues have also drafted sections of *Writing Matters:* Amy Rupiper Taggart from North Dakota State University drafted "Designing in Context: Academic and Business Documents"; Ted Johnston, formerly of El Paso Community College, and Maggie Sokolik, University of California, Berkeley, drafted "Language Matters: Guidance for Multilingual Writers" and the EFL Notes that appear throughout *Writing Matters;* Sandra Jamieson, Drew University, and Bruce R. Thaler drafted many of the exercises; and a number of instructors—David Hooper, of Western Washington University; Tom Howard, of Colgate University; Ann Marie Leshkowich, of College of the Holy Cross; Leslie Yoder, of Southwestern College; and Paul Yoder, of University of Arkansas at Little Rock—kindly contributed sample exercises designed to help students learn the art of analyzing arguments.

McGraw-Hill has supported the project from beginning to end. My thanks go out to David Patterson, Managing Director; Claire Brantley, Executive Brand Manager; Lisa Pinto, Lead Product Developer; Kelly Villela, Editorial Director; Nanette Giles, Executive Market Development Manager; and Marisa Cavanaugh, Marketing Manager. My special thanks go to Michael O'Loughlin, my brilliant Senior Product Developer, whose energy, patience, and intelligence have made a third edition that shines.

In addition, *Writing Matters* has benefited greatly from the efforts of an extended editorial team: David Chodoff, Janet Byrne Smith, Elizabeth Murphy, and Francesca King. It has been a pleasure to work with an outstanding production team: Jennifer Shekleton, Samantha Donisi-Hamm, Sandy Schnee, Debra Kubiak, DeAnna Dausener, Shawntel Schmitt, Mark Schaefer, Stacey Dong Miskell, and Melissa Sacco. In particular, I would like to thank the copyediting and proofreading team of Gary Morris and Karen Robito, whose careful eyes saved me from many embarrassing errors, and Lisa Bruflodt, our fabulous production editor, who juggled schedules and personalities with aplomb.

Contents

Part Two   Reasoning Matters
Reading, Thinking, and Arguing 111

Part Five **Documentation Matters**
Creating Citations and Informational Notes 299

Part Six   Genre Matters
Writing in and beyond College 451

Part Eight   Grammar Matters
Writing with Clarity 595

Part Nine — **Language Matters**
Guidance for Multilingual Writers 733

Part Ten **Detail Matters**
Punctuation and Mechanics 777

Part One

Writing
Matters

Planning, Drafting,
Revising, Editing,
Proofreading,
and Formatting

Self

Assessment
To fulfill your responsibility to your AUDIENCE, ask yourself the following questions:

As you research, develop, and write your project, ask yourself the following questions, revising as necessary to improve your work.

- Have you chosen a topic that is appropriate and interesting to your reader?
- Does your title prepare your reader for what follows?
- Will your reader find the reasons you supply logical and compelling?
- Have you supplied enough relevant evidence to persuade your reader to accept (or at least to consider) your position?
- Will your reader find your project logically organized?
- Have you provided transitions to guide your reader?
- Is your project written at an appropriate level for your reader?
- Is your tone appropriate to your reader?
- Have you revised, edited, and proofread your project so that your reader will find the writing clear, correct, and powerful?

Self

Assessment
To fulfill your responsibility to your TOPIC, ask yourself the following questions:

As you research, develop, and write your project, ask yourself the following questions, revising as necessary to improve your work.

- Have you explored your topic thoroughly and creatively?
- Have you conducted research (when needed), using the most in-depth and reliable sources available to you?
- Have you provided logical reasons that support your thesis?
- Have you provided sufficient evidence to support your claims?
- Have you used visuals when they are the most effective way of presenting supporting evidence or examples?
- Have you assessed your sources carefully and presented evidence from reliable sources?
- Have you represented ideas borrowed from sources accurately and fully?

Lydia Nichols

Prof. Concannon

Writing 205

30 April 2016

Holy Underground Comics, Batman! Moving Away from the Mainstream

When most people think of comic books, predictable images usually come to mind: caped heroes, maniacal villains, deeds of incredible strength, and other typical elements of super-powered adventures. Undeniably, characters like Batman, Superman, and Spider-Man are the most prominent features of the comic book landscape, in terms of both popularity and revenue (Wright xiv). However, there is more to comic books than superpowers and secret identities. Underground comics (also known as comix), printed by small publishers or by individual artists, are very different from what is usually expected in the genre. While far less well-known than their superhero counterparts, underground comics often offer an innovative and more sophisticated alternative to mainstream titles.

Almost from the beginning, comic books were associated with superheroes. The first comic books appeared in the early 1930s, nearly four decades after comic strips such as *Yellow Boy* began appearing in the major newspapers. However, Les Daniels, who has written extensively on conventional and underground comics, points out that comic books did not gain widespread popularity until June of 1938, when writer Jerry Siegel and artist Joe Shuster debuted their character Superman in *Action Comics* #1 (9). Daniels reports that Superman was an immediate success,

> Introduction: Initiates contrast, moves from familiar to unfamiliar, concludes with thesis

> In-text citation—book

> Thesis: Establishes topic, purpose, and author's position

> Topic sentence: Prepares reader for historical overview

> Signal phrase identifies source and establishes credibility

This project appears in full on pp. 350–62.

Writing Matters | Writer's Responsibilities Checklists

Self

Assessment
To fulfill your responsibility to OTHER WRITERS, ask yourself the following questions:

As you research, develop, and write your project, ask yourself the following questions, revising as necessary to improve your work.

- Have you given credit to those from whom you have borrowed words or ideas, whether you have summarized, paraphrased, or quoted material or whether your source is printed or online?

- Have you avoided patchwriting by paraphrasing borrowed material fully, putting the text into your own words and sentence structures?

- Have you represented the ideas of other writers accurately and fairly?

- Have you treated other writers respectfully, even when you disagree with them?

- Have you considered alternative viewpoints?

- Have you addressed alternative perspectives that conflict with your own position?

Self

Assessment
To fulfill your responsibility to YOURSELF, ask yourself the following questions:

As you research, develop, and write your project, ask yourself the following questions, revising as necessary to improve your work.

- Have you used the writing assignment to learn something new and to expand your scope as a writer?

- Have you represented your ideas clearly, powerfully, and accurately?

- Have you integrated your own ideas or your own synthesis of sources to provide a text that is original and interesting?

- Have you used language inclusively, avoiding bias and representing yourself as a respectful person?

- Have you written in a voice that is true to yourself and in keeping with your context (academic, business, public) and genre (college essay, presentation, newsletter)?

- Have you revised, edited, and proofread your project to make sure your presentation reflects the effort you have put into the writing?

- Is your project the best representation of yourself that you can make it?

and the character quickly inspired the creation of copycat superheroes in other comic books. The protagonists of these comics each had their own strengths and vulnerabilities, but the stories all shared a basic formula: individuals with extraordinary abilities battling against evil and struggling to maintain a secret identity. These superhero comics, although similar to each other, set the comic book industry on its feet, paving the way to profits and sustained success. Over the decades and even today, superhero comics are what are typically seen on store shelves.

Topic sentence: Supported by quotation and summary

While writers and artists over the years have certainly done inventive work in superhero comics, some similarity in mainstream titles was for many years unavoidable due to the creation in 1954 of the Comics Code Authority (CCA), an organization formed by a number of the leading comic book publishers to regulate the content of comics ("Good Shall Triumph"). It set very explicit standards, dictating what content was allowed in comic books and what content was expected. Some parts of the code were incredibly specific and controlling:

Block indentation for long quotation; ellipses mark cut

> The letters of the word "crime" on a comics magazine shall never be appreciably greater in dimension than the other words contained in the title. The word "crime" shall never appear alone on a cover. ... Restraint in the use of the word "crime" in titles or subtitles shall be exercised. (qtd. in "Good Shall Triumph")

Indirect source: Author unknown, so title used

Quotation marks for brief quotation

Other rules were more general—vague enough to allow the CCA a free hand in shaping content. One read, "Respect for parents, the moral code, and for honorable behavior shall be fostered" (qtd. in "Good Shall Triumph"). The CCA also regulated

Paragraph uses combination of summary, paraphrase, and quotation

Websites: no page numbers in citations

This project appears in full on pp. 350–62.

1 Writing Responsibly in the Information Age

© PeopleImages/iStockphoto.com

"I just can't write." We've all heard the lament; most of us have uttered it at least once. Some mistakenly believe it is a basic truth: Just as some people don't have an "ear" for music, others don't have the "gift" for writing. This is an inaccurate comparison, though: no one is a born writer. There are no three-year-old children who are amazing writers. Acclaim for writers may come early, but their "gift" comes from reading, from the practice of writing, and in many cases, from the study of writing. Expert writing, in other words, involves a high level of training. Writing is a skill that is learned and practiced.

Successful writing holds out the promise of self-expression, even self-discovery. It is also a valuable asset in the workplace: A report from the National Commission on Writing revealed that American corporations expect their salaried employees to be able to write clearly, correctly, and logically. Eighty percent of finance, insurance, and real estate employers take writing skills into consideration when hiring.

Whether drafting business e-mails or making PowerPoint presentations, texting friends or commenting on an Instagram picture, writing in a personal journal or even composing a paper for a college course, we write to develop and evaluate beliefs and ideas, to move others, to express ourselves, and to explore possibilities. For all these reasons and more, writing matters.

> **More about**
> Writer's responsibilities checklists, 2–5 (*Writing Matters* tutorial preceding this chapter)

FIGURE 1.1 **The media revolution** In the fifteenth century, few could read (or had access to) the Gutenberg Bible. Today, readers can view its pages on their phones, but to do so they must be multiliterate: Not only must they be able to read and write, but they must also know how to access multiple media online.

1a Writing Today

Long before Johannes Gutenberg introduced the printing press in the fifteenth century, a *page* was seen as a sheet of paper covered with text, and *literacy* meant the ability to read and write a text, whether written on the page or carved in stone. But as the Internet revolution changes our understanding of what a page is, it also expands our concept of literacy (Figure 1.1). Today, a page can be a sheet of paper, but it can also be a screen in a website or an e-mail on a smartphone; it can include not only words, but also images and sound files, links to other web pages, and animations. The ability to understand, interpret, and use these new kinds of pages—by contributing to a class wiki or making an online presentation, for example—requires not just print literacy but multiple literacies (visual literacy, digital literacy, information literacy).

Like most people reading this book, you are probably already multiliterate: You "code shift," switching from medium to medium easily because the "literacies" required for each medium are not entirely separate. Whether penning a thank-you note, searching a library database, reading an advertisement, composing a college paper, or texting your best friend, you analyze and interpret, adjusting your message in response to your purpose, audience, context, and medium. When texting a friend you may ignore the conventions of punctuation and capitalization, for example, but you would not do so when writing a résumé.

This handbook focuses on print literacy because it remains central to communication; yet *Writing Matters* also addresses digital, visual, oral, and information literacies because they have become impossible to separate from one another and from traditional print literacy. As a reader, you must be able not only to decipher written language but also to interpret visuals—drawing meaning from advertisements, for example, and subjecting them to the scrutiny of a careful shopper. As a writer, you may incorporate graphics into papers in economics and psychology; contribute to class blogs or Twitter discussions; search online databases and electronic library catalogs; or create presentations using Prezi. As both a reader and a writer, you will be expected to manage all the information you receive and transmit. Being multiliterate *means* being information literate.

More about
Writing business memos, 501–02
Creating Power-Points, 191
Creating websites, 179–85
Writing in literature and other humanities, 452–74 (ch. 22)
Writing in the sciences and social sciences, 475–89 (ch. 23)
Reading critically, 112–35 (ch. 7)
Interpreting visuals, 123, 126, 130
Incorporating visuals, 101, 322–23, 341–42, 347–49, 394–95

1b The Writer's Responsibilities

Your opportunities to express and even create yourself in words come with responsibilities to your readers, to the topics you address, to the other writers from whom you borrow and to whom you respond, and perhaps especially to yourself as a writer with ideas and ideals to express.

1. Your responsibilities to your audience

Audience members make a commitment to you by spending their time reading your work. To help them feel that this commitment was worthwhile, you can do the following:

- Choose a topic that your audience will find interesting and about which you have something you want to say.

- Make a claim that will help your audience follow your thoughts.

- Support your claim with thoughtful, logical, even creative evidence drawn from sources that you have evaluated carefully for relevance and reliability.

- Write clearly so that your audience (even if that audience is your composition teacher) does not have to struggle to understand. To write clearly, build a logical structure, use transitional techniques to guide readers, and correct errors of grammar, punctuation, and spelling.

- Write appropriately by using a tone and vocabulary that are right for your rhetorical situation—your topic, audience, context, and genre.

- Write engagingly by varying sentence structures and word choices, avoiding wordiness, and using repetition only for special effect.

2. Your responsibilities to your topic

Examples of writers who did not take seriously their responsibility to their topic are everywhere. Here are three:

- A six-year-old child who won tickets to a Hannah Montana concert with an essay about her father's Iraq War death; her father had *not* been killed in Iraq. She lost those tickets.

- Jayson Blair, a *New York Times* reporter who concocted "eyewitness" stories about events in far-away places without leaving his apartment; he was forced to resign.

- The president of Raytheon Company, who plagiarized large sections of his book *Swanson's Unwritten Rules of Management* from a book published in 1944; he was fined a million dollars by the company's shareholders.

> **More about**
> Writing Respon-
>   sibly, tutorial
>   preceding ch. 1
> List of Writing
>   Responsibly
>   boxes, pages
>   facing inside
>   back cover
> Devising a topic,
>   24–30
> Finding informa-
>   tion, 210–32
>   (ch. 13)
> Using support-
>   ing evidence,
>   45–47
> Evaluating sources,
>   233–46 (ch. 14)
> Organizing,
>   38–43
> Providing transi-
>   tions, 60–61
> Correcting gram-
>   mar, 595–731
>   (part 8, Gram-
>   mar Matters)
> Correcting
>   punctuation,
>   777–863 (part
>   10, Detail
>   Matters)
> Writing with flair,
>   519–594 (part 7,
>   Style Matters)

You treat your topic responsibly when you explore it thoroughly and creatively, rely on trustworthy sources, and offer supporting evidence that is accurate, relevant, and reliable. You show respect for your topic when you provide enough evidence to persuade readers of your claims and when you acknowledge viewpoints that do not support your position. In a college writing project, not fulfilling your responsibilities to your topic might lead to a bad grade. In the workplace, it could have great financial, even life-and-death, consequences: The Merck pharmaceutical company, for example, was accused of suppressing evidence that its drug Vioxx could cause heart attacks and strokes. As a result, Merck faced a host of lawsuits, trials, and out-of-court settlements.

> ### Writing
> ### Responsibly | **Your Responsibilities as a Writer**
>
> When you write, you have four areas of responsibility:
> 1. To your audience
> 2. To your topic
> 3. To other writers
> 4. To yourself

> *More about*
> Avoiding hypothetical evidence, 46
> Avoiding altering images inappropriately, 84–87

3. Your responsibilities to other writers

You have important responsibilities to other writers whose work you may be using.

Acknowledge your sources   Writing circulates easily today, and vast quantities of it are available online, readily accessible through search engines such as Bing and Google and databases such as JSTOR. It may seem natural, then, simply to copy the information you need from a source and paste it into your own text, as you might if you were collecting information about a disease you were facing or a concert you hoped to attend. But when you provide readers with information, ideas, language, or images that others have collected or created, you also have a responsibility to *acknowledge* those sources. Such acknowledgment gives credit to those who contributed to your thinking, and it allows your readers to read your sources for themselves. Acknowledging your sources also protects you from charges of plagiarism, and it builds your authority and credibility as a writer by establishing that you have reviewed key sources on a topic and taken other writers' views into consideration.

To acknowledge sources in academic writing, you must do *all* of the following:

> *More about*
> Using a search engine, 214–17
> Using an online database, 218–23
> Using an electronic library catalog, 223–28

> *More about*
> When to quote, paraphrase, or summarize, 253–64
> Using quotation marks, 810–19 (ch. 51)
> Formatting block quotations, 346–347, 392, 812
> Adjusting quotations using brackets and ellipses, 816, 828, 831–32

1. When quoting, copy accurately and use quotation marks or block indention to signal the beginning and end of the copied passage; when paraphrasing or summarizing, put the ideas fully into your own words and sentences.

2. Include an in-text citation to the source, whether you are quoting, paraphrasing, or summarizing.

> **More about**
> Citing and
>   documenting
>   sources,
>   299–449
>   (part 5,
>   Documentation
>   Matters)
> Avoiding
>   plagiarism and
>   "patchwriting,"
>   251–57, 275–77

3. Document the source, providing enough information for your readers to locate the source and to identify the type of source you used. This documentation usually appears in a bibliography (often called a list of works cited or a reference list) at the end of college research projects.

Writing Responsibly around the World Concepts of plagiarism vary from one culture or context to another. Where one may see cooperation, another may see plagiarism. Even if borrowing ideas and language without acknowledgment is a familiar custom for you, writers in the United States (especially in academic contexts) must explicitly acknowledge all ideas and information borrowed from another source.

___

Obtain copyright clearance While plagiarism is concerned with acknowledging sources of ideas or language, copyright focuses on the right to compensation for the use of writers' words and ideas in a public context. When writers use a substantial portion of another writer's text, they must not only acknowledge the source but may also need to obtain the original author's permission, often in exchange for a fee.

As a student, your use of sources is covered under the *fair use* provision of US copyright law, which allows you to include copyrighted material without permission when you are doing your college assignments. What counts as fair use cannot be expressed in percentages or checklists. The Center for Social Media at American University offers a "Code of Best Practices in Fair Use for Media Literacy Education" that you can find online. It explains that if you copy someone else's text or music files and avoid paying for it, you are violating copyright. But if you are using parts of a text or a song for educational purposes, and if you are not interfering with the copyright owner's ability to profit from the material, you are making fair use of it

Quick Reference **Your College's Plagiarism Policy**

Most colleges publish their plagiarism policies in their student handbook, which is often available online. **Find your plagiarism policy** by searching the student handbook's table of contents or index. Or search your college's website, using key terms such as *plagiarism, cheating policy, academic honesty,* or *academic integrity.* Before writing a research project, **read your school's plagiarism policy** carefully. If you are unsure what the policy means, talk with your adviser or instructor. In addition to the general policy for your college, **read your course syllabi** carefully to see what specific guidelines your instructors may provide there.

and do not need the copyright owner's permission. Because plagiarism and copyright are separate issues, though, you must always acknowledge your source, even when no permission is needed.

Copyright protections also apply to you as a writer: Anything you write is protected by US copyright law—even your college assignments.

Treat other writers fairly Your responsibility to other writers does not end with the need to acknowledge your use of their ideas or language. You must also represent *accurately* and *fairly* what your sources say: Quoting selectively to distort meaning or taking a comment out of context is irresponsible. So is treating other writers with scorn.

It is perfectly acceptable to criticize the ideas of others. In fact, examining ideas under the bright light of careful scrutiny is central to higher education. But treating the people who developed the ideas with derision is not. Avoid *ad hominem* (personal) attacks, and focus your attention on other writers' ideas and their expression of them.

More about
Bias, 566–69
Ad hominem, 162

4. Your responsibilities to yourself

You have a responsibility to yourself as a writer. Writers represent themselves on paper and screen through the words and images (and even sounds) they create and borrow, so submitting a project as your own that someone else has written is a form of impersonation—it does not represent you. Make sure that the writing "avatar," or **persona,** you create is the best representation of yourself it can be. Encourage readers to view you with respect by treating others—not only other writers but also other people and groups—respectfully and without bias. Earn your audience's respect by synthesizing information from sources to produce new and compelling ideas and by using language clearly, correctly, logically, and with flair.

If you graduate from college having learned to be an effective writer, you will have learned something employers value highly. More importantly, though, you will have fulfilled a key responsibility to yourself.

More about
Synthesis, 127–29
Common sentence problems, 78–83 (Grammar Matters tutorial preceding ch. 33)
Style, 519–594 (part 7, Style Matters)
Grammar, 595–731 (part 8, Grammar Matters)
Punctuation and mechanics, 777–863 (part 10, Detail Matters)

Writing Responsibly   Taking Yourself Seriously as a Writer

Many students enter writing classes thinking of themselves as "bad writers." This belief can be a self-fulfilling prophecy: students fail to engage because they already believe they are doomed to fail. Remember that writing is not an inborn talent but a skill to be learned. Instead of thinking of yourself as a bad writer, think of yourself as a writer-in-progress, someone who has something to say and who is learning how to say it effectively. If you speak or have studied another language, think of yourself as someone who is learning to draw on that experience.

to SELF

→ **EXERCISE 1.1 Assessing the writer's responsibilities**

Read "Plagiarism Cheats Students," written by Salt Lake Community College student Jeff Gurney for his college newspaper, *The Globe*. To what extent do you agree with Gurney's argument? What reservations do you have about it? What other writers' responsibilities might a revision of the article take into account?

Student Model Newspaper Article

Plagiarism Cheats Students

By JEFF GURNEY

In the world of higher education, your growth as a student comes with a heavy price. Many hours are spent reading, researching and writing for required reports in most of your classes. This means staying up many nights until almost dawn and drinking a lot of coffee.

Or at least this is how it should be. Unfortunately, an amazing number of students are getting into buying ready-made reports. There are many places that you can go online and pick the type of paper you want. For a fee they will send you the paper and all you have to do is change a few sentences. Once that part is done all you need to do is turn it in.

This is the way some students have made it through college. Then the professors got smart and noticed that there were a lot of papers that sounded pretty much the same or had just about the same content.

Along come services like Turnitin. com where the professor tells you to first send the report online, and for a fee, usually paid for by the school, your paper is compared to many different papers and texts that are in a massive database. The service can tell in percentages how much content in your paper was gleaned from other sources.

This service also provides [instructors] with the results of the scan and tells them what your scores are in each of several categories.

Over the past few years there have been several writers working for very prominent media services that have been caught plagiarizing, and surprisingly they were using quite a bit of other people's stuff. The most amazing thing about this misuse is that they worked for trusted publications and broke that trust for money.

In a 2011 survey conducted by the Pew Research Center ("The Digital Revolution and Higher Education"), a majority of college presidents reported their belief that plagiarism rates are at an all-time high. While firm data on rates of plagiarism are hard to pin down, educators' perceptions and concerns raise an important question:

What is the reason we go to college? Are you attending SLCC merely to get a better job, or to learn something in the process for that job? An unknown author once said, "If it were easy then everybody would have done it." This is the ideal that those that started higher education probably had in mind. It is much more valuable, that diploma in hand, when you earn it yourself.

Text Credits

2 Planning Your Project

© image100/Alamy RF

Just as an architect creates a blueprint to show how to fit together the concrete footings, steel beams, and electrical wiring of a building, so, too, does a writer create a plan that takes into account the project's purpose, audience, context, and genre. Just as an architect must choose the right materials and devise plans to complete the project on budget and on schedule, a writer must select an engaging topic, devise ideas that will resonate with the reader, fulfill the terms of the assignment, and do it all on time.

2a Analyzing Your Writing Situation

A first step in planning a writing project is to consider your *writing situation* (or *rhetorical situation*):

- What is your **purpose**? What might you accomplish with the text?

- Who is your **audience**? Who will be reading the text you produce and why?

- What **topics** might interest them, and why? What information about the topic might the audience be expected already to know, and what might you need to explain?

- What **tone** is appropriate to your purpose and audience?

- What are the **context** (academic, business, personal) and **genre** (or type) of writing you will produce (research report, résumé, Facebook status update)? How will your context and genre affect the way you write this project?

13

Throughout the writing process—planning, drafting, revising, and editing—you can refine or reconsider your initial decisions.

1. Establish a purpose.

Writers write for a variety of reasons, or *purposes*: to entertain, inform, or persuade an audience; or for the writer's own self-expression or learning.

- **To entertain.** Entertaining your readers (by providing them with an engaging reading experience) is a goal all writers share, but it is unlikely to be your primary purpose in academic or business writing.

More about
Description, 59

- **To express feelings or beliefs.** In *expressive* writing, an experience is often conveyed through *description*, and the language is richly evocative. The purpose of the following paragraph is expressive; the writer's goal is to convey the feelings and experiences of a small would-be ballerina.

> She stood in the doorframe shivering. She was a tiny girl, about four years old, and her wispy blonde hair was tied back with a pink satin ribbon. Leaning against her mother's leg, she gazed into the unfamiliar room. Other girls her age were twirling and jumping with confidence, laughing at their reflections in the mirrors, spinning on the slippery wooden floors. The girl's mother handed her the ballet shoes, gave her a quick peck on the cheek, and stepped back into the snowstorm. Alone now, the girl retreated to the wall and slid into a dark corner. She bent her knees against her chest and wrapped her arms around her legs. There she sat.
>
> —Amanda Godfrey, McHenry County College, "Ballet Blues"

In most college courses, an expressive purpose is unlikely to be primary, but it may well play a secondary role, as you draw on your own experiences to illustrate a point.

Writing about Personal Experiences Depending on your cultural background or educational experiences, writing about personal issues and experiences may seem odd in an academic writing course. Instructors at US colleges and universities, however, sometimes assign expressive essays as a way to get their students to write about something they already know. If you are uncomfortable writing on a personal topic, discuss the issue with your instructor.

- **To inform.** An *informative* (or *expository*) text may explain a concept, describe a sequence of events or a process, or analyze a relationship. Scientific, technical, journalistic, and business writing are typically informative. The abstract below, which comes from a psychology research project, is expository because it informs the reader of the results of a psychological study:

> This study explores the potential influence of stereotypical appearances on male subjects' stated opinions regarding entertainment perceived as "feminine." The findings show that participants were more likely to give a favorable ranking of a "chick flick" in the presence of a counter-stereotypical male than in the presence of a stereotypical male. The discussion focuses on possible explanations for participant behavior, with a theoretical basis in gender role conflict.
>
> —Heather DeGroot, James Madison University, "The Power of Wardrobe: Male Stereotype Influences"

Student Models
Informative projects:
"Rethinking Alternative Energy," Michael Wedd, 101–106
"The Power of Wardrobe," Heather DeGroot, 396–405
"Nature vs. Nurture," Robyn Worthington, 481–89

- **To persuade or argue.** Texts that try to convince readers to adopt beliefs or opinions or to take action have a *persuasive* (or *argumentative*) purpose. Editorials, book and movie reviews, grant proposals, and much academic writing all have a persuasive purpose. The paragraph below comes from an editorial. It draws on evidence from studies to support its claim that Head Start is a worthwhile program:

> Head Start, the federally funded pre-kindergarten program, has been under attack recently as a waste of money, because some say the effects don't last long enough to make a difference later in life. I beg to differ. Studies show that eighth graders who were in Head Start do as well as kids who received education from a private pre-school. Poor children who do not attend Head Start do no better than their parents. To raise our population out of poverty, children must learn at an early age to have confidence, have goals and strive for them, and receive the best education they can. Head Start provides a good start.
>
> —Lynn Holmlund, Bentley College, "Going Public: Head Start"

More about
Analyzing and crafting arguments, 136–64 (ch. 8)

- **To learn.** As writers struggle to find the words to express a complex thought, they are actually struggling to understand what they are writing about. "How do I know what I think until I see what I say?" the writer E. M. Forster is quoted as saying. Writing a summary of a source involves pushing oneself to understand that

More about
Summary, 247–64 (ch. 15)
Rogerian argument, 136–64 (ch. 8)

source. Explaining its relationship to another source involves thinking critically about both sources. Many college writing assignments are designed not only to have you practice your writing techniques but also to help you grasp the material you are writing about. The work of psychologist Carl Rogers inspired a method of argument, *Rogerian argument*, whose purpose is not so much to persuade an audience but to explore possible interpretations of and solutions to difficult topics.

→ **EXERCISE 2.1 Analyzing purpose**

Read the following passages and determine whether the primary purpose of each passage is expressive, informative, or persuasive:

Camels do not store water in their humps. They drink furiously, up to twenty-eight gallons in a ten-minute session, then distribute the water evenly through-out their bodies. Afterward, they use the water stingily. They have viscous urine and dry feces. They breathe through their noses, and keep their mouths shut. They do sweat, but only as a last resort, after first allowing their body temperatures to rise 10 degrees Fahrenheit. As they begin to dehydrate, the volume of their blood plasma does not at first diminish. They can survive a water loss of up to one-third of their body weight, then drink up and feel fine. Left alone, unhurried and unburdened, they can live two weeks between drinks.

—William Langewiesche, *Sahara Unveiled*

Gentlemen, I want you to suppose a case for a moment. Suppose that all the property you were worth was in gold, and you had to put it in the hands of Blondin, the famous rope-walker, to carry across the Niagara Falls on a tight rope. Would you shake the rope while he was passing over it, or keep shouting to him, "Blondin, stop a little more! Go a little faster!"? No. I am sure you would not. You would hold your breath as well as your tongue and keep your hand off until he was safely over. Now the Government is in the same situation. It is carrying an immense weight across a stormy ocean. Untold treasures are in its hands. It is doing the best it can. Don't badger it! Just keep still, and it will get you safely over.

—Abraham Lincoln, "Reply to Critics of His Administration"

Have you ever had to ask for help, knowing your children will suffer unless you get it? Think about asking for a loan from a relative, if this is the only way you can imagine asking for help. I will tell you how it feels. You find out where the office is that you are supposed to visit. You circle that block four or five times. Thinking of your children, you go in.

Everybody is very busy. Finally, someone comes out and you tell her that you need help. That never is the person you need to see. You go see another person, and after spilling the whole shame of your poverty all over the desk between you, you find that this isn't the right office after all—you might repeat the whole process, and it never is any easier at the next place.

—Jo Goodwin Parker, "What Is Poverty?"

2. Identify and address your audience.

A text is seldom written for the writer alone. Rather, it is intended for an *audience*, and this fact shapes the text in large and small ways. That is why, for a piece of writing to be effective, the writer must make a careful analysis of the intended reader (or readers).

Before putting fingers to keyboard, consider the characteristics of your audience, such as age and gender, occupation and interests, educational background, abilities, sexualities and identities, political or cultural affiliations, and ethnic or religious background. Then, consider the audience's expectations:

Writing Responsibly Seeing and Showing the Whole Picture

As a writer, you have a responsibility to look beyond your own experiences and beliefs, beyond your own self-interest. As you explore an issue, give thorough, respectful attention to interpretations that contradict or conflict with yours. Figure out what motivates the supporters of opposing positions. Consider whether your own opinion should be revised. Then, as you write, no matter which position you support in your text, let your audience see all the viewpoints and the reasons for them.

to AUDIENCE

- Are your readers already well informed about the topic, or are they reading your text to learn about something new to them?
- Are your readers eager to learn about your topic, or do they have only a passing interest?
- Do readers hold strong opinions about your topic, or are they likely to be open-minded?

Next, consider what will make your writing most effective for this audience:

- **What information will your audience need in order to understand and appreciate what you are saying?** A general audience will need you to define all specialized terms as you use them, as well as to provide any background information necessary for them to understand the topic. A specialist audience, on the other hand, may be bored by too much explanation, but these readers will still need you to define any terms you are using in an unusual sense and to provide background information about aspects of the topic likely to fall outside of their area of expertise. An instructor, while an expert, may expect you to write for a nonspecialist reader.

- **What kinds of language, examples, or evidence will be most effective?** Someone arguing for the legalization of marijuana in front of a group of college students will make very different choices than will someone arguing the same position in front of an audience filled with their parents or with police officers.

One way to write for an audience is to picture a few specific people (representative of your audience) and then to think about what each of them will need in order to understand and appreciate what you are saying.

 Getting Help in Understanding Your Audience If you have a different cultural or linguistic background than your prospective readers—whether you are a native English speaker or not—try to find classmates, peers, instructors, tutors, or advisers who may share experiences with the readers you have in mind. They might be able to help you determine how much background information your readers will need and what kinds of evidence they will find most effective.

The excerpt below shows a writer crafting a text with her audience in mind:

More about
Writing letters,
497–18 (ch. 25)

Dear Governor:

Your effort to improve education has been quite extensive. Throughout these past few years the creation of after-school programs that have offered tutoring for students has been possible because of your involvement. You have also formed the National Teachers Academy in Illinois, which works to improve the quality of teaching in schools. In addition, you secured several hundred million dollars that gave libraries the ability to replace many outdated books. Although you have made some great accomplishments for education, the conditions of our schools still call for much improvement. By striving to implement a voucher system, you could cause a nationwide education reform, and give every child a chance at a quality education. . . .

—Amanda Godfrey, McHenry County College

By imagining the governor's reactions, what he might appreciate and what he might resist, Godfrey knows to start her letter by listing the actions he has already taken to improve the state's schools. *Then* Godfrey argues for a new school voucher program.

In much of your college writing, you will have an audience of one—your instructor. To satisfy that audience, begin with a careful analysis of what the instructor hopes you will learn from the assignment. These objectives may be specified in the assignment or in the course syllabus, but sometimes you will simply need to ask. Generally, your instructor will be a specialist reader who wants to be reassured that you have done the reading, understood the issues, and synthesized the information from classroom lectures, discussions, and assigned reading. In addition, most instructors want to see that you can express yourself clearly and correctly in writing. To accomplish these goals, provide the following:

- Important background information
- Definitions of key terms
- Explanations of key concepts
- Analysis of the issues
- Synthesis of evidence from assigned reading and classroom discussion to support claims
- Synthesis of *counterevidence* (opposing or alternative interpretations or opinions) from assigned reading and classroom discussion, to provide a whole picture
- Citations and a list of works cited or references for source-based writing

3. Match your tone to your purpose and your audience.

When you speak, your *tone* of voice, gestures, facial expressions, and body language all convey your attitude. Are you patient, annoyed, angry, pleasantly surprised? All of these attitudes are conveyed in a moment by the pitch of your voice or the look on your face. Writers convey their attitude toward their readers and their subject through their tone. In writing, tone is conveyed primarily through *level of diction* (formal or informal) and the *connotation* (emotional resonance) of the words you choose. To write at a formal level of diction, use standard American English; avoid regionalisms (such as *y'all*), colloquial language (such as *what up*), and slang (such as *hot* rather than *good* or *exciting*); and write in complete sentences (*Are you coming?* rather than just *Coming?*).

> **More about**
> Reading to comprehend, 112–18
> Reading to reflect, 118–23
> Reading to write, 123–31
> Analysis, 124–26
> Synthesis, 127–29

> **More about**
> Citing and documenting sources, 304–62 (MLA style, ch. 18), 363–405 (APA style, ch. 19), 406–34 (*Chicago* style, ch. 20), 435–50 (CSE style, ch. 21)

> **More about**
> Developing a thesis, 34–38
> Level of diction, 565
> Connotation and denotation, 570–72

Although most college instructors will expect you to adopt a formal level of diction, the individual decisions you make will vary from course to course and discipline to discipline. In some courses, using the first-person pronoun *I* might be perfectly acceptable or even required, but for others (such as economics and sociology) it might be considered too informal.

More about
Dictionaries
  for second-
  language learn-
  ers, 581

More about
Writing in liter-
  ature and the
  other human-
  ities, 452–74
  (ch. 22)
Writing in the
  sciences and
  social sciences,
  475–89 (ch. 23)
Exploratory argu-
  ments, 136–40
Considering alter-
  native view-
  points, 148–49

Recognizing Differences in Connotation A word in your first language may share a literal meaning with a word in another language but have a very different connotation. The word *ambitious* ("eager for success"), for example, can be positive or negative in English; in Spanish, *ambición* is generally negative. If you are not sure how key words are used by your prospective readers, consult a cross-language or bilingual dictionary or check with classmates, a writing tutor, or your instructor.

Whatever the particular demands of your course, all disciplines expect you to adopt a measured tone. In general, opt for connotatively neutral language: Shrill or sarcastic prose will suggest to your audience that your opinions spring from your heart and not your head. This does not mean that emotional topics are off limits or that you may not express your beliefs, but temperance (moderation, self-restraint) is highly valued in academic discourse. Your instructor will expect you to have looked at all sides of an issue carefully before drawing a conclusion and to exhibit respect for those with whom you disagree.

Make It **Your Own**

Draft a paragraph on one of the topics below as if you were writing to knowledgeable adults (perhaps even college professors). Carefully consider your purpose and your audience as you do so. Next, revise the paragraph to address an audience of high school students. Finally, revise it to appeal to a general audience.

1. The importance of participating in local government
2. Restrictions on language, dress, and behavior in public schools
3. Cell phone etiquette
4. Individual participation in recycling projects

Work **Together**

Working in pairs or small groups, compare your paragraphs with those of your classmate(s). Are the purpose and audience clear for each? Discuss the connotations of specific words, assess the level of formality of each sample paragraph, and point to words or sentences that make the diction more formal or less formal.

Next, write a paragraph reflecting on this process. Consider the similarities and differences you observed among the paragraphs and the things that surprised you. Make a note of the challenges you faced as you drafted your paragraphs and how you responded to those challenges. List the strategies you plan to use next time you write for a specific audience.

4. Consider context and genre.

As earlier sections on addressing an academic audience have implied, the *context* (or setting) in which your text is to be read will affect all your writing decisions. So, too, will the *genre* (or type) of writing you produce.

The contexts in which you are likely to write, now and in the future, are *academic, business, public,* and *personal*. Like academic writing, business writing generally adopts a formal level of diction and uses words with neutral connotations. Public writing, which ranges from blog posts to press releases and reports, generally maintains a formal level of diction (it is directed to a wide-ranging audience), but its tone may be more impassioned than would be appropriate in an academic or business context. An informal tone is most appropriate in a personal context, but even then, the audience makes a difference: A casual, bantering tone and highly informal level of diction might be appropriate in a text message to a friend, while a warm but slightly more formal tone might be appropriate for an e-mail to a grandparent. Nor is the distinction between public and private communications always clear: a post in a lifestyle blog might be public and widely circulated, but it might also be quite informal. Whenever you write in an unfamiliar context, consulting examples can help you hit the right note.

In literature classes, you may have learned that poetry, drama, fiction, and nonfiction were the four major literary genres, but genre extends beyond literature. If you are unfamiliar with the genre in which you will be writing, read several examples to determine what they have in common. This handbook contains sample documents in a variety of genres. Your instructor may also be able to provide examples, or you could locate examples in your library or on the Internet. Whether you are writing a business e-mail, a scientific report, a grant proposal, or a letter to the editor, the expectations readers have for this type of writing will affect every choice you make.

> *More about*
> Business writing,
>   497–518
> Public writing,
>   499–502

Student Models
Editorial (public), 12
Essay (academic),
   47–51, 101–06,
   131–34, 495–96,
Research project
   (academic), 349–62,
   396–405, 424–34,
   448–49, 481–89
Essay exam (aca-
   demic), 495–96
Memo (business),
   502–03
Résumés (business),
   508, 510
Business News Article
   (business), 515

Professional Models
Editorials (public),
   120–21
Article (public), 116–18
Review (public),
   472–474
Letter (business), 501
Press release (public),
   514

2b Analyzing an Assignment

Recognizing the purpose of an assignment is crucial to success. If you are asked to *argue* for or against the goals of the plain speech movement of the 1920s, for example, and, instead, you *describe* those goals, you will probably not get an *A*. When analyzing an assignment, look for words that indicate purpose.

The audience for an assignment is, of course, your instructor, and the instructor's goal in assigning the project is to assess your knowledge of the facts, to gauge how well you have synthesized this information with other knowledge, and to assess your ability to express your understanding in writing. Occasionally, your instructor may ask you to imagine another audience—the readership of a particular magazine, for example.

Frequently, an assignment will specify the approach you should take. If you are asked to analyze, your instructor will expect you to break a topic, issue, or text into its component parts and, perhaps, evaluate each one. If your instructor asks you to summarize a reading assignment, you will be expected to write the main idea and key supporting points briefly, in your own words and using your own sentence structures.

Sometimes, an assignment will specify the genre, although the genre may be taken for granted. A biology instructor teaching a laboratory class may assume that you understand that a laboratory report is required. If you are not sure what the genre of the assignment is, or what it requires, ask your instructor.

> **More about**
> Analyzing,
> 124–26, 271–73
> Summarizing, 115

Quick Reference Analyzing the Purpose of an Assignment

If the assignment asks you to . . .	The purpose is . . .	The approach is . . .
describe, explain	informative (expository)	to put into words what something looks, sounds, feels, smells, or tastes like; to discuss *how* something functions
assess, evaluate, argue	persuasive	to make a judgment based on evidence or offer an interpretation based on close reading, and to explain *why*
analyze, consider, discuss	informative or persuasive	to break a topic, reading assignment, or issue into its component parts and explain how it works; to reflect critically on the pros and cons of an issue, offer an interpretation based on a close reading, and sometimes explain why you have reached this conclusion

Finally, an assignment will generally include a due date. In order to meet that date, you will have to create a realistic schedule. Start by listing the steps in the writing process in reverse order on a sheet of paper or in a new computer file so that you can work back from the due date. Next, list all your other obligations: other assignments, studying for exams, work, rehearsals or team practices, family and social obligations. Then work backward to figure out how much time you can allot to each task. The more obligations you have, the more time you will need to leave between steps. Finally, write the intermediate due dates on a calendar—a date book, the calendar on your computer, or your phone. For each of these due dates, write down not just the name of the project ("English paper") but also the specific action that you need to have taken by that date ("outline English paper"). A schedule for a five-page project that does not require research might look like that shown in Figure 2.1.

More about
Time management, 198
Online assignment calendar, 198

SEPTEMBER

Sunday	Monday	Tuesday	Wednesday	Thursday	Friday	Saturday
		19 Track meet	20	21 Comp. assignment distributed	22 Analyze Comp. assignment and writing situation	23 Work Date with the "girls"
24 Generate ideas, develop topic, draft thesis for comp. paper	25 Review notes, draft outline for comp. paper	26 Study for Econ quiz	27 Write first draft, make appt. at Writing Center	28 Econ quiz	29 Bring draft to class for peer review	30 Work

OCTOBER

Sunday	Monday	Tuesday	Wednesday	Thursday	Friday	Saturday
1 Lunch with Mom & Dad	2 Bring essay to Writing Center	3 Revise comp. essay	4	5	6 → Revise comp. essay	7 Work Proofread & edit comp. paper
8 Format & print comp. paper	9 Comp. paper due	10 Study for psych midterm	11	12	13 → Psych midterm!	14 Work

FIGURE 2.1 A sample calendar Your calendar will differ depending on the complexity of the assignment, the time you have to complete it, and your other obligations.

→ **EXERCISE 2.2 Analyzing an assignment**

Read the following assignments; indicate whether their purpose is informative, persuasive, or both; and underline the words that indicate purpose.

1. Describe two or three medical services available to families in your community, and explain how a family nurse-practitioner could use these services.
2. Evaluate the constitutionality of judicial review, explaining its origins and offering several examples from US Supreme Court decisions.
3. Analyze the impact an increase in the price of higher education in the United States would have on the market for higher education in India.
4. Assess the main arguments of Handlin's *Boston's Immigrants* (1941) in light of the other assigned course reading. Are they still persuasive? Why or why not?

Make It **Your Own**

For an upcoming writing assignment or one already under way, analyze the assignment and set up a schedule that takes into account all your other obligations.

2c Generating Ideas

For some writing projects, especially in college or business, your *topic* will often be assigned. When you are required to come up with a topic on your own, ask yourself these questions:

More about
Finding informa-
tion, 210–32
(ch. 13)
Reading and
thinking criti-
cally, 112–35
(ch. 7)

- What topics are appropriate to the assignment?
- What topics will interest, exasperate, or intrigue me *and* my reader?
- What topics do I have special access to or knowledge about?

You will be most engaged when you choose a topic that interests you, but your reader will be most engaged when you offer some special knowledge or insight into what you are writing about. You can create that special knowledge by doing research, but you can also create special knowledge by thinking critically about your topic.

Invention techniques, like those outlined below, can help you devise and develop a topic. No single strategy works for everyone, and most writers use several methods. If you have tried some of these before, experiment with the others. Drawing on new techniques may increase your creativity.

Generating Ideas in English or Your First Language If English is not your first language, you might find it helpful to keep a journal, freewrite, or brainstorm in English. If you get stuck, try using words and phrases from your first language. But be careful when returning to your notes to translate not merely your *words* but also your *ideas* into English appropriate for your readers.

1. Keep an idea journal or commonplace book.

In the nineteenth century, the philosopher Ralph Waldo Emerson wrote his essays from ideas he had jotted down in a notebook. In the twenty-first century, writers often use apps or online tools such as Evernote, Google Docs, or OneNote to store ideas. Whatever medium you use, you may find that keeping an *idea journal* or a *commonplace book* (or both) is an effective part of the creative process.

Like a diary, an idea journal is something to write in every day. Unlike a diary, it is not a record of your life but rather of your thoughts. A commonplace book records the ideas (quotations, summaries, paraphrases) of others that you might find useful in the future. You can also use your commonplace book to record your reactions to those ideas. As you jot notes in your commonplace book, record your sources and use quotation marks to separate carefully the words of others from your own.

> *More about*
> Keeping a reading journal, 121–23
> Keeping a research log, 202–03

> *More about*
> Avoiding accidental plagiarism, 251–52, 253–57

Writing Responsibly Note Taking and Plagiarism

Many people have unintentionally plagiarized sources because of a faulty note-taking system, saying that they did not record the source when taking notes or that they failed to put quotation marks around passages they copied. To avoid finding yourself in such a situation, consider putting all quotations, summaries, and paraphrases in one column of your journal or commonplace book and your own comments and reactions in another. That way, even if you forget to put quotation marks around a quotation or to record a page number, you will not be lulled into believing the words or ideas were your own—and your sources will get proper credit.

to OTHER WRITERS

Make It **Your Own**

Keep an idea journal for one week. Write in it daily about the topics discussed in your classes, and at the end of the week read through your notes. What topics have arisen repeatedly? Which are most engaging? What ideas could be developed into a project?

2. Freewrite.

Have you ever found yourself sitting in front of a blank screen, knowing you had to begin writing but just not being able to get started? Try *freewriting:* writing the first thing that enters your head and then continuing to write nonstop for ten to fifteen minutes (or for a set number of pages). What you write about does not matter; if you draw a blank, just write (or type) the same word over and over again until something comes to you.

To be useful, freewriting must be fast and spontaneous. If you find that you cannot resist correcting and revising, turn the brightness down until your screen is very dim or even black. Here is a sample of freewriting for Michael Wedd's essay:

Student Model **Freewrite**

> Drawing a blank about what to write about. Maybe should go to the park
> for a run. Need to figure out schedule for next sem. Can't decide b/w bio
> and environ science. Oooh, that reminds me I need to find out if I can
> recycle my old notebooks somewhere.

Once the time has elapsed, read through what you wrote. Even among random thoughts you might find a usable idea. Michael Wedd's essay topic—the environmental movement—appears in this freewriting snippet, for example. But the exercise is also beneficial for freeing the mind and exorcising writer's block.

A variation of freewriting is *focused freewriting.* Instead of starting from the first idea to pop into your head, start from something specific: your topic, a quotation, a memory, an image. If you stray from the topic, just keep writing, trying to circle back to it.

3. Brainstorm

Brainstorming (or *listing*) is writing down everything you can think of on a topic. Brainstorming helps get ideas percolating and provides a record of that percolation. Here is a snippet of Michael Wedd's brainstorm on the environmental movement:

Student Model Brainstorm

- *Types of alternative energy: solar, wind, hydro.*
- *Advantages/disadvantages of each.*
- *Alt energy may benefit consumers; might harm wildlife.*
- *Who is for it, against it. Their different arguments.*
- *Where is alt energy movement strongest, weakest? Why?*
- *Why alternatives to fossil fuels needed.*
- *History of oil exploration and development of alternatives.*

After you have amassed a useful number of items, sort through the material to make connections: Move items around or draw lines to connect related items. Then brainstorm about the idea groups that seem most important, interesting, or challenging.

4. Cluster.

Clustering (or *mapping*) is a visual method for identifying and developing ideas. To create a cluster or idea map, follow these steps:

1. Write your topic in the middle of the page, and draw a circle around it.
2. Write other ideas related to your topic around the central idea bubble, and draw a circle around each of those.
3. Draw connecting lines from the word bubbles to the central topic or to the other word bubbles to show the relationships among the ideas.

When creating a cluster, keep two things in mind:

1. Keep your topic and idea notes brief—if you write more than a word or two, the diagram will quickly become difficult to read.
2. Use a pencil—you will probably make many changes as you work.

The cluster diagram on the next page (Figure 2.2) shows some of Michael Wedd's ideas for his project on alternative energy.

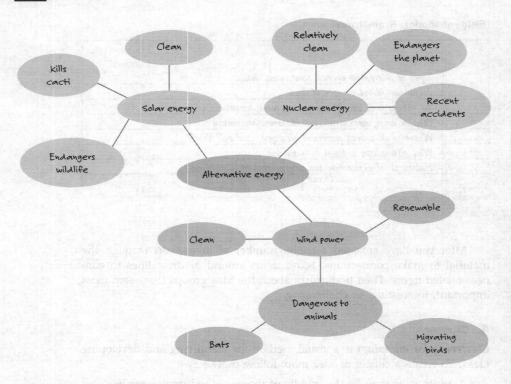

FIGURE 2.2 A sample cluster diagram

Tech	**Brainstorming with Word Clouds**

Your word choices echo the ideas and opinions that resonate most with you. You might process some of your early brainstorming through programs like Wordle, to get "word clouds" of your most frequently used words. The visualization of that information may help you figure out what you're emphasizing, which can help lead you to your thesis.

5. Answer the journalists' questions.

The *journalists' questions*—*who, what, where, when, why,* and *how*—not only can help you generate ideas about your topic but also can help you figure out what you need to learn in order to write the paper. When considering a topic, ask yourself questions like these:

- **Who** are the key figures?
- **What** did they accomplish, or what are the issues?
- **Where** and **when** did the main events occur?
- **Why** did they do what they did, or why did these events transpire as they did?
- **How** did it happen?

As a college student, you will also benefit from adding two additional questions to the journalists' list:

- What is the **significance**?
- What are the **consequences**?

The journalists' questions tailored to Michael Wedd's topic are shown in Figure 2.3.

Student Model Journalists' Questions

	Who is affected by the building of wind farms? Who will benefit from their being built?
	What other sources of energy do we have? What impact do they have on the environment? What impact will the wind farms have?
	Where are wind farms being built?
	When will the wind farms go online? When will the courts rule on the challenges to these wind farms?
	Why is there disagreement within the environmental community about whether wind farms should be built?
	How will the issues be resolved? How can animals be protected?

FIGURE 2.3 **The journalists' questions**

6. Discuss your topics with friends and classmates.

Sometimes just batting ideas around with friends or classmates can help you generate ideas. This can be as casual as a late-night chat with your roommate or texting with a friend ("What do you think about . . . ?"), or it can be as formal as a scheduled brainstorming session with a collaborative writing group. Whatever approach you take, keep the discussion open enough that people feel free to speak their minds but focused enough that your discussion does not drift too far from your topic, and always be ready to record ideas.

7. Use the Internet, the library, and classroom tools.

More about
Blogs, 217–18
Evaluating
  online sources,
  239–43

Surfing the Internet can provide direction and stimulate ideas when you are faced with a new topic. Start by searching a *subject directory,* a collection of websites organized into groups by topic and arranged hierarchically from most general to most specific to get a sense of the range of related subtopics. Subject directories are useful for narrowing or expanding your topic. For very current topics, searching a news site or locating a specialized blog can also be useful.

The reference sources provided by your college library are another resource for generating ideas. Browse through general encyclopedias and dictionaries to get a sense of how your topic is usually discussed, or turn to specialized dictionaries or encyclopedias to get a more detailed introduction. Some reference sources may be available online through your college library's website.

More about
Reference
  sources, 210–14

Finally, because you will often be writing about topics that were introduced in class, you can get ideas often by reading (or rereading) course materials, such as your textbook, class notes, and any handouts your instructor has distributed. Any of these may provide context or help you identify a topic that interests you.

More about
Note taking,
  124–31, 251–52
Annotating,
  118–21

Make It **Your Own**

Use focused freewriting, brainstorming, or clustering to develop one of the ideas that came out of your weeklong experiment with keeping an idea journal (p. 25) or an idea from the reading in one of your classes.

2d Narrowing or Broadening a Topic

Once you have devised a topic, consider whether you can do justice to it in the assigned length. In most cases, you will need to narrow your topic further; occasionally, you may have to broaden it.

1. Narrow your topic.

To narrow an overly general topic, use brainstorming or one of the other idea-generating techniques to develop a list of subtopics. Michael Wedd wanted to write about alternative energy, but the topic was so big, he could not cover it in a three- to five-page project; he had to narrow it. Some of his possible subtopics are listed in the brainstorming example below.

Student Model **Brainstorm**

	The green movement has been around for a while but has been gaining in recognition in recent years.
	Many aspects of the green/environmentalist movement: climate change, preservation, endangered species, alternatives to fossil fuels, etc.
	People can feel very strongly about these issues. Some modify how they eat and what they buy; some join groups like Greenpeace and are willing to be arrested and/or put themselves in danger to fight for change.
	Are there conflicts within the green movement? What might they entail?

2. Broaden your topic.

While you are much more likely to have to narrow your topic, you may occasionally find yourself struggling to come up with something to say about the topic you have selected, in which case your topic may be too narrow. If, for example, you were thinking about exploring whether social workers in your town are pressured to overreport their contact hours with Medicare patients, but you were finding too little research on this topic, you could broaden your topic by expanding the region (from social workers in your town to social workers throughout the country), or you could broaden the type of caregivers you studied by including medical personnel (doctors, nurses, and technicians) and social workers. The idea-generating techniques discussed in *section 2c* can help you broaden, as well as narrow, your topic.

2e Working with Others: Planning a Collaborative Project

In academic and professional contexts, collaborative work is common. Working in a group can be challenging, but there are several steps you can take to make collaborative work more satisfying and less frustrating.

1. Form a cohesive group.

Start group projects by establishing rapport. A few small steps taken at the outset can help:

- Meet face-to-face, at least at the start.
- Start your first meeting by having group members introduce themselves and mention some detail—hometown, favorite book, a special interest or talent—to help everyone get to know one another.
- Make an effort to learn everyone's name.
- Discuss members' skills and challenges. Learn what each member brings to the project: Is there a good proofreader in the group? A good designer? A good researcher? A good organizer? Consider, as well, accessibility issues within the group: Do any members have physical limitations that should be taken into account when assigning duties and schedules?
- Distribute the contact information, such as e-mail addresses and phone numbers (with best times to call), for every group member at the end of the first session.

2. Anticipate pitfalls.

Anyone who has participated in a collaborative project knows that pitfalls abound: One person is consistently late, another lets other team members do all the work, a third dominates the proceedings, and a fourth is resentful but never says a word. Before starting a project, work together to figure out the likely pitfalls and to decide in advance how the group will respond:

- What will you do if someone does not complete assigned work?
- What will you do if someone does assigned work badly?
- How will you want the instructor to grade the completed project, if it is a class assignment?

Once you have developed a list of potential problems and how the group will resolve them, put it in writing, have everybody sign the document, and distribute copies to all members. This written agreement not only will provide a record but also will remind all members of their responsibilities to the group. If something does go wrong, address the problem immediately; do not let it fester.

self

Assessment

To ensure your group is effective, pause regularly to reflect on every member's contribution. Be sure every member participates in the following tasks:

- ☐ Deciding on a topic
- ☐ Drafting a thesis statement
- ☐ Brainstorming ideas
- ☐ Organizing the project
- ☐ Assigning tasks

3. Devise a schedule and assign tasks.

The writing process for individual projects applies to collaborative projects as well. Some additional steps include the following:

- Select a recorder. That role can be performed by one person or can rotate among group members.

- Brainstorm project ideas, making sure everyone participates.

- List component tasks (such as coordinating the group; researching the topic; drafting, revising, and editing the text; identifying or creating appropriate visuals).

- Establish dates by which each task needs to be completed, and construct a timetable.

- Divide the work among group members, taking into account people's talents, interests, and schedules and the difficulty of each task. Keep in mind that some phases of the project should be done by the entire group. (See the Self-Assessment checklist above.)

- Plan periodic meetings to discuss progress and problems.

- Distribute a schedule of meetings and due dates.

> **More about**
Analyzing the writing situation, 13–21
Devising a topic, 24–30
Drafting, 44–47
Revising globally and locally, 88–95
Drafting and revising visuals, 79–87 (ch. 5)
Proofreading and formatting, 99–101

Text Credits

p. 16: Langewiesche, Willisam, *Sahara Unveiled: A Journey Across the Desert,* copyright © 1996 by William Langewiesche (Random House, 1996); Parker, Jo Goodwin, "What Is Poverty?" in *America's Other Children: Public Schools Outside Suburbia,* edited by George Henderson. (University of Oklahoma Press, 1971).

3 Organizing and Drafting Your Project

© epa european pressphoto agency b.v./ Alamy Stock Photo

Before producing a new line of clothing or an automobile, designers sketch the product, planning and arranging the shapes before dressing them in colors and textures. Writers, too, begin with a plan. They take into account the writing situation (purpose, audience, topic, context, and genre), then sketch their ideas in words and arrange them in sentences and paragraphs. Both designers and writers sometimes erase initial ideas and revise early efforts. For both, until that first sketch is penned, the finished work is merely an idea.

3a Crafting an Effective Thesis

A *thesis* is a brief statement (one or two sentences) of the central claim you will make. It gives your audience an indication of the focus and direction of your writing project. Drafting a preliminary thesis statement as early as possible and then testing, revising, and even replacing it as you learn more about your topic and develop your project will help you evaluate, focus, and clarify your ideas.

Stating the Main Idea In some contexts and cultures, it is appropriate to imply the main idea rather than state it explicitly. However, readers in the United States, especially in academic and business contexts, will usually expect you to express your main idea clearly and directly, usually at the beginning of your written document or project.

1. Devise a thesis statement.

Before you begin to draft a thesis, review your notes. Do any ideas jump out? If not, return to the idea-generating stage. If so, focus on an aspect of your topic that will engage you and your reader and that is appropriate to your purpose, context, and genre. Next, ask yourself probing questions about your topic and then answer them. Review your answers, looking for ones that identify your topic and make a claim about it. Choose one that will allow you to bring your own insights to the topic, and use that as your preliminary thesis. Here are some sample questions and answers, with the claim highlighted in yellow and the topic underlined:

> More about
> Generating ideas,
> 24–30

Questions	Answers
Should members of political parties be barred from overseeing presidential elections?	Members of political parties should be barred from overseeing presidential elections to avoid even the suspicion of electoral manipulation such as occurred in Florida in 2000 and Ohio in 2004.
What drove the ivory-billed woodpecker to near-extinction in the United States?	The direct effects of the two world wars led to the near-extinction of the ivory-billed woodpecker.
What kinds of privacy violations or other social mischief occur with social networking sites like Snapchat, Instagram, and Facebook?	Social networking sites open new avenues for privacy violations and other social dangers, such as publication of incriminating photographs, stalking, and contact with inappropriate new "friends."
What motivates students to plagiarize, and what can we do to reduce the number of incidents?	Reducing the incidents of plagiarism among college students requires understanding its causes, which include late-night desperation, fear of a bad grade, lack of interest in a course, ignorance of citation requirements, and societal norms.

Student Model
Exploratory argument:
"Why Students Cheat,"
Tom Hackman,
150–56

If you are not sure how to answer your question, use idea-generating techniques to develop possibilities.

> EXERCISE 3.1 Selecting a topic and developing a preliminary thesis

Make a list of at least five topics that interest you. Select two of the topics (or two from the following list) and write one or more questions for each. Then answer those questions to create a preliminary thesis.

Optional Topics

1. Violence in college sports
2. Compulsory military service

3. Standardized testing
4. Passenger screening in airports

Underline each of your two topics, and circle your claims.

2. Revise a thesis statement.

A well-crafted thesis statement should indicate your topic and make a claim that is appropriate to your purpose, and it should do so in language that will engage the reader. Only rarely does a writer accomplish all of these objectives in the first draft of the thesis. Most writers need to revise the thesis statement repeatedly as they draft.

Purpose: Informative The thesis of an *informative* essay makes a *claim of fact*, a claim that can be verified. To be engaging, an informative thesis must make a claim of fact that is not yet widely known to or accepted by the audience, and it must be specific enough that the writer can explore it in depth.

> *More about*
Claims of fact,
    140–41
Common knowl-
    edge, 250–51

DRAFT THESIS
Topic
This paper is about conflicts within the environmental movement.

This draft thesis establishes a topic but does not make a claim of fact, and it is far too general to explore in depth.

REVISION 1—FOR AN INFORMATIVE PROJECT
Topic
There are many conflicts within the environmental movement.

This thesis statement establishes the topic and makes a claim of fact, but the claim is too broad. Because the writer has not specified which conflicts she has in mind, she would potentially have to explain all possible conflicts within the environmental movement to satisfy the promise of the thesis.

self Assessment

When revising a thesis, ask yourself the following questions. If the answer to any question is no, make the revisions necessary to strengthen your thesis.

- ☐ Does your thesis identify your **topic**?
- ☐ Does it indicate your **purpose** (informative or persuasive)?
- ☐ Does it make a **claim** (or assertion) that you can support—a claim of fact (a verifiable issue) for an informative project, or a claim of judgment or value (a belief or opinion that can be supported by evidence) for a persuasive project?
- ☐ Will it **interest** your readers?

REVISION 2—FOR AN INFORMATIVE PROJECT

Among the conflicts within the environmental movement is that between those who want to reduce global warming by replacing fossil fuels with alternatives like wind energy and solar energy, and those who fear that new energy-generating plants will harm local wildlife.

Topic

The thesis statement now narrows the claim—makes it specific—so that it focuses solely on one area of conflict within the environmental movement. It will intrigue readers interested in environmental issues and will inform those who know little about the conflicts.

Purpose: Persuasive The thesis of a *persuasive* writing project must make a *claim of value* (a belief about the way the world should be) or *judgment* (an opinion or a provisional decision that is not widely shared). The claim must be one that can be supported with evidence. The revised informative thesis above clearly specifies a topic and will probably intrigue readers, but it is not appropriate for a persuasive project because it makes a claim of fact, not a claim of value or judgment.

> *More about*
> Claims of value,
> 141
> Claims of judg-
> ment, 142–44

REVISION 3—FOR A PERSUASIVE PROJECT

As serious and time-sensitive as the issue of climate change is, alternative energy is not a solution if it will be just as harmful to wildlife as conventional energy.

Topic

This thesis still specifies the topic, but it now also makes a *claim of judgment* ("alternative energy is not a solution"). Because it is narrow, focusing on just one issue ("alternative energy [that] is . . . harmful to wildlife"), it can be explained in a brief essay. And because it demonstrates the importance of the topic ("As serious and time-sensitive as the issue of climate change is"), it is likely to interest readers.

Because it makes clear that there are multiple legitimate opinions about the issue, it invites readers to engage with the problem.

Your thesis statement should focus on a claim you can support and that will interest your reader. Evaluate whether the evidence you provide for your thesis statement actually supports the claim. If it does not, either find more pertinent evidence or revise your thesis statement so that it is supported by your evidence. Also consider the counterevidence to your claim: information or perspectives that contradict it or doubts you have about it. Is the counterevidence more credible than the evidence? If so, you may want to change your claim.

> **EXERCISE 3.2 Revising a thesis statement**
>
> Revise the thesis statements you drafted in Exercise 3.1, and explain why you made your revisions.

┌─ Make It **Your Own** ──────────────────────────────────────┐

For a project that you are currently working on in this or another class, draft and revise your thesis statement so that it makes a claim you can support convincingly.

└──┘

More about
Reorganizing a
draft, 89–92

3b Organizing Your Ideas

Most writing projects will be improved by your attention to organization both *before* and *after* the first draft. Organizing beforehand makes the project easier to draft; reviewing the structure after you have written a draft can show you where your thesis needs more evidence or explanation, whether the project is logically organized, and whether any of the evidence is irrelevant or insufficient.

1. Review your prewriting and make a list of ideas.

More about
Keeping a
  journal, 25
Freewriting, 26
Brainstorming,
  26–27
Clustering, 27–28
Journalists' questions, 28–29

Start organizing by reviewing all the preparatory writing you have done. Then write your preliminary thesis statement at the top of a clean sheet of paper or in a new electronic document. Below the thesis statement, list all the reasons you believe it is true or at least plausible.

2. Arrange your ideas into logical groupings.

More about
Cluster diagrams,
28

Read through your list of reasons for believing your thesis. How are they related? Create a cluster diagram or table to group ideas by topic. Or create a *tree diagram* to arrange ideas from most general to most specific: Write your main idea at the top of the page and let subsequent ideas branch off below it (Figure 3.1).

3. Consider your project's overall shape.

More about
Organizing para-
graphs, 55–57,
66–68

Essays and many other writing projects typically have three basic parts:

- Introduction
- Body
- Conclusion

FIGURE 3.1 **Tree diagram** A tree diagram can help you organize your thoughts before you begin writing.

In its simplest form, the typical essay becomes a "five-paragraph theme": one paragraph for the introduction, three for the body, and one for the conclusion. Of course, college writing seldom takes such a tidy form. Instead, it is more likely to unfold in this manner:

Introduction   The introduction is typically brief (one to three paragraphs, depending on the overall length of the project). Often the thesis statement appears in the introduction, where it can shape the reader's expectations of what follows. What goes into the introduction depends on your purpose, audience, context, and genre, but it should entice readers to carry on and should prepare them for what follows.

> **More about**
> Writing the introduction, 69–71

Body   The body is the longest portion of the project, with its length depending on the complexity of ideas being conveyed and the amount of explanation needed to convince the audience. Each paragraph in the body should typically make one main point, expressed in a topic sentence. The body paragraphs should supply explanations and evidence that support the topic sentence; and each topic sentence should support or develop the thesis. In most types of academic writing, counterevidence is included in the body: explain why, although it is credible, you find the evidence more convincing.

> **More about**
> Relevance, 53, 233–34
> Unity, 53–58
> Coherence, 58–65
> Development, 65–69
> Evidence, 45–47
> Conclusion, 71–75

Conclusion   Like the introduction, the conclusion is usually rather brief (one to three paragraphs, depending on the length of the project). Just as the introduction should entice readers, so the conclusion should convince them that they have spent their time well.

4. Choose an organizational strategy.

Once you have collected and organized your notes, choose the order in which to present your ideas that best fits your thesis and supporting materials. One or more of the following basic organizational patterns may provide useful models for you:

More about
Description, 65
Narration, 66
Exemplification, 65–66
Comparison-contrast, 66–68
Cause-effect, 68
Analysis, 68
Definition, 68–69

Chronological organization Use *chronological* (or *time*) order to tell a story (narrative) or explain a process (process analysis).

Spatial organization Organize your project spatially—from left to right, inside to outside, top to bottom—when describing a scene or structure.

Logical organization This is probably the most common organizational scheme for academic projects: Begin with an introduction that includes a general statement—the thesis—and then proceed to the body, where specific evidence is provided. With indifferent or skeptical readers, consider reversing this order: Begin with something specific—an interesting anecdote, some dramatic statistics, a provocative illustration—that will gain your audience's interest, attention, or sympathy, and then move on to the general conclusion.

If you are writing for an audience likely to balk when faced with new ideas or ideas that challenge their beliefs, organize your project from *familiar to unfamiliar*. To startle your readers into seeing a familiar issue in a new light, use *unfamiliar-to-familiar order*.

You may choose to organize your body paragraphs in *climactic order*, from least to most exciting. You might even save your thesis until the end.

EXERCISE 3.3 Reviewing organizational strategies

Read the student models beginning on pages 41 and 42. What organizational strategies does each use? What organizational changes would you recommend?

5. Choose an outlining technique that is appropriate for you.

Outlines, whether formal or informal, not only guide you as you draft, but also allow you to experiment with ways of sequencing your supporting paragraphs.

An informal outline An *informal* (or *scratch*) *outline* is simply a list of the ideas in your project in the order you want to present them. You can jot down your ideas in words, phrases, complete sentences, even pictures—whatever you need to jog your memory about what to put next. Here is a sample scratch outline for Michael Wedd's draft essay on conflicts within the environmental movement.

Student Model Informal (or Scratch) Outline

Intro
Green/environmental movement: brief explanation
Growing importance and awareness in recent years → conflict within the movement about how to handle these issues
Thesis: A major goal of the green movement is to find fossil fuel alternatives, but some members are concerned that wind, solar, and nuclear power sites will also harm the environment.
Body
Benefits/importance of alternative energy: types of alternative fuel being proposed: wind, solar, nuclear
Problems with alternative energy sources: harmful to animals, their habitats, and safety for humans
Conclusion
Conflicts might be inevitable, but we have to move forward, find creative compromises, use less energy

A formal outline (topic or sentence) A *formal outline* uses roman numerals (I, II, III), capital letters (A, B, C), arabic numerals (1, 2, 3), lowercase letters (a, b, c), and indentions of five spaces (or half an inch) to indicate level of generality, with roman numeral headings being most general and lowercase letters most specific. Each level of a formal outline should include at least two entries.

A *topic outline* uses words and phrases to indicate the ideas to be discussed. A *sentence outline* uses complete sentences. Some writers prefer a topic outline because it is easier to construct. Others prefer a sentence outline because it provides a starting point for drafting. Which type of outline you choose depends entirely on your own preferences, the complexity of your project, and your instructor's expectations.

> Student Models
> Essays by Michael Wedd:
> First draft, "Issues with Alternative Energy," 47–51
> Final draft, "Rethinking Alternative Energy," 101–06

Student Models Topic Outline and Sentence Outline

Compare a section of a topic outline with a section of a sentence outline for a later draft of Michael Wedd's essay:

Thesis: A major goal of the green movement is to find fossil fuel alternatives, but some members are concerned that wind, solar, and nuclear power sites will also harm the environment.

Topic Outline

I. Changing perspectives on alternative energy to include risks as well as benefits

   A. Benefits of alternative fuel
      1. Fewer greenhouse gas emissions/less warming
      2. Sustainable renewable energy sources: the sun, wind, and water

   B. Drawbacks
      1. Bad for environment: scenery, humans
      2. Destruction of animal habitats, extinction
      3. Future problems unknown without tests

Sentence Outline

I. The issue of global warming is urgent and serious, but we ought to consider the costs of alternative energy production that we deploy

   A. There are numerous potential benefits of using alternative fuel sources.
      1. Alternative energy produces fewer carbon dioxide and other greenhouse gas emissions, improving air quality and slowing the rate of global warming.
      2. Renewable energy sources, including the sun, wind, and water, are sustainable; they cannot be depleted and therefore can be used for the foreseeable future.

   B. Although there are many advantages to alternative fuel sources, there are drawbacks as well.
      1. New structures can have negative consequences on their surroundings, ranging from ruining picturesque views to endangering human health.
      2. Animal habitats may be destroyed, leading to extinction of species.
      3. The long-term effects of building new facilities is still largely unknown and could present even greater problems in the future.

6. Check your outline for unity and coherence.

Once you have completed your outline, review it critically for *unity* and *coherence*. Unity is achieved when all the supporting paragraphs are relevant to the thesis and when all the evidence and explanations are relevant to the main idea of the supporting paragraph. Coherence is achieved when the supporting paragraphs, with all their evidence and explanations, are organized logically so that readers can move from idea to idea without having to pause to figure out the relationships among the parts.

More about
Coherence,
58–65
Unity, 53–58

➤ EXERCISE 3.4 Creating an informal outline

Using the thesis statement below, arrange the ideas in the list that follows into an informal (or scratch) outline for an essay.

Thesis: Effectively combating plagiarism, in all its forms, requires a fuller understanding of how and why students break the rules.

List of Ideas

- Many honest students plagiarize accidentally because they don't know the rules.
- One commonly held myth is that plagiarism is the result of slothfulness.
- The Internet makes it harder for students to separate their words from those of others and to keep track of where ideas come from.
- Some students plagiarize because they lack interest in the course or paper topic.
- What is considered acceptable source use in some cultures is called plagiarism in others.
- Plagiarism is often treated as a crime committed through laziness.
- High-achieving students sometimes plagiarize to maintain high grades.

➤ EXERCISE 3.5 Creating a topic outline

Use the ideas in Exercise 3.4 to create a formal topic outline. Then compare the two outlines you created for this list of ideas and note how they differ. Review them for unity and coherence; then write a paragraph describing other possible organizations you could have used and explaining why you selected these.

3c Preparing to Draft

When the moment comes to combine words and sentences into paragraphs and paragraphs into a draft of your project, set aside some time and find a place where you can concentrate. Begin drafting by reviewing the writing you have done while generating ideas, drafting your thesis, and creating an outline. Even in the best circumstances, you may encounter writer's block, but by using appropriate techniques, you should be able to get past it. If you get stuck, try the strategies outlined in the Quick Reference box on page 45.

1. Get ready: Allocate enough time and find a good place to write.

Ideally, set aside a substantial block of time for writing your first draft. How you define *substantial* depends on how long or complex your project will be: An hour or two might be enough for a three- to five-page essay; a longer project will require more. If you are unable to find an uninterrupted block of time, work in smaller chunks over several days. Do not delay starting just because you have only short bits of time available.

Next, consider what place is best for you: a study carrel in the library or a table at a sidewalk café? Whatever your preference, focus on the task at hand by turning off your phone and closing your Internet browser.

2. Start writing.

The writing you have done while analyzing your writing situation and devising your topic, drafting your thesis, and organizing your ideas will provide you with a starting point. Begin by reviewing this material, and then try one of the following methods (or a combination of them):

- **Method 1: Fill in your outline.** Use your outline as scaffolding, filling it in and fleshing it out until it becomes a first draft.

- **Method 2: Start with what you have.** Instead of beginning at the beginning, start writing whatever parts of the project you feel confident about—an interesting example, a descriptive passage in support of one of your ideas, or even just a sentence or a phrase that captures a relevant thought. Continue writing out-of-order thoughts until you can stitch them together and fill in the gaps.

- **Method 3: Write straight from your brain.** Type your thesis statement at the top of a computer file, and then just start writing. This may produce a very brief, general first draft, but it will be one that actually speaks from what you have to say. You can supplement it later.

Whatever method you choose, do not worry about the language you use to present your ideas. Just get words on paper. You can smooth out the kinks later, when you revise and edit.

3. Overcome writer's block.

Gene Fowler—a newspaper columnist, novelist, and screenwriter—once said, "Writing is easy: All you do is sit staring at a blank sheet of paper until drops of blood form on your forehead." Fortunately, there are techniques to help you avoid writing trauma.

Quick

Reference   Overcoming Writer's Block

- **Take a break.** Doing something else, like taking a walk or doing your laundry, can help.
- **Write something else.** Just the act of writing can help unblock you.
- **Write what you can.** You do not have to start at the beginning and keep writing until you get to the conclusion. Instead, write the parts you *can* write, even if you cannot yet string them together.
- **Start from what you already have.** Use your outline, brainstorming, and other notes to jump-start your writing.
- **Write a message to yourself.** Write a note to yourself: "What I want to say is . . . ," and then finish the sentence.
- **Talk, text, or e-mail.** Tell a tutor, instructor, classmate, or friend what your project will be about. Then use your own words as a starting point for writing.
- **Change your situation.** Switch media—from pencil and paper to word processor, or vice versa—or change the setting in which you are writing.
- **Avoid perfection.** It is the rare writer who produces a masterpiece on the first try. If you cannot avoid focusing on problems, turn off your computer screen so that you cannot see what you have written until it is time to start revising.

> *More about*
> Finding information, 210–32 (ch. 13)

3d Drafting: Explaining and Supporting Your Ideas

To draft a thesis statement for your project, you asked yourself a question and wrote a tentative answer. The body of your project will explain *why* you believe that your answer is true and why your readers should agree with you. The topic sentence (or main idea) in each supporting paragraph will form the backbone of your project, and your evidence and counterevidence will be the flesh that covers the skeleton.

Specific evidence is needed to make your writing convincing and interesting. Some kinds of evidence you can draw on include the following:

- Facts and statistics
- Expert opinion
- Examples
- Observations
- Case studies
- Anecdotes
- Passages from the text you are studying

Writing Responsibly — Made-up Evidence

In 2014, two stem cell experts resigned their positions at the Riken Center for Developmental Biology, one of Japan's leading research institutes, following revelations by the journal *Nature* that their lab had falsified data; one of the researchers later committed suicide. A few years earlier, noted anesthesiologist Scott S. Rubin had been fired by Massachusetts' Baystate Medical Center, then sent to prison and ordered to pay $420,000 in restitution, for falsifying data. Such punishments are increasingly common, but, as the more recent Riken incident shows, they are not always a deterrent. Millions of research dollars have been wasted, professional reputations destroyed, and hopes for cures dashed by scientists who faked results in studies on challenges as diverse as cancer, AIDS vaccines, obesity, and pain treatment. Commentators have noted that competition is often a factor in such cases. For too many professionals, the desire for acclaim has become more important than the desire for truth.

The highly competitive academic environment may tempt you, too, to make up "facts" to support a thesis in a project. It is easy to alter data, invent statistics or quotations, or manipulate an image so that it "shows" what you want it to. Resist the temptation: The short-term benefits are not worth it. Not only are you likely to get caught—fabricated evidence often *sounds* fake—but you are also sacrificing the opportunity to learn something about your topic and about the writing process.

to TOPIC

The paragraph below uses facts and examples:

Topic sentence

Support: Facts/ Examples

The physical demands on competitive cyclists are immense. One day, they will have to ride two hundred kilometres through the mountains; the next day there might be a long, flat sprint lasting seven hours. Because cyclists have such a low percentage of body fat, they are more susceptible to infections than other people. (At the beginning of the Tour, Armstrong's body fat is around four or five percent; this season Shaquille O'Neal, the most powerful player in the N.B.A., boasted that his body-fat level was sixteen percent.)

—Michael Specter, "The Long Ride," *The New Yorker*

This paragraph uses facts and statistics:

> One of the most important, if often unnoticed, features of American life in the late twentieth century was the aging of the American population. After decades of steady growth, the nation's birth rate began to decline in the 1970s and remained low through the 1980s and 1990s. In 1970, there were 18.4 births for every 1,000 people in the population. By 1996, the rate had dropped to 14.8 births. The declining birth rate and a significant rise in life expectancy produced a substantial increase in the proportion of elderly citizens. Almost 13 percent of the population was more than sixty-five years old in 2000, as compared with 8 percent in 1970. The median age in 2000 was 35.3, the highest in the nation's history. In 1970, it was 28.0.
> —Alan Brinkley, *American History: A Survey*

Topic sentence

Support: Facts and statistics

As you draft, ask yourself: Have I supplied *enough* evidence to persuade my reader? Does the evidence convincingly explain my belief in the thesis?

> **More about**
> Relevance, 53,
> 233–34

Tech **Protecting Your Work**

Because terrible things happen to computer files all the time, it is important to **save early and often,** and to **save your file in multiple locations:** Copy it to a secure location in the cloud, save it on a flash drive, or e-mail a copy to yourself. Remember to date each version of a file so you know which is the most recent and so you have a backup of your research.

 EXERCISE 3.6 Analyzing evidence

Analyze the two sample paragraphs in this section and list the types of evidence provided. Note whether there is sufficient evidence to support the topic sentence and explain your response.

Make It **Your Own**

For a project that you are working on, produce a first draft using one of the drafting methods described in this section.

Student Model First Draft

The first draft of Michael Wedd's essay on conflict within the environmental movement appears on the pages that follow. Note that in this draft he does not worry about polished writing or even perfect grammar and spelling. He knows he can make changes as he revises. For now, his focus is on getting his ideas down in a logical order and on supporting his thesis. Consider what he will need to do as he revises to fulfill his responsibilities to his reader, his topic, other writers, and himself.

Student Model
Draft thesis, 35
Revised thesis, 36–38
Outlines, 40–42
Final draft, 101–106

Michael Wedd

Professor Dunn

English 102

19 Sept. 2016

Issues with Alternative Energy

The rise of Alternative Energy Industries has been challenging, controversial, and turbulent these days. With the availability of many forms of alternative energy systems globally (wind, solar, nuclearetc.), it is worth pausing for a minute to ask some questions. People are talking at many levels of society about both the costs and the benefits of alternative energy. The problematic relationships between Alternative Energy Industries and the things they claim to be protecting are emerging as a key focus of these debates.

Environmentalists are conflicted when it comes to alternative energy. Most agree that fossil-fuel-based power plants are damaging the climate and making life harder for many of the worlds species. One of the primary benefits of alternative energy sources is that they are in practically limitless supply. They are producing energy all the time anyways. Obvious benefits aside, the structures needed to produce these forms of alternative energy can have bad affects on their surrounding environments (Pulitzer, Cherry, DW, McCurry). The issue of global warming is urgent and serious and we ought to consider the costs of alternative energy production that we deploy. Alternative energy might be putting the environment in danger. Maybe its time to question the way we as a society use these alternatives.

First draft, so not concerned with spelling, style, grammar, or title

Thesis statement makes a claim of fact, appropriate if purpose is informative but not if purpose is persuasive.

Facts and specifics needed to better support writer's points

Sources cited even in first draft

Topic sentence introduces first example and prepares reader for discussion about problems with wind energy.

Wind energy seems to be a harmless, passive, and effective way of producing energy, but upon closer inspection it also has its drawbacks. Wind turbines are killing birds and other airborne creatures at fast rate. A report by *The American Bird Conservancy* states that "[t]he United States now has 48,000 wind turbines installed from coast to coast, with many more planned. Those turbines killed nearly 600,000 birds in 2012, from Golden Eagles to migratory songbirds" ("Bird Strikes"). These wind turbines reach hundreds of feet into the air and threaten birds. By 2030, "a ten-fold increase in turbines is expected to boost annual bird mortality to 1.4 to 2 million."

Quotation not cited.

Topic sentence introduces an example of another kind of alternative fuel: solar energy

Solar energy is another alternative that at first seems benign but is actually putting airborne wildlife in grave danger. At the $2.2 billion-dollar Ivanpah solar facility in the CA desert, which is part of the largest solar energy complex in the world, birds are being burn mid-flight and plummeting to earth like meteorites. A report by the Pulitzer Center states that "[u]nsuspecting birds fly through Ivanpah's airspace, where the superheated air between the heliostats and the towers can reach temperatures as high as 900 degrees Fahrenheit. flesh catches fire as the birds are ignited in midair" (Pulitzer). The way we are generating solar electricity is producing high risks for a number of animals.

Abbreviations generally avoided in prose

Topic sentence introduces discussion of nuclear fuel, with its advantages and disadvantages.

The most controversial of these alternative energy sources is the atom. Japan's 2011 Fukushima nuclear meltdown is still recent. Naoto Kan believes that the Japanese gov. isn't taking the dangers of nuclear power seriously enough after the recent meltdown. He was quoted in *Deutche Welle* saying, "Unfortunately, I have the impression that neither the Japanese public nor the experts have learned the right lessons from the disaster" (DW). We must carefully consider the dangers of nuclear power before embracing it as the clean energy of the future.

People acknowledge how important it is to check global warming and diversify our energy portfolio, but it is crucial that we also protect the flora and fauna with which we share this planet. It's not enough to be environmentally conscious about the sources from which we draw our energy; we also need to be careful about how we harvest from them. The solution to this will have to include ideas for not only increasing renewable energy production safely but also of reducing global consumption equilaterally.

Conclusion

Contractions may be too informal for college writing.

Works Cited

Bird Strikes. American Bird Conservancy.

"The Fall Of Icarus: Ivanpah's Solar Controversy." *Pulitzer Center*.

"Former Japanese PM Naoto kan: 'Fukushima radically changed my Perspective' Asia *DW.COM* 25.02.2015. DW.COM.

Mccurry, Justin. "Japan Restarts First Nuclear Reactor since Fukushima Disaster." The Guardian August 11th, 2015. *The Guardian*.

Cites sources even in first draft

Citations need revision to follow MLA style.

➤ EXERCISE 3.7 Analyzing a draft

Create a topic outline for Michael Wedd's draft above. (Tip: Outlines of the first part of his draft appear on pages 41 and 42.) Based on your outline, how unified is his draft? How cohesive is it? Now consider the evidence he provides: Is there enough? Is it specific enough?

3e Writing with Others: Collaborative Projects

The work of many academic courses is conducted collaboratively, as are many workplace writing projects. Collaboration may mean that each team member is responsible for a separate part of the project, but often projects are *coauthored:* Group members work together to draft a thesis, devise an outline, and even write the text.

Drafting collaboratively can be a difficult process to manage, but it can also be rewarding and creative. The following principles will help keep the experience a happy one:

- If possible, keep groups small; smaller groups can reach the "critical mass" needed for creativity without the many management difficulties (such as finding a time to meet) that larger groups face.

- As with planning, it is important to the drafting process that each member has an opportunity to contribute. Make an effort to restrain overbearing members and to encourage reluctant participants.

- Treat everyone's writing respectfully. Some group members may be more skilled than others, but insightful ideas may be coaxed from initially unimpressive material.

- Whether your group is collaborating over e-mail or courseware such as Blackboard, in a Google Hangout, or face-to-face, make sure everyone has a copy of the latest draft and schedule following each session.

> *More about*
> Planning a collaborative project,
> 31–33
> Peer response,
> 96–98

┌ Make It **Your Own** ─────

Use the material in this chapter to analyze a project you are working on or have recently completed. Identify the thesis statement or main idea; then analyze how well each paragraph supports it. Does the evidence support each paragraph's main point? If so, write a note in the margin explaining how; if not, revise the paragraph. Finally, make a topic outline and use it to check for unity and cohesion.

Text Credits

p. 46: Specter, Michael, "The Long Ride," *The New Yorker,* July 15, 2002; **p. 47:** Brinkley, Alan, *American History: A Survey,* 13th Edition. (New York: McGraw-Hill Education, 2008); **p. 48:** Courtesy of Michael Wedd.

4 Crafting and Connecting Paragraphs

© SuperStock/Getty

American landscape architect Frederick Law Olmsted understood that an alluring landscape consists of more than just individual trees, flowers, and lawns. "Service must precede art," he said, arguing that city parks had to be functional as well as beautiful. He created, out of rough Manhattan farmland, a deceptively natural-looking oasis that appears always to have been there. Olmsted's hills and bridges, paths and ponds were as essential to Central Park as the park itself became to the city of New York.

Similarly, a writing project will be most effective—and a pleasure to read—when each paragraph is essential to the whole. When is a paragraph essential? It is essential when it is relevant, unified, coherent, well developed, interesting, and carefully connected to the paragraphs that come before and after it. A paragraph will be an essential part of the whole when it is all of the following:

- **Relevant.** It should support the main claim of the project (the *thesis*) and, when needed, remind readers of what that thesis is and how this paragraph supports it.

- **Unified.** It should have a clear point (*topic*) and include only the material that explains that point.

- **Coherent.** It should include connections that make clear how the sentences are related to each other.

- **Well developed.** It should supply the information your readers need to be persuaded of your claim.

- **Connected.** It should begin and end so that your readers can see how it relates to the paragraphs that precede and follow it.

- **Interesting.** It should make your readers want to move on to the next paragraph and follow the development of your ideas.

4a Writing Relevant Paragraphs

A *relevant* paragraph not only describes the general topic of your project but also contributes to the reader's understanding of or belief in the main claim of the project (the *thesis*). Compare this paragraph to the essay's thesis:

> Second, by calling hip-hop a "lethal genre," Staples places it into a category separate from other works of art that are not as "virulent." Yes, many hip-hop lyrics are violent, but that does not distinguish the songs from many other artistic works. Edgar Allan Poe, considered one of America's greatest writers, wrote numerous stories about murder and death, including "The Tell-Tale Heart," whose narrator is a confessed killer. *The Talented Mr. Ripley*, a novel by Patricia Highsmith, and the movie based on this novel, make Tom Ripley, an unrepentant murderer, a sympathetic character. Sculptor Kiki Smith depicts mutilated or deformed bodies in her art (see fig. 1), and, instead of being criticized, she is considered one of today's most important sculptors. No one would claim, I think, that Kiki Smith influences her viewers to commit mayhem. Clearly, hip-hop artists are not alone in depicting horrible people and events; they should not be singled out for doing so, and it should not be assumed that their audience will blindly follow suit.

FIG. 1 Kiki Smith, *Untitled* (1993).

—Alea Wratten, SUNY–Geneseo,
"Reflecting on Brant Staples's Editorial 'How Hip-Hop Music Lost Its Way and Betrayed Its Fans'"

Thesis:
. . . [Staples's] argument fails to be persuasive for several reasons: He doesn't account for the influence positive role models have, he ignores the fact that art frequently depicts violence without dire consequences to its consumers, and he overlooks the broad spectrum of hip-hop to focus on only a single strand.

Topic Sentence

Concession/rebuttal

Example 1

Example 2

Example 3

Concluding Sentence (also recalls thesis)

Student Model
Alea Wratten's complete essay, 131–34

4b Writing Unified Paragraphs

Paragraphs are ***unified*** when they focus on a single main idea. Unifying a paragraph is easiest when it includes a ***topic sentence***, a single sentence (sometimes two) that clearly states the main idea of the paragraph. That way, you can check each supporting sentence against this main idea and eliminate all those that are not relevant.

1. Focus the paragraph on a central idea and delete irrelevant details.

All the sentences in a supporting paragraph should support or explain the paragraph's main idea or topic, and each supporting paragraph should provide evidence for or develop further your project's main idea.

Topic Sentence

Irrelevant: Focus of ¶ is on how writer came to inherit, not writer's or city attorney's reaction or library's location—cut

Relevant: Explains why writer inherited library

> Last year I inherited a library—not just the books, but the whole building. I didn't see it as a boon at first; I saw it only as a legal nuisance. In the 1950s, my grandfather, I discovered, had donated the library to the town. Fifty years later, when the townspeople built a new library and decided to sell the old building, they discovered that they couldn't: The deed specified that if they ceased to use the building as a library, it would revert to the owner or his heirs. When the city attorney found the deed, he called every member of the town council. I was that heir. So now I owned the library in which I had spent so many hours as a girl. The building stands on a shady corner in what was once a quiet town.

When revising, hone your paragraphs until they focus on a single supporting idea: No matter how much you may like a certain sentence, if it does not support the main idea of the paragraph, it must be cut.

→ EXERCISE 4.1 Unifying a paragraph

Underline the topic sentence or main idea of the sample paragraph below. Then cross through any sentences that do not support that main idea.

> As we consider American dietary habits we also need to think about how people learn about nutrition. How do we know if our favorite foods are good for us? The national shift to convenience food is a problem too, because we don't know what is in it. Few people know that since 1909 Americans doubled the amount of sugar we eat (Amrock 8). Schools teach about the Federal Dietary Recommendations, but they change. First we had a Food Pyramid, and now we have a plate with different sized portions of food types. Davis and Saltos explain that it changes as understanding of nutrition grows (34). How can we trust something that keeps changing? The Food Pyramid said 6–11 servings of grains and only 3–5 of vegetables (www.nal.usda.gov/fnic/Fpyr/pmap.htm), but now portions of grains and vegetables are the same size (choosemyplate.gov). Having fewer vegetables was easier and popular with kids. Some people cut fat or carbohydrates to lose weight. My friends just exercise a lot or count calories. People can also get nutritional information from websites, but not all of them are healthy. The Harvard School of Public Health has an interactive website that clarifies nutritional information ("Knowledge for Healthy Eating").

→ EXERCISE 4.2 Writing unified paragraphs

Using the topic sentence and some of the supporting details given below, write a unified paragraph. Be selective: Not all the supporting details provided may be relevant.

> **Topic sentence:** Over the last four decades, the average American has increased the amount of food eaten from 16.4 pounds to 18.2 pounds per week and Americans' obesity rate has doubled.

Possible Supporting Details

1. The government recommends that fruits and vegetables should make up half of what we eat (choosemyplate.gov).
2. The US Department of Agriculture (USDA) compiles food consumption figures.
3. Corn syrup consumption in the US increased by 387% from 1970 to 2005 (Wells & Buzby 17).
4. What we eat is as important as how much we eat.
5. In 2005, 86 pounds of added fats and oils were consumed per person in the United States; we consumed 53 pounds in 1970 (Wells & Buzby 12).
6. In 1970, US consumption of added sugars and sweeteners was 119 pounds per person and by 2005 that number was 142 pounds (Wells & Buzby 17-18).
7. According to Schlosser, half of the US food budget is spent on fast food.
8. The National Health Nutrition Examination Survey (NHANES) tracks obesity.
9. In 2014, NHANES found that 80 million adult Americans (36.5%) were obese.

2. Place the topic sentence appropriately.

Topic sentences can appear at the beginning, middle, or end of a paragraph, but they typically appear at the beginning or end.

Topic sentence at beginning of paragraph   The most common placement for a topic sentence is at the beginning of the paragraph:

> Environmentalists paint a bleak picture of aquaculture. The David Suzuki Foundation, for example, maintains that fish waste contained in the fishery pens kills organisms living in the seabed. Yvon Gesinghaus, a manager of a tribal council in British Columbia, Canada, also notes that the scummy foam from the farms collects on the beaches, smothering the

Topic sentence

clams that provide the natives with food and money. George K. Iwama, Biksham Gujja, and Andrea Finger-Stich point to the destruction of coastal habitats in Africa and Southeast Asia to make room for shrimp ponds.

—Adrianne Anderson, Texas Christian University

In the paragraph above, the main idea is spelled out in the first sentence, so readers can easily see the relationship between the main idea and the supporting evidence and explanations that follow.

Topic sentence at end of paragraph   Writers may place the topic sentence at the end of a paragraph to draw a conclusion based on the evidence presented and to enhance dramatic effect.

When I was a little girl, Walt Disney's *The Little Mermaid* was my favorite movie, and Ariel (the title character) was my favorite character. I watched this movie three times a day, repeating Ariel's lines word for word. I wanted to be like her—cute and little and sweet and lovable, with big eyes and a tiny waist. But when I watched *The Little Mermaid* for the first time in more than seven years, I noticed things I had overlooked as a child. Was Ariel unhealthily thin? Was she more childlike than a full-grown woman should be? Was Ariel too willing to make sacrifices for Prince Charming? Maybe *The Little Mermaid* wasn't the innocent entertainment I had once thought.

Topic sentence

—Heidi Johnson, North Dakota State University

Holding the topic sentence until the end of the paragraph and starting with dramatic statistics or (as in the example above) a thought-provoking anecdote may stimulate your readers' interest before you draw your conclusion. Remember, though: The relationship between evidence and claim must be clear, or you might leave your readers puzzled.

Topic sentence in middle of paragraph   Occasionally writers place the topic sentence somewhere in the middle of the paragraph:

Biology is destiny—or at least more and more people seem ready to believe that it is. Perhaps this is because recent scientific advances—gene splicing, in vitro fertilization, DNA identification of criminals, mapping the human genome—have been repeatedly echoed and amplified by popular culture. From science fact to science fiction (and back again), the gene has become a pervasive cultural symbol. It crops up not just in staid scientific journals and PBS documentaries, but also with increasing regularity in political discourse, popular entertainment, and advertising.

Topic sentence

—Jeff Reid, "The DNA-ing of America," *Utne Reader*

In cases where the main idea appears in the middle of the paragraph, it acts as a linchpin: In this example, the paragraph begins with examples of genetic advances, and it ends with a sentence supporting the widespread cultural importance of these genetic tests. The topic sentence links these two different kinds of support.

3. Decide whether to leave the main idea unstated.

Some paragraphs (especially descriptive and narrative ones) may leave the main idea unstated. The main idea of the paragraph below, for example, is implied by the details and the word choices. The words and phrases that suggest the main idea are highlighted.

> The sound of discreet footsteps echoed in my ears as our choir followed a monk through one of the dark, damp archways into a grand hall furnished with ancient tables and chairs; it had been immaculately preserved by the family that had inhabited the old palace, which now served as a monastery, school, and museum. From the hall we passed into a room filled with religious relics that had belonged to the old prince. In another room, brown music manuscripts in Beethoven's and Haydn's own handwriting lay in crystal cases. In a third, bright tapestries woven from gold thread hung from the shiny stone walls, and sparkling crown jewels bedecked glass cabinets. We passed quickly through room after room filled with rusty (or bloodstained?) torture devices. Just before we reached an open-air walkway, we passed doors that seemed to belong to dwarves: They were entrances to the rooms of children who attended school here.
>
> —Christina Huey, Georgia Southern University

In this paragraph, the implied main idea—something like "Everything in the monastery seemed strange and remarkable"—comes through without Huey's having to state it explicitly. Write such paragraphs with the explicit thesis statement clearly articulated in your own mind, so that you don't include irrelevant material that might make the paragraph incomprehensible.

EXERCISE 4.3 Identifying the topic sentence

Identify the topic sentence (main idea) in the following paragraphs:

1. Rock music had always been a vehicle to express frustration, rebellion, and obloquy, but as the 1970s proceeded, these themes were often softened to achieve mass acceptance. The notion of rock as mainstream entertainment was gaining ground steadily. David Bowie, for example, who in an earlier era might have been considered too inaccessible a figure for television audiences, turned up as a smiling guest on Cher's variety show in 1975. Rock was

becoming a common language, the reference point for a splintered culture. In March 1976, presidential candidate Jimmy Carter told a lecture audience that Bob Dylan, Led Zeppelin, and the Grateful Dead were among the artists who had inspired him to work hard as governor of Georgia, and once he won the election, Carter continued to court rock by inviting numerous musicians to the White House.

—Ken Tucker, "The Seventies and Beyond," in *Rock of Ages: The Rolling Stone History of Rock & Roll,* p. 520

2. We spend so much of our lives hiding and pretending to be someone we're not. It's incredibly liberating to let your appearances reflect who you are, and what you're going through. Imagine looking in the mirror and saying: yep, I look like *me*. I've had some pretty insane haircuts, most recently including long hair with designs shaved into the sides, a curly little pixie, and an awkward mohawk. But even the mohawk (which really didn't look great) represented me well, because I was just coming out of a major breakup. My ex's lifestyle had required that I show up places wearing dresses, heels, and a blow-out, looking pretty and "appropriate." It never felt right to me, and by cutting my hair like a weirdo, I released my old identity and let my true Self show through better. I am odd and wild, creative, boyish, and happy; it's thrilling and liberating to actually express that, instead of hiding it.

—Jessi Kneeland, "8 Lessons on Unconditional Self-Love (aka: Crazy Hair Don't Care)," *Remodel Fitness*

Make It **Your Own**

Select a paragraph from a recent or current writing project. Underline the topic sentence or main idea; then cross through any sentences that do not support it.

4c Writing Coherent Paragraphs

A paragraph is *coherent* when readers can understand the relationships among the sentences without having to pause or ponder. Readers are most likely to find a paragraph coherent when all the sentences in the paragraph are relevant, when the paragraph is clearly organized, and when transitional words and phrases link sentences.

1. Organize your paragraphs logically.

There are many ways to organize a paragraph logically. Most paragraphs follow deductive order: They begin with a topic sentence (the most general statement in the paragraph), and the supporting evidence follows:

> I'd known Sam for all of a month before I got him a dog in 2006. Belle, now nine years old, is half Border Collie, a female pup out of our friend Thad's Australian Shepherd. Neither of us had any experience with making a pup into a stock dog. But one thing I *did* know before my impulsive purchase was the value of an obedient working dog. After several summers on cattle ranches, I'd seen just how handy it was to send dogs into thickets where cattle shaded up. I'd watched them work a cow that didn't want to stay with the herd until she turned back and joined them. One cowboy with a good dog or two could easily handle several hundred cattle, the same number it might take five people to drive. (Hiring day help could set you back around five hundred bucks). And well-intended but inexperienced cow hands can end up in the wrong place, but a seasoned dog is rarely mistaken about where the cattle need to go.

Topic sentence

Supporting evidence

> —Laura Jean Schneider, "Ranch Diaries: One Dog Can Be Worth Three Hands," *High Country News*

A less common option is to organize the paragraph inductively, so that it begins with the supporting details and concludes with the topic sentence:

> His trademark character Mr. DOB (who appears in the sculpture *DOB in the Strange Forest*) is reminiscent of both Mickey Mouse and Sonic the Hedgehog. But there's something heavier going on here. It's hinted at in the manic eyes of Murakami's characters. It's unleashed fully in the show's centerpiece painting *Tan Tan Bo Puking,* aka *Gero Tan,* where the cartoon character subject is bearing fearsome jagged teeth, and the whole lot is melting. It's like cartoon Dali, sure, but it's also another reminder that Japan experienced the flesh-melting horror of atomic attack.

Supporting evidence

Topic sentence

> —Daniel Etherington, "Nasty Cartoons from Japan," bbc.co.uk

The painting referred to in the paragraph above is shown in the background of Figure 4.1.

A third option is to organize the paragraph by increasing order of emphasis or interest:

> Monotonously the trucks sway, monotonously come the calls, monotonously falls the rain. It falls on our heads and on the heads of the dead up the line, on the body of the little recruit with the wound that is so much too big for his hip; it falls on Kemmerich's grave; it falls in our hearts.

Least emphatic

Most emphatic

> —Erich Maria Remarque, *All Quiet on the Western Front*

© *Richard Stonehouse/Camera Press/Redux*

FIGURE 4.1 **The painting *Tan Tan Bo Puking*—aka *Gero Tan*—and sculptures by artist Takashi Murakami**

A fourth option is to organize the paragraph by posing a problem or question and then resolving it:

Question

Answer

So why exactly is the protagonist drawn to the dreams of the past? It may be because those dreams are not the trivialities of modern times. They are not about realizing suddenly that you are standing at your locker naked or unable to get to the airport in time for your flight. Instead, the dreams of the past are dreams of death, of unknown gods, of devouring monsters.

—Michael Parr, McHenry Community College, "The Importance of Dreaming in Sylvia Plath's 'Johnny Panic and the Bible of Dreams'"

2. Use transitions within (and between) paragraphs.

In addition to omitting irrelevancies and being well organized, a coherent paragraph provides guideposts that point readers from one sentence to the next. These are *transitional words and phrases.* They alert readers to the significance of what you are saying and point up the relationships among your ideas. The following paragraph uses transitional words and phrases to guide readers through a comparison of two books:

Baron's book, which is written in the relentlessly melodramatic style of *Jaws*, describes cougars spreading inexorably eastward.

By contrast, Elizabeth Marshall Thomas, in *The Tribe of Tiger: Cats and Their Culture,* argues that cougars were never fully exterminated in the East and instead survived in remote areas by being especially stealthy around humans. The difference is significant. If you accept Marshall Thomas's argument, then the eastern seaboard sounds a great deal like pre-cougar-resurgence Colorado. Indeed, the herds of deer plaguing the unbroken strip of Eastern suburbs makes a replay of the Boulder situation likely—but on a far larger scale. Already, bears and coyotes are invading the Eastern suburbs. Can cougars and wolves be far behind?

—Peter Canby, "The Cat Came Back," Harper's

> Contrast

> Cause-effect

> Emphasis

> Time

Make sure you choose the appropriate transition for the situation, and vary your selection to avoid ineffective repetition. (For some sample transitions, see the Quick Reference box on the next page.)

> **More about**
> Avoiding repetition, 523–24

3. Repeat words, phrases, and sentence structures.

Repetition—especially repetition used for padding—can annoy readers, but repetition used consciously, to knit sentences into a cohesive paragraph or to call attention to an idea, can be an asset. The following paragraph repeats words and phrases (*deer hunting, hunting, deer season*) to emphasize the point made in the final sentence, where the writer uses the word *deer* on its own.

> **More about**
> Developing without padding, 95
> Effective repetition, 558–59

> I don't object to deer hunting: let everyone have his sport, I say. I don't for a moment doubt the value, importance, and dignity of hunting for those who do it. Deer hunting teaches skill, discipline, and patience. More than that, it teaches the moral lesson of seriousness—that certain things must be entered into advisedly, done with care, and done right. That hunting provides an education I am very willing to believe. And yet deer season is for me a sad couple of weeks. Because with all its profound advantages for the hunter, the fact remains that deer season is a little tough on the deer.

—Castle Freeman, "Surviving Deer Season:
A Lesson in Ambiguity," Atlantic

> Repeated structure

> Repeated words

> Key concept

The paragraph above repeats sentence structures ("I don't object," "I don't . . . doubt"; "Deer hunting teaches," "It teaches") but largely relies on the repetition of words (*deer, hunting, season*) for emphasis. The paragraph below uses related concepts (the word *gangster,* the names of gangsters and others from the FBI's Most Wanted list), but it mainly relies on repetition of phrase and sentence structures to lend emphasis.

> When he said he'd been a gangster, they smiled. Sure you were, pops. When he said he'd been Public Enemy Number One—right after John Dillinger, Pretty Boy Floyd, and his old protégé Baby Face Nelson—people

> Key concept

Repeated structure

Examples of concept

turned away and rolled their eyes. When he said he and his confederates had single-handedly "created" J. Edgar Hoover and the modern FBI, well, then he would get bitter and people would get up and move to another table. He was obviously unstable. How could you believe anyone who claimed he was the only man in history to have met Charles Manson, Al Capone, and Bonnie and Clyde?

—Bryan Burrough, *Public Enemies*

4. Use pronouns, synonyms, and equivalent expressions.

Pronouns (I, you, he, she, it, we, they), *synonyms* (words that mean the same thing), and equivalent expressions not only help writers avoid having to repeat the same word over and over (unintentional repetition) but also create coherence by establishing links to words and phrases that appeared earlier.

Quick Reference | Sample Transitional Expressions

To add to an idea: *again, also, and, and then, besides, further, furthermore, in addition, incidentally, likewise, moreover, next, still, too*

To indicate cause or effect: *accordingly, as a result, because, consequently, hence, since, then, therefore, thus*

To indicate chronology (time sequence): *after, afterward, as long as, as soon as, at last, before, earlier, finally, first, formerly, immediately, in the first place, in the interval, in the meantime, in the next place, in the last place, later, latter, meanwhile, next, now, often, once, previously, second, shortly, simultaneously, since, sometime later, subsequently, suddenly, then, third, today, tomorrow, until, until now, when, years ago, yesterday*

To conclude: *all in all, finally, in brief, in conclusion, in other words, in short, in sum, in summary, that is, to summarize*

To concede: *certainly, granted, of course*

To compare: *alike, also, in the same way, like, likewise, resembling, similarly*

To contrast: *after all, and yet, although, but, conversely, despite, difference, dissimilar, even so, even though, granted, however, in contrast, in spite of, instead, nevertheless, nonetheless, notwithstanding, on the contrary, on the other hand, otherwise, regardless, still, though, unlike, while this may be true, yet*

To emphasize: *after all, certainly, clearly, even, indeed, in fact, in other words, in truth, it is true, moreover, of course, undoubtedly*

To offer an example: *as an example, for example, for instance, in other words, namely, specifically, that is, thus, to exemplify, to illustrate*

To indicate spatial relationships: *above, adjacent to, against, alongside, around, at a distance from, behind, below, beside, beyond, encircling, far off, farther along, forward, here, in front of, inside, near the back, near the end, nearly, next to, on, over, surrounding, there, through, to the left, to the right, to the north, to the south, up front*

Writing
Responsibly Guiding the Reader

As a writer, you have a responsibility to guide your reader from point to point, high-lighting the relationships among your words, sentences, and paragraphs. Do not leave readers to puzzle out the relationships among your ideas for themselves. Few academic readers in the United States will think that explicit claims and transitions insult their intelligence.

                                                                to AUDIENCE

The following paragraph, for example, uses several equivalent expressions for the word *gossip* as well as the pronoun *it* to refer to this concept:

> The first law of gossip is that you never know how many people are talking about you behind your back. The second law is thank God. The third—and most important—law is that as gossip spreads from friends to acquaintances to people you've never met, it grows more garbled, vivid, and definitive. Out of stray factoids and hesitant impressions emerges a hard mass of what everyone knows to be true. Imagination supplies the missing pieces, and repetition turns these pieces into facts; gossip achieves its shape and amplitude only in the continual retelling. The best stories about us are told by perfect strangers.
>
> —Tad Friend, "The Harriet-the-Spy Club," *New Yorker*

| Key concept |
| Repeated structure |
| Pronouns |
| Equivalent expressions |

5. Combine techniques.

The example paragraphs in *section 4c* used more than one technique to achieve coherence. When revising your own paragraphs, draw on a variety of techniques to make your paragraphs cohere.

▶ EXERCISE 4.4 Analyzing coherence

For each of the following paragraphs, identify how the paragraph is organized, underline the transitional words and phrases, and circle the words that are repeated or the pronouns or synonyms that replace them.

1. Readers of this novel can attribute multiple meanings to the word *paradise* depending on whose point of view they are looking from. The founders of Ruby consider *paradise* to consist of preserving the history of the Old Fathers and remaining isolated from outsiders, but this view proves faulty and falls apart. On their journey toward seeking comfort, the women of the convent realize that *paradise* means coming to terms with one's past instead of running from it or letting it determine who they are, and this

understanding leads them to show compassion and mercy toward those who have harmed them.

—Sonu Ray, Drew University, "Journey to *Paradise:*
Discovering Its Gateway"

2. The group worshipped unharassed until 1667. At that time, the Court acted on the complaints of the orthodox churches of the area against Myles and his followers. In an order from the Plymouth Court dated July 2, 1667, the members were fined five pounds each for "setting up of a public meeting without the knowledge and approbation of the Court to the disturbance of the peace of the place" (King 30–31). The Court offered them three alternatives: They could discontinue their worship services, leave the town, or petition the Court for an alternate site of worship. Mr. Myles moved his church to New Meadow Neck, just south of Rehoboth, which is today in Barrington, Rhode Island.

—Robyn Worthington, Bristol Community College, "The Covenant between
Church and Town in Swansea, Massachusetts"

3. First, use the cork borer to cut 2 cylinders out of the potato and then slice the cores into pieces 2 cm long. It is a good idea to place the slices in a beaker to prevent them from drying out. There should be two potato cylinders for each treatment. Weigh the two cylinders for each treatment and record the weight in grams: that is your initial weight. Next, blot the cylinders with a paper towel and put each of the sets of cylinders into 100 ml beakers (there should be five) and place 50 ml of each solution in the beakers.

—Stephanie Warnekros, Johnson County Community College, "Osmosis in
Potato Cubes"

→ **EXERCISE 4.5 Unscrambling the "Gettysburg Address"**

The sentences below make up the final paragraph of Abraham Lincoln's "Gettysburg Address," but they have been scrambled. Without checking the original, use the clues within the paragraph to restore Lincoln's sentences to their proper order. Then list the coherence techniques that helped you put the paragraph back together again.

1. It is rather for us to be here dedicated to the great task remaining before us—that from these honored dead we take increased devotion to that cause for which they gave the last full measure of devotion—that we here highly resolve that these dead shall not have died in vain—that this nation, under God, shall have a new birth of freedom—and that government of the people, by the people, for the people, shall not perish from the earth.

2. The world will little note, nor long remember, what we say here, but it can never forget what they did here.

3. But, in a larger sense, we cannot dedicate—we cannot consecrate—we cannot hallow—this ground.

4. The brave men, living and dead, who struggled here, have consecrated it, far above our poor power to add or detract.
5. It is for us the living, rather, to be dedicated here to the unfinished work which they who fought here have thus far so nobly advanced.

Make It **Your Own**

Select a paragraph from a current or recent writing project and assess its coherence. List the techniques you used to weave the sentences together into a paragraph and note what you could do to make it even more coherent.

4d Developing Paragraphs Using Patterns

Using *patterns*—description, narration or process analysis, exemplification, comparison and contrast, cause and effect, analysis, and definition—can help you develop your paragraphs (and your whole project) into a cohesive and unified whole.

Description   When describing, include details that appeal to the senses (sight, sound, taste, smell, touch) and organize them spatially (from left to right, top to bottom, near to middle to far) to mimic how we normally take in a scene. Spatially organized paragraphs rely on indications of place or location to guide the reader by the mind's eye (or ear or nose).

> A few moments later French announces, "Bottom contact on sonar." The seafloor rolls out like a soft, beige carpet. Robison points to tiny purple jellies floating just above the floor. Beyond them, lying on the floor itself, are several bumpy sea cucumbers, sea stars with skinny legs, pink anemones, and tube worms, which quickly retract their feathery feeding arms at *Tiburon's* approach. A single rattail fish hangs inches above the bottom, shoving its snout into the sediments in search of a meal.
> —Virginia Morell, "OK, There It Is—Our Mystery Mollusk,"
> *National Geographic*

Sensory description

Indications of place or location

Exemplification: Explaining through example   Exemplification works by providing examples to make a general point specific:

> For many years I believed that women had only one thing to learn from men: how to get the attention of a waiter by some means short of kicking over the table and shrieking. Never in my life have I gotten the attention of a waiter, unless it was an off-duty waiter whose car I'd accidentally scraped

in a parking lot somewhere. Men, however, can summon a maître d' just by thinking the word "coffee," and this is a power women would be well-advised to study. What else would we possibly want to learn from them? How to interrupt someone in midsentence as if you were performing an act of conversational euthanasia? How to drop a pair of socks three feet from an open hamper and keep right on walking? How to make those weird guttural gargling sounds in the bathroom?

Example 1

Example 2

Example 3

—Barbara Ehrenreich, "What I've Learned from Men:
Lessons for a Full-Grown Feminist," *Ms.*

Step 1

Step 2

Narration and process analysis   A paragraph that tells a story or describes a process unrolls over time. Include each step or key moment, and describe it in enough detail that readers can envision it.

Step 3

Step 4

Step 5

Step 6

Step 7

The very first trick ever performed by Houdini on the professional stage was a simple but effective illusion known generally as the "Substitution Trunk," though he preferred to call it "Metamorphosis." Houdini and his partner would bring a large trunk onto the stage. It was opened and a sack or bag produced from inside it. Houdini, bound and handcuffed, would get into the sack, which was then sealed or tied around the neck. The trunk was closed over the bag and its occupant. It was locked, strapped, and chained. Then a screen was drawn around it. The partner (after they married, this was always Mrs. Houdini) stepped behind the screen which, next moment, was thrown aside—by Houdini himself. The partner had meanwhile disappeared. A committee of the audience was called onstage to verify that the ties, straps, etc. around the trunk had not been tampered with. These were then laboriously loosened; the trunk was opened and there, inside the securely fastened bag, was—Mrs. Houdini!

—Ruth Brandon, *The Life and Many Deaths of Harry Houdini*

The sequence of events in the Substitution, or Metamorphosis, trick is depicted in Figure 4.2.

Library of Congress, Rare Book and Special Collections

FIGURE 4.2 A visual process analysis

Comparison-contrast: Showing similarities and differences   A paragraph that is developed using comparison-contrast points out similarities or differences (sometimes both). A comparison-contrast paragraph can proceed by either the ***block method*** or the ***alternating method.*** In the block method, the writer groups all the traits of the first item together before discussing the second item.

In the alternating method, the writer proceeds point by point, discussing each common or divergent trait of both items before moving to the next trait. In the block method, readers must remember everything you have said about item A while they read about item B, so the more complex your material, the more your readers are likely to need the alternating method.

Block Method	Alternating Method
A	A
A	B
A	
	A
B	B
B	
B	A
	B

The first paragraph below uses the alternating method; the second uses the block method.

Asante kente cloth is made from strips in a single weave with alternative double-woven panels such that when the strips are sewn together, the effect is similar to a checkerboard. It is noted for its vivid colors and the abstract motifs woven into the strips, unlike Ewe kente, in which the colors are more subdued and the motifs are more lifelike. Like adinkra, the motifs used in Asante kente cloth weaving have specific names; however, the cloth is usually named for the colors and design of the background, which is often striped. As with adinkra, kente is named for historic figures and events and also for Asante values. The design *kyeretwie*, or leopard catcher, for example, symbolizes courage, while *aberewa* ben, or "wise old woman," indicates the respect accorded older women in Asante society.

— Boatema Boateng, "The Copyright Thing Doesn't Work Here: Adinkra and Kente Cloth and Intellectual Property in Ghana"

> colors and motifs
> colors and motifs
> names based on motifs
> names based on cloth
> symbolism
> values

Europeans interpreted the simplicity of Indian dress in two different ways. Some saw the lack of clothing as evidence of "barbarism." André Thevet, a shocked French visitor to Brazil in 1557, voiced this point of view when he attributed nakedness to simple lust. If the Indians could weave hammocks, he sniffed, why not shirts? But other Europeans viewed unashamed nakedness as the Indians' badge of innocence. As remnants of a bygone "golden age," they believed, Indians needed

> "barbarism"

> "innocence"

clothing no more than government, laws, regular employment, or other corruptions of civilization.

—James West Davidson et al., *Nation of Nations*, 5th ed.

Cause-and-effect: Reasons and consequences A cause-and-effect paragraph explains why something happened or what its consequences are:

Causes

Effects

Here is a modest suggestion for what Twitter can do to fix one of the problems that most annoy me and I imagine many other users: the problem of crackpot, abusive tweets. The paradox of Twitter is that the more followers you have (I currently have over 20,000), the more abusive tweets you are likely to get calling you various scatological names or passing along insane conspiracy theories. Some of this is bearable, but after a while you want to take a hot bath and never go back into the cesspool again. I'm not suggesting that these offensive tweets comprise the bulk of what's on Twitter—far from it. I would have stopped using it long ago if that were true. But it's more of a chore than it should be to find the good stuff in your feed among all the abusive attacks that are out there.

—Max Boot, "Abusing Anonymity," *Commentary*

Analysis: Dividing a whole into its parts Analysis divides a single entity into its component parts:

United States

Great Plains

Prairie

The central United States is divided into two geographical zones: the Great Plains in the west and the prairie in the east. Though both are more or less flat, the Great Plains—extending south from eastern Montana and western North Dakota to eastern New Mexico and western Texas—are the drier of the two regions and are distinguished by short grasses, while the more populous prairie to the east (surrounding Omaha, St. Louis, and Fort Leavenworth) is tall-grass country. The Great Plains are the "West"; the prairie, the "Midwest."

—Robert D. Kaplan, *An Empire of Wilderness*

Definition: Explaining the meaning of a word or concept Like those in a dictionary, a definition explains the meaning of a word or concept by grouping it into a class and then providing the distinguishing characteristics that set it apart from other members of that class:

Term to Be Defined	Class	Distinguishing Characteristics
Argument is	a way to discover truth	by examining all sides of the issue.

Extended definitions (definitions that run to a paragraph or more) analyze in detail what a term does or does not mean. They go beyond a desktop dictionary, often using anecdotes, examples, or reasons for using the word in this particular way:

> The international movement known as *theater of the absurd* so vividly captured the anguish of modern society that late twentieth-century critics called it "the true theater of our time." Abandoning classical theater from Sophocles and Shakespeare through Ibsen and Miller, absurdist playwrights rejected traditional dramatic structure (in which action moves from conflict to resolution), along with traditional modes of character development. The absurdist play, which drew stylistic inspiration from dada performance art and surrealist film, usually lacks dramatic progression, direction, and resolution. Its characters undergo little or no change, dialogue contradicts actions, and events follow no logical order. Dramatic action, leavened with gallows humor, may consist of irrational and grotesque situations that remain unresolved at the end of the performance—as is often the case in real life.
>
> —Gloria Fiero, *The Humanistic Tradition*, 5th ed.

| Term to be defined |
| Class |
| Distinguishing characteristics |

Make It **Your Own**

Write two paragraphs. For each, choose one of the patterns of development discussed in this section. Check to make sure that they are unified and that they use appropriate transitions to guide the reader.

Work **Together**

Exchange paragraphs with a classmate and make a note of which patterns you see. Mark any places where the paragraph lacks coherence or needs additional transitions.

4e Writing Introductory Paragraphs

Introductory paragraphs shape readers' attitudes toward the rest of the text. Yet writers often have a hard time producing these paragraphs. Many writers find it helpful to draft the body of the project before tackling the introduction.

Avoid Praising the Reader in Your Introduction In some contexts and cultures, writers win the approval of readers by overtly praising their taste, character, or intelligence, whether the writing is intended to be wholly personal or not. Generally, however, this is considered inappropriate for a college project, and academic and professional writers in the United States avoid referring directly to the reader and occasionally will actually challenge the reader's beliefs.

Whether you write the introduction first or last, it should prepare the reader for what follows. In many cases, this means including the thesis in the introduction. A common placement for the thesis statement is at the end of the introduction—this is the *funnel introduction.*

Regardless of whether you include your thesis in your introduction, hold it until your conclusion, or merely imply your main idea, your introduction should identify and convey your stance toward your topic, establish your purpose, and engage readers to make them want to read on. One or more of the following strategies can help you write an effective introduction:

- Begin with a vivid quotation, a compelling question, or some interesting data.
- Start with an engaging—and relevant—anecdote.
- Offer a surprising but apt definition of a key term.
- Provide background information.
- State a commonly held belief and then challenge it.
- Explain what interesting, conflicting, difficult, or misunderstood territory the project will explore.

(For some opening gambits to avoid, see the Quick Reference box on page 71.)

In the introductory paragraph that follows, the writer uses several effective strategies: She begins with a question that challenges the audience to examine some common assumptions about the topic, she provides background information that her readers may lack, and she concludes with a thesis statement that explains why reading her text should be important to the audience.

Opening question	Many people enjoy sitting down to a nice seafood dinner, but how many of those people actually stop to think about where the fish on their plate came from? With many species of wild fish disappearing
Answer that provides background information	because of overfishing, increasingly the answer will be a fish farm. But while fish farming can help to supply the demand, it can threaten the environment and cause problems with wild fish. It can also threaten the health of consumers by increasing the risk of disease and increasing the
Thesis	quantity of antibiotics consumed. In fact, as a careful and conscientious consumer, you would do well to learn the risks involved in buying and eating farm-raised fish before one winds up on your dinner plate.

—Adrianne Anderson, Texas Christian University

Quick Reference | Seven Don'ts for Introductions

Avoid common problems that can undermine your introduction's success:

1. **"In my paper I will . . ."** While announcing your topic is acceptable in some academic disciplines (in the sciences, for example), announcing what your project is or will do is usually unnecessary and boring. Also avoid referring to your own text by its title.

2. **"In this paper I hope to . . ."** **or "In this paper I will try to . . ."** These openers share the shortcomings of *"In my paper I will . . ."*; they also state something your instructor already assumes, and they undermine your credibility by emphasizing your lack of confidence.

3. **"I don't know much about this topic, but . . ."** Introductions that apologize for your amateur status undermine your credibil-ity as a writer and give readers an excuse to stop reading.

4. **"I have a lot of expertise in this topic."** Refrain from claiming more prestige or credit than is your due.

5. **"According to *Merriam-Webster's Third Unabridged Dictionary*, . . ."** While starting with a definition can be an effective opening strategy, merely providing readers with a definition they could easily find for themselves is tedious.

6. **"Ever since the beginning of time, . . ."** Start your project at the beginning of your material, not before recorded history.

7. **"The greatest problem facing our society today . . ."** Do not make claims that your project cannot support with concrete evidence.

Brief essays may require only a one-paragraph introduction, but longer projects often need more. A text of twenty pages may have an introduction that runs several paragraphs, and introductions to books are generally the length of a short chapter. While there are no firm rules about the length of the introduction, they should be in proportion to the project's length.

4f Writing Concluding Paragraphs

As with the introduction, the conclusion is a part of the project that readers are likely to remember. In fact, because it is the last thing the audience will read, it is what they will probably remember best. Thus, it demands a writer's best work.

The shape of the conclusion is often what might be called an *inverted funnel:* While the introduction often starts at a general level and then narrows down to the thesis, a common strategy for the conclusion is to start out specific—with a restatement and development of the thesis (in different words)—and then to broaden out. The restatement of your thesis should add perspectives that you have developed in the body of your project and not be a simple paraphrase of what appeared in your introduction. The final draft of Michael Wedd's project (pp. 101–106) demonstrates the technique:

Thesis in the introduction

Despite how serious and pressing the issue of global warming is, we must be careful to consider not only the benefits but also the costs of the forms of alternative energy production that we deploy. If alternative energy ends up putting the environment—and in some cases humanity directly—in jeopardy, then we need to rethink the ways in which we use it.

Thesis in the conclusion

Clearly, environmentally conscious citizens acknowledge how important it is to check global warming and diversify our energy portfolio, but it is crucial that we also protect the flora and fauna with which we share this planet.

In Wedd's introduction, the thesis raises a problem and indicates the possible conflicts. In Wedd's conclusion, the *if* is gone, replaced by *clearly*. The body of Wedd's project has described the conflicts as being very real, so in his conclusion he can state his thesis in much more definite terms.

The purpose of the conclusion is to provide readers with a sense of closure and to make them feel that reading the text was worthwhile. To achieve closure and convey the importance of the project, try one or more of the following strategies:

- Return to the anecdote, question, or quotation with which you began.

- Summarize your findings (especially in long or technical projects).

- Discuss how what you have learned has changed your thinking.

- Suggest a possible solution (or solutions) to the problems raised in the text.

- Indicate additional research that needs to be conducted or what the reader can do to help solve the problem.

- Leave readers with a vivid and pertinent image, quotation, or anecdote.

(For some strategies to avoid when writing your conclusion, see the Quick Reference box on the next page.)

The concluding paragraph below provides an example of an effective conclusion.

> The farmers of nineteenth-century America could afford to do here what they had not dared to do in the Old World: hope. This hope—for greater economic security, for more opportunity for themselves, their children, and their grandchildren—is the optimism and idealism that has carried our country forward and that, indeed, still carries us forward. Although the American dream has evolved across the centuries, it survives today and is a cornerstone of American philosophy. It is what underlies our Constitution and our laws, and it is a testimony to the vision of the farmers who founded this nation.
>
> —Leonard Lin, University of Southern California, "The Middle Class Farmers and the American Philosophy"

Makes reader feel time reading was well spent by showing importance of American dream

Restates thesis (American dream = hope for greater security, opportunity)

Achieves closure by recurring to introduction with mention of American dream

Quick Reference   Five Don'ts for Conclusions

Avoid common problems that can undermine your conclusion's success:

1. **Don't offer additional support for your thesis in your conclusion.** Such conclusions undermine the feeling of closure and leave readers wanting and expecting more.

2. **Don't end with a generality or a cliché.** Almost nothing will more undermine the readers' sense that they have spent their time well than ending with something trite.

3. **Don't apologize for the shortcomings of your project.** Such an ending will leave readers feeling they have wasted their time. If your project is truly bad, you should have revised your draft, not shared its shortcomings

with readers; if it is not, you have nothing to apologize for.

4. **Don't repeat your introduction.** It may be useful to return to the anecdote or statistics with which you began, but merely repeating your introduction or thesis will insult your audience. They do not want to read the same text a second time.

5. **Don't announce what your project has done or shown ("In my paper, I have shown . . .").** In a long or complicated text, a summary can be useful to readers, but your readers will be reminded of what your text has done when they read your summary; there is no need to announce it.

EXERCISE 4.6 Writing introductory paragraphs

Revise the following introductory paragraph to make it more effective:

People aged 50 and older cannot see as well at night as younger people. The small muscles that control the size of the pupil get weaker with age, and with age there may be a loss of rods, which are crucial for night vision. This affects older people's ability to adapt to the dark. This can cause problems when driving at night after the bright headlights of a car pass or just walking from well-lit to dark parts of a home. Older people need to recognize their decreased ability to see at night and to take measures that will help them be safe in the dark, whether driving, walking outdoors, or getting around the home. This paper presents the reasons why night vision is weaker in older people and some methods of compensating for this problem.

EXERCISE 4.7 Writing concluding paragraphs

Revise the following concluding paragraph to make it more effective:

To summarize the point of this essay, the majority of experts acknowledge that every one of the world's seven species of marine turtles is threatened by extinction. At present humans are causing more turtle deaths than natural forces. A key cause is habitat destruction and alteration. Coastal development is rapidly eliminating access to beaches for female turtles to nest and lay eggs. Another important cause is predation for turtle meat, eggs, hides, and shells. Incidental capture in fisheries increases the loss of turtles. Masking the threat is the slow maturation of turtles, which can hide the effect of overexploitation for many years. We need to greatly expand our knowledge of marine turtle life history patterns and the true conservation status of turtle populations, as well as the level and types of exploitation. With this knowledge we need to formulate and implement effective management and conservation strategies to preserve viable marine turtle populations. If we do not, time will run out for one of the most intriguing creatures on the face of the earth.

Make It **Your Own**

Review the introduction and conclusion of a current or recent writing project. What strategies did you use? Referring to the Quick Reference boxes and the strategies discussed in this chapter, revise your introduction and conclusion.

Work **Together**

Exchange your revised introductions and conclusions and note what strategies your classmate used in the revision. Did they work? What strategies might make these paragraphs more powerful?

Before reviewing your classmate's comments, write a paragraph reflecting on this process. What did you learn about effective introductions and conclusions by reading and evaluating someone else's? Did your classmate use any strategies you might try? Next, review the comments you received and make a note of any revisions that you plan to make.

4g Connecting Paragraphs

Readers need to know not only how sentences connect to one another but also how paragraphs are connected. One way to connect paragraphs is by using one of the patterns of development (*section 4d*) for the project, just as you would do with individual paragraphs. You can also link paragraphs using these transitional devices:

- Providing transitional expressions (and sentences)
- Repeating words and phrases strategically
- Using pronouns and synonyms to refer back to words and ideas
- Creating parallel sentence structures

A final way to create coherence among paragraphs is by referring back to the project's main idea.

The following speech by President-elect John F. Kennedy, delivered on January 9, 1961, to the General Court of the Commonwealth of Massachusetts, uses all of these strategies to create a unified and cohesive text:

Professional Model Speech

The City Upon a Hill

By JOHN F. KENNEDY

I have welcomed this opportunity to address this historic body, and, through you, the people of Massachusetts to whom I am so deeply indebted for a lifetime of friendship and trust.

For fourteen years I have placed my confidence in the citizens of Massachusetts—and they have generously responded by placing their confidence in me.

Now, on the Friday after next, I am to assume new and broader responsibilities. But I am not here to bid farewell to Massachusetts.

For forty-three years—whether I was in London, Washington, the South Pacific, or elsewhere—this has been my home; and, God willing, wherever I serve this shall remain my home.

It was here my grandparents were born—it is here I

Words chosen to emphasize the speaker's bond with his audience hope my grandchildren will be born.

I speak neither from false provincial pride nor artful political flattery. For no man about to enter high office in this country can ever be unmindful of the contribution this state has made to our national greatness.

Its leaders have shaped our destiny long before the great republic was born. Its principles have guided our footsteps in times of crisis as well as in times of calm. Its democratic institutions—including this historic body—have served as beacon lights for other nations as well as our sister states.

For what Pericles said to the Athenians has long been true of this commonwealth: "We do not imitate—for we are a model to others."

And so it is that I carry with me from this state to that high and lonely office to which I now succeed more than fond memories of firm friendships. The enduring qualities of Massachusetts—the common threads woven by the Pilgrim and the Puritan, the fisherman and the farmer, the Yankee and the immigrant—will not be and could not be forgotten in this nation's executive mansion.

They are an indelible part of my life, my convictions, my view of the past, and my hopes for the future.

Allow me to illustrate: During the last sixty days, I have been at the task of constructing an administration. It has been a long and deliberate process. Some have counseled greater speed. Others have counseled more expedient tests.

But I have been guided by the standard John Winthrop set before his shipmates on the flagship Arabella three hundred and thirty-one years ago, as they, too, faced the task of building a new government on a perilous frontier.

"We must always consider," he said, "that we shall be as a city upon a hill—the eyes of all people are upon us."

Today the eyes of all people are truly upon us—and our governments, in every branch, at every level, national, state and local, must be as a city upon a hill—constructed and inhabited by men aware of their great trust and their great responsibilities.

For we are setting out upon a voyage in 1961 no less hazardous than that undertaken by the Arabella in 1630. We are committing ourselves to tasks of statecraft no less awesome than that of governing the Massachusetts Bay Colony, beset as it was then by terror without and disorder within.

History will not judge our endeavors—and a government cannot be selected—merely on the basis of color or creed or even party affiliation. Neither will competence and loyalty and stature, while essential to the utmost, suffice in times such as these.

For of those to whom much is given, much is required. And when at some future date the high court of history sits in judgment on each one of us—recording whether in our

---

Margin annotations:

Evidence for the claim that follows: Massachusetts is a model for the world

thesis

Example supports his claim

Central motif: the city on a hill

Sets up key terms that will dominate his conclusion

Transitional words clarify and emphasize his statements

Repeats his key terms to explain his main claim

brief span of service we fulfilled our responsibilities to the state—our success or failure, in whatever office we may hold, will be measured by the answers to four questions:

First, were we truly men of courage—with the courage to stand up to one's enemies—and the courage to stand up, when necessary, to one's associates—the courage to resist public pressure, as well as private greed?

Secondly, were we truly men of judgment—with perceptive judgment of the future as well as the past—of our own mistakes as well as the mistakes of others—with enough wisdom to know that we did not know, and enough candor to admit it?

Third, were we truly men of integrity—men who never ran out on either the principles in which they believed or the people who believed in them—men who believed in us—men whom neither financial gain nor political ambition could ever divert from the fulfillment of our sacred trust?

Finally, were we truly men of dedication—with an honor mortgaged to no single individual or group, and compromised by no private obligation or aim, but devoted solely to serving the public good and the national interest.

Courage—judgment—integrity—dedication—these are the historic qualities of the Bay Colony and the Bay State—the qualities which this state has consistently sent to this chamber on Beacon Hill here in Boston and to Capitol Hill back in Washington.

And these are the qualities which, with God's help, this son of Massachusetts hopes will characterize our government's conduct in the four stormy years that lie ahead. Humbly I ask His help in that undertaking—but aware that on earth His will is worked by men. I ask for your help and your prayers, as I embark on this new and solemn journey.

EXERCISE 4.8 Identifying paragraph-building techniques

Review John F. Kennedy's "City Upon a Hill" speech as follows:

1. Check each paragraph for relevance, unity, and coherence. Highlight topic sentences and identify the patterns used to develop paragraphs. (Patterns may be mixed.) Note examples of strategies described in this chapter.
2. Identify and review the introductory and concluding paragraphs. Note the techniques used to begin and end the speech.
3. Identify the methods Kennedy used to weave the paragraphs into a unified and cohesive whole: Circle the repeated words, underline the transitional expressions, and draw a box around the pronouns and synonyms that refer back to earlier passages.

Make It **Your Own**

Select a current or recent writing project and review it using the three steps described in Exercise 4.8. Write your observations in the margin and note any revisions you might make to develop your ideas more fully. If this is a project you are currently drafting, use this review to help you revise it.

Text Credits

p. 56: Jeff Reid, "The DNA-ing of America," *Utne Reader*, Sept.-Oct. 1995, pp. 26–27. Reprinted from *Utne Reader*. www.utne.com. Copyright © 1995 Ogden Publications, Inc. Used by permission; **Ex. 4.3:** "The Seventies and Beyond" from Stokes, Geoffrey, Tucker, Ken, Ward, Ed, *Rock of Ages: The Rolling Stone History of Rock and Roll* (Rolling Stone Press/Fireside, 1986) **p. 58:** Jessica Kneeland, "8 Lessons on Unconditional Self-Love (aka: Crazy Hair Don't Care)" Remodel Fitness. http://jessikneeland.com/8-lessons-on-unconditional-self-love-crazy-hair-dont-care/ Copyright © Jessica Kneeland. Used by permission of the author; **p. 59:** Laura Jean Schneider, "Ranch Diaries: One Dog Can Be Worth Three Hands" *High Country News*, September 8, 2015. Copyright © 2015 High Country News. Used with permission; **p. 59:** Daniel Etherington, "Nasty Cartoons from Japan." www.bbc.co.uk, November 14, 2002. Copyright © bbc.co.uk/news; **p. 59:** Remarque, Erich Maria, *All Quiet on the Western Front*, translated by A.W. Wheen. Copyright © 1929, 1930 by Little, Brown and Company; copyright renewed 1957, 1958 by Erich Maria Remarque. (New York: Little, Brown & Co., 1929); **p. 60:** Peter Canby, "The Cat Came Back," *Harper's*, March 2005. Copyright © 2005 by Peter Canby for *Harper's*. Reprinted by permission of International Creative Management, Inc.; **p. 61:** Castle Freeman, "Surviving Deer Season: A Lesson in Ambiguity," *Atlantic Monthly*, December 1995. Used with permission of the author; **p. 62:** Burrough, Bryan, *Public Enemies: America's Greatest Crime Wave and the Birth of the FBI*, 1933-34. Copyright © 2004 by Bryan Burrough (New York: Penguin Group (USA) Inc., 2004); **p. 63:** Tad Friend, "The Harriet-the-Spy Club," *The New Yorker*, July 31, 2000. Reprinted by permission of International Creative Management, Inc. Copyright © 2000 by Tad Friend for the New Yorker; **p. 65:** Virginia Morell, "OK, There It Is-Our Mystery Mollusk," from "Monterey Menagerie," *National Geographic*, June 2004. Copyright © 2004 by Virginia Morell. Reprinted by permission of the author; **p. 66:** Brandon, Ruth, *The Life and Many Deaths of Harry Houdini*. Copyright © 2003 by Ruth Brandon (New York: Random House, 2003); **p. 66:** Barbara Ehrenreich, "What I've Learned from Men: Lessons for a Full-Grown Feminist," published in *Ms.* 1985. Copyright 1985 by Barbara Ehrenreich. Reprinted by permission of International Creative Management; **p. 67:** Boateng, Boatema, *The Copyright Thing Doesn't Work Here: Adinkra and Kente Cloth and Intellectual Property in Ghana*. Copyright © 2011 by the Regents of the University of Minnesota. Pg. 23; **p. 67:** Davidson, James West et al., *Nation of Nations: A Narrative History of the American Republic* 5th Edition (New York: McGraw-Hill Education, 2007); **p. 68:** Boot, Max, "Abusing Anonymity" *Commentary*, February 23, 2016. Copyright © 2016 Commentary, Inc. Used with permission; **p. 68:** Kaplan, Robert D. *An Empire of Wilderness: Travels into America's Future*. Copyright © 1998 by Robert D. Kaplan. (New York: Random House, Inc. 1998); **p. 69:** Fiero, Gloria, *The Humanistic Tradition*, 5th Edition (New York: McGraw-Hill Education, 2005); **p. 75:** John F. Kennedy, "City Upon a Hill" speech delivered to a Joint Convention of the General Court of the Commonwealth of Massachusetts, The State House, Boston, January 9, 1961.

5 Drafting and Revising Visuals

WDCN/University College London/Photo Researchers, Inc.

Visuals can bring life to a written text: A Facebook page, a political ad, a website—all would be boring without images. Visuals play a much more important role than mere decoration, however; they also help us understand the world. The colors in these PET scans, for example, inform researchers about the portions of the brain that are activated while a subject is listening to words (top) or repeating them (bottom). Images from the Hubble Space Telescope make the theoretical real: They inform viewers about the universe that surrounds our home planet.

5a Deciding Whether to Illustrate College Writing Projects

In personal writing, visuals are often used to entertain or express the writer's thoughts or feelings. In business and public writing, visuals can make an arguable claim and provide evidence for it. In academic writing, visuals may engage or persuade readers, but their primary role is to aid understanding. A photograph of a painting you are analyzing for an art history course, a graph comparing voter turnout among age groups for a political science project, a video or animation that describes the course of a disease for a biology assignment—all these would be appropriate illustrations in an academic text.

To determine whether a visual is appropriate in a college project, ask yourself these questions:

> **More about**
> Purpose, 14–17
> Audience, 17–20
> Context and
>   genre, 21

- **Does this visual reinforce my purpose?** The primary purpose of visuals in academic writing is to inform. They may have a secondary persuasive purpose—evidence should be chosen that the reader will find convincing—but the primary purpose will be informative.

Student Models
Visual support, 133, 152, 353, 354, 356, 404–05, 428, 489

■ **Is this visual appropriate to my audience, context, and genre?** To determine whether illustrations are appropriate, look at articles from journals in your field or ask your instructor.

Photographs in Job Applications In Europe and Asia it is common to include a personal photograph with a job application. In the United States, however, it is generally considered inappropriate for a résumé to include a photograph (or a physical description of the job candidate). In fact, US employers are barred by law from asking applicants personal questions, such as their age, marital status, race, religion, or sexual orientation.

■ **Does the "tone" of the visual match that of the text?** While a caricature might be an amusing or pungent feature of a political magazine or poster, it would not be appropriate in most college projects (Figure 5.1).

FIGURE 5.1 **Caricature versus photograph** Unless you were analyzing the political content of such an image, a caricature would not be appropriate in a college project. Caricature are too often insulting. In this case, the caricature ridiculed a wartime enemy.

© Mim Friday / Alamy Stock Photo

5b Using Visuals as Evidence

In academic writing, visuals are used primarily as evidence. Choose the right type of illustration for the information you wish to convey.

1. Information graphics

Information graphics—such as tables, bar graphs, line graphs, and pie charts—convey and depict relationships among data.

Tables Tables, such as Table 5.1, organize large amounts of information in rows and columns for easy viewing. The information in a table can be textual, graphic, or numeric, but it is usually numeric. Tables are frequently the best choice for presenting data on more than four variables or data that include decimals.

Bar graphs and pie charts Bar graphs and pie charts allow comparison of data in two or more categories. A bar graph (Figure 5.2) uses bars of different colors and heights (or lengths). A

Reference   Matching Visual Evidence to Claims

- **Tables** display large amounts of information, data that include decimals, or information on multiple variables that are difficult to convey in a graph.
- **Pie charts** convey significant divisions in a single entity that add up to 100 percent.
- **Bar graphs** compare two or more variables.
- **Line graphs** show changes among variables over time.
- **Diagrams** model processes or locations.
- **Maps** represent geographic locations; may also include data.
- **Photographs** provide readers with a reference point or example, or depict a process (two or more photographs needed).
- **Movie stills** provide a reference point, offer an example, show a process (two or more stills needed).
- **Screenshots** provide a reference point or example from an electronic resource, such as a website.

TABLE 5.1	CHILDREN 3 TO 21 YEARS OLD SERVED IN FEDERALLY SUPPORTED PROGRAMS FOR THE DISABLED, BY TYPE OF DISABILITY (2006–09)			
Type of Disability	**2005–06**	**2006–07**	**2007–08**	**2008–09**
Autism	3.3	3.9	4.5	5.2
Developmental delay	5.1	5.0	5.4	5.5
Emotional disturbance	7.1	6.9	6.7	6.5
Hearing impairments	1.2	1.2	1.2	1.2
Intellectual disability	8.3	8.0	7.6	7.4
Multiple disabilities	2.1	2.1	2.1	2.0
Orthopedic impairments	1.1	1.0	1.0	1.1
Other health impairments	8.5	9.1	9.7	10.2
Specific learning disabilities	40.7	39.9	39.0	38.2
Speech or language impairments	21.9	22.1	22.0	22.0
Visual impairments	0.4	0.4	0.4	0.4
Traumatic brain injury	0.4	0.4	0.4	0.4

Source: US Dept. of Educ., Inst. of Educ. Sciences, Natl. Center for Educ. Statistics, *Digest of Education Statistics*, 2010.

Student Models
"Why Students Cheat," Tom Hackman, 150–56
"Nature versus Nurture," Robyn Worthington, 481–89
"The Power of Wardrobe: Male Stereotype Influences," Heather DeGroot, 396–405

pie chart (Figure 5.3) uses segments of a circle to depict portions of a whole. Choose a pie chart when comparing percentages that add up to 100. Both bar graphs and pie charts work best with a small number of categories where the differences among them are clear. Tom Hackman, Robyn Worthington, and Heather DeGroot use bar graphs to supply evidence succinctly.

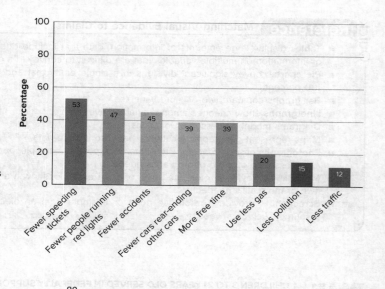

FIGURE 5.2 Benefits of self-driving vehicles The bar graph shown here displays the breakdown in the opinions of 1,133 US youths ages 8–18 when surveyed about the pros and cons of self-driving cars. While the majority felt that self-driving cars would be dangerous, they also cited numerous benefits. (Data from Nielsen's Youth Viewpoint on Self-Driving Cars study conducted online by the Harris Poll, Oct. 2015. www.nielsen.com.)

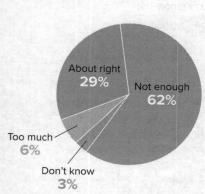

FIGURE 5.3 Americans' opinion about government aid to the middle class This pie chart breaks down the views of 1,500 adults who responded to a question in a national survey conducted in December 2015 by the Pew Research Center. Because the information to be conveyed is relatively simple (there are just four different percent-ages), it can easily be conveyed in a pie chart that totals 100. (Data from Pew Research Center, Dec. 8–13, 2015. www.pewresearch.org.)

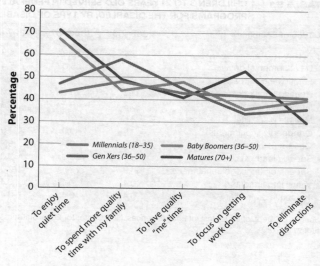

FIGURE 5.4 Reasons for "unplugging" Respondents (2,193 US adults) to a national online survey were asked to number in order of importance the reasons they occasionally disconnected from tech and social media. This line graph allows readers to see at a glance the top five reasons and the differences among generations. (Data from the Harris Poll, Jan. 2016. www.harrisinteractive.com.)

Line graphs   Line graphs (such as Figure 5.4) are especially useful in illustrating change over time. The more lines, the more types of data can be compared (but the more complex the graphic). As with bar graphs and pie charts, line graphs work best when you are comparing only a few variables. With more variables, the more difficult it will be to convey the information clearly.

2. Images

Academic writers use images (such as photographs, screenshots, film stills, and architectural renderings) as references, as when writing about a work of art or a scene from a movie, and they use them as examples. The photograph in Figure 5.5 would provide an effective example in a project exploring the connections between the women's movement of the 1970s and Vietnam War protests.

Just as a historian might include an image of an 18th-century map to show readers the area studied by the first European explorers of the Pacific Northwest, Mallory Reese includes an image of women's sports equipment to illustrate the concept of "pink marketing." Alea Wratten uses a photograph of a sculpture as a visual example. Lydia Nichols uses illustrations from superhero and underground comics to demonstrate the differences between these two types of comic books. Heather DeGroot shows photographs of a proctor in stereotypical, counterstereotypical, and "control" outfits.

Student Models
"Ride the Wave,"
  Mallory Reese,
  516–18
"Reflecting on Brent
  Staples's Editorial, ..."
  Alea Wratten, 131–34
"Holy Underground
  Comics, Batman!"
  Lydia Nichols,
  349–62
"The Power of Ward-
  robe: Male Stereo-
  type Influences,"
  Heather DeGroot,
  396–405

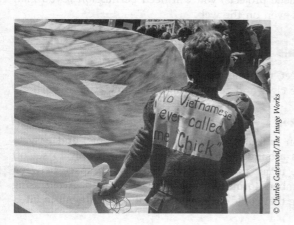

© Charles Gatewood/The Image Works

FIGURE 5.5 Photographs in history
Photographs are frequently used in history projects to supply visual evidence.

EXERCISE 5.1 Using visuals as evidence

For one of the thesis statements you revised in Exercise 3.2, describe the type of visuals you might use as support.

> **More about**
> Placing visuals
> on the page,
> 347–48 (MLA),
> 394–95 (APA)

Writing
Responsibly   Exploitative Images

When using images in your academic work, keep in mind that ethical writing cannot include images that might be seen as emotionally manipulative of the reader, nor as those that might emotionally exploit those whom they depict. As you review your selection of images, think about what is useful for developing your topic; how much respect you are extending to the people depicted; and how those people might feel about your use of the image.

to TOPIC

5c Deciding Whether to Copy Visuals or to Create Them

Original artwork, like original thoughts, can often be more effective than material "quoted" from others. Some illustrations, however, must come from an outside source, either because the subject is inaccessible (as with a historical photograph) or because the software needed to create the visual is beyond the writer's ability.

Whenever you borrow images from an outside source, be sure to identify your source, either in the figure caption (for most illustrations) or in a source note (for tables). While you are not required to obtain permission to use a visual in your college projects, you will need permission if you plan to publish your project, even on the web.

5d Revising Visuals

As you revise your project, reconsider not only your words but your visuals, too. Make sure they are clear and accurate and that they avoid distortion.

1. Avoid visual clutter.

Revise your information graphics so they are clean, simple, and easy to understand. Omit lines around cells in a table; use them only to set off headings or to indicate major divisions (Table 5.2). Leave space between columns, and align numbers to make graphics easier to read. Avoid using special views or shading that could make your visual more difficult to interpret (Figure 5.6).

2. Keep visuals clear and accurate.

Double-check the numbers in tables and figures to make sure totals are accurate and that percentages in a pie chart total 100. (If rounding the

Tech	**Consider the Size of Your Document**

Submitting an illustrated document brings with it certain concerns:

- If you will be submitting your project on paper, make sure you have access to a printer of sufficient quality that it can handle your graphics.
- If you will be submitting your project electronically, think about how large a file your e-mail program—

and that of your recipient—can handle. Because image files dramatically increase the size of a document file, you may wish to compress them before sending.

- If you will be delivering your project online, make sure to optimize your graphics for the web so that they load quickly into the reader's browser.

numbers up or down has caused inaccuracy, indicate this in a note.) Label all parts of your tables and figures (columns, rows, vertical and horizontal axes, "slices" of a pie chart) so that readers can understand them without having to read the text. Avoid abbreviations that might be unfamiliar or confusing (Figure 5.6).

Johnsville Tigers Batting Statistics

NAME	AB	R	H	SO	BA
Tamika	12	2	5	7	.416
Alyssa	14	0	1	13	.071
Travis	12	5	7	5	.583
Jose	15	3	5	10	.333
Akira	13	6	8	5	.615
Walid	14	7	7	7	.500
Taylor	5	4	1	4	.200
Leslie	11	2	4	7	.363
Chloe	9	3	5	4	.555
Derek	8	7	6	2	.250
Maria	14	4	6	8	.571
Ahmed	12	5	3	9	.250
Carlos	12	4	4	8	.333
Antoine	14	6	5	9	.357
B.J.	5	2	2	3	.400
Sasha	15	7	6	9	.400

NAME	AT BATS	RUNS	HITS	STRIKE OUTS	BATTING AVERAGE
Tamika	12	2	5	7	.416
Alyssa	14	0	1	13	.071
Travis	12	5	7	5	.583
Jose	15	3	5	10	.333
Akira	13	6	8	5	.615
Walid	14	7	7	7	.500
Taylor	5	4	1	4	.200
Leslie	11	2	4	7	.363
Chloe	9	3	5	4	.555
Derek	8	7	6	2	.250
Maria	14	4	6	8	.571
Ahmed	12	5	3	9	.250
Carlos	12	4	4	8	.333
Antoine	14	6	5	9	.357
B.J.	5	2	2	3	.400
Sasha	15	7	6	9	.400

TABLE 5.2 Less is more Instead of enhancing clarity, lines around cells and abbreviations in headings in the table on the left can make the visual more difficult to read.

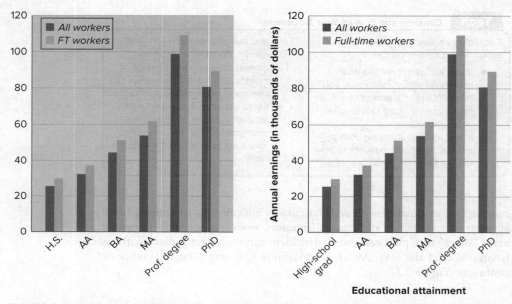

FIGURE 5.6 Clarity and precision The bar graph at left will be more difficult for readers to interpret than the graph at right: "Full-time" is abbreviated to FT and "high-school" to H.S., which could be confusing; no indication is given that the dollar amounts are in thousands; and the shading and the box around the legend make the figure unnecessarily busy.

3. Avoid distortion.

Make sure the information supplied in visuals is complete. The graph on the left in Figure 5.7 distorts the disparity in number of Democratic and Republican voters by starting the scale at 104. Changing the vertical axis in the revised graph on the right more accurately reflects the difference. Cropping photographs to eliminate background or to focus on the main action is acceptable, but cropping to distort information is unethical, as is using image-processing programs to change or distort an image.

> **More about**
> Logical appeals
>   (logos), 144–45
> Emotional
>   appeals
>   (pathos), 146–47

4. Do not manipulate.

Advertisements may use photographs that tug on readers' heartstrings (Figure 5.8). An academic audience, however, will expect images that stir the emotions to be supported by arguments grounded in logic.

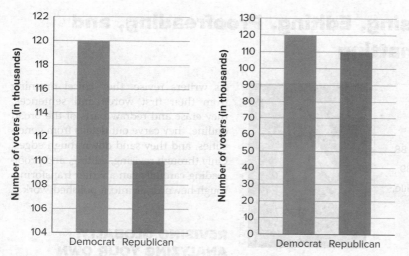

FIGURE 5.7 Distortion in scale By starting the vertical scale at 104, the graph at left distorts the difference in the number of voters. The graph at right more accurately depicts the differences.

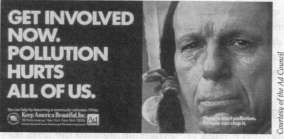

Courtesy of the Ad Council

FIGURE 5.8 Manipulative images in advertising This famous advertisement, showing a tearful Iron Eyes Cody, makes a powerful emotional argument in favor of protecting the environment, but it does not offer a reasoned position that would be expected in an academic or professional context.

6 Revising, Editing, Proofreading, and Formatting

© Scala / Art Resource, NY

As writers revise, they chisel meaning from their first words and sentences, they erase and redraw parts of the broad outline, they carve out details from generalities, and they sand down rough edges. Only through revising, editing, and proofreading carefully can a writer transform a rough-hewn draft into a polished work.

REVISING GLOBALLY: ANALYZING YOUR OWN WORK

Revising globally means learning to re-see—looking at the big picture to address elements like thesis, evidence, audience, context, genre, and ethical responsibilities. The first step toward assessing these aspects of your writing is to take a step backward to gain the distance needed for being objective about your own work. The second is to dive in, adjusting focus and organization, making changes to address your audience more effectively, and developing your ideas more fully.

6a Gaining Perspective

Writers generally feel a sense of "ownership" toward the texts they compose. This helps them produce an authentic voice and a commitment to the ideas they express. Yet that sense of ownership can hold a writer back from making needed changes. To gain the objectivity they need, writers can draw on a wide range of techniques, such as those described in the Quick Reference box on the next page.

Quick

Reference   Seven Ways to Gain Objectivity about Your Draft

1. **Allow time between drafts.** A few days or even a few hours between drafts can provide the distance you need.
2. **Clear your mind.** Do something to get your mind off your project, such as going for a run or playing a quick game of Guitar Hero.
3. **Learn from other readers.** Having others read and react to your draft will give you a sense of what your text is (and is not) communicating.
4. **Analyze the work of a fellow writer.** Most tutors and teachers will tell you that they learn as much from the coaching experience as do the people whom they coach.
5. **Listen to your draft being read aloud.** Every time your reader stumbles, pauses, or has to reread a passage, mark the spot. Then figure out what caused the interruption and revise accordingly.
6. **Outline your draft.** Once your outline is complete, read it through carefully. If any sections seem unconnected to the thesis or to the sections before or after, reorganize.
7. **Compare your text to others in the target context and genre.** When writing in an unfamiliar context or genre, consider reading professional texts to help you see what does and does not work in your own writing.

> *More about*
> Peer revising,
> 96–98

6b Revising Your Draft

Begin revising by rereading the text. Read your project through to the end before making any changes. Then reread and take notes. As you work through each paragraph, focus on the global issues of thesis, evidence, organization, and development. Most writers revise for just one issue at a time, rereading for each issue. At this stage you should skip over local issues such as spelling and punctuation; do not let them distract you.

1. Thesis and introduction

Because writers often discover and develop their ideas as they compose, the draft thesis may not capture the evolving project's main idea. (Often, the true thesis appears in the conclusion of the first draft.) This might mean you should adjust your evidence to your thesis. More frequently it means you should revise your thesis to match the evidence offered in your draft. Check your draft, too, to be sure that the introduction indicates your purpose—your reasons for writing—and your attitude toward your material. Are you skeptical? Enthusiastic? Still figuring it out?

> *More about*
> Drafting a thesis,
> 35–36
> Revising a thesis,
> 36–38
> Drafting an intro-
> duction, 69–71

In addition to revising your thesis, consider your introduction. Is the length proportionate to the whole project? A three-paragraph introduction is fine for a seven-page paper, but if the whole project is only four paragraphs long, the introduction should be very short. Does the introduction provide necessary background, a relevant anecdote, or compelling statistics that will give the audience a context for the thesis?

2. Evidence and counterevidence

More about
Organizing arguments, 157–59

In rereading your text, you may have had concerns about the evidence you offered in support of your thesis. Perhaps you noticed something weak, irrelevant, or overly general, or that you just did not supply enough evidence. If you need more or better evidence, go back to the idea-generating stage or do additional research. Perhaps your draft talked only about the evidence for your thesis, while ignoring conflicting information and alternative interpretations. An effective argument shows both evidence and counterevidence and explains why the writer believes the evidence is more valid or useful than the counterevidence.

3. Audience

More about
Audience, 17–20
Introduction,
  69–71
Development,
  45–46, 65–69
Connotation,
  19–20, 572
Level of formality,
  19–20, 565–66
Conclusions,
  71–73

After rereading your text, consider how your readers will react. Have you won them over? Think about your introduction. Does it make your audience want to keep reading? Next, consider the evidence in your body paragraphs. Will it persuade the people who will be reading your project? Now consider your word choice. Is the language appropriate to those people? An academic or business audience will expect a more formal tone but will not need you to define specialized terms; a general audience may be more engaged by an informal tone and may need specialized terms clearly defined. Finally, review your conclusion. Does it provide readers with a feeling of closure? There are many ways to create this sense of closure. Tailor the conclusion to the needs of your readers. For a long or complex text, readers may need a summary; for a persuasive one, readers may want to take action, so offer any suggestions you might have.

4. Organization

More about
Unity, 53–58
Coherence,
  58–65
Transitions,
  277–79, 783

Rereading your text may have alerted you to problems with organization. When revising, make sure that your project is both unified and coherent. In a unified text, all the paragraphs support the thesis, and all the details in each paragraph support the paragraph's main idea.

Writing
Responsibly / The Big Picture

A useful way to think about revising is to focus on your responsibilities to your audience, your topic, other writers, and yourself:

- Have you provided your audience with a worthwhile reading experience?
- Have you covered your topic fully and creatively?
- Have you represented borrowed ideas accurately and acknowledged all your

sources, whether you have quoted, summarized, or paraphrased?

- Have you developed a stance that readers will find credible, represented your ideas clearly and powerfully, and written in a voice that is a reflection of your best self?

to SELF

Assessment

As you revise, check your draft for the following elements. If the answer to any question is no, make the revisions necessary.

Introduction
- ☐ **Thesis** Does my thesis state my main claim? Does my thesis match the evidence in my draft? Does the introduction indicate my purpose and attitude toward my topic?
- ☐ **Evidence and counterevidence** Does my introduction indicate the complexity of my topic and how I will support my thesis?
- ☐ **Audience** Does my introduction provide needed background information? Will the introduction be engaging or compelling for the people reading my project?
- ☐ **Organization** Does my introduction give readers a sense of how the body of my project will develop my ideas?

Body Paragraphs
- ☐ **Thesis** Does my whole draft explain why I believe the thesis? Is each body paragraph relevant to my thesis? Is the evidence in each paragraph relevant to the paragraph's topic?
- ☐ **Evidence and counterevidence** Is the evidence I supply relevant? Do I supply enough evidence? Is the evidence compelling? Do I show counterevidence to my thesis? Do I credit my sources?
- ☐ **Audience** Will my readers need more (or less) information? Are my tone and word choices appropriate for this audience?
- ☐ **Organization** Does my organizational pattern suit my evidence? Does each paragraph lead logically to the next?

Conclusion
- ☐ **Thesis** Is my conclusion focused on a relevant issue that shows the importance of my topic? Does it reinforce my purpose?
- ☐ **Evidence and counterevidence** Does my conclusion avoid introducing new supporting evidence?
- ☐ **Audience** Does my conclusion provide an action plan, reflection, or necessary summary?
- ☐ **Organization** Does my conclusion follow logically from my body paragraphs?

> **More about**
> Relevance, 53,
>   233–39
> Generating ideas,
>   24–30
> Developing para-
>   graphs, 65–69
> Finding informa-
>   tion, 210–32
>   (ch. 13)

When revising, be prepared to delete ideas, facts, and even whole paragraphs—no matter how much you like them—if you notice that they do not support your thesis.

In a coherent text, the relationship among the paragraphs is clear and logical. Sometimes a text lacks coherence because the writer has not included transitional words and phrases that signal the relationships among ideas. Sometimes it lacks coherence because a step in the argument has been omitted or the ideas are not fully supported. It may lack coherence because the relationships among the paragraphs are unclear.

6c Reconsidering Your Title

Once you have revised your draft globally, revisit your title. It should prepare the audience for what it will read in your text. For most college projects, your title should accurately reflect not only the topic but also your approach to it:

Note how these
writers use a
descriptive phrase
(underlined) to make
their titles more
specific.

- The Power of Wardrobe: <u>An Analysis of Male Stereotype Influences</u>
- <u>Transcending Stereotypes</u> in Hurston's *Their Eyes Were Watching God*

You might also use a clever turn of phrase, a quotation, or a question to intrigue your readers and draw them into your project (Figure 6.1):

Note how these
writers indicate their
approach in their
titles (highlighted).

- Holy Underground Comics, Batman! <u>Moving Away from the Mainstream</u>
- My View from the Sidelines: <u>A Close Reading of Gary Snyder's "Front Lines"</u>

© Erich Lessing/Art Resource, NY

FIGURE 6.1 The importance of a title The title plays an important role in guiding your audience. Without knowing the title of this painting, a viewer might have seen this as a depiction of trees. By calling it *Farmhouse in Normandy*, the artist, Paul Cézanne (1839–1906), shifts the viewer's focus from the dense foliage in the foreground to the small building in the background on the left.

A question in your title can also suggest your approach (analysis, comparison-contrast, cause-effect).

- Differing Intentions? Comparing Raphael's Painting with a Print of Raphael's *Saint Cecilia*

Make It **Your Own**

Review a writing project you have gotten back from an instructor, and write a paragraph explaining how you fulfilled your responsibilities . as a writer. (See "The Big Picture," p. 91.) Are there any global issues you would revise now if you had the opportunity? Explain.

REVISING LOCALLY: EDITING WORDS AND SENTENCES

Your writing is a reflection of you—your ideas and your attitude toward your topic and audience. Revise locally to make your words and sentences reflect your meaning and create a *persona* that is appropriate for your purpose, audience, context, and genre.

> **persona** The apparent personality of the writer as conveyed through tone and style

6d Choosing Your Words with Care

When revising, reconsider your word choices. Each word should reflect your intended meaning; it should have the right *denotation.* Be very careful to use the word that expresses your exact meaning: If readers have to guess your intent, they may not guess correctly, and they may be annoyed by having to figure it out.

In addition to denotations, words carry *connotations*—emotional associations that affect readers' interpretations. Compare *freedom fighter* with *terrorist*. Both words have roughly the same denotation; both refer to people who use violence to achieve political ends. The connotative difference, however, is enormous.

Next, consider the level of formality that is appropriate to your audience, context, and genre: A text message to a friend may be filled with slang and acronyms, but this informality is rarely appropriate in academic or professional writing. Writers who intend to sound sophisticated by trotting out a word like *progenitor* to mean *parent* may instead make themselves sound pompous.

All writing benefits from avoiding biased language—language that unfairly or offensively characterizes groups or individuals.

> **More about**
> Denotation, 19–20, 571–572, 574
> Connotation, 19–20, 572, 574
> Levels of formality, 19–20, 565–66
> Biased language, 566–69
> General and specific language, 562–69

More about
Common sen-
tence problems,
78–83 (Grammar
Matters tutorial
preceding
ch. 33)
Sentence types,
625–27
Sentence variety,
552
Writing concisely,
520–28
(ch. 26)
Style, 519–94
(part 7)
Grammar, 595–731
(part 8)
Punctuation and
mechanics,
777–863
(part 10)

Finally, consider whether you have combined general, abstract language with specific, concrete words; explaining broad issues requires abstract language, but specific words will make your writing more compelling.

6e Editing Your Sentences

When revising, reconsider the structure of your sentences:

1. Are they grammatically correct?
2. Are they varied, and do they emphasize the most important information?
3. Are they as concise as they can be without losing meaning or affecting style?

In most contexts (academic and business, in particular), readers expect sentences to be formed according to the conventions of English grammar. Nongrammatical sentences may confuse, distract, or even annoy readers. Edit your prose to conform to standard written English.

Once you are sure that your sentences are clear and correct, shape them to reflect your emphases. A good way to begin editing for style is to read your draft out loud—or better still, get a friend to read it to you. Listen to the rhythm of your sentences. Do they all sound alike? If so, your sentences probably use the same sentence structure, or they all begin the same way.

To correct this problem, consider the information in your sentences. Combine related information in a single sentence by putting the most important information in the independent (main) clause and additional information in the subordinate (dependent) clause. If the information is of equal weight, use compound sentences and parallel structures to emphasize this balance. Where appropriate, use questions, commands, and exclamations for variety or emphasis.

In addition to writing varied sentences, hone them to eliminate clutter and polish them to add luster to your ideas. Try these strategies to revise for wordiness:

More about
Writing concisely,
520–28
(ch. 26)
Coordination and
subordination,
529–41 (ch. 27)
Parallelism,
542–50 (ch. 28)
Variety and
emphasis,
551–61 (ch. 29)

- Eliminate empty expressions, intensifiers, roundabout expressions, and redundancies.
- Eliminate ineffective repetition.
- Favor the active voice.

Writing Responsibly

Making Your Text Long Enough without Wordiness

When your text is too short, you may be tempted to pad it with wordy sentences, but that might make it hard (and boring) to read. Instead, try these tips:

- Revisit your thesis: Is it too narrow? If so, explore strategies for broadening it.
- Check your evidence: Have you offered facts, statistics, expert testimony, and examples to support your thesis? If not, return to the library or its website to search for more information. Have you explained your evidence so that your audience will understand it? Have you

specified exactly how your evidence supports your thesis?

- Analyze your counterevidence: Are you showing your audience the whole range of perspectives or only the data that support your thesis? Most audiences will appreciate knowing not just why you believe your thesis but also why you believe it even though there are other reasonable interpretations of the issue.

to TOPIC

Writing concisely for the web is particularly important, as most users prefer pages that are easy to scan.

Because not every writer makes the same kinds of mistakes, a personalized editing checklist can come in handy. To create one, try the following:

1. Review the last five texts that you have produced, looking for the kinds of common sentence errors noted in the Grammar Matters tutorial preceding chapter 33 (part 8).
2. Make a list of the issues you find (or that your instructor marked).
3. Reorganize the list so that the type of mistake you make most frequently is at the top.

Each time you write, use the top five items on your editing checklist to guide your local revisions. Over time, you are likely to find that you make fewer of these errors and can add some of your less common mistakes.

NOTE Instructors often use symbols to indicate the most common mistakes. Learn these symbols so that you can correct errors your instructor identifies and improve your draft.

> **More about**
> Empty phrases, 521
> Roundabout and redundant expressions, 522–23
> Ineffective repetition, 523–24
> Using the active voice, 559–60

> **More about**
> List of editing symbols, inside back cover

REVISING WITH OTHERS

As writers we can be touchy. We pour ourselves into our texts and feel hurt that others might not understand or appreciate what we have written. Little wonder, then, that we often feel defensive when others read our work before it is finished. Yet paradoxically, getting feedback from a real, live audience is one of the best ways to make sure readers—who do not have you standing by to explain—will understand your writing, will be convinced by your evidence, will be persuaded by your conclusion, and will form a high opinion of you as a responsible, authoritative writer.

6f Revising with Peers

One way to get feedback from readers is to solicit comments from your peers. In business, this might mean sharing your text with coworkers online or via e-mail. In school, this usually means sharing your draft with your classmates face-to-face, through a class blog or wiki, or in an online writing environment like Connect Composition 2.0, which accompanies this book (mcgrawhillconnect.com). Whether in a business or academic context, the role of writer and peer editor carries its own responsibilities.

1. The writer's role

When readers respond to your text, adopt a stance that is both engaged and receptive:

- **Talk.** Before readers begin to comment, explain what you are trying to accomplish and what you would like help with.

- **Listen.** As others respond to your draft, listen instead of arguing or defending. If readers seem uninformed or inattentive, figure out how you can revise the text so that even an uninformed or inattentive reader can understand what you are trying to say.

 Peer Review with Multilingual Students Many students are nervous about working in peer groups. But participation can reduce people's fears by showing that everyone makes mistakes and benefits from their experience with diversity. Group work helps non-native speakers of English become more familiar with the rules and idiosyncrasies of English—resolving difficult issues of idiom and word choice, for example—and more trustful of native speakers' natural abilities with their language.

Native English-speaking students may also be hesitant to work in groups with peers from different language backgrounds. However, workplaces, like college, are increasingly diverse. Enhancing the generally excellent practice of peer response, it may be especially useful for native English speakers to hear from multilingual peers whose diverse experiences with language may provide insightful perspectives on topic, organization, word choice, grammar, and style.

- **Question.** If your readers are not addressing your concerns or are speaking in generalities, ask them to point to specific passages. Ask yourself what underlying issue they are trying to get at. Do not settle for a disappointing response.

- **Write.** Take notes as your readers talk. What they say may be vivid at the time, but you will be surprised by how quickly you forget the details.

- **Evaluate.** You are the person who must make the final decision. Be open to advice, and consider whether there may be a better way of solving the problem.

2. The peer reviewer's role

As a reader of a classmate's draft, keep the following guidelines in mind:

- **Stay positive.** Tell the writer what is working well, along with what could be improved (Figure 6.2).

- **Talk to the writer.** Listen and respond to the writer's concerns, whether conducting the session face-to-face or electronically.

- **Look at the big picture, but be specific.** Focus on what the writer is trying to achieve, but back up general comments by pointing to

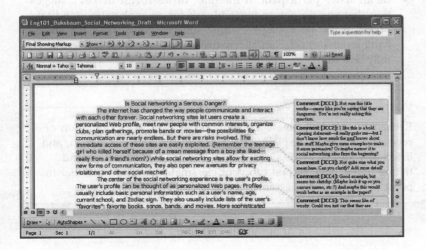

FIGURE 6.2
Electronic peer review If conducting peer review electronically, remember that there is a person on the receiving end of your comments. Stay positive, helpful, and friendly, and link each comment to something specific in the text.

specific passages in the text and explaining as best you can why they do not work for you.

► **Be a reader and a fellow writer—not a teacher, editor, or critic.** Your job is not to judge the text or to rewrite it, but to participate in its composition by helping the writer recognize and resolve issues.

6g Revising with a Tutor or an Instructor

More about
Time manage-
ment, 22–23,
198

Many colleges sponsor a writing center that offers free tutoring or online services such as NetTutor. Many instructors also allow students to submit a rough draft of their projects for comment. Take full advantage of these opportunities, and when you do, follow these guidelines:

- **Be prepared.** Bring a copy of your assignment, your textbook or handbook, any sources you are using, and whatever writing you have already done on the assignment, even if that writing is very informal or a work in progress.

- **Be open to advice.** Bring your own list of issues or concerns about the text or project, but also be receptive to broader issues or suggestions. Your tutor or instructor may have concerns that go beyond your list and that require you to rethink your assumptions, revise your thesis, or revisit the library for additional research.

- **Be an active participant.** If the tutor or instructor makes a sugges- tion that you do not understand, ask for an explanation (and take notes). If you do not agree with a suggestion, consider the under- lying issue and offer an alternative resolution. Then revise thought- fully and fully.

Work **Together**

Exchange with a classmate a writing project you are working on or recently completed. Explain what you are trying to accomplish, and listen to your classmate's comments, asking for clarification and taking notes. Now respond to your classmate's draft. Remember to point to specific words, sentences, and paragraphs.

Make It **Your Own**

Using comments you received from your classmate, revise your draft. After completing the process, write a paragraph discussing which of your peer's suggestions made the biggest difference in your revision, and why. If you did not find the process helpful, discuss what you or your classmate might have done to make it more productive.

PROOFREADING AND FORMATTING

6h Proofreading

When revising, your focus is on your ideas and how you express them; when proofreading, you concentrate on correcting errors.

To proofread effectively, divorce yourself from the content you know so well, so that you can see the text as it actually appears on the page. An effective way to achieve this distance is to print out your draft and read the hard copy line by line from the bottom up. Mark each correction on the printout as you read; enter them one by one, and then check to make sure that you have made each correction without introducing additional errors. Another option for proofreading is to work in teams: One person reads the text (including punctuation marks) out loud, while the other person marks errors on the printout.

> *More about*
> Using a dictionary, 582–84
> Usage glossary, G14–G19
> Homonyms and near homonyms, 585–87

Writing **Responsibly** Beware the Spelling Checker!

While spelling checkers and autocorrect can be very helpful in catching typos, they cannot always distinguish between homonyms (*they're, their*) or other frequently confused words (*lay, lie; affect, effect*). They may even lead you astray, suggesting words that are close to the word you mistyped (*defiant* for the misspelled *definate*) but worlds away from the word you intended (*definite*). As a writer, you have a responsibility to use words that communicate what you want to say and to not leave your reader guessing. Do not completely rely on automated spelling correction; also use a dictionary to double-check the program's suggestions, check usage in the usage glossary, and proofread your text carefully yourself. Only you can know what you *meant* to say!

to SELF

self Assessment   A Checklist for Proofreading

Before you submit your text to your instructor, check the following elements. If you answer no to any of the questions, make the revisions necessary.

Spelling
- ☐ Did you spell-check your project?
- ☐ Did you read through the text carefully, looking for misused words?
- ☐ Did you check specifically for words you frequently confuse or misspell?

Punctuation
- ☐ Did you check sentence punctuation, especially use of the comma and the apostrophe?
- ☐ Did you make sure that all quotations have quotation marks or block indentation, that you provided end punctuation for all your sentences, and that end punctuation and in-text citations are correctly placed?
- ☐ Did you check specifically for errors you regularly make (for example, comma splices or fused sentences)?

Other Errors
- ☐ Did you make sure that remnants of previous corrections—an extra word, letter, or punctuation mark—do not remain?
- ☐ Did you check that you have included all in-text citations where needed (for summaries, paraphrases, quotations, or ideas you have borrowed for a research project)?
- ☐ Did you check that all in-text citations are included in the reference list or list of works cited, and make sure that all formats are correct and consistent?

Proofreading When English Is Not Your First Language If you have difficulty proofreading a project, try reading it aloud; this may help you recognize errors. Also, ask your instructor if you can have a friend, classmate, or tutor help you proofread. A visit to the writing center may result in some helpful tips or practice, as well.

Make It **Your Own**

Customize the proofreading checklist in the Self-Assessment on this page to reflect your own needs by adding the errors you have made on your last two or three writing projects.

Work **Together**

Working in pairs, trade printed copies of a writing project. Have the other student read the text out loud while you mark corrections. When the process is complete for one text, trade roles with your partner and repeat the process.

More about
Visual design,
166–74 (ch. 9)
MLA format,
345–49
APA format,
392–96

6i **Formatting an Academic Text**

The Quick Reference box on this page provides guidelines for formatting an academic text. More coverage of formatting and incorporating visuals appears elsewhere in this book.

More about
Prewriting and
earlier drafts
of "Rethinking
Alternative
Energy":
Freewriting,
101–106
Brainstorming,
26–27, 30, 31
Cluster diagram-
ming, 27–28
Journalists' ques-
tions, 28–29
Thesis, 34–37
Tree diagram,
38, 39
Outline, 40–41
First draft, 47–51

Quick **Reference** Formatting Academic Texts

- Leave 1- to 1.5-inch margins.
- Indent the first line of each paragraph by half an inch.
- Use a standard font, such as Times New Roman or Cambria, in 12-point size.
- Use headings, headers, page numbers, and paragraph indents to help readers navigate the text easily.
- Format headings of the same level the same way throughout the project.
- Use figure and table numbers to guide the reader from text to visual.
- Use a style guide that is appropriate to your discipline.
- Keep your design simple; focus on content.

Student Model Final Draft

You have seen the essay by Michael Wedd (Columbia College) as it developed, from freewriting and brainstorming, to drafting a thesis statement, outlining, and first draft. Now consider his final draft. If you compare this to his earlier draft, you will see how he has revised globally and locally to tighten his thesis, develop his evidence, and make his introduction and conclusion more compelling.

Michael Wedd

Professor Dunn

English 102

5 Oct. 2016

Rethinking Alternative Energy

The rise of alternative energy industries has been challenging, controversial, and turbulent. With the availability of many forms of alternative energy systems globally, it is worth pausing for a minute to ask some questions. Conversations are taking place at many levels of government and society about both the costs and the benefits of alternative energy. The problematic relationships between alternative energy industries and the environment they claim to be protecting are emerging as a key focus of these debates.

Environmentalists are conflicted when it comes to alternative energy. Most agree that fossil-fuel-based power plants are damaging the climate and making life harder for many of the world's species. Which forms present the best alternative to fossil-fuels, though, remains a difficult question. One of the primary benefits of energy sources such as the wind, sun, and water is that they are in practically limitless supply. They are producing harvestable energy every day. Despite the clear benefits of these sources, some environmental activists, government regulators, and members of the general public are concerned about the risks. The structures needed to produce these forms of alternative energy can have grave effects on their surrounding environments, ecosystems, wildlife, and in the case of nuclear power plants, on human beings, too

Thesis statement

(Cherry; Deverakonda; "Former Japanese"; McCurry). Despite how serious and pressing the issue of global warming is, we must be careful to consider not only the benefits but also the costs of the forms of alternative energy production that we deploy. If alternative energy ends up putting the environment—and in some cases humanity directly—in jeopardy, then we need to rethink the ways in which we use it.

Topic sentence

counterevidence

evidence

Wind energy seems to be a harmless, passive, and effective way of producing energy, but upon closer inspection it also has its drawbacks. Wind turbines are killing birds, bats, and other airborne creatures at an alarming and quickening rate. The American Bird Conservancy (ABC), a group whose mission is to protect bird species and their habitats throughout the Americas, targets wind turbines as a growing threat to birds. An ABC report states that "[t]he United States now has 48,000 wind turbines installed from coast to coast, with many more planned. Those turbines killed nearly 600,000 birds in 2012, from Golden Eagles to migratory songbirds" ("Bird Strikes"). These wind turbines, which are being built increasingly larger to increase their productivity, reach hundreds of feet into the air and threaten birds, some of which are endangered. The group predicts that by 2030, "a ten-fold increase in turbines is expected to boost annual bird mortality to 1.4 to 2 million." Wind turbines put bats at great risk, too. Steven Cherry, a reporter with The Iowa Center for Public Affairs Journalism—a state-wide political watchdog group—highlighted some of these risks in a recent article. He explains, "Wind turbine blades catch the [bats] in a vortex wake that ruptures their lungs, causing them to drown in their blood, experts have found" (Cherry). He lists the Northern long-eared bat, which is an endangered species, as a common casualty. Wind turbines should not be marketed as a safe, "clean" form of alternative energy while their blades are being bloodied by hundreds of thousands of airborne creatures annually in the United States alone.

counterevidence

Transition

Topic sentence

Solar energy is another alternative that at first seems benign but is actually putting airborne wildlife in grave danger. At the $2.2 billion-dollar Ivanpah solar facility in the California desert, which is part of the largest solar energy complex in the world, birds are being scorched mid-flight and plummeting to earth like meteorites. A report by the *Pulitzer Center* states that "[u]nsuspecting birds fly through Ivanpah's airspace, where the superheated air between the heliostats [mirrors] and the [boiling] towers can reach temperatures as high as 900 degrees Fahrenheit. Flesh catches fire as the birds are ignited in midair" (Deverakonda). Researchers with the U.S. Fish & Wildlife Service, who visited Ivanpah in 2012, were quoted as referring to the complex as a "mega-trap" for a number of wildlife species (Deverakonda). Solar energy is one of the most abundant and seemingly limitless sources of harvestable energy in our solar system, but the ways in which we are capturing it are producing high risks for a number of animal species.

evidence

Topic sentence

The most controversial of these alternative energy sources is the atom. Nuclear energy accounts for significant portions of the world's alternative energy portfolio, but recent events cast a dark shadow on the industry. Japan's 2011 Fukushima nuclear meltdown is still in recent memory. Its physical effects are predicted to reach decades into the future, and its psycho-social effects could last much longer. Japan's powerful nuclear lobby is attempting to rekindle their reactors, though, despite the long shadow cast by Fukushima's triple-meltdown. *The Guardian* reports that "Japan's revamped Nuclear Regulation Authority (NRA) said the new safety checks meant there would be no repeat of the Fukushima catastrophe" (McCurry). Naoto Kan, former prime minister of Japan, believes that the Japanese government is not taking the dangers of nuclear power seriously enough, though. He was quoted in *Deutche Welle*, a German broadcasting service, saying, "[u]nfortunately, I have the impression that neither the Japanese public nor the experts have learned the right lessons from the disaster. If the accident had been a bit more severe, we would have had to evacuate ... [an area of] 250 kilometers for a long period of time" ("Former Japanese"). Nuclear energy holds potential as an alternative source, but with the aftershocks of both the Chernobyl crisis of the 1970s and 1980s and the more recent Fukushima disaster still affecting people and whole ecosystems today, we must carefully consider the dangers of nuclear power before embracing it as the clean energy of the future.

Restates thesis more specifically

Transition

Clearly, environmentally conscious citizens acknowledge how important it is to check global warming and diversify our energy portfolio, but it is crucial that we also protect the flora and fauna with which we share this planet. It is not enough to be environmentally conscious about the sources from which we draw our energy; we must also consider the ways in which we harvest from those sources, and the tangible effects that alternative energy infrastructure can have on its surroundings. Instead of merely replacing fossil-fuel sources with renewable ones, it is also important that we ask whether it is possible to scale back energy consumption as well. It will be a long time before alternative energy production can meet the accelerating global demand. The solution to this problem will have to include ways of not only increasing renewable energy production safely but also of reducing global consumption substantially.

Concludes by emphasizing importance of issue

Works Cited

"Bird Strikes." *American Bird Conservancy*, 2016, abcbirds.org/.

Cherry, Steven. "Wind Energy Industry Spun into Bat Preservation Effort." *The Iowa Center for Public Affairs Journalism*, 30 June 2015, iowawatch.org/2015/06/30/wind-energy-industry-spun-into-in-bat-preservation-effort/.

"The Fall of Icarus: Ivanpah's Solar Controversy." *Pulitzer Center on Crisis Reporting*, 5 Mar. 2015. Web. 1 Sept. 2015.

Deverakonda, Akshay. "The Fall of Icarus: Ivanpah's Solar Controversy." *Pulitzer Center on Crisis Reporting*, 5 Mar. 2015, pulitzercenter.org/reporting/united-states-california-ivanpah-solar-electric-generating-system-birds-controversy-sharp-seminar.

"Former Japanese PM Naoto Kan: 'Fukushima Radically Changed My Perspective.'" *Deutsche Welle*, 25 Feb. 2015, www.dw.com/en/former-japanese-pm-naoto-kan-fukushima-radically-changed-my-perspective/a-18275921.

McCurry, Justin. "Japan Restarts First Nuclear Reactor since Fukushima Disaster." *The Guardian*, 11 Aug. 2015. Web. 1 Sept. 2015, www.theguardian.com/environment/2015/aug/11/japan-restarts-first-nuclear-reactor-fukushima-disaster.

List of works cited follows MLA style.

→ EXERCISE 6.1 Assessing a revision

Compare the final version of Michael Wedd's essay (above) with the earlier version (pp. 48–50). Which changes are global and which are local? Is there anything more that you would suggest he do with this essay before submitting it? Explain.

6j Creating and Submitting a Portfolio

Some instructors (and prospective employers) may ask you to submit a writing portfolio. A portfolio may contain any of the following:

- A collection of texts that show your best work
- A collection of texts (such as a proposal, a formal report, a set of instructions, a website) that demonstrate the range of work you have produced
- A collection of texts from a single project (such as journal entries, freewriting and brainstorming, outline, first draft, revised draft) that show your writing process

What you include depends on the portfolio's purpose, audience, and context: You may create a portfolio of your best work to demonstrate your writing skills for admission to a course (a creative writing course, for example); you may create a portfolio showing the range of writing you have done to apply for a job; or you may create a portfolio to demonstrate the process you followed for a composition class.

As you select the contents, consider your audience:

- What kinds of writing projects will interest your readers?
- How many examples will your readers expect you to include? Will they want to see multiple examples of the same type of work, or is one example sufficient? Will they be interested in work you have created in electronic media, or will they focus exclusively on your writing?
- How will they want you to submit the portfolio—electronically or in print?

Once you have selected the items to be included, think about how you want to arrange the contents. A portfolio that shows your writing process should be arranged chronologically; a portfolio that includes a range of your work might be arranged from strongest to weakest; and a portfolio that includes your best work might be arranged in order of interest to your audience. While the contents of a portfolio will vary, in general, include the following:

Title page or home page For a printed portfolio, include a title page with the following information:

- Title (for example, "One Writer's Journey through Sophomore Composition" or "Portfolio for Application to Stockbridge Writers' Group")
- Identifying information (name, course, contact information)
- Date of submission

For an electronic portfolio, include this information in a separate document or on the home page.

Table of contents or menu with hyperlinks For a printed portfolio, include a table of contents listing the items in the order in which they are arranged, number the pages sequentially, and provide page references in your table of contents. An electronic portfolio should include a menu with hyperlinks to the contents.

Personal statement Whether submitted electronically or in print, a portfolio usually includes a personal statement that describes the contents of the portfolio and explains your choice and arrangement of selections and what the selections demonstrate about you as a writer. For portfolios submitted electronically, consider embedding links to your writing selections from your personal statement as well as from the menu.

Make It **Your Own**

Review three recent writing projects and consider what they reveal about you as a writer. Think about the process you used to write them, the choices you made as you worked on them, and your level of satisfaction with the finished pieces. Then write a two-page reflective essay that could be used as the basis for a personal statement to introduce them in a portfolio. Use specific examples from these texts to support your claims.

Submission Submitting a printed portfolio is straightforward: You assemble the contents, make sure each page is clearly labeled with your name and a brief title, place the contents in a folder or three-ring binder with your identifying information on the front, double-check the contents against the table of contents, and hand it in.

More about Creating a website, 179–85

Submitting an electronic portfolio offers more options: You might create an electronic folder that contains your documents and either save the documents to a disc and mail it or attach the folder to an email. Alternatively, you might create a website, post the contents to a server, and send the URL to recipients. Consult your recipient in advance to determine the best method of electronic submission.

Student Model Personal Statement

Consider the following personal statement. Notice how Syracuse University student Rachana Ky lists the items he included in his writing portfolio, briefly describes his reasons for selecting them, and points out what he believes are the strengths of each.

Dear Professor Howard:

Here is my writing portfolio, the culmination of the semester's work. The selections I have included are the literacy development essay and ethnography from Writing 205 (Sophomore Composition) and a paper on the Parthenon from Architecture 133 (History of Architecture). The purpose of including these papers is to show how I write on a range of assignments, from the personal to the purely academic. The literacy development essay was based on my own life experience. The ethnography describes my observations in the weight room but is more objective than the literacy development essay. The Parthenon essay is the most objective of the three, focusing on a topic about which I have no personal knowledge.

Each of these three pieces of work reflects different qualities or characteristics that reveal me as a writer. The literacy development essay describes my intellectual growth. This piece was written for a broad audience. To show my own growth, I used simple, direct language in the early parts of the essay and more sophisticated language later. My development is best reflected through the verb choices: From simple forms of "to be" and "learned," I moved on to "flogged," "balked," and "superseded."

My ethnography strives to capture the mood of the weight room, and I used descriptive language to convey the smell of body odor, the feel of extreme exertion, and the look of the sweaty, muscular bodies. I also tried to capture the different mind-sets of those using the weight room, from steroidal bodybuilders to svelte women striving for better abs.

The paper on the Parthenon shows my writing when it is limited to the language of architecture. It describes the Parthenon, what it meant to the people who built it, and the history of the building (what remains and how pieces of it were dispersed across the Western world). I notice that in this essay, my word choices were fairly simple, but I was still able to get my point across without using all the fancy words used by architecture critics.

I believe the introduction to each paper is strong. In general, when I cannot come up with a good start to a paper, I notice that I have problems developing the rest of the essay, so I work hard to develop an introduction that creates a sense of what my paper will discuss and how. The first two samples in particular, where I was not limited to following a certain style, have particularly engaging introductions that, I hope, have captured the reader's imagination.

I look forward to hearing your thoughts about the enclosed.

Rachana

Rachana Ky

Part Two

Reasoning
Matters

Reading, Thinking, and Arguing

7   Thinking and Reading Critically   112

8   Analyzing and Crafting Arguments   136

7 Thinking and Reading Critically

© Tom Merton/OJO Images/Getty Images

When you read critically, you peel back a text to uncover its meaning. You begin with comprehension, just getting the gist of the text. Next comes reflection, when you annotate and analyze the text. As you prepare to write, you explore not only what is written but also what is left unstated, and you draw on your own experience and other texts to hone your evaluation. The process of peeling a text, as you would the layers of an onion, is what drives and deepens the intellectual process.

7a Comprehending

In our day-to-day lives, we read constantly, and the texts range from brief tweets to thousand-page books. Some texts, like street signs (Figure 7.1), are simple messages of just a few words or images; they are designed to communicate information quickly, simply, and clearly.

Most of the texts you read in college were written to inform or educate you about an issue or topic. They may also have a

Writing Responsibly | Engaging with What You Read

When conducting research, you have a responsibility to engage with the texts you read. If you are struggling, begin by determining what barrier is keeping you from making a connection with the text: Is the language too challenging? Is the topic unfamiliar or too familiar? Is your concentration poor because you did not eat lunch? Then try to overcome the barrier: Use a dictionary to acquaint yourself with the unfamiliar vocabulary; consider the material as a primer or a recapitulation of an important topic; eat a sandwich.

to TOPIC

secondary purpose: to persuade you to accept a position on that issue or topic. Because most college-level reading assignments attempt to engage you in the complexities of an issue, you should read the text several times. You will get the most out of complex texts if you preview the text, read through it quickly to get the gist, write a brief summary, and, most importantly, enjoy what you read!

© Roger Wright/Getty Images

 Reading for Comprehension Many people think the key to better reading is to read slower. Native and non-native English speakers may slow their *speech* to help their listeners comprehend, but the same idea may not work for *reading*. In fact, research shows that reading faster can help increase your comprehension, because you associate ideas more readily.

1. Preview the text.

The more you know about a text before you begin reading, the more efficiently you will be able to read. Unless you are reading a work of literature—a novel, a poem, or a play—resist the urge to dive in and read the text from beginning to end. Instead, start by *previewing*:

© Design Pics Inc/Alamy Stock Photo

- **Note the title and subtitle.** The title sets the stage for the work and may reveal its topic, its approach, and even its tone.

- **Read the abstract, introduction, conclusion, and sidebars**. Many scholarly journals place an *abstract,* or summary, at the beginning of each article; abstracts also appear in article database entries. Other texts may offer overviews of main ideas and important questions in introductions, prologues, conclusions, boxes, or sidebars. Textbook chapters often conclude with study questions that provide a framework for thinking about key topics.

- **Read first sentences and paragraphs.** In short texts, read the first sentence of each paragraph; in longer texts, read the first paragraph of each section. From this you will gain a preliminary sense of the topic and argument of the text.

- **Note the key terms.** In textbooks, important terms are often indicated in italic or boldfaced type and may also be listed at the end of the chapter or in a glossary. Terms are generally defined in the body or margins of a text; the text may also have a glossary.

- **Read the headings and subheadings.** If the text is organized into sections with headings, skim them for an outline.

FIGURE 7.1 Everyday texts Street signs convey information through words, shapes, and images. They are simple, so we can act on them immediately, almost without thinking.

- **Scan figures and illustrations.** Figures may signal important ideas. Visuals convey complex processes quickly and are often accompanied by a succinct explanation (Figure 7.2).

2. Get the gist.

> **More about**
> Paraphrasing and
> patchwriting,
> 253–57

After previewing the text, you are ready to read it once through from beginning to end to get the *gist,* or basic idea. If the text you are reading is persuasive or argumentative, the gist may be expressed in a *thesis statement.* Often this will be signaled in the introduction and then developed and expanded throughout the text. As you read, circle words or phrases you have questions about, but press on without looking them up—yet. When you have finished, close the book and write down what you remember. Try to *paraphrase,* to state the ideas in your own words, rather than quoting from the text. If you can accurately paraphrase the text's major points without quoting or *patchwriting,* you have grasped its literal meaning. If you cannot, read the text again, close the book, and try again to paraphrase.

> **patchwriting** Using the language or sentence structure of the source; not putting the content into fresh words

D. melanogaster ♂

D. biarmipes ♂

a.

b.

12th ed., New York, McGraw-Hill Education, 2016, p. 269

FIGURE 7.2 Preview figures and illustrations Previewing figures and illustrations, and reading their captions, can provide insight. This figure and its caption, for example, describe a distinguishing characteristic of an insect, pointing to an emphasis on evolution.

Wing spot in *Drosophila biarmipes* a. Male *D. biarmipes* have a spot on the leading edge of their wings that is not present in their close relative, *D. melanogaster.* **b.** *D. biarmipes* males flash the spot on their wings to attract the attention of females during a courtship dance.

3. Summarize the text.

Student Model
"Reflecting on Brent
Staples's Editorial
'How Hip-Hop Music
Lost Its Way and
Betrayed Its Fans,'"
Alea Wratten, 131–34

When you feel you have a good (though not necessarily perfect) grasp of the text, *summarize* it. A paraphrase may be as long as (or longer than) the passage it restates, but a summary shortens it by restating only the main idea (the *thesis*) and major supporting points (the *evidence*). Your summary should be at least 50 percent shorter than the text it restates; many summaries are only 10 percent (or less) as long as the original. The summary on the next page captures the main idea and major supporting points of the Brent Staples editorial that Alea Wratten writes about later in this chapter. The original editorial, which starts on page 120, is about 730 words; this summary is about 140 words, a bit less than a quarter of the original.

Student Model Summary

> Summary of "How Hip-Hop Music
> Lost Its Way and Betrayed Its Fans"
>
> In this editorial, *The New York Times* writer Brent Staples claims that both rap music and the way it is marketed perpetuate racial stereotypes and glorify violence, materialism, and sexism. Citing the example of an actual gang war in the 1990s, Staples argues that rival rappers use their music to insult each other and initiate violence. 50 Cent, for instance, timed a post–radio-interview gun battle to coincide with the release of his album *Massacre*. Staples worries that rap will influence inner-city kids, who already face poverty and violence, to adopt the glamorous "gangsta" lifestyle and maybe even wind up in prison. He also blames producers like Jimmy Iovine and Dr. Dre for the direction hip-hop has taken. Staples ends by saying that he feels the public will not stand for much more of this; if hip-hop continues in this vein, he thinks, it won't last.

For any complex reading assignment, writing a summary will help you to remember the main points of the text, and the summary you create will also provide a useful reference. As with paraphrasing, avoid patchwriting: The more you can write about a topic in your own words, the better you will understand it.

4. Enjoy the text.

You are most likely to comprehend a text when you enjoy it, and you are far more likely to enjoy it if you *think about* the text as you read. Engage with it as you would with a message from a friend or with the trailer for a new movie. The pleasure of reading often comes from noticing the details: a nice turn of phrase, a subtle joke, or a clever comparison. Enjoyment does not require total agreement with—or even a complete understanding of—every word on the page. It does require active engagement and an open mind. Allowing yourself to take pleasure in reading can also improve your academic performance and your ability to connect (or *synthesize*) what you read with material from other classes and your own life.

> **More about**
> Synthesis, 127–29,
> 263–64

EXERCISE 7.1 Comprehending and Engaging with the text

Look at the title of the article below, and then write a sentence indicating what you think the essay will be about, based on the title alone. Next, read the essay and summarize the text. Identify the author's point of view on the topic and give an example to support your claim. Finally, write one or two sentences explaining what you found surprising, interesting, or challenging about this essay, and why.

Professional Model Essay

The Moral Absurdity of Denying Financial Aid to Undocumented Students
By Eric Johnson

Financial-aid nights offer a fascinating window into the state of the world. Spending long hours talking with students, parents, guidance counselors, and legal guardians in a rural high school or a downtown community center, I am always struck by the chasm that separates bloodless policy discussions from lived reality.

A few months ago, I went to a national conference where the hot topic among aid administrators was retirement savings, and whether "excessive" assets ought to be counted as a college resource. Meanwhile, about half of working adults have no retirement savings at all, and more than half of those approaching retirement age have less than $25,000. Not surprisingly, I don't field many questions about excess capital in 401(k)s.

But the most jarring gulf between policy and practice emerges around immigration. While national leaders preach mass deportation or debate a long and arduous path to legal status, school counselors and college administrators are confronted every day with the wrenching fallout of a failed system.

For me, it almost always comes in the form of a quiet plea, offered as a financial-aid night wraps up. After all of the questions about summer jobs and custody issues have been asked and answered in front of the crowd, a student will linger, waiting patiently to speak with me away from the audience.

Whenever this happens, the students tell me about growing up nearby, about working hard in school, about their grades and their extracurriculars. They tell me about the classes they've loved, about the teachers or counselors who've encouraged them. They tell me about dreams of becoming an engineer, or a nurse, or a computer programmer.

Colleges work hard to recruit kids like those: self-motivated, sharp, and ready to succeed in one of our tougher disciplines. Policy makers profess to want them, too. Every politician who has wandered past a microphone in recent years—Republican or Democratic, urban or rural, moderate or radical—has called for more graduates in science and mathematics, more young people with solid career ambitions and the drive to succeed in higher education. Our economy needs those students, I am well assured.

But all too often, with manifestly qualified students standing before me and asking for the chance to earn a degree, I am charged with slamming the door. "I'm sorry," I have to tell them. "But there's not much we can do if you're undocumented."

By the time they're talking to me, the students have come to expect disappointment. Brought to this country years ago, spirited across a border they were too young to comprehend by parents who wanted better for them, the children are beginning to understand their outlaw status. They've begun to realize that our laws treat them as indefinite accomplices to a crime committed when they were toddlers.

So now, even though they might have lived an entire remembered existence within my state, I have to tell them that they're nonresidents, at least when it comes to college tuition, and that they won't be eligible for financial aid. Those are the policies; those are the choices we have democratically made for shepherding these blameless children.

The best I can do is scribble down a first name and an email address; I will pass them along to one of the nonprofit groups that tries to find options for undocumented students. And I apologize that there's not a better, more persuasive answer for why undocumented children are allowed to graduate high school—indeed, are legally compelled to attend school in the United States—but effectively are barred from our public colleges.

Immigration is a legitimately tough issue. I don't know the best way to handle those who came here illegally—the adults who made decisions and crossed borders, and have now lived in the United States for years or decades. Their situation is politically and morally fraught.

The fate of their children should not be. No reasonable doctrine holds children responsible for the sins of parents, yet that is exactly what most states are doing when it comes to tuition and aid for undocumented young people. If the daughter of a drug addict shows up at my financial-aid night seeking aid and advice, I congratulate her on overcoming a tragic obstacle. But the daughter of a fieldworker who hiked across the Arizona desert a decade ago? I'm supposed to turn her away.

At least 20 states have recognized the moral absurdity in that situation. Legislatures in several states, including Florida and Utah, have decided to offer in-state tuition to undocumented students who meet basic criteria. A handful of states—including California, Minnesota, and Texas—even allow access to state financial aid. But in most of the country, a closed door prevails.

Federal legislation that would replace that confusing patchwork with a more humane system, the Dream Act, has been stymied for nearly five years. Meanwhile, yet another class of ambitious, talented, and innocent Dreamers will soon graduate without a clear path to college.

The cost of that squandered opportunity is mounting. Not only in the teachers, nurses, engineers, and entrepreneurs we're missing, but in the generational leadership we're going to need in a demographically changing America.

These are our children. They grew up in our towns, they speak our language, and they have worked and learned in our schools. To leave them permanently exiled within their own world is not a policy—it is an abdication. And it will come to haunt us, as too many of these aid-night conversations already haunt me.

Chronicle of Higher Education, 21 Feb. 2016.

Make It **Your Own**

Find a photograph in a printed or online newspaper (or use one from this book), and write a one- or two-paragraph description of it. Be sure to indicate your first impression and what the photo depicts. Then insert a copy of the image after your description so that readers will see the description *before* they see the image.

Work **Together**

Trade descriptions with a classmate. Without looking at the photograph, try to form a mental picture of the image. Now look at the photograph. Discuss how well the description captured the image and what you would change. Did the description change what you noticed or how you responded to the image?

7b Reflecting

Once you have the gist of a text, let *reflection* help lead you to full comprehension. Annotating the text is a good starting-place for reflection; writing about the text in your reading journal may spur reflection, too.

1. Annotate the text.

A useful first step in reflecting upon a text is to reread it with a pencil or pen in hand (or a computer at the ready). Careful annotations will also be

Tech **Annotating Online Texts**

When you read from a screen instead of a page, consider saving the text to your hard drive, flash drive, or cloud server so you can annotate it in your word processor or PDF reader.

self

Assessment

When annotating an image, analyze the following elements. Be sure to answer each of these questions and take the suggested steps to offer a thorough critique.

☐ **Tone.** Does it strike you as warm, amused, angry, dispassionate? Point to specific parts of the image that convey the tone.

☐ **Responses.** What responses does the image elicit from you, and why? Again, tie your responses directly to elements of the image.

☐ **Biases.** Do you detect any assumptions or biases? If so, explain what they are and how the visual indicates them.

☐ **Connections.** Does this image remind you of another visual or printed text? If so, in what ways? (Be specific.) Identify any connections between the visual and your own experience.

useful later, when you are studying for an exam or composing a project that discusses the text. As you annotate, focus on some or all of the following:

- **Definitions.** Look up and write down definitions of unfamiliar words.

- **Concepts.** Underline the most important, interesting, or difficult concepts.

- **Tone.** Note the writer's tone—sarcastic, sincere, witty, shrill.

- **Biases.** Look out for the writer's biases and unstated assumptions (and your own). Does the text ignore or misrepresent important counterevidence? Does it contain loaded or hurtful language?

- **Fallacies.** Is the text illogical or misleading?

- **Responses.** Jot down your own reactions and insights, as well as any questions you have about the text.

- **Connections.** Make connections with other texts you have read or with your own experiences.

More about
Tone, 19–20, 138, 565, 570–72
Bias, 566–69
Avoiding logical fallacies, 159–63
Note taking, 251–64
Working bibliography, 204–09

Read footnotes and any text in parentheses: They seldom contain the main claims or supporting evidence, but they can provide key background information, references to additional scholarship on a topic, and juicy tidbits the writer felt moved to share.

Professional Model Editorial

Read the following newspaper editorial by Brent Staples. The annotations to this editorial, which appeared in *The New York Times*, reflect Alea Wratten's thoughts, insights, and struggles with a text she would later write about. The comments define unfamiliar vocabulary, note reflections, and make connections.

> *I loved "Just Walk on By" (same author)*

> *There are certainly negative images out there, but there are many positive African American role models, too (including Staples).*

> *virulent— extremely infectious or damaging. Why is rap the most "virulent" music?*

> *Central argument—raises an important issue but over-generalizes.*

> *"palette" compares music to painting*

> *misogyny—hatred of women*

> *Is this logic backwards? Sometimes gangsta rappers are violent, but does their music describe the violence or cause it?*

How Hip–Hop Music Lost Its Way and Betrayed Its Fans

By BRENT STAPLES

African–American teenagers are beset on all sides by dangerous myths about race. The most poisonous one defines middle class normalcy and achievement as "white," while embracing violence, illiteracy and drug dealing as "authentically" black. This fiction rears its head from time to time in films and literature. But it finds its most virulent expression in rap music, which started out with a broad palette of themes but has increasingly evolved into a medium for worshiping misogyny, materialism and murder.

This dangerous narrowing of hip–hop music would be reason for concern in any case. But it is especially troubling against the backdrop of the 1990s, when rappers provoked a real–world gang war by using recordings and music videos to insult and threaten rivals. Two of the music's biggest stars—Tupac Shakur and the Notorious B.I.G.—were eventually shot to death.

People who pay only minimal attention to the rap world may have thought the killings would sober up the rap community. Not quite. The May cover of the hip–hop magazine *Vibe* was on the mark when it depicted fallen rappers standing among tombstones under the headline: "Hip–Hop Murders: Why Haven't We Learned Anything?"

The cover may have been prompted in part by a rivalry between two rappers that culminated in a shootout at a New York radio station, Hot 97, earlier this spring. The events that led up to the shooting show how recording labels now exploit violence to make and sell recordings.

At the center of that Hot 97 shootout was none other than 50 Cent, whose given name is Curtis Jackson III. Mr. Jackson is a confessed former drug dealer who seems to revel in the fact that he was shot several times while dealing in Queens. He has also made a career of "beef" recordings, in which he whips up controversy and heightens tension by insulting rival artists.

He was following this pattern in a radio interview in March when a rival showed up at the station. The story's murky, but it appears that the rival's entourage met Mr. Jackson's on the street, resulting in gunfire. Mr. Jackson's on–air agitation was clearly timed to coincide

> *How much have things changed since then?*

> *The "rap community" isn't entirely gangsta rap; there are other kinds of rap hip-hop out there.*

> *Too strong? Rap sometimes glamorizes, but it can raise awareness, too.*

> *Many people "learned" or were not involved in the violence: Kanye West, Chuck D., Public Enemy, etc.*

> *True—recording labels are marketing an image.*

> *Example: 50 Cent and the release/ marketing of "The Massacre"*

with the release of "The Massa—cre," his grotesquely violent and misogynist compact disc. The CD cover depicts the artist stand—ing before a wall adorned with weapons, pointing what appears to be a shotgun at the camera. The photographs in the liner notes depict every ghetto stereo—type—the artist selling drugs, the artist in a gunfight—and includes a mock autopsy report that has been seen as a covert threat aimed at some of his critics.

The "Massacre" promotion raises the ante in a most destruc—tive way. New artists, desperate for stardom, will say or do anything to win notice—and buzz—for their next projects. As the trend esca—lates, inner—city listeners who are already at risk of dying prema—turely are being fed a toxic diet of rap cuts that glorify murder and make it seem perfectly normal to spend your life in prison.

Critics who have been angered by this trend have pointed at Jimmy Iovine, the music impresario whose Interscope Records reaped millions on gangster rap in the 90s. Mr. Iovine makes a convenient target as a white man who is lording over an essentially black art form.

But also listed on "The Massacre" as an executive producer is the legendary rapper Dr. Dre, a black man who happens to be one of the most powerful people in the busi—ness. Dr. Dre has a unique vantage point on rap—related violence. He was co—founder of Death Row Records, an infamous Califor—nia company that marketed West Coast rap in the 1990s and had a front—row seat for the feud that led to so much bloodshed back then.

The music business hopes to make a financial killing on a recently announced summer concert tour that is set to feature 50 Cent and the mega—selling rap star Eminem. But promot—ers will need to make heavy use of metal detectors to suppress the kind of gun—related vio—lence that gangster artists cel—ebrate. That this lethal genre of art has grown speaks volumes about the industry's greed and lack of self—control.

But trends like this reach a tipping point, when business as usual becomes unacceptable to the public as a whole. Judging from the rising hue and cry, hip—hop is just about there.

Margin annotations

No concrete proof that 50 Cent planned a gun—fight to promote his album. Is the inference fair? I think so.

Is it the mar—keting or the art itself that is "misogynistic" and "supremely violent"? Note: Listen to this song.

In many neigh—borhoods, kids grow up seeing people going to prison all the time, so for them it is normal.

I wonder who these other crit—ics are?

impresario—entertainment manager or pro—moter

Good example of author's point—even in the name of the record company.

A pun?

Can art be "lethal"?

tipping point—the moment when something rare becomes much more common

Hip-hop is still popular. Does he just mean against gangsta rap?

→ EXERCISE 7.2 Annotating a text

Using the annotations to the Brent Staples editorial above as a model, annotate the essay by Eric Johnson (pp. 116–118).

2. Keep a journal.

Articulating your responses in a *journal* is a good way to build a deeper understanding and a sense of taking part in—not just taking in—what you read. A journal entry can do any of the following:

- Analyze the writer's purpose: Is it to entertain, inform, persuade?

More about
Purpose, 14–16
Generating ideas,
    24–30
Outlining, 40–42
Synthesizing, 127–29,
    263–64

- Develop insights through freewriting.
- Brainstorm reasons for supporting or opposing the claims.
- Organize your ideas through clustering or outlining.
- Synthesize ideas from the text with ideas of your own or ideas from other sources.

A double-entry reading journal provides a column for quotations, summaries, or paraphrases and a column for your responses. This technique can help you avoid plagiarism by keeping your own ideas separate from the ideas you have found in the text.

The entries from the reading journal below reflect one student's thoughts about the Eric Johnson essay that appears in Exercise 7.1.

Student Model **Double-Entry Reading Journal**

Quotation/Summary/Paraphrase	Response
"Every politician who has wandered past a microphone in recent years—Republican or Democratic, urban or rural, moderate or radical—has called for more graduates in science and mathematics..." (par 6)	*This sentence made me laugh. Maybe it's a cynical line, but it's a great way to introduce a key point. It helps the reader "see" how every politician has an opinion on this issue.*
"No reasonable doctrine holds children responsible for the sins of their parents." (par 12)	*I don't think the author sees illegal immigration as a sin. Instead, by using this familiar term, he draws our attention to how undocumented children are penalized for their parents' legal status.*
Children of drug addicts can get financial aid, but children of undocumented immigrants can't in many states. Both are praised for their success in overcoming challenges, but only one is helped to get to college. (par 12)	*This is definitely worth following up. I'll google to find articles on this, in case it affects Maritza's plans for college next year. The author doesn't use exact numbers but I can find out and include them in my research project.*
The author says "a closed door prevails" (most states don't give undocumented students financial aid) and he is "charged with slamming the door" (students ask him for financial aid, but he can only say no). (par 13, par 7)	*I like the image of the closed door. It's used twice in the essay. That reinforces the point that undocumented students are literally shut out of the education system.*

> **EXERCISE 7.3 Writing a journal entry**

Using the journal entry on the previous page as a model, write a journal entry on either the Johnson essay (pp. 116–118) or the Staples editorial (pp. 120–121). If you quote any material, note where it comes from, in case you have to cite it later.

> **EXERCISE 7.4 Writing about an image**

Find a striking photograph online or in a magazine, newspaper, or textbook. Using the sample below as a model, write a journal entry about the image, relating your thoughts, feelings, and reactions to the photograph as a whole or to specific parts of it.

7c Preparing to Write

Critical readers are often readying themselves for the next step: writing. Having something interesting to say about a reading selection will come from *analyzing* the text carefully; *interpreting* the text to find or create a new, deeper meaning; *synthesizing* what you have learned from the text with what you have learned elsewhere; and *critiquing,* or evaluating, the text.

© Boris Roessler/dpa/Corbis

The colors in this photo are vibrant; robe concealing the woman in the foreground is almost the same shade of blue as the blue blouse that Preety Zinta is wearing.

Is the subject the woman in the foreground, covered head to toe, or the glamour shots of models and actresses (especially Preety Zinta) in the background? Preety Zinta almost looks like the woman's reflection. Her set expression reveals very little, almost as little as the covered woman's.

It's interesting to wonder what the woman in the foreground is thinking. Does she want to uncover her head (like Preety Zinta) or is she shocked by Zinta's flowing hair and red lipstick?

The contrast here makes me think about what these photos say about the way women are perceived and treated in various cultures.

More about
Analysis, 66, 68
Evaluating claims, 136–44
Evidence, 45–46
Analyzing works of literature, 452–74 (ch. 22)

1. Analyze.

To comprehend a text fully, you must *analyze* it: Take it apart, consider its components, figure out how the parts fit together, and assess how the text as a whole convinces its audience of its claims. When analyzing a text, consider the following:

- The major claims a text makes. Are all the claims backed by evidence (such as examples, facts, and expert testimony)?

- The type and quality of the evidence offered to support the claims. How appropriate and satisfying is the evidence? Is it sufficient to support the claims?

- The presence or absence of counterevidence. Does the text inform its audience of weaknesses in its claims or evidence, or offer alternative perspectives?

- The sources the author draws on (if any). How reliable are they, and what is the author's attitude toward them?

- The organization of the argument (classical, Rogerian, Toulmin). What does the organization suggest about the writer's purpose?

More about
Purpose, 14–16
Audience, 17–20
Organization:
 classical, Rogerian, Toulmin, 156–59
Rhetorical
 appeals (logos, ethos, pathos), 144–47
Tone, 19–20, 138, 565, 570–72
Style, 519–94
 (part 7, Style Matters)

- The rhetorical appeals used in the text. Where can you see the author appealing to logos (rational, logical claims or evidence), ethos (where the texts shows the expertise or credibility of the author or the sources), or pathos (drawing on the audience's emotions or sympathy)? How appropriate are the rhetorical appeals for the audience, context, and purpose?

- The tone and style. What do these reflect about the author's purpose in writing this piece or attitude toward the topic or audience?

- The logical pattern used in the text, which provides information about the author's purpose. Exploratory arguments are likely to use *inductive logic,* citing particular examples and then drawing a general conclusion. Persuasive arguments are likely to use *deductive logic,* offering generally accepted truths from which conclusions can be drawn about specific instances. How appropriate are the logical patterns for the audience, context, and purpose?

Quick Reference   Steps in Developing Critical Understanding

- **Analyze.** Divide a text into its component parts to understand *how* it reaches its audience.
- **Interpret.** Dig below the surface to draw conclusions based on the author's assumptions, motives, and omissions, as well as the circumstances in which the text was written.
- **Synthesize.** Connect ideas in a text to relevant ideas in other texts or experiences; analyze the relationships among ideas or draw comparisons and contrasts.
- **Critique.** Evaluate based on evidence gathered through careful reading, analysis, interpretation, and synthesis.

Student Model   Claims and Evidence Analysis

In analyzing the Staples editorial (p. 120), Alea Wratten identified its main claim and the explanations and evidence provided to support that claim:

Major claims:

1. Today's hip-hop music spreads a dangerous myth that an authentic black experience is violent.

2. This has serious consequences for listeners.

Evidence:

- Lyrics promote racism, sexism, violence

- Behavior of hip-hop artists promotes violence: Deaths of Tupac Shakur, Notorious B.I.G.

- 50 Cent's insulting rivals and shootout at Hot 97 to promote record

- Violent imagery on cover of The Massacre and in liner notes

- Dr Dre-cofounder of Death Row Records, executive producer of 50 Cent's record

- Need for metal detectors at concerts

Student Model   Advertisement Critique

An analysis of an advertisement—focusing on the claims it makes, the relation between image and text, and the reaction the advertisement is trying to elicit from the reader—appears on the next page.

This advertisement for Adopt Us Kids, sponsored by the Ad Council, appeared in a variety of magazines. It makes two explicit claims: "You don't have to be perfect to be a perfect parent" and "There are thousands of teens in foster care who would love to put up with you." These two claims suggest a third: *Readers should consider adopting a child in foster care.* The ad relies on the assumption that people don't adopt because they worry they won't be good parents.

You don't have to be perfect to be a perfect parent.
There are thousands of teens in foster care who would love to put up with you.

1 888 200 4005 · adoptuskids.org

The image of a flawed but still inviting birthday cake illustrates the first claim. This cake may sag a bit, but it's been placed in an elegant serving dish and lit up with polka-dotted candles. Atop the cake is the number 16—a milestone age that people associate with sweet sixteen parties and driver's licenses.

The specificity of this age implies a particular person, and an engaged reader can't help but wonder about all the kids in foster care who turn sixteen without this rite of passage, the luxury of a birthday cake, or the love of a parent who'd buy or make one. The image elicits our emotional response, but the written text articulates and clarifies its message: What matters in parenthood is effort and love, not perfection. Omission is also used powerfully here; what is *missing* from the photograph—a child—might be missing from a reader's life, too.

2. Interpret.

More about
Identifying
   assumptions, 150
Identifying
   stakeholders,
   236, 238
Interpreting,
   263–64, 271–73

After analyzing the text to determine how it works, consider the significance or meaning of the elements you have identified, and draw inferences about what may be below the surface of the text. Use the following questions to help guide your *interpretation* of a text:

- What assumptions does the writer make about the subject or audience? Why are such assumptions significant?

- What does the text omit (evidence, opposing views), and what might these omissions indicate?

- What conclusions can you draw about the author's attitude from the tone? What motives can you infer from the author's background or previous publications?

- Who published this text or sponsored the research, and what influence might these sponsors have upon the way the information, arguments, or evidence is presented?

- In what context was the text written—place, time, cultural environment—and how might this context have influenced the writer?

Student Model Prewrite

In prewriting for her critical response essay, Alea Wratten considered Staples's assumptions, omissions, and possible motivations:

> Staples treats hip-hop and rap as synonyms. He refers to the "dangerous narrowing" of this kind of music, but there is no discussion of what this narrowed from. He gives examples of rappers whose albums glorify violence, but not of hip-hop artists with other themes. Also, while Staples states twice that rap is misogynistic, he doesn't provide any lyrics or examples to prove it. Is he relying on his readers to know enough about rap to know this is true? I don't think so—people who read *The New York Times* are probably mostly white, middle-aged, and well off, not the kind of folks who are usually into hip-hop. And he mustn't think his readers really know about hip-hop because he has to tell them what *Vibe* is ("the hip-hop magazine"). So are these gaps typical of newspaper editorials? They do have to be short, so not a lot of room for examples. And since they're directed toward a general audience, they're more likely to use this kind of dramatic language. Or is this an indication of a blind spot about hip-hop? This is something I think a lot of people from the Beatles or Motown generation—like my mom!—share.

3. Synthesize.

College assignments often ask you to *synthesize*—to connect what you have read to ideas in other texts or to the world around you. You may begin to synthesize early on, as you read and annotate the text. You will probably develop these connections in your reading journal and as you draft and revise your project.

More about
Synthesizing,
263–64
Comparing and
contrasting,
66–67

To synthesize, ask yourself the following questions:

- What else have you read or experienced that this text may explain, illustrate, clarify, complicate, or contradict?

- How do the author's other writings amplify, clarify, complicate, or contradict the selection you are writing about?

- What outside forces (historical events, socioeconomic forces, cultural shifts) might influence or underlie the text?

- What claims or points in each text do you find especially compelling? How do compelling points in one text connect to ideas in the other(s)?

- What claims could these texts, taken together, provide evidence for?

- How is your understanding of a topic enhanced or your thinking changed by putting these texts together? What might others gain by seeing these texts together?

Writing Responsibly

Drawing Inferences

An inference is only as good as what it is based on. Inferences based on facts are fair; those based on personal values and beliefs or on a faulty understanding of the text are apt to be one-sided and unfair. Aim for the former and avoid the latter.

to TOPIC

An excerpt from prewriting for Alea Wratten's essay draws connections between Brent Staples's editorial "How Hip-Hop Music Lost Its Way and Betrayed Its Fans" and the hip-hop music she listens to.

Staples uses examples of gangsta rappers like 50 Cent and Eminem to support his claim that hip-hop promotes negative stereotypes and violence. Sure, 50 Cent's music may try to make violence look cool, but not all hip-hop is ultra-violent. Kanye West is a big star, and he has gone platinum with positive, even spiritual messages. Lauren Hill, Kam, KRS One, Arrested Development, Chuck D, and Public Enemy are just a few of the artists in my music collection who set positive examples for listeners.

Wratten's inferences are fair: They are based on facts (other hip-hop stars who are successful without violence) and on her analysis of Staples's omissions.

Make It **Your Own**

College assignments often ask you to synthesize ideas found in two or more texts. Using the questions on page 128 as a guide, write a 350- to 500-word essay that synthesizes "The Moral Absurdity of Denying Financial Aid to Undocumented Students" (Exercise 7.1, p. 116) with the information below and any other texts or experiences that are relevant.

> We teach boys to be such men as we are. We do not teach them to aspire to be all they can. We do not give them a training as if we believed in their noble nature. We scarce educate their bodies. We do not train the eye and the hand. We exercise their understandings to the apprehension and comparison of some facts, to a skill in numbers, in words; we aim to make accountants, attorneys, engineers; but not to make able, earnest, great-hearted men. The great object of education should be commensurate with the object of life. It should be a moral one: to teach self-trust; to inspire the youthful man with an interest in himself; with a curiosity touching his own nature; to acquaint him with the resources of his mind, and to teach him that *there* is all his strength, and to inflame him with a piety towards the Grand Mind in which he lives.
>
> —Ralph Waldo Emerson, "Education"

4. Critique.

A *critique* is a well-informed evaluation. It may be positive, negative, or a bit of both. A movie review, for example, is a critique; it provides readers with an evaluation to help them decide whether or not to see the film. A reviewer's opinion alone is usually not enough to sway a would-be audience member. The reviewer must also provide evidence for the judgment by describing the performances, the screenplay, or the director's vision. Similarly, critiques written

Writing **Responsibly** Understanding Criticism

In everyday speech, *criticism* is often used simply to mean "finding fault." But in academic disciplines, *criticizing* means "evaluating a work's merits based on a careful and fair analysis." Approach the task of critique skeptically yet with an open mind, and provide evidence for the judgments you make. If you are used to thinking about published texts as absolutely authoritative sources of information, it is important for you to realize that *all* texts present only partial views that can always be challenged.

to OTHER WRITERS

Professional Model
Review, 472–74

for college courses offer judgments based on careful analysis of the text's component parts. They may also be informed by other texts, your own knowledge and experience, or both.

As you prepare to write a critique, consider the following issues:

- **The writer's aims.** What are the author's goals? Are they achieved? Are they worth achieving?

- **The writer's claims.** What are the writer's claims? How much are you persuaded by them? Why?

- **The writer's evidence.** How credible is the evidence? How reliable and relevant is the evidence? How sound is the reasoning?

- **The writer's authority.** What expertise or life experience does the writer bring to the topic, and is it relevant?

self Assessment | Preparing to Write about a Visual

When exploring a visual, especially if writing about it, ask yourself the following questions. What evidence supports your answers?

Analysis

- **Parts and patterns.** What are the relationships among the parts? Does the image include or imply a comparison or contrast, a cause or effect?

- **Purpose.** Is the visual's purpose to inform, persuade, entertain, or express emotion? If the visual is persuasive, what does it claim and how does it support this claim?

- **Attitude.** What is the artist's attitude toward the subject or audience? On what basis can you make this inference?

- **Context.** Where is the image set? When was it created? Who produced or sponsored it, and why? How do accompanying words inform your reading?

Interpretation

- **Assumptions.** What values does the image assume or promote? How do those values match, contrast with, or challenge those of its audience?

- **Omissions.** Is something missing? Has the visual been cropped to eliminate background? If so, how does this affect your understanding?

- **Audience.** Who is the intended audience? Where was the visual originally published, or where did you find it? How was the image received by its original audience?

Synthesis

- **Other sources.** How is this image similar to or different from others that you know? Have you read or studied anything that could help you understand this visual?

- **Background.** What knowledge or personal experiences do you have that might deepen your understanding?

Critique

- **Aims.** Based on your analysis, what were the artist's aims, and were they achieved?

- **Claims.** What claims is the artist making, and are you persuaded?

- **Authority.** What expertise or experience does the artist bring?

Also consider your own goals and position:

- **Your aims, claims, and evidence.** Why are you writing the critique? What claims are you making? What evidence will you use to support those claims?

- **Your authority.** What authority do you have, and why might readers value your judgment and evaluation? You may not be an expert, but your opinion can be interesting and persuasive if it is based on thoughtful analysis.

- **Your audience.** What are your readers' interests and knowledge about the subject? What background information will you need to provide? Will they be sympathetic to your claims, or will you have to work hard to persuade them?

More about
Claims, 140–44
Evidence, 45–46
Authority, 145,
  236, 238
Relevance, 233–34
Reliability, 234–39
Audience, 17–20

> **EXERCISE 7.5 Analyzing a speech**

Analyze the speech by John F. Kennedy on pages 75–77. In two or three paragraphs, describe the speaker's assumptions and attitude. Also consider how circumstances (the "son of Boston" leaving his home state of Massachusetts for Washington, DC; the recent presidential election) might have affected its reception.

Work **Together**

In groups of three or more, compare your syntheses. How effectively do your classmates' syntheses draw connections between the two texts? In what ways are they similar to and different from your own? Discuss the strategies you used to complete this synthesis and any revisions that could make them more effective. Make a note of strategies you might use in the future.

Student Model **Critical Response Essay**

In the essay that follows, Alea Wratten (SUNY–Geneseo) analyzes Brent Staples's editorial "How Hip-Hop Music Lost Its Way and Betrayed Its Fans" and draws on her knowledge of hip-hop to create this critical response.

Reflecting on Brent Staples's Editorial "How Hip-Hop

Music Lost Its Way and Betrayed Its Fans"

Hip-hop is among today's most popular forms of American music. You can hear it walking through the mall, during TV commercials, and in nearly anyone's music collection (including mine). Despite, or perhaps because of, this popularity, Brent Staples, in his *The New York Times* editorial, "How Hip-Hop Music Lost Its Way and Betrayed Its Fans," calls hip-hop a "lethal genre of art" (26), claiming the music brainwashes and endangers black kids, who will identify blackness with the criminal underworld depicted in these songs. He claims that hip-hop "has evolved into a medium for worshiping misogyny, materialism, and murder" (26) and that it is only getting worse. Staples raises some excellent concerns about the dangers of marketing violence to young people, but ultimately his argument fails to be persuasive for several reasons: He does not account for the influence positive role models have, he ignores the fact that art frequently depicts violence without dire consequences to its consumers, and he overlooks the broad spectrum of hip-hop to focus on only a single strand.

First, it is distressing that Staples, who himself presents a positive role model for black teens, would assume that black teens would be likely to identify with violent, misogynistic lyrics, associating success and respect for the law with whiteness and poverty, crime, and sexism with blackness. Staples, who grew up poor and black, was likely smarter than this, and so are today's black teens. They see successful black men and women all around them—an African American president, the nation's wealthiest and most popular talk show host, an influential editorial writer for *The New York Times*, not to mention scores of business men and women, actors,

Introduction: Brief summary of editorial to which it is responding

Thesis: Acknowledges strengths of Staples's editorial but also lists three problems

Topic sentence: Analyzes assumption that black teens use rap stars as models

Counterevidence

comedians, and sports figures—all of whom are role models that black teens might identify with and aspire to become. With this range of possible models before them, it is unlikely that many black teens would be deluded about the world because they had listened to offensive hip-hop lyrics.

Second, by calling hip-hop a "lethal genre," Staples places it into a category separate from other works of art that are not as "virulent." Yes, many hip-hop lyrics are violent, but that does not distinguish them from many other artistic works. Edgar Allan Poe, considered one of America's greatest writers, wrote numerous stories about murder and death, including "The Tell-Tale Heart," whose narrator is a confessed killer. *The Talented Mr. Ripley*, a novel by Patricia Highsmith, and the movie based on this novel, make Tom Ripley, an unrepentant murderer, a sympathetic character. Sculptor Kiki Smith depicts mutilated bodies in her art (See Figure 1), and, instead of being criticized, she is considered one of today's most important sculptors. No one would claim, I think, that Kiki Smith influences her viewers to commit mayhem. Clearly, hip-hop artists are not alone in depicting horrible people and events; they should not be singled out for doing so, and it should not be assumed that their audience will blindly follow suit.

© Kiki Smith, courtesy Pace Gallery

Fig. 1. Kiki Smith, *Untitled*, 1993. Paper and papier-mâché. Pace Wildenstein Gallery, New York.

Topic sentence: Analyzes assumption that hip-hop is different from other art forms

Body: Analyzes author's assumptions, claims, and evidence, and provides counterexamples based on knowledge of hip-hop and other information

Counterexamples

Visual counterexample

133

Topic sentence: Challenges assumption that all hip-hop is *gangsta*

Finally, tarring all of hip-hop with one brush is a mistake. While gangsta rap continues to be very popular, hip-hop includes many bands and artists who write uplifting and socially aware lyrics. Kanye West, for instance, currently among hip-hop's biggest stars, offers a positive, spiritual message in his music, a message of which

Counterexamples

Staples would likely approve. In his song "Family Business," West explains, "I woke up early this mornin' with a new state of mind / A creative way to rhyme without usin' nines and guns / keep your nose out the sky, keep your heart to God / and keep your face to the risin' sun" (West). And West is not alone: Lauren Hill, Kam, KRS One, Arrested Development, Chuck D, and Public Enemy are just a few of the musicians and bands in my music collection that explore hip-hop's more socially responsible side. These artists show that the strand of hip-hop that Staples accuses of providing a "toxic diet" (25) for listeners is just one of many.

Conclusion: Acknowledges violent and misogynistic lyrics in hip-hop but offers different interpretation

Some of the most popular hip-hop songs do revolve around violent or sexist themes. It is important to remember, though, that these themes draw attention to conditions in the communities out of which hip-hop developed. They bring important social problems of poor communities to the attention of a wide audience—black and white. So hip-hop may offer more than just a catchy beat; it is also a way for artists to express themselves and a form of art that tells their stories.

Works Cited

Staples, Brent. "How Hip-Hop Music Lost Its Way and Betrayed Its Fans." Editorial. *The New York Times* 12 May 2005: A25. Print.

West, Kanye. "Family Business." *The College Dropout*. Roc-a-Fella, 2004. CD.

→ EXERCISE 7.6 Writing a critique

Find an editorial in a printed or online newspaper. First, read the editorial using the techniques discussed in this chapter and write a summary noting the editorial's main idea and major supporting points. Then write a paragraph-long critical response to it using analysis, interpretation, synthesis, and critique.

→ EXERCISE 7.7 Interpreting a graphic

Bar graphs like the one here regularly appear in newspapers and magazines with no accompanying story. Based on the graphic alone, write a one- to two-paragraph story to accompany it.

What is the main claim of the graphic? What evidence does it use to support its main claim?

How to Earn Millennials' Loyalty

What companies can offer Millennials, based on most important factors of employer choice (excluding salary)*.

Work-life balance
16.8%

Opportunities to progress/ be leaders
13.4%

Flexibility (i.e., remote working flexible hours)
11%

Sense of meaning from work
9.3%

Professional development training programs
8.3%

*Percentage share of importance
Source: The 2016 Deloitte Millennial Survey

Text Credits

pp. 114 From Mader, *Biology, 12th ed.*, New York, McGraw-Hill, 2016, p. 269. Used with permission. **pp. 116:** Johnson, Eric, "The Moral Absurdity of Denying Financial Aid to Undocumented Students" *The Chronicle of Higher Education*, February 21, 2016. Copyright © 2016 by The Chronicle of Higher Education. Used with permission **pp. 120–121:** Staples, Brent, "How Hip-Hop Music Lost Its Way and Betrayed Its Fans," *The New York Times*, online edition, May 12, 2005. © 2005 The New York Times. All rights reserved. Used by permission and protected by the Copyright Laws of the United States. The printing, copying, redistribution, or retransmission of the Material without express written permission is prohibited. **p. 127:** Courtesy of Alea Wratten. **p. 129:** Emerson, Ralph Waldo, "Education," *The Complete Works of Ralph Waldo Emerson, Volume X: Lectures and Biographical Sketches* (1884).

8 Analyzing and Crafting Arguments

© Greg Craybas

Our culture often confuses *arguing* with *fighting*. While arguments can indeed lead to fights, they usually do not. We're also accustomed to hearing about "both sides" of an argument, which is a misleading concept: arguments are discussions that usually have *many* sides, many points of view, many pros and cons that cannot easily be weighed against each other. This chapter introduces several different forms of argument, ranging from exploration to persuasion, that are appropriate in academic and professional settings, and it explains how you can enter into argument as a critical thinker, not just a fighter.

8a Persuading and Exploring

Arguments may be *persuasive* or *exploratory*. Classical and Toulmin arguments are thesis driven and claim based, seeking to persuade the audience. Rogerian arguments are thesis seeking and inquiry based; they explore a complex problem and look for the best course of action.

A persuasive argument articulates and advocates for a *claim of judgment*. It will be most effective when it provides compelling explanations and evidence in support of the claim and when the writer's tone is reasonable. The advertisement in Figure 8.1 makes a persuasive argument.

Many academic writing assignments are designed to elicit an exploratory argument. The writer's purpose in such assignments is to examine a complex situation, consider the available evidence, and arrive at the best solution. This "best solution" may be provisional; it may not be the permanent answer to the situation, but only the best one available at this time. Exploratory arguments are useful for assessing complex issues and developing well-informed opinions about them, even if such opinions are provisional, subject to change when new information or a better interpretation becomes available. They are thus essential to navigating contemporary life, in which we daily encounter problems too complex for a tidy solution—problems that nevertheless demand that we make a judgment and go forward on that basis. The evolving research, politics, and ideologies of climate change are one example of a contemporary situation too complex for easy judgment.

An exploratory argument begins by examining the evidence, which it then uses to arrive at a well-founded recommendation for the best course of action. This recommendation is expressed in the thesis.

Takeout can eat up your savings.

Pack your own lunch instead of going out. $6 saved a day x 5 days a week x 10 years x 6% interest = $19,592. That could be money in your pocket. Small changes today. Big bucks tomorrow. Go to feedthepig.org for free savings tips.

Courtesy of the Ad Council

FIGURE 8.1 **Arguing to persuade** This advertisement argues that taking your lunch to work saves money over time; it first asserts this claim, then backs it up with evidence.

1. Reason with inductive logic.

Exploratory arguments are likely to use *inductive logic:* They cite particular examples or specific instances and then draw a conclusion or claim. For instance, imagine that, over a period of months or years, you take exams, sometimes after a good night's sleep and sometimes after staying up late cramming. Reflecting back on your experience, you draw the conclusion that you get better grades on tests after getting a good night's sleep before an exam. This is inductive reasoning. *Counterevidence*, material that contradicts or offers alternatives to your claim, plays an essential role in exploratory argument. An argument that assesses a complex situation but includes only the evidence that supports its thesis is not exploratory; rather, it attempts to hide the messiness of the situation. Only by dealing with the whole range of evidence can an exploratory argument arrive at a plausible recommendation.

To incorporate both evidence and counterevidence into your argument, explain each item thoroughly, and explain why you find the evidence more persuasive than the counterevidence. As you are drafting your argument, keep your mind open: if, as you are brainstorming and drafting your project, you realize that the counterevidence actually is more persuasive than the evidence, you can change your thesis.

2. Reason with deductive logic.

Persuasive arguments are likely to use *deductive logic.* They start from a general premise to draw conclusions about specific instances. Continuing with the example from the section above, consider this general premise: "Test-takers do their best work after a good night's sleep." From this premise, you might draw the conclusion that, before your next psychology exam, you should get a good night's sleep. If the general premise is true, then the conclusion is inescapable, but is the general premise true?

Imagine that you have not read the assigned chapters and that you have put off studying for the exam. In that case, all the sleep in the world is unlikely to improve your performance, and studying for the exam late into the night might be your best option. When writing or assessing arguments based on deductive logic, be sure to consider alternative explanations for the conclusion and to examine carefully the assumptions underlying the premises.

In this excerpt from his journal, student William Archer explores two possible ways to understand the Vietnam War in the context of a class discussion of tragedy; he begins with a question, considers the evidence, and weighs his findings to arrive at a tentative position:

> Should the Vietnam War be viewed more as a Greek or Christian tragedy? Viewing the war as a Christian tragedy would suggest that if certain things had been done differently, a more positive outcome might have resulted; officials made mistakes (moral and strategic) that led to their downfall (and the deaths of soldiers), and those mistakes could have been avoided. Viewing the war as a Greek tragedy would imply that nothing those involved did could have made any difference; officials had character flaws and destinies that ultimately led to their downfall.
>
> There is valid evidence to support either claim. Someone could take the Christian tragedy outlook and argue that had the United States chosen to maintain democratic principles instead of overthrowing President Diem, then we might have avoided the war altogether. Others could take the Greek tragedy outlook and claim that under our government's built-in fear of the spread of communism, war in Southeast Asia was inevitable.

Writing Responsibly — The Well-Tempered Tone

In public discourse, especially in public blogs, the "zinger," or clever put-down, is often used to trump an opponent. Sarcasm also thrives: Some bloggers take a sarcastic tone toward whatever they oppose. But if you want your argument (and yourself) to be taken seriously— especially in academic and business circles—and if you want to persuade people who do not already agree with you, establishing a fair, even-tempered tone and avoiding sarcasm are crucial. Use logic and sound evidence, not snide comments, to make your point.

to SELF

For now, I view the war more as a Greek tragedy; given the historical context following World War II, a proxy war between key powers was bound to happen somewhere in the region. I wonder what would have happened if the United States had chosen a different Southeast Asian nation to "draw the line" with?
—William Archer, Colgate University

Academic writing like Archer's is frequently exploratory in its early stages and becomes persuasive as the argument develops. Working this way often yields a more thoughtful, considered position than does beginning from a predetermined position.

 Exploratory versus Persuasive Approaches to Argument For personal or cultural reasons, you may be more comfortable seeking consensus than stating an opinion. Seek help in formulating a Rogerian or Toulmin argument, or if you want to write an exploratory argument, check with your instructor to be sure this approach is acceptable.

> **EXERCISE 8.1 Choosing an approach to argument**

Consider the assignments below and decide whether each calls for a persuasive or exploratory argument; be prepared to explain your answer.

1. Using Kate Chopin's "The Story of an Hour," (1) identify a theme argued by the story; (2) provide support from the story to demonstrate that this is in fact one of the story's themes; (3) describe how the story uses setting, symbolism, or point of view to develop this theme; and (4) explain why the story's theme is important given its original context. (English 116, Southwestern College-Chula Vista)

2. Write about global change and how ecosystem ecology applies to that issue. Discuss one of the following aspects of global change: (1) climate change; (2) land-use change; (3) species invasions; or (4) altered biodiversity. Reference at least one paper from the primary literature, and discuss both what is known about your topic as well as what uncertainties remain. (Biol 416, Western Washington University)

3. Darwin, Marx, Nietzsche: Which one of the three was the most important "challenge" to the orthodoxy of his day? Why? Do you feel that the impact of the three was largely the same or significantly different? Why? (CORE 152, Colgate University)

> *More about*
> Analyzing an
> assignment,
> 22–24, 196–97

Work **Together**

In small groups, discuss your analysis of the assignments in Exercise 8.1. Come to a consensus (if possible) about each assignment and present your conclusions to the class. Finally, consider the process by which your group worked toward consensus: Was the debate more persuasive or exploratory?

8b Making Claims

> **More about**
> Prejudice, 142–43

Just about every text—speeches, advertisements, websites, journal or magazine articles—has a main point or thesis that makes a claim (Figure 8.2). When faced with any kind of text, begin your critical evaluation by determining whether the thesis makes a claim of *fact, opinion,* or *belief,* or whether it simply expresses a *superstition* or *prejudice.*

1. A claim of fact can be verified.

A text whose main claim is a statement of fact is *informative* (or *expository*):

> **More about**
> Informative purpose, 15, 36–37

Susan B. Anthony and Martha Carey Thomas worked for women's voting rights in the United States.

Denmark became a constitutional monarchy in 1849.

The square root of 4 is 2.

© McGraw-Hill Education/Mark Dierker, photographer

FIGURE 8.2 Sugar Shock Claims can be advanced visually as well as in writing. This visual makes a claim about the relationship between sugary sodas and health. Bring the same critical acumen to assessing the claims made through visuals that you bring to assessing print texts.

More about
Warrants, 158

Quick Reference **Devising an Arguable Thesis**

In an argument, make sure your thesis makes a claim of judgment or value:

Claim of Judgment (Opinion)
The use of email in the workplace reduces personal interactions among colleagues.

Claim of Value (Personal Belief)
Electronic communications ruin interpersonal relationships.

Claim of Fact
Email has surpassed the telephone as the most popular way to communicate in the workplace.

Also, consider qualifying your position with words like *often*, *sometimes*, *some*, and *most* to avoid committing yourself to a stronger position than you can effectively defend. Do not, however, use these qualifiers as a way of making claims that cannot be supported.

A *claim of fact* is not debatable and cannot be the central claim in an argument. For this reason, claims of fact are sometimes called *weak claims*.

Superstitions are claims with no basis in fact:

A wish made on a falling star will come true.

The Chicago Cubs will never win a World Series because of the curse of the Billy Goat.

If you don't forward this email to five friends, you'll suffer ten years of bad luck.

2. A claim of value is based on moral or religious beliefs.

Values are fundamental principles that an individual or a group holds to be inarguably true; they are based on a moral or religious belief system:

Humans should not eat animals.

All people should be treated fairly under the law.

Stealing is unjustifiable.

People tend to defend their beliefs with great passion, and *claims of value*, like the three statements above, are frequently at the heart of argumentative (or persuasive) texts. As you craft your own argument or read the arguments of others, carefully assess the relationship between a claim of value and the assumptions (or warrants) underlying it, whether you are assessing an argument or crafting one.

3. A claim of judgment reflects a reasoned opinion.

The holder of an opinion regards it as the most plausible answer *for now*, based on an evaluation of the available information:

Graduates with engineering degrees are likely to find high-paying jobs.

The healthiest diet is low in carbohydrates.

The Adam Ezra Group is destined to have a number-one hit song.

Supplied with identical facts, not everyone will hold the same opinion. For this reason, the main claim of an argumentative text is often based on an opinion, or *claim of judgment.* Sometimes it makes a *claim of policy* (a claim about what we should do or how we should solve a problem). Sometimes it makes a *claim of causation* (a claim about the causes or effects of a problem).

When opinions are not provisional or temporary, they become *prejudices,* usually expressed in stereotypes:

Athletes are poor students.

Women are too emotional to be president.

Blondes are dumb.

> **More about**
> Counterevidence, 137
> Sweeping generalizations, 159–60

Prejudice is by its very nature unfair because it ascribes qualities to an individual based on generalities about a group, generalities that are themselves often inaccurate. Whenever you suspect that a prejudice is operating as a

Writing
Responsibly   Choosing an Engaging Topic

In addition to making sure your topic is arguable, you should also ask yourself the following questions:

1. Is my topic fresh?
2. Do I have something to add?
3. Is it worth reading (and writing) about?

Thinking critically about saturated topics (such as abortion and gun control) is difficult. Instead of articulating your own argument, you can easily wind up offering a rehash of other people's.

The topics about which you can write most interestingly are those on which you have a distinctive perspective. Almost any eighteen-year-old can write passionately about the legal drinking age, for example, but to justify resuscitating tired topics, you must have something original to add. Whatever topic you choose, you will have your best shot at engaging your readers and doing justice to your topic when you write about something you and your readers find compelling.

to TOPIC

claim, examine the evidence—and more importantly, the counterevidence—for the claim. Often a prejudice is based on an overgeneralization, and counterevidence is easy to come by. A claim based on prejudice never makes an ethical thesis in an argument.

When writing an argument, ask yourself the following question: Do I take a position on which reasonable people could disagree? A claim of fact (or a widely held opinion) is not debatable; reasonable people would not disagree about the number of Electoral College votes needed to win a US presidential election (270) or about the temperature at which water boils at sea level (212 degrees Fahrenheit).

Because claims of value (personal conviction or belief) depend on shared assumptions, they are often difficult to support with persuasive evidence. Writers typically find it difficult, if not impossible, to conduct an open-minded exploration of such issues. Writing about claims of value is an important way of exploring and sharing your beliefs, but if your assignment is to craft a persuasive argument, focusing on a claim of value can make your task extremely difficult.

EXERCISE 8.2 Assessing claims

Determine whether each of the following topics makes a claim of judgment, a claim of fact, or a claim of value. Explain each of your answers in a sentence or two.

EXAMPLE

It is illegal in this town for grocery stores to use plastic bags.

This is a claim of fact because it can be verified.

1. Grocery stores should charge customers for plastic bags to encourage people to recycle their old bags or to use canvas sacks instead.
2. Expecting customers to provide their own bags is ridiculous.
3. In some areas of the country, subsidizing solar energy is a waste of government money.
4. Solar panels have become much less expensive over the last ten years.
5. It is too difficult to be a vegetarian.

EXERCISE 8.3 Assessing thesis statements

Determine whether the following thesis statements are arguable or not, and explain why.

EXAMPLE

Theodore Roosevelt's sickly and weak physical condition as a child had a critical influence on many of his later personal and political decisions.

This is arguable because we have extensive factual information about Roosevelt's childhood physical condition as well as his later personal and political decisions, and a writer can form a knowledgeable and defensible opinion about the importance of the connection between them.

1. Using animals for drug experimentation is barbaric, cruel, and immoral.
2. Exposure to secondhand smoke significantly increases the risk of lung cancer and heart disease in nonsmokers, as well as several respiratory illnesses in young children.
3. Bilingual education is not effective in areas with large non-English-speaking populations of the United States.
4. Advertisements cause significant harm to people and our society as a whole.
5. Many invasive plants now threatening native species in the United States were deliberately planted by home gardeners.

Make It **Your Own**

Draft an arguable thesis for one of the topics in Exercise 3.1 (p. 35) or 3.2 (p. 38). If you prefer, select a different topic.

8c Choosing Evidence Rhetorically

An argument will be only as persuasive as the explanations and evidence, or *grounds*, that support the claim. Support can appeal to your readers' intellect, it can draw on the authority of a figure they respect, or it can appeal to their emotions. Each of these is a *rhetorical appeal.* The ancient Greeks called these appeals logos, ethos, and pathos. Each has a place in responsible writing. As you develop your evidence, you have a responsibility, to your audience and to yourself, to make rhetorical appeals that your audience will find appropriate and persuasive.

1. Appeal to your readers' intellect (logos).

Logos refers to evidence that is rational and consistent; it appeals to readers by engaging their logical powers. Academic writing, such as the excerpt from Rachel Bateman's essay below, relies heavily on reasoned support and concrete evidence:

> Research suggests that violence in the media adversely affects a particularly vulnerable subset of children (usually males): those with Attention Deficit Disorder or information-processing disorders. These children

have a hard time understanding the moral context of violence when it is used as entertainment; they may not differentiate enough between an action sequence in a movie and a face-to-face interaction in their daily lives (Gerteis 1993). Television viewing of children with these disorders should be carefully monitored, and role-models—parents, doctors, and teachers—should work with these kids to help them better understand the meaning and consequences of real-life violence.

—Rachel Bateman, University of Kansas,
"A Closer Look at the Causes of Violence"

A logical appeal can effectively reach a wide range of readers—from sympathetic to hostile—by reinforcing or challenging opinions with reasoned support.

Visuals that provide strong, quantifiable evidence—facts, data, statistics—appeal to the reader's intellect. This evidence may be displayed in a graph, chart, or map or in a before-after photo pair (Figure 8.3). They are effective for convincing a skeptical audience and are appropriate in all types of texts, especially academic texts, where logical reasoning is highly valued.

Logos and Ethos in the United States In academic and business writing in the United States, argument relies primarily on rational appeals. Mentioning highly revered traditional authorities or sources (such as important political figures or religious works) is not considered a sufficient form of support. Instead, evaluate the arguments and supporting evidence of these authorities, and include their work as support only if it directly contributes to your argument.

Source: Dr. Lonnie G. Thompson, Distinguished University Professor, Byrd Polar and Climate Research Center, The Ohio State University, via NASA

Source: Dr. Lonnie G. Thompson, Distinguished University Professor, Byrd Polar and Climate Research Center, The Ohio State University, via NASA

FIGURE 8.3 Melting Qori Kalis Glacier, Peru, 1978–2011 These photographs make a logical appeal: They provide factual (verifiable) evidence for global warming.

2. Appeal to your readers by establishing your credibility (ethos).

Establishing a credible *ethos*—good character, sound knowledge, or good reputation—encourages readers to have confidence in what you say. Maxine Paetro, for example, establishes her credentials before she expresses her judgments:

> As the executive recruiter for several major ad agencies, I've eyeballed more than 40,000 cover letters. Some were winners. Some should have been deleted before ever seeing the light of print.
>
> —Maxine Paetro, "Mission: Employable," *Mademoiselle*

Ethical appeals (ethos) can be very effective with wavering readers. When people are undecided about an issue, they often want to learn more about it from a person of good character who has considered all possibilities and provides sound judgments.

3. Appeal to your readers' emotions (pathos).

> **More about**
> Making a presentation, 187–94 (ch. 11)
> Tone, 19–20, 138, 565, 570–72

Using *pathos* to support a claim means stirring the audience's emotions in an effort to elicit sympathy and, thus, agreement. Pathos often relies on examples, stories, or anecdotes to persuade readers. It also uses a tone that stimulates readers' feelings. Visuals that appeal to the readers' emotions or beliefs (Figures 8.4 and 8.5) make an emotional (or *pathetic*) appeal. Use pathos cautiously: Arguments that appeal solely to readers' emotions can be manipulative, even unethical, unless they are backed by strong logical evidence. In addition, many academic disciplines respect only logos and ethos as rhetorical appeals.

Many emotional appeals make use of visuals, especially photographs, because of the immediate impact they can have on the hearts of audience members. Photographs that tug on the readers' emotions are common in advertising but rare in academic or business writing, where judgments are more likely to be made on a logical basis.

Writing Responsibly

Establishing Yourself as a Responsible Writer

As a writer, you can establish your ethos not only by offering your credentials, but also by providing readers with sound and sufficient evidence drawn from recognized authorities on the topic, thereby demonstrating your grasp of the material. By adopting a reasonable tone and treating alternative views fairly, you demonstrate that you are a sensible person. By editing your prose carefully, you establish your respect for your readers.

to SELF

FIGURE 8.4 **Loss of sea ice poses a threat to the polar bear** This photograph makes a strong emotional appeal—we fear for the safety and well-being of the polar bear—but it would be out of place in an academic text without statistics that show a clear relationship between diminishing polar bear populations and reduced ice coverage caused by global warming.

© GeoStock/Getty Images RF

© PA Wire/PA Photos/AP Images

FIGURE 8.5 **Visual pathos** Charitable organizations like Save the Children often use pathos to elicit donations.

▶ EXERCISE 8.4 Assessing logos, ethos, and pathos

Examine the evidence Brent Staples offers in his editorial (pp. 120–121). Classify it as logical, ethical, or emotional. Now classify the evidence in Alea Wratten's critique of the Staples editorial (pp. 132–134) in the same way. Finally, write a paragraph explaining which of these two texts you find more persuasive and why.

Writing Responsibly Preparing Oral Arguments

When you write formal arguments for college courses, rational and ethical appeals are often more appropriate to your context and genre. But when you deliver a speech, presentation, or other form of oral argument, supplement logical and ethical appeals with vivid emotional appeals that your audience will remember. Be sure to support emotional appeals with logical and ethical appeals: After telling a moving story about an individual, use statistics or an expert's opinion to show how the issue affects others. Without logical evidence and ethical appeals, an emotional appeal is merely manipulative.

to AUDIENCE

Student Models
Illustrated projects: 132, 152, 350, 397, 425, 482

➤ EXERCISE 8.5 Assessing visual appeals

Write a paragraph in which you argue that illustrations in one of the student projects in this book make a logical, ethical, or emotional appeal.

8d Considering Alternative Viewpoints

To address an issue in all its complexity, you must consider alternative viewpoints. When reading or writing an argument, consider *counterevidence:* the doubts you or other reasonable people might have or the objections that opponents might raise. Ask friends or colleagues to help you brainstorm alternative positions or search for alternative voices in print and online sources. When assessing an argument, consider whether the writer has taken these alternative viewpoints into consideration and how well the writer responds to critics' concerns.

Responses to alternative viewpoints can take several approaches:

- You can provide counterevidence that refutes the opposition. Consider a supporting paragraph from Alea Wratten's response to the Bret Staples editorial on the ill effects of hip-hop music:

Refutation

Counterevidence

. . . While gangsta rap continues to be very popular, hip-hop includes many bands and artists who pen uplifting and socially aware lyrics. Kanye West, for instance, currently among hip-hop's biggest stars, offers a positive, spiritual message in his music, a message of which Staples would likely approve. . . . And West is not alone: Lauren Hill, Kam, KRS One, Arrested Development, Chuck D, and Public Enemy are just a few of the musicians and bands on my iPod that explore hip-hop's more socially responsible side. These artists show that the strand of hip-hop that Staples accuses of providing a "toxic diet" for listeners is just one of many.

—Alea Wratten, SUNY–Geneseo, "Reflecting on Brent Staples's Editorial"

Student Model
Critique: 131–34

- You can acknowledge alternative views and explain why your position is still the most reasonable *despite* this counterevidence. In the introduction to her essay, Shona Sequiera creates an appealing tension by indicating what both her counterevidence and her evidence will be:

Although *Their Eyes Were Watching God* has been widely criticized for painting too romantic a picture of African American life, Hurston's heroine Janie is ultimately able to transcend oppressive stereotypes and successfully come into her own. Her journey towards self-identity and self-knowledge harbors the celebratory ethnic notion that black is not just a color but a culture as well.

Concession

Explanation of why opposing position is less important than the writer's

—Shona Sequiera, Connecticut College, "Transcending Stereotypes in Hurston's *Their Eyes Were Watching God*"

- You can revise your thesis to include concessions, exceptions, or qualifiers such as *some* or *usually*:

While the media may have an effect on some young adults, bursts of violence, like those at Columbine High School, Virginia Tech, and Northern Illinois University, are far more complex and have many more underlying causes than anti–media violence activists usually acknowledge: Mental illness, alienation, availability of weapons, and defects in school security are also components of the motivation to become violent.

Concession

Qualifier

—Rachel Bateman, University of Kansas, "A Closer Look at the Causes of Violence"

EXERCISE 8.6 Assessing the strength of a conclusion

Reread the student essay by Alea Wratten that appears at the end of Chapter 7 (pp. 132–134). Does the writer include enough evidence to persuade you of her claim? Does she consider evidence that undermines her claim? How reasonable is her tone? Write a paragraph discussing these issues. Draw specific evidence from the essay to support your claims.

8e   Discovering Assumptions and Common Ground

In order to persuade an audience of the truth of a claim, the writer must move it to accept certain common assumptions. For Tom Hackman to convince us that colleges and universities should take the motivations for plagiarism into consideration when devising academic integrity policies, we must first assume that plagiarism is a widespread problem and that it is wrong. If you do not share these basic assumptions (and most of us do), then you would not be convinced that rethinking plagiarism policies is worth the time and trouble. When W.E.B. DuBois said in 1903, "The problem of the twentieth century is the problem of the color-line—the relation of the darker to the lighter races of men in Asia and Africa, in America and the islands of the sea," he may have assumed that his statement would lead to social change. That would depend, however, on whether his audience *wanted* equality between the races. DuBois knew that some of the audience did not agree with that principle, so his book, *The Souls of Black Folk*, offers evidence in support of the need for change.

As you read and write arguments, consider carefully the assumptions, or **warrants,** that underlie the claims being made: On what common ground must both reader and writer stand before they can discuss a topic productively? What must both writer and audience agree is true without argument or evidence? What information should you share that might help move your audience to endorse your principles?

Student Models
Persuasive arguments,
131, 350, 463, 482

 EXERCISE 8.7 Identifying main claim and evidence
Read (or reread) the essay "The Moral Absurdity of Denying Financial Aid to Undocumented Students" (pp. 116–118), identify the main claim, and assess the evidence provided in support of this claim.

Student Model   Exploratory Argument

In the following exploratory argument, Tom Hackman, a student at Syracuse University, first analyzes plagiarism and then uses his analysis as the basis of a claim that universities should take these differences into consideration when devising their plagiarism policies.

Tom Hackman

Professor Howard

Writing 109

28 November 2016

Why Students Cheat: The Complexities and Oversimplifications of Plagiarism

Introduction:
Explains why
topic matters

The system of American higher education is founded on principles of honesty and academic integrity. For this reason, nearly all those invested in this system—students, instructors, and administrators—recognize that plagiarism cannot be tolerated. They also agree that a lot of plagiarism is occurring. A survey published in *Who's Who Among American High School Students* (reported by Newberger) indicated that 15% of top-ranked high schoolers plagiarize. Practices among higher education students are not much better. According to research by Donald L. McCabe, a professor at Rutgers University who has done extensive work on cheating, 70% of college students "copied almost word for word from a source and submitted it as their own work" (41). A 2006 study by Hard et al. showed that plagiarism was common among the 421 students who participated in their research. Fig. 1 illustrates the various forms this plagiarism took.

Background:
Describes extent
and severity of
plagiarism

There is a commonly held myth about how most plagiarism occurs. Late at night, a student sits staring at a computer screen. A paper is due the following morning, and research needs to be done, notes need to be taken, and, in the end, an essay needs to be written and edited. Instead of completing this immense task, though, the student succumbs to the temptations of plagiarism—"cutting and pasting" from sources, downloading an essay from the Internet, or simply buying a paper from

Counter-
evidence:
Describes
alternative
perspectives

151

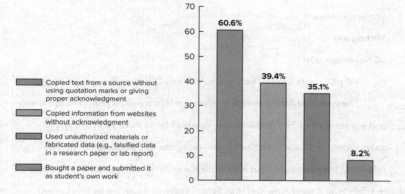

Copied text from a source without using quotation marks or giving proper acknowledgment

Copied information from websites without acknowledgment

Used unauthorized materials or fabricated data (e.g., falsified data in a research paper or lab report)

Bought a paper and submitted it as student's own work

Fig. 1   Common types of plagiarism and the percentage of students who commit them. (Data and categories from Hard et al. 1069)

another student. In this myth, students are too apathetic and slothful to complete their assignments on their own; instead, they cheat.

Undeniably, some plagiarism occurs because students find it easier than simply doing the work required. The mind of a plagiarist, however, cannot be fit so easily into a single stereotype. The argument that laziness is the main cause of plagiarism is at best incomplete, and moreover it seems fed by unfair stereotypes of modern students as bored by academic rigor, more interested in video games or their Facebook page than the hard work of learning.

In fact, some plagiarism grows from the opposite of these characteristics. High-achieving students, for example, fear what a bad grade will do to their

Acknowledges the legitimacy of the counterevidence

Evidence: Expert opinions, examples

otherwise stellar GPA. Such students treat the attainment of impressive marks as a necessity and will betray the very academic system they revere in order to sustain their average.

Other students plagiarize more from lack of interest in a particular course than general idleness. Students who view writing papers as hoops they must jump through to graduate, for instance, are more likely simply to download a paper from an online "paper mill" than write one themselves. For them, a college writing class is something to be endured, rather than an opportunity for learning. Russell Hunt, a professor at St. Thomas University in Canada, explains this attitude in point 2 of his article:

> If I wanted to learn how to play the guitar, or improve my golf swing, or write HTML, "cheating" would be the last thing that would ever occur to me. It would be utterly irrelevant to the situation. On the other hand, if I wanted a certificate saying that I could pick a jig, play a round in under 80, or produce a slick webpage (and never actually expected to perform the activity in question), I might well consider cheating. . . .

Students draw a distinction between their interests and their academic assignments. They rationalize their plagiarism as a way to escape an "unfair" academic obligation. Websites such as essaytown.com, which will write a paper to order, cater to students like these, who consider at least some aspects of academia essentially useless.

Many other instances of plagiarism are committed by students with honest intentions but who are ignorant of citation methods. Writing for his college

Quotes authority to support claim; notes the author's credentials

Provides example that illustrates claim

153

newspaper, Nam Tran describes widespread confusion among college students about what constitutes plagiarism. Even students who recognize the importance of citation may not know how to cite their sources correctly. A student who omits the source of a paraphrase in a paper would probably be surprised to learn that he or she is often considered as guilty of plagiarism as the student who downloads an essay.

The Internet has compounded confusion with regard to citation. The Internet is a place of free exchange where information moves from computer to computer with the click of a mouse. In this environment, ownership and citation become hazy. And as Rhodri Marsden, who writes about technology and the arts for *The Guardian*, notes, the more information becomes available on the Internet, the more material is available for easy plagiarizing. Many students find it is easy and "natural" to take text from an online source—for instance, by highlighting the text, copying it, and pasting it into a word processing document. Because it can be difficult to keep track of everything they have read, the chances of accidental plagiarism (forgetting to cite the copied text) increase. So, too, does the likelihood of "patchwriting," which researchers Pecorari and Petric define as substituting synonyms or moving sentences around, but not fully putting the borrowed text into the writer's own words. While patchwriting can be done deliberately, Pecorari and Petric identify a subset of patchwriters who don't realize they're doing anything wrong (278). Li's research supports the existence of this subset; the Chinese senior professors in that study actively discouraged plagiarism, but some of their doctoral students thought patchwriting was acceptable. Finally, some students will also be tempted to commit intentional plagiarism, choosing to leave a block of copied text uncited.

Evidence: quotes authority and provides author's credentials

Paraphrases authority to corroborate claim

Despite the many varieties and causes of plagiarism, college instructors and administrators too often treat the issue simply as a crime committed by the laziest of pupils. Birchard quotes a dean of Canada's Simon Fraser University, who voices a typical view: "We have a zero tolerance policy for cheating.... And we hope the severity of the penalties sends a strong message to other students who might be tempted to cheat or cut academic corners." Granted, there is ultimately no excuse for plagiarism, and any honest student should share the goal of eliminating it from academic life. Yet a less simplistic response to plagiarism would ultimately be more productive than the widespread law-and-order mentality that now exists.

The motivations behind plagiarism, and the situations that give rise to it, are varied. Importantly, much plagiarism occurs without the guilty student understanding that what he or she is doing represents academic dishonesty. Effectively combating plagiarism, in all its forms, requires a fuller understanding of how and why students break the rules. Academic policy writers must realize that plagiarism is not a single offense but a general term for a lack of citation, and plagiarism must be recognized as dynamic behavior, with many motivations, including social expectations, desires for high GPAs, disregard for the value of learning or intellectual property, and unawareness of citation standards. A regular user of a paper mill website has far different attitudes than a nonciting Chinese exchange student (or professor). The various categories of plagiarism threaten academia to varying extents and therefore demand a flexible response based upon the specifics of each incident. Only through this approach will plagiarism, in all its forms, be reduced.

Works Cited

Birchard, Karen. "Canada's Simon Fraser U. Suspends 44 Students in Plagiarism Scandal." *The Chronicle of Higher Education*, vol. 53, no. 8, 24 Oct. 2002, p. 46. *EbscoHost*, chronicle.com/article/Canadas-Simon-Fraser-U/116779.

Hard, Stephen F., et al. "Faculty and College Student Beliefs about the Frequency of Student Academic Misconduct." *The Journal of Higher Education*, vol. 77, no. 6, Nov.-Dec. 2006, pp. 1058-80.

Hunt, Russell. "Four Reasons to Be Happy about Internet Plagiarism." *Teaching Perspectives*, Dec. 2002, stu.ca/~hunt/4reasons.htm.

Li, Yongyan. "Text-Based Plagiarism in Scientific Writing: What Chinese Supervisors Think about Copying and How to Reduce It in Students' Writing." *Science and Engineering Ethics*, vol. 19.2, June 2013, pp. 569–83.

Marsden, Rhodri. "The Big Steal: Rise of the Plagiarist in the Digital Age." *The Guardian*, 21 Mar. 2014, www.theguardian.com/technology/2014/mar/21/rise-plagiarism-internet-shia-labeouf.

McCabe, Donald L. "Cheating: Why Students Do It and How We Can Help Them Stop." *American Educator*, Winter 2001, pp. 38–43.

Newberger, Eli H. "Why Do Students Cheat?" *School for Champions*. School for Champions, 6 Dec 2003. school-for-champions.com/character/newberger_cheating2.htm#.Vvl8THpxBqs.

Pecorari, Diane, and Bojana Petric. "Plagiarism in Second-Language Writing." *Language Teaching*, vol. 47.3, July 2014, pp. 269–302.

Tran, Nam. "Plagiarism Policies Lead to Confusion among Students." *The Daily Nebraskan*, 9 Oct. 2015, dailynebraskan.com/news/plagiarism-policies-lead-to-confusion-among-students/article_2c875fa2-6e2c-11e5-ad00-cfbdd1242e21.html.

8f Organizing Arguments: Classical, Rogerian, and Toulmin Models

As with any writing, an argument is most effective when it is carefully organized. The following are three widely used models for organizing arguments. Each one serves certain purposes of argument.

Before choosing a structure, study the following models; one may work well for your project. If you combine elements from more than one, do it for rhetorical reasons rather than convenience; organize your argument with your purpose and audience foremost in your mind.

> *More about*
Organizing,
38–40
Explaining and
  supporting your
  ideas, 45–46
Purpose, 14–16
Audience, 17–20

1. The classical model

The *classical model* of argumentation derives from the work of ancient Greek and Roman orators. It is well suited to persuasive arguments and is composed of five parts, usually presented in this order:

1. **Introduction.** Acquaint readers with your topic, give them a sense of why it is important and why you are qualified to address it, suggest the purpose of your argument, and state your main claim (or *thesis*) in one or two sentences.

2. **Background.** Provide whatever basic information your audience will need to understand and appreciate your position. You might include a brief review of major sources on the subject or offer a chronology of relevant events.

3. **Evidence.** This is the heart of your argument, and it should be the longest section in your project—at least 50 percent of the whole. In it, explain to readers why you believe what you do, and offer well-chosen evidence to support your claims. Depending on your rhetorical situation, you might appeal to your readers through their logic (*logos*), through their respect for you and your sources (*ethos*), or through their emotions (*pathos*). Support your argument with *logos*, *ethos*, or *pathos* depending on rhetorical considerations such as your purpose, your audience, and the genre in which you are writing. If your project is multimedia, you might want to include information graphics to support logical appeals. A well-chosen and accurately formatted list of works cited will help your appeals to *ethos*, especially if, in your text, you point to the high credentials of your sources. Images and videos can effectively move an audiences's emotions, as they identify with (or reject) what they see.

4. **Counterevidence.** Describe and explain alternative viewpoints, treating opponents fairly.

> *More about*
Deduction,
137–39

5. **Conclusion.** Leave readers with a strong sense of why they should agree with you: suggest solutions, call for action, or reemphasize the value of your position. If your argument is complex, it may also be helpful to summarize it briefly here.

2. The Rogerian model

The purpose of *Rogerian* argument is to build common ground on complex issues, not to "win" an argument. It was developed by Carl Rogers, a twentieth-century psychologist who hoped this method would make discussion more productive. The Rogerian model is composed of the same five parts as the classical model, but in a different order:

1. **Introduction**
2. **Background**
3. **Counterevidence**
4. **Explanations and evidence**
5. **Conclusion**

In a Rogerian argument, the counterevidence appears before the evidence because the presentation of counterevidence helps establish the complexity of the issue. Instead of refuting the counterevidence, the writer explores its legitimacy first and then explains why he or she nevertheless believes the thesis. Tom Hackman's essay earlier in this chapter follows the Rogerian model.

3. The Toulmin model

The model for arguments developed by philosopher Stephen *Toulmin* includes five parts, but the parts are somewhat different from those of classical and Rogerian argument:

1. **Claim:** your thesis, the central argument
2. **Grounds:** the reasons you believe the claim and evidence supporting your claim
3. **Warrants:** any assumptions that explain how the grounds support the claim
4. **Backing:** supporting evidence for the warrants; they require their own supporting evidence because they are themselves claims
5. **Rebuttal:** counterevidence and your response to it

Like classical argument, the Toulmin model is persuasive. Like classical argument, Toulmin presents the main claim and evidence before counterevidence.

One distinctive feature of Toulmin argument is that it places counterevidence last, and it also refutes the counterevidence, leaving less doubt that the main claim is the best perspective. It also recognizes that assumptions underlie all claims and brings those assumptions to the surface, making the search for common ground easier (or at least clarifying the terms of the discussion).

More about
Revising, 88–98
Claims of value,
  judgment,
  142–43
Explanations
  and evidence,
  45–46
Appeals, 144–48
Counterevidence,
  137, 148–49
Persuading and
  exploring,
  136–39

8g Avoiding Logical Fallacies

When assessing an argument that seems persuasive, keep an eye out for logical *fallacies*. Familiarizing yourself with logical fallacies will help you avoid them as you write your own argument, and it will help you evaluate the trustworthiness of sources you are consulting. Because inductive arguments depend on examples and the conclusions you draw from them, fallacies like the following can creep in:

- **Hasty generalization (jumping to conclusions).** *Look at her, running that stop sign! She's a terrible driver!*

  A hasty generalization occurs when a general conclusion is based on insufficient evidence: Since even the best drivers occasionally make mistakes, this one piece of evidence is not enough to incriminate this driver.

- **Sweeping generalization.** *Women are terrible drivers! My girlfriend ran a stop sign the other day and almost got us both killed!*

Writing
Responsibly   Visual Claims and Visual Fallacies

Courtesy of The Advertising Archives

In academic writing, you might use a visual to *support* a claim, but you should be cautious about using a visual to *make* a claim. Visual claims are effective sales tools (they are common in advertisements), but they are likely to commit a visual fallacy, such as *overgeneralization*—drawing a conclusion based on too little evidence. (Is it reasonable to assume that *all* women using a certain brand of soap will look like a movie star simply because one celebrity claims to use the product?) This ad may also commit the fallacy of false authority. (Is the actress an authority on whose expertise we can rely when buying soap?) As this vintage ad indicates, such consumer-manipulating arguments are not new.

to TOPIC

Sweeping generalizations apply a claim to *all* cases when it actually applies to only a few or maybe to none. Stereotypes are often based on a sweeping generalization. (Whenever words like *all*, *every*, and *none* are used in an argument, take a closer look; these often signal that a sweeping generalization is coming.)

- **False analogy.** *Our candidate's victories over his enemies during the war will ensure his victory over his political opponents in the election.*

A false analogy draws a connection between two items or events that have few or no relevant common characteristics. This false analogy does not explain how the two things resemble each other: Why would a military victory guarantee a political victory? Is the political process really like a military campaign? Are opposition candidates really like enemy soldiers?

- **Stacking the deck (special pleading).** *Got dandruff? Our shampoo contains MarvEll, guaranteed to end your dandruff problems!*

An argument that stacks the deck focuses only on supporting evidence and ignores counterevidence that casts reasonable doubt upon it. In this case, the dandruff-killing properties of the shampoo may also make your hair brittle, but the ad would not mention that fact.

- **False authority.** *My mother says that ice cream is more nourishing than a bowl of oatmeal.*

Unless your mother is a nutritionist, her word alone is insufficient. An argument that appeals to a false authority draws evidence from someone who is *not* an expert on the topic.

- **Bandwagon appeal.** *Mom and Dad, you have to buy me an SUV; all my friends have one!*

The bandwagon appeal implies that the majority opinion is the right opinion and invites you to climb aboard. Some bandwagon appeals may be based on poll results, lending them the impression of reliability. But poll results merely report what the majority of respondents *believe* to be true. Many European Americans in 1860 believed that holding other people in slavery was acceptable, which goes to show that the majority can be wrong.

The power of deductive arguments depends on the validity of the conclusion or the appeal of the premises, so watch out for arguments based on dubious logic or hidden or missing premises:

- **Begging the question (circular reasoning).** *You must believe me because I never lie.*

An argument that begs the question uses the conclusion (in a disguised form) as one of the premises in the argument. In this example, the second half of the sentence repeats the conclusion rather than offering a premise from which it can be derived.

- **Non sequitur (irrelevant argument).** *You can solve a lot of problems with money, so the rich must be much happier than we are.*

A non sequitur (which means "it does not follow" in Latin) draws a conclusion from a premise that does not follow logically. The conclusion in the statement above equates money with happiness, but anyone with money will tell you that the two do not go hand in hand.

- ***Post hoc, ergo propter hoc* (false cause).** *This ring must be lucky: I wore it for the first time today, and I pitched a perfect game.*

Post hoc, ergo propter hoc means "after this, therefore, because of this" in Latin. In a *post hoc* fallacy, the speaker wrongly assumes that the first event caused the second: Just because the player wore a ring while pitching a perfect game does not mean that the ring is "lucky"; maybe he was just having a good day or the other team's hitters were weak.

- **Either-or fallacy (false dilemma).** *You're either for us or against us!*

The either-or fallacy allows, misleadingly, for only two choices or sides in an argument, never allowing for other options, never acknowledging compromise or complexity. (A visual false dilemma occurs in the image shown in Figure 8.6.)

FIGURE 8.6 Either-or fallacy on a website This image from an anti–gun control website suggests that there are only two ways to protect yourself. A third option might be to call the police. (Source: http://bbvm.wordpress.com/2009/03/12/two-ways-to-shield-yourself-from-a-violent-attack-see-women-of-caliber/)

Two ways to shield yourself from a violent attack.

Illustration by Oleg Volk, olegvolk.net

self

Assessment

As you revise your argument, consider the following features. If your answer to any of these questions is no, make the necessary revisions.

☐ **Claim.** Do you take an arguable position based on an opinion or belief on which reasonable people could disagree? Have you modified it to avoid making a stronger claim than you can effectively support? Does your introduction show why your topic is important?

☐ **Evidence.** Do you supply evidence in support of your claim? Do you use rational, ethical, or emotional appeals that are appropriate to your topic, purpose,

and audience? Do you use visuals, where appropriate, to make or support claims?

☐ **Counterevidence.** Have you acknowledged alternative interpretations of your evidence, as well as evidence that undermines your claims? Have you explained why your position is the most reasonable despite these objections?

☐ **Organization.** Have you followed an appropriate model of argument, such as a classical, Rogerian, or Toulmin model? Is the organizational structure appropriate to your overall aim—persuasion or exploration?

- **Red herring.** *Reporter: "Mayor, what do you have to say about the dangerous decay of the city's flood walls?" Mayor: "I'm proud of the accomplishments in my administration: We have a much larger, better equipped police force than when I took office."*

According to the *Oxford English Dictionary*, a red herring is a smoked fish with a distinctive odor used to train dogs to follow a scent. As early as 1884, it was used to mean an irrelevance used to distract attention from the real issue. In the example above, the mayor is trying to dodge a difficult question by changing the subject.

- **Ad hominem (personal attack).** *His views on how to resolve the parking problem on campus are ridiculous! What would you expect from a member of a frat that has its own parking lot?*

An ad hominem (personal) attack attempts to undermine an opposing viewpoint by criticizing the motives or character of the individual offering the alternative view. When writers use ad hominem attacks, they focus their critiques on aspects of a person's character without connecting character flaws to the issues in question.

- **Guilt by association.** *Tiffany is the most treacherous person I ever met. If Makoto is Tiffany's friend, he can't be trusted.*

Guilt by association dismisses or condemns people because of the relationships they have. Just because Tiffany is untrustworthy (if indeed she is) does not mean that everyone who befriends her is also untrustworthy.

- **Slippery slope.** *If we exempt one person from the physical education requirement, everybody will want an exemption.*

  The slippery slope fallacy implies that one event will initiate an unstoppable sequence of events. But as any skier can tell you, a slippery slope does not always mean that you will slide uncontrollably to the bottom of the hill. It is not impossible to exempt some students (those with a good excuse) while requiring the rest to take gym.

> **EXERCISE 8.8 Locating logical fallacies in political websites**
>
> Locate three logical fallacies in the websites of political figures—the president, your city's mayor, a senator from your home state, a candidate running for an upcoming election. (Go beyond the home page, deeper into the site, at least twice.) In a paragraph, name the fallacy and explain how the text (or visual) commits it.

8h Using the Appropriate Tone and Style

Disagreement is an integral part of contemporary culture; we encounter it daily in school, at work, online, and amongst our friends. We might call these disagreements "arguments," but often they are simply quarrels based almost exclusively on appeals to *ethos* and *pathos*. The comments that are posted in response to virtually any article online illustrate this sort of discourse. On the ESPN sports website, for example, readers will see *logos* as commenters cite the statistics of a player, team, or match, but they will also see a great deal of ad hominem and red herring logical fallacies when commenters attack the character or lifestyle of the person with whom they disagree.

It is important to exercise respect for the people, situations, and cultures you are writing about; don't adopt a tone of superiority to them. Similarly, salty language is often used to emphasize claims or to discredit others, but it adds nothing to an argument. State your opinions and feel free to critique others when writing in academic and professional contexts, but state your disagreement explicitly and in reasoned language.

Work **Together**

Exchange your revised project with a fellow student. Read each other's work carefully. Does it commit any of the fallacies listed on pages 159–163? If so, mark them and explain what makes them fallacies. If the project is fallacy-free, explain why its claims are logical.

Make It **Your Own**

Write a paragraph reflecting on the material in this chapter and your responses. What did you learn about effective argumentation and logic by reading and evaluating other people's writing? What surprised you? Have you noticed the use of ethos, logos, or pathos in your daily life, or caught any logical fallacies? If so, what effect did these things have on the argument being made? Has your opinion of argument changed as a result of your increased understanding of it? End with a checklist of five specific issues to check as you revise future projects.

Text Credits

pp. 150, 409: W.E.B. DuBois, *The Souls of Black Folks* (Chicago: A.C. McClurg & Co., 1903). **pp. 151:** Hackman, Tom.

Part Three

Media
Matters
Designing, Writing, and Presenting

9 Designing Printed and Electronic Documents

© Werner Forman/Art Resource, NY

The early Peruvians wove this design to represent and honor their sun god. They used proximity to connect the head and tail to the figure's torso. They used the alignment of short yellow and red lines and the repetition of shapes (straight lines at right and left, red and yellow emblems above and below) to create the background against which the figure stands out. They used contrast of white outline against brown background to define the figure, and they inserted a rectangle in the center of the figure, which contrasts with the rest because it is filled in by color. This contrasting element attracts the eye and draws attention to the figure's core. According to renowned designer Robin Williams, these four principles—proximity, alignment, repetition, and contrast—are the pillars on which effective design rests.

9a Understanding the Four Principles of Design

Robin Williams explains how the four principles of design work:

- **Proximity** (or nearness) suggests that content is related.

- **Alignment,** arrangement in a straight line (vertical, horizontal, or diagonal), creates connections among parts and ideas.

- **Repetition** of a design element lends unity (oneness).

- **Contrast** among design elements calls attention through difference.

Handwriting font calls attention to page title through contrast

Yellow rule and white font of title contrast with dark blue background

Grayed portrait of Adams contrasts with colored background; juts out of yellow frame to call attention to subject of site

Same color used for outline around central portion of screen and quotation to link outer and inner elements

Quotation aligns with portrait to associate the man with his words

Proximity of quotation to image associates the man with his words

Stacked links align to show similarity (all 3 are links to similar content types)

Thumbnail images contrast with surrounding type to call attention to exhibition and timeline; blue and red type contrast with background and surrounding type

Tan of panel repeated in logo for the library and type below the panel

Proximity suggests similarity of information in stacked links

Proximity links thumbnail image to text (and icon)

Boston Public Library

FIGURE 9.1 **An effective web page design** The four principles of design make this page from the Boston Public Library's website as attractive as it is functional.

In an effective design, such as that in the web page in Figure 9.1, these four principles work together to direct readers to the most important information and to highlight relationships among the elements on the page or screen.

EXERCISE 9.1 Analyzing a design

Find a web page, brochure, or advertisement (in print or online) that you think makes good use of words and graphics, and in two or three paragraphs explain how it uses the four principles of design.

9b Planning Your Design Project

To figure out how best to apply the four principles of design to your project, begin with a careful consideration of your rhetorical situation:

- **Topic.** What is your topic, and how can you reflect that topic through your design?

- **Audience.** Who will your audience be, what kind of expectations do they bring with them, and what kind of relationship do you have (or want to have) with them?

More about
Purpose, 13–16
Audience, 17–20
Context and
genre, 21

- **Purpose.** Is your purpose to inform, to persuade, to express yourself, or to entertain, and how should this be reflected in your design?

- **Context.** In what context (academic, business, public) or setting (over the Internet, in person) will your project be received, and how might this affect its design?

- **Genre.** What type of project (résumé, business letter, essay, lab report) will best fulfill your purpose, and what design conventions are associated with this genre?

- **Circulation.** Will this document be distributed in print or digitally? If digitally, in what sort of media? Should it operate on a variety of electronic devices? Consider audience and context as you make these decisions.

More about
Organizing,
38–43

Next determine how the pieces of information you want to convey relate to one another:

- What information is most and least important?

- Does some of the information support a broader claim or provide evidence for this claim?

- How might you convey or reinforce your ideas visually?

> **EXERCISE 9.2 Analyzing a document**

Return to the web page, brochure, or advertisement that you used in Exercise 9.1. Analyze its purpose, audience, context, and genre. What (if any) principles of design can you identify at work in the document? What design principles would you recommend be applied in a revision of the document?

Make It **Your Own**

For an organization you are involved with or endorse, plan a promotional web page, brochure, or advertisement to solicit members or advertise an event. How will the purpose of your document affect its design? What audience will you appeal to? What information will they need, or what information will persuade them to join or attend an event?

9c Applying the Principles of Design

Once you have organized your project, you are ready to begin designing it.

1. Create an overall impression.

Start by considering the overall impression you want to give the reader: Should the design be conservative or trendy, serious or playful? Let your decision about the style of your project guide you in your choice of colors, fonts, and visuals.

2. Plan the layout.

Next consider the overall *layout*, the visual arrangement of text and images. An effective layout should use proximity, alignment, repetition, and contrast to make the relationships among the elements clear. Keep your layout simple, and use it to direct the reader's eye to the most important pieces of information.

3. Format the document.

Once you have sketched your layout, you are ready to create a cohesive and attractive design by using the following elements:

Fonts Word processors give writers a wide range of fonts (or typefaces) to choose from. Serif fonts (fonts with a little tail on the ends of letters, like Cambria and Times New Roman) are easier to read when printed on paper, while sans serif fonts (such as Arial and Calibri) are easier to read on screen and are preferred for web publishing.

In addition to selecting the font family, you can set your font in a variety of styles, including **boldface,** *italics,* underlining, or color. Use color or **boldface** for emphasis and contrast, but do so consistently and sparingly: The more they are used, the less attention they will call to themselves. Since *italics* and underlining often have a specific meaning, avoid using them except when necessary. Apply the core design principles of repetition and contrast to your font choices: repeat the same font for consistency and use a different font to produce contrast.

When choosing a font size, make sure it will be easy to read (especially if you are using it for the body of your

> **More about**
> Colors, 172–73
> Fonts, 169–70
> Visuals, 79–87, 173–74
> White space, 170–71

> **More about**
> Using italics and underlining, 842–47

Writing Responsibly

Selecting Fonts with Readers in Mind

Not all readers have perfect vision. If your audience might include members over forty (or under twelve), use a font size of at least 12 points to make the reading experience easier and more pleasant. If your audience might include visually impaired people, increase your font size even more.

to AUDIENCE

More about
Using information
responsibly,
247–64 (ch. 15)

Writing Responsibly | Establishing a Consistent Font

When you copy material from a source, you have the responsibility of citing the source, indicating that it is a direct quotation, and providing full information about the source in a bibliography. When you cut and paste your direct copy from an electronic source, you also have the responsibility of converting its font to the one you are using for your main text. Otherwise, when the font suddenly shifts from black to blue, or from Times to Arial, the audience may be distracted from your message.

to OTHER WRITERS

More about
Page layout:
MLA style,
345–49 (ch. 18)
APA style,
392–96 (ch. 19)
Chicago style,
423 (ch. 20)
CSE style,
447–48 (ch. 21)

project). Generally, a 10- or 12-point type will be legible to most readers, but print out a page of text to check the font size: 10-point type in one font may look larger than 12-point in another.

The font you choose can also add contrast, or it can group items through repetition: If most of your text is in a serif font, a sans serif font (or the same font in bold or a different color) can call attention to a heading. Use the same style, size, color, and type of font for all the headings at the same level and for all text of the same type. Ensure consistency by using the Styles option on your word processing program.

Keep in mind, too, that the fonts you use (especially in headings) can reinforce the overall impression you are trying to create. A typeface such as 𝔒𝔩𝔡 𝔈𝔫𝔤𝔩𝔦𝔰𝔥, for example, might be appropriate in a poster announcing the first meeting of the Shakespeare Society. Be careful: For a text-heavy document, legibility is more important than drama. More than a few words in an ornate font like *Edwardian Script* or **Haettenschweiler** will be hard to read. Setting lengthy passages on a website in a serif font may also make the text difficult to read on screen, though such fonts can be used effectively for headings online. With digital documents, you will also need to establish legible contrast between background and text.

NOTE For college writing, check the style guide for your discipline to make sure these design decisions will be acceptable.

FIGURE 9.2 Using white space to group elements To group information into a unit for readers, add white space above a heading or around a figure and its caption.

White space The portion of a page or screen with no text or images, the *white space,* does not literally have to be white (Figure 9.2). The margins at top, bottom, left, and right of a page provide white space, as does the extra space before

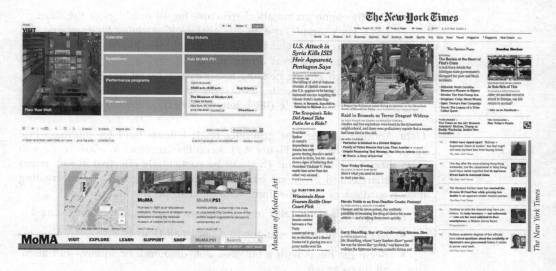

FIGURE 9.3 **Formatting a web page** The web pages from the Museum of Modern Art in New York (left) and *The New York Times* (right) use font size, style, color, and white space to highlight information and make the page attractive. A news page is by necessity crowded with information, so it also uses lists, boxes, and bullets to make the page easier to navigate. The museum uses boxes and shading to organize and distinguish content, and it also reserves white space for pop-up information, such as maps and links to lectures and membership.

a paragraph or around a heading. Extra white space above or around text or a graphic organizes elements into a section. Using the same amount of white space around headings at the same level or visuals of the same type lends consistency to your layout. Adding extra white space lends emphasis through contrast. Ample white space makes a page inviting and easy to read; without it, a page looks crowded, and the eye has difficulty finding the focal point (Figure 9.3).

Headings Writers often use headings and subheadings to group text and guide readers. They can help readers comprehend a text's structure at a glance. The principles of repetition and contrast are crucial with headings:

> **More about**
> Parallelism,
> 542–50 (ch. 28)

- Set all headings of the same level in the same font, style, and color, and align them in the same way on the page or screen:

  First-level heading (title)

  Second-level heading (major section)

  Third-level heading (subsection)

- Use the same grammatical structure for all headings of the same level. For example, use all *-ing* phrases (*Containing the Economic Downturn, Bailing Out Wall Street*) or all *noun phrases* (*Economic Downturn Ahead, Wall Street Bailout*).
- Distinguish among heading levels by setting all headings of the same level in a specific font, style, or color or by placing them differently on the page (flush left, centered).

Lists Another strategy for grouping related items (and for adding white space) is to use lists (see Figure 9.3). Keep lists succinct to allow readers to skim them for information. They can be particularly effective in web pages to summarize and break up blocks of text on the screen. When creating lists, regardless of your medium, remember to do the following:

- Keep list items parallel (use all phrases or all sentences, for example).
- Keep the number of items in a list small (four to six).
- Begin list items with a bullet—a dot, diamond, or square—and align all items at left.
- Use numbered lists to indicate steps in a process and bulleted lists to group related information.

While lists are common in professional writing (as in résumés and PowerPoint presentations), they are used sparingly in most academic writing.

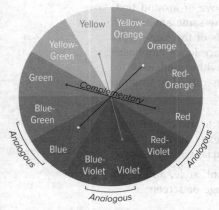

FIGURE 9.4 **The color wheel** Colors opposite each other on the color wheel are complementary; colors adjacent to each other are analogous.

Color Color, through contrast, calls the reader's attention to what is important in the text: Headings; bullets or numbers in lists; boxes, charts and graphs; or illustrations often appear in color so that readers will notice them. Use color judiciously:

- Use a limited color palette. Too many colors in close proximity will create a hodgepodge effect.
- Use a pleasing color palette. Analogous colors, those adjacent to each other on a color wheel (Figure 9.4), create a softer, more harmonious look. Complementary colors, those opposite each other on the color wheel, contrast with each other, each making the other color look brighter.

Writing
Responsibly | **Designing for Those with Impaired Color Vision**

Most people with a color-vision impairment are unable to distinguish between red and green: Both colors appear gray. A smaller number are unable to distinguish between blue and yellow. To be sure that those with a color-vision impairment can obtain important information, avoid the red/green or blue/yellow color combination, or use labels or underlining in addition to color.

to OTHER WRITERS

- Use readable color combinations. Make sure colors contrast enough with their background that they are legible.

- Use appropriate colors. Consider the associations colors and combinations of colors carry: pastels for new babies, bright yellow and black for warnings, green for nature. Consider your audience carefully as you choose colors; their associations vary from one culture to another. White, for example, is the color for weddings in the United States; in China, it is red.

- Use colors consistently. The repetition of colors will group items of the same type.

4. Add visuals.

Visuals are the first thing readers notice when they look at a text. For this reason, they are integral to documents geared toward the general public and must thus catch the eye of potential readers. Visuals are appropriate in some academic genres—in economics, for example, graphs are used frequently—but they are not customary in all academic disciplines. Ideally, any visuals you include in a document should be visually compelling. This does not mean that you should choose images just because they will capture the reader's attention. To be effective, images must be compelling *and* must expand your readers' understanding of your text. They must also be appropriate to your writing situation.

Place visuals on a page as soon as possible after the text discussion that refers to them. In academic and professional writing, include a reference to the figure or table in your text, numbered in order of appearance (such as figure 1 or table 2). Provide a caption that includes this number and, wherever possible, adds information that is not included in the text. The overall effect is usually best if images are placed at the top or bottom of the page and are either centered or placed flush with the left or right margin.

More about
Visual arguments, 136–64 (ch. 8)
Visuals in college writing assignments, 79–80

More about
Incorporating visuals, 322–23, 345–49 (MLA), 394–95 (APA)
Choosing the right type of visual, 80–83
Revising visuals, 84–87
Academic writing, 452–96
Professional writing, 497–518

Reference   Including Visuals (Images and Graphics)

	Images	Graphics
Type	Photographs, drawings and sketches, screen-shots, film stills.	Tables, flowcharts, pie charts, line and bar graphs, diagrams, timelines, maps.
Purpose	Depict or explain an event, object, or process, or illustrate a concept.	Convey complex information in an easily readable form.
Audience	Use images to draw readers in.	Use graphics to help readers understand complex data, trends, processes.
Context and Genre	In academic and professional contexts and genres, use images to provide evidence, to help readers grasp a point, or to provide an example. In personal and public writing, use images for these purposes, as well as to capture interest, make an argument, or reinforce a point.	In every context and genre, use graphics to help readers understand complex data quickly.

→ EXERCISE 9.3 Analyzing layout

Return once again to the design you analyzed in Exercises 9.1 and 9.2. In one or two paragraphs, analyze its layout. Consider its overall impression (trendy or conservative, playful or serious); its use of white space, lists, color, and headings to create proximity, alignment, repetition, and contrast; its use of fonts and visuals, and how the visuals function (do they reinforce product identity, provide an example, offer additional information, further the argument, demonstrate a process?). Has your assessment of the document's purpose, audience, context, and genre changed as you studied it more closely?

Make It **Your Own**

Using the plan you developed for the Make It Your Own exercise on page 168, sketch the web page, brochure, or advertisement you planned. Consider the overall impression that would be most appropriate given your writing situation.

Work **Together**

In groups of three or four, critique the documents you produced in the Make It Your Own exercise above. How well has each designer used proximity, alignment, repetition, and contrast? How well does each design express the purpose of the group or event? How well does it appeal to the target audience?

10 Writing for Multiple Media

IN THIS CHAPTER

a. Writing and answering email, 175

b. Creating websites and web pages, 179

c. Writing in social media, 185

Photographs in the Carol M. Highsmith Archive, Library of Congress, Prints & Photographs Division

Like contemporary artists, writers today have an array of media to choose from: pen and paper, email, instant message, website, blog, wiki, tweet, Snapchat, Instagram. From these many choices, they must select the medium that will be most appropriate to their message, their purpose, and their audience. They must also choose a medium that will help them meet their responsibilities as writers. This chapter offers guidelines for matching medium to message, for deciding on the most appropriate style and tone, and for meeting your responsibilities to yourself and your readers.

10a Writing and Answering Email

Writers today have a wide range of choices for informal messaging on applications such as Facebook and Twitter, in addition to the texting enabled by cell phone apps. If your boss or instructor initiates a conversation on one of these informal platforms, you should of course feel free to reply in that medium. Unless your boss or instructor indicates otherwise, though, choose email as your most appropriate means of professional communication. Email offers a convenient and speedy way to communicate in writing, but its very speed creates the need for special care. Before you press the Send button, consider whether you have selected and arranged your words to create an appropriate *tone*. If you have doubts, revisit your message or consider making a phone call or paying a visit in person instead.

1. Write email.

More about
Tone, 19–20, 138,
565, 570–72
Business emails,
memos,
502–03
Acronyms, 564,
850–51

To deal efficiently with the volume of email most of us get, even personal email should take on the characteristics of the traditional business memo: limiting the number of recipients, providing an appropriate subject line, getting right to the point, and sticking to a single topic.

Recipients Include in the To line only those recipients who need to take action on the message; include in the cc line anyone who must be kept informed but from whom you do not need a reply.

Subject line Provide a short, descriptive title in the subject line of your email: "A question about tomorrow's assignment." The subject line should reflect the content of the message; alter it, in a reply or when forwarding a message, only when doing so is necessary or useful.

Salutation Many professional communities use formal salutations ("Dear Dr. Mansfield") in their emails; others do not. Pay attention to emails you have previously received from the people to whom you are writing, and follow their lead. When in doubt, include the formal salutation.

Task-Oriented Emails Get Right to the Point The tone of an email should be appropriate to the task. An email to a professor or business associate should not be as informal as a note to a friend. Indeed, in formal settings in the United States, emails that are task oriented frequently dispense with formalities and personal touches and get right to the point following the greeting. In some cultures, such messages would be considered rude. Members of some professional communities in the US view them as efficient and timesaving.

Quick Reference Consider Your Writing Situation When Composing Email

Purpose and Focus

The primary purpose of most email messages is to inform, so focus on a single issue, state it briefly in the subject line, repeat it in the first paragraph, and keep the email brief.

Audience and Context

While email is generally somewhat informal, adjust your tone and level of formality to the context in which you are writing and in which your words will be read. Unless you are writing to a close friend, avoid emoji, emoticons, gifs, stickers, and conversational acronyms—IMO for "in my opinion" or FWIW for "for what it's worth"—and nonstandard capitalization, grammar, punctuation, and spelling. If you are replying to an earlier message, select "reply" rather than starting a new email, to avoid creating filing problems for your audience.

Writing Responsibly

Maintaining Confidentiality in Email

You may have noticed the bcc ("blind carbon copy") option in the header of your email messages. Any recipient you list in this line will receive a copy of your message but will not be identified to other recipients. Sending blind copies can be ethical or unethical: Use the Bcc option to keep the email addresses of recipients private, as when sending a message to a group of people who do not know one another. Do not blind-copy a recipient to deceive your correspondent into believing a message is confidential. So your readers will not mistakenly believe they are the only recipient of a message, mention in the body of the message that it is being shared with others. If you wish to forward another's email, first obtain permission.

to OTHER WRITERS

Organization and length State your purpose in the first paragraph, and keep the paragraphs short. If an email must be long, use numbered lists, headings, and transitions to make the organization clear and to help the recipient quickly grasp the content.

Style To avoid embarrassing mistakes, treat the writing context as being slightly more formal than you think it is.

Design Some email programs allow for text styling such as boldface and italics; others allow only plain text. When you are not sure whether your recipient will see formatting, use the following conventions:

1. For book titles and other text you would normally italicize, place an underline before and after the title: _Lone Survivor_ by Marcus Luttrell.

2. For emphasis, place an asterisk before and after the word to be highlighted: *Recommendations*.

3. Place URLs on a separate line to make it easy for your readers to copy and paste them into the address bar of their web browser.

4. Avoid special characters, like dashes, that may disappear or become garbled in transmission.

Some discussion groups require that messages be sent in plain text. In general, format paragraphs in block style, with no indention of the first line, and separate paragraphs with a blank space. Choose a standard sans serif font such as Arial or Verdana in a 10- or 12-point font size. Keep the font black.

> *More about*
> URLs, 240
> Block style letters, 498–99
> Font types and styles, 169–70
> Discussion groups, 185–86, 217–218

Closing If your email begins with a formal salutation, provide a pleasant or complimentary closing ("Yours truly," "Best wishes," "Sincerely"), as well.

Contact information After your name, list contact information such as your mailing address, telephone number, or website address.

More about
Spelling, 580–94
(ch. 32)
Punctuation,
769–834
(ch. 47–53)
Capitalization,
835–841
(ch. 54)

Revision Edit for grammatical and typographical errors and be sure you included your attachments. If your emotions are involved, delay sending for an hour or even a day, until you are calm and reasonable. Hostile email can establish you as an unreasonable person; it may also circulate beyond your intended recipients, doing even more harm.

Archiving Consider whether sent messages need to be preserved. You may find it helpful to "tag" emails—establish topical archive folders for your correspondence (Figure 10.1). Merely saving email messages in your inbox will make them difficult to find later and may use up limited storage space.

2. Answer email.

Answering email messages involves not only the issues related to writing email but also the following:

Timing Read and reply to your email regularly—every day, if possible. If replying to a particular email will take more time than you have, send an immediate reply so that the sender knows you received the message, and indicate when you will respond. If you are going to be away from email for a day or more, add an auto-reply message to alert correspondents.

Context Before answering, read all the messages that have been sent to you on that topic. If your email program allows, sort your messages by subject

Writing Responsibly — Making Considerate Attachments

When your recipients receive your email with attachments, they may download it to their computers. Before you attach your file, give it a name that will make sense when it appears on the recipients' hard drive. Often this will mean including your name in the file name, along with a label identifying the text, such as "Rivera Graphs.doc." In the body of your email, name and describe your attachments; otherwise your recipients may be hesitant to open them for fear of phishing and viruses. While you may be able to email large files as attachments, your recipients' servers may not accommodate them. Consider zipping (compressing) big files or sending them through a free third-party program such as Dropbox, Google Drive Windows OneDrive, or Hightail.

to OTHER WRITERS

Writing
Responsibly / Understanding Email and Privacy

Email is never private. A confidential message to a close friend may get forwarded to others, intentionally or accidentally; messages sent from a company computer may be read by your boss or your company's compliance team; and even deleted messages can be accessed by hackers or the government. For your own peace of mind, do not write messages that might harm your reputation or those of others.

to SELF

to be sure that you have read everything in the thread you are responding to. So that your recipient has a context for what you are saying, quote pertinent passages from the email to which you are responding, or refer your reader to an earlier message in the thread.

Recipients Most people get more email than they can handle, so always consider carefully before selecting "reply all." Does everybody on the list really need to be included?

→ **EXERCISE 10.1** Analyzing an email message

Analyze an email message you wrote to a boss, an instructor, or an older family member (parent or grandparent, aunt or uncle): Is it focused on a single topic? Does it include an appropriate subject line? Is the message logically organized? Is it of an appropriate length? Is the tone appropriate given the recipient of the message? Does the message avoid errors of grammar, spelling, punctuation, and mechanics? In one or two paragraphs, explain how you might revise the message. Next, rewrite the email for a different audience and, asking the same questions, describe the differences.

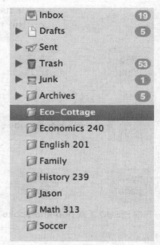

Inbox	19
▶ Drafts	5
▶ Sent	
▶ Trash	53
▶ Junk	1
▶ Archives	5
Eco-Cottage	
Economics 240	
English 201	
Family	
History 239	
Jason	
Math 313	
Soccer	

FIGURE 10.1 **Folders for archived email**

10b Creating Websites and Web Pages

"Writing for the web" can involve a wide range of social media work, such as maintaining a Twitter feed or Facebook page. Or it can mean creating a *website*, a collection of files located at a single address, or URL, on the World Wide Web.

1. Plan your site.

Every website begins with a *home page*, the page designed to introduce visitors to the site. Many writers turn to a blogging platform such as

WordPress to host not only a traditional blog but also websites. However you create your website, the home page should include the website's title, the date the site was created or last updated, contact information, a copyright or Creative Commons notice, and clear navigation to site content, either through navigation bars or a site map.

Unlike print documents in which reading traditionally proceeds *linearly* (the document is arranged so that all readers begin at page 1 and read through to the end), most websites are *networked* (users may enter the site at any page and follow their own path through the site). Just how easy it is for users to find their way around your site depends on its structure and on the navigation tools you provide.

FIGURE 10.2 **A hub-and-spoke structure**

Site structure When creating a website, consider how the various pages will relate to one another and how users will move among them. A site that includes a home page and a handful of *web pages*—documents that, like the home page itself, may include text, audio and still images, and database files—with loosely related content may work best with a hub-and-spoke structure (Figure 10.2). If your website will offer a series of pages with related content, a hierarchical arrangement, with links from home page to lower-level pages and from page to page, may be more useful (Figure 10.3).

Reference   Creating a Website? Consider Your Rhetorical Situation

Purpose and Focus

Readers scan websites quickly, so keep your sentences brief and clear and your focus tight. Images, sound files, and design should reflect your purpose and capture readers' attention.

Context and Audience

Consider any restrictions of your host (site sponsor) as you plan your site. Consider, too, the needs and expectations of your readers, but remember that unintended readers may also see what you post on the open Web, so avoid language or content that you or others might find embarrassing or offensive.

Genre

If you will be providing information that will remain current for a long time, create a website that you update once or twice a year; if your site requires daily or weekly updates, create a blog; if you want readers to contribute to the site's content, create a wiki.

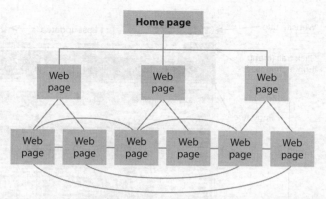

FIGURE 10.3 **A hierarchical, treelike structure, with additional links**

Navigation tools Navigation tools include the following:

- **Menus.** Placed at the top, bottom, left, or right side of the web page, menus list main sections of your website and are consistent from page to page.

- **Breadcrumb trails.** Used to show the path you took to the page you are on, breadcrumb (or "click") trails offer users an easy way to jump back to higher-level pages.

- **Links.** Used to jump from place to place on a web page or from web page to web page, links appear as highlighted words or images on a web page.

The website shown in Figure 10.4 offers these navigation tools.

Home page While the contents of your home page will depend on the purpose, audience, context, and genre of your site, users will benefit from the following:

- **Title.** The home page (and each additional web page) should include a title that clearly and succinctly indicates the type of information your site will include.

- **Date created, last updated.** Providing a copyright date or indicating when you last updated the site lets readers know how current your site is and enables users to create a complete bibliographic citation. This will not be necessary on blogs because the reverse chronological structure places the most recent update at the top.

FIGURE 10.4 Website navigation tools and helpful features The Massachusetts Bay Transportation Authority's Webby–award-winning site includes menus, search boxes, and even a click trail that reinforces the sponsoring organization's identity by resembling stops on a subway map. It appeals to its target audience by placing convenient links to schedules and maps, rider tools, and subway advisories on its home page (*left*) and featuring photographs of Boston's iconic landmarks.

Massachusetts Bay Transportation Authority

- **Link to a site map**. A site map is a table of contents for the site; it helps users find the information they are looking for quickly and easily.

- **Search function.** A natural-language search box that provides an alternative to the site map or navigation bar.

- **Link to contact information.** Provide a link to your basic contact information, including an email address, your name, and your role. To avoid possible cyberstalking, reveal only as much information as you are willing for the entire world to know, and establish a separate email address exclusively for correspondence from your website.

- **Copyright or Creative Commons notice.** All material published on the web is automatically protected by copyright. Remind readers of this fact by including a copyright notice: "Copyright © 2017 Paul Jefferson." For the copyright date, use the year in which you created or last updated the page. An increasingly popular alternative notice is a Creative Commons License. Browse the Creative Commons website (http://creativecommons.org/) to learn more about this project.

> **EXERCISE 10.2 Examining the navigation tools and home page of a website**
>
> Analyze your school's website or another website you visit regularly. In a paragraph or two, discuss the strengths and weaknesses of the site's structure and navigation tools. What tools do you use regularly and why? Now study the website's home page. Which elements discussed in this chapter are included? Which would you like to see added, and why?

3. Design your site.

Communicating on the web is inescapably visual, and the design of your website will influence both how clear and accessible your site is and how receptive users are to your message. To make your site visually effective, plan it carefully and apply the principles of design (proximity, alignment, repetition, and contrast). When choosing a template, evaluate the available options carefully and select one that follows the four principles of design.

Incorporating image, sound, and video files Web pages more easily attract an audience when they include multimedia files—images, graphics, sound, or video. Images and graphics should do more than ornament the page,

More about
Four principles of design, 166–67

PDF Portable Document Format; created by Adobe, PDF format allows a document to be opened in different systems without losing its formatting however; they should also provide useful information, set an appropriate tone, or suggest useful perspectives on the content of the page. When adding images and graphics to your site, consider how much is enough. Just as a visually bland web page can fail to stir readers' interest, a visually cluttered page can distract them.

Since not every site visitor will actually play the files (and some may not be able to see or hear the files), provide a written description of any that are crucial to your point. A description may also pique visitors' curiosity enough for them to click the link or file you provide. Most video files can and should be hosted elsewhere (YouTube and Vimeo are two possibilities) and embedded on your site to push content across multiple platforms.

Ensuring accessibility Design your site so that it is accessible to all users. For blind audience members who are using screen readers, provide visual descriptions of images. For deaf audience members, caption your videos. The free captioning tool Amara is one option, and the basic captioning function offered by *YouTube* will let you upload a transcript and sync the text to the dialogue. If you are attaching PDFs to your site, keep in mind that they are inaccessible to blind users: they are an image of text rather than text itself, so screen readers cannot read them. WebAIM.org offers helpful details on designing for PDF accessibility.

Tech **Use a Lower Resolution to Avoid Memory-Hogging Image Files**

Including high-resolution image files or a large quantity of lower-resolution image files can make loading a web page so time-consuming that visitors become exasperated and give up.

Avoid this problem by reducing the size of your images. Most image files will look fine online at 72 dots per inch, and .jpg and .gif are generally acceptable image file types.

> **More about**
> Writing concisely,
>   520–28
>   (ch. 26)
> Deciding to illus-
>   trate, 79–80
> Designing printed
>   and electronic
>   documents,
>   166–74 (ch. 9)
> Evaluating web-
>   sites, 239–43
> Editing and proof-
>   reading, 93–95,
>   99–100

4. Revise and edit your website.

A website full of errors will undermine your credibility with readers long before they ever assess the content on your site, so check your website carefully before bringing it "live":

- Since most readers scan websites for information, make sure your prose is clear and concise.

- Check that visual, audio, and multimedia files add value and meaning and are not merely ornamental, intended just to catch the eye.

- Check that your design is attractive and consistent.

- Check that image, audio, and other media files load properly.

- Check all links to make sure they work.

- Ask friends to read pages: Users with different platforms, browsers, and devices will run into different problems.

- Edit and proofread your site carefully for errors in spelling, grammar, punctuation, and mechanics. Whether consciously or unconsciously, readers' opinions of writers' credibility can be affected by the quality (or lack) of editing and proofreading.

> ## Writing Responsibly
> ### Checking Accessibility
>
> As you work online, avoid *ableism*. Always design your project so that its text, image, audio, and video components are accessible to impaired users. It may be helpful to run your material through an accessibility checker. The Assistive Technology Resource Center (atrc.colostate.edu) provides a list of programs, some of which are free.
>
> to AUDIENCE

5. Maintain your website.

Once your website is up and running, check it every month or so:

- Make sure the site continues to run on different browsers.

- Delete, replace, or repair broken links at least once a month.

- Make sure image files appear; if a small icon appears instead, check that the image file is in your server folder and that its URL is typed correctly (including the file extension, such as .jpg or .gif).

10c Writing in Social Media

Online communication is woven deeply into the fabric of contemporary life: email, texting, wikis, blogs, and an array of social apps, from Twitter to Snapchat, are in classrooms, professional settings, and homes. The very familiarity of these media can lull writers into making errors that they later regret. Writers must always adapt their style and tone to their *rhetorical situation*; now the medium and the app are part of a writer's rhetorical situation, too. As writers move from the Yik Yak app to the Mail app, the style and tone of what they write must also make the instantaneous change. Moreover, the nature of the conversations taking place within an app can vary dramatically, as well; compare a Twitter thread about a celebrity's love life with a Twitter conversation about copyright law to see the differences.

> **More about**
> Rhetorical situation, 8

Writing
Responsibly — Flaming

More about
Ad hominem and
other logical fal-
lacies, 159–63

The quick interactivity and the anonymity of online media present a special challenge: keeping your temper. **Flaming**—writing a scathing response to someone with whom you disagree—is a great temptation, but it shuts down reasoned discourse, instead encouraging ad hominem attack. Flaming may convey a sense of power for your having found a biting way to put down an opponent, but it also minimizes the likelihood of anyone's listening to or being influenced by you.

to OTHER WRITERS

More about
Discussion lists,
217–18
Blogs, 217–18
Documenting
posts to dis-
cussion lists,
336 (MLA),
387 (APA), 420
(*Chicago*), 446
(CSE)
Citing blogs and
blog posts,
336 (MLA),
387 (APA), 420
(*Chicago*), 446
(CSE)

Many of the principles described in *sections 10a* and *10b* for email and website writing also apply to these other forms of online writing. Think about your purpose, and tailor your writing style and tone to your intended audience. Before sending or posting your message, consider how your audiences might interpret it, and make any necessary adjustments.

The goal of online discussions, as with live discussions, is to learn collaboratively through give and take; however, because participants are not physically present, the temptation to go off on a tangent may be great. To avoid this, focus on responding directly to the comments of other participants and summarizing the discussion before moving on. Your online voice can be casual, but strive to keep your comments clear and to maintain a voice that is friendly and polite, even when you disagree.

When participating in a discussion in *asynchronous media* (media that do not require participants to sign on at a specific date and time), take advantage of the opportunity to reflect on and proofread your comments before posting them. Asynchronous discussions usually require participants to make a commitment to sign on regularly and to make comments at least once a week.

More about
Collaborative
writing projects,
31–33, 51

In *synchronous media* such as instant messaging and chat, where communication occurs in real time, participants must make a commitment to sign on at a specific time and to focus attention on the discussion while it is occurring. Reflection and careful proofreading are not possible, but synchronous discussions are useful for brainstorming and for developing a sense of community.

11 Presenting with Multiple Media

Hurricane Katrina
August 29, 2005

Photo: NOAA

© Paramount Classics/courtesy Everett Collection

"Future generations may well have occasion to ask themselves, 'What were our parents thinking? Why didn't they wake up when they had a chance?'" So speaks Al Gore in this presentation on global warming. He gave his presentation to groups large and small across the country and around the world. It was captured in the classic documentary *An Inconvenient Truth,* which has been seen by millions of viewers. Very few of us ever have an opportunity to reach out to such a large audience on a topic of global importance. Still, we are often called upon to present our ideas at school, at work, and in our communities. If we can present them clearly and compellingly, using multiple media when they will help us reach listeners, we, too, can effect change.

11a Identifying Your Purpose, Audience, Context, and Genre

> **More about**
> Purpose, 14–16
> Audience, 17–20
> Context and genre, 21

As with any writing project, begin planning a presentation by considering your *purpose, audience, context,* and *genre.* In an academic or business context, your primary *purpose* is likely to be the same as for a written text: to present information or to persuade others to accept your position or to take action. Even more so than a written text, an oral presentation is likely also to have a secondary purpose: to engage the imagination or emotions of the audience so that members can more readily identify with and remember the key points.

When addressing classmates or colleagues, you will probably have a sense of the needs and expectations of your *audience*. When addressing an unfamiliar group, ask yourself why the group has assembled and what they hope to get out of your presentation. It may be useful to ask the event organizers what kind of audience to expect.

The *context*, or setting, in which you deliver your presentation will affect the kinds of equipment you will need, the types of multimedia aids you create, and the relationship you can establish with your audience. When addressing a small group in a college classroom, for example, you will probably not need any special equipment, whereas in larger settings you may need a projector, a sound system, and special lighting.

Finally, consider the *genre* of your presentation. As a college student, you are most likely to be asked to contribute to or lead a class discussion, or to give a presentation online or in person to a class, student group, or social service organization. In business, you may be asked to train colleagues or make a sales pitch to potential customers in person or online.

 Contributing to Class Discussion In US schools, active participation in class is an important part of the learning experience, and it may even play a role in instructors' grades. If you are uncomfortable with the idea of speaking in class, let your instructor know. If students in your class seem uncomfortable when they speak, remember that you are responsible for being an effective listener as well as a speaker. That means listening patiently and respectfully at all times.

11b Devising a Topic and Thesis

> *More about*
Devising a
  topic, 24
Narrowing,
  expanding a
  topic, 30–31
Devising a thesis,
  35–36

A presentation, like a written text, begins with an appropriate topic and a well-focused thesis. Your topic and approach should engage you and your audience and offer special insight. Craft a thesis that conveys your purpose and that will engage and guide your audience.

11c Organizing the Presentation

It is more difficult for people to understand and remember ideas they have heard than those they have read. Organize your talk to help your audience hold your main points in memory while the presentation unfolds.

1. Introduction

Use your introduction (10–15 percent of your presentation) to develop a rapport with your audience and to establish the key points of your presentation. Your introduction should accomplish the following:

> *More about*
> Introductions,
> 69–71

- Specify your topic and approach, and convey why it should matter to your audience.

- Engage your audience: A compelling anecdote, startling statistics, or an apt quotation are all good opening gambits.

- Establish your credentials: Knowledge, experience, or the research you have conducted all give you special expertise.

- Provide a brief overview of your main points so that the audience will know in advance what they should be listening for.

2. Body

The body (75–85 percent of your presentation) should explain the points that you previewed in your introduction. It should be clearly and logically organized, so listeners know where you are going and where you have been. Use transitions such as "first," "second," and "third" to guide your audience, and provide a brief summary of the main points you made earlier ("As I explained a few minutes ago …") and a preview of the points you are about to discuss ("Next I will show how …").

> *More about*
> Organizing,
> 38–43, 53–58,
> 267–70
> Transitions, 60–61
> Explaining and
> supporting
> ideas, 45–46,
> 65–69, 271–73
> Using visuals
> as evidence,
> 80–83
> Finding informa-
> tion, 210–32
> (ch. 13)

For each claim you make, supply appropriate, relevant evidence, such as specific examples drawn from your reading or your experience. Facts and statistics can be very effective as long as you do not burden your audience with more numbers than it can process. (Presenting statistics in information graphics can help.) Engaging anecdotes or stories that use concrete, descriptive language, on the other hand, are more easily remembered.

3. Conclusion

Keep your conclusion brief (5–10 percent of your presentation). Use it to reinforce the main point of the presentation: Repeat the main idea and key points, end with a brief but powerful statement, or return to the opening anecdote, example, or statistic.

> *More about*
> Conclusions,
> 71–73

11d Preparing and Rehearsing the Presentation

For an oral presentation, the following methods of delivery are common, and many presenters combine them when appropriate:

- **Speaking off-the-cuff.** If you are an expert on a topic about which your audience knows little, you may be able to speak engagingly and informatively with little special preparation.

- **Reading a written presentation aloud.** If your material is highly technical or if you are anxious about speaking, reading your presentation may work. Since you will lose eye contact with the audience and risk losing their attention, build in opportunities to speak without a script to engage your listeners.

- **Speaking from your notes.** Speaking from notes will keep you organized and prevent you from forgetting important points while allowing you to make eye contact with the audience.

1. Prepare a speaking outline.

> *More about*
> Topic outlines,
> 41–42, 268–70

When speaking from notes, create a speaking outline by jotting notes on a topic outline about where to pause, when to increase the urgency in your voice, and when to advance to the next slide or visual aid. Add content notes, too, but keep them brief, including only as much information as you need to remind yourself of the point you want to make.

2. Use language effectively.

Well-chosen language can help listeners understand and remember your main points. As you draft and rehearse your presentation, do the following:

> *More about*
> Abstract versus
> concrete lan-
> guage, 572–74
> Eliminating wordi-
> ness, 521–24
> Figures of
> speech, 574–77
> Parallelism,
> 542–50 (ch. 28)
> Repetition (inten-
> tional), 558–59

- Use clear, familiar language.

- Choose concrete words. When abstract words are needed, support them with concrete examples.

- Eliminate wordiness.

- Keep sentences relatively short.

- Include vivid figures of speech, such as metaphors and similes, that link an unfamiliar notion to a familiar or striking one.

- Use parallelism and repetition to emphasize your main points.

3. Create visual, audio, and multimedia aids.

Visual, audio, and multimedia aids can enhance your presentation by clarifying or providing additional information, by showing what you are describing, and by countering stage fright (directing attention away from you). When using visual or multimedia aids during a presentation, make sure the aids are relevant, that you explain them clearly and succinctly, that you do not provide so many that the audience pays attention to them rather than to you, and that you speak to your audience, not to your visual aids.

> *More about*
> Using visuals as
> support, 80–83

Presentation software such as Microsoft PowerPoint, Google Slides, or Apple Keynote usefully projects visual, audio, and multimedia aids. However, overuse of presentation software or poor preparation of slides can overwhelm or distract the audience. (For advice on effective use of presentation software, see the Self Assessment box on the next page.)

4. Rehearse your presentation.

Practice your presentation out loud in front of a mirror, a group of friends or family, or a video camera. Reading the slides word-for-word can bore your audience, so learn your material well. Use at least two or three practice sessions to make sure of the following:

- You are comfortable with the content of your presentation.

- Your presentation is the right length (long enough but not too long).

- Your delivery is polished: You are familiar with the pronunciation of all words and names, you know when to pause or gesture, and you are comfortable making eye contact with the audience (or with yourself in the mirror).

> *More about*
> Visual design,
> 166–74 (ch. 9)
> Matching visual
> to information,
> 80–83

Quick Reference   **Overcoming Presentation Anxiety**

The following tips may help you get through your presentation with a minimum of nerves.

- Envision your success: Picture yourself calm and relaxed at the podium; imagine your sense of accomplishment at the end of the presentation.
- Take several slow, deep breaths, or tighten and relax your muscles just before you take the podium.
- Ignore your racing heart or clammy hands. Instead, use the adrenaline surge to add energy to your presentation.
- Focus on your message: Get excited about what you have to say, and you will bring the audience with you.
- Accept the fact that you may stumble, and be prepared to go on.

Self Assessment — Ten Steps to Using Presentation Software Effectively

When preparing a presentation, reflect on your work. Ask yourself the following questions, revising and practicing as necessary.

- ☐ **Did you review your outline to determine where slides would enhance your presentation?** Do not overwhelm your presentation by creating a slide for every moment.
- ☐ **Did you begin with a title slide?** This slide should include the title of your presentation, your name, and any other useful identifying information, such as your college or business affiliation and your Twitter handle.

- ☐ **Did you keep text brief, design uniform, and contents varied?** The audience should be listening to you, not reading your slides. To make slides easy to absorb, maintain a consistent design. To enhance interest, vary the other components (images, information graphics, video clips).
- ☐ **Did you add blank slides?** Go to a blank slide when no illustration is relevant.
- ☐ **Did you check that slides are visually pleasing?** Keep slides uncluttered and balanced; limit your use of animations (the way text or images enter a slide).
- ☐ **Did you proofread your slides?** Make sure all text is clear, and correct all misspellings and all mistakes of grammar, punctuation, and mechanics.
- ☐ **Did you learn your software's commands?** Keystroke commands allow you to advance or return to slides, use the animation effects, and end the slide show.
- ☐ **Did you practice your presentation with your slides in advance?** Use animations to bring information forward, and do not leave slides up after you have moved on to the next topic.
- ☐ **Did you check your equipment in advance?** Make sure that cords are long enough, that you can lower the lights and cover windows, and so forth.
- ☐ **Did you practice giving your presentation without your slides?** Murphy's Law—whenever something *can* go wrong, it *will* go wrong—applies to presentation software. If the power fails or your computer dies, you should still be able to go on with the show.

- You deploy and discuss visual aids with grace.

- You have good posture and avoid nervous fidgeting and irritating mannerisms (such as the repetition of "um" or "like").

If possible, rehearse in the space where you will be making your presentation to determine how loudly you will have to speak, to test placement of visual aids or screens, and to check your equipment.

Adjusting Your Gestures to Appeal to a Multicultural Audience Gestures vary from culture to culture. As you prepare to give formal presentations, pay attention to the gestures commonly made by classmates or other peers who represent your prospective audience. How do they differ from gestures you are accustomed to? Are you aware of any gestures you should not use while speaking to a multicultural audience?

11e Delivering the Presentation

When the time comes to make your presentation, approach the podium, wait for your audience to settle down, and then begin:

- **Connect with the audience.** Introduce yourself, thank the audience for attending, and smile.

- **Maintain eye contact with the audience.** As you speak, look out at the audience, turning to the left, the right, and center, so all members of the audience feel included.

- **Control your pacing, volume, and tempo.** Speak slowly and clearly. Pause between sections of your presentation. Vary the tone of your voice. If you sense that you are losing your audience, slow your pace, increase your volume, or step closer to the audience.

- **Avoid ableism.** Assume that some members of your audience have impaired hearing or vision. Speak loudly and clearly enough for hearing-impaired audience members. Make your graphics large enough to be easily read, and don't choose a background design that interferes with readability.

Writing
Responsibly | **Listening Actively**

When attending a presentation, be fair to the speaker by listening actively:

- Give the speaker your undivided attention.
- Make an effort to understand the speaker's point of view.
- Set aside prejudices based on the speaker's appearance, accent, rate of speech, or apparent level of comfort.
- Listen for the speaker's main points.
- Identify and assess the evidence presented.

to OTHER WRITERS

11f Speaking Responsibly

As you prepare your presentation, keep your responsibilities as a speaker in mind:

More about
Biased language,
  566–70
Logical fallacies,
  159–63
Patchwriting, 248,
  253–57
Signal phrases,
  277, 278,
  304–05 (MLA),
  364–65 (APA)
Revising visuals,
  84–87
Contextualizing
  sources, 277–79

- **Know your material and your purpose.** For an informative speech, be sure your information is current and your examples pertinent. For a persuasive speech, adopt a position that you believe in, one for which you can offer compelling, concrete evidence.

- **Acknowledge counterevidence and alternative interpretations.** Do not alter quotations unfairly or misuse statistics. Avoid words and images that manipulate your audience or that rely on logical fallacies.

- **Use signal phrases.** Since your audience will not have access to your written text, acknowledge sources with signal phrases such as "Alison Ling's research shows. . ." and be prepared to provide a list of works cited if requested.

- **Practice before presenting.** Respect the time and attention of your audience by practicing your presentation until you can deliver it with confidence and grace.

Work **Together**

With two to four classmates, listen to a complete speech posted on YouTube or a website such as American Rhetoric (http://american-rhetoric.com/). As you listen, take notes on the main point of the speech, the organization of the speech, the transitions or other sign-posts the speaker used, and the speaker's language and delivery. Compare your notes. What did you notice that other group members did not (and vice versa)?

Part Four

Research Matters

Finding, Evaluating, and Citing Sources

12 Planning a Research Project

> *More about*
> Purpose, 14–16
> Audience, 17–20

© Ian Cartwright, collage, Self-Portrait, 2001

To create this collage, the artist had to devise a plan, gather the right materials, and assemble them to create a unified whole. Yet it took more than just the right materials; it took an idea that would unify them and engage the viewer. Similarly, when you write a research project, you not only must devise a plan and gather supporting information, but you also must have a vision. The goal of your project should be to present the research in your text in a way that engages and even enlightens the reader. The quality of your *planning*, the first stage of the research process, is crucial to the success of this endeavor.

12a Analyzing the Assignment's Purpose, Audience, and Method of Development

Most research projects will have one of these purposes:

- **To inform:** to explain an issue, compare proposed solutions, or review the research on a specific topic
- **To persuade:** to argue for a claim
- **To inquire:** to explore a complex topic, searching for the best possible solution

Study your assignment carefully and talk with your instructor to figure out which purpose your project is intended to serve. If your purpose is *to discover and describe the features of your topic* (the merits and risks of nuclear power generation, for example), you should not be making an argument on the topic. If you are asked *to explore a topic, take a position, and defend it* (researching nuclear power generation, say, and deciding whether it is necessary), you will need to include description but focus on making an argument.

If you are asked *to explore a situation and make a recommendation* (such as on a state initiative to build a nuclear power plant), your research will be inquiry-based. Again, you will need to describe the situation, but your focus will be on weighing the pros and cons and then recommending a *provisional* course of action, one based on the best information available but subject to revision as new information comes to light.

Sometimes, college research assignments specify the method of development to use: comparison-contrast, cause-effect, and so on. One of the most frequently used methods of development is *analysis*—the writer divides the issue, proposal, or event into its component parts; explains how the parts work together; and discusses the implications.

As a writer, you have a responsibility to shape your project with the needs and expectations of your audience in mind, so consider who that audience will be. For most college assignments, your audience will include your instructor and perhaps your fellow students. Your instructor will want to see not only that you understand the material covered in class, but also that you can interpret it, analyze it, and think creatively and critically about it. Fellow students may need you to define terms or provide background.

> *More about*
> Arguing for a
>   claim, 140–44
> Methods of
>   development,
>   65–69
> Interpretation,
>   analysis, syn-
>   thesis, and
>   critique, 68,
>   123–35,
>   263–64, 271–73
> Generating ideas,
>   24–30

→ EXERCISE 12.1 Writing with your audience in mind

For each of the assignments listed below, determine whether the purpose is informative, persuasive, or inquiry-based. Then choose one assignment and write a paragraph about how you would approach it if you were writing for an academic audience, for the readers of your college newspaper, and for a website appealing to readers already interested in the topic.

1. Analyze the effect that monitoring Internet searches at the library would have on patrons.
2. Argue for or against the monitoring of Internet searches at libraries.
3. Evaluate the treatment options for gambling addictions—which option seems most effective, and why?
4. Describe the symptoms of a gambling addiction.
5. Explain how genetic engineering is currently used to diagnose and control disease in humans.
6. Argue for or against the use of genetic engineering to control disease in humans.
7. Compare the results of homeschooling and traditional classroom education on academic success in college.
8. Explain the effects of homeschooling on children.
9. Define "reality television."
10. Support or refute this statement: Network news is reality television.

Reference   **Factors in Planning a Research Project**

- When is the project due?
- How long is the project to be?
- What type of research is required?
- What types of sources are more useful: scholarly books and articles only, or a mix of scholarly and popular sources?

- How many sources will you need to answer your research questions fully and accurately?
- On what criteria will the project be evaluated?
- What other work and activities will compete for your time and attention?

12b Setting a Schedule

> *More about*
> Setting a realistic schedule,
> 22–24

Set a schedule for your research project that allows time for each of the following steps:

- Analyzing the assignment, taking its scope and purpose into consideration

- Analyzing your audience to determine what your reader will expect from you

- Choosing a topic that is appropriate to your assignment and your audience

- Narrowing your topic to one that can be fully explored within the time you have available to devote to it

- Framing research questions and developing a hypothesis that will structure and focus your research project

- Creating a working bibliography to keep track of the information you will need for documenting your sources later

- Annotating your working bibliography so that you can remember what these sources cover and how you expect to use them

Check with your instructor if you do not know the answer to these questions.

Tech   **Using an Assignment Calculator**

To set a realistic schedule, try using an online assignment calculator like the one offered by the University of Minnesota Libraries (www.lib.umn.edu/apps/ac). Such tools divide the writing process into steps and suggest a date by which each step should be completed. Check your own library's website to see whether a time management calculator is provided, or search for one by typing "assignment calculator" into the search box of a search engine such as Bing or Google.

┌─ Make It **Your Own** ─────────────────────────────────

For a research project you have been assigned, answer the questions
in the Quick Reference box on the previous page, and then set up
a schedule for each stage of your research project. Be sure to leave
time for other assignments and for unexpected delays.

12c Choosing and Narrowing a Research Topic

When the choice is up to you, select a topic that will interest your readers
and you, ideally one about which you already have some knowledge and
insight. Idea-generating techniques such as freewriting and brainstorming can
help you devise a topic that will be of interest to your readers, and they can
help you narrow your topic so that you can write about it specifically and
insightfully. For college research projects, conducting preliminary research or
reviewing assigned reading or class notes may be the most helpful in choosing and narrowing your topic. You might try putting your general topic into
the search box of a library catalog or database to see what topics arise in the
results that are returned. A search in the database PsycARTICLES on "peer
influence," for example, generated topics from smoking and group initiation
to copycat crime among juvenile offenders.

> *More about*
> Generating ideas,
>   24–30
> Narrowing a
>   topic, 30–31

If you are choosing a topic that you want to learn more about, consider whether the purpose of your assignment is to write an informative,
persuasive, or exploratory research project. If your topic is one you do not
know much about, your research will include familiarizing yourself with the
basic data and issues surrounding that topic. That will work well if your
purpose is to inform your audience of what you have learned. If, however,
your purpose is to persuade an audience of one position on your topic or
to explore the complexities of the topic and make recommendations, you
will need to conduct additional research. Unless you have been given an
information-based assignment or have a lot of free time to devote to this
project, you may want to choose a topic you are already familiar with.

┌─ Make It **Your Own** ─────────────────────────────────

Use two or more of the idea-generating techniques in chapter 2,
section 2c, to devise and narrow a research topic for this or another class.

> **Student Models**
> Research projects:
>   "Holy Underground
>   Comics, Batman!"
>   Lydia Nichols,
>   349–62
> "The Power of Ward-
>   robe," Heather
>   DeGroot, 396–405

12d Drafting Research Questions and Hypotheses

After you have tentatively chosen a topic but before you begin searching
for sources, list a number of questions about your topic that research might

answer. These are your *research questions.* Next, write the answers you expect to find. These answers are the *hypotheses* that your research will test. The following examples show research questions and hypotheses for Lydia Nichols's project on underground comics and for Heather DeGroot's project on the effects of wardrobe on social influence.

> **Research question:** What are the characteristics that distinguish underground comics from mainstream comics?
>
> **Hypothesis:** Unlike mainstream comics, underground comics focus on topics that challenge social mores, have an author or author team that has creative control, and appeal to an adult readership.

> **Research question:** Does the clothing a man wears influence the behavior of other men?
>
> **Hypothesis:** The clothing a man wears will influence the behavior of other men when he is in a position of authority relative to the rest of the group.

As you conduct your research, you will continually revise your research questions and hypotheses; the more you learn, the more you know about what questions can be answered and what hypotheses are most plausible. You will also reduce the number of questions you are asking. Your finished project will probably answer only one of the questions you generated at the beginning of the process, and your *thesis* will probably come directly from the hypothesis that you generated to answer that question.

> *More about*
> Devising a thesis, 34–36
> Revising a thesis, 36–38

EXERCISE 12.2 Devising research questions and hypotheses

Devise a research question for one of the assignments you analyzed in Exercise 12.1. Then answer it to create a research hypothesis. (You may need to use the idea-generating techniques discussed in chapter 2.) If your research question cannot be readily answered through research, divide it into several more specific questions that can be.

┌ Make It **Your Own** ─

Create three to five questions that could guide your research on the topic you devised and narrowed in the second Make It Your Own activity on page 199. Remember that your questions must be answerable through research. If they are too broad, divide them into more specific questions. Then turn one of your questions into a hypothesis.

Writing Responsibly | Using Printed Sources

With so much information available online, you might think that you no longer need to consult printed materials. However, many classic and scholarly books are not yet available digitally, and your library may not subscribe to the electronic versions of important newspapers, magazines, and scholarly journals. Dedicate yourself to finding the best information available, whether you access it through a search engine, through an online database like *Academic Search Premier* or *Web of Science*, or through trips to your library's stacks. Most libraries display the latest issues of journals and magazines together in a section of the library called "current periodicals." Ask a librarian to point you to them.

to TOPIC

12e Choosing Research Sources Strategically

Your research project must reflect real research, instead of just creating the appearance of it. The sources you choose are key to fulfilling your responsibilities to your reader, your topic, and yourself. When choosing sources, ask yourself these questions:

- Have you visited your library and its academic databases (not just Google) to see what kinds of resources are available?

- Have you consulted, for background, general reference sources that provide basic facts about your topic?

- Have you consulted, for an authoritative overview, specialized reference sources that discuss the debates and issues about your topic?

- Have you found in-depth analyses and arguments written by experts on your topic, and have other experts on the topic peer reviewed the source before publication?

- Have you located—after finding a journalist, blogger, or website discussing research results—the research report itself, instead of settling for secondhand information?

- Are your sources either up-to-date or classics that established the principles for studying the topic you are researching?

- Have you consulted enough sources to develop a broad understanding of your topic?

- Have you consulted sources that offer a variety of perspectives on your topic, rather than just searching for sources that agree with your hypothesis?

More about
Reliability, 234–39
Scholarly versus popular sources, 235–36, 237
Counterevidence, 148–49
Finding online sources, 214–18
Finding articles in journals, magazines, and newspapers, 218–23
Finding books, 223–26
Finding government documents, 226–27
Finding multimedia sources, 227
Field research: interviews, observational studies, surveys, 229–32

- Have you consulted the best sources, even if they are not available online?

- Have you conducted experiments, observations, surveys, or interviews, when relevant, to develop information of your own?

You may need help to determine whether a source is up-to-date or reliable or to locate sources online or in your library's print collection. When you do, consult a research expert: a reference librarian.

Work **Together**

Skim Lydia Nichols's "Holy Underground Comics, Batman!" (pp. 350–62) or Heather DeGroot's "The Power of Wardrobe: Male Stereotype Influences" (pp. 397–405). Then, with a classmate, evaluate the writer's choice of sources. What types of sources were consulted? How authoritative are they? Would you suggest any strategic changes in source choices? Why or why not?

Make It **Your Own**

For the research hypothesis you devised in the Make It Your Own activity on page 200, make a list of sources that would allow you to uncover useful information. Write a paragraph about these sources, answering the questions following the bullets in *section 12e*.

12f Establishing a Research Log

A *research log* is a journal in which you record research questions and hypotheses; your working thesis; your search terms; information from sources; your interpretation, analysis, synthesis, and critique of sources; and your ideas for where to go next.

1. Set up the research log.

A research log can be compiled in any of the following media: index cards, a notebook, or a file in a computer, tablet, or phone.

Before you set up your research log, consider the advantages and disadvantages of each medium: Although some may think index cards are old-fashioned in the digital age, they are easy to arrange in outline order or to "storyboard" when it comes time to write. Notebooks are easy to carry around and more difficult to lose than note cards. Keeping notes on index cards or in a notebook forces you to interact with your sources, rather than just cutting and pasting information

> **Tech**   **Back Up Your Electronic Research Log**
>
> Do not be a victim of a computer crash: If you keep your research log in electronic form, be sure to back up your files after every session, and store the backup files in a separate place—on a cloud server, for example. If you cannot save your files to a second device, email the files to yourself or print out the new material after each session.

into a word processing file. Keeping a research log on a computer (especially a laptop or tablet) or phone makes it possible to search your notes electronically, to rearrange them into outline order, and to copy material from your notes directly into your project. A phone is likely to be with you at all times, and you can sync note-taking apps such as OneNote and Evernote with your computer.

2. Define the components of a research log.

Divide your research log into sections for different categories of notes:

- The research assignment
- Purpose statement and audience profile
- Your research schedule
- A list of possible research questions
- Your working hypothesis
- Notes taken while reading sources
- Your own ideas
- Your working bibliography

Make It **Your Own**

> Using the information you have generated in the other Make It Your Own activities in this chapter (pp. 199, 200, 202), establish a research log.

Writing
Responsibly   **Avoiding Accidental Plagiarism**

> The wonderful ease of cutting and pasting from digital sources is matched by the terrible ease of falling into unintentional plagiarism. If you are maintaining an electronic research log, it is especially important to mark clearly what you have copied directly from a source and what you have paraphrased, summarized, or commented upon. Consider supplementing your electronic research log with a folder for printouts and photocopies, and check your text against it.
>
> to SELF

> *More about*
> Taking notes to avoid plagiarism, 251–52
> Patchwriting, 253–57

12g Building and Annotating a Working Bibliography

Start your research by gathering potential sources and reviewing them to discover whether they are relevant and reliable. Then set up a *working bibliography* to record those that might be useful. Annotate each entry so that you can remember why you thought the source was worth examining.

1. Identify the components of a working bibliography.

DOI (digital object identifier) A permanent tag that does not change over time or from database to database

A working bibliography should include the information you will need for locating and documenting your sources. You will want to note the following: names (author, editor, publisher), titles (book, article, journal, website), sources (URL, DOI), version (issue, volume), dates (publication, access), and, if required by the documentation style you follow, medium (print, Web, DVD, Kindle e-book). See the Quick Reference box on this page for additional guidance.

As you construct the entries in your working bibliography, follow the documentation style that you will use in your project. Scholars in literature typically use MLA style (ch. 18), scholars in psychology and other social sciences

Quick **Reference** Components of a Working Bibliography

To locate and document . . .	include in the working bibliography . . .
a printed book or an article or chapter in a printed book	the call number, the name of the author or editor, the title of the book, the title of the article or chapter (if relevant), the publisher, the place of publication, the date of publication, and the medium of publication (for example, Print).
an e-book or an article or chapter in an e-book	all of the above minus the call number, plus the DOI or URL; include the e-book format (for example, Kindle e-book, Nook e-book) as the medium.
a printed article	the name of the author, the title of the article, the title of the journal, the volume and issue number of the journal, the year of publication, the page numbers of the article, and the medium of publication (in this case, Print).
an article accessed through a database	all of the above, plus the name of the database, the DOI or, if there is no DOI, the URL for the journal's home page, and the date you last accessed the file. If no page numbers are provided, include paragraph numbers or section name. (The medium will be Web.)
an article in an online journal	all of the above. (The medium will be Web.)
a web page, wiki entry, or entry in a blog or discussion list	the name of the author, the title of the web page or entry title, the title of the website or blog, the sponsor, and the publication date or the date you last accessed the file. (The medium will be Web.)

> **Tech** | **Citation Management Software**
>
> Citation management software—such as the proprietary Mendeley and Ref-Works and the open source Zotero—can format the entries in your bibliography no matter what documentation style you choose. Your library may make such software available to you for free.
>
> Use the documentation chapters in this handbook to test your program for accuracy; not every program performs to perfection, and you are the writer and the person responsible for providing your audience with error-free documentation that does not cause confusion.

typically use APA style (ch. 19), scholars in the humanities (except for literature) typically use *Chicago* style (ch. 20), and scholars in the sciences typically use CSE style (ch. 21). (If you are not sure which documentation style to use, consult your instructor.) Using the appropriate style in the planning stage will save you time later, when you are formatting your finished project.

Saving a copy of an e-file or photocopying a printed document is prudent in case the source becomes unavailable later. Some instructors may also require you to submit copies of your sources with your final project. A PDF generally captures an article as it looked (or would have looked) in print, while an HTML copy provides the text, often without the formatting, page numbers, or illustrations. If both a PDF and an HTML file are available, select the PDF, which will enable you to cite the page numbers of the article and see any illustrations.

> *More about*
> Publication information, 300–03 (Documentation Matters tutorial preceding ch. 18)
> Digital object identifiers (DOI), 204, 374–75, 382–83, 386, 416, 442

2. Recognize the title of the source and name of the publisher.

For many projects, you will be using sources found through library databases or on the web. As you construct your working bibliography, you may be challenged to figure out the title of your source or the name of the publication. Often it is difficult to identify which is the name of the publication and which is the sponsor of the publication. This is even more confusing when the sponsor is identified as "Publisher" (as in Figure 12.3, p. 208). Another problem arises when the name of a subsection of the publication looks like the name of the publication or the title of the source.

The following strategies should be helpful in your search for accurate information to include in your working bibliography:

- **Explore links.** Links labeled "about" or "contact us" often contain revealing information. You can also try clicking on the website logo.

- **Look for a bibliographic entry.** Many library databases not only provide you with the source itself but also with a model bibliographic entry for it. You may have to convert the model from

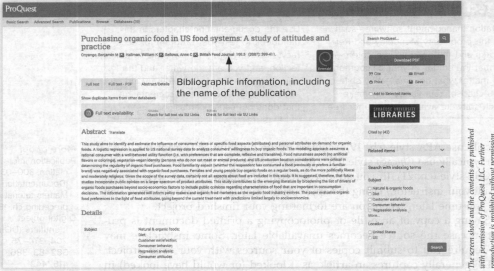

FIGURE 12.1 **Locating the title in the model bibliographic information** In this source retrieved from a database, it is only in the bibliographic information that the name of the publication, *The British Food Journal*, appears.

one style (APA, for example) to another (perhaps MLA), but from the model you will at least know the correct name of the publication. Figure 12.1 shows a search result from a library database. It seems clear that the source title is "Purchasing Organic Food in US Food Systems: A Study of Attitudes and Practices." The name of the publication, however, is not as clear. Is it *ProQuest* or *Emerald*? Fortunately, a bibliographic citation immediately follows the title, and that identifies the publication as *The British Food Journal*.

- **Look for a click path**. Many online publications have a small bar that shows where the current page appears in the site's organization. The current page usually will be on the right-hand side of the click path, with increasingly larger categories to the left.

- **Look for a volume and issue number.** The name of the publication usually accompanies this information (Figures 12.3 and 12.4).

- **Look for the name of an organization or university.** These are usually the sponsor of the publication, rather than the name of the publication

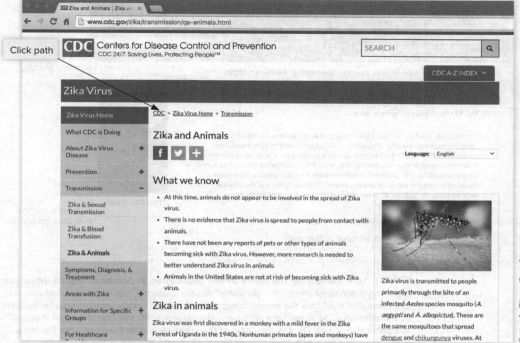

FIGURE 12.2 Locating the publisher by following the click path The name of the website *Centers for Disease Control and Prevention* (abbreviated to *CDC*) is the first item on the left of the click path, followed by the name of the site subsection, "Zika Virus Home," and that subsection's subsection, "Transmission." The title of this source, "Zika and Animals," appears below the click path.

itself. Once you have eliminated the sponsor, keep looking around the page for the name of the publication. Figure 12.3 shows the process.

- **Look at the top of the page.** Websites often place the sponsor's or database's name at the top, followed by the name of the publication, and then by the title and author of the source (Figure 12.4).

3. Annotate the working bibliography.

An annotated entry in a working bibliography includes not only the information you will need to document and locate the source, but also a brief note that summarizes the source and indicates how you might use it in your project. Annotating sources now will save you time later when you begin synthesizing and reporting your research.

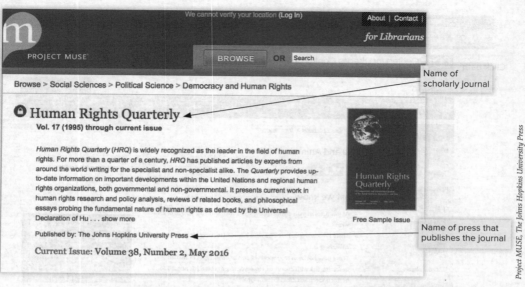

FIGURE 12.3 Identifying the name of the publication in database results When you are citing a scholarly article, the "publisher" in your citation is the name of the journal, not the press that publishes the journal. Interpreting database results requires your being alert to the difference. As is the case with many database results, this one shows an image of the publication cover. On it is the name of the scholarly journal *Human Rights Quarterly*. If you are citing an article from *Human Rights Quarterly*, this title is the information you need. Below it is the notation "Published by: The Johns Hopkins University Press." Don't let that confuse you. (Click on that link, and you will find a list of all the scholarly journals published by that press.)

Student Model
Research project: "Holy Underground Comics, Batman!" Lydia Nichols, 349–62

Below is a sample entry from a working bibliography for Lydia Nichols's research project:

Author names

Publication info:
–Title of journal
–Volume, number, year of publication

Fenty, Sean, et al. "Webcomics: The Influence and Continuation of the Comix Revolution." *ImageTexT* vol. 1, no. 2, 2004, www.english.ufl. edu/imagetext/archives/v1_2/group/index.shtml.

An article in a peer-reviewed online journal. Good history of Underground Comics movement; definitions. Covers importance of comics on the Internet. Compares & contrasts Underground Comics and webcomics. Mentions *The Comics Journal*—check that out.

Article title

URL

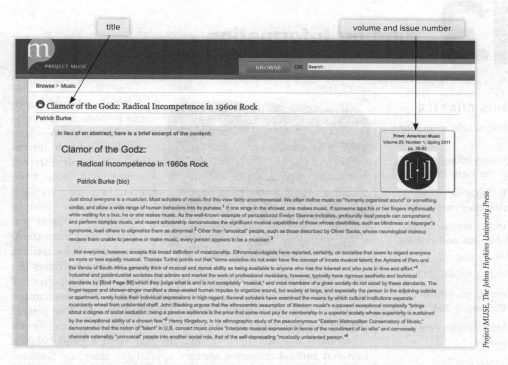

title

volume and issue number

Project MUSE, The Johns Hopkins University Press

FIGURE 12.4 Locating the title by finding volume and issue numbers and by the organizational path At the top is the database name, *Project Muse*. Below that is the organizational path, which often identifies the database, publication, and volume and issue number. Some databases and publications put the name of the publication, volume, and issue number in the banner, as in this case. Further down is the title of the source, "Clamor of the Godz: Radical Incompetence in 1960s Rock," and under that, the author's name.

Make It **Your Own**

For the research project that you have been working on through the Make It Your Own assignments in this chapter, create a working bibliography of at least ten sources. Choose a mix of source types, including at least three books, three scholarly articles, and one or more newspaper or magazine articles, reference works, websites, pamphlets, government publications, or visual, multimedia, or audio sources. Then locate and annotate the five most promising sources, recording complete publication information and taking preliminary notes on what the source covers and how it might be useful to your research project.

> **More about**
> Finding information, 210–32 (ch. 13)
> Scholarly versus popular sources, 235–36, 237

13 Finding Information

© James Yang/Illustration Source

A simple Internet search can provide ready access to information—some excellent, much unreliable. A simple Internet search will not, however, help you strike a good balance among the types of sources you consult in your research. A web search for sources too easily becomes an issue of quantity, collecting "enough sources." The inexperienced researcher may tend to choose brief, quickly available online resources that are easy to read but that lead to a shallow project relying on general facts or pieces that do not fit. Experienced researchers use advanced techniques that yield a good balance between general reference sources, specialized reference sources, popular opinion, and expert insight. They also go beyond the open web to find scholarly resources—the print, electronic, and multimedia gems.

13a Finding Reference Works

Unless you are already an expert on your research topic, your search for sources should include both general and specialized reference works such as dictionaries, encyclopedias, biographical sources, bibliographies, almanacs, yearbooks, and atlases. General reference sources, written for newcomers to the topic, can do the following:

> **More about**
> Reliability, 234–39
> Scholarly versus popular sources, 235–36, 237

- Introduce you to your topic and help you determine whether it will sustain your interest
- Provide an overview and basic facts

Your search should also include specialized, subject-specific reference works written for researchers wanting in-depth understanding of the topic; these can:

- Introduce you to the issues and debates on your topic
- Help you get a sense of subtopics you might want to explore
- Provide lists of reliable sources on the topic
- Introduce and define special terminology, which will help you develop a list of keywords that you can use in further searching for sources

You will find reference works listed in your library's catalog. You may also be able to link to electronic reference sources through your library's home page or databases. As you search reference works, you may have to generate keywords for increasingly general search terms: If you cannot find good overview sources on "bats AND wind turbines," for example, you may have to search separately for "dangers of alternative energy sources" or "wildlife AND alternative energy." If you cannot find good overview sources on "ghostwriting," you might try the larger category of "plagiarism" or the even larger category of "ethics." Reference sources on related issues that include your topic may help you understand and explain the context for your research or its importance.

> *More about*
Searching a
library catalog,
223–26

1. Use dictionaries and encyclopedias.

In addition to whatever online tools they may use, most writers keep a collegiate dictionary at hand to verify spellings, look up definitions, and gather additional brief information about words. An *unabridged* dictionary provides more: more words, more examples of usage, more complete descriptions of the word's roots in other languages. The most extensive unabridged dictionary is the *Oxford English Dictionary* (or *OED*), a multivolume work providing the entire history of English words and showing the ways in which their meanings have changed over time. Unabridged dictionaries, including the *OED*, may be available in print or online.

> *More about*
Selecting a dictionary, 580–82
Using a dictionary
582–84

Specialized dictionaries are written for students and scholars in specific academic fields. In addition to defining terms, subject-specific dictionaries may also provide a comprehensive introduction to the topic, as well as a list of further resources. If, for example, you want a deeper understanding of what *absolutism* means to a political scientist, you can turn to a source like the *Blackwell Dictionary of Political Science,* which offers a long paragraph explaining the term, followed by three recommended sources on the topic.

Writing Responsibly
Using Wikipedia Responsibly

Wikipedia (www.wikipedia.org) is an online encyclopedia created and revised by users. Its ongoing updates make its entries more up-to-date than those in most other encyclopedias. Most Wikipedia updates, however, are done by a relatively small number of people whose average age is 27, which means most entries are not validated by experts—unlike a source such as the *Encyclopedia Britannica.* Approach Wikipedia with care, and verify the information you find there. Wikipedia is not an authoritative source for most college-level research projects, and its use in your project could subject you to the sort of ridicule that a US presidential candidate encountered when she cited Wikipedia in a campaign ad.

to TOPIC

Encyclopedias such as the *Concise Columbia Electronic Encyclopedia* and Wikipedia are available for free online. Others, such as *The New Encyclopedia Britannica,* are available in print but may be free of charge through your library's website.

> **More about**
> Reliability,
> 234–39

General encyclopedias provide a useful introduction to your topic, and some may offer a list of further resources. Specialized encyclopedias, on the other hand, provide not only an introduction to the topic, but also a sense of how scholars in the field approach the topic. They are also likely to provide a brief list of authoritative sources. If your library makes *Reference Universe* or *Credo* available, you can search across many of the library's reference works online and the contents of much of its print reference holdings.

Quick Reference Dictionaries and Encyclopedias

Specialized Dictionaries

The Bedford Glossary of Critical and Literary Terms
Dictionary of American History
Dictionary of American Literary Characters
Grove Dictionary of Art
Dictionary of 20th-Century World Politics
Public Policy Dictionary

Specialized Encyclopedias

The Advertising Age Encyclopedia of Advertising
Cambridge Encyclopedia of the English Language
Encyclopedia of African-American Culture and History
Encyclopedia of American Cultural and Intellectual History
Encyclopedia of Bioethics
Encyclopedia of Government and Politics
Encyclopedia of Latin American History and Culture
Encyclopedia of Religion
Garland Encyclopedia of World Music
McGraw-Hill Encyclopedia of Engineering
McGraw-Hill Encyclopedia of Science and Technology
Routledge Encyclopedia of Philosophy
Women's Studies Encyclopedia

2. Refer to almanacs and yearbooks.

Almanacs and yearbooks are annual publications offering facts and statistics, such as when each phase of the moon will occur and annual per capita income of nations. The best-known general-purpose almanac is the *World Almanac and Book of Facts,* which has been published annually since 1923. Subject-specific almanacs and yearbooks, such as the *Almanac of American Politics* and the *Yearbook of Immigration Statistics,* provide a wide body of statistical and tabular data on specific topics. Today, much of the information once most readily found in an almanac or yearbook is now available online at sites such as the *CIA Factbook* and the Research Tools page at the *Economist* magazine's website.

Quick **Reference**

Almanacs and Yearbooks
Almanac of American Politics
Americana Annual
Britannica Book of the Year
Congressional Quarterly Almanac Plus
Facts on File Yearbook
Information Please Almanac
Statistical Abstract of the United States
UNESCO Statistical Yearbook

3. Check out biographical reference works.

Biographical reference sources can provide you with the facts and events of people's lives (both the famous and the fairly obscure), such as their education, their accomplishments, and their current position. They can also help you understand the historical context in which the person lived or in which his or her works were produced. Numerous biographical resources are available to researchers; two of the most commonly consulted are the *American National Biography* and the *Oxford Dictionary of National Biography* (British).

Quick **Reference**

Biographical Reference Sources	**Bibliographical Resources**
Baker's Biographical Dictionary of Musicians	*Bibliographic Guide to Education*
Biographical Dictionary of American Indian History to 1900	*Bibliographic Guide to Psychology*
Cambridge Biographical Encyclopedia	*Bibliographic Guide to the History of Computing, Computers, and the Information Processing Industry*
Cambridge Dictionary of American Biography	
Fifty Major Thinkers on Education	*Film Research: A Critical Bibliography*
McGraw-Hill Encyclopedia of World Biography	*Information Sources in the Life Sciences*
Mexican American Biographies: A Historical Dictionary, 1836–1987	*Information Sources of Political Science*
	International Bibliography of the Social Sciences
Notable American Women: A Biographical Dictionary	*MLA International Bibliography of Books and Articles on the Modern Languages and Literatures*
Notable Black American Women	*Sociology: A Guide to Reference and Information Sources*
Webster's New Biographical Dictionary	

Writing
Responsibly   **Going beyond Reference Sources**

> Because both general and specialized reference works provide background informa-
> tion to orient you to your topic, they are an essential starting point in your research.
> For a college-level research project, however, reference works are only the begin-
> ning; to fulfill your responsibilities to your topic and audience, you must go beyond
> these sources to find books, articles, and websites that treat your topic in depth.
>
> to TOPIC

4. Use bibliographies.

Bibliographies list sources on a particular topic, providing the information
needed to locate the source. They often provide an abstract or brief summary of each source, so you can tell whether it is likely to be relevant to
your research.

13b Finding Information on the Web

Engines like Google and Bing search billions of web pages for whatever
words the user enters and then return links in order of relevance, as determined by the search engine's criteria. (Google, for example, ranks its results
based on a frequently changing, proprietary algorithm that considers factors
such as the number of other pages that link to a site, its purpose, as well as
advertising.) The results retrieved can differ based on the criteria the search
engine uses to rank relevance, as well as on the web pages it indexes. For
that reason, running a search on multiple engines is a good idea. A list of
alternative search engines appears in the Quick Reference box on page 216.

Before using a search engine for the first time, read about how it works.
Look for links (often at the bottom of the page) called "About" or "Help"
to find answers to frequently asked questions (FAQs) or for advice about
how best to conduct a search on that site. Look, too, for advanced search
options; these will help you focus your search.

1. Use keywords.

The most common way to begin a web search is with a simple keyword
search. A search on Google using the term "underground comics" (the topic
of Lydia Nichols's project at the end of chapter 18) yielded more than 2
million hits (Figure 13.1).

This kind of searching is very easy, and it yields plenty of results—too
many. No one could look at all 2 million results, and most are not even

FIGURE 13.1
A simple keyword search on Google

relevant. To narrow the results to a more manageable number, and to focus more closely on sites that will be relevant to your research, you can group terms using quotation marks or use a combination of terms. A search on "underground comics" and "history," for example, reduced the number of hits from 2 million to 34,300—still too many but a definite improvement.

More about Relevance, 233–34

2. Use advanced search options.

You can narrow search results further with advanced search options (Figure 13.2), which can limit results by language, file type (Word, rich text, PDF, or Excel), domain (.org, .gov, .edu, or .com), and other options. Limiting the search on "'underground comics' history" to sites with the domain .edu, for example, reduced the number of hits to 1,420.

3. Use metasearch engines.

Because search engines index different web pages and use different methods to rank sites, using more than one engine increases your odds of finding useful resources. To search multiple sites simultaneously, use *metasearch engines,* which return the top search results from several search engines at

FIGURE 13.2 An advanced search on Google

once, with duplicate entries deleted. (A list of metasearch engines appears in the Quick Reference below.) Searching on the terms "underground comics" and "history" on InfoSpace, for example, produced three pages of hits (not 3 million).

> **More about**
> Devising a topic,
>   24–30, 199
> Narrowing or
>   broadening a
>   topic, 30–31

> **EXERCISE 13.1** Conducting a simple keyword search

Using the topic you selected for Exercise 12.1 (p. 197), generate three or more keywords and use them to conduct keyword searches on two of the search engines listed in the Quick Reference box below. Write a paragraph comparing your results: Did each search engine generate the same number of results? How do the top ten results differ? What about the next ten?

Quick Reference Search Engines

Search Engines
Ask: www.ask.com
Bing: www.bing.com
Gigablast: gigablast.com
Google: www.google.com
Lycos: www.lycos.com

Metasearch Engines
Info.com: www.info.com
Infospace: infospace.com
Search.com: www.search.com
Yippy: Yippy.com

EXERCISE 13.2 Conducting an advanced keyword search

Return to the same search engines you used in Exercise 13.1 and use the same keywords, but this time select the advanced search feature to narrow your search to sites within the domains .edu, .gov, and .org. Write a paragraph comparing the results from the advanced search with those from the simple search you conducted in Exercise 13.1.

Make It **Your Own**

Review the sources generated in Exercises 13.1 and 13.2 and create a working list of sources you might use for a project on the topic. Write a paragraph explaining why this combination of sources seems appropriate.

Make It **Your Own**

For a research project you are developing, create a list of keywords. Use the advanced search option of one of the search engines listed in the Quick Reference Box on the previous page to help you find .edu, .gov, or .org sources for these keywords. Bookmark any sources that seem as if they will be useful, and make a note of the search term and the title in your research notebook. Write one sentence about why that source might be useful for your project.

13c Finding Reliable Interactive Media

In addition to conventional websites, a variety of other electronic sources—including blogs, discussion lists, and groups on social networking sites like Facebook and Twitter—can offer you insight into your topic. Such sources are often contributed to by experts, so they have become an important source for up-to-the-minute news.

Of course, not all blogs, discussion lists, and groups are equally author-itative. Evaluate the reliability of such sites by finding out the qualifications of the writers, and verify the information you glean from such sources by consulting additional sources.

To find a blog or discussion list on your topic, use a specialized search engine (such as Blogarama and Google Groups). You can also enter your keyword with "blog," "listserv," "newsgroup," or "chat room" in a search engine.

News alerts and RSS feeds collect news stories on topics you specify. Registering for alerts at sites such as Google (www.google.com/alerts)

More about
Documenting
a blog, 336
(MLA), 387
(APA), 420
(*Chicago*), 446
(CSE)
Documenting a
discussion list,
336 (MLA), 387
(APA), 420
(*Chicago*), 446
(CSE)
Reliability,
234–39
Netiquette, 504

will bring daily updates on your chosen topics to your email box. To read RSS feeds, use a website like Feedly or Inoreader to subscribe to site feeds.

Sites for sharing information, whether in print or other media, are being born and expiring (or at least fading in popularity) almost every day; as this book goes to press, YouTube, Pocket, Pinterest, and Instagram are widely used for sharing information and media files on topics of common interest, but new possibilities constantly arise.

> **EXERCISE 13.4** **Researching electronic sources**
>
> Find a blog or discussion group on the topic you explored in Exercises 13.1 and 13.2. Who are the contributors to this site? Conduct a web search to learn about contributors.

13d Finding Articles in Journals and Other Periodicals Using Databases and Indexes

Periodical is the umbrella term for magazines, newspapers, and scholarly journals that are issued at regular intervals—daily, weekly, monthly, quarterly. A search engine such as Google or Ask can point you to articles published online in magazines, newspapers, and some journals, but many articles in academic journals are not available for free on the web, and many magazines and newspapers require subscriptions before you can access their content. For a comprehensive listing of articles published in periodicals, turn to the databases available through your college library's website. (You may be prompted to sign in.)

Library databases are organized so that you can search for articles by author, title, subject, date, and other fields. Some databases provide only an *abstract,* or summary, but many provide the complete text, either in a *PDF* (sometimes called "full text PDF") file, which shows the article more or less as it would have appeared in print, or in an *HTML* (sometimes called "full text") file, which provides the text but not the formatting or illustrations that would have appeared in the printed text.

1. Choose an appropriate database.

Most college libraries provide a wide variety of databases. Most will offer an all-purpose database like *ProQuest Central, Academic Search Premier,* or *Academic OneFile* that indexes both popular magazines and scholarly journals, as well as discipline-specific databases, such as *Education Source, PsycARTICLES,* and *Science Direct.* They may also offer *LexisNexis*

Writing
Responsibly / Really Reading Real Sources

As you choose your sources, it may seem efficient to select only those that are short and easy to read. Resist this temptation; fulfill your responsibility to your topic by pushing beyond easy, basic information. If you controlled for page length in your source selection, you would be writing your research project from uninsightful sources that would produce shallow, uninteresting claims. Instead, when your source selection is finished, include substantial sources that treat complex questions in complex ways. Reading these sources will be a greater challenge, but you will be able to produce richer, more successful writing from them.

to TOPIC

Academic, which indexes news reports from around the world. A reference librarian can help you learn which databases available at your library will best suit your research needs.

More about
Writing situation,
13–21

Tech | **Using *Google Scholar***

Google Scholar (scholar.google.com) allows users to search the web for scholarly materials—articles in academic journals, theses, books, and abstracts.

More about
Evaluating
sources,
233–46 (ch. 14)

Pros	Cons	
■ *Google Scholar* can help you locate material that you would otherwise need both your library's catalog and subscription databases to find.	■ Google has its own definition of *scholarly*, so some hits may be to works your instructor may not consider authoritative.	■ Because of Google's search and ranking methods, the most recent sources may not be included, or they may appear at the end of the list. (You can include a date range in Advanced Scholar Search.)
■ It may even link to your own library's digital holdings (see the preferences settings in *Google Scholar*).	■ You may be shifted to sites where you will be asked to pay for full-text versions of the source. (Always check your library's holdings or try interlibrary loan—a system for borrowing from another library—before paying for access.)	
■ It links to many citation management software types.		
■ It indicates how many online sites have cited the source and provides links to those citations.		

When searching for articles, be sure to consider the types of sources that are most appropriate to your topic and writing situation. In particular, consider whether you should use popular sources, scholarly sources, or a combination of the two.

Student Model
Research projects:
"The Power of
    Wardrobe," Heather
    DeGroot, 396–405
"Holy Underground
    Comics, Batman!"
    Lydia Nichols,
    349–62

For Heather DeGroot, writing for her psychology class, *PsycINFO* (a database that indexes articles from psychology journals) was a good starting place for her periodicals search. For Lydia Nichols, researching the characteristics of underground comics, a general database (such as *ProQuest Central* or *Academic Search Premier*), which indexes both popular and scholarly sources, was a good place to start.

2. Search the database.

Searching a database is much like using a search engine such as Google or Bing. You type in a search term and hit Enter (or Return) to generate a list of articles that include your keywords. Unlike a search engine, however, the database limits its search to selected publications, and because you are provided with full information about these sources, it is easier to assess their reliability.

To make sure the results of a database search are relevant, narrow your search by combining search terms and using the advanced search options the database makes available. Typing "comic books" in the search box of a database like *Academic Search Premier* generates a list of over 17,000 items—fewer than with a Google search but still far too many to be helpful. As with a web search engine, combining terms ("comic books AND underground") narrows the search. The search could be narrowed further by using the database's search options. The menu bars on the left and right in Figure 13.3 show some of the options for narrowing a search.

NOTE Databases differ from vendor to vendor and are updated frequently, so check your library's Help screens or ask a librarian for advice.

If narrowing your search by combining terms and using the database's narrowing options is not getting you the results you need, try the following:

- Conduct your search again with alternative or refined search terms. Check your database's subject or topics list (sometimes

> *More about*
Relevance,
    233–34
Citation manage-
    ment programs,
    205

Tech **Hidden Benefits of Library Databases**

In addition to their superiority in finding sources, a library database may be linked to RefWorks or another citation management software to which your library subscribes. When you choose a source in the database, the software makes a bibliographic entry in whatever style—MLA, APA, and so forth—you select.

Narrow results to articles that focus on one of these terms

Narrow results to a specific publication (such as *The New York Times* or *ART News*)

Click article title for full citation

Click "Add to folder" to save the citation

Click to locate related images

Article available in full text: PDF and HTML

Click on the magnifying glass to read an abstract (summary) of the article

EBSCO Information Services

called Thesaurus) for the terms with which your topic was indexed and use those terms in your search.

- Narrow (or expand) your search using Boolean logic. (See the Quick Reference box on the next page.)

- Return to the library's database menu to run your search on other databases.

As you find promising sources, create entries for them in your working bibliography, or follow directions on the database for emailing entries to yourself.

Just as metasearch engines allow you to send your keyword search out to several search engines simultaneously, some database vendors allow you to search simultaneously through all their databases. Increasingly, libraries

FIGURE 13.3
Search results for "underground comics AND genre"

> **More about**
> Creating a working bibliography, 204–09

Tech **HTML versus PDF**

Articles accessed through a database are often available in both HTML and PDF versions. The HTML (often called *full text*) version will download much more quickly, but the PDF (often called *full text PDF*) version may be a duplicate of the article as it appears in the publication, including illustrations and page numbers, which you can then include in your reference list or list of works cited.

Quick Reference · Conducting a Boolean Search

Most databases (and search engines like Google and Bing) narrow a search with Boolean logic, which relies on the words *and, not,* and *or* to expand or narrow a search and parentheses or quotation marks to group words. Most databases also use wildcard characters (* or ?) to stand in place of letters, allowing you to search for different forms of a word at the same time. Check Help screens or consult a reference librarian to learn how to use Boolean logic in searching your library's databases.

AND

Comics AND History

Narrows a search by by retrieving items that include *both* terms.

Comics | History

OR

Comics OR History

Expands a search by retrieving items that include *either* term.

Comics | History

NOT

Comics NOT History

Narrows a search by retrieving items that include one term but not the other.

Comics | History

" "

"graphic novel"

Quotation marks group terms to retrieve pages with these words in this order.

( )

(comics OR comix) AND (underground)

Parentheses group terms so complex alternatives can be retrieved.

* / ?

comi* (or comi?) to search for comic, comics, and comix simultaneously

Wildcard characters allow you to search for more than one version of a word at the same time by replacing the letters that are different in each word with an asterisk (*) or question mark (?).

are also offering *federated searching,* which allows you to search across many databases simultaneously. Check your library's website to see what multiple-database searching options are available to you.

3. Find copies of articles.

Once you have generated a list of articles from your database search, you are ready to retrieve copies of the articles. Some articles you can access directly from the database search page (look for links saying something like "Find It in Full Text") and you can then print them, download them to your hard drive, or email them to yourself. The first article from the search screen in Figure 13.3, for example, is available online.

For some articles, however, only an abstract will be available through the database; in a few cases, only a bibliographic citation may be available. While it may be tempting to skip articles that you cannot have delivered instantly to your desktop, you may miss out on important sources of information, especially classics published before the Internet revolution. To find articles you cannot link to from the database, consult your library's website (or a librarian) for a list of journals available through your library or through interlibrary loan.

→ EXERCISE **13.5** Conducting a database search

Using one or more keywords that you generated in Exercise 13.1, conduct a search using a general database such as *ProQuest Central* or *Academic Search Premier.* Now conduct the same search using an appropriate subject-specific database. (Ask your instructor or a librarian for help in determining which databases might be appropriate.) Compare the results: How many articles were returned on each search? How many of the same articles were listed on the first two pages of results?

→ EXERCISE **13.6** Locating an article

For one of the searches you performed in Exercise 13.5, find an article that is not available as a link from the database results page. Then write a paragraph describing the steps you took to find it.

13e Finding Books Using Library Catalogs

While reference works can give you an overview or direct you to other sources, it is in books that you are most likely to find extensive, in-depth treatments of your topic—especially in the humanities and some social

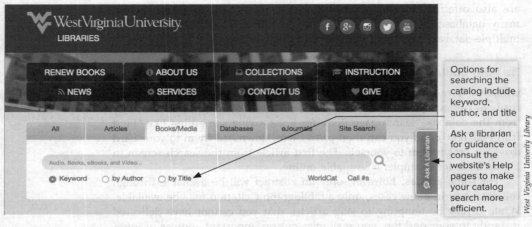

FIGURE 13.4 A library website Students at West Virginia University and other colleges and universities around the country can search for print and digital sources from their library's catalog.

sciences. One or two well-chosen books, supplemented by a selection of journal articles and other sources, can round out your research and deepen your understanding of your topic.

1. Search the catalog.

Libraries index all their holdings in catalogs, which in most cases you can access through your library's website. Most library catalogs allow users to search for resources by author, title, and subject heading. Some include additional search options such as call number or keyword (Figure 13.4). Because catalogs differ from library to library, check the Help or Search Tips screen before beginning a search. If your library's catalog allows keyword searching, you may find it useful to conduct a "keyword anywhere" search, using your search terms. Most library catalogs include tables of contents for anthologies and edited books, so a keyword search may yield useful results.

NOTE Some catalogs may require you to specify the category (such as author or title) in which you wish to search. If you do not, the program may default to a category you are not expecting. For example, if you are looking for books *about* Herman Melville and do not specify that you are searching by subject, your library's program may default to searching for books *by* Melville and provide you with a list of books by him as well as about him.

> **More about**
> Keyword search-
> ing, 214–17

Search a library's catalog much as you do a search engine or a periodical database: Type a keyword or a combination of words in the search box and hit Enter. Whereas Google and other web search engines allow you to use any keyword related to your topic, library catalogs use a preset list of subject headings to index library books. When searching a library's catalog by subject, use these preset headings. To find the subject headings the library has used, go to a catalog entry for a book on your topic that you have already identified as relevant. The book's record will list the subject headings used (Figure 13.5). Clicking on them will bring you to a list of related subject headings and to other books cataloged using the same terms. Repeat the process with other useful books to add subject terms.

2. Browse the stacks or the catalog.

Many researchers enjoy browsing library stacks to find books on their topic: Since books on a topic all share the first part of a call number, they are shelved close together. If you are free to wander in your library's stacks, check for other books on your topic shelved close to those you have identified as

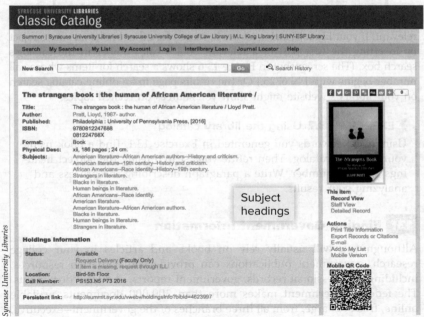

FIGURE 13.5 **Finding subject headings in a library record**

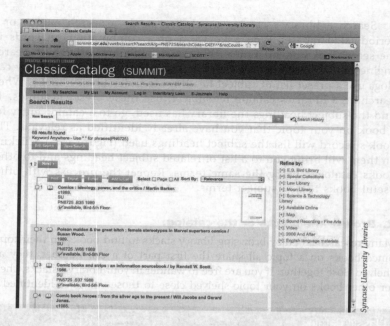

**FIGURE 13.6
Browsing by call number**

Syracuse University Libraries

relevant. If your library catalog allows it, search for other books on your subject by inserting the first part of a relevant book's call number in the catalog's search box. (The screenshot in Figure 13.6 shows a search for items whose call number begins with PN 6725.) Or the results page in an online catalog search on your library's website might show you sources on related topics.

> **EXERCISE 13.7 Using the library catalog**
> Using the keywords you generated in Exercise 13.1, find a book using your library's catalog. Then refine your search using the subject headings and call number. Write a paragraph describing the process and analyzing your results.

13f Finding Government Information

Although you will usually rely on books and articles in your college research, government publications can provide you with rich resources, including congressional records, government reports, and legal documents. The federal government makes more than 300,000 documents available online, free of charge, from all three branches of the government—executive,

Quick Reference Accessing Government Information Online

The websites for the following all provide access to government documents and datasets online:

European Union
FedStats
FedWorld Information Network
FirstGov
Library of Congress
National Institutes of Health
Organization for Economic Cooperation and Development
State and Local Government on the Net
United Nations
US Bureau of Labor Statistics
US Census Bureau
US Government Printing Office

legislative, and judicial. Most state and local governments also post their documents on the web, as do many governments around the world. If you are researching a social, legal, or political issue or if you need up-to-date statistics about almost any group, you may find valuable information in government publications. To locate government documents, conduct an advanced web search limited to the domain .gov or search databases such as *CQ Press Electronic Library* and *LexisNexis Congressional*.

13g Finding Multimedia Sources

Photographs, graphs, charts, and drawings have long been a staple of research in disciplines such as art history, film studies, history, geography, geology, political science, sociology, and psychology. With research in all disciplines now being shared through multimedia presentations and websites, the use of multimedia resources has also expanded. To find multimedia resources, start with your library's catalog. Besides the video clips you can find on YouTube and Hulu, you may also find appropriate multimedia resources online at the sites hosted by the organizations listed in the Quick Reference box on this page.

NOTE Because you need to cite your media sources, remember to add them to your working bibliography.

More about
Working bibliography, 204–05

Reference **Multimedia Resources**

Academy of American Poets
American Rhetoric: The Power of Oratory in the United States
Archive.org
Library of Congress
MIT Open Courseware
National Aeronautics and Space Administration (NASA)
National Park Service
New York Public Library
Perry Castañeda Library Map Collection, University of Texas
Smithsonian Institution

Make It **Your Own**

For a research assignment for this or another class, create a working bibliography of at least ten items. Include at least one of the following:

- Website
- Article in a scholarly journal
- Article in a newspaper
- Article in a magazine

- Subject-specific reference book
- Book
- Government publication
- Media resource

Which are available online? Which can you locate in your library?

Work **Together**

In small groups or as a class, take a tour of the library. (You will need to arrange this in advance.) Come prepared with a topic, and ask a librarian for advice on how best to conduct a database search or find resources on your topic in the library's catalog. Explore the library's multimedia offerings, and check out at least one book on your topic. Finally, prepare a brief report listing at least three things you learned about the library that you did not know before your visit.

13h Conducting and Reporting Field Research

Field research is often part of a research project in which the writer begins by reviewing information from secondary sources (reports of others' research) and then adds to the body of information by conducting a fresh inquiry. The most common types of field research are interviews, observational studies, and surveys.

1. Interviews

Expertise and the knowledge that comes with experience can often be gained only through an interview. Media such as email, text messaging, video chat, and even the telephone extend your range of possible interviewees, but face-to-face interviews give you an opportunity to read the other person's body language (facial expressions and bodily gestures) which can provide insight and direction for follow-up questions.

Instructors with special expertise in your subject make good subjects for an interview; government agencies, businesses, and public service organizations can also connect you with experts. When researching cultural or historical events, consider interviewing participants such as attorneys in a legal case, your soldier-cousin for her experience in Iraq, organizers of a demonstration for immigrants' rights.

These tips can help you make the best use of your time:

Before the Interview

- Consider your purpose, and shape your questions accordingly.
- Select your interviewee with care, and contact that person for an appointment.

Writing
Responsibly | Conducting Interviews Fairly

- To project professionalism, show up for the interview on time and prepared.
- Ask only for information that your expert alone could provide, not information you could easily gather on your own.
- Tell the interviewee up front how you will use the information you gather, and get her or his written consent.

- Ask for permission to record the interview, and confirm any quotations you may want to use.
- Offer the interviewee an opportunity to review your notes or your draft document. (You need not change your notes or document in response, but you should acknowledge any difference of opinion.)

to SELF

- Conduct background research on the topic and on the person whom you are interviewing, and develop ten to fifteen open-ended questions. (Ask "How would you rate the job the president of the Student Senate is doing, and why?" *not* "Is the president of the Student Senate doing a good job?") Avoid questions that prompt an interviewee to provide a particular answer. (Ask "How do you think the stock market will react in the coming year, and why?" *not* "How far will the stock market fall in the coming year?")

During the Interview

- Set your interviewee at ease, but remain politely neutral.
- Use your prepared questions and listen carefully to the answers; also listen for surprises and ask follow-up questions.
- Take extensive notes or, if permitted, record the interview.
- Avoid interrupting the interviewee or talking about yourself.

After the Interview

- Reflect on your notes while the interview is still fresh, recording your thoughts and any additional questions you would like to ask; then phone or email the interviewee once for follow-up. (Multiple follow-up messages are likely to annoy.)
- Make a transcript of the interview, and send a copy to your interviewee for comment or confirmation.
- Send a thank-you note within twenty-four hours of your interview, and then send the interviewee a copy of your finished project with a note of appreciation.

Writing Responsibly
Avoiding Manipulation and Bias in Observations

- Ask permission to observe organized groups. Let the group's leader decide whether all should be informed, but reveal your purpose if asked.
- Resist manipulating the site or the community to get the results you want.
- Move around the scene to change your perspective.

- Provide groups the opportunity to read and respond to your study before you submit it. (You need not change your report, but you should acknowledge differences of opinion.)
- Alert readers to the limitations of your study or to ways your own experiences and perspectives may have influenced your observations.

to TOPIC

2. Observational studies

Observational studies are common in the social sciences, particularly in psychology, sociology, and anthropology. Consider the following before beginning an observational study:

- **Your hypothesis.** What do you expect to learn? You can refine your hypothesis as your observations continue, but starting out with a hypothesis will help guide your observations and note taking.

- **Your role.** Will you participate in the group or observe the group from outside? The role you play will influence your perspective and affect your observations. Consider the steps you can take to minimize bias.

- **Your methods.** Establish categories for the observations you expect, and adjust them in response to your observations. Make notes immediately after a research session rather than during it, so your presence will be less obtrusive.

> *More about*
> Devising a
> hypothesis,
> 199–200

3. Surveys

Surveys are used frequently in politics and marketing but are useful in many types of research to assess beliefs, opinions, and behavior. When developing a survey, consider these issues:

- **Your hypothesis.** What do you expect to learn from your survey?

- **Your target population.** What group will you reach and how will you contact them? Strive to include a broad and representative range of respondents.

- **Your survey.** What type of questions will you ask, how many questions will you include, and how will you administer the survey?

Tech   **Online Surveys**

A variety of web-based survey tools allows you to conduct surveys online. The following are among the most popular:

- Google Docs
- SurveyMonkey
- SurveyGizmo
- Zoomerang

Each allows users to create and send out a basic survey to a limited number of respondents for free.

You might also consider conducting your survey with the help of social media such as Facebook or Twitter.

Most surveys offer true-false, yes-no, and multiple-choice questions because these are easier to tabulate. Still, a few open-ended questions may deepen your sense of the respondents' feelings, and quotations can be used in your project. Whatever type of questions you ask, be sure your answer options are fair and that they offer an adequate range of choices. Because respondents are not likely to spend more than a few minutes answering questions, surveys should be brief: One to two pages is a reasonable limit.

Writing
Responsibly　Reporting Results Fairly

As you integrate the results of your field research into your larger project, explain how you chose your research participants, how many you invited, and how many agreed to participate. Do not, however, name or indirectly identify your participants unless they have agreed to their identity being made public.

When you quote from an interview or survey, indicate how typical the quotation is. Did you choose it just because it supports your thesis, or is it typical of the majority of responses?

to AUDIENCE

Evaluating Information

CLOTHING

"Do you have this in sheep?"

© *Marty Bucella/CartoonStock, Ltd.*

In Aesop's fable "The Wolf in Sheep's Clothing," the wolf uses a sheep's skin to lull his intended dinner into a false sense of security. Texts, too, can be a kind of wolf in sheep's clothing. They can appear to be wonderful resources, full of interesting facts and persuasive arguments, while hiding misinformation and faulty reasoning. For this reason, it is crucial that researchers dig below the surface to evaluate their sources carefully for relevance and reliability. Just as a wolf can hide under a sheep's clothing, a book should not be judged by its cover!

14a Evaluating for Relevance and Reliability

Evaluating sources means assessing how *relevant,* or useful, a source is to your research and determining the source's *reliability—* how much you can count on it.

1. Relevance

When considering a potential source, first consider its relevance: Does the source offer information that could enrich your understanding of your topic, provide background information or evidence to support your claims, or suggest alternative perspectives? Before taking the time to read the text, determine its likely relevance by *previewing* it:

- **Check the publication date.** Recently published works are most likely to be of the greatest relevance, as they will probably provide the most up-to-date information. Be alert, though, to classics; they contain information or ideas on

233

which researchers still rely. Classics will be cited frequently by other reliable sources; your instructor can also help you identify them.

- **Read the abstract, foreword, introduction, or lead** (first paragraph in a newspaper article). These usually provide a summary, overview, or key facts discussed in detail in the source.
- **Read the headings and subheadings.** These will provide an outline of the work.
- **Scan figures and illustrations.** These might signal important ideas and explain complex processes.
- **Read the conclusion.** The conclusion (the last few paragraphs in a journal or magazine article or the final chapter of a book) often reiterates the central idea and argument, important questions, and major findings.
- **Consult the index.** Check it for key terms in your research.

2. Reliability

Judging reliability is not a simple, yes-or-no litmus test. Instead, it is a balancing act: You rate a source on a variety of criteria; the more criteria on

abstract A summary of the text's main claims and most important supporting evidence

More about
Previewing a text, 113–14
Finding the copyright date, 300–03 (Documentation Matters tutorial preceding ch. 18)
Primary versus secondary sources, 455–57

Quick Reference — Judging Reliability

Scholarly work. Was the source published in a scholarly journal or book, or in a popular magazine, newspaper, or book?

Expertise. Is the author an authority on the subject?

Objectivity. Do tone, logic, quality of the evidence, and coverage of the opposition suggest that the source is unbiased?

Scope. Does the author attempt to test his or her own assumptions and explore alternatives?

Citations. Does the text cite sources, and is it cited in other texts?

Scrutiny. Was the text subjected to scrutiny by someone else before you saw it? For example, was it selected by the library, reviewed by another scholar, or fact-checked for accuracy?

Presentation. Is the text clearly written, well organized, and carefully edited and proofread?

Domain. Does the main portion of the URL end in .edu or .org, suggesting a noncommercial purpose, or does it end with .com, suggesting a commercial purpose?

Site sponsor or host. Is the site's host identified? Does the host promote a viewpoint or position that might bias the content?

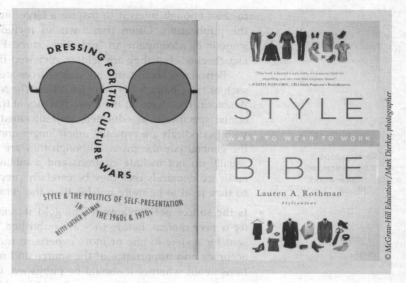

FIGURE 14.1 **Popular versus scholarly books** *Style Bible: What to Wear to Work* (Bibliomotion) is a popular-press book aimed at a general audience: professional men and women who want to dress stylishly but appropriately at the office. *Dressing for the Culture Wars: Style & the Politics of Self-Presentation in the 1960s & 1970s* (University of Nebraska Press), on the other hand, is a scholarly book about the ways in which changes in fashion and style influenced the political climate and social norms of an era; its target audience is intellectuals and scholars in fields such as women's studies and cultural studies.

which you can rate the source highly, the more reliable it is likely to be. Here are several criteria to consider:

- **Is the author an expert on the topic?** Does the author have advanced training in the subject? You can determine this by reading about the author in a biographical reference work, by finding other works the author has published, by considering the author's academic background, by searching the author's name on the web, or by determining whether the author has been cited in the footnotes or bibliographies of other reliable sources.

- **Is it a scholarly source?** The intended audience of a source significantly affects the reliability of the source. A *scholarly source* is intended for an audience of experts on the topic. Although it may be challenging for you to read, it will contain the most detailed, insightful information available—well worth your effort. Scholarly sources (Figure 14.1) include articles published in academic journals and books published by scholarly presses. They usually include citations to other sources and full bibliographic information for them, either in notes or in a bibliography.

In contrast, articles in magazines and books published by the *popular press* are selected for a general audience and are intended to raise enough interest to inspire a large number of people to buy the publication. Often these articles include advertisements that sometimes accompany an "objective" story. Popular sources may be fact-checked, but they are seldom reviewed by experts.

Between scholarly and popular sources are intellectual periodicals such as the *Chronicle of Higher Education, The New Yorker,* and *Scientific American.* They have all the characteristics of the popular press but are aimed specifically at educated, well-informed audiences. Articles in such periodicals are typically much longer and more detailed than in the general popular press. Although they are not peer reviewed and usually do not include citations and a bibliography, their intended audience demands that they be carefully prepared and fact-checked, so they tend to be more reliable than the general popular press.

❯ *More about*
Biographical reference works, 213–14

- **Is the source peer reviewed?** The gold standard of source reliability is *peer review*. Before they are published, scholarly sources are sent for review to one or more experts in the field who check the accuracy and importance of the source and make recommendations about whether it should be published. On the home page of a peer-reviewed periodical, you should be able to find the words *peer review* or *editorial board*. If the source is published by a university press, it will be peer reviewed, but not all peer-reviewed sources are published by university presses.

❯ *More about*
Tone, 19–20, 138, 565, 570–72
Opinion versus belief, 140–43
Types of evidence, 45–50
Bias, 566–69

- **Does the source seem objective?** Does the source have an objective tone, make reasonable claims supported by logical evidence, include counterevidence, and treat it with respect? Or does it contain emotionally loaded language, make exaggerated claims, support those claims with faulty logic and questionable or scanty evidence, or omit counterevidence? An author may care deeply and write passionately about a subject, but if he or she characterizes groups unfairly or offensively or treats the individuals making up the group as if they are all the same, then you should suspect bias.

- **Is the type of source appropriate to your purpose?** Does your source offer a detailed exploration of the debates about your issue, or does it offer just basic facts or a condensed overview? You cannot write an insightful argument based only on a shallow understanding of your issue.

- **Does the author or publisher have a vested interest?** How does the author stand to benefit from the work? Most authors will benefit in some way: through sales of the book or through the prestige of publishing. But consider whether the author or publisher will

Quick

Reference   Typical Characteristics of Scholarly and Popular Sources

Scholarly

- Articles are written by scholars, specialists, researchers
- Use technical terminology
- Tend to be long—typically, ten pages or more
- Include citations in the text and a list of references
- Are reviewed by other scholars before publication
- Acknowledge any conflicts of interest (such as research support from a pharmaceutical company)
- Generally look serious; unlikely to include color photographs, but may include charts, graphs, and tables
- Published by professional organizations

Popular

- Articles are written by journalists or professional writers
- Avoid technical terminology
- Tend to be brief—as little as one or two pages
- Seldom include citations or a list of references
- Generally fact-checked but not reviewed by panel of experts
- Unlikely to acknowledge potential conflicts of interest
- Often published on glossy paper with eye-catching color images
- Published by commercial companies

© McGraw-Hill Education / Mark Dierker, photographer

© McGraw-Hill Education / Mark Dierker, photographer

Writing
Responsibly   Keeping an Open, Inquiring Mind

Read sources with an open mind, use reliable sources, avoid exaggerated claims and logical fallacies, and criticize unreasonable or poorly supported conclusions but not the people who hold them. As a researcher, you have a responsibility to avoid bias. Consider all sides of an argument, especially those that challenge the positions you hold. Use difficult sources, too: Do not reject a source because it is written for a more expert audience than you. Find the time to study it carefully and gain at least a provisional understanding of it.

to TOPIC

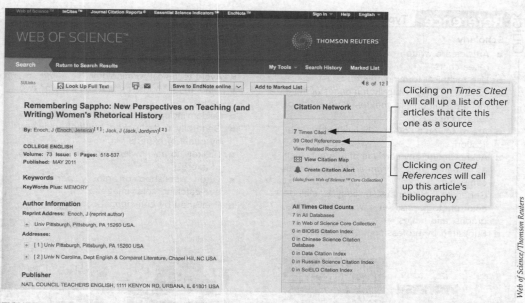

FIGURE 14.2 Determining reliability by assessing citations Both the number of times an article has been cited and the citations in the article itself are useful ways of determining an article's reliability.

benefit in some other way: Is the author promoting a product or process from which she will benefit financially? Will the author or publisher gain adherents to a political position? Check the author's or publisher's website for advertisements and to see whether a mission statement reveals an agenda.

- **Does the text cite its sources?** Most scholarly articles and books and some popular books will include a bibliography, and some journal databases will list the article's sources in the citation. Reputable newspapers and magazines will check a writer's sources, though they often go unnamed, identified only as a "White House source" or a "source close to the investigation."

- **Do other scholars cite the text?** Also important is the number of times a source has been cited by other scholarly works. Some journal databases indicate the number of times an article has been cited by other articles indexed by that database (Figure 14.2).

Writing Responsibly

Online Plagiarism

The ease with which users can cut and paste information from one site into another means you must be wary of online sites, especially if they are self-sponsored. Unreliable sites frequently copy directly from other, more reliable sites. If you sus- pect plagiarism, copy a passage and paste it into a search engine's search box. Do any of your hits use the same (or very similar) language? The best way to avoid using material plagiarized from another site is to evaluate sites carefully for reliability.

to SELF

Citation indexes such as *Web of Science, Scopus, Microsoft Academic Search*, and *Google Scholar* also provide this information. If you find very few citations to your source, check the publication date: Sources published within the previous three years may not yet have been cited. Citation frequency does not itself determine reliability; it is just one test.

- **How did you find the source?** Sources located through your college library are more likely to be reliable than are sources located through a Google search because library sources are selected in consultation with subject-matter experts, in response to reviews, or after considering where the source was published. A source published solely on the web (unless in a scholarly journal published online) is not likely to have been subjected to the same level of scrutiny. Google searches will return such sites, but library databases will not. Finding a source on a library database is not a guarantee of reliability, but it is one indicator.

- **Is the source well written and edited?** Has the writer approached the task with a sense of responsibility—by writing, organizing, editing, and proofreading the material carefully? Is the page design easy to follow? Are the visuals appropriate to the audience and purpose and free from manipulation or distortion?

14b Evaluating Online Texts: Websites, Blogs, Wikis, and Discussion Forums

Anyone can create a website, post a blog, or contribute to an open wiki or discussion forum. This freedom makes the web exciting, but it also means researchers should evaluate online sources with special care. In addition

> *More about*
> Websites, 179–85,
> 217–23
> Interactive media,
> 185–86, 217–18

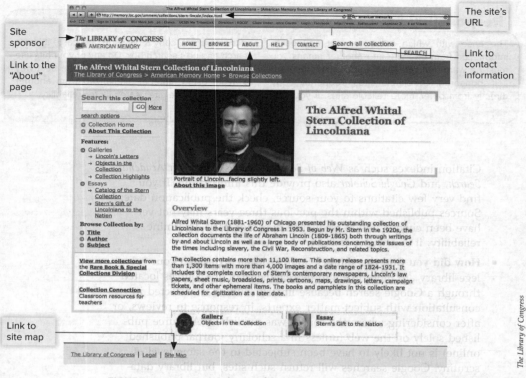

Site sponsor

Link to the "About" page

Link to site map

The site's URL

Link to contact information

FIGURE 14.3 A web page The URL appears at the top of the browser window. Note that the Library of Congress's website indicates the sponsoring organization prominently and provides links to pages providing information about the organization and site.

to the general criteria listed above, consider these factors when evaluating websites:

URL A site's *URL* (short for *universal resource locator,* its web address) appears at the top of the browser window (Figure 14.3). Every item on the web has a URL, and all URLs end with an extension, or *domain,* that indicates the type of site it is. The most common domains are these:

- **.com** (commercial): sites hosted by businesses

- **.edu** (educational): sites sponsored by colleges and universities

- **.gov** (governmental): sites sponsored by some branch of federal, state, or local government

- **.net** (network): typically, sites sponsored by businesses selling Internet infrastructure services (such as Internet providers) but also sometimes chosen by businesses that want to appear technologically sophisticated or organizations that want to indicate that they are part of a network

> **Tech**   **Identifying Personal Websites**
>
> A URL that includes a personal name (jsmith) plus a tilde (˜) or percent sign (%) or words like "users" or "members" is likely to be personal (not sponsored by a larger organization). Before using information from a personal site, investigate the author's credentials carefully.

- **.org** (organization): usually sites sponsored by nonprofit groups (though sometimes the nonprofit status of these groups may be questionable)

Sites sponsored by educational, governmental, and nonprofit organizations are likely to be reliable, but your evaluation of a website should never end with its URL. Businesses usually offer information intended to sell products or services, yet commercial sites can nevertheless be highly informative. A site ending in .edu may just as easily have been constructed and posted by a student as by an expert, and much of the information posted on university websites is designed to entice new students and is thus a type of advertising. Nonprofit organizations are not trying to sell a product, but they are usually seeking support. Government sites, too, while often a source of highly reliable information, are unlikely to publish information that will undermine the administration's agenda. The reliability of information from all sites (indeed, all texts) must be evaluated with care.

Sponsor As with any publication, the credentials of a website's creator are an important factor in assessing reliability, but websites frequently lack an identified author. Instead, they have *sponsors*—corporations, agencies, and organizations that are responsible for creating content and making it available. To determine who sponsors a site, jump to the home page, link to pages called "About" or "Contact us," or click on the website's logo (see Figure 14.3). Often, deleting the portion of the URL following the domain (.com, .edu, .org) will take you to the home page. If the website yields little information, try conducting a web search on the site's name; you might even try including the word "scam" or "fraud" in that search. You can also go to the WhoIs site (whois.net) to search for information about your website.

Open or moderated? The reliability of online discussion forums depends in large part on their contributors. Sources to which anyone can contribute should be screened carefully; nonexpert enthusiasts can post inaccurate information, and people can deliberately insert distorted "truths." For example, Wikipedia once had to block certain web addresses on Capitol Hill to

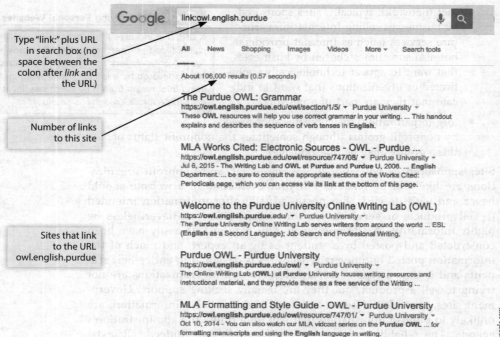

Type "link:" plus URL in search box (no space between the colon after *link* and the URL)

Number of links to this site

Sites that link to the URL owl.english.purdue

google.com

FIGURE 14.4 Using the links to a page to assess reliability

keep congressional staffers from altering—and falsifying—the biographies of their bosses or their bosses' political opponents.

Wikis and web forums in which prospective contributors are screened by the site's owner, or *moderator,* are more likely to be reliable. The wiki *Encyclopedia of Life,* for example, promises to provide reliable information because it will be created and moderated by a consortium of highly regarded scientific institutions. Some scholars are even writing wiki textbooks to which they invite other experts to contribute.

Links An additional step in assessing the reliability of a website is to determine the number and type of sites that link to it. From the Google search page, you can determine the number of times a site has been linked to and review the linked sites (Figure 14.4): Type "link:" plus the URL in the search box and click Search or hit Return. Popularity alone does not guarantee reliability (the site may just be fun to read or authored by a celebrity) but when coupled with other criteria, it can be one indication of reliability.

14c Evaluating Visual Sources

Visual texts such as information graphics (tables, graphs, flowcharts) and photographs convey their messages powerfully yet sometimes so subtly that uncritical viewers may accept their claims without even realizing that a claim is being made. As with printed texts, researchers need to evaluate visual texts carefully to determine whether the source is both relevant and reliable. To determine relevance and reliability, consider the following:

> *More about*
> Visual arguments,
> 136–37, 140–41,
> 144–47, 159, 161,
> 173–74

- What are the credentials of the visual's creator?
- How authoritative is the source in which the visual appeared?
- On what date was the image created or the photograph taken?
- What purpose(s) does the visual serve? Is it to entertain, to inform, or to persuade?
- Who is its intended audience?

> *More about*
> Purpose, 14–17
> Avoiding
>   distortion,
>   manipulation,
>   86, 148

- How accurate are the title, headings, labels, and any other text that appears with the visual? How does the text influence how you "read" the visual? How relevant is the visual to the accompanying text?
- What is in the foreground and background, and what is your eye drawn to?
- To what social, ethnic, or national groups do the subjects belong, and is this relevant?
- What emotions does the visual depict? What emotions does it elicit from you or other viewers?
- Has the visual been manipulated or cropped to omit or distort information? (See Figure 14.5.)

For graphics, also consider the following:

- What do the data represent?
- What relationships does the graphic show?
- How up-to-date is the information in the graphic?
- Are the data complete? Are there any gaps in years covered or groups represented?
- Are the data presented fairly?
- Is the source of the data unbiased?

FIGURE 14.5 **The power of an image** Although many Americans knew that President Roosevelt had been partially paralyzed by polio, only two photographs were taken of the president in a wheelchair. Were photographers protecting FDR's privacy or suppressing important information?

Franklin D. Roosevelt Presidential Library and Museum

EXERCISE 14.1 Evaluating reliability

Using the criteria discussed in *section a* in this chapter, write a paragraph in which you rate the reliability of the article excerpted below. Be sure to explain why you rated the article as you did.

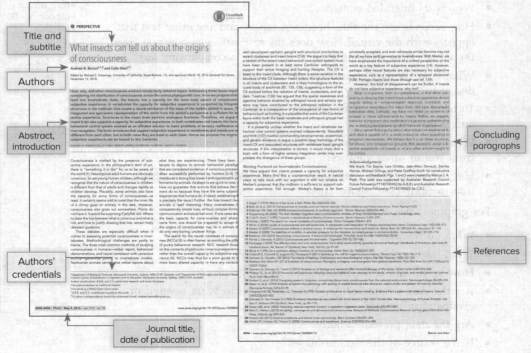

EXERCISE 14.2 Evaluating web pages

Using the criteria discussed in *sections 14a* and *14b,* evaluate the two web pages shown on this page. Which would you consider the more reliable source on plagiarism, and why?

→ EXERCISE **14.3** Evaluating a graph

Using the criteria discussed in *section 14c,* write a paragraph evaluating the graph below. Be sure to support your assessment with specific evidence.

PINCHED FOR TIME: MORE WOMEN THAN MEN
Percentage of Americans Who Always Feel Rushed

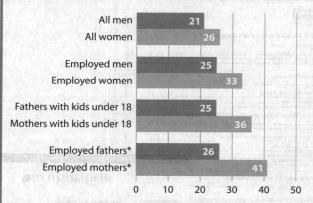

*Employed fathers, employed mothers refers to employed parents with children under age 18.
Employed does not include people who identify as retired but also work for pay.*
Source: Pew Research Center

Make It **Your Own**

Using the criteria in this chapter, write a paragraph evaluating three sources in the working bibliography that you began in the Make It Your Own exercise in chapter 12, page 209, or that you found for a research project in this or another class.

Work **Together**

In small groups, discuss your evaluations from Exercises 14.1, 14.2, and 14.3. Where do you agree or disagree in your evaluations, and why?

Text Credit

p. 246: Data from the Pew Research Center.

15

Using Information Responsibly: Taking Notes and Avoiding Plagiarism

Doris Kearns Goodwin

Chris Hedges

Plagiarism stories are always in the news cycle. Former star *New York Times* writer Chris Hedges submitted an article to *Harper's* magazine and was rejected for using unattributed quotations from another journalist's research.[1] Harvard historian Doris Kearns Goodwin was accused of plagiarizing portions of her book *The Fitzgeralds and the Kennedys*. She admitted that she had carelessly included some sentences word for word from her sources without putting those sentences in quotation marks. Her publisher was forced to make a financial settlement with the writer whose sentences she lifted, and as with Hedges, Goodwin's credibility was severely undermined.[2]

Plagiarism is of such widespread concern that scholarly research and corporations are devoted to it. A computer science professor at Emory University designs software to determine whether some forms of *patchwriting* (often categorized as a type of plagiarism) are not academic misconduct but effective writing techniques.[3] Corporations like Turnitin.com are devoted to "catching" plagiarism, and instructors, publishers, and colleges pay substantial sums of money for that service. Even Wikipedia employs Turnitin to check its entries.[4]

---

[1]Ketcham, Christopher. "The Troubling Case of Chris Hedges." *New Republic*, 12 June 2014.
[2]Lewis, Mark, "Doris Kearns Goodwin and the Credibility Gap." *Forbes*, 27 Feb. 2002.
[3]Williams, Kimber. "Interdisciplinary Project Analyzes 'Patchwriting' through Math, Computer Science." *Emory News Center*, 13 Oct. 2015.
[4]Schaffhauser, Dian. "Wikipedia Edits Get Student Paper-Style Plagiarism Check." *T/H/E Journal*, 17 Nov. 2015.

Nor is the issue exclusive to the United States. The Ventures Africa website acknowledges widespread plagiarism in Nigeria but asserts that the problem is global.[5] *The Moscow Times* reports that a study in Russia revealed that 21% of the graduate theses in Russian universities included significant plagiarism.[6] Among students, scholars, journalists, and writers and publishers worldwide, the issue of plagiarism often arises. Its frequency does not, however, mean that it is an acceptable practice. Plagiarism is always regarded negatively and is usually penalized. This chapter is designed to help you understand it and keep it out of your own work.

Plagiarism involves the presentation of another person's work—a paper or story, a photograph or graphic, a speech or song, a web page or email message—without indicating that it came from a source. Buying a paper or "borrowing" a sentence (without citation and quotation marks) are both classified as plagiarism.

Sometimes plagiarism may be inadvertent—Kearns Goodwin, for example, claimed that she had copied passages word for word into her notes and then forgot that these passages were not her own.[7] Whether intentional or not, such borrowings are still considered unacceptable.

Student plagiarism may not be reported in *The New York Times,* but to many instructors, it is even more objectionable than the cases discussed here, because when students are given a writing assignment, they are expected to learn something about the topic and about writing itself, and plagiarism prevents this learning.

Also be alert to the possibility of *patchwriting,* copying and only partially changing the language of a source. The National Council of Writing Program Administrators classifies patchwriting as a misuse of sources. Sometimes, though, instructors and college policies classify it as plagiarism. In either case, patchwriting is not good writing. It is sometimes unintentional, the result of inaccurate note taking, misunderstanding the source, incorrect use of or omitting quotation marks, or incomplete paraphrasing. Whether plagiarism occurs intentionally or unintentionally, writers are always held responsible for it. You should make every effort to avoid it.

Inform yourself in detail about what your instructor and your college (or your employer) define as ethical writing; although everyone rejects plagiarism, the definition of what constitutes plagiarism can vary subtly from one discipline or profession to another. Still, as you follow the guidelines for writing described in this chapter (and throughout this book), you can be confident that the work you produce will represent its sources responsibly.

citation The acknowledgment of sources in the body of a research project

documentation Information in a footnote, bibliography, reference list, or list of works cited that allows readers to locate the source cited in the text

---

[5]Odunmorayo, Emmanuel. "It's About Time We Recognize That Plagiarism Is a Global Problem, Not Peculiar to Nigeria Alone." *Ventures Africa,* 3 Nov. 2015.

[6]"21% of Theses Defended by Russian University Rectors Contain Plagiarism." *Moscow Times,* 23 Nov. 2015.

[7]Kirkpatrick, David. "Historian Says Borrowing Was Wider Than Known," *The New York Times,* 23 Feb. 2002.

Plagiarism and Culture Attitudes toward and definitions of plagiarism vary from one culture to another. Some individualist cultures, like that of the United States, see words and ideas as personal property that can be "stolen" by plagiarists. Some collectivist cultures view information as a shared good. Whether your home culture tends to be more individualist or collectivist, when writing for a US academic audience, be especially careful to mark borrowed language as quotation, to provide a citation whenever you borrow language or ideas, and to document sources fully.

15a Valuing Research

One of the keys to avoiding plagiarism is understanding why instructors value source acknowledgment: Seeking the truth is the heart of all academic work. To achieve this goal, academic researchers—from architects to anthropologists, psychologists to physicists—build on the work of others. They must be able to trace ideas to their source because one faulty piece of information can invalidate a whole research project. That is why failing to credit previous researchers is considered such a serious breach of academic discipline, and cheating in all its forms—from distorting an opponent's position to doctoring a quotation, manipulating an image, falsifying data, or taking credit for someone else's work—is punished so severely.

For students, conducting research and learning to write clearly and accurately has another value: It develops the intellectual, rhetorical, and ethical skills and practices needed in college, at work, and in one's community. Plagiarism prevents that learning.

15b Using Information Ethically: What You Do and Do Not Have to Acknowledge

The first step toward avoiding plagiarism is approaching your writing tasks with a clear sense of what you are and are not expected to cite and document.

1. What you *do* have to cite: Quotations, paraphrases, summaries, and *un*common knowledge

You must document quotations, paraphrases, summaries, and information that is unlikely to be known by nonexperts:

- **Quotations.** Enclose short quotations in quotation marks, and indent long quotations as a block. Name the author either in

More about
Using quotation marks, 810–19 (ch. 51)
Block indention for long quotations, 308, 346–47 (MLA), 392 (APA)
Citing sources, 304–321 (MLA), 363–73 (APA), 406–23 (*Chicago*), 435–37 (CSE)
Documenting sources, 321–44 (MLA), 374–91 (APA), 407–23 (*Chicago*), 435–47 (CSE)
Using signal phrases, 275–87, 307, 305

a signal phrase ("Professor Jones argues") or in a parenthetical citation, and include the page number. (In some styles, you may include this information in a footnote or endnote.) Then document the source in your bibliography, references list, or list of works cited.

- **Paraphrases and summaries.** Provide a citation each time you use a source, even when you are not quoting. As with quotations, cite the author and page number in the text, and include full source information in your bibliography, references list, or list of works cited.

- **Ideas and information.** Acknowledge the source of any information or ideas that are *not* common knowledge. As with quotations, paraphrases, and summaries, cite the author and page number in your text and provide full source information in your bibliography, references list, or list of works cited. A piece of information from the Internet needs to be cited every bit as much as does a piece of information gleaned from a journal article or book.

2. What you do *not* have to cite: Common knowledge (facts, dates, events, cultural knowledge)

You do *not* have to cite *common knowledge* (unless it is included in a quotation)—even if you learned the information from a source. Common knowledge is general information that is available in a number of different sources and that is considered factual and incontestable. Here are some examples:

Facts

- On average, the Earth is about 93 million miles from the sun.
- Labor organizer "Mother" Jones worked on behalf of the United Mine Workers of America.

Dates

- The spring equinox occurred on March 20 in 2016.
- US women won the right to vote on August 26, 1920, when the Nineteenth Amendment was passed.

Writing
Responsibly Using Illustrations and Avoiding Plagiarism

> **More about**
> Citing media illustrations, 341–42 (MLA), 388–89 (APA), 421 (*Chicago*)

The web contains a variety of images, videos, and sound files that you can download to your word processor: A click of the mouse, and they are yours. Or are they? Keep full records of who created them, where you found them, and on what date you downloaded them so that you can cite them fully.

to OTHER WRITERS

Events

- James Earl Ray was convicted of the assassination of civil rights leader Martin Luther King Jr.

- Francis Crick, James Watson, and Maurice Wilkins are credited with discovering the structure of DNA.

Cultural Knowledge

- The composer Wolfgang Amadeus Mozart was a child prodigy.

- Elvis Presley made the song "Hound Dog" a smash hit, although he did not write it.

Everything outside of these categories should be cited in the text of your project and documented in a footnote or in your bibliography, references list, or list of works cited.

15c Making Notes That Help You Avoid Plagiarizing

Inadvertent plagiarism is a growing problem for researchers today because cutting and pasting material from online sources into notes is so easy. It is easy to lose track of which material has been borrowed, and it is easy to lose track of which material came from which source. The following strategies for maintaining good research notes can help you avoid problems:

- **Keep two sets of notes—bibliography and content.** For every source you consult, create a bibliographic note in your working bibliography and create content notes in a separate section of your research log.

- **Indicate the source and page number for all content notes.** Keying your notes to a source page will help you find the source passage when you return to the notes later and will also allow you to cite the source fully.

- **Make a fresh file, blog entry, or notebook section for notes on each source, and include the author and page number in each note.** Separating notes helps you avoid confusing one source with another.

- **Use columns or different colored fonts or cards to mark different types of notes.** If done consistently, using one column or color for your own comments, another for quotations, and a third for summaries and paraphrases can provide a useful visual cue for identifying source material and avoiding unintentional plagiarism.

More about
Research log,
202–03
Working bibliography, 204–09

- **Create a Favorites list or bookmark useful web pages.** When taking notes on a computer, bookmark or create a Favorites list for sites you have visited, so you can track your sources.

Tech **Bookmarking and Listing Favorites**

If you will not always be working from a single computer, set up bookmarks on a social bookmarking site like Pinterest or Digg, which allow you to store, tag, and share bookmarks.

15d Making Notes That Help You Research

Research note making involves the following activities:

> **More about**
> Annotation,
> 118–21
> Summarizing, 115,
> 257–60
> Patchwriting,
> 253–57
> Quoting,
> 260–62, 273
> Analyzing,
> 124–26,
> 263–64, 271–73
> Interpreting,
> 126–27,
> 263–64, 271–73
> Synthesizing,
> 127–29,
> 263–64, 271–73
> Critiquing,
> 129–31,
> 263–64, 271–73

- Annotating sources
- Summarizing sources accurately and without patchwriting
- Paraphrasing sources accurately and without patchwriting
- Recording quotations that you may want to use later
- Analyzing sources by dividing them into their component parts
- Interpreting the meaning of sources
- Synthesizing information from one source with information from other sources
- Critiquing or evaluating sources
- Recording source information, including the page number on which the material appears

---

Writing
Responsibly **Highlighting versus Making Notes**

While highlighting is a useful way to signal important information in a source, it is not a substitute for writing your own notes about a text. Highlighting can help you mark what is important, but annotating will push you to engage with the text and save you from leafing through page after highlighted page, looking for a passage that you faintly recall having read. So even though it may seem more time-consuming than highlighting, making notes will actually serve you better in the long run.

to SELF

15e Paraphrasing without Patchwriting

A *paraphrase* restates someone else's ideas in fresh words and sentences. Paraphrase a source when you want to do the following:

- Understand the logic of complex passages
- Convey ideas from a source in your own words
- Mention examples and details from the source

After summarizing, paraphrasing is the technique you should use most often when making notes from sources.

 Making Notes in English If you are a non-native writer of English, you may want to save time by copying passages in English into your notes word for word or by copying your own translation of the material into your notes. However, your English language skills will improve more quickly if you make an effort to paraphrase, and you will also be less likely to commit unintentional plagiarism. Remember that writing with sources in US academic and professional settings often means using your sources critically—another reason to avoid simply copying them.

Because you are including all of the writer's main ideas, a paraphrase is often as long as, and sometimes even longer than, the original. Like a summary, a paraphrase must not use the same language as the original (except for keywords), and the order of ideas and the sentence structures must be fresh as well. Just as you would cite the source of a quotation, you must also cite the source when you paraphrase.

Writers who are inexperienced with paraphrasing often patchwrite: They replace some terms with synonyms, delete a few words, or alter the grammar slightly, but they do not put the passage fully into fresh words and sentences. Patchwriting commonly happens as writers work with sources on complex, unfamiliar topics. Good writers rewrite their patchwriting, turning it into effective paraphrase; in doing this, they push themselves toward a better understanding of the source.

To paraphrase without patchwriting, follow these steps:

1. Read the source until you feel you understand it. Think about the overall meaning of the passage you are borrowing. Figure out whether there are any key terms that must be retained in your paraphrase.
2. Close the text and walk away. Do something else for a few minutes or a few hours.

3. Come back to your desk and write what you remember. If you cannot remember anything, repeat steps 1 and 2.
4. Check your paraphrase against the source to make sure you have correctly represented what it said. If you have closely followed any of the source language (other than key terms), either copy exactly and supply quotation marks or revise your note.

When your paraphrase is complete, check to be sure that you have done *all* of the following:

- Used synonyms rather than the words of the source where possible; used key terms and technical language from the source when no synonym is reasonable.

- Quoted specialized terms the first time used but not thereafter.

More about
Varying sentence
length and
structure, 552

- Used different sentence structures from those in the original passage. If you find yourself borrowing the sentence structures of your source, try dividing or combining sentences or varying their length and structure to alter their rhythm and blend them into your own text.

- Cited the source of the paraphrase in your text, usually by bookending the paraphrase with a signal phrase and a page reference in parentheses.

- Documented the source in your bibliography, reference list, or list of works cited.

The following examples illustrate techniques for revising passages to avoid patchwriting:

Passage from Source

With these caveats, we argue more limitedly that digital technology offers new avenues of aesthetic experimentation for comic artists and that the internet has given some comic artists a modest prosperity that they would not have without the internet as a means of distribution. (Sean Fenty et al., "Webcomics: The Influence and Continuation of the Comix Revolution," *ImageTexT*, vol. 1, no. 2, 2004, par. 2, www.english.ufl.edu/imagetext/archives/v1_2/group/.)

First author + et al.

Note with Patchwriting

Picks up language from source

Uses synonym or word in another form

Paragraph reference (use only when source numbers its paragraphs)

Fenty et al. argue that digital technology provides comic artists with an opportunity for artistic experimentation and that some have more success than they would have without the Internet (par. 2).

Note without Patchwriting

> According to Fenty et al., comic artists use the computer to experiment and the internet to publish their works, allowing them more creative options and earning them more money than they made in the pre-Internet era (par. 2).

Notice that the patchwritten note relies heavily not only on the language but also on the sentence structure of the source. The note without patchwriting captures the main ideas of the passage without borrowing sentence structures or more than a few keywords from the original.

Here is another example:

Passage from Source

Until recently, the Church was one of the least studied aspects of the Cuban revolution, almost as if it were a voiceless part of Cuban society, an institution and faith that had little impact on the course of events. (Super, John C. "Interpretations of Church and State in Cuba, 1959–1961." *The Catholic Historical Review*, vol. 89, no. 3, 2003, pp. 511–29.)

Note with Patchwriting

> Super 511
>
> According to Super, the Catholic Church until recently was not much studied as an aspect of the Cuban revolution. It was as if the Church was voiceless in Cuban culture, as if it had little influence on events (511).

Author
Picks up language from source
Uses synonym or word in another form
Page reference

Note without Patchwriting

> Super argues that scholarship on the Cuban revolution is only beginning to recognize the influential role of the Church (511).

The revised note still retains key terms from the source: "Cuban revolution" and "Church" appear in both the original passage and the revised note because there can be no synonyms for proper nouns (names). But the passage no longer draws heavily on the source's sentence structure, organization, or word choices.

Writing from sources without patchwriting is an advanced skill; learning how to avoid patchwriting requires conscious, ongoing effort. You will find it hard at first, but it gets easier with practice. Remember, if you find yourself leaning heavily on the wording of the source in your first-draft paraphrases, revise them. Work for greater comprehension of the text by looking up unfamiliar words or thinking about concepts you do not understand. Then turn away from the source and write from your head rather than from the source. As long as you are looking at the source and asking yourself, "How else can I say this?" you are playing with words rather than comprehending the source.

→ **EXERCISE 15.1 Correcting a paraphrase to avoid patchwriting**

Study the following source and the first draft of a paraphrase that follows. Circle words in the note that appear in the source, and underline synonyms or words in another form. Then revise the note to avoid the patchwriting.

Passage from Source

The War Department's decision to enlist the movie industry's help after Pearl Harbor was not inevitable. The Signal Corps had used movies to train soldiers since 1929, just as the studios were making the transition from silent pictures to talkies, and in the 1930s, Roosevelt and his team had come to understand the power of short films and newsreels to sell the New Deal. But for much of the decade before Pearl Harbor, Hollywood and Washington had remained, in a way, competing principalities, each impressed by and distrustful of the clout held by the other. Hollywood feared the near-constant threat of censure, investigation, and regulation from the capital; Washington watched the growth of a medium that had become unrivaled in capturing the attention of the American people and, by degrees, learned to acknowledge, if sometimes unhappily, its power. But the beginning of the war marked the government's first attempt at a sustained program of filmed propaganda, and its use of Hollywood filmmakers to explain its objectives, tout its successes, and shape the war as a narrative for both civilians and soldiers constituted a remarkable, even radical experiment.

—Mark Harris, *Five Came Back: A Story of Hollywood and the Second World War*

Draft Note

Harris

It was not inevitable for the War Department to decide to get help from the movie industry after Pearl Harbor. Movies had been used for military training and political propaganda since 1929, yet Hollywood and the government were wary of each other.

→ **EXERCISE 15.2 Paraphrasing without patchwriting**

Using the guidelines for paraphrasing without patchwriting in *section 15d* in this chapter, choose a key sentence from the passage in Exercise 15.1 and paraphrase it. Then compare your paraphrase with the original. Is your paraphrase accurate? Does it avoid patchwriting? Revise your paraphrase until it is accurate and written completely in fresh words and sentence structures.

Make It **Your Own**

From a source for a research project (or from another college-level text), choose three sentences you consider important. Then paraphrase them following the guidelines in *section 15d*. Attach a copy of the source to your paraphrase.

Work **Together**

In groups of two or three, compare the original source with the paraphrases that each group member wrote for the Make It Your Own exercise above. Did group members paraphrase accurately? Did they avoid patchwriting? Discuss any sentences that may lean too heavily on the language or sentence structure of the original source. What might the writer do to avoid patchwriting? If the paraphrase avoids patchwriting, identify the paraphrasing strategies each writer used.

15f Summarizing

An effective *summary* briefly restates the main claims and supporting evidence of a source. By forcing you to identify the main claims and understand them well enough to state them accurately in fresh words, writing an accurate summary helps you understand a difficult text. Most of your content notes should summarize your sources.

In general, a summary should be at least 50 percent shorter than the material you are summarizing, but most summaries go far beyond that: A single paragraph, for example, might summarize a 25-page essay. Your summary should be only as long as needed to capture the main claim and major supporting evidence accurately. To summarize a source, follow these steps:

1. Read the source, underlining key terms and looking up words that you do not know. For short sources, one or two careful readings may be enough; for longer or more complex sources, you may need to reread the source several times.

2. Annotate the source. Underline or highlight the thesis or main idea of the source, and identify the main supporting ideas. For a longer source, creating an outline may be helpful.
3. Write down, without looking at the source, the thesis or main claim in a sentence or two. For each group of supporting paragraphs, write a one- or two-sentence summary in your own words.
4. Combine your sentences into a paragraph, editing to omit repetition and using transitions to make logical connections between sentences clear.
5. Check your summary against the source. Have you used fresh words and sentence structures? If not, this may be a sign that you do not yet understand the source. Go back and read the material again, and revise your summary to avoid patchwriting.
6. Credit the original source when you incorporate your summary into your project. Use a signal phrase to indicate where the summary begins and a page reference (in parentheses) to indicate where it ends.

More about
Transitions, 60–61
Placing signal phrases and page references, 277–78, 304–06, 364–65

Student Model Summary

Below is an example of an effective summary of an original source:

Passage from Source

Before exploring these connections, however, webcomics must be more clearly defined. Many people are only familar with webcomics through Scott McCloud's explanation of them in *Reinventing Comics,* where he took on the role of a spokesperson for webcomics. While McCloud offered an initial study on

self Assessment

When you summarize, check for these elements. Have you done *all* of the following?

- ☐ Made clear that you are writing a summary of a source, not your own ideas.
- ☐ Cited the source you are summarizing.
- ☐ Rearranged the ideas of the source so that they make sense in your own text. For example, if the source presents a cause and its effects, you can present the effects first and the causes second, if that will work better in your project.
- ☐ Provided transitions to clarify relationships among ideas.
- ☐ Kept your own ideas, examples, and interpretations out (unless you were

asked to analyze, respond, or interpret in addition to summarizing).
- ☐ Included page citations wherever you are summarizing an identifiable part of the source.
- ☐ Maintained the balance of the ideas in the source, without emphasizing one more than it was emphasized in the source.
- ☐ Made sure that your omissions and deletions do not alter or distort the meaning of the source.
- ☐ Documented the source in your bibliography, reference list, or list of works cited.

webcomics, this paper does not operate within a McCloudian definition of comics, where he expounds upon their potential to revolutionize all comics production. In this paper, the term webcomics must be distinguished from hyperbolic proclamations about the internet as an inevitable site of radical aesthetic evolution and economic revolution for comics. The problems with McCloud's claims about the liberatory and radical properties of the internet have been addressed by others, like Gary Groth in his article for *The Comics Journal,* "McCloud Cuckoo Land." Our argument does not claim that the internet is a superior comic medium, free of those "tiny boxes" and "finite canvases" that seem to trouble McCloud (online). Further, we recognize that the internet has not offered a level playing field, free of corporate domination, "a world," to quote McCloud's *Reinventing Comics,* "in which the path from selling ten comics to selling ten thousand comics to selling ten million comics is as smooth as ice" (188, Panel 1). With these caveats, we argue more limitedly that digital technology offers new avenues of aesthetic experimentation for comic artists and that the Internet has given some comic artists a modest prosperity that they would not have without the internet as a means of distribution. (Sean Fenty et al., "Webcomics: The Influence and Continuation of the Comix Revolution," *ImageTexT,* vol. 1, no. 2, 2004, par. 2, www.english.ufl.edu/imagetext/archives/v1_2/group/.)

Summary

Scott McCloud claims that the Internet will free underground comic artists from the restrictions of print distribution and make it possible for underground comic artists to reach huge audiences. Fenty, Houp, and Taylor, on the other hand, focus on the possibilities for experimentation on the web and argue that the web provides better opportunities to make money publishing underground comics than does print. (Fenty et al., par. 2)

Notice that the writer of the summary captures the main idea of the source in her own words and sentence structures. Her summary is about one quarter the length of the original material.

→ **EXERCISE 15.3 Summarizing accurately**

Write one or two sentences summarizing the following passages:

1. Norms facilitate social interaction by providing guidance (What should I do?), predictability (What is supposed to happen?), and coordination (Whose job is it to do what?). These functions were indispensable for ancestral groups of nomadic humans who roamed extreme terrains from the burning heat of Africa to the crushing cold of Northern Europe. Norms had to regulate co-living in small spaces, joint hunting, food sharing, and seasonal and generational migration. Then, a qualitative jump in moral life occurred when humans settled down 12,000 years ago, as a plethora of new norms had to regulate

novel behaviors. As humans began to practice agriculture and settle in fixed communities, they needed norms to govern possessions (e.g., land, dwellings), new forms of production, (e.g., crops, tools to harvest them), and the vast expansion of social roles (e.g., king, carpenter, servant). Today, norms govern an almost infinite number of cultural behaviors, such as eating, speaking, dressing, moving, and working. We may speculate that humans know more social and moral norms than they know words in their native language.

—Bertram Malle, "Teaching Robots to Behave Ethically"

2. Our brain uses two different types of cognitive processing when doing these two operations: typing and writing. As tested on a group of undergrads, the research proved that laptop users type almost everything they hear without processing the meaning or devoting much thought to what it is they're taking notes on. Basically, when you type, all you're doing is mindlessly transcribing, and that does not require much cognitive activity. When you take notes by hand, however, you obviously can't write down every single word your professor utters. So you listen, summarize, and list only the key points. Your brain is more engaged in the process of comprehension and so the information processed this way is remembered better.

—Elena Prokopets, "Here's Why You Should Take Notes by Hand (Instead of with a Laptop)"

> **More about**
> Using quotation
>   marks, 810–19
>   (ch. 51)
> Indention for lon-
>   ger quotations,
>   308, 346–47
>   (MLA), 392 (APA)
> Deciding when to
>   create or bor-
>   row visuals, 84
> Obtaining permis-
>   sion, 10–11, 230
> Ellipses in quo-
>   tations, 816,
>   831–32
> Brackets in
>   quotations,
>   816, 828
> Interviews,
>   229–30
> Surveys, 231–32
> Writing about lit-
>   erature, 452–74
>   (ch. 22)

15g Quoting

A *quotation* is someone else's words transcribed exactly, with quotation marks or block indention to signal that it is from a source. Quote from a source under the following circumstances:

- When your source uses particularly vivid or engaging language
- When you want to reproduce a subtle idea that might be difficult to paraphrase or summarize without distortion
- When your source conveys technical information that is difficult to paraphrase
- When you want to convey ideas in an expert's own words
- When you want to analyze or highlight the specific language used in your source (as when studying a work of literature or a historical document)
- When you want to emphasize an important point

When making notes, copy quotations word for word, and double-check them against the source. Whether you transcribe a quotation or cut and paste it into your notes, put quotation marks around it to avoid any confusion later. In your writing project, adjust quotations to integrate them into your own sentences, using ellipses to signal cuts and brackets to indicate any words you have added or changed. In your notes, the quotation should appear exactly as it did in the source.

When working with primary sources such as interviews and surveys that you have conducted or works of literature you are studying, you are likely to use quotations extensively. In contrast, secondary sources such as newspaper articles, scholarly articles, and books are already quoting, summarizing, and paraphrasing their sources, so you should limit the number of direct quotations you copy from them. Use summary and paraphrase instead.

If you find that you are copying a lot of quotations but are paraphrasing little and summarizing even less, you may not be fully comprehending what you are reading. In these situations, try the following:

- Read the source again.
- Look up words you do not understand.
- Consult reference sources that can provide background knowledge.
- Discuss the source with your instructor, classmates, or friends.

More about
Evaluating sources, 233–46 (ch. 14)

Good scholarship requires that you work to understand the whole source rather than just quoting from the sections that you believe you understand or that you think sound authoritative. Understanding the difficult parts is important, for they may well change the meaning of what you thought at first you understood.

Writing Responsibly / Using Quotations Fairly

We have all seen ellipsis-laden quotations praising a new movie, and we have all wondered whether a crucial word or words might have been omitted: "This is the . . . movie of the year!" could well have been "This is the *worst* movie of the year!" in the original review. That is one reason to be skeptical when reading such advertisements. (Another is the advertiser's desire for the movie to succeed at the box office.)

In academic writing, you can adjust a quotation to bring the punctuation or grammar into line with your own text, or to remove extraneous information, as long as your changes are indicated with ellipses or brackets and you do not distort the author's point. Protect your credibility and be fair to your source by altering quotations accurately.

to OTHER WRITERS

Student Model **Reading Note**

The following reading note correctly uses quotation marks to signal material taken word for word from the source, yet it indicates that the writer does not fully understand what she is writing about.

Draft Note

Milne 140

The "free-black community . . . of Five Points" is not reflected in "the areas of Block 160 that were excavated." "All that survived . . . were the remains of their ancestors interred in the mostly forgotten burying ground, a few intriguing and unusual items discarded in the defunct privies and cisterns, and a handful of church addresses." But "it is probable that many members of this community remained in the neighborhood, living 'off-the-grid.' . . . "

This note is merely a string of quotations, sewn together with a few of the note-taker's own words. Using these notes as is would produce a research project that would similarly be a mosaic of quotation, difficult to read and lacking the researcher's insight and critical judgment. Rereading the source in order to gain a better understanding of it enabled the writer to summarize with much less quotation. The following revision is much easier to read, as well:

Revised Note

Milne 140

Very few items belonging to members of the African American population in Five Points have been excavated, most likely because members of this community were not part of mainstream society—they were "living 'off the grid'" (140)—not because they had all moved away.

> **More about**
> Integrating bor-
> rowed ideas
> and words, 273,
> 276–79

Other chapters in this text discuss the mechanics of using quotation marks and integrating quotations into your text. Consult these sections before you begin your research, as you make notes on sources, and as you draft and revise your text. Applying these principles will enable you to be responsible to the writers from whom you borrow, to your readers, and to yourself.

Assessment

self

When analyzing, interpreting, synthesizing, and critiquing a source, ask yourself the following questions. If the answer is not clear, reread and reevaluate the source, as necessary.

Analysis

☐ What is the purpose of the source?

☐ Who is the intended audience?

☐ What major claims does the source make?

☐ What evidence (facts, statistics, examples, expert testimony) does the source use to support these claims?

Interpretation

☐ What assumptions does the author make about the subject or audience, and why are such assumptions significant?

☐ What does the source omit (evidence, opposing views), and what might these omissions indicate?

☐ What conclusions can you draw about the author's attitude from the text's tone? What motives can you infer from the author's background?

☐ Who published this text or sponsored the research, and what influence might these sponsors have upon the way the information, arguments, or evidence is presented?

☐ In what context was the text written— place, time, cultural environment—and how might this context have influenced the author?

☐ What expertise or life experience does the author bring to the subject, and is it relevant to the topic?

Synthesis

☐ Do any other sources make a similar (or opposing) claim, reach a similar (or opposing) conclusion, or offer similar (or opposing) evidence?

☐ Do any other sources identify similar causes or effects?

☐ What else do you know about this topic?

Critique

☐ What are the aims of the source, how worthwhile are they, and how well are they achieved?

☐ What claims does the source make? Are you persuaded by them? Why or why not?

☐ How credible is the evidence? Is evidence based on verifiable facts? How relevant is the evidence?

☐ How logical is the source? Does the author commit any fallacies?

☐ How fairly does the source treat alternative viewpoints?

> **More about**
> Analysis, interpretation, synthesis, and critique, 123–35, 271–73

15h Using Analysis, Interpretation, Synthesis, and Critique in Your Notes

In addition to recording information from sources, the note-taking stage is also the time to start analyzing, interpreting, synthesizing, and critiquing what you read. The Self-Assessment box above lists questions to ask yourself as you read and take notes on your sources.

The following note for Lydia Nichols's research project provides a summary of the source while also including her own assessment of it:

Student Models
Research projects: "Holy Underground Comics, Batman!" Lydia Nichols, 349–62

"The Power of Wardrobe," Heather DeGroot, 396–405

Student Model　Summary Note with Writer's Assessment

Summary that includes analysis and interpretation

Critique

Synthesis

Heller

Provides a history of *Zap* comics from the first issue by Robert Crumb in 1968 to the most recent issue in 1994. Describes *Zap* as founding the underground "comix" movement in reaction to the superhero comics that adhered to the 1950s Comics Code and spurred on by late 1960s cultural challenges to the status quo, but doesn't go into detail or identify any comics it inspired. Identifies artists who joined forces with Crumb, and highlights their contributions. Discusses censorship battle over *Zap* #4, which was accused of violating community standards of decency. But not sure what happened: Bookstore owner was fined, but article doesn't indicate what other legal troubles it caused. Later issues continued to be sexually explicit, but they also satirized contemporary mores and included "comic documentary" similar to comic books published during World War II. Article provides a good overview of the history of *Zap* comics (including showing all 14 covers); it assumes that readers will already know a good deal about the history of comics. "Good Shall Triumph" and "Comic Book Code" provide more info. about the Comics Code Authority, but I would like to know more about early examples of documentary comics. Heller is obviously a fan of *Zap* comics (I read online that he was an art director at *The NY Times*) but I would like to know more about what motivated Crumb and the others to rebel.

Work **Together**

Read the research project in chapter 18 (pp. 350–62) or 19 (pp. 350–62). In small groups of two or three, use the criteria in the bulleted list in *section 15g* to categorize the writer's use of quotations. Has she used quotations effectively? Why or why not?

Make It **Your Own**

Create a content note on a source for an upcoming research project. First, paraphrase or summarize the source, following the instructions in *sections 15e* and *15f*. Then ask yourself three or more of the questions in the Self-Assessment box on p. 263 and create a note on the source. Bring it to class.

Text Credits

16 Writing the Research Project

© STScI/NASA

The Hubble Space Telescope, taking pictures of the cosmos since 1990, has provided enough data to keep scientists busy for years, long after the telescope stops functioning. So far, scientists have published over six thousand articles based on what they have learned from Hubble. These articles have given us a clearer idea of the age of our universe, a better understanding of how galaxies evolve, and information about what happens when stars collapse. Until these articles were published, the Hubble merely provided pretty pictures to the rest of us.

Like the scientific articles published from the Hubble data, your college research projects are an opportunity to share what you have read and studied; they are an opportunity to provide readers with a synthesis of the information you have gleaned from a variety of sources and to present what you have learned, filtered through the lens of your understanding. They are the culmination of your research and an expression of yourself.

16a Drafting a Thesis Statement

As you began your research, you chose and defined a *topic* that would be appropriate to your purpose and of interest to your

> *More about*
Assessing the
  writing situation,
  13–21, 196–97
Devising a thesis,
  34–37, 199–200
Choosing a topic,
  24–30, 199
Using evidence,
  45–46
Finding informa-
  tion, 210–32
  (ch. 13)
Acknowledging
  alternative
  views, 148–49
Organizing,
  38–43, 53–58,
  157–59, 267–70
Drafting, 44–47,
  271–73
Summary, para-
  phrase, and
  quotation,
  257–62, 273
Avoiding patch-
  writing, 253–57,
  275–79
Relevance,
  233–34

Quick Reference Drafting the Research Project

- **Thesis.** Draft a one- or two-sentence thesis statement that grows out of your research questions and hypothesis. Revise your thesis as you draft your project.
- **Organization.** List and explain the reasons you believe your thesis statement or why you think it is the most reasonable way to address a difficult issue. Sort research notes into separate piles for each of your reasons. Draft an outline that organizes your material so that readers can follow your logic and maintain interest to the end.
- **Analysis, interpretation, synthesis, critique.** Divide ideas into their component parts and think about what they mean. Then combine ideas from sources with your own ideas to come up with something fresh. Decide how well sources have achieved their authors' goals and whether those goals were worthwhile.
- **Evidence and counterevidence.** Incorporate evidence, making sure it is relevant. Use summaries, paraphrases, and a few quotations as support. Acknowledge contradictory evidence and explain why your position is still reasonable despite this. (If your position does *not* seem reasonable in light of counterevidence, revise your thesis.) Make sure you provide enough evidence—and the appropriate types of evidence—to persuade your readers.
- **Citation and documentation.** Cite your sources in the body of your text. Use quotation marks for all direct copying. Replace any patchwriting with paraphase. Document sources in a list of works cited.

reader. You then framed *research questions* and turned them into a *hypothesis* that you tried to test and confirm through your research. Now, with research data in hand, you are ready to draft a *thesis statement* that will serve as the focus of your project.

This thesis should be a one- or two-sentence statement that grows out of your research hypothesis (or hypotheses), revised in light of what you learned through your research process. It should be a statement that you are prepared to defend, using the information you gleaned from sources and your own ideas, and it should convey your *purpose*.

Student Model Thesis Statement

Read the research question, hypothesis, and thesis statement for the student research essay by Lydia Nichols:

Research question: What are the characteristics of underground comics?

Hypothesis: The characteristics of underground comics are a focus on topics that challenge social mores ❶, an author or author team ❷ that has creative control, and an adult readership ❸.

Thesis statement: While far less well-known than their superhero counterparts, underground comics offer an innovative and sophisticated alternative to mainstream titles.

> Hypothesis answers research question by listing three distinguishing traits.

> Thesis statement makes purpose clear: uses comparison of comic types to persuade readers that underground comics are more innovative and sophisticated. It transforms specifics of hypothesis into a broader, more engaging claim.

As you draft your research project, you may discover that the counter-evidence is overwhelming or that the body of your draft offers a different answer to your research question than the one in your thesis. (Frequently, the true thesis takes shape in the conclusion of the first draft.) So be prepared to revisit your thesis as you draft, revising or even replacing it as necessary.

Make It **Your Own**

For a research project that you are working on, draft (or revise) a thesis statement. Does the thesis statement concisely assert your main claim? Will it appeal to your readers? Does it convey your purpose?

16b Organizing Your Ideas

The process of organizing your ideas begins with assembling the materials you will need. These include the following:

- Your research log and any other notes you have taken
- Any photocopies or printouts of sources
- A copy of your thesis statement
- Any supplies you may need (flash drives, pens, pencils, highlighters, stick-on notes, index cards, a notebook)

> *More about*
> Research log, 202–03
> Annotating, 118–21
> Generating ideas, 24–30
> Making notes, 121–23, 251–52, 260-63

1. Organize your ideas and notes.

With your preliminary thesis statement drafted and supplies at hand, you are ready to begin organizing your ideas and notes.

1. Start by listing the reasons you believe your thesis is true. While these reasons may be derived from your research sources, they should be *your* reasons, stated in your own words. (The strategies for generating ideas can help.)

2. Review the notes you took while reading sources: Do they provide evidence that supports your reasons for believing your thesis? Organize your notes according to which of your reasons they support: Separate index cards into piles, or cut and paste notes into separate computer files for each supporting point.

3. Review your notes again, looking for counterevidence that undermines your thesis or that points to alternative interpretations. Organize this material and consider how it might change your own point of view. If (as is usually the case) your understanding of your topic has changed during the course of your research, revise your preliminary thesis to reflect your current beliefs.

4. Assess your evidence: The size of a computer file or stack of index cards will indicate how much information you have collected in support of each of your reasons for believing the thesis. If a set of notes looks skimpy, find more supporting evidence, revise your thesis, or delve deeper into your reasons for believing your thesis.

2. Outline your project.

After you have organized your ideas and notes, outline your project to determine the most effective order for presenting your ideas. Some writers prefer a sentence outline because it aids drafting. (Each sentence in the outline

> **More about**
> Scratch outlines,
> 40–41
> Sentence out-
> lines, 41–42
> Topic outlines,
> 41–42

Writing
Responsibly | Acknowledging Counterevidence

While sorting your notes, be sure to retain *counterevidence*—evidence that *undermines* your claims. If some of your research contradicts or complicates your thesis or supporting reasons, do not suppress it. Instead, revise your thesis or supporting reasons on the basis of this counterevidence, or acknowledge the counterevidence and explain why the reasons for believing your thesis are more convincing than those that challenge it. Your readers will appreciate your presentation of multiple perspectives.

to AUDIENCE

becomes the topic sentence of a paragraph.) Others, eager to start writing, prefer a scratch (informal) outline that simply lists their reasons and the major supporting points in order of presentation. Still others prefer a topic outline: It is quicker to write than a sentence outline, but its formal structure of roman numerals and letters makes the structure of the draft clearer.

Student Model Outline

The topic outline below shows the structure of the first part of Lydia Nichols's research project. Note that the roman numeral sections list Nichols's reasons; the capital letter and arabic numeral sections list the evidence in support of her reasons.

Thesis: While far less well-known than their superhero counterparts, underground comics offer an innovative and sophisticated alternative to mainstream titles.

I.   Success of superhero comics in the late 1930s led to homogenization

    A. Superhero defined

    B. Superman debuted June 1938

    C. Copycat superheroes ride Superman's success

Overall organization: Chronological (1930s, 1950s, 1960s)

II. Further homogenization in the 1950s, with creation of Comics Code Authority (1954)

    A. Specific rules of CCA code—example: letters of the word "crime" cannot be bigger than other letters on the cover

Uses example to support claim

    B. General rules of CCA code

       1. Show respect for parents, morality (good triumphs over evil)

       2. Portray criminals, crimes negatively

       3. Religion treated respectfully

       4. No profanity

    C. Violators not distributed (EC Comics and others); conformers gained market share

III. Homogenization, superhero domination undermined by appearance of underground "comix" in late 1960s

A. Underground comix defined

1. Not submitted to CCA for approval

2. Satirized conservative beliefs

3. Included political and sexual content (fetishism)

4. Challenged social norms

5. Offered insightful commentary on society

6. Example: Robert Crumb's *Zap*, first issue released in 1968

B. Underground comix contrasted with CCA-approved comics

1. *Amazing Fantasy* (1962) (Visual: Cover of *Amazing Fantasy* #15)

a. Comics Code Authority approval stamp in upper-right corner of *Amazing Fantasy*

b. Traditional superhero

c. Traditional drawing

2. *Snarf* (1976) (Visual: *Snarf* #6)

a. Not CCA-approved (no stamp)

b. Depicts regular guy fighting real problems (big oil—an important issue in the mid-1970s)

c. Takes on political issues

d. Drawing crude

Uses definition to support claim

Supports claim by showing and analyzing contrasting visuals

Make It **Your Own**

For a research project that you are working on, do the following:

- List the evidence (including visual evidence, if any) that makes you believe your thesis.

- Decide on the best order in which to present your material, and make an outline (sentence, scratch, or topic) from which to work.

16c Drafting Your Research Project

When drafting your research project, your goal is to draw on information in sources to support your own ideas, weaving that information into your sentences and paragraphs so that it supports your ideas without overwhelming them. Draw on your analysis of sources, your own interpretations of what you have read, and your synthesis of ideas from sources. To support your claims, incorporate summaries, paraphrases, and quotations from your notes, using signal phrases to identify the sources of borrowed ideas and to provide context for your sources.

> ### Make It **Your Own**
>
> For a research project that you are working on, compose a first draft. As you write, reread the tips in the Quick Reference box below as necessary. You will revise this draft later, so you should not worry about errors and gaps in the draft.

1. Use analysis, interpretation, and synthesis to evaluate and support your claims.

When you read sources and took notes, you analyzed your material to divide it into its component parts, and you interpreted what you read to determine

---

Quick Reference | Writing the First Draft

As you begin writing, keep in mind that you are composing a draft—what you write will be revised—so do not worry about whether you are saying it "right." A few writers' tricks will help you produce that first draft:

- Keep your thesis statement in front of you to help you stay focused as you write.
- Start with the sections that are easiest to write, and then organize and fill in the gaps later.
- Begin writing without looking at your sources or notes. Then consult sources and notes for evidence to support what you have drafted.
- When incorporating quotations, paraphrases, or summaries, identify which source the material comes from (including the page number) to avoid having to track down this information later and, perhaps, plagiarizing inadvertently.
- Draft with a notepad next to you or another file open on your computer, so you can jot down ideas that come to you while drafting.
- Include visuals that support your points and that help your reader understand what you are writing about.

More about
Drafting, 44–47

Student Model
Research project:
"Holy Underground
Comics, Batman,"
Lydia Nichols,
349–62

its meaning. You also synthesized sources: You may have identified ideas in one source that were supported by information in others, described areas of agreement (or disagreement) among sources, or explained which sources were most persuasive and why. The work you have already done to analyze, interpret, and synthesize sources is what you will draw on as you draft your research project. Use it to show readers how your sources support, complicate, or destabilize your thesis; do not expect readers to figure this out without your help.

Examine the paragraph below from Lydia Nichols's essay on underground comics to see how she uses analysis, interpretation, and synthesis to support her own claims.

Sentence 1: Nichols's claim (topic sentence) offers her interpretation.

Sentences 2, 3, 4, and 5 synthesize information from sources to support her claim.

Sentence 6 provides her own analysis to support her claim.

Sentence 1 continues her own analysis to support her claim.

In the 1960s, in contrast to mainstream CAA-approved superhero comics, alternatives began to appear. According to Steven Heller, an art director at *The New York Times* and a founder of the Masters in Graphic Arts Program at the School for Visual Arts in New York, Robert Crumb's *Zap* (1968) initiated the "underground comix revolution" (101). Crumb and other like-minded artists did not submit their comics for CAA approval. Though this limited the distribution of their work, it allowed them artistic freedom. From its first issue, *Zap* satirized mainstream, conservative beliefs and did not shy away from sexual or political content (Heller 101–02). Beneath the crude humor of *Zap* and similar comics lay insightful commentary on society and its principles, which many readers found to be a refreshing change from mainstream superhero titles.

Besides Zap, other well-known underground titles of the era include *Subvert* and *Weirdo*. Gilbert Shelton's hilariously nonconformist *Fabulous Furry Freak Brothers* and Crumb's most recognizable hero, the sketchy guru *Mr. Natural*, starred in their own, often X-rated, comic books (see fig 2.).

Illustration provides an example that supports Nichols's claim, and caption offers interpretation of what the reader is seeing there.

© McGraw-Hill Education/Mark Dierker, photographer

Fig 2. Examples of late-'60s underground comics. In defiance of the authoritarian standards of the Comic Code Authority and influenced by '50s humor magazine *Mad*, underground artists pushed the boundaries of humor, propriety, and good taste.

Instead of merely stringing together material from sources, Nichols integrates her own ideas with information from sources to craft a paragraph that readers will find persuasive. She analyzes primary sources (examples of underground comics) to determine what makes them visually exciting, she interprets her sources to determine which support her claim, and she synthesizes evidence to make her case.

2. Use summary, paraphrase, and some quotations to support your claims.

So that your research project will not seem like a series of quotations strung together with a few words of your own, use quotations sparingly. Put borrowed ideas into your own words, by either paraphrasing or summarizing. Use quotations only when the language is particularly vivid or technical, when you want to demonstrate the ethos (credibility) of the speaker, or when you are analyzing the language of the source. In the sample paragraph on the previous page, Lydia Nichols uses a combination of quotation and summary to support her claims. She quotes Heller because the phrase "underground comix revolution" is especially vivid, but she goes on to summarize Heller's ideas to convey his argument concisely.

NOTE When summarizing or paraphrasing, work to avoid patchwriting, and when quoting, use quotation marks or indent longer quoted passages as a block.

> *More about*
> Quoting, para-
>   phrasing, or
>   summarizing,
>   249–63
> Signal phrases,
>   277–78, 306–08,
>   364–65
> Avoiding
>   patchwriting,
>   253–57
> Quotation marks,
>   810–19 (ch. 51)

3. Acknowledge your sources.

Even while working on your first draft, you should acknowledge information you have gathered from sources—quotations, paraphrases, summaries, illustrations, data, or other information—by citing them in the text and providing full documentation in a list of works cited, a reference list, or a bibliography. Both citation and documentation are necessary to avoid plagiarism and demonstrate your ethos as a writer. No matter which citation and documentation style you use, your entries should be complete and consistent so that readers can locate your sources and enter into the conversation you have contributed to in your research project.

> *More about*
> Citing sources,
>   304–321 (MLA),
>   363–405 (APA),
>   406–34
>   (*Chicago*),
>   435–49 (CSE)
> Documenting
>   sources, 321–44
>   (MLA), 374–91
>   (APA), 407–423
>   (*Chicago*),
>   435–47 (CSE)

16d Revising, Proofreading, Formatting, and Publishing Your Project

More about
Global revision,
  88–93
Local revision
  (editing), 93–95
Peer editing,
  96–98
Proofreading,
  99–100
Formatting,
  101, 345–49
  (MLA), 392–96
  (APA), 423–24
  (*Chicago*),
  447–48 (CSE)

Once you have composed a first draft, however rough it may be, you can begin the process of shaping and polishing it—the process of *revision*. First, attend to big-picture (global) issues, such as clarifying your purpose, making sure your project is cohesive and unified, and making sure your ideas are fully developed. Next, attend to local issues, such as making sure your word choices reflect your meaning and are at the appropriate level, that you have varied your sentences, and that your prose is concise.

Once revision is complete, edit your text to correct errors of grammar, punctuation, and mechanics. Then proofread carefully—remember that spell-check software can help, but it cannot replace a careful human proofreader. Finally, format your project following the requirements of your discipline.

Text Credit
p. 267: Courtesy of Lydia Nichols

17 Citing Expertly

© McGraw-Hill Education/Mark Dierker, photographer

When you research a topic, you explore sources that express a variety of perspectives; you choose those that enhance your understanding of the topic; and then you describe those sources' ideas in ways that will allow readers to understand what the sources have contributed to your point of view.

Source citations are necessary in a researched project, yet simple citations do not help readers see how you are using your sources. For your readers, the clarity of your project comes when you go beyond just naming the source. When you cite expertly, you use accurate signal verbs, show source boundaries, emphasize your own voice, provide context for the source, and accurately integrate altered quotations. Expert citation makes your conversation with sources, like the image or message in a glass paperweight, "transparent": Others can see how your ideas developed and how you are relating to your sources and the information in them.

Citations are an essential part of academic writing. They identify the sources you are using—the other writers with whom you are "talking." At more expert levels of researched writing, *rhetorical citations* accomplish this task and more: They provide helpful information about your sources; they reveal your attitude toward, and judgment of, your sources; and they highlight your own contributions to the "conversation" that takes place between you and your sources.

More about
Using information
responsibly,
247–64
In-text citation
304–321 (MLA
style, ch. 18)
Ethos, 145–46

17a Integrating Source Material Responsibly

When writing from sources, your most basic responsibility is to let your audience know whenever your text is drawing on a source. This protects you from charges of plagiarism. It also fulfills a responsibility to your audience, by letting readers know who is speaking in your text. It fulfills a responsibility to yourself, as well: Careful citation increases your writerly ethos; it makes you a more credible, respected writer. In MLA style, *in-text citation—* whether through parenthetical references, signal phrases, or a combination of the two—accomplishes all of this.

Having a Conversation with Sources You may consider published sources to be authorities, but an important aspect of academic writing is learning how to be critical even of authoritative material. You are free to agree or disagree with any source, but it is important that you use sources to support your claims, rather than simply repeating a source's language and ideas.

1. Parenthetical citations

You can cite your sources by using the author's last name and relevant page number(s) in a *parenthetical citation.*[1] Place that citation at the end of the material from your source:

> Quotation marks indicate the beginning and end of the source's exact words
>
> Source author (last name only)
>
> Page in source

"His name was Mark Zuckerberg, he was a sophomore, and although Eduardo had spent a fair amount of time at various Epsilon Pi events with him, along with at least one prepunch Phoenix event that Eduardo could remember, he still barely knew the kid" (Mezrich 15).

Mezrich, Ben, The Accidental Billionaires: The Founding of Facebook, A Tale of Sex, Money, Genius and Betrayal (New York: Doubleday,

When you are paraphrasing or summarizing material, you should also use parenthetical citation to acknowledge that your material comes from a source:

---

[1] The terms *parenthetical citation, parenthetical note,* and *parenthetical reference* are often interchangeable.

> Who wouldn't envy the genius and wealth of the person who
> invented Facebook? But who wouldn't pity a person who has no close
> friends? Mark Zuckerberg may have great wealth, but he has few
> confidantes (Denby 98).

Source author (last name only)

Page in source

2. Signal phrases

To incorporate borrowed material smoothly into your prose, introduce it with a *signal phrase.* One part of the signal phrase is an identification (usually the name) of the writer from whom you are borrowing. The other part is a verb; choose one that conveys your sense of the writer's intention.

In choosing your signal verb, consider the attitude or position of the writer you are quoting. Is the writer making a claim? Is she or he agreeing or disagreeing or even conceding a point? Or is the writer's position neutral? It is easy to choose a neutral verb, such as *writes, says,* or *comments.* Whenever possible, though, go beyond these neutral verbs to indicate the writer's attitude:

> Oscar Wilde quipped, "A poet can survive everything but a misprint."

> *More about*
> Verb tense,
> 672–75

For the quotation above, *quipped* (which means "uttered a witty remark") is clearly appropriate, given the cleverness of the sentence quoted. *Snarled,* on the other hand, would not be appropriate: Although Wilde's quip may have an edge to it, few would agree that the comment conveys the anger or viciousness associated with the verb *snarl.*

To maintain your audience's interest, vary the signal words you use, while avoiding verbs that might misrepresent the writer's intentions. (A list of signal verbs appears in the Quick Reference box on p. 278.) You can also vary your placement of the signal phrase:

> E. M. Forster asked, "How do I know what I think until I see what I say?"

> "How do I know what I think," E. M. Forster asked, "until I see what I say?"

> "How do I know what I think until I see what I say?" E. M. Forster asked.

> *More about*
> Paraphrasing,
> 249–57
> Summarizing,
> 257–60
> Using quotation
> marks, 260–62,
> 810–19

17b Showing Source Boundaries

When the material from your source is a quotation, it is easy for the audience to see the source boundaries: The quotation marks indicate where your use of source material begins and ends. When you are paraphrasing or

Quick

Reference Signal Verbs

Neutral Signal Verbs		Signal Verbs That Indicate:		
		Claim/Argument		**Concession**
analyzes	introduces	argues	finds	acknowledges
comments	notes	asserts	holds	admits
compares	observes	believes	maintains	concedes
concludes	records	charges	points out	grants
contrasts	remarks	claims	proposes	
describes	reports	confirms	recommends	
discusses	says	contends	suggests	
explains	shows	demonstrates		
focuses on	states			
illustrates	thinks		**Disagreement**	**Agreement**
indicates	writes	complains	questions	agrees
		contradicts	refutes	concurs

Writers in literature and the other humanities typically use present tense verbs in signal phrases; writers in the sciences use the present or past tense, depending on the context.

criticizes	rejects	confirms
denies	warns	supports
disagrees		

summarizing the source, the place where you begin to use source material may not be clear. Signal phrases help solve the problem; you can place a signal phrase at the beginning of the source material and a parenthetical reference at the end.

Consider this example:

Signal phrase includes source author (full name on first reference)

Quotation marks indicate the beginning and end of the source's exact words

Page in source

Who wouldn't envy the genius and wealth of the person who invented Facebook? But who wouldn't pity a person who has no close friends? David Denby describes Mark Zuckerberg as having great wealth, but he has few confidantes. "*The Social Network* is shrewdly perceptive about such things as class, manners, ethics, and the emptying out of self that accompanies a genius's absorption in his work" (98).

In the example above, it is clear that the first two sentences are the writer's statement of her own ideas, the third sentence is a paraphrase from the Denby source, and the fourth a quotation from Denby. Notice that when the author's name is included in the signal phrase, it does not need to be included in the parenthetical reference.

1. Unpaginated source material

Many sources are accessed electronically and have no page numbers. For an unpaginated source, include only the author's last name in the parenthetical reference:

> "Facebook, which surpassed MySpace in 2008 as the largest social-networking site, now has nearly 500 million members, or 22 percent of all Internet users, who spend more than 500 billion minutes a month on the site" (Rosen).

Source author (last name only)

Rosen, Jeffrey, "The Web Means the End of Forgetting," The New York Times Magazine, July 21, 2010

When you are copying from the source, the quotation marks show where the copying begins and ends.

When you are paraphrasing or summarizing from an electronic source with no page numbers, however, you must work subtly with the material to show your audience where the source use begins and ends. Usually you can do this by using the author's name in the parenthetical reference, and describing the author in a signal phrase:

Signal phrase describes source author

> A writer for *The New York Times* explains how damaging Facebook material can be when one searches for a job (Rosen).

Parenthetical reference identifies source author (last name only)

17c Emphasizing Your Voice

Just as important as signaling source boundaries is the need to signal your own voice. Your readers want to know clearly when it is *you* talking. In the following example it is not clear where the student writer stops drawing from the Rosen source and begins to state his own ideas:

| Signal phrase | Rosen explains, "Seventy percent of US recruiters report that they have rejected candidates because of information found online, like photos and discussion-board conversations and membership in controversial groups." With 500 million people on Facebook, the dangers are widespread. It is ironic that this phenomenon of personal data revealed to the world was begun by a person who himself had poor social skills. |

Rosen, Jeffrey, "The Web Means the End of Forgetting," The New York Times Magazine, July 21, 2010

The use of a signal phrase with a parenthetical reference clarifies the boundaries of the information from Rosen:

| Signal phrase describes source author

Parenthetical reference identifies source author (last name only) | A writer for *The New York Times* explains, "Seventy percent of US recruiters report that they have rejected candidates because of information found online, like photos and discussion-board conversations and membership in controversial groups." With 500 million people on Facebook, the dangers are widespread (Rosen). It is ironic that this phenomenon of personal data revealed to the world was begun by a person who himself had poor social skills. |

> **More about**
> First-person pronouns, 458–59, 709–10

The final sentence in this passage is an interesting one, and the student writer wants to emphasize that it is his own insight. That could be done with first-person singular phrases such as "I believe" or "in my opinion."

Yet in some genres and writing situations (including many college assignments), first-person singular is inappropriate. Fortunately, there are more sophisticated ways to handle the task. One option is to speak in the first-person plural, subtly drawing the audience into the conversation:

A writer for *The New York Times* explains, "Seventy percent of US recruiters report that they have rejected candidates because of information found online, like photos and discussion-board conversations and membership in controversial groups." With 500 million people on Facebook, the dangers are widespread (Rosen). We cannot escape the irony that this phenomenon of personal data revealed to the world was begun by a person who himself had poor social skills.

> Parenthetical reference shows end of source material

> First-person plural suggests shift to student writer's voice

It is even more effective to comment upon the source or its information:

A writer for *The New York Times* explains, "Seventy percent of US recruiters report that they have rejected candidates because of information found online, like photos and discussion-board conversations and membership in controversial groups." With 500 million people on Facebook, the dangers are widespread (Rosen). Such information suggests an irony: This phenomenon of personal data revealed to the world was begun by a person who himself had poor social skills.

> Parenthetical reference shows end of source material

> Transition to student writer's interpretation of source material

In this version, the writer's voice is implicitly clear. He uses the adjective *such* to point to the previous material and then provides his interpretation. Demonstrative pronouns (*this, that, these, those*) can also be used as a transition to the student writer talking about source material.

17d Providing Context

Readers appreciate knowing not only when you are speaking and when your sources are, but also *who* your sources are and why you chose them. *Rhetorical citations* provide this information smoothly: Your citations can explain why you chose the source, what kind of source it is, when the source was published, and what its argument is.

More about
Evaluating
sources,
233–46 (ch. 14)

1. Explain your choice of sources.

Unless your readers are familiar with your sources, they may have no reason to respect them and thus no reason to believe your claims. You can avoid this problem with rhetorical citations that not only name your source but also indicate why you respect the source, as this writer does:

> **Signal phrase includes student writer's opinion of the source**
>
> Gary Wolf provides a helpful, wide-ranging overview of our motivations for gathering and sharing data about ourselves, offering examples like this: "*Foursquare,* a geo-tracking application with about one million users, keeps a running tally of how many times players 'check in' at every locale, automatically building a detailed diary of movements and habits; many users publish these data widely."

In the example above, the writer establishes that the source can be respected for its thorough treatment of the topic.

The selection below acknowledges the shortcomings of the source while also asserting its usefulness:

> **Signal phrase becomes extended explanation of student writer's opinion of the source**
>
> Mezrich has made up parts of his story about Zuckerberg's rise, while claiming he is sticking as closely as possible to reality. Yet his fiction is worth reading; it shows how people perceive Harvard and its geniuses: "There was something playful about those eyes—but that was where any sense of natural emotion or readability ended. His narrow face was otherwise devoid of any expression at all. And his posture, his general aura—the way he seemed closed in on himself, even while engaged in a group dynamic, even here, in the safety of his own fraternity—was almost painfully awkward" (15).
>
> **Page in source**

2. Identify the type of source.

Is your source a newspaper column? A blog? A scholarly article? The differences among types of sources are important. If you want up-to-the-minute information, a newspaper or blog is likely to have it. If you want carefully researched, accurate information, a scholarly journal article is a good choice. Your readers want to know that you have made appropriate source choices, and you can provide such information in rhetorical citations:

<table>
<tr>
<td>Signal phrase describes and identifies source author and his credentials</td>
<td>Writing in The New York Times, journalist Gary Wolf provides a wide-ranging overview of our motivations for gathering and sharing data about ourselves, offering examples like this: "Foursquare, a geo-tracking application with about one million users, keeps a running tally of how many times players 'check in' at every locale, automatically building a detailed diary of movements and habits; many users publish these data widely."</td>
</tr>
</table>

3. Identify the date of publication.

For many topics, the date of publication is important. The number of people who use the Foursquare application, for example, changes constantly. Providing the date on which such information was published helps readers know how fresh the numbers are and how accurate they might still be:

<table>
<tr>
<td>Signal phrase includes publication date of time-sensitive information</td>
<td>In a 2010 article in The New York Times, journalist Gary Wolf says, "Foursquare, a geo-tracking application with about one million users, keeps a running tally of how many times players 'check in' at every locale, automatically building a detailed diary of movements and habits; many users publish these data widely."</td>
</tr>
</table>

Wolf, Gary. "The Data-Driven Life." The New York Times Magazine, April 28, 2010.

4. Identify the larger discussion in the source.

For the most successful, persuasive writing from sources, you need to *read* the sources, rather than just pulling sentences from them. That allows you

More about
Critical reading,
112–35
Avoiding plagia-
rism, 247–64
(ch. 15)

not only to position the quotation, paraphrase, or summary in your text, but also to indicate how it contributed to the source text's discussion. Build a brief source summary into rhetorical citation:

Extended signal phrase includes summary of the source

In a 2010 article in *The New York Times*, journalist Gary Wolf provides a wide-ranging overview of our motivations for gathering and sharing data about ourselves, offering examples like this: *"Foursquare,* a geo-tracking application with about one million users, keeps a running tally of how many times players 'check in' at every locale, automatically building a detailed diary of movements and habits; many users publish these data widely."

The phrase "overview of our motivations for gathering and sharing data about ourselves" summarizes the source.

Citation is not only ethical but rhetorical; in addition to protecting you against charges of plagiarism, it also creates a sophisticated, readable document that audiences are likely to trust.

EXERCISE 17.1 Integrating and identifying source material

Read Lydia Nichols's essay "Holy Underground Comics, Batman! Moving Away from the Mainstream" (pp. 350–59) and note how she integrates her source material. Use one of four different colored highlighting markers to identify each of the different rhetorical moves she uses:

- Parenthetical references that are the only acknowledgment of the source in the sentence (that is, any sentences that have no signal phrases or other cues; just the parenthetical reference)

- Signal phrases

- Phrases that clearly signal her own voice speaking

- References to context: explaining her choice of source, the type of source, or the date of publication

When you have finished highlighting, use what you have learned in this chapter to evaluate how Nichols integrates her sources. What changes would you recommend if she were to revise this essay? Include the page reference in this book where she can read an explanation of each.

Make It **Your Own**

Choose a source-based project you have already written or a draft in progress, and working on a printout of your project, use one of four different colored highlighting markers to identify each of the four different rhetorical moves described in Exercise 17.1

Work **Together**

When you have completed the highlighting, exchange your work with another student and use his or her highlighting and what you have learned so far in this chapter to evaluate the ways he or she integrates sources. For any revisions you recommend, be sure to include the page reference in this book where an explanation can be found.

Now review your own work and the comments and suggestions made by your reader and look for patterns. Which types of signals do you use most? Which do you use least? Make a checklist of issues and use it to help you revise in the future.

If this is a project you are currently drafting, revise to include some of these rhetorical cues in the sections where you seem to have the least transparency regarding sources. Before you look at your project again, write a brief reflection on this process. What did you learn about how sources can be used effectively by reading and evaluating someone else's work? Did your fellow student use any strategies that you think you might try? Did he or she use sources in a way that you would prefer to avoid?

17e Integrating Altered Quotations

Sometimes you may need to alter a quotation so that it fits into your sentence. In her draft for her project on underground comics, Nichols deletes words from one source's quotation because those words do not help her make her point. As long as the meaning is not significantly changed, writers may do any of the following to fit quoted material more fluidly into their own sentences:

- Quote short phrases rather than full sentences
- Add or change words for clarity
- Change capitalization
- Change grammar

> **More about**
> Using ellipses in quotations, 816, 831–32
> Using square brackets in quotations, 816, 828

All added or changed words should be placed in square brackets; deleted words should be replaced with ellipses. The example below shows a responsible alteration of a quotation:

Quotation Integrated into Student Text	Original Quotation
Certain portions of the Comic Book Code were incredibly specific and controlling, such as the rule that forbade "[t]he letters of the word 'crime' on a comics magazine . . . [to] be appreciably greater in dimension than the other words contained in the title" (qtd. in "Good Shall Triumph over Evil").	The letters of the word "crime" on a comics magazine shall never be appreciably greater in dimension than the other words contained in the title.

A capital letter was changed to a lowercase letter, double quotation marks were changed to single, one word was added and a couple of others were omitted, but the overall meaning of the passage remains the same.

Imagine, however, that the writer had made these changes instead:

Quotation Unfairly Altered	Original Quotation
Certain portions of the code allowed some flexibility. Consider, for example, the rule that allowed "[t]he letters of the word 'crime' on a comics magazine . . . [to] be appreciably greater in dimension than the other words contained in the title" (qtd. in "Good Shall Triumph over Evil").	The letters of the word "crime" on a comics magazine shall never be appreciably greater in dimension than the other words contained in the title.

Clearly this alteration of the quotation is not acceptable, as it changes the meaning of the passage completely.

→ **EXERCISE 17.2 Integrating quotations**

Read the passage below. Then, in the following quotations, circle the numbers for those that alter the quotation fairly, and cross through the numbers of those that change the meaning of the quotation.

> The meeting of Normans and Anglo-Saxons at Hastings was the most decisive battle of the Middle Ages and one of the determining days in the making of the West. Hastings changed Britain, which had been dominated since the end of Roman rule by invading tribes from the Continent and the North—Angles, Saxons, and Vikings. This day more than any other turned Britain away from its Scandinavian past and toward

Europe. Hastings inaugurated the era of the knight, the social domi-
nance of those who fought with lance on horseback.

—Howard R. Bloch, *A Needle in the Right Hand of God*.
Random House, 2006, p. 7.

1. Bloch maintains that the Battle of Hastings "turned Britain away from
    its Scandinavian past" and from Europe as well (7).
2. The Battle of Hastings, notes Bloch, gave the "invading tribes from
    the Continent and the North" new power over Britain (7).
3. "[T]hose who fought with lance on horseback" became dominant
    after the Battle of Hastings, observes Bloch (7).
4. Bloch concludes that the fight between the Romans and the invading
    tribes from the Continent and the North was "the most decisive battle
    of the Middle Ages" (7).

self Assessment

**As you revise projects that use sources, review your draft, revising as
necessary, to be sure you:**

☐ Cite your sources. Did you name any from which you are paraphrasing,
  summarizing, or quoting?

☐ Use signal verbs. Did you convey the attitude of your source?

☐ Use signal phrases and parenthetical references. Did you show where
  each source use begins and ends, even when it is unpaginated?

☐ Emphasize your own insights. Did you comment on or analyze the
  source, rather than just repeat it?

☐ Provide relevant contextual information. Did you identify the type of
  source, its date of publication, and its publisher?

☐ Reveal your reasoning. Did you explain why you chose and trusted your
  sources?

Make It **Your Own**

Choose a source-based project you have already written or a draft
in progress, and use the material in this chapter and the tips in
the Self-Assessment box above to help you review the ways you
use and incorporate source material. Make a note of changes that
would strengthen your use of source material, and add any new
items you identify to the checklist in the Self-Assessment.

Writing **Responsibly**

Explaining Your Choice of Sources

Make It Your Own! When college writers share their opinion of their sources, their text is more interesting and convincing. Rather than just quoting from your sources, tell *why* you are quoting them, and your writing will be more persuasive.

In much of your college writing, you select and work with sources: You decide how to use sources to help convey your thesis. Your basic responsibility is to acknowledge those sources, cite them correctly, and provide full publication information about them at the end of your project. When you talk *about* your sources—tell what you think of your source and its information—you invite your audience into your thinking processes and portray yourself as an experienced academic writer.

When college writing instructors involved in the Citation Project studied research projects from US colleges, they noticed how few students talked about their sources. Most of the projects just pulled out information—usually a brief quotation—from sources, as if all the sources were alike. The nature of the sources and the student's thoughts about them remained invisible to the audience. The following example, from a project on sexism and sexual violence, shows the drab result:

First draft

Student's voice	Hostility toward women can be seen even in the ancient West. Stevenson observes,
Quotation	"Livy's underlying message, it would seem, is that Roman men have to regulate public contributions by prominent women, and not accept female advice too easily, without prolonged	citation
	consideration" (189).

The material from the Stevenson source is accurately quoted and cited, and the sentences flow. But the passage provokes questions rather than insights. Who are Stevenson and Livy? Where did this source come from? Why did the writer choose it? Why should the writer's audience respect Stevenson's opinions? What else did the source say? What was the context in which the quotation appeared? These are the kinds of questions readers ask, and answering them will bring your text to life:

Revised draft

Student's voice	Hostility toward women can be seen even in the ancient West. Tom Stevenson, a classics	Citation
Credentials of author and publisher	scholar at the University of Queensland, writes in the scholarly journal *Classical World* that the Roman historian Livy described women who supported their menfolks' success, which	
	might seem to be a compliment to the women. But notice that the women aren't having their	Summary of the remainder of the source
	own successes. Furthermore, all of Livy's women are either described too briefly, or they are	
	flawed. Even as Stevenson provides this analysis, he also cautions against being too simplistic	Counter-evidence

Revised draft continued

> Citation
>
> about Livy's portrayal of women; some of their faults were because their men were flawed. Still, Stevenson concludes, "Livy's underlying message, it would seem, is that Roman men have to regulate public contributions by prominent women, and not accept female advice too easily, without prolonged consideration" (189).
>
> Quotation

Source: Stevenson, Tom. "Women of Early Rome as *Exempla* in Livy, *AB Urbe Condita,* Book1." *Classical World,* vol. 104, no. 2, Winter 2011, pp. 175–89.

Now, not only is the material from the source accurately quoted and cited, but Levy has been identified, and Stevenson's credentials and the authority of the publication have been established, along with a description of his argument.

Sometimes you choose to use a source because you like its argument or presentation of information, even if it may not be particularly scholarly. In these cases, too, you should let your audience know why you have chosen the source:

> Information about why the writer chose this source
>
> Summary of some information in the source
>
> Citation
>
> One good way to understand the treatment of women in contemporary society is to consult news media. They are not reports of research written by experts, but rather are sources that reflect and shape popular opinion. *Time* magazine publishes an article on date rape because it believes this is an issue that readers will or should care about. It also reports on current events. So it is *Time* that reports on a congressional bill intended to reduce sexual violence in colleges. Why is the bill needed? The answer is in the shocking numbers the magazine cites: "One in five college women will be the victim of a sexual assault (and 6% of men)" (Webley).
>
> Student's voice
>
> Quotation

Source: Webley, Kayla. "It's Not Just Yale: Are Colleges Doing Enough to Combat Sexual Violence?" *Time,* 18 Apr. 2011, time.com/time/nation/article/0,8599,2065849,00.html?xid=fblike.

Assessment

self

Review your work with each source. Have you done the following?

☐ Identify the author of the source and his or her credentials. Did you show what makes you trust this person? ▶ *Analyzing and crafting arguments, 136–64*

☐ Identify the publisher of the source and its credentials. Did you show what makes you trust this organization? ▶ *Finding information, 210–32*

☐ Consider the date of publication. Did you provide and comment on the publication date, if it affects your trust in the source?

☐ Summarize the source. Did you indicate how the selection you have drawn from contributed to the argument the source was making? ▶ *Evaluating information, 233–46*

☐ Provide additional discussion. Did you help your audience understand the reasons you chose this source and your selections from it?

Writing **Responsibly**

Understanding and Representing the Entire Source

Make It Your Own! For a research project to be worthwhile, it should represent the overall arguments of its sources—more than just a few sentences—so that readers can understand what the sources were saying and how they fit together.

Each time you write from sources, push yourself to work with them in more substantial ways. Take the time to read each source—the entire source—carefully. Next, **summarize** it, as a way of processing the information: Restate, concisely and in fresh language, the main claims (and the most important supporting evidence) of an entire source. Then when you draft your research project, blend in summaries of your important sources, so that your readers understand how they, too, contribute to your discussion.

Page Cited

DATA FROM **The Citation Project**

Researchers found that although most college writers quote from the first pages of a source, the best research projects drew from the entire source.

You can also draw from sources by quoting or paraphrasing brief passages. But if you simply paste a quotation into your draft, how much do you or your audience actually understand the source or even the passage you are quoting? **Paraphrasing** is a better alternative, because it pushes you to think about the passage: to know the material well enough to restate it in your own words. Changing just a few words in the passage, however, is not paraphrasing; it is **patchwriting**: a mixture of your words and the source's. This is an error interpreted by many readers as plagiarism.

Because quoting and patchwriting do not require much comprehension and are easy to do, inexperienced college writers rely on them too heavily. Frequently, too, the quotations come from the first few pages of the source—which some students feel is all they have to read. Researchers with the Citation Project found that the majority of college writers' citations came from the first two pages of the source (see chart) and felt the quality of these projects suffered. That is because, in most sources, the first few pages discuss only general findings, while the insightful, detailed examples and evidence that are important to a good analysis or argument are deeper in the text.

When a writer provides only isolated quotations from sources ("dropped quotations"), the result may be uninformative, like this passage from a project about social media and individual identity:

First draft

Student's voice People value their personal lives and try to separate their private and public selves. Many are aware of being different people in the workplace, in school, on a date. All this may be changing, though. "The fact that the Internet never seems to forget is threatening, at an almost existential level, our ability to control our identities; to preserve the option of reinventing ourselves and starting anew; to overcome our checkered pasts" (Rosen).

Quotation

Parenthetical citation

Notice how, in this draft, readers are given no information about the source; they are presented only with one sentence from it. This causes the reader to wonder: Does the writer understand the source, or has she simply found a "killer quote" that supports her argument? Because the writer provides only the isolated quotation, it is not even clear what her purpose is in including it.

Now consider how this passage is transformed by adding a summary and contextualized quotations:

Revised draft

> People value their personal lives, and many deliberately work to keep their private and public selves separate. Many of us are aware, too, of being different people in the workplace, in school, on the athletic field, on a date. Some value these differences, happy to switch from dedicated intellectual in the classroom to enthusiastic player on the soccer field.
>
> All this may be changing, though. Writing in *The New York Times*, journalist Jeffrey Rosen points out that we may no longer be in control of the multiple identities that were previously taken for granted. In our online lives, what we post on Facebook and Twitter can easily merge with what we post on a school blog, in our comments on a news story, or in our pictures on Flickr. Rosen explains that even in untagged pictures, our faces can be identified through facial-recognition technology. He also describes the privacy-protecting laws that are in development and the companies that offer services to clean up our online reputations. Most central to my research, though, is his explanation for this claim: "The fact that the Internet never seems to forget is threatening, at an almost existential level, our ability to control our identities; to preserve the option of reinventing ourselves and starting anew; to overcome our checkered pasts."

Margin notes: Student's voice | Signal phrase providing information about the author | Summary of the parts of the source relevant to the student's argument | Summary of the remainder of the source | Student's voice | Quotation (no page reference because source is unpaginated)

Source: Rosen, Jeffrey. "The Web Means the End of Forgetting." *The New York Times,* 21 July 2010, www.nytimes.com/2010/07/25/magazine/25privacy-t2.html?pagewanted=all&_r=0.

The writer has shown responsibility to her source, her topic, and her audience. Because she has taken the time to read and understand the source, she is able to summarize it to show what its main claims are. Her audience now knows how the quotation was used in the source and how it supports her argument. With this brief summary, the writer has also explained her ideas clearly and established a "conversation" between herself, her source, and her audience—that is, rather than just "using" sources, she is thinking about them, interacting with them, and giving her audience enough information that they can do the same.

self | Assessment

Review and revise your work with each source. Have you done the following?

☐ Read, understand, and accurately represent the whole source. Did you look for the details deeper in the source?

☐ Summarize the main ideas of the source. Did you put the source's ideas in your own words, fairly and accurately? ▶ *Paraphrasing, 253–57*

☐ Incorporate your summary into your source analysis. Did you use the best examples and evidence?

☐ Locate the most relevant passages. Did you cite from *throughout* the source?
   ▶ *Critical reading, 111–35*

Writing **Responsibly**

Choosing and Unpacking Complex Sources

Make It Your Own! Research projects that rely heavily on short, simple sources tend to be simplistic and awkward. If you find, read, and write about lengthy, complex sources, you will produce superior scholarship.

Everyone wants to be efficient, yet college writers trying to save time may inadvertently do themselves and their audience a disservice when they write. While incorporating research into their projects, too many writers choose only short, simple sources that can be read quickly (see chart), and the quality of their writing suffers.

Researchers with the Citation Project were struck by the extent to which the quality of students' research projects was reduced by the shallowness of their sources. More than half of the projects' citations were to a source no longer than five pages, resulting in projects that were simplistic and unimpressive. They lacked the complex information and in-depth opinions that are essential to good research and interesting writing.

Length of Source Cited
DATA FROM **The Citation Project**

Length of Source	Percent of citations (n = 1,911)
1–2 pages	26
3–5 pages	24
6–12 pages	22
13–30 pages	14
31 or more pages	14

Researchers found that while most college research writers choose short, simple sources, the best writers work from lengthy, complex sources that bring details and insight—and not just basic facts—to the topic.

Writers relying on short sources work with too small a toolbox. Their projects will have very little to say if there is very little to draw on. Sources that are more extensive, in contrast, explore the interesting complexities and important debates about their topic. Such sources give writers—and the writers' audience—things to think about and talk about. They provide essential research material that leads to rich analysis and well-grounded argument.

Simply choosing lengthy sources is not enough, however. You should also "unpack" your sources—share with your audience the complexities and insights of your sources. Note how, in the following example, from an article on unnecessary medical procedures, complexity is lacking when the writer simply drops a quotation into his text and lets it speak for him:

First draft

Student's voice

Every time a person goes to the doctor, he or she should be aware of the risks of unnecessary medical testing. A doctor from San Francisco says, "[M]ost experts agree that overuse needs to be curbed. If it isn't, we could face a future public health problem of rising cancer rates, thanks to our medical overzealousness" (Parikh).

Signal phrase

Parenthetical citation

Quotation

The writer offers a quotation that supports his argument, and he has cited the quotation correctly. He has also provided some information about the writer of the source. However, because this quotation stands alone, readers of this student's project may think that the source made this statement as a simple directive: *Overuse of medical tests should stop.* In fact, the source offered a detailed review of the reasons for the overuse of CT scans, as well as a thoughtful set of recommendations.

Such information deserves to be represented. It is part of your responsibility to your audience and topic to show the whole picture that the source offers. Consider how much more interesting, informative, and persuasive the passage becomes when it provides more information and context:

Revised draft

Student's voice	Every time a person goes to the doctor, he or she should be aware of the risks of unnecessary medical testing. San Francisco Bay Area pediatrician Rahul Parikh says that CT scans are a dangerously overused test, putting children in particular risk for cancer due to the radiation levels in the procedure. "[M]ost experts agree that overuse needs to be curbed. If it isn't, we could face a future public health problem of rising cancer rates, thanks to our medical overzealousness," says Parikh. He notes, though, that the test is quick and easy. Moreover, television medical shows give people a general awareness of tests like the CT scan, and thus patients may demand it even when it is not medically necessary. Doctors, too, have a reason for overusing the test: It is financially profitable. In addition to recommending that the test be administered less often, Parikh advocates adjusting the radiation dose when the CT scan is administered to children.

Annotations:
- Signal phrase
- Quotation
- Signal phrase
- Summary that clarifies the argument of the source
- Summary of the source's complex treatment of the topic
- Signal phrase

Source: Parikh, Rahul. "How TV Illustrates a Disturbing Medical Trend." *Salon,* 18 Apr. 2011, www.salon.com/2011/04/18/poprx_unncessary_tests/.

Notice that in the first draft, it sounds as if the doctor quoted is talking about all medical testing; the second draft shows that in fact Parikh was talking about a specific test, the CT scan. Choosing extensive sources, paying attention to the complexity of the material, and incorporating that complexity into your project not only increases the sophistication of your own writing; it can also save you from misrepresenting the source.

Assessment

Review your work with each source, revising as necessary, to be sure you:

☐ Choose lengthy, detailed sources. Did you find material that provides insights and debates on the topic? ▶ *Finding information, 210–32*

☐ Discuss the complexities of your sources' treatment of their topic. Did you go beyond simple, basic facts? ▶ *Analyzing, interpreting, synthesizing, and critiquing, 263–64; "Understanding and Representing the Entire Source," 290–91*

☐ Explain any material you quote. Did you give background on every source? ▶ *Relevance and reliability, 233–39*

Writing **Responsibly**

Blending Voices in Your Text

Make It Your Own! Good researched writing is more than collecting the ideas of others; it is instead an exploration of how the sources have helped researchers develop their own ideas. You will produce better work if, as you draft your project, you let your readers see *your* thinking.

Whenever you write from sources, you are blending the voices of your sources with one another and with your own. Although *voice* sometimes refers to the difference between passive and active voice, it also refers to who is talking in the text—the writer or the source.

Your audience wants to know whose voice it is "hearing." When you quote, it knows you are importing the voice of the source. When you **paraphrase** (rewrite the information in fresh language), your audience hears you talking. But when you **patchwrite** (copy from sources and make minor changes to its language, but not actually paraphrase), you lead your audience to the mistaken belief that it is hearing you when in fact it is neither your voice nor the source's, but rather an inappropriate mixture of the two. To blend voices successfully, you need to avoid patchwriting and show the beginning and end of your use of sources.

Most readers consider it plagiarism when a writer patchwrites. Regardless of whether he or she classifies it as plagiarism, no reader considers patchwriting good writing. The following passage from a source discussing the history of child psychology, followed by a student's first-draft writing from that source, illustrates the issue:

Passage from source

> In the 1910s and later, as child psychology became an academic discipline, teachers increasingly looked to educational researchers rather than librarians as the central experts in children's reading.

Patchwriting

> From the 1910s on, child psychology became a discipline, and teachers more and more thought that educational researchers rather than librarians were the main experts in children's reading (248).

The patchwriting follows the original sentence, deleting a few words and substituting some others, but still dependent on the language and arrangement of the source sentence. Not knowing that this is a blend of two voices—the writer's and the source's—the reader is misled to think this is the student's voice.

Paraphrase

> Child psychology emerged as an academic discipline in the early twentieth century, prompting teachers to look to researchers for expertise about children's reading. Librarians were no longer the primary authority on the topic (248).

The paraphrase appropriately uses keywords from the original, such as *discipline* and *child psychology*, but it otherwise uses fresh language and fresh sentence arrangement to restate the source.

Ground your own writing in paraphrase and summary, include some quotation, and avoid patchwriting altogether. This will allow your voice, rather than those of your sources, to dominate your text. This strategy requires your conscious effort and practice. Writing true paraphrase is an advanced skill that many college writers do not practice (see chart), but those who master this skill write the most successful research projects.

To let your readers know when you are paraphrasing or summarizing, use a signal phrase at the beginning of the source use and a parenthetical citation at the end. If your use of sources is lengthy, you can also occasionally mention the source or the author as you write, just to remind your readers that they are reading your summary or paraphrase of a source:

Students' Use of Sources
DATA FROM **The Citation Project**

- Summarizing 6%
- Patchwriting 16%
- Direct quotation 46%
- Paraphrasing 32%

Percent (*n* = 1,911)

Researchers found that while most college research writers use quoting and patchwriting, the best projects were by those who use summary and paraphrase.

Marking where the source use begins and ends

Signal phrase at beginning of source use → McDowell explains that the academic discipline of child psychology, which emerged in the early twentieth century, looked to researchers for expertise about children's reading. Librarians were no longer the leading authorities on the topic. Both librarians and child psychologists were interested in children's reading patterns, but for different reasons. The librarians, ← Paraphrase of a sentence from the source

Signal phrase within the source use → McDowell says, wanted to understand what sorts of texts would interest children so they could get them into the library. Child psychologists, in contrast, wanted to understand the children themselves. Both groups collected information about children's reading, but they did it in different ways. The librarians observed children's reading and reported on their observations, while the child psychologists conducted scientific research (248-49). ← Summary of two pages in the source

← Parenthetical citation at end of source use

Source: McDowell, Kathleen. "Toward a History of Children as Readers, 1890–1930." *Book History,* vol. 12, 2009, pp. 240–65.

self Assessment

Review your work with each source, revising as necessary, to be sure you:

☐ Use paraphrase and summary. Did you avoid overreliance on quotations?
  ▶ *Summarizing, 257–58; paraphrasing, 253–57; patchwriting, 248*

☐ Paraphrase while avoiding patchwriting. Did you restate source material in fresh language and fresh sentences? ▶ *Taking notes and avoiding plagiarism, 251–52*

☐ Use signal phrases and parenthetical citations. Did you let your audience know where your paraphrase and summary begins and ends? ▶ *Voice, 279–81*

Writing **Responsibly**

Acknowledging Indirect Sources

Make It Your Own! Confusing direct and indirect sources is a common problem. Fortunately, the procedures for correctly representing indirect sources in your research projects are not hard to learn, and following them will subtly enhance your writing.

When you cite sources, you do not just inform your audience about where you obtained your information; you let your audience know who is speaking in the source. If your source quotes or uses ideas from another writer, that other writer is for you an indirect source[1]. You are not reading that other writer yourself but are reading what he or she said. If you want to use that material from the indirect source, you should acknowledge the indirect source as well as the source that was talking about it. This is a sophisticated technique that takes practice to master; researchers with the Citation Project discovered that citing indirect sources accurately was a challenge for first-year college writers, separating them from experienced writers.

The following example, from a project exploring the Graduate Equivalency Diploma (GED) alternative to traditional high schools, shows how the problem occurs:

Student's first draft

Paraphrase of passage in source
Quotation from source

> Nontraditional high school students in the GED Options Pathway program shouldn't be labeled "GED kids"; they should be judged on their individual accomplishments. "This is supposed to be the land of the free and equal opportunity and all that stuff" (Peterson).

In-text citation

Peterson, who is cited in the sample above, is the writer of the newspaper story in which the quotation appears. However, Peterson does not speak the sentence in quotation marks. That sentence is being spoken by another source, whom Peterson is quoting in the following passage:

Passage from source

> The program does use the Graduate Equivalency Degree, or GED, as a tool. The students all have to pass the test's five sections, but when they complete the program they earn a regular high school diploma. This is an important point for Robbins, and she stresses that her students will get to graduate with their classes.
>
> "In fact, I'm trying to get everybody to quit calling them those GED kids," she said. "Number one, they've labeled them. That irritates me. This is supposed to be land of the free and equal opportunity and all that stuff. Don't label my kids. Let them prove what they can do. Let the test scores speak."

Quoted passage

---

[1]The terms *indirect source* and *indirect quotation* are often used interchangeably.

When you are drawing on material from a source that is quoting, paraphrasing, or summarizing another, your citations should accurately indicate who is speaking and should also indicate where you found the material. This can be accomplished in a parenthetical citation, a signal phrase, or a combination of the two:

Parenthetical citation: Name the speaker, write "qtd. in" (quoted in), then name the source's author

Paraphrase of passage in source

Quotation from source

> Students in the GED Options Pathway program should not be labeled "GED kids"; they should be judged on their individual accomplishments. "This is supposed to be the land of the free and equal opportunity and all that stuff" (Robbins, qtd. in Peterson).

Parenthetical citation identifies speaker and source

Signal phrase: Name both the speaker and the source in your text

Signal phrase identifies source and speaker

> Journalist Erica Peterson reports teacher Anastasia Robbins's beliefs: Students in the GED Options Pathway program should not be labeled "GED kids"; they should be judged on their individual accomplishments. "This is supposed to be the land of the free and equal opportunity and all that stuff," says Robbins.

Paraphrase of passage in source

Quotation

Combination of signal phrase and parenthetical citation:

Signal phrase identifies the speaker

Quotation

> Teacher Anastasia Robbins believes that students in the GED Options Pathway program should not be labeled "GED kids"; they should be judged on their individual accomplishments. "This is supposed to be the land of the free and equal opportunity and all that stuff" (qtd. in Peterson).

Paraphrase of passage in source

Parenthetical citation identifies speaker and source

Source: Peterson, Erica. "W.Va. Program Gives High-Risk Students an Option." *West Virginia Gazette*, 24 Apr. 2011, www.wvgazettemail.com/News/201104240499.

Providing the name of the person being quoted (regardless of whether it is a person who was interviewed or another author) is all you need for acknowledging your indirect source; that name should not be in the list of works cited at the end of your project, since you did not read the original article or interview that person. The source you were reading, though, should be both cited in your project and included in your list of works cited.

self

Assessment

Review your work to be sure that whenever you work from an indirect source, you:

☐ Cite the direct source. Did you name the source in which you found the material and include only the direct source in your list of works cited? ▶ *Direct versus indirect sources, 711–12*

☐ Use parenthetical citation, signal phrases, or a combination of both to acknowledge the name of the speaker in the indirect source and the author of the source in which you found the material. Did you make clear who is speaking? ▶ *Signal phrases, 277–81*

Text Credits

p. 277: Forster, E. M., *Aspects of the Novel* (Edward Arnold, 1927). **pp. 286–287: 17.2** Bloch, R. Howard, *A Needle in the Right Hand of God: The Norman Conquest of 1066 and the Making and Meaning of the Bayeux Tapestry* Random House, 2006, p. 7.

Part Five

Documentation
Matters

© Image Source/Getty Images RF

Book (Printed)

MLA style:

author   title   publication information

King, Laura A. *Experience Psychology.* McGraw-Hill Education, 2016.

               imprint-publisher   publication date

APA style:

author   title   publication information

King, L.A. (2016). *Experience psychology.* New York, NY: McGraw-Hill Education.

publication   place of   imprint-publisher
date   publication

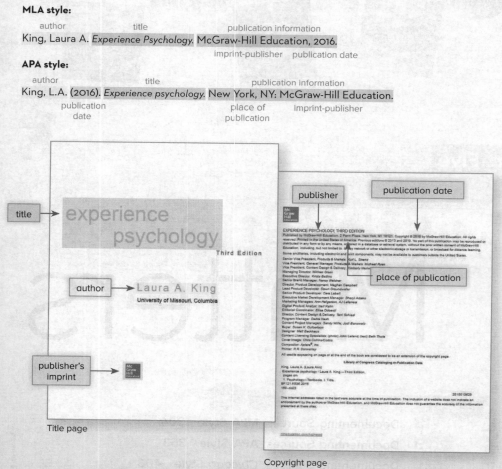

Title page

Copyright page

Look for the information you need to document a printed book on the book's title page and copyright page. In APA style, if more than one location for the publisher is listed on the title page, use the first. (For more about documenting a book, see pp. 321–30 for MLA style, pp. 374–81 for APA style.)

Journal Article (Printed)

MLA style:

author · title and subtitle (article)

Chaubal, Mekhala, and Tatum Taylor. "Lessons from 5Pointz: Toward Legal Protection of Collaborative,

Evolving Heritage." *Future Anterior*, vol. 12, no. 1, 2015, pp. 77–97.

vol.↑ · year · pages

APA style:

author · year · title and subtitle (article)

Chaubal, M. & Taylor, T. (2015). Lessons from 5pointz: Toward legal protection of collaborative, evolving

heritage. *Future Anterior, 12*(1), 77–97.

vol.↑ · pages

Journal table of contents · First page of article

Look for the information you need to document a journal article on the cover or table of contents of the journal and on the first and last pages of the article. (For more about documenting an article from a printed or online periodical, see pp. 330–34 for MLA style, pp. 381–68 for APA style.)

Journal Article from an Online Database

MLA style:

author   title and subtitle (article)

Joselit, Jenna Weissman. "The Brooklyn Thrill-Kill Gang and the Great Comic Book Scare of the 1950s."

        journal   issue ▼

American Jewish History, vol. 100, no. 1, Jan. 2016. *Web of Science*, doi:10.1353/ajh.2016.0015.

                vol.▲   pub. date   database

APA style:

author   year   title and subtitle (article)

Joselit, J. W. (2016). The Brooklyn Thrill-Kill Gang and the great comic book scare of the 1950s.

        journal

American Jewish History, *100*, 155–56. doi:10.1353/ajh.2016.0015

             vol.▲   pages

Database screen: full record of article

Look for the information you need to document an article you accessed through an online database on the search results screen, the full record of the article, or the first and last pages of the article itself. (For more about documenting an article accessed through an online database, see pp. 331–33 for MLA style, pp. 382–84 for APA style.)

Short Work on a Website

MLA style:

author — web page title — website title

Wulf, Karin. "The Importance of Academic (History) Writing." *The Scholarly Kitchen,*

pub. date — URL for web page

27 Jan. 2016, scholarlykitchen.sspnet.org/2016/01/27/the-importance-of-academic-history-writing/.

APA style:

author — web page title — pub. date — website title — retrieval statement

Wulf, K. *The scholarly kitchen.* (2016, January 27). The importance of academic (history) writing. Retrieved

URL for web page

from https://scholarlykitchen.sspnet.org/2016/01/27/the-importance-of-academic-history-writing/

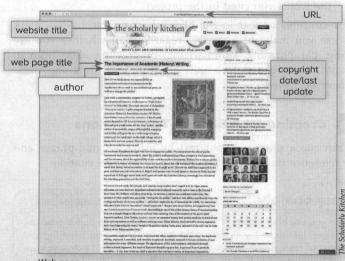

website title

the scholarly kitchen

URL

web page title

The Importance of Academic (History) Writing

author

copyright date/last update

The Scholarly Kitchen

Web page

Frequently, the information you need to create a complete entry in the list of works cited is missing or difficult to find on web pages. Look at the top or bottom of the web page or home page or for a link to an "About" or "Contact Us" page. (For more about documenting online sources, see pp. 334–37 for MLA style, pp. 386–88 for APA style.)

18 Documenting Sources: MLA Style

Developed by the Modern Language Association (MLA), MLA style guidelines are used by many researchers in the humanities—especially in languages and literature—to cite and document sources and to format researched projects in a uniform way. These guidelines are revised every few years, to accommodate writers' needs in a time of ongoing changes in the technologies used for researching and writing from sources. The *MLA Handbook* (8th ed.) requires that writers acknowledge sources in two ways:

- **Citation:** In the body of your project, provide an in-text citation for each source used.
- **Documentation:** At the project's end, provide a list of all the works you cited in the project.

In-text citations appear in the body of your project. They mark each use you make of a source, regardless of whether you are quoting, paraphrasing, summarizing, or drawing ideas from it. They also alert readers to a shift between *your* ideas and those you have borrowed.

> *More about*
> Documenting a
>   Source: MLA
>   Style and APA
>   Style, 300–03
>   (*Documentation
>   Matters* tutorial
>   preceding this
>   chapter)
> Popular academic
>   styles per dis-
>   cipline, 457,
>   476–477
> APA style,
>   363–405
>   (ch. 19)
> *Chicago* style,
>   406–434
>   (ch. 20)
> CSE style,
>   435–50 (ch. 21)

18a Creating MLA-Style In-Text Citations

You can cite a source in your text by using a signal phrase and page reference (in parentheses) or a parenthetical citation:

Writing Responsibly | Citing and Documenting Sources

When you cite and document sources, you demonstrate how thoroughly you have researched your topic and how carefully you have thought about your sources, which encourages your audience to believe you are a credible researcher. In your citations and documentation you acknowledge any material that you have borrowed from a source and you join the conversation on your topic by adding your own interpretation. Accurate entries in the body of your project and list of works cited allow your audience to find and read your sources so that they can evaluate your interpretation and learn more about the subject themselves. Accurate entries also demonstrate the care with which you have written your research project, which further reinforces your credibility, or ethos.

to AUDIENCE

- *Signal phrase.* Include the author's name and an appropriate verb in your sentence before the borrowed material, and put the page number(s) in parentheses after the borrowed material. Often you will use just the author's surname, and you should never use the author's first name alone.

More about
Signal verbs,
275–87 (ch. 17)

> signal phrase
> While encouraging writers to use figurative language, journalist Constance Hale cautions
> page no.
> that "a metaphor has the shelf life of a fresh vegetable" (224), illustrating the
> warning with her own lively metaphor.

Qualifications of
source author

Using a signal phrase allows you to integrate the borrowed material into your sentence, to put the source in context by adding your own interpretation, and to describe the qualifications of the source author. For these reasons, most summaries, paraphrases, and quotations should be introduced by a signal phrase.

- *Parenthetical citation.* Include in parentheses the author's surname plus the page number(s) from which the borrowed material comes:

> While figurative language can make a passage come alive, be aware that metaphors
> parenthetical note
> have "the shelf life of a fresh vegetable" (Hale 224).

Parenthetical citations are useful when you are citing more than one source, when you are establishing facts, or when the author's identity is not relevant to the point you are making.

NOTE The works-cited entry is the same whether you use a signal phrase or a parenthetical citation:

More about
Creating works-
cited entries,
321–44

> author   title   publication info
> Hale, Constance. *Sin and Syntax.* Broadway, 2001.

---

1. Include enough information to lead readers to the source in your list of works cited.

Whether you are using a signal phrase or a parenthetical citation, in-text citations should provide enough information for readers to locate the source in the

More about
What you do and
  do not need to
  cite, 364–66
Signal phrases,
  276–87
Signal verbs
  (list), 278
Integrating bor-
  rowed material
  into your text,
  276–77

Quick Reference | **General Principles of In-Text Citation**

- Cite not only direct quotations but also paraphrases, summaries, and infor-mation gathered from a source, whether printed or online.
- In most cases, include the author's surname and a page reference. For one-page and unpaginated sources (such as websites), provide only the author's name.
- Place the name(s) either in a signal phrase or in a parenthetical citation. A signal phrase makes it easier to integrate borrowed information or the author's credentials into your own prose. A parenthetical citation is appro-priate when establishing facts or citing more than one source for a piece of information.
- For two or more sources by the same author, include the title—either a complete title in the text or an abbreviated title in the parenthetical citation.
- Whenever you add a title or abbreviated title, insert a comma between the surname and the title, but not between the title and the page number. In parenthetical citations, do not insert punctuation between the author's surname and the page number.

List of works cited. In most cases, providing the author's surname and a page reference is enough. Occasionally, however, you may need to provide more information:

Example 6, 312

- If you cite more than one source by the same author, mention the title of the work in the text or include a shortened form of the title in the in-text citation. (You may also want to mention the title of the work, if it is relevant to the point you are making.)

Example 7, 312

- If you refer to sources by two different authors who have the same surname, mention the authors' first names in the text, or include the authors' first initials in the in-text citation.

Occasionally, you may need to include less information. For example, you would omit a page number when you are summarizing an entire source, when your source is just one page long, or when your source, such as a web page, is not paginated.

Example 8, 312
Example 16a, 318

2. Place in-text citations to avoid distracting readers and show them where borrowed material starts and stops.

When you incorporate a quotation, paraphrase, summary, or idea from a source into your own text, carefully consider the placement of the in-text citation, keeping the following goals in mind:

Tech **Page References and Web Pages**

Despite the term *web page*, most websites do not have page numbers in the sense that printed books do. Your browser may number the pages when you print a web page from a website, but this numbering appears only on your printed copy. Different computers and printers break pages differently, so your printed page 5 might be someone else's page 4 or 6. For this reason, in-text citations of most web pages include only the author's name. If a website numbers its paragraphs, provide that information in place of a page reference.

- To make clear exactly which material is drawn from the source
- To avoid distracting your reader

Signal phrase When using a signal phrase, bookend the borrowed information: Insert the author's name before, and the page number after, the cited material.

> Daniels, who has written several books about DC Comics' creations, notes that underground comics artists are not controlled by corporate interests that discourage daring material (165).

signal phrase

Page number

Parenthetical citation When using a parenthetical citation, place the note at a natural pause—at the end of a phrase, clause, or sentence—right after the borrowed material and before any punctuation.

More about
Phrases, 619–22
Clauses, 622–25
Sentences, 625–27

Following a sentence

> Common themes of underground comics include sex and sexual identity, politics, and social issues (Daniels 165).

Following a clause

> Other common themes of underground comics include sex and sexual identity, politics, and social issues (Daniels 165), as shown in Robert Crumb's *Snarf* comics.

Following a phrase

> The themes of underground comics, such as sex and sexual identity, politics, and social
>
> issues (Daniels 165), are all demonstrated in Robert Crumb's *Snarf* comics.

More about
Block quotations,
315, 346–47

Block quotations When the text you are quoting takes up more than four lines of your project, indent the borrowed material as a block by one-half inch from the left margin, and place the parenthetical citation one space after the closing punctuation mark. No quotation marks should be used when indenting quoted material as a block.

Example

> signal phrase
> Howard and Kennedy assert that parents and school officials tend to ignore
>
> hazing until an incident becomes public knowledge. They describe a concrete
>
> incident that demonstrates their claims:
>
> 1/2" → In general, the Bredvik school community (parents, teachers, coaches, and stu-
>
>   dents) condoned or ignored behaviors that could be called "hazing" or "sexual
>
>   harassment." However, when the incident was formally brought to the attention of
>
>   the larger, public audience, a conflict erupted in the community over how to frame,
>
>   understand, and react to the event. (347–48)

3. Adjust in-text citations to match your source.

The exact form of an in-text citation depends on the source. Does it have one author, several authors, or no authors? Is the source paginated? Is the source a novel, a story in an anthology, or a PowerPoint presentation? The examples below cover the most common source types. (A list of in-text citation examples in MLA style appears on page 310.) For more unusual sources, study the general principles as outlined here and in the *MLA Handbook*, 8th ed. (available in any library), and adapt them to your special circumstances.

Writing
Responsibly Using Signal Phrases to Demonstrate Your Relationship with Sources

More about
Integrating sup-
porting material,
276–77
When to use
signal phrases,
277, 278

As you consider using a source, think about *why* you want to use it. Does it provide a supporting reason or illustration? Does it provide an authoritative voice? Does it make a point that contrasts with your own? Then include a signal phrase that reflects your answer to that question.

Tom Bergin, who covers the oil and gas industry for Reuters, provides one example of the consequences of offshore drilling.

Neurobiologist Catherine Levine agrees with this point of view.

The views of meteorologist John Coleman contrast dramatically with those of the majority of climate scientists.

to TOPIC

1. One author
a. Signal phrase

Cahill cautions responsible historians against disparaging the Middle Ages. Medieval Europe's reputation as a time of darkness, ignorance, and blind faith is "largely (if not wholly) undeserved" (310).

page no.

b. Parenthetical citation

The Middle Ages are often unjustly characterized as a time of darkness, ignorance, and blind faith (Cahill 310).

2. Two authors
Include the surnames of the two authors in your signal phrase or parenthetical citation; use *and*, not an ampersand (&), in the parenthetical citation.

To write successfully about their families, authors must have motives beyond merely exposing secret histories (Miller and Paola 72).

MLA In-Text
Citations Index

1. One author
2. Two authors
3. Three or more authors
4. Group, government, or corporate author

MLA In-Text
Citations Index

3. Three or more authors For sources with three or more authors, insert the Latin phrase *et al.* following the first author's surname.

NOTE *al.* is an abbreviation, so it requires a period; *et* is a complete word, so it does not. There should be no punctuation between the author's name and *et al.* Do not italicize this Latin phrase in your citation.

et al. Abbreviation of the Latin phrase *et alii*, "and others"

> 1st author's surname + et al. in signal phrase
> Visonà et al. stress that symbols used in African art are not intended to be iconic but instead to suggest a wide variety of meanings. The authors liken this complexity to "a telephone line that carries multiple messages simultaneously" (19).

> Symbols used in African art are not intended to be iconic but rather to
>
> 1st author + et al.
> suggest a complex range of meanings (Visonà et al. 19).

Do the same in your list of works cited.

Example 3, 324

4. Group, government, or corporate author When a government agency, corporation, or other organization is listed as the author, use that organization's name in your in-text citation. The MLA suggests incorporating names into your sentence in a signal phrase to avoid long parenthetical citations.

> government agency as author
> The Federal Emergency Management Agency indicates that Kansas City is located in a
>
> region of frequent and intense tornado activity (4).

If a parenthetical citation makes more sense in the context, use common abbreviations (such as "Dept." for *Department*) to shorten the name where you can.

5. Unnamed author If the author is unnamed and the work is alphabetized by title in the list of works cited, use the title in your in-text citation. Abbreviate long titles in parenthetical citations.

> One nineteenth-century children's book vows that "when examined by the microscope,
>
> the flea is a pleasant object," and the author's vivid description of this sight—a body
>
> "curiously adorned with a suit of polished armor, neatly jointed, and beset with a great
>
> number of sharp pins almost like the quills of a porcupine"—may win readers' curiosity,
>
> title
> if not their sympathy (*Insects* 8).

If you do abbreviate the title, start your abbreviation with the word by which the title will be alphabetized in your list of works cited. Also, only if the author is listed specifically as "Anonymous" should you use that designation.

Example 4, 324

6. Two or more sources by the same author When you draw on two or more sources by the same author, differentiate between those sources by including titles.

---

book title
In her book *Nickel and Dimed*, social critic Barbara Ehrenreich demonstrates that

people cannot live on the then-current minimum wage (60). Perhaps, as she notes in her

blog entry title
blog entry "'Values' Voters Raise Minimum Wages," they will be a little better able to

hold their own in the six states (Arizona, Colorado, Montana, Missouri, Nevada, Ohio)

that have recently raised their minimum wage.

---

7. Two or more authors with the same surname When you cite sources by two different authors with the same surname, differentiate them by including their first names (the first time you mention them in a signal phrase) or by including their first initials (in a parenthetical reference or subsequent in-text citations).

Including citations is important not only because they give credit but also because they

"organize a field of inquiry, create order, and allow for accountability" (S. Rose 243).

This concern for acknowledging original sources dates back to the early eighteenth

century: Joseph Addison was one of the first to argue for "the superiority of original to

imitative composition" (M. Rose 114).

---

8. Entire source (including a one-page source) Mention an entire source— whether it is a film or a website, a book or an article, a painting or a graphic novel—in your text using the information that begins the entry in your list of works cited.

Example 41b, 339

> The film *The Lady Eve* asks whether love is possible without trust.

Example 10, 326

9. Selection from an anthology If your source is a selection from an anthology, reader, or other collection, your citation should name the author of the selection—not the editor of the anthology. In the example below, Faulkner is the author of the selection "A Rose for Emily," a story that appears in a literature anthology edited by Robert DiYanni.

MLA In-Text Citations Index

> Southern fiction often explores the marked curiosity that women of stature and mystery
> author of selection
> inspire in their communities. Faulkner's "A Rose for Emily," for example, describes the
> title character as "a tradition, a duty, and a care; a sort of hereditary obligation upon
> the town . . ." (79).

10. Multivolume source If you use information from more than one volume of a multivolume work, your in-text citation must indicate both the volume and the page from which you are borrowing. (This information can be omitted if you use only one volume of the work, since your works-cited entry will indicate which volume you used.)

Example 15b, 328

> author
> Esteemed journalist Ida Tarbell writes that in 1847 Abraham Lincoln was a popular
> man of "simple, sincere friendliness" who was an enthusiastic—though awkward—
> pg. no vol. no. ch. no.
> bowler (210; vol. 1, ch. 13).

Abbreviations for the words *volume* and *chapter* are used. No abbreviations before the page number is needed.

11. Literary source Because many classics of literature—novels, poems, plays—are published in a number of editions (printed and digital) with pagination that varies widely, your citation should provide your readers with the information they will need to find the passage, regardless of which edition they are reading.

a. Novel Include the chapter number (with the abbreviation *ch.*) after the page number (or location reference for digital books) from your edition.

> Joyce shows his protagonist's dissatisfaction with family, faith, and country through the
>
> adolescent Stephen Daedalus's first dinner at the adult table, an evening filled with
>
> pg. no. ch. no.
> political and religious discord (274; ch. 1).

If the novel has chapters grouped into parts or books, include both the part or book number and the chapter number, using the appropriate abbreviation (*pt.* for *part* or *bk.* for *book*).

> Even though New York society declares the Countess Olenska beyond her prime,
>
> Newland Archer sees in her the "mysterious authority of beauty" (Wharton 58; bk. 1, ch. 8).

b. Play When citing plays, use act, scene, and line numbers (in that order), not page numbers or location numbers (used in digital editions). Do not label the parts. Instead, separate them with periods.

> When the ghost of Hamlet's father cries, "Adieu, adieu, adieu! remember me," Hamlet
>
> wonders if he must "remember" his father through vengeance (1.5.91).

c. Poem For poetry, use line numbers, rather than page or location numbers. With the first reference to line numbers, use the word *line* or *lines*; omit it thereafter.

Shakespeare ends Sonnet 55 with a gesture to his lover (lines 13–14), but it seems an

afterthought to a sonnet that meditates on death: "Like as the waves make

towards the pebbled shore, / So do our minutes hasten to their end" (1–2).

1st ref

later ref

For long poems that are divided into sections (books, parts, numbered stanzas), provide section information as well, omitting the section type (such as *book* or *part*) and separating the section number from the line number(s) with a period. If you provide more than four lines of the poem, treat the material as you would a block quotation.

Lord Byron's *Don Juan* (1818–1824) begins with a cheeky criticism of heroism, indicating

the poem's irreverent outlook on life that is to come.

> I want a hero: an uncommon want,
>
> When every year and month sends forth a new one,
>
> Till, after cloying the gazettes with cant,
>
> The age discovers he is not the true one;
>
> Of such as these I should not care to vaunt,
>
> I'll therefore take our ancient friend Don Juan—
>
> We all have seen him, in the pantomime,
>
> Sent to the devil somewhat ere his time. (11.1–8)

sec

lines

> **More about** block quotations, 346–47

Use arabic (*1, 8*), not roman (*i, viii*), numerals, and omit spaces.

12. Sacred text Cite sacred texts (such as the Bhagavad-Gita, the Talmud, the Qur'an, and the Bible) not by page number but by book title (abbreviated in parenthetical citations), chapter number, and verse number(s), and separate each section with a period. Do not italicize titles of sacred books or put them in quotation marks, and do not italicize the name of the sacred text, unless you are referring to a specific edition.

sacred text

In the Bible's timeless love poetry, the female speaker concludes her description of her

lover with this proclamation: "This is my beloved and this is my friend, / O daughters

book   ch. verse

of Jerusalem" (Song of Sol. 5.16).

No space →

specific edition

The New Oxford Annotated Bible offers a moving translation of the timeless love

book

poetry in the Song of Solomon. The female speaker concludes her description of her

lover with this proclamation: "This is my beloved and this is my friend, / O daughters

ch. verse

of Jerusalem" (5.16).

13. Motion picture, television or radio broadcast The information you include in an in-text citation for a motion picture or for a television or radio broadcast depends on what you are emphasizing in your project. When you are emphasizing the work itself, use the title; when you are emphasizing the director's work, use the director's name; when you are emphasizing an actor's work, use the actor's name. Start your works-cited entry with whatever you have used in your in-text citation.

Example 41b, 316

title

While *The Lady Eve* is full of slapstick humor, it is mainly remembered for its snappy

dialogue, at once witty and suggestive.

actor's name

Barbara Stanwyck's portrayal of Jean Harrington is at once sexy and wholesome.

14. Indirect source When you can, avoid quoting from a secondhand source. When you cannot use the original source, mention the name of the person you are quoting in your sentence. In your parenthetical citation, include *qtd. in* (for *quoted in*) plus the name of the author of the source in which you found the quotation.

> Handel's stock among opera-goers rose considerably over the course of the twentieth
> author quoted
> century. In 1912, an English music critic, H. C. Colles, maintained that "it would be diffi-
> cult, if not impossible, to make any one of Handel's operas tolerable to a modern
> source of quotation
> audience" (qtd. in Orrey 62). Today, however, Handel's operas are performed around
> the world.

In your list of works cited, include the *indirect* source (*Orrey*), not the source being quoted (*H. C. Colles*).

15. Dictionary or encyclopedia entry In the citation of a dictionary or encyclopedia entry, omit the page number on which you found the item. For a dictionary entry, place the defined word in quotation marks, followed by the abbreviation *def.* Follow this with the letter or number of the definition you wish to reference.

> Another definition of *honest* is "respectable" ("Honest," def. 6), but what, if anything,
> does truth have to do with respectability?

In the parenthetical citation for an encyclopedia entry, include the entry's full title in quotation marks.

> More about
> Parts of a dictionary entry, 582–84

> The study of ethics is not limited to philosophers, as its "all-embracing practical nature"
> makes it an applicable or even necessary course of study in a wide variety of disci-
> plines, from biology to business ("Ethics").

If you are citing two entries with the same title from different reference sources, add an abbreviated form of the reference work's title to each entry.

While the word *ethics* is commonly understood to mean "moral principles" ("Ethics,"

def. 4, *Random House Webster's*), to philosophers it is "the evaluation of human con-

duct" ("Ethics," *Philosophical Dict.*).

16. Website or other online source Cite electronic sources such as websites, online articles, e-books, and emails as you would print sources, even though many of these sources do not use page numbers.

a. Without page, paragraph, screen, or slide numbers Unless there is another numbering system at work (such as numbered paragraphs, screens, or slides), cite the author without a page reference.

When first published in 1986, Alan Moore's *Watchmen* revolutionized the comic book.
                                                                    author only
Today, even its harshest critics acknowledge the book's landmark status (Shone).

You may credit your source more elegantly by mentioning the author in a signal phrase and omitting the parenthetical citation altogether.

                                        signal phrase
Reading Alan Moore's *Watchmen* in 2005, critic Tom Shone found it "underwhelming,"

but he admitted that in 1986 the comic book was "unquestionably a landmark work."

b. With paragraph, screen, or slide numbers If an electronic source numbers its paragraphs, screens, or slides, you can reference these numbers as you would pages (with an appropriate identifying abbreviation—*par.* or *pars.*, *screen* or *screens*).

The Internet has also become an outlet for direct distribution through artist websites, making independent titles not only more accessible to consumers but also more affordable for individual artists to produce and market (Fenty et al., par. 1).

c. In a PDF file Online documents offered as a PDF (portable document format) file include all the elements of the printed document, including the page number. Since pages are fixed, you can and should cite page numbers.

More about PDF files, 183, 184, 205, 218, 221

17. Personal communication (email, letter, interview) As with other unpaginated sources, when citing information from a letter, email message, interview, or other personal communication, you should include the author's name in a signal phrase or parenthetical citation. Also indicate the type of source you are citing.

MLA In-Text Citations Index

14. Indirect source
15. Dictionary or encyclopedia entry
16. Website or other online source
17. Personal communication
18. Table, chart, or figure
19. Government document
20. Legal source

Many people have asked why teachers cannot do more to prevent school shootings;
source type
in an email to this author, one instructor responds: "As creative writing teachers untrained in psychology, can we really determine from a student's poetry whether he or
author of email
she is emotionally disturbed—even a threat to others?" (Fox).

18. Table, chart, or figure If a copy of the visual you are discussing is *not* included in your project, include relevant information in the text (artist's name or table title, for example), and include an entry in your list of works cited.

Examples 47–51, 341–42

There is no experience quite like standing in front of a full-size painting by Jackson Pollock. His paintings have an irresistible sense of movement to them, the particular quality of which is unique to his work. This is especially evident in *One (Number 31, 1950)*, which once hung on the fourth floor of New York's Museum of Modern Art.

TABLE 1 | THE DEMISE OF THE THREE-DECKER NOVEL

Year	No. of 3-deckers published
1894	184
1895	52
1896	—
1897	4
1898	0

Source: Information from John Feather, *A History of British Publishing*. Crown Helm, 1988, p. 125.

FIGURE 18.1 Table in MLA style

If a copy of the visual *is* included in your project, reference it in your text and include the source information in a table's source note (Figure 18.1) or in a figure's caption (see the figure caption on p. 353 in the student model project at the end of this chapter).

19. Government document Because government documents are alphabetized in the list of works cited by the name of the nation that produced them, mention the country as well as the agency in your text.

> Example 52, 342–43

Just as the nation was entering World War II, the United States War Department published a book outlining what it had learned about reading aerial photographs.

> Example 53, 343

20. Legal source Laws, acts, and legal cases are typically referred to by name either in your sentence or in a parenthetical citation. Laws and acts are neither italicized nor enclosed in quotation marks.

In 2008 the U.S. Congress passed the Combat Bonus Act.

Legal cases are italicized in your text, but not in the list of works cited.

In 1963 the Supreme Court ruled that poor defendants should receive legal representation, even if they could not pay for it themselves (*Gideon v. Wainright*).

21. Multiple sources in one sentence When you use different information from multiple sources within a single sentence, give separate citations in the appropriate place.

MLA In-Text
Citations Index

20. Legal source
21. Multiple
    sources in one
    sentence
22. **Multiple
    sources in
    one citation**

Other common themes of underground comics include sex and sexual identity, politics,

and social issues (Daniels 165), as shown in Crumb's work, which is well known for its

satirical approach to countercultural topics (Heller 101-02).

22. Multiple sources in one citation When you draw information from more than one source, follow the borrowed material with a list of all relevant sources, separated by semicolons.

Jamestown was once described as a failed colony populated by failed colonists, but

new findings suggest that the colonists were resourceful survivors (Howard; Lepore 43).

Entire source—no
page reference

18b Preparing an MLA-Style List of Works Cited

The list of works cited, which comes at the end of your research project, includes information about the sources you have cited in your text. (A bibliography that includes sources you read but did not cite in your research project is called a *list of works consulted*.) Your list of works cited provides readers with the information they need to locate the material you used in your project. The format of each entry depends in part on the type of source it is. (See the Quick Reference box on pp. 322–23 for a list of MLA-style examples included in this chapter.)

MLA Works-
Cited Entries

1. **One author**
2. Two authors
3. Three or more
   authors

Books—Printed and Electronic

In a printed book, most or all of the information you need to create an entry in the list of works cited appears on the title and copyright pages, which are located at the beginning of the book. In an online or e-book, print and electronic publication information often appears at the top or bottom of the first page or screen or is available through a link.

Annotated visual
of where to find
author, title, and
publication informa-
tion, in tutorial pre-
ceding this chapter,
300–03

1. One author

a. Printed The basic entry for a printed book looks like this:

Author's surname, First name. *Title: Subtitle.* Publisher, date of publication.

Quick

Reference Examples of MLA-Style Works-Cited Entries

MLA Works-Cited Entries

1. One author

2. Two authors

3. Three or more authors

Here is an example of an actual entry in the list of works cited:

author   title   publication information
Morrison, Toni. *Home.* Knopf, 2012.
                   pub. date

b. Database Some books are available in online, full-text archives, or databases, such as Bartleby.com. When you are documenting a book you accessed through a database, add the name of the database and include the complete URL for that book within the database.

Wharton, Edith. *The Age of Innocence.* D. Appleton, 1920.
    database
    Bartleby.com, www.bartleby.com/1005/.
    URL

MLA Works-Cited Entries

1. One author
2. Two authors
3. Three or more authors

c. E-book The citation for an electronic version of a book is the same as for a printed book except for the inclusion of the specific type of e-book version you read: Nook ed., Microsoft Reader ed., Kindle ed., and so on.

version
Morrison, Toni. *Home.* Kindle ed., Knopf, 2012.

2. Two authors List authors in the order in which they appear on the title page. Only the first author should be listed with surname first.

author 1   author 2
Zimmerman, Julie, and Olaf F. Larson. *Opening Windows onto Hidden Lives: Women,*

Country Life, and Early Rural Sociological Research. West Virginia UP, 2010.

author 1   author 2
Anderson, Poul, and Karen Anderson. *Innocent at Large.* Project Gutenberg, 3 Apr.

2016, www.gutenberg.org/files/51650/51650-h/51650-h.htm.

3. Three or more authors List the first author, surname first, and add *et al.* Be sure to do the same in your in-text citation.

More about et al., 156

Andersen, Thomas Hestbaek, et al. *Social Semiotics: Key Figures, New Directions.*

Routledge, 2015.

Example 3, 310–11

Collinson, Diané, et al. *Fifty Eastern Thinkers.* Routledge, 2000, routledgeonline

.com:80/religion/Book.aspx?id=w035&SiteId=ROL.

MLA Works-Cited Entries

4. Unnamed (anonymous) author Start the entry with the title.

title
Terrorist Hunter: The Extraordinary Story of a Woman Who Went Undercover to Infiltrate

the Radical Islamic Groups Operating in America. HarperCollins, 2003.

Alphabetize the entry in your list of works cited using the first significant word of the title (not an article like *a, an,* or *the*). Only if the author is listed specifically as "Anonymous" should you use that designation in the works-cited entry (and in your text).

Anonymous. *Go Ask Alice.* Prentice Hall, 1971.

5. Author using a pen name (pseudonym) If the author is using a pen name (or *pseudonym*), document the source using the author's pen name and insert the author's actual name in parentheses following the pseudonym.

Keene, Carolyn (Edward Stratemeyer). *The Secret of the Old Clock.* Grosset & Dunlap, 1930.

6. Two or more works by the same author Alphabetize the entries by the first important word in each title. Supply the author's name only with the first entry. For subsequent works, replace the author's name with three hyphens.

> Ritter, Kelly. *Before Shaughnessy: Basic Writing at Yale and Harvard, 1920–1960.*
>
> Southern Illinois UP, 2009.
>
> ---. *Reframing the Subject: Instructional Film and Class-Conscious Literacies.* U of
>
> Pittsburgh P, 2015.

7. Group or corporate author Treat the sponsoring organization as the author.

> corporate author
> Blackfoot Gallery Committee. *The Story of the Blackfoot People: Nitsitapiisinni.* Firefly,
>
> 2002.

8. Edited book or anthology When citing the book as a whole, treat the editor as the author and insert the word *editor* (or *editors* if there is more than one editor) after the name. For more than two editors, use the first editor's name (surname first), followed by a comma and the words *et al., editors.*

> Hage, Erik, editor. *The Melville-Hawthorne Connection: A Study of the Literary Friend-*
>
> *ship.* McFarland, 2014.
>
> Callahan, Vicki, and Virginia Kuhn, editors. *Future Texts: Subversive Performance and*
>
> *Feminist Bodies.* Parlor, 2016.
>
> Sarto, Guida, et al., editors. *The Cambridge Companion to Boccaccio.* Cambridge UP,
>
> 2015. *University Publishing Online,* dx.doi.org/10.1017/CCO9781139013987.

9. Author and editor or translator List the author first. After the title, include the words *Edited by* or *Translated by* (as appropriate) before the editor's or translator's name. If the book was accessed online, add the information shown in item 1b–c.

> Larsson, Asa. *Sun Storm.* Translated by Marlaine Delargy. Delacorte, 2006.

10. One or more selections from an edited book or anthology If your source is a selection (such as a chapter, story, poem, or image) in an edited book or anthology, think of that book or anthology as a *container*, and provide full information about both your source and its container. Start your entry with the selection's author and title.

author | title (selection)
Faulkner, William. "A Rose for Emily." *Literature: Reading Fiction, Poetry, and Drama*,
pages (selection)
edited by Robert DiYanni, 6th ed., McGraw-Hill, 2007. pp. 79-84.

When documenting a longer work, such as a novel or a play, that is included in the anthology or collection, italicize the work's title.

title (selection)
Ives, David. *Sure Thing. Literature: Reading Fiction, Poetry, and Drama.* . . .

If you are citing more than one selection in the anthology or collection, include an entry for the collection as a whole.

DiYanni, Robert D., editor. *Literature: Reading Fiction, Poetry, and Drama*, 6th ed.

McGraw-Hill, 2009.

Then, for each selection you use from the anthology, include only the author and title of the selection, the surname of the anthology's editor, and the page numbers of the selection.

Faulkner, William. "A Rose for Emily." DiYanni, pp. 79-84.

For a scholarly article included in an edited book, include the article's original publication information first, *Reprinted in,* and then the publication information for the anthology.

original publication info
Stock, A. G. "Yeats and Achebe." *The Journal of Commonwealth Literature*, vol. 5, no. 3,
reprint publication info
1970, pp. 105-11. Reprinted in *Things Fall Apart*, by Chinua Achebe. Edited by Francis

Abiola Irele. Norton, 2008, pp. 271-77.

If the book was accessed online, add the information shown in item 1b–c.

11. Edition other than the first Insert the edition number (*2nd ed., 3rd ed.*) or edition name (*Rev. ed.* for "revised edition") before the publication information. The edition number or name should appear on the title page.

Feather, John. *The Information Society: A Study of Continuity and Change.* 6th ed.,

Facet, 2013.

12. Imprint (division) of a larger publishing company Name only the main publisher.

> Betcherman, Lita-Rose. *Court Lady and Country Wife: Two Noble Sisters in*
> 　　　　　　　　　　　　　　　　　publisher
> *Seventeenth-Century England.* HarperCollins, 2005.

13. Introduction, preface, foreword, or afterword Begin with the name of the person who wrote this section of the text. Then provide a descriptive label (such as *Introduction* or *Preface*), the title of the book, and the name of the book's author. (If the author of the section and the book are the same, use only the author's surname after the title.) Include the page numbers for the section.

> Howard, Rebecca Moore. Foreword. *Authorship Contested: Cultural Challenges to the*
>
> *Authentic, Autonomous Author,* edited by Amy E. Robillard and Ron Fortune.
>
> Routledge, 2016, pp. xiii–xii.

If this section has a title, include it before the descriptive label.

> 　　　　　　　　　　　　　afterword's title
> Burton, Larry W. "Countering the Naysayers: Independent Writing Programs as
> 　　　　　　　　　　　　　　　　　　　　Label
> *Successful Experiments in American Education.*" Afterword. *A Field of Dreams:*
>
> *Independent Writing Programs and the Future of Composition Studies,* edited by
>
> Peggy O'Neill, et al., Utah State UP, 2002, pp. 295-300.

14. Entry in a reference work Format an entry in a dictionary or encyclopedia as you would a selection from an edited book or anthology. For signed articles, include the author's name. (Articles in reference works often carry the author's initials only, so you may need to cross-reference the initials with a list of contributors in the front or back of the book.) If an article is unsigned, begin with its title.

a. Printed For familiar reference works, omit publication information other than the edition and year of publication. If the entries are arranged alphabetically, omit a page reference.

> "Culture." *Oxford English Dictionary.* Compact 2nd ed., 1991.
>
> Green, Michael. "Cultural Studies." *A Dictionary of Cultural and Critical Theory,*
>
> Blackwell Publishers, 1996.

b. Online For online reference works, include the full URL of the site you referenced.

> "Culture." *Merriam-Webster Online Dictionary*, 2016, www.merriam-webster.com/
>
> dictionary/culture.

c. CD or DVD Although CDs have largely been replaced by the Internet, you may still need to use them. If the CD or DVD is published in versions rather than editions, include the version number before the publication information. Including the medium (CD, DVD) is not necessary, but if your source contains multiple discs, include the disc number you used (such as *disc 1*) after the publication date.

> Cooley, Marianne. "Alphabet." *World Book Multimedia Encyclopedia*,
>   version
>   version 6.0.2, World Book, 2002.

15. Multivolume work

a. Multiple volumes Indicate the span of years in which the volumes were published, as well as the total number of volumes, followed by the abbreviation *vols.* Specify the volume from which you borrowed a particular passage or idea in your in-text citation.

Example 10, 313

>   pub. dates
> Tarbell, Ida M. *The Life of Abraham Lincoln*. Lincoln Memorial Association, 1895-1900.
> no. of vols.
> 2 vols.

b. One volume If you used only one volume, include the number of the volume you used before the publication information, and give only the publication date of that volume.

>   vol. used   pub. date
> Tarbell, Ida M. *The Life of Abraham Lincoln*. Vol. 1, Lincoln Memorial Association, 1895.

16. Book in a series

If the book you are citing is part of a series, the series title will usually be noted on the book's title page or on the page before the title page. Insert the series title (with no quotation marks or italics) after the publication date. If books in the series are numbered, include the number following the series title.

> Todorov, Tzvetan. *Mikhail Bakhtin: The Dialogical Principle*. Translated by Wlad
>   series title   no.
> Godzich, U of Minnesota P, 1995. Theory and History of Literature 13.

17. Republished book If a book has been republished, its original date of publication will appear on the book's copyright page. If the original publication date may be of interest to your readers, include it before publication information for the version you consulted. If the book was edited or an introduction was added, include that information before the republication information.

Burroughs, William S. *Naked Lunch*. 1959. Edited by James Grauerholz and

Barry Miles, Grove, 2001.

18. Title within a title Omit italics from any title that would normally be italicized when it falls within the main title of a book.

Birmingham, Kevin. *The Most Dangerous Book:* The Battle for Ulysses. Penguin Books, 2014.

If the title within the title would normally appear in quotation marks, retain the quotation marks and italicize both titles.

19. Sacred text Italicize the title of the edition you are using. Editors' and translators' names follow the title.

The New Oxford Annotated Bible. New Revised Standard Version, edited by Michael D.

Coogan et al., 3rd ed., Oxford UP, 2010.

The Holy Qur'an. Edited and translated by Abdullah Yusuf Ali, 10th ed., Amana, 1997.

20. Missing publication information Certain sources may not include page numbers, date of publication, or publisher. Provide as much information about your source as you are able to locate. The following source does not contain printed page numbers or a publication date. Therefore, these items are not included in the citation.

Barrett, Edgar, editor. *Football West Virginia 1960*. West Virginia.

21. Pamphlet, brochure, or press release Follow the format for book entries. For a press release, include day, month, and year of publication, if available.

Example 1, 321

Worcester Police Department. *Preparations Underway for St. Patrick's Day Parade*. City

of Worcester, MA, 10 Mar. 2016, www.worcesterma.gov/wpd-press-releases/-

preparations-underway-for-st.-patrick-s-parade# idIPWSypnuVJtYkjrIA9vDrQ.

> Example 46, 341

If the item was emailed or published online, document it as you would a book published online.

22. Conference proceedings Include the title of the conference, the sponsoring organization (if its name is not cited in the conference title), and the date and location of the conference, if that information is not already included in the publication's title.

> sponsor
> Bizzell, Patricia, editor. *Proceedings of the Rhetoric Society of America:*
>   title (conference)   date
> *Rhetorical Agendas: Political, Ethical, Spiritual.* 28–31 May 2004,
>   location
> U of Texas—Austin. Erlbaum, 2005.

For a paper delivered at a conference, include the word *Lecture* at the very end of the citation.

23. Dissertation Include the word *Dissertation*, the school to which the dissertation was submitted (abbreviate *University* to *U*), and the year it was submitted. For published dissertations, italicize the title.

> Brackins, Genevieve. *Mothering Amidst and Beyond Hegemony in Margaret Atwood's*
>   *The Handmaid's Tale and* Toni Morrison's *Beloved.* Dissertation, Florida State U,
>   2014. *ProQuest,* fsu.digital.flvc.org/islandora/object/fsu%3A253602.

For unpublished dissertations, put the title in quotation marks.

> Brommer, Stephanie. "We Walk with Them: South Asian Women' Organizations
>   diss. submission info.
>   in Northern California Confront Domestic Abuse." Dissertation, U of California—
>   Santa Barbara, 2004.

Periodicals—Printed and Electronic

Newspapers, magazines, and scholarly journals are types of *periodicals* that publish collections of texts such as stories, articles, poems, and images at regular intervals—daily, monthly, or at set intervals during the year. Most researchers today find articles in periodicals by searching their library's **databases**—online indexes that provide citation information as well as an abstract (or summary) and sometimes an electronic copy of the article itself—in either PDF or HTML format. (A PDF file shows the article more or less as it would have appeared in print; an HTML file includes the text of the article but not the illustrations or formatting of the print version.) As you construct your works-cited entry for a selection in a periodical, think of that periodical as the selection's *container*, and provide full information about both the selection and the container. Include not only the title of the article (in quotation marks) but also the title of the periodical (in italics). The other publication information you include depends on the type of periodical you are documenting.

24. Article in a scholarly journal The information you need to create an entry for a printed journal article is on the cover or in the table of contents of the journal and on the first and last page of the article. For articles downloaded from a database, the information you need appears on the screen listing the articles that fit your search terms, on the first and last page of the file you download, or in the full record for the article you select. For articles that appear in journals published solely online, you may find the information you need on the website's home page, in the journal's table of contents, or on the first screen of the article. Access dates for database and online articles should come from your notes.

a. Printed The basic entry for an article in a printed journal looks like this:

> Surname, First name. "Article Title." *Journal Title*, vol. #, (issue) no. #, year, pp.

Here is an example of an actual entry:

> Weaver, Karen. "Trophies, Treasure, and Turmoil: College Athletics at a Tipping Point."
>
> *Change*, vol. 47, no. 1, 2015, pp. 36–45.

b. Accessed through a database When you document an article from a scholarly journal that you accessed through an online database, add the name of the database (in italics), and add the full URL or DOI for the article.

> Weaver, Karen. "Trophies, Treasure, and Turmoil: College Athletics at a Tipping Point."
>
> *Change*, vol. 47, no. 1, 2015, pp. 36–45. *Taylor & Francis Current Content Access*,
>
> doi:10.1080/00091383.

c. Online To document an online journal article, follow the model for a printed journal article. After the publication information, add a comma and provide a complete URL or DOI for the article. (The parts that are different from a printed journal article are highlighted.)

> Woolums, Viola. "Gendered Avatar Identity." *Kairos*, vol. 16, no. 1, 2001, kairos
>
> .technorhetoric.net/16.1/topoi/woolums/.

MLA Works-Cited Entries

Annotated visual of where to find author, title, publication, and other information, tutorial on pages preceding this chapter, 300–03.

25. Article in a magazine (weekly, monthly)

a. Printed Provide the issue's publication date (month and year or day, month, and year) and the page range for the article, but not the magazine's volume or issue number, even when they are available.

> Fuller, Alexandra. "Her Heart Inform Her Tongue: Language Lost and
> Found." *Harper's Magazine*, Jan. 2012, pp. 60-64.
>
> (pub. date) (pgs.)

> Gladwell, Malcolm. "Thresholds of Violence." *The New Yorker*, 19 Oct. 2015, pp. 30-37.

If the article appears on nonconsecutive pages (the first part appears on p. 2 but the rest of the article is continued on p. 10), include a plus sign after the first page number (2+).

b. Accessed through a database

> Fuller, Alexandra. "Her Heart Inform Her Tongue: Language Lost and
> Found." *Harper's Magazine*, Jan. 2012, pp. 60-64. *EBSCOhost, www.ebsco.com/*
> *ezproxy/fuller_01/12.*
>
> (database)

c. Online

> Carr, Nicholas. "Is Google Making Us Stupid?" *The Atlantic*, July/Aug. 2008,
> www.theatlantic.com/magazine/archive/2008/07/is-google-making-us-stupid/
> 306868/.
>
> (website)

> Thomas, June. "Is Social Acceptance Killing Queer Cinema?" *Slate*, 27 Nov. 2015,
> www.slate.com/blogs/outward/2015/11/27/gay_movies_two_hollywood_reporter_
> cities_think_2015_s_queer_films_are_terrible.html.
>
> (website)

26. Article in a newspaper The information you need to create an entry for a printed newspaper article is on the masthead of the newspaper (at the top of the first page) and on the first and last page of the article. For newspaper articles downloaded from a database, the information you need appears on the screen listing the articles that fit your search terms or on the first and last page of the article itself. Articles that appear in online versions of the newspaper usually contain all the information you need at the top of the first screen. Use conventional capitalization of titles even when your original source does not.

Annotated visual of where to find author, title, publication, and other information, tutorial on pages preceding this chapter, 300-03

a. Printed For an article in a daily newspaper, include the date (day, month, year). If the paper paginates sections separately, include the section number, letter, or name immediately before the page number.

More about
Title capitalization, 838–39

Richtel, Matt, and Julie Bosman. "To Serve the Young, E-Book Fans
                          date sec. & pg.
      Prefer Print." *The New York Times*, 21 Nov. 2011, p. B1.

MLA Works-Cited Entries

23. Dissertation
24. Article in a scholarly journal
25. Article in a magazine
26. **Article in a newspaper**
27. Article on microform
28. Review (printed or online)

If the section number or letter is not part of the page number, add the abbreviation *sec.* and the section name, number, or letter. If the section is named, add the section name before the abbreviation *sec.* If no author is listed, begin the entry with the title of the article. If the article continues on a nonconsecutive page, add a plus sign after the first page number (*A20+*). If the newspaper's masthead specifies an edition (such as late edition or national edition), include that information after the date.

                                          section, nonconsecutive. pg.
Keller, Julia. "Viral Villainy." *Chicago Tribune*, 22 Mar. 2009, final ed., sec. 6, pp. 1+.
                       edition

If the name of the city in which the newspaper is published does not appear in the newspaper's title, include it in brackets after the title.

Speciale, Samuel. "Majority of Students Apply to Only One College, Federal Study
      Says." *Gazette-Mail* [Charleston], 26 Nov. 2015, p. B1.

For well-known national newspapers (such as *The Christian Science Monitor, USA Today,* and *The Wall Street Journal*), no city or state is needed. If you are unsure whether the newspaper is well known, consult your instructor or a reference librarian.

b. Accessed through a database For a newspaper article accessed through a database, add the database name and include the full URL or DOI for the article.

Maiman, Bruce. "In Praise of Common Courtesy." *The Sacramento Bee*, 15 Apr.
               database
      2014, p. 11A. *Access World News,* sacbee.com/opinion/op-ed/bruce-maiman.

c. Online For an online newspaper article, include the full URL or DOI.

Netburn, Deborah. "Theaters Set Aside Tweet Seats for Twitter Users."
      website
      Los Angeles Times, 6 Dec. 2011, latimesblogs.latimes.com/technology/2011/12/

      theaters-tweet-seats-twitter.html.

Do not italicize a website name unless it is also the name of a periodical.

MLA Works-
Cite Entries

27. Article on microform Many libraries still store some back issues of periodicals on microform, a photograph of a periodical printed on plastic and viewed through a special microform reader. Your entry for an article on microform is the same as for a printed article.

If your source is preserved on microform in a reference source such as NewsBank, add the title of the reference source and any access numbers (such as fiche and grid numbers) following the publication information.

28. Review (printed or online) Begin with the reviewer's name (if provided), followed by the title of the review (if any) and the label *Review of*. Then include the title and author of the work being reviewed. Finally, include the title of the periodical and its publication information. If the review was accessed online, add information as shown in item 24b–c, 25b–c, or 26b–c.

reviewer   title (review)   title (book)

Grover, Jan. "Unreliable Narrator." Review of *Love Works Like This: Opening*

author

One's Life to a Child, by Lauren Slater. *Women's Review of Books,* vol. 19, nos.

10-11, 2002, p. 40.

29. Editorial (printed or online) Often editorials are unsigned. When that is the case, begin with the title of the editorial (if any). Then insert the label *Editorial* and follow with the periodical's publication information.

editorial title   label

"Making Tax Season Worse." Editorial. *Columbus Dispatch,* 28 Feb. 2015, p. 11A.

If the editorial was accessed online, add information as shown in item 24b–c, 25b–c, or 26b–c.

30. Letter to the editor (printed or online) Begin with the author's name, followed by the label *Letter to the editor* and the periodical's publication information.

letter author   label

Park, John. Letter to the editor. *Time,* 5 Dec. 2011, p. 9.

If the letter to the editor has a title, add it (in quotation marks) after the author's name. If the letter to the editor was accessed online, add information as shown in item 24b–c, 25b–c, or 26b–c.

Other Electronic Sources

While it is usually easy to find the information you need to create a complete entry for a book or an article in a periodical, websites can be a bit trickier. Most of the information you need will appear on the site's home page, usually at the bottom or top of the page, or on the web page you are documenting. Sometimes you may need to look further: Click on links such as "About us" or "More information." Frequently, websites do not provide complete information, so include as much as you can.

31. Website The basic entry for a website looks like this:

Author's surname, First name. *Website title.* Publisher, Publication date, URL.

Here is an example of an actual entry:

editor   title (website)
McGann, Jerome J., ed. *The Complete Writings and Pictures of Dante Gabriel Rossetti:*

A Hypermedia Archive. Institute for Advanced Technology in the Humanities,

publisher
U of Virginia, and Networked Infrastructure for Nineteenth-Century Electronic

publication date   URL
Scholarship, 2008, www.rossettiarchive.org/index.html.

If no author or editor is listed, begin with the website's title.

32. Web page or short work on a website If your source is part of a larger website, think of the larger site as a *container*, and provide full information about both your source and its container. Add the title of the web page to the entry for a website.

page title
Callaghan, Jennefer. "Adorno, Theodor." *Postcolonial Studies @ Emory.* Dept. of English,

Emory U, Oct. 2012, scholarblogs.emory.edu/postcolonialstudies/6/01/65/.

33. Home page (academic)
a. Course

title (page)
"Philosophy of the Program: The Basics Underscoring the Approach to Composition

title (website)   publisher
Classes at Labette Community College." *Department of English,* Labette Community

College, 2014, www.labette.edu/english/philosophy.html.

b. Department

English Dept. U of California—Santa Barbara, 2013, www.English.ucsb.edu/.

Do not italicize a sponsor's name unless the sponsor is itself a publication.

34. Discussion list posting Treat the subject line (*thread*) as the title, and include the name of the list, the sponsoring group, and the date of the posting.

Ballard, Donna Kim. "Punctuation Question." *Writing Program Administration Discussion*

List, 19 June 2014.

35. Article on a wiki Usually wikis are written and edited collaboratively, so there is no author to cite. Instead, begin the entry with the article title. When a wiki article is signed, begin the entry with the author's name.

Quigley, Nina, and Madeline Moore. "History of Sweatshop Protests at SU, 2000–2001."

SyrGuide. 11 June 2014, syrguide.com/guide/2014/06/11/history-of-sweatshop-

protests-at-su-2000-2001/.

36. Blog

a. Blog

Browsings. Harper's Magazine, 28 Nov. 2015, harpers.org/blog/2015/11/.

b. Blog posting

Luther, Jason. "Our Failed Writing Center: A Response." *Taxomania!,*

11 Nov. 2011, taxomania.org/blog/our-failed-writing-center-a-response/.

c. Comment on a blog posting

Danderson, Mark. Comment on "Some Tough Love for Authors." *The Scholarly Kitchen,*

25 Oct. 2011, 3:12 p.m., scholarlykitchen.sspnet.org/2011/10/25/some-tough-love-for-

authors/#comments.

If the comment's author uses a screen name, use that; if the actual name is available and of interest to readers, provide that as well, following the screen name, in square brackets. Also, if there is a time stamp included with the comment, include that as part of your citation.

37. Pseudonyms and online usernames If the author/speaker uses a different name than the writer's actual name, use the pseudonyms or online username.

@NASA. "Behemoth black hole found in an unlikely place: the center of a galaxy in

cosmic backwater." *Twitter,* 7 Apr. 2016, 3:30 p.m., twitter.com/NASA/

status/717851257403211778.

38. App (for an e-device)

Minecraft Pocket Edition. Version 0.14.0, Mojang AB. Accessed 8 Apr. 2016.

39. Video game (for devices such as *Xbox* or *Wii*)

Guitar Hero Live. Xbox One. Activision, 2015.

- game: *Guitar Hero Live.*
- platform: Xbox One.
- publisher: Activision,
- release date: 2015.

Audio and Visual Sources

The information you need to create an entry for most audio and visual sources will appear on the cover, label, or program of the work or in the credits at the end of a film. The person you list in the "author" position—the director, performer, artist, or composer—will vary depending on what you have emphasized in your research project. If you are writing about a director's body of work, put the director's name first; if you are writing about a performance, put the performer's name first. If it is the work itself that you are writing about, put the title of the work first. (This decision should be mirrored in your in-text citation.) However you choose to organize the entry, indicate the role of those whom you list, using phrases such as *performance by*, *directed by*, and *conducted by*.

As with any other entry, italicize the titles of complete or longer works (such as albums, films, operas, and original works of art) and place quotation marks around the titles of shorter works or works published as part of a larger whole (such as songs on a CD or a single episode of a television show). Publication information includes the name of the distributor, production company, or network, as well as the date on which the audio or visual was created, recorded, or broadcast. If you found the audio or visual source online and there is no date of publication, also include the date on which you accessed it.

40. Motion picture

a. Film

Good Deeds. Directed by Tyler Perry. Lionsgate, 2012.

- title: *Good Deeds.*
- director: Directed by Tyler Perry.
- distributor: Lionsgate,
- release date: 2012.

If other artists besides the director are relevant to your project, list them between the director and the distributor.

Good Deeds. Directed by Tyler Perry, performances by Perry and Thandie Newton, Lionsgate, 2012.

- performers: performances by Perry and Thandie Newton,

If your project stresses the director, performer, or other contributor, place that information at the beginning of the citation.

> Perry, Tyler, director. *Good Deeds*. Performances by Perry and Thandie Newton, Lions-
>
> gate, 2012.

b. Video or DVD Include the original release date, when relevant, before the distributor.

> *The Lady Eve*. Directed by Preston Sturges, performances by Barbara Stanwyck and Henry
> orig. release distributor
> Fonda. 1941. Universal Home Entertainment, 2006.

c. Internet download Include the source you used to download the video, as well as the film's URL.

> *Juno*. Screenplay by Diablo Cody, directed by Jason Reitman, performances by Ellen
>
> Page and Jason Bateman. Fox Searchlight, 2007. *iTunes*, www.itunes.com/.

d. Online video clip Cite a video clip on YouTube or a similar site as you would a web page. If the name of the uploader appears, include it after the website (*uploaded by*). Since these types of videos are not always stable, you may want to include the date you accessed the material.

> performer video clip title website
> Ok Go. "This Too Shall Pass—Rube Goldberg Machine Version." *YouTube*,
> date posted date accessed
> 2 Mar. 2010, www.youtube.com/watch?v=qybUFny7y8w. Accessed 8 Apr. 2016.

e. DVD extras Add the title of the extra (in quotation marks).

> DVD extra
> "The Making of *Winter's Bone*." *Winter's Bone*. Directed by Debra Granik, performances
>
> by Jennifer Lawrence and John Hawkes. Lionsgate, 2010.

41. Television or radio broadcast If your source is an episode in a series, think of that series as a *container*, and provide full information about both your source and its container. Start your entry with the title of the series or episode. Follow that with a list of the relevant contributors and include the network on which the series or episode aired. Because the director may change from episode to episode, other contributors, such as the creator or producer, may be more relevant. Include the date of the program. If your project emphasizes an individual, begin with that person's name.

a. Series

series title
How I Met Your Mother. Created by Carter Bays and Craig Thomas, produced by

network
Bays et al., performances by Josh Radnor and Alyson Hannigan. CBS,

broadcast dates
19 Sept. 2009–31 Mar. 2014.

b. Episode

"There Will Be a Future." *Narcos,* performance by Wagner Moura, season 1, episode 5.

Netflix, www.netflix.com/watch/80025317?trackId=14170104&tctx=0%2C4%2C-

316dcd53-46a2-4312-bf21-cdfc24d01eb6-43631335.

c. Single program

Persuasion. By Jane Austen. Adapted by Simon Burke, performances by Julia Davis and

Rupert Penry-Jones, PBS, 13 Jan. 2008.

d. Podcast For a podcast, add the full URL for the file.

"The Giant Pool of Money." *This American Life,* narrated by Ira Glass, Natl. Public Radio,

9 May 2008, www.thisamericanlife.org/radio-archives/episode/355/the-giant-

pool-of-money.

42. Musical or other audio recording Begin with whichever part of the entry is more relevant to your project—the name of the composer or performer, or the title of the CD or song. Place the title of shorter works, such as a song, in quotation marks. Italicize the titles of longer works, such as the title of an opera, but not the titles of symphonies identified only by form, number, and key, such as Brahms's Symphony no. 1.

a. CD, LP, audiobook

Adamo, Mark. *Little Women.* Performances by Stephanie Novacek et al., conducted

prod. co. & release date
by Patrick Summers, Ondine, 2001.

Brahms, Johannes. Symphony no. 1. Performance by Chicago Symphony Orchestra,

conducted by Georg Solti, Decca, 1992.

b. Song or selection from a CD or LP or a chapter from an audiobook

Vetiver. "Last Hurrah." *Complete Strangers*, Easy Sound Recording Company, 2015.

c. Compressed music file (MP3, MP4)

Beyoncé. "Formation." *Tangerine*, Parkwood/Columbia, 2016, listen.tidal.com/artist/1566.

Example 32, 335

d. Online sound file or clip For a sound recording accessed online, combine the format for a web page with the format for a sound recording.

"The General Prologue, The Knight's Portrait, II, 43–78." *The Riverside Chaucer*,

3rd ed., 2000. *Baragona's Literary Resources*, alanbaragona.wordpress.com/the-

criyng-and-the-soun/the-general-prologue-the-knights-portrait-ii-43-78-baragona/.

43. Live performance The entry for a performance is similar to that for a film. Include the venue and city of the performance and the date of the performance you attended. If your project emphasizes the composer, writer, or performer, begin the entry with that information. If the performance is untitled, include a descriptive label.

a. Ensemble

The Importance of Being Earnest. By Oscar Wilde, directed by Jerry Chipman,

group   perf. date

performance by Brian Everson et al., Theatre Memphis, 27 Jan. 2012, Lohrey Stage,

Memphis.

b. Individual

performer   label

Hartig, Caroline. Clarinet recital, 18 Nov. 2011, Brigham Young U, Provo.

44. Musical composition To document a musical composition itself rather than a specific performance, recording, or published version of it, include only the composer and the title of the work (in italics unless the composition is identified only by form, number, and key).

composer   untitled symphony

Schumann, Robert. Symphony no. 1 in B-flat major, op. 38.

45. Lecture, speech, or debate Treat the speaker as the author; place the title in quotation marks (if there is one); and indicate the occasion and sponsoring organization (if relevant), location, date, and mode of delivery (such as *Lecture* or *Address*). If the lecture, speech, or debate is untitled, replace the title with a brief descriptive label.

speaker   title   sponsor
Capri, Frank. "The Peace Movement of the 1960s." 92nd Street Y,

location date
New York. 14 Mar. 2010. Lecture.

46. Table For a table included in your project, place source information in a note below the table. For a table that you are discussing but that does not appear in your project, include an entry in your list of works cited following the model below.

Example 18, 319–20

title   label   website
"Senate Salaries since 1789." Table. *United States Senate*, 7 June 2012, www.senate.gov/

artandhistory/history/common/briefing/senate_salaries.htm.

47. Work of art For a work of art included in your project, place source information in the figure caption. For a work that you discuss but that does not appear in your project, include an entry in your list of works cited following the models below.

Example 18, 319–20

a. Original work

artist   title   date of   location
             production
Pollock, Jackson. *One (Number 31)*. 1950. Museum of Modern Art, New York.

b. Reproduction of a work of art

Lichtenstein, Roy. *Whaam!* 1963. *Responding to Art: Form, Content, and Context.* By

Robert Bersson, McGraw-Hill, 2004.

48. Comic or cartoon For a cartoon reproduced in your project, provide source information in the caption. For cartoons that you discuss without providing a copy of the image in your project, include an entry in your list of works cited following these models:

a. Cartoon or comic strip

artist   title   publication information
Thaves, Bob. "Frank and Ernest." *Evening Sun*, [Norwich]. 26 Nov. 2015, p. 14.

b. Comic book or graphic novel

authors   title

Pekar, Harvey, and Joyce Brabner. *Our Cancer Year*, illustrated by Frank

pub. info.

Stack, Running Press, 1994.

Example 18,
319–20

49. Map or chart For a map or chart reproduced in your project, provide source information in the caption. For a map or chart discussed but not included in your project, include an entry in your list of works cited following the model below.

"The Invasion of Sicily: Allied Advance to Messina (23 July-17 August 1943)." *The West Point*

Atlas of American War, vol. 2, edited by Vincent J. Esposito. Praeger, 1959, p. 247.

50. Advertisement For an advertisement reproduced in your project, provide source information in the caption. For an advertisement discussed but not included in your project, include an entry in your list of works cited following the models below.

label

Earthlink Cable Internet. Advertisement. *Metro*, 17 Apr. 2007, p. 11.

date accessed

Infiniti. Advertisement. *Yahoo.com*. Accessed 20 Apr. 2016.

date broadcast

Domino's Pizza. Advertisement. *Comedy Central*, 2 Aug. 2006.

Miscellaneous Sources—Printed and Electronic

Example 7, 325
Example 19, 320

51. Government document If no author is listed, use the name of the governing nation and the government department and agency (if any) that produced the document, as you would for a work with a corporate author.

nation   department

United States, War Department. *Advanced Map and Aerial Photograph Reading*.

Government Publishing Office, 1941.

For congressional documents, include the number and session of Congress and the number and type of document.

a. Printed

United States, Congress, House. *Combat Bonus Act*. Government Publishing Office, 2008.

110th Congress, 2nd session, House Report 6760.

b. Online

> United States, Congress, House. *Combat Bonus Act.* Library of Congress, 31 July 2008,
>
> www.congress.gov/bill/110th-congress/house-bill/6760.

52. Legal source

> United States, Supreme Court. *Gideon vs. Wainwright.* 1963. *FindLaw,* caselaw.findlaw
>
> .com/us-supreme-court/372/335.html.

53. Letter (published)
a. Single letter Cite a single letter as you would a selection from an edited book or anthology but add the recipient's name, the date the letter was written, and the letter number (if there is one).

Example 10, 326

>   author   recipient   date written
> Brooks, Phillips. "To Agnes." 24 Sept. 1882. *Children's Letters: A Collection of Letters*
>
> *Written to Children by Famous Men and Women,* edited by Elizabeth Colson and
>
> Anna Gansevoort Chittenden, Hinds, 1905, pp. 3-4.

b. Collection of letters Cite as you would an edited book or anthology.

Example 8, 325

54. Interview Treat a published interview as you would an article in a periodical. Treat an interview broadcast on radio or television or podcasted as you would a broadcast. For an unpublished interview you conducted, include the name of the person interviewed, the label *Personal interview, Telephone interview,* or *Email interview,* and the date on which the interview took place.

Examples 24–25,
331–32
Example 42,
339–40

>   person
>   interviewed   label   date
> Harberg, Amanda. Personal interview. 11 Feb. 2016.

55. Personal correspondence To document personal correspondence, such as a letter, include a descriptive label such as *Letter to the author.*

a. Letter
>   letter writer   label   date written
> Gould, Stephen Jay. Letter to the author. 13 Nov. 1986.

b. E-mail
>   e-mail author   subject line   date sent
> Elbow, Peter. "Re: bibliography about resistance." Received by Rebecca Howard, 12 Apr. 2016.

c. Memorandum Very few institutions send out printed memos anymore, but if you need to document one, treat it as you would an email message.

d. Instant message (IM)

> Grimm, Laura. Message to the author. 14 June 2012.

56. Diary or journal

a. Single entry, published Treat an entry in a published diary or journal like an article in an edited book or anthology, but include a descriptive label (*Diary entry*) and the date of composition after the entry title.

b. Single entry, unpublished

> author   title   label   entry date
> Zook, Aaron. "Sketches for *Aesop's Foibles* (new musical)." Journal entry. 1 May 2016.

c. Diary or journal, published Treat a complete diary or journal as you would an edited book or anthology.

18c Using MLA Style for Informational Notes

In addition to in-text citations, MLA style allows researchers to include informational notes to provide relevant, but potentially distracting, content or to provide bibliographic information about one or more sources. MLA style recommends using a list of endnotes at the end of the project. To identify informational notes in the text, include a superscript (above-the-line) arabic number that corresponds to the note number in the list of endnotes. Include an entry for each source in your list of works cited.

> Graphic novels, such as Spiegelman's *Maus* and Harvey Pekar and Joyce Brabner's *Our Cancer Year* (1994), have successfully addressed some of the most highly charged and sensitive subjects in modern society.[1] . . . Comics like Tomine's provide a subject or situation that readers can identify with more easily than, say, Superman's battles with Brainiac.[2]

Notes Heading (centered), new page

←½"→1. These are iconic comics; Smith goes so far as to call *Maus* "one of the most

important comics in the history of the medium" (509).

　　2. For an intriguing argument that the world of classic comic book superheroes

is not so different from our own—including a discussion of how comics before World

War II commented on then current events—see Wright 1-28.

　　Use *content notes* to provide information that clarifies or justifies a point in your text, but avoid notes that include interesting digressions that could distract your readers. Lydia Nichols's essay at the end of this chapter includes a content note. You can also use content notes to acknowledge the contributions of others (tutors, classmates, and so on) to the preparation of your project.

　　Bibliographic notes can add information about a source or point readers to other sources on the topic. If several sources provide the same information, cite the most valuable source in your text, and list the others in a bibliographic note. Then include the full citation of all these sources in your list of works cited.

18d Formatting a Paper in MLA Style

The care with which you cite and document your sources reflects the care you have taken in writing your research project. Continue that care by formatting your project in the way your readers expect. For most writing projects in literature and composition, follow the MLA's formatting guidelines.

1. Margins and spacing

Set one-inch margins at the top, bottom, and sides of your paper. Double-space the entire paper, including long quotations, the list of works cited, and any endnotes. Indent the first line of each paragraph by half an inch, and do not add an extra space between paragraphs. Use a hanging indent for each entry in the list of works cited: The first line should be flush with the left margin with subsequent lines indented half an inch. (For more on creating a hanging indent in a word processing program, see the Tech box on page 347.)

Student Model
Research project, MLA
style, 349–62

> **Tech** Creating a Header
>
> Most word processing software allows you to insert a header. In Microsoft Word, select "Header" from the Insert tab. Any information you type into the header space will then appear at the top of every page of your manuscript. You can also choose to insert page numbers to paginate your project automatically.

More about
Choosing a type-
face and type
size, 169–70

2. Typeface

Choose a standard typeface, such as Times New Roman or Arial, in an easily readable size (usually 12 points).

3. Header

MLA style requires that each page of your project include a header, consisting of your surname and the page number. Place the header in the upper right-hand corner, a half inch from the upper edge and one inch from the right edge of the page.

4. Identifying information

No title page is required in MLA style. Instead, include the following identifying information in the upper left-hand corner of the first page of your research project, one inch from the top and left edges of the paper:

- Your name
- Your instructor's name
- The number of the course in which you are submitting the paper
- The date

If your instructor requires a title page, ask for formatting instructions or follow the model on page 397.

More about
Crafting a title,
92–93

5. Title

Center the title of your project and insert it two lines below the date. Do not put quotation marks around your title or italicize it. Drop down two more lines before beginning to type the first paragraph of your research project.

More about
Block quotations,
308, 315,
351, 812
Sample block
quotations, 308
(prose), 315
(poetry)

6. Long quotations

Set quotations of prose longer than four lines of your text as a block: Omit the quotation marks, and indent the entire quotation one-half inch from the left margin of your text. When quoting four or more lines of poetry, indent

Tech   Indentation

The major style guides (MLA, APA, *Chicago*, CSE) were initially written before the widespread use of personal computers, when most writers still worked on typewriters. To create a paragraph or hanging indent on a typewriter, the typist would hit the space bar five times or set a tab. Now, just about everyone creates writing projects on a computer, where paragraphs and hanging indents are created using the Ruler or Paragraph Dialog box.

Ruler

Almost from the beginning, comic books were associated with superheroes. The first comic books appeared in the early 1930s, nearly four decades after comic strips

Move the top triangle to the right to create a paragraph indent

"The Comic Book Code." *Culture Shock*, PBS, 2000, www.pbs.org/wgbh/ cultureshock/flashpoints/visualarts/comiccode.html. "Comics History: Underground Comix and the Underground Press." *Comiclopedia* Lambiek, 2016, www.lambiek.net/comics/underground.htm.

Move the bottom triangle to the right to create a hanging indent

Paragraph Dialog Box

all the lines one-half inch from the left margin; keep the same indentation and line breaks that were in the original poem, and include the line numbers of the passage quoted. If a line of the poem is too long to fit on a single line of your page, indent the continuation by an extra quarter of an inch.

7. Tables and figures

Tables and figures (photographs, cartoons, graphs, and charts) are most effective when they appear as close as possible after the text in which they are first discussed. (If placing figures and tables appropriately is awkward, consider including them in an appendix at the end of your project.) Labeling your tables and figures, both in the text and in your caption, will help readers connect your discussion with the illustration:

> Sample tables and figures, 80–87, 319-20, 354, 356

- Refer to the visual in your text using the word *table* or the abbreviation *fig.*, and number tables and figures in a separate sequence using arabic numerals (table 1, table 2; fig. 1, fig. 2). MLA style uses lowercase for in-text references to tables and figures unless they begin a sentence: "Table 1 presents 2010 data, and table 2 presents 2012 data."

Writing
Responsibly | Of Deadlines and Paperclips

Instructors expect students to turn in thoughtful, carefully proofread, and neatly formatted papers on time—usually in class on the due date. Another expectation is that the writer will clip or staple the pages of the paper *before* it is submitted. Do justice to yourself by being fully prepared.

to SELF

- Accompany each illustration with the word *Table* or the abbreviation *Fig.,* the appropriate number, and a brief, explanatory title. Customarily, table numbers and titles appear above the table, and figure numbers and titles appear below the figure. Generally, they use the same margins as the rest of the paper.

- If additional information is needed, provide an explanatory caption after the number and title. (Remember that your text should explain what the figure or table demonstrates. That information should not be repeated in the caption.)

- If you borrow the illustration or borrow information needed to create the illustration, cite your source. Any photographs or drawings you create yourself should identify the subject but do not need a citation. Citations usually appear below the table in a source note or in the figure caption. If you document the illustration in a figure caption or source note, you do not need to include an entry in your list of works cited.

8. Printing and binding

If you are submitting a hard copy of your project, print it using a high-quality printer (make sure it has plenty of ink), on opaque 8½ × 11–inch white paper. Most instructors do not want you to enclose your project in a binder. Unless your instructor tells you otherwise, staple or paperclip the pages together in the upper left-hand corner.

9. Portfolios

Many instructors ask students to submit the final draft of the research project in a portfolio, which may include an outline, preliminary notes and drafts, a working or annotated bibliography, and a personal statement describing their writing process and what they have learned from the experience (Figure 18.2).

> *More about*
Outlining, 40–42,
   268–70
Note taking,
   121–23, 251–52,
   260–63
Writing a first
   draft, 44–47
Working or
   annotated
   bibliography,
   204–09

FIGURE 18.2 Page 1 of Lydia Nichols's personal statement Nichols created a visual personal statement to explain how her interest in underground comics developed.

Student Model **Research Project: MLA Style**

In the student model research project that follows, Lydia Nichols fulfills her responsibilities to topic and audience. She uses comparison-contrast to support her claim that underground comics are more innovative than their mainstream cousins, and she provides a historical overview to fill in the background her readers lack. Her research draws on a variety of print and online sources, and she uses visuals to support some of her points.

½" 1"

1"

Lydia Nichols

Prof. Concannon

Writing 205

30 April 2016

Identifying information (double-spaced)

Header: Author's surname, page number

Double-space between date and title

Title (centered)

Holy Underground Comics, Batman! Moving Away from the Mainstream

Double-space between title and 1st line

½" When most people think of comic books, predictable images usually come to mind: caped heroes, maniacal villains, deeds of incredible strength, and other typical elements of super-powered adventures. Undeniably, characters like Batman, Superman, and Spider-Man are the most prominent features of the comic book landscape, in terms of both popularity and revenue (Wright xiv). However, there is more to comic books than superpowers and secret identities. Underground comics (also known as *comix*), printed by small publishers or by individual artists, are very different from what is usually expected in the genre. While far less well-known than their superhero counterparts, underground comics often offer an innovative and more sophisticated alternative to mainstream titles.

Almost from the beginning, comic books were associated with superheroes. The first comic books appeared in the early 1930s, nearly four decades after comic strips such as *Yellow Boy* began appearing in the major newspapers. However, Les Daniels, who has written extensively on conventional and underground comics, points out that comic books did not gain widespread popularity until June of 1938, when writer Jerry Siegel and artist Joe Shuster debuted their character Superman

Introduction: Initiates contrast, moves from familiar to unfamiliar, concludes with thesis

In-text citation—book

Thesis: Establishes topic, purpose, and author's position

Topic sentence: Prepares reader for historical overview

Signal phrase identifies source and establishes credibility

1"

in *Action Comics* #1 (9). Daniels reports that Superman was an immediate success, and the character quickly inspired the creation of copycat superheroes in other comic books. The protagonists of these comics each had their own strengths and vulnerabilities, but the stories all shared a basic formula: individuals with extraordinary abilities battling against evil and struggling to maintain a secret identity. These superhero comics, although similar to each other, set the comic book industry on its feet, paving the way to profits and sustained success. Over the decades and even today, superhero comics are what are typically seen on store shelves.

Body: Begins with historical overview

While writers and artists over the years have certainly done inventive work in superhero comics, some similarity in mainstream titles was for many years unavoidable due to the creation in 1954 of the Comics Code Authority (CCA), an organization formed by a number of the leading comic book publishers to regulate the content of comics ("Good Shall Triumph"). It set very explicit standards, dictating what content was allowed in comic books and what content was expected. Some parts of the code were incredibly specific and controlling:

Topic sentence: Supported by quotation and summary

> The letters of the word "crime" on a comics magazine shall never be appreciably greater in dimension than the other words contained in the title. The word "crime" shall never appear alone on a cover. ... Restraint in the use of the word "crime" in titles or subtitles shall be exercised. (qtd. in "Good Shall Triumph")

Block indentation for long quotation; ellipses mark cut

Indirect source: Author unknown, so title used

Other rules were more general—vague enough to allow the CCA a free hand in shaping content. One read, "Respect for parents, the moral code, and for honorable behavior shall be fostered" (qtd. in "Good Shall Triumph"). The CCA also regulated

Quotation marks for brief quotation

the presentation of criminals and criminal acts, themes of religion and race, and dialogue, especially profanity. While the CCA had no legal authority, major magazine distributors refused comics that did not have CCA approval. Many comic publishers, such as EC Comics (*Vault of Horror*, *Tales from the Crypt*), were virtually forced out of business as a result of the CCA, though the banned titles would eventually gain the appreciation and respect of collectors and aspiring comic book artists such as Art Spiegelman, author of the graphic novel *Maus* (1986) ("Comic Book Code"). Other publishers, including DC Comics, made their artists abide by CCA rules in order to continue selling to a wide audience ("Good Shall Triumph"). The result was that the comics with the largest distribution were those that conformed to the CCA's strict rules about appropriate language, subjects, and tone. To see an example of a comic book cover both before and after the code took effect, look at fig. 1 (on the next page). The *Batman* cover (left), published by DC Comics in 1940, is code free, while the cover for *Captain Steve Savage and His Jet Fighters* (right) includes the CCA stamp in its upper-right corner. Captain Steve Savage made his first appearance in January 1950, not long after the start of the Korean War—but pre-code. Issues of the comic book ran without the CCA stamp until 1954, when the CCA took effect; after that, all issues (and reissues—it appears certain covers were recycled) featured the stamp prominently.

In the 1960s, in contrast to mainstream CCA-approved superhero comics, alternatives began to appear. According to Steven Heller, an art director at *The New York Times* and a founder of the Masters in Graphic Arts Program at the School for Visual Arts in New York, Robert Crumb's *Zap* (1968) initiated the "underground comix

> Paragraph uses combination of summary, paraphrase, and quotation

> Websites: no page numbers in citations

> Signal phrase identifies source and establishes credibility

Fig. 1. Batman (with his sidekick, Robin, the Boy Wonder) flies into Gotham in his own comic book (left) in 1940, before the institution of the Comics Code Authority, while Captain Steve Savage (right), ace fighter pilot, shoots down an enemy plane. The CCA stamp ("Approved by the Comics Code Authority") is in the upper-right corner.

Figure number links visual to text discussion

Source information in caption

revolution" (101). Crumb and other like-minded artists did not submit their comics for CCA approval. Though this limited the distribution of their work, it allowed them artistic freedom. From its first issue, *Zap* satirized mainstream, conservative beliefs and did not shy away from sexual or political content (Heller 101–02). Beneath the crude humor of *Zap* and similar comics lay insightful commentary on society and its principles, which many readers found to be a refreshing change from mainstream superhero titles.

Fig. 2. Examples of late '60s underground comics. In defiance of the authoritarian standards of the Comics Code Authority and influenced by '50s humor magazine *Mad*, underground artists pushed the boundaries of humor, propriety, and good taste.

> **Caption explains how visual supports claim**

Besides *Zap*, other well-known underground titles of the era include *Subvert* and *Weirdo*. Gilbert Shelton's hilariously nonconformist *Fabulous Furry Freak Brothers* and Crumb's most recognizable hero, the sketchy guru *Mr. Natural*, starred in their own, often X-rated, comic books (see fig. 2, above). Comiclopedia, an online encyclopedia of comic artists maintained by the legendary Dutch comic shop Lambiek, notes that many underground comics were inspired by *Mad* magazine founding father Harvey Kurtzman, who also gave Crumb and Shelton their first break in his *Help!* magazine.

> **Topic sentence: Claim supported by visual, analysis; figure number links discussion to visual**

> **Figures analyzed in text**

Underground comics continue to be less well-known than superhero comics, but they are better-respected among mature readers for their bold and inventive

> **Topic sentence: Claim supported by examples**

content. Graphic novels, such as Spiegelman's *Maus* and Harvey Pekar and Joyce Brabner's *Our Cancer Year* (1994), have successfully addressed some of the most highly charged and sensitive subjects in modern society.[1] Both of these show the

Content note

subtlety and wide range of topics that underground comics explore. Daniels notes underground comics frequently explore themes of sex and sexual identity, politics, and social issues (165), as shown in Crumb's work, which Heller describes as taking a satirical approach to countercultural topics (101–02).

Mainstream superhero comics are set on an epic scale—depicting amazing feats, heroic battles between good and evil, and the like—while underground comics tend to focus on everyday life. Steven Weiner, who reviews graphic novels for *Library Journal*, called Adrian Tomine, for example, "a master of pseudorealistic stories" due to his ability to present an ordinary situation as profoundly interesting and complex (58; see fig. 3, page 356). Comics like Tomine's provide a subject or situation that readers can identify with more easily than, say, Superman's battles with Brainiac.[2] The United Nations' World Food Programme (WFP) recognized the broad appeal of the genre when it hired *The New York Times* bestselling graphic novelist Joshua Dysart to travel to Iraq and create a graphic novel highlighting the humanitarian work of the WFP and the people it tries to help. The resulting comic, *Living Level 3*, received worldwide attention when it was serialized in *The Huffington Post* in January 2016.

Topic sentence: Claim supported by example, visual, quotation

Bibliographic note

The quirky perspectives of underground artists would be impossible in mainstream comics because the structure for producing and publishing mainstream comics limits the input of the artists working on them. The modern comic book industry is a huge business, selling not only comics but also related merchandise

Fig. 3. Comic whose characters face realistic challenges--the loss of a loved one, parental guilt--that readers can easily relate to. From Adrian Tomine, *Optic Nerve* #6, Drawn and Quarterly, Feb. 1999, p. 22.

such as T-shirts, toys, and video games, not to mention tickets to comic book-inspired movies. Story decisions involving major characters such as Batman and the Hulk have to be made with profits in mind. Because mainstream comic publishers often change the creative teams working on their titles (Herndon 23) and because teams can

Citation: Placement clarifies which information comes from which source include dozens of members (McCloud 180), individual artists can have only so much impact on a particular character or story. Most mainstream comics are the result of work done by many different people.

Transition

In contrast, the individual artist in the underground realm has almost total control in creating his or her comic book. The creative teams working on underground titles are usually very small, and they rarely change (Herndon 23).

Signal phrase

Daniels notes that underground comic artists are not controlled by corporate interests that discourage daring materials that might not sell (165, 180). This freedom allows for the uninhibited creativity that distinguishes underground comics from their more commercially oriented counterparts.

Information from two passages, same source

Topic sentence: Claim supported by summary, quotation, visual evidence

Underground artists not only push the envelope in terms of content but they also incorporate experimental visual devices, earning critical praise for breaking away from traditional comic layouts in favor of more artistic perspectives. Artists such as Daniel Clowes argue that comic art can be more evocative than film, especially in the use of nonlinear storytelling techniques (Hignite 18). *The New York Times* columnist

Signal phrase identifies source and establishes credibility

John Hodgman agrees: Discussing a moment of existential crisis in Kevin Huizenga's *Ganges #1,* he writes, "I have never seen any film or read any prose that gets at that frozen moment when we suddenly feel our mortality, when God is seen or denied, as effectively as a comic panel" (18). Artist Chris Ware, in graphic novels like *Jimmy Corrigan: The Smartest Kid on Earth* and *Building Stories,* manipulates the borders and frames in his comics so extensively that even reading his works can feel like an art to be mastered. The demands his comics place on the reader create an interaction between viewer and artist that is unheard of in the pages of superhero titles.

While Ware and Clowes demonstrate how the page can be used to create innovative and complicated layouts, other underground artists excel at creating simple, striking visuals. Unlike mainstream comics, which depict dynamic scenes through loud, flamboyant colors, underground comics often achieve their effects through simplicity. Frequently, they are printed in black and white or with limited colors, with characters rendered in clean, bold lines. The clarity and lack of clutter in such art allows for immediate, striking storytelling (see fig. 3, page 7).

> Reference to earlier figure

Obviously, most underground comics are not intended for young children. Yet because of the childish connotations of the word "comic," most adults overlook the fascinating work that underground comic artists do. The association of comics with superheroes and children has made reading comics a source of shame or embarrassment for many adults. As Clowes comments, "I think that the average reader is far more open to a well-designed book than a standard comic book. ... Very few would feel comfortable reading a standard comic book pamphlet" (qtd. in Highnite 17). Artists such as Scott McCloud have changed this perception of comic books by offering a broader definition of what a comic is. According to McCloud, comics are "juxtaposed pictorial and other images in a deliberate sequence" (12). This definition includes not only what one might find in the latest Spider-Man comic, but also all of the experimental work that McCloud and his underground colleagues are creating.

> Establishes credibility

> Signal phrase and parenthetical page reference bookend apt quotation

McCloud and others have succeeded in bringing underground comics to a wider audience. Since the 1980s, underground comics have been finding their way into gallery and museum exhibitions, where the craftsmanship of the individual comic book artist can be better appreciated (Hignite 18). Major newspapers like *The New York Times* have begun featuring underground comics in their pages, including serialized graphic novels such as *George Sprott (1894-1975)* and *Watergate Sue*. The market for underground comics has also expanded through Internet venues such as eBay, where interested readers can find not only new titles but also classic comix otherwise available only in specialty shops. The Internet has also become an outlet for direct distribution through artists' websites, making independent titles not only more accessible to consumers but also more affordable for individual artists to produce and market (Fenty et al., par. 1). While underground comics may never sell as well or be as large a part of popular culture as Superman and his ilk, their creators will likely continue to be heroes to anyone seeking courage, creativity, and artistic quality in their comics.

Conclusion: Provides closure

Revisits thesis, states why underground comics provide more sophisticated alternative

Notes Heading (centered), new page

1. These are iconic comics; Smith goes so far as to call *Maus* "one of the most
   important comics in the history of the medium" (509).

2. For an intriguing argument that the world of classic comic book superheroes is not
   so different from our own—including a discussion of how comics before World
   War II commented on then current events—see Wright 1-28.

Signal phrase and parenthetical citation within note

Works Cited

Heading (centered), new page; entries alphabetized by author (or title if no author)

Web page: No author

"The Comic Book Code." *Culture Shock*, PBS, 2000, www.pbs.org/wgbh/
cultureshock/flashpoints/visualarts/comiccode.html.

"Comics History: Underground Comix and the Underground Press." *Comiclopedia*,
½" Lambiek, 2016, www.lambiek.net/comics/underground.htm.

Journal article published only online; paragraphs numbered

Daniels, Les. *Comix: A History of Comic Books in America*. Outerbridge, 1971.

Fenty, Sean, et al. "Webcomics: The Influence and Continuation of the Comix
Revolution." *ImageTexT*, vol. 1, no. 2, 2004, 22 pars., www.english.ufl.edu/
imagetext/archives/v1_2/group/index.shtml.

Online scholarly project: No authors—alphabetized by title

" 'Good Shall Triumph over Evil': The Comic Book Code of 1954." *History Matters:
The U.S. History Survey Course on the Web*. American Social History Project /
Center for Media and Learning, CUNY, and the Center for History and New
Media, George Mason, 2006, historymatters.gmu.edu/d/6543/.

Journal article: Accessed through database

Heller, Steven. "Zap Comics." *Print*, May/June 2000, pp. 100-05. *Academic OneFile*,
www.ebscohost.com/ezproxy/zap_comics/print/2000_0506/.

Newspaper article: Accessed through database

Herndon, L. Kristin. "Mainstream Culture Is in Trouble, and Superman's Not Gonna Save
It. But the Simpsons Might." *Art Papers*, vol. 21, no. 6, 1997, pp. 22-25. *Art Index*,
ebscohost.com/tag/SIMPSONS,%20The%20(TV%20program)&offset=400.

Hignite, M. Todd. "Avant-Garde and Comics: Serious Cartooning." *Art Papers*, vol. 26,
no. 1, 2002, pp. 17-19.

Hodgman, John. "Comics Chronicle." *The New York Times*, 4 June 2006,
www.nytimes.com/2006/06/04/books/review/04hodgman.html.

Book (printed): Popular press

McCloud, Scott. *Understanding Comics, the Invisible Art*. Harper Perennial, 1994.

Smith, Philip. "Spiegelman Studies Part 2 of 2: *Breakdowns, No Towers* and the Rest of the Canon." *Literature Compass*, vol. 12, no. 10, Oct. 2015, pp. 509–16. *Wiley Online Library*, doi:10.1111/lic3.12263.

Weiner, Stephen. "Beyond Superheroes: Comics Get Serious." *Library Journal*, vol. 7, no. 2, 2002, pp. 55-58. *Academic OneFile*, ebscohost.com/c/articles/5992770/beyond-superheroes-comics-get-serious.

Wright, Bradford W. *Comic Book Nation: The Transformation of Youth Culture in America.* Johns Hopkins UP, 2001.

Specialized reference work: Accessed through database

Book (printed): Scholarly press, *University Press* abbreviated to *UP*

Text Credits
p. 308: Howard, Adam, "Breaking the Silence: Power, conflict and contested frames within an affluent high school" *Anthropology & Education Quarterly* 37(4) December 2006. **p. 313:** Faulkner, William, "A Rose for Emily," *The Forum*, April 30, 1930. **p. 315:** William Shakespeare, "Sonnet 55". **p. 350:** Courtesy of Lydia Nichols. **p. 356:** Adrian Tomine, 8-panel cartoon "Optic Nerve #6," p. 22, from *Drawn and Quarterly*, February 1999. © 1999 by Adrian Tomine. Reproduced by permission.

19 Documenting Sources: APA Style

> *More about*
> Documenting a Source:
>   APA Style, 300–03
>   (*Documentation Matters*
>   tutorial preceding ch. 18)
> MLA style, 304–62 (ch. 18)
> *Chicago* style, 406–34
>   (ch. 20)
> CSE style, 435–49 (ch. 21)

Developed by the American Psychological Association, APA style is used by researchers in psychology and many other social science disciplines, such as education, social work, and sociology. The *Publication Manual of the American Psychological Association* (6th ed.) requires that sources be cited in two ways:

- **Citation:** In the body of your project, provide an in-text citation for each source used.

- **Documentation:** At the project's end, provide a reference list.

19a Creating APA-Style In-Text Citations

In-text citations appear in the body of your project. They mark each use you make of a source, regardless of whether you are quoting, paraphrasing, or drawing on an idea. In-text citations should include just enough information for readers to locate the source in your reference list, which appears at the end of the project. They should also alert readers to shifts between *your* ideas and those you have borrowed from a source.

Writing Responsibly | Citing and Documenting Sources

When you cite and document sources, you demonstrate how thoroughly you have researched your topic and how carefully you have thought about your sources, which encourages your audience to believe you are a credible researcher. In your citations and documentation, you acknowledge any material that you have borrowed from a source, and you join the conversation on your topic by adding your own interpretation. Accurate entries in the body of your project and list of references allow your audience to find and read your sources so that they can evaluate your interpretation and learn more about the subject themselves. Accurate entries also demonstrate the care with which you have written your research project, which further reinforces your credibility, or ethos.

to AUDIENCE

Quick

Reference General Principles of In-Text Citation

- Cite not only direct quotations but also paraphrases, summaries, and information gathered from a source, whether printed or online.
- Include the author's surname and the year of publication. You may place the name(s) in a signal phrase or in a parenthetical citation.
- Place parenthetical citations after the borrowed material; if the author is named in a signal phrase, insert the year of publication, in parentheses, immediately following the author's name and the page reference at the end of the borrowed passage.
- For works with no author, use the first few words of the title in the author position.
- For works with multiple authors, use the word *and* before the last author in a signal phrase; replace the word *and* with an ampersand (&) in a parenthetical citation.
- Include a page or paragraph number when borrowing specific information but not when summarizing an entire source.

1. Place in-text citations so that readers know where borrowed material starts and stops.

> **More about**
> What you do and
> do not need to
> cite, 364–66
> Signal phrases,
> 275–87 (ch. 17)
> Integrating bor-
> rowed material
> into your text,
> 275–77

When you incorporate a quotation, paraphrase, summary, or idea from a source into your own prose, carefully consider the placement of the in-text citation, keeping the following goals in mind:

- To make clear exactly which material is drawn from the source
- To avoid distracting your reader

You can cite a source in your text in two ways:

- *Signal phrase.* Include the author's name (often just the surname) and an appropriate verb in your sentence, and place the date of publication, in parentheses, immediately following the author's name.

> Psychologist G. H. Edwards (1992) found that subtypes or subcategories of beliefs emerge from within gender categories.

A signal phrase often makes it easier for readers to determine where your ideas end and borrowed material begins. It also allows you to integrate the borrowed material into your sentence and to put the source in context by adding your own interpretation and the qualifications of the source author. For these reasons, most of your summaries, paraphrases, and quotations should be introduced by a signal phrase.

- *Parenthetical citation*. In parentheses, provide the author's surname, followed by a comma and the year in which the source was published. Place the note immediately after the borrowed material.

> Subtypes or subcategories of beliefs emerge from within gender categories
>
> (Edwards, 1992).

Parenthetical citations are most appropriate when citing more than one source or establishing facts.

NOTE The reference list entry is the same, regardless of whether you use a signal phrase or a parenthetical citation:

More about
Creating reference list entries, 374–91

> author   pub. year   title
> Edwards, G. H. (1992). The structure and content of the male gender role
>   publication info.
>   stereotype: An exploration of subtypes. *Sex Roles, 27*, 553-561.

Provide enough information in your in-text citation for readers to locate the source in the reference list. In most cases, the author's surname and the date of publication are sufficient. Occasionally, you may need to provide more information. When citing works by authors with the same surname, also include the authors' initials.

Examples 1–2, 366–68

Example 11, 371
Example 7, 378

> While subtypes or subcategories of beliefs may emerge from within gender
>
> categories (Edwards, G. H., 1992), broader categories of beliefs emerge from
>
> within cultural groups (Edwards, C. P., 1988).

Example 2, 367   When quoting from a source, include page numbers.

> The stereotype effect occurs when "individual members . . . are judged in a direction
>
> consistent with group-level expectations . . ." (Biernat, 2003, p. 1019).

APA In-Text Citations

1. One author, paraphrase or summary
2. One author, quotation
3. Two authors

2. Adjust in-text citations to match your source.

The exact form of an in-text citation depends on the type of source you are citing. The examples that follow cover the most common types. For more unusual sources, study the general principles outlined here and adapt them to your special circumstances or consult the *Publication Manual of the American Psychological Association,* 6th ed. (available in any library).

1. One author, paraphrase or summary The APA does not require that writers include a page reference for summaries and paraphrases, but your instructor may. If your instructor does want you to include a page reference, follow the model for a quotation on the next page.

a. Signal phrase

signal phrase
From her interviews with vegans, Cherry (2015) found that the majority had adopted

that lifestyle before the age of 18.

b. Parenthetical citation

The majority of vegans participating in a sociological study reported having adopted

that lifestyle before the age of 18 (Cherry, 2015).

2. One author, quotation If you are borrowing specific language from your source, include the author's name, the year of publication, and a page reference.

NOTE The APA suggests, but does not require, that writers include a page reference for summaries and paraphrases when readers may need help finding the cited passage. Your instructor may require that you always include one, so be sure to ask. If your instructor *does* want you to include a page reference, follow examples 2a–b.

a. Signal phrase In a signal phrase, insert the year of publication immediately after the author's name and a page reference at the end of the cited passage. This not only provides source information but also makes clear what part of your text comes from the source.

Cherry (2015) reports that simply self-identifying as a vegan is not enough to sustain

the lifestyle; the 23 vegans interviewed placed great value on their social networks with

other vegans (p. 67).

APA In-Text Citations

1. One author, paraphrase or summary
2. One author, quotation
3. Two authors
4. Three to five authors

b. Parenthetical citation In a parenthetical citation, include all three pieces of information at the end of the passage cited.

Simply self-identifying as a vegan is not enough to sustain the lifestyle; the

23 vegans interviewed placed great value on their social networks with other vegans

(Cherry, 2015, p. 67).

---

3. Two authors List two authors by surnames in the order listed by the source; be sure to use this same order in your reference list entry. In a signal phrase, spell out the word *and* between the two surnames; in a parenthetical citation, replace the word *and* with an ampersand (&).

---

signal phrase (*and* spelled out)
Iezzoni and Long-Bellil (2012) observe that "with limited exceptions, physicians have

little training in addressing the wide-ranging needs of persons with disabilities" (p. 136).

Most physicians, the authors observe, "have little training in addressing the

              parenthetical citation (ampersand)
wide-ranging needs of persons with disabilities" (Iezzoni & Long-Bellil, 2012, p. 136).

---

4. Three to five authors When a source has three, four, or five authors, list them all in your first in-text citation.

The research of Oller, Pearson, and Cobo-Lewis (2007) suggests that bilingual children

may have a smaller vocabulary in each of their languages than monolingual children

have in their sole language.

APA In-Text
Citations

1. One author,
paraphrase or
summary
**2. One author,
quotation**
3. Two authors
**4. Three to five
authors**
5. Six or more
authors
6. Group or
corporate
author

In subsequent citations, list only the first author, representing the others with the abbreviation *et al.* In APA style, this abbreviation should not be underlined or italicized.

> The bilingual children in the study were all Spanish-English speakers (Oller et al., 2007).

NOTE *al.* is an abbreviation, so it requires a period; *et* is a complete word, so it does not. There should be no punctuation between the author's name and *et al.*

et al. Abbreviation of the Latin phrase *et alii*, "and others"

5. Six or more authors If the source has six or more authors, use only the surname of the first author plus *et al.* unless confusion will result.

acronym A word formed from the first letters of words in a name or phrase, such as NASA from National Aeronautics and Space Administration

> The study demonstrates that positive stories about honesty, such as "George Washington and the Cherry Tree," have a positive effect on children's honesty, whereas negative stories, such as "Pinocchio," do not (Lee et al., 2014).

6. Group or corporate author Provide the full name of the group in your signal phrase or parenthetical citation. If you are going to cite this source again in your project, use the group's name in a signal phrase and insert an abbreviation of the name in parentheses. In subsequent in-text references, use only the abbreviation.

APA In-Text Citations

3. Two authors

4. Three to five authors

5. Six or more authors

6. Group or corporate author

7. Unnamed (anonymous) author

8. Two or more sources in one citation

>   full name   acronym
> In 2003 the National Commission on Writing in America's Schools and Colleges (NCWASC) demanded that "the nation's leaders . . . place writing squarely in the center of the school agenda, and [that] policymakers at the state and local levels . . . provide the resources required to improve writing" (p. 3). The NCWASC also noted that . . .

Alternatively, include the full name in a parenthetical citation, and insert the abbreviation in square brackets afterward.

If writing is to improve, our society "must place writing squarely in the center

of the school agenda, and policymakers at the state and local levels must

provide the resources required to improve writing" (National Commission on
 full name   abbreviation
Writing in America's Schools and Colleges [NCWASC], 2003, p. 3).

More about
Quotation marks
 with titles,
 812–13
Italics with titles,
 842–43

7. Unnamed (anonymous) author When no author is listed for a source, use the first few words of the reference list entry (usually the title) instead.

On average, smokers shave about 12 minutes off their life for every
                                          title
cigarette smoked ("A Fistful of Risks," 1996, pp. 82–83).

Set titles of articles or parts of books in quotation marks and titles of books and other longer works in italics.

8. Two or more sources in one citation When the information you are drawing on comes from more than one source, follow the borrowed material with a list of all relevant sources, separated by semicolons. List the sources in alphabetical order, the same order in which they appear in the reference list.

Introducing domestic animals into the prison environment has beneficial effects on

female inmates (Cooke & Farrington, 2015; Jasperson, 2010).

---

9. Two or more sources by the same author in one citation When citing two or more sources by the same author in a single citation, name the author once but include all publication years, separating them with commas.

Wynn's work explores the ability of human infants to perform mathematical functions,
pub. year 1   pub. year 2
such as addition and subtraction (1992, 2000).

Human infants have shown surprising abilities to perform mathematical
pub. year 1   pub. year 2
functions, such as addition and subtraction (Wynn, 1992, 2000).

10. Two or more sources by the same author in the same year When your reference list includes two or more publications by the same author in the same year, add a letter following the year (*2006a, 2006b*). Use these year-and-letter designations in your in-text citations and in your reference list.

> Example 6, 376

For history students whose first language is not English, a writing-to-learn pedagogy
letter assigned
has a positive effect on the acquisition of historical reasoning (Smirnova, 2015b).

11. Two or more authors with the same surname If your reference list includes works by different authors with the same surname, include the authors' initials to differentiate them.

Rehabilitation is a viable option for many juvenile offenders, whose

immaturities and disabilities can, with institutional support and guidance,
first initial + surname
be overcome as the child matures (M. Beyer, 2006).

If a source has more than one author, include initials for the first author only.

12. Reprinted or republished work Include both dates in your in-text citation, with the original date of publication first.

orig. year
Danon-Boileau (2005/2006) takes a cross-disciplinary approach to the study
                                    reprint year
of language disorders in children.

13. Sacred or classical source Cite sacred texts, such as the Bible, the Talmud, or the Qur'an, in the body of your research project using standard book titles, chapter numbers, and verse numbers, and indicate the version you used.

In the Song of Solomon, the female speaker concludes her description of her lover with

this proclamation: "His mouth is sweetness itself, he is all delight. / Such is my lover,
                                                          ch.   version
and such my friend, O daughters of Jerusalem" (5:16, Revised Standard Version).
                                                            verse

For classical works, cite the year of the translation or version you used: (Plato, trans. 1968).

14. Indirect source When you can, avoid quoting from a secondhand source (source material you have learned about through its mention in another source). When you cannot locate or translate the original source, mention the original author's name in a signal phrase. In your parenthetical citation, include *as cited in* followed by the name of the author of the source in which you found the information, and conclude with the year of that source's publication.

Bonilla-Silva (as cited in Utheim, 2014) locates the origin of US "colorblind racism"

in the 1960s.

In the reference list, provide only the source you used: For the example above, include a reference list entry for Utheim, not Bonilla-Silva.

15. Website or other online source Frequently, the information you need to create a complete in-text citation is missing. Electronic sources may lack fixed page numbers: Page 5 in one browser may be page 4 or 6 in another. Use page numbers only when they are fixed, as in a PDF file. When paragraph numbers are provided, include those (with the abbreviation *para.*) instead of a page number.

More about
PDF files, 183, 184, 205, 218, 221

> The Internet has also become an outlet for direct distribution of underground comics through artist websites, making independent titles more affordable to market (Fenty, Houp, & Taylor, 2004, para. 1).

When the source includes neither fixed page numbers nor paragraph numbers, cite the source by author name and publication date only. If the author is unnamed, use the first few words of the title.

Examples 27–28, 387

> Cell-phone use while driving can impair performance as badly as drinking alcohol does ("Driven to Distraction," 2006, para. 1).

If no date is provided, use *n.d.* for *no date.*

> Barrett (n.d.) unwittingly reveals the sexism prevalent on college campuses in the early 1960s through his account of a football game.

16. Personal communication (email, letter, interview) For sources such as personal email messages, interviews, and phone calls that your readers cannot retrieve and read, mention the communication in your text or provide a parenthetical citation, but do not include an entry in the reference list.

> The author herself was much more modest about the award (S. Alexievich, personal communication, April 13, 2016).

19b Preparing an APA-Style Reference List

The reference list, which comes after the body of your research project, lists the sources you have cited in your text. The format of each entry in the list depends in part on the type of source you are citing, such as a printed book, an article in an electronic journal or accessed through a database, or an audio recording. (See the Quick Reference box on pp. 376–77 for a list of APA-style reference list examples.)

Books—Printed and Electronic

> Annotated visual of where to find author, title, and publication information, in tutorial preceding ch. 18, 300–03

In a printed book, the information you need to create a reference list entry appears on the title and copyright pages at the beginning of the book. In an online book or e-book, print and electronic publication information appears at the top or bottom of the first page or is available through a link.

1. One author

a. Printed The basic entry for a printed book looks like this:

Author's surname, Initial(s). (Year of publication). *Title: Subtitle*. Place of publication (city,

state [abbreviated]): Publisher.

Here is an example of an actual citation:

> For books, only first word of title and subtitle (plus names) are capitalized.

Pollock, J. (2012). *Crime and justice in America: An introduction to criminal justice*. Mary-

land Heights, MO: Anderson Publishing.

> **More about**
> Digital object identifiers, 204, 374–75, 382–83, 386, 416, 442
> URLs, 240–41

b. E-book Works published electronically or made accessible online are now frequently tagged with a digital object identifier (DOI). Unlike a URL that may change or stop working, a DOI is a permanent identifier that will not change over time or from database to database. If the e-book you are documenting is tagged with a DOI, use that identifier instead of publication information or URL, and add a description of the source type in brackets after the title. If no DOI has been assigned, replace publication information with the URL from which the electronic file can be obtained. If you accessed the source on a device such as a Kindle or Nook, no URL should be included.

Carter, J. (2003). *Nasty people: How to stop being hurt by them without stooping to*

their level [Adobe Digital Editions version]. doi:10.1036/0071410228

> **Tech** **Citing Electronic Sources: Digital Object Identifiers (DOIs) and URLs**
>
> Because URLs change and links break, the APA now recommends using a digital object identifier (DOI), a permanent identifying code, whenever available; use a URL, or web address, only when no DOI is available. Most electronic books and articles in academic journals now include a DOI. When your citation ends with a DOI or URL, do *not* add a period after it. Break a DOI or URL (if necessary) only after a slash or before a dot or other punctuation mark; do not add a hyphen.

von Hippel, E. (n.d.). *Democratizing innovation.* Retrieved from http://web.mit

.edu/evhippel/www/democ.htm

If no publication date available, use n.d.

2. Two authors When there are two authors, list them in the order in which they appear on the title page.

author 1   author 2
Raskin, H., & Rabiner, D. (2012). *College drinking and drug use.*

New York, NY: Guilford.

Use an ampersand (&) between names.

3. Three to seven authors When the book has three to seven authors, list all their names.

James, J., Burks, W., & Eigenmann, P. (2011). *Food allergy.* Philadelphia, PA:

Saunders.

Use an ampersand (&) between the last two names.

4. Eight or more authors When the book has eight or more authors, list the first six authors followed by three ellipsis points and the last author's name.

Masters, R., Skrapec, C., Muscat, B., Dussich, J. P., Pincu, L., Way,

L. B., . . . Gerstenfeld, P. (2010). *Criminal justice: Realities and challenges.*

New York, NY: McGraw-Hill.

5. Unnamed (anonymous) author Start the entry with the title followed by the publication date. Alphabetize the entry in the reference list using the first significant word in the title (not an article such as *a, an,* or *the*).

And still we conquer! The diary of a Nazi Unteroffizier in the German Africa

Corps. (1968). University, AL: Confederate Publishing.

APA Reference List Entries

1. One author
2. Two authors
3. Three to seven authors
4. Eight or more authors
5. Unnamed (anonymous) author
6. Two or more books by the same author
7. Two or more authors with the same surname and first initial

APA Reference List Entries

Example 10, 371

6. Two or more books by the same author For multiple books by the same author (or authors), arrange the entries in order of publication (from least to most recent). If the publisher is a university whose state name is included in its title, you may leave out the state.

> Benson, T. (2003). *Writing JFK: Presidential rhetoric and the press in the Bay of*
>
> *Pigs crisis*. College Station: Texas A&M University Press.
>
> Benson, T. (2015). *Posters for peace: Visual rhetoric and civic action*. University Park:
>
> Penn State University Press.

When books were written by the same author(s) in the same year, alphabetize the entries by title and add the letter *a* following the publication date of the first entry, *b* following the publication date of the second entry, and so on.

Dobrin, S. I. (2011a). *Ecology, writing theory, and new media: Writing ecology.* New York, NY: Routledge.

Dobrin, S. I. (2011b). *Postcomposition.* Carbondale: Southern Illinois University Press.

Works written by a single author should be listed *before* sources written by that same author plus a coauthor, regardless of publication dates.

Kress, G. (2010). *Multimodality: A social semiotic approach to contemporary communication.* New York, NY: Routledge.

Kress, G., Jewett, C., Ogborn, J., & Tsatsarelis, C. (2015). *Multimodal teaching and learning: The rhetorics of the science classroom.* New York, NY: Bloomsbury.

APA Reference List Entries

5. Unnamed (anonymous) author
6. Two or more books by the same author
7. Two or more authors with the same surname and first initial

APA Reference
List Entries

6. Two or more
   books by the
   same author
7. Two or more
   authors with
   the same
   surname and
   first initial
8. Group or
   corporate
   author
9. Author and
   editor or
   translator
10. Edited book or
    anthology

No state
abbreviation if state
included in name of
university press

When citing multiple sources by an author and various coauthors, alphabetize entries by the surname of the second author.

> Sternberg, R., Grigorenko, E., & Jarvin, L. (2009). *Teaching for wisdom, intelligence,*
>
> *creativity, and success.* New York, NY: Skyhorse Publishing.
>
> Sternberg, R., & Sternberg, K. (2016). *Cognitive psychology* (7th ed). Belmont,
>
> CA: Wadsworth.

7. Two or more authors with the same surname and first initial When your reference list includes sources by two different authors with the same surname and first initial, differentiate them by including their first names in brackets.

> Cohen, A. [Andrew]. (1994). *Assessing language ability in the classroom.*
>
> Boston, MA: Heinle.
>
> Cohen, A. [Anne]. (1973). *Poor Pearl, poor girl! The murdered girl stereotype in*
>
> *ballad and newspaper.* Austin: University of Texas Press.

8. Group or corporate author List the sponsoring organization as the author. Use the full name, and alphabetize it in the reference list according to the name's first significant word (ignoring articles such as *a, an,* or *the*). If the same group or corporation is also listed as the publisher, replace the name of the publisher with the word *Author.*

> Fabian Society, Commission on Life Chances and Child Poverty. (2006).
>
> *Narrowing the gap: The final report of the Fabian Commission on Life*
>
> *Chances and Child Poverty.* London, UK: Author.

9. Author and editor or translator If the source originally appeared earlier than the edited or translated version, add the date of original publication at the end of the entry. If the work has an editor, use the abbreviation *Ed.* For a translator, use the abbreviation *Trans.*

Alvtegen, K. (2010). *Shame* (S. Murray, Trans.). New York, NY: Felony and

Mayhem. (Original work published 2006)

10. Edited book or anthology Put the editor's name in the author position.

Brownell, K., & Gold, M. (Eds.). (2012). *Food and addiction: A comprehensive handbook.*

New York, NY: Oxford University Press.

For a book with a single editor, change the abbreviation to *Ed.*

11. Selection from an edited book or anthology Begin with the selection's author, followed by the publication date of the book and the selection's title (with no quotation marks or other formatting). Then insert the word *In*, the editors' names, and the title of the book or anthology (italicized). Next include page numbers for the entire selection (even if you used only part of it). Conclude the entry with the publication information for the book in which the selection appeared.

selection author   selection title   editors
Smither, N. (2000). Crime scene cleaner. In J. Bowe, M. Bowe, & S
                                                    selection pg. nos.
Streeter (Eds.), *Gig: Americans talk about their jobs* (pp. 96–103).

New York, NY: Crown.

12. Edition other than the first Insert the edition number (*2nd ed., 3rd ed.*) or edition name (*Rev. ed.* for "revised edition") after the book's title. (The edition number or name usually appears on the title page.)

Nier, J. A. (2013). *Taking sides: Clashing views in social psychology* (4th ed.).

New York, NY: McGraw-Hill.

13. Introduction, preface, foreword, or afterword The sixth edition of the *Publication Manual of the APA* does not provide an example of an entry for an introduction, preface, foreword, or afterword, but based on other examples, such an entry might look like the one below:

foreword's author   label   book's author   book's title
Andretti, M. (2008). Foreword. In D. Daly, *Race to win: How to become a*
                          pg. nos. (foreword)
complete champion (pp. 2–3). Minneapolis, MN: Quayside-Motorbooks.

Example 11, 379

14. Entry in an encyclopedia or other reference work Format an entry in a reference work as you would a selection from an edited book. For signed articles, include the author's name. (Articles in reference works often carry the author's initials only, so you may need to cross-reference the initials with a list of contributors in the front or back of the book.) If an article is unsigned, begin with its title.

APA Reference List Entries

a. Printed

entry author   entry title

Treffert, D. A. (2000). Savant syndrome. In A. E. Kazdin (Ed.), *Encyclopedia*

entry page nos.

of psychology (pp. 144–148). New York, NY: Oxford University Press.

b. Online

Kontos, A. (2014). Assimilation. In Eklund, R., & Tenenbaum, G. (Eds.), *Encyclopedia of*

URL

sport and exercise psychology. Retrieved from https://us.sagepub.com/en-us/nam

/encyclopedia-of-sport-and-exercise-psychology/book237359

15. Multivolume work

Tomasello, M. (Ed.). (1998–2003). *The new psychology of language: Cognitive and*

functional approaches to language structure (Vols. 1–2). Mahwah, NJ:

Erlbaum.

16. Republished book

Huxley, E. (2006). *Red strangers*. New York, NY: Penguin Group. (Original work published 1939)

Example 13, 372

17. Sacred or classical source No entry in the reference list is needed for a sacred source, such as the Bible, the Talmud, or the Qur'an, or a classical source, such as Plato's *Republic*.

18. Dissertation or thesis Indicate whether the work is a doctoral dissertation or a master's thesis. If the dissertation or thesis was accessed through a database service, include the name of the database from which it was obtained and provide any identifying number. If it was obtained from a university or personal website, include the URL.

a. Published

Pervil, I. (2016). *Ways of thinking about illness representations of cancer* (Doctoral dissertation). Available from ProQuest Dissertations and Theses Global database. (DAI-B 77/03E).

Lillie, A. S. (2008). *MusicBox: Navigating the space of your music* (Master's thesis, Massachusetts Institute of Technology). Retrieved from http://thesis.flyingpudding.com/documents/Anita_FINAL_THESIS.pdf

b. Unpublished

Luster, L. (1992). *Schooling, survival and struggle: Black women and the GED* (Unpublished doctoral dissertation). Stanford University, Stanford, CA.

c. Abstracted in DAI If you used the abstract in the *Dissertation Abstracts International* database, include that information in the entry. Remember, though, that reading the abstract is no substitute for reading the actual source.

Kelley, E. (2008). Parental depression and negative attribution bias in parent reports of child symptoms. *Dissertation Abstracts International: Section B. Sciences and Engineering, 69*(7), 4427.

Periodicals—Printed and Electronic

A periodical is a publication issued at regular intervals—newspapers are generally published every day, magazines every week or month, and scholarly journals four times a year. For periodicals, include not only the title of the article (with no quotation marks or italics) but also the title of the periodical

> Annotated visual of where to find author, title, publication, and other information, in tutorial preceding ch. 18, 300–03

> **More about** Formatting author information: Examples 1–11, 366–71

APA Reference List Entries

> **More about** Digital object identifiers (DOIs), PDFs, 183, 184, 205, 218, 221, 374–75, 386

(in italics, all important words capitalized). Other publication information you include depends on the type of periodical you are citing.

19. Article in a scholarly journal The information needed to create a reference list entry for a printed journal article appears on the cover or in the table of contents of the journal and on the first and last page of the article. For articles downloaded from a database, the information appears on the search results screen, in the full record of the article, or on the first and last page of the downloaded file. For articles that appear in journals that are published solely online, the needed information may be on the website's home page, in the journal's table of contents, or on the first page of the article.

a. Printed The basic citation for an article in a printed journal looks like this:

Author's surname, Initial(s). (Year of publication). Article title. *Journal Title, vol no., pages.*

Here is an example of an actual citation:

Wright, S. (2011). Invasive species and the loss of beta diversity. *Ethics and the Environment, 16,* 79–98.

If the article is published in a journal that starts each issue with page 1, provide the issue number after the volume number (not italicized, in parentheses).

Sui, C. (2007). Giving indigenous people a voice. *Taiwan Review,* 57(8), 40.

b. Online or accessed through a database More and more, researchers access journal articles electronically, either through online journals or through databases that provide access to articles in PDF or HTML format. Articles accessed electronically now frequently include a digital object identifier (DOI). The DOI is a permanent code that does not change from library to library or from database to database. The DOI makes URLs unnecessary. Whenever a DOI is provided, include it at the end of your reference list entry. The basic citation for an article in an online journal or accessed through an online database that has a DOI is the same as for a printed journal article except that the DOI appears at the end of the citation.

Luo, Y. (2011). Do 10-month-old infants understand others' false beliefs?

DOI

Cognition, 121, 289–298. doi:10.1016/j.cognition.2011.07.011

For an article in an online journal that does *not* provide a DOI, include the phrase *Retrieved from* followed by the URL for the journal's home page.

Janyam, K. (2011). The influence of job satisfaction on mental health of factory

workers. *The Internet Journal of Mental Health, 7*(1). Retrieved from http://

www.ispub.com/journal/the_internet_journal_of_mental_health/

20. Special issue of a journal

special issue title

Lowe, B., Souze-Monteiro, D., & Fraser, I. (Eds.) (2015). Changing food consumption

label

behaviors [Special issue]. *Psychology & Marketing, 32*(5).

21. Article in a magazine

a. **Printed** Provide the full publication date of the issue (year, month, and day or year and month). If the volume and issue number of the magazine are available, include that information as you would for a journal article.

Greene, K. (2011, December). Our data, ourselves. *Discover*, 42–47.

Goodwin, D. (2015, September). Neuroscience needs hackers.

Scientific American, 313(3), 24.

b. **Online or accessed through a database** Include the URL for the magazine's home page.

Washington, H. (2015, November). Catching madness. *Psychology Today*. Retrieved

from: https://www.psychologytoday.com/magazine/archive

Example 20, 383

If the magazine is available in a printed edition but the article is only available online, include the phrase *Supplemental material* in brackets after the article's title.

> Daniller, A. (2007, December). Psychology research done right [Supplemental material].
>
> *GradPSYCH*. Retrieved from http://gradpsych.apags.org

22. Article in a newspaper The information you need to create a reference list entry for a printed newspaper article is on the masthead of the newspaper (at the top of the first page) and on the first and last page of the article. For newspaper articles downloaded from a database, the information you need appears on the search results screen, the full record of the article, or the article itself. For articles that appear in online versions of the newspaper, the information you need is usually at the top of the first page of the article. Include "*The*" if it is part of the newspaper's name.

a. Printed

>   author   pub date   title
> Smith, E. (2015, November 17). Preventive side of justice reform.
>   newspaper   sec./pg. no.
>   *The Sacramento Bee*, p. 1B.

If the title of a newspaper does not include its place of publication, supply the city and state, in square brackets, following the title.

> Esch, M. (2011, July 1). New York may ban gas drilling in watersheds, state
>
> land. *The Evening Sun* [Norwich, NY], pp. 1, 3.

If the pages of the article are not continuous, provide all page numbers.

> Apuzzo, M., & Lipton, E. (2015, November 25). Rare alliance on sentencing begins to
>
> fray. *The New York Times*, pp. A1, A17.

To cite a newspaper article downloaded from a database, follow the model for a printed newspaper article, but omit the page numbers, and change the comma after the newspaper's title to a period.

b. Online or accessed through a database Follow the format for a printed newspaper article, but omit the page reference and include the words *Retrieved from* and the URL for the newspaper's home page.

Smyth, J. C., & Thompson, D. (2011, December 10). Public retirement ages

come under greater scrutiny. *The Denver Post*. Retrieved from http://www

.denverpost.com

23. Review (printed or online) Follow the model for the type of periodi-cal in which the review appeared. In the author position, insert the name of the author of the review; if the review is titled, insert that title in the title position (no italics or quotation marks); and add in brackets the label *Review of the book* (or *Review of the film,* and so forth) followed by the title and author of the reviewed work. End with publication information for the periodical in which the review appeared.

Examples 20 and 20–23, 383–85

review author   review title   label
Oryzysyn, D. (2014, June 10). Writers on death and grief [Review of the book

Dying in character, by J. Berman]. *Death Studies, 38*(10)

doi:10.1080/07481187.2013.869466

Comma between title, author

If the review is untitled, substitute the label *Review of the book,* the book's title, and the book's author in brackets.

Hurdley, R. (2011, September). [Review of the book *Gripes: The little*

quarrels of couples, by J. Kaufmann]. *Cultural Sociology,* 5, pp. 452–453.

Comma between title, author

24. Letter to the editor (printed or online) Follow the model for the type of periodical in which the letter appeared, and insert the label *Letter to the editor* in brackets following the letter's title.

Examples 20 and 20–23, 383–85

letter author   label
Dennett, D. (2015, March 20). [Letter to the editor]. *Times Literary Supplement, 5842,* p. 6.

If the letter is titled, put that information (no italics or quotation marks) right before the *Letter to the editor* label.

25. Abstract (printed or online) It is always better to read and cite the arti-cle itself. However, if you relied only on the abstract, or summary, cite only the abstract to avoid misrepresenting your source and your research.

Loverock, D. S. (2007). Object superiority as a function of object coherence and task

difficulty [Abstract]. *American Journal of Psychology, 120,* pp. 565–591.

APA Reference List Entries

22. Article in a newspaper

23. Review (printed or online)

24. Letter to the editor (printed or online)

25. Abstract (printed or online)

26. Website

Tebeaux, E. (2011). Technical writing and the development of the English

paragraph 1473-1700. *Journal of Technical Writing and Communication,*

41, 219-253. Abstract retrieved from http://www.ebscohost.com

Other Electronic Sources

Annotated visual
of where to find
author, title, and
publication infor-
mation, in tutorial
preceding ch. 18,
300–03

While it is usually easy to find the information you need to create a complete citation for a book or an article in a periodical, websites can be a bit trickier. Most of the information you need will appear on the site's home page, usually at the bottom or top of that page, or on the web page you are citing. Sometimes, however, you may need to look further. Click on links with titles such as "About us" or "More information." Frequently, websites do not provide complete information, in which case include as much information in your entry as you can.

Example 15, 373

26. Website In general, when mentioning an entire website in a research project, you do not have to include an entry in your reference list. However, if you quote or paraphrase content from the site or interact with it in a substantial way, include it, following this model:

APA Reference
List Entries

Author's surname, Initial(s). (Copyright date or date last updated). *Website title.*

Retrieved from + URL

Here is an example of an actual citation:

Gilbert, R. (2001). Shake your shyness. Retrieved from http://shakeyourshyness.com

Tech   Checking URLs and DOIs

DOIs. If your entry includes a DOI, check its accuracy before submitting your project by visiting crossref.org and inserting the DOI into the search box.

URLs. Just before submitting your project, test all the URLs. Sometimes web addresses change or content is taken down. If the URL you provided no longer works, search for the work online by title or keyword; you may find it "cached" on the web even though the owner of the original site has taken the work down. Then use the URL for the cached version in your bibliographic entry.

If no author is cited, move the title to the author position. If the web page is untitled, add a description in brackets. If no date is provided, insert *(n.d.)* following the author's name.

Example 5, 375

27. Web page Provide the title of the page (with no formatting) and the URL for the specific page you are citing.

web page title
American Psychological Association. (2011). Treatment for binge eating.
URL for web page
Retrieved from http://www.apa.org/

28. Discussion list posting Treat the subject line (or *thread*) as the title, and include the label *Discussion list post* (in brackets).

date posted   subject line   label
Pace, T. (2015, August 24). Genre and workplace writing. [Discussion list post].
URL
Retrieved from https://lists.asu.edu/cgi-bin/wa?A1=ind1508&L=WPA-L#51

If the name of the list is not included in the URL, add it to the retrieval statement: *Retrieved from Early Childhood Education Discussion List: http://www.dmoz.org/Reference/Education/Early_Childhood*

29. Article on a wiki Cite a wiki article as you would a web page. Because wikis are written and edited collaboratively, there is no author to cite; begin with the article's title. If the date of the most recent update is not noted, include the abbreviation *n.d.* (*no date*) in its place. Always include a retrieval date and direct URL.

retrieval date
Battered person syndrome. (n.d.). Retrieved April 22, 2012, from http://
URL
psychology.wikia.com

30. Blog Include a screen name if the author's name is not provided.
a. Blog posting

post author   post date   post title   label
(post)
Bell, V. (2015, November 7). A medieval attitude to suicide [Web log post].
URL
Retrieved from http://mindhacks.com/2015/11/07/a-medieval-attitude-to-suicide/

APA Reference List Entries

25. Abstract (printed or online)
26. Website
27. Web page
28. Discussion list posting
29. Article on a wiki
30. Blog
31. Computer software
32. Presentation slides

> **More about**
> Reliability, 233–43

b. Comment on a blog posting

comment author [avatar]   date posted   subject line (thread title)
Medicinehorse179. (2015, November 17). Re: No more type I/II error confusion
         label   URL
[Web log comment]. Retrieved from http://mindhacks.com/

31. Computer software Provide an entry for computer software only if it is unfamiliar to your readers and it is necessary to a computation you have made.

    title   label
Power Researcher [Computer software]. Atlanta, GA: Uniting Networks.

If the software you are citing is available in more than one version, add a version number in parentheses between the title of the software and the identifying label.

32. Presentation slides The sixth edition of the *Publication Manual of the APA* does not provide an example of an entry for presentation slides, but based on other examples such an entry might look like the one below:

                                        label
Stolley, K., & Brizee, A. (2015). *Visual rhetoric for student writers* [PowerPoint slides].

    Purdue OWL. Retrieved from https://owl.english.purdue.edu/owl/

Audio and Visual Sources

The information you need to create an entry for most audio and visual sources appears on the cover, label, or program of the work or in the credits at the end of a film or television show. As with other citations, italicize the titles of longer works, such as CDs and films, and do not format or add quotation marks to the titles of shorter works, such as single songs or single episodes of television programs.

33. Motion picture

                                  release   title
Grazer, B. (Producer), & Howard, R. (Director). (2001). *A beautiful mind*
                      distributor
    [Motion picture]. United States: Warner Bros.

34. Online video or video blog (vlog)

if no author identified, begin entry with source title
25 things psychology tells you about yourself. (2014, December 8). [Video file].

    Retrieved from: https://www.youtube.com/watch?v=ic9fnTpoYdk

35. Television or radio broadcast
a. Series

Garcia, R. (Executive producer). (2008–2009). *In treatment* [Television series].

New York, NY: HBO.

b. Episode

Reingold, J. (Writer), & Barclay, P. (Director). (2009). Mia: Week three

[Television series episode]. In R. Garcia (Executive producer), *In treatment*.

New York, NY: HBO.

c. Podcast

Vedantam, S. The science of compassion [Audio podcast]. *The Hidden Brain*. Retrieved

from http://www.npr.org/series/423302056/hidden-brain

36. Musical or other audio recording
a. CD, LP, or audiobook

Rockefeller, J. (2014, November 11). The introvert personality:

The advantage of introverts in an extrovert world [Audio book].

Retrieved from http://www.amazon.com/

b. Selection or song on a CD, LP, or audiobook

writers © date   performers
Dilly, D., & Wilkin, M. (1959). The long black veil [Recorded by H. Dickens & A. Gerrard].

On *Pioneering women of bluegrass* [CD]. Washington, DC: Smithsonian/
recording date
Folkways Records. (1996).

37. Lecture, speech, conference presentation, or poster session

Guilko, T. (2015, October 4). *From baby boomers to Generation Y: Motivation across the*

ages. Paper presented at the British Psychological Society's Division on Occupa-

tional Therapy Conference, Oxford, UK.

APA Reference List Entries

33. Motion picture
34. Online video or video blog (vlog)
35. Television or radio broadcast
36. Musical or other audio recording
37. Lecture, speech, conference presentation, or poster session
38. Work of art
39. Advertisement

38. Map

U.S. Census Bureau, Geography Division (Cartographer). (2001). *Mean center of*

   population for the United States: 1790 to 2000 [Demographic map].

   Retrieved from http://www.census.gov/geo/www/cenpop/meanctr.pdf

Miscellaneous Sources—Printed and Electronic

39. Government publication
a. Printed

                                                                    title
Child Welfare Information Gateway. (2015). *Adoption options: Where do I start?* Washington,

   DC: U.S. Department of Health and Human Services, Children's Bureau.

If the source includes a publication number, add that information in parentheses after the title.

b. Online

U.S. General Accounting Office. (1993, September 21). *North American Free Trade Agree-*

   ment: A focus on the substantive issues (Publication No. GAO/T-GGD-93-44).

   Retrieved from http://www.gpoaccess.gov/gaoreports/search.html

40. Report (nongovernmental)

Head, A. (2014, July 29). *Trends from the lifelong learning interviews with recent*

   graduates. Project Information Literacy Progress Report. Retrieved from

   http://projectinfolit.org/publications

41. Data set

U.S. Department of Justice, Federal Bureau of Investigation. (2007, September). *2006*

   Crime in the United States [Data set]. Retrieved from http://www.data.gov/raw/310

42. Fact sheet, brochure, pamphlet

Information Services Department, Hong Kong Special Administrative Region Govern-

   ment. (2015, February). *Agriculture and Fisheries* [Fact sheet]. Retrieved from

   http://www.gov.hk/en/about/abouthk/factsheets/

If no author is listed, move the title to the author position. If no publication date is available, insert *n.d.* (for *no date*) in its place.

43. Conference proceedings Cite conference proceedings either as an edited book or as the special issue of a journal, depending on how they were published.

Example 10, 371
Example 21, 383–84

44. Legal source (printed or online)

case title (abbreviated)   *U.S. Reports*   decision
     vol.   no.   date
Lynn v. Alabama, 493 U.S. 945 (1989). Retrieved from *Open Jurist* website:
                 URL

     http://openjurist.org/493/us/945/lynn-v-alabama

45. Interview (published or broadcast)

interview subject   broadcast date
    Hoffman, B. (2015, November 28). What information do intelligence agencies need to

    keep US safe? Interview by S. Simon. Retrieved from http://www.npr.org

    /sections/interviews/

46. Personal communication (email, letter, interview) Cite personal communications that are not available to the public in the body of the research project, but do not include an entry in the reference list.

19c Using APA Style for Informational Notes

In addition to in-text citations, APA style allows researchers to include informational notes. These notes may provide supplementary information, acknowledge any help the writer received, or call attention to possible conflicts of interest.

Example 16, 380

    To add supplementary information, include a superscript (above-the-line) arabic number in the text and at the beginning of the note (either at the bottom of the page for a footnote or in a list of notes at the end of the project).

The participants in each condition were told at the beginning of the experiment that they were

participating in a memory-recall task. They were to identify what they could remember from a clip from the

movie *Pretty Woman* (Milchan, Reuther, & Marshall, 1990),[1] a stereotypical "chick-flick."

Notes

½"
←——→ ¹This romantic comedy starring Julia Roberts and Richard Gere (dir. Garry Marshall) was extremely

popular, grossing nearly $464 million worldwide, according to the site Box Office Mojo (http://www.boxoffi

cemojo.com/movies/?id=prettywoman.htm). Nevertheless, participants had not seen the film before

participating in the experiment.

> Sample title
> page, 397

Add notes to acknowledge help or possible conflicts of interest to the title page, four lines below the date.

19d Formatting a Paper in APA Style

Student Model
Research project,
APA style: "The Power
of Wardrobe,"
Heather DeGroot,
396–405

The care with which you cite and document your sources reflects the care you have taken in writing your research project. Continue that care by formatting your project in the way your readers expect. For most writing projects in the social sciences, follow the APA's formatting guidelines. The *Publication Manual of the APA* offers guidance for writers submitting projects for publication in scholarly journals, so not all its formatting requirements are appropriate for student projects. Ask your instructor about making reasonable modifications.

1. Margins and spacing

- Set margins of at least one inch at the top, bottom, and left- and right-hand sides of your paper.

> *More about*
> Block quotations,
> 812

- Indent the first line of each paragraph half an inch.

- Indent quotations of forty or more words as a block, half an inch from the left margin.

- Double-space the entire paper, including the abstract, title page, block quotations, footnotes, figure captions, and the reference list. Set the text so that the right margin is uneven (ragged), and do not hyphenate words at the ends of lines.

- Insert two spaces after punctuation at the end of a sentence.

- Use a hanging indent for each reference list entry: The first line should be flush with the left margin with subsequent lines indented half an inch.

Sample reference list, 403

2. Typeface, header, and page number

Use a standard typeface such as Times New Roman or Arial in a readable size (usually 12 points). Include a header, or *running head,* consisting of the first two or three words of the title (no more than fifty characters) in the upper left-hand corner of the page, half an inch from the upper edge. Include the page number half an inch from the top and one inch from the right edge of the page. Use your word processor's header feature to insert the running head and number the pages automatically.

More about
Choosing a type-
face and type
size, 169–70

3. Title page

- Insert the title, typed in upper- and lowercase letters, centered on the top half of the page.
- Insert a blank line and then type your name.

More about
Crafting a title,
92–93
Notes acknowl-
edging help
or conflicts,
391–92, 397

Tech   Indention

The major style guides (MLA, APA, *Chicago*, CSE) were initially written before the widespread use of personal computers, when most writers still worked on typewriters. To create a paragraph or hanging indention on a typewriter, the typist would hit the space bar five times or set a tab. Now, just about everyone creates writing projects on a computer, where paragraph and hanging indentions are created using the Ruler or Paragraph Dialog box.

Ruler

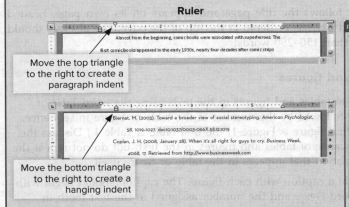

Almost from the beginning, comic books were associated with superheroes. The first comic books appeared in the early 1930s, nearly four decades after comic strips

Move the top triangle to the right to create a paragraph indent

Biernat, M. (2003). Toward a broader view of social stereotyping. *American Psychologist,* 58, 1019-1027. doi:10.1037/0003-066X.58.12.1019

Coplan, J. H. (2008, January 28). When it's all right for guys to cry. *Business Week,* 4068, 17. Retrieved from http://www.businessweek.com

Move the bottom triangle to the right to create a hanging indent

Paragraph Dialog Box

Sample title page, APA style, 397

Sample abstract, APA style, 397

Sample figure captions, APA style, 404

> **Tech** **Creating a Header**
>
> Word processing programs allow you to insert a header automatically. In Microsoft Word, select "Header and Footer" | under the View menu. If you have any questions about creating a header, consult your program's Help directory.

- Papers for submission to a scholarly journal include the author's university or college affiliation; student writers usually include the course number, the name of the instructor to whom the project will be submitted, and the date of submission, each centered on separate lines.

- If you need to acknowledge help you received—for example, in conducting your research or interpreting your results—include a note on the title page, four lines below the identifying information.

4. Abstract

The abstract generally includes a one-sentence summary of the most important points in each section of the project:

- Introduction—problem you are investigating

- Methods—number and characteristics of the participants and your research methods

- Results—your outcomes

- Discussion—implications of your results. This section concludes your text.

The abstract follows the title page and appears on its own page, headed with the word *Abstract* centered at the top of the page. The abstract should be no more than 150–250 words.

5. Tables and figures

- Refer to tables and figures in the text, using the word *Table* or *Figure* followed by the number of the table or figure in sequence. (The first figure is Figure 1; the first table is Table 1.) Discuss the significance of tables and figures in the text, but do not repeat the information that appears in the table or figure itself.

- Include a caption with each figure. The caption should begin with the word *Figure* and the number assigned in the text (both in italics). The caption, which follows the figure, should describe the figure briefly but not repeat the information in your text. If you borrowed the figure or the data to create the figure, include the source information at the end of your caption.

- Include the word *Table* and the table number (no italics) on one line and, on the next line, the table title (in italics). The table itself should appear below the table number and title. If you borrowed the table or the data to create the table, include source information below the table, preceded by the word *Note* (in italics, followed by a period).

- In research projects submitted for publication, tables should appear, each on a new page, after the reference list or endnotes (if any). Figures (graphs, charts, photographs, maps, and so on) should appear, each on a new page, following the tables. In college research projects, however, your instructor may prefer to see tables and figures in the body of your research project, as close as possible following their first mention in the text. Check with your instructor before formatting your project.

Sample figures, APA style, 404–405

6. Reference list

- Center the heading "References" at the top of the page.

- Use a hanging indent for each reference list entry: The first line should be flush with the left margin, with subsequent lines indented half an inch.

- Alphabetize the entries in the reference list by the surname of the author or, if no author is listed, by the first important word in the title (ignoring *A, An,* or *The*).

- Italicize all titles of books and websites, but do not enclose titles of articles or book chapters in quotation marks.

More about Italics with titles, 842–43

Writing
Responsibly   Of Deadlines and Paperclips

Instructors expect students to turn in thoughtful, carefully proofread, and neatly formatted papers on time—usually in class on the due date. Another expectation is that the writer will clip or staple the pages of the paper *before* the paper is submitted. Do justice to yourself by being fully prepared.

to SELF

More about
Capitalization,
838–39
Proper nouns,
837–38

- Capitalize the first word, the first word following a colon or a dash, and proper nouns in titles of books, articles in periodicals, websites and web pages, films, and so on. Capitalize all major words in journal titles: *Psychology, Public Policy, and Law; Monitor on Psychology.*

7. Printing, paper, and binding

Print your project using a high-quality printer (make sure it has plenty of ink), on opaque, 8½ × 11–inch white paper. Most instructors do not want you to enclose your paper in a binder, but if you are in doubt, ask. If it is not submitted in a binder, paperclip or staple the pages together.

Student Model Research Project: APA Style

More about
Writing in the sciences and social sciences, 475–89 (ch. 23)
Appendixes, 480–81

In the sample student research project that follows, Heather DeGroot examines the influence that gender stereotypes can have on behavior. She fulfills her responsibilities to topic and audience by drawing on a variety of relevant and reliable sources to provide the background that her readers will need, by including visuals that help her readers understand her project, and by following the format for an APA-style research project, the format her readers expect. By acknowledging her sources, she fulfills her responsibility to the other writers from whom she has borrowed information. By conducting her primary research with care, by thanking Patrick Brown for the assistance he provided, by acknowledging the limitations of her project, and by revising, editing, and proofreading her project carefully, she demonstrates her own credibility as a researcher and writer.

Running head: Shortened title   pg. no.

The words *Running head,* followed by a colon, may not be needed for college research projects in APA style.

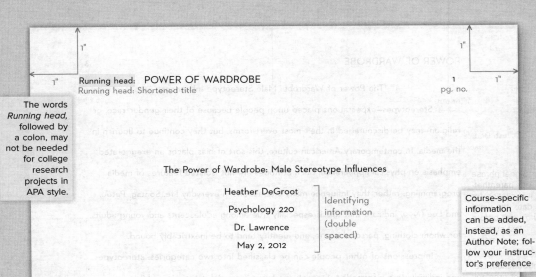

The Power of Wardrobe: Male Stereotype Influences

Heather DeGroot

Psychology 220

Dr. Lawrence

May 2, 2012

Identifying information (double spaced)

Course-specific information can be added, instead, as an Author Note; follow your instructor's preference

Author Note

I would like to thank Patrick Brown for playing the proctor in each of the three conditions.

Abstract   Heading (centered, 1" from top), new page

Abstract: Summary of problem, methods, results, discussion

This study explores the potential influence of stereotypical appearances on male subjects' stated opinions regarding entertainment perceived as "feminine." Results are based on responses from 26 undergraduate males. Data were analyzed using one-way variance tests and Tukey HSD post hoc tests. The findings show that participants were more likely to give a favorable rating to a "chick-flick" in the presence of a counterstereotypical male ($M = 8.67$, $SD = 1.53$) than in the presence of a stereotypical male ($M = 5.31$, $SD = 1.97$) or control proctor ($M = 5.20$, $SD = 1.99$). Results suggest that participants may have experienced gender role conflict.

397

The Power of Wardrobe: Male Stereotype Influences   *Title (centered)*

¶ indent: ½"

Stereotypes—expectations placed upon people because of their gender, race, or religion—may be discouraged in their most overt forms, but they continue to flourish in the media. In contemporary American culture, this sort of bias places an exaggerated emphasis on physical appearance. Such attitudes are not isolated features of media programming; rather, they influence many interactions in everyday life. Sontag, Peteu, and Lee (1999) indicate that this is especially true among adolescents and young adults, for whom clothing, personal image, and identity tend to be inextricably bound.

Impressions of other people can be classified into two categories: stereotypes and individuating information. Stereotypes focus on social categories, while individuating information is the focus of other factors, including personality, actions of the individual, and so forth (Kunda & Thagard, 1996). The stereotype effect, as defined by researcher Monica Biernat (2003), is "a finding that individual members (comparable in all ways except their category membership) are judged in a direction consistent with group-level expectations or stereotypes" (p. 1019). Under such circumstances, people are judged more by the category in which one can group them than by their qualities or skills as individuals. However, according to Kunda and Thagard (1996), the division of these types of judgment is not always clear. This was the influence for their impression-formation theory in which stereotypes, traits, and behaviors are all constrained by positive and negative associations. In their research, they found that appearance was crucial in this process.

The influential power of stereotypes is particularly interesting when gender boundaries are crossed. In a 2003 study, researchers Vescio, Snyder, and Butz found that while membership in a socioeconomic class or "power position" (p. 1062) tended

Text: Double-spaced

Signal phrase with parenthetical citation for date; the word and used before last author's name

Introduction: De-Groot provides background, definitions, hypothesis.

Signal phrase with parenthetical citation for date, page number included with quotation

Date of publication in text, so not in parentheses following author names

to give participants a biased or predetermined opinion about the beliefs and behaviors (such as work ethic) by which a person in another category lived, gender exerted at least as great an influence on the manner in which people were categorized. Mansfield (2006) demonstrated that males in power positions were likely to be viewed differently than females in the same positions.

Would these findings remain consistent if only one gender were used in the study? That is, can we identify intra-gender roles or stereotypes that similarly affect perception and beliefs about individuals? A study by G. H. Edwards (1992) found that beliefs regarding men and women transcend gender, with subtypes or categories (such as for men, businessman, athlete, or loser) emerging within each sex. Typically, such seeming variations represent varying degrees of a supposed normative "masculinity," rather than truly distinct expressions of a male gender role. Rudman and Fairchild (2004) write that "for men, a lifetime of experience observing one's peers being teased or ostracized for 'effeminate' behavior may evoke strong normative pressures toward highly masculine self-presentations" (p. 160). Plummer (2001) indicates that boys begin pressuring one another to conform in childhood, telling each other to toughen up or to stop acting like a baby.

Direct quotation from PDF; page number included

The purpose of this study is to observe whether male participants are likely to be influenced by a stereotypically "male" opinion. Are college-aged males more swayed by the "jock" or "cool guy on campus" than by those with an "average Joe" or a "metrosexual" appearance? Hypothetically, male participants should more likely be swayed by the opinions of the stereotypical male than by those of the control group ("average Joe") or the experimental group (counterstereotypical).

Hypothesis

POWER OF WARDROBE

Methods First-level heading (centered, boldface)

Participants Second-level heading (left, boldface)

Methods:
DeGroot explains
how study was
conducted

Twenty-six undergraduate males from a large southeastern university (mean

age = 19) participated in this study in order to fill a course requirement in their general

psychology classes.

Procedure

Projects for pub-
lication: Tables
and figures
follow reference
list or endnotes.
College projects:
Ask your instruc-
tor—tables and
figures may be
included in the
text, following
the first refer-
ence to them.
Figures for this
project appear
on pp. 404–405

The participants were randomly assigned to one of three conditions in the study: the

stereotypically "male" proctor group, the counterstereotypical proctor group, and the control

group. The proctor was the same person in each condition, but his appearance was different

in each (Figure 1). In the stereotypically male proctor condition, the proctor wore an outfit

consisting of team sports apparel: a baseball cap, a basketball jersey, shorts, and sneakers.

In the counterstereotypical condition, he wore a long-sleeved, light pink button-down shirt

(tucked in), creased khaki pants, and dress shoes. In the control condition, the proctor wore

a short-sleeved blue polo shirt (not tucked in), khaki shorts, and sneakers.

The participants in each condition were told at the beginning of the experiment

that they were participating in a memory-recall task. They were to identify what

they could remember from a clip from the movie *Pretty Woman* (Milchan, Reuther, &

Ampersand used
in parenthetical
citation

Marshall, 1990), a stereotypical "chick-flick." During the ten-minute film clip, which was

constant for each of the three conditions, the proctor read scripted lines such as "Oh!

I love this part!" and "I'm seriously such a sap, but this film is just so good!" The script

was a constant in each of the three conditions.

After the clip was viewed by all, the proctor handed out a questionnaire to

conduct the "memory-recall task." The questionnaire contained diversion questions such

as "What color is the dress that Vivian (Julia Roberts's character) wears in the scene?"

and "What game do Edward and Vivian play after the performance?" At the end of the questionnaire, the participants rated the movie on an opinion scale from 1 to 10, with 10 being the highest overall liking.

After the experiment was over, participants in each condition were debriefed as a group and were dismissed from the study.

Results

A one-way analysis of variance (ANOVA) was conducted on the data in order to determine whether males are more influenced by a stereotypically "male" proctor in comparison to the counterstereotypical and control-group proctors. The analysis demonstrated that at least one group was significantly different from the others, $F(2, 23) = 4.08$, $p < .05$. Tukey HSD post hoc tests were performed to measure the difference between the groups individually. The Tukey HSD revealed that the participants were more likely to give a favorable movie rating under the influence of the counterstereotypically masculine proctor ($M = 8.67$, $SD = 1.53$) than the stereotypically masculine proctor ($M = 5.31$, $SD = 1.97$) or the control proctor ($M = 5.20$, $SD = 1.99$) (see Figure 2).

There were no significant differences in movie ratings between those in the stereotypically masculine proctor's group and those in the control proctor's. These results were contrary to the study's initial hypothesis, and they suggest that male participants are more likely to defy gender roles in the presence of a counterstereotypical proctor than in the presence of a stereotypically masculine proctor.

Discussion

The study elicited something beyond stereotypical responses from the participants. In fact, the participants may have experienced gender role conflict. Instead of scoring favorably

Results: DeGroot summarizes data and research findings; includes figures, pp. 244.

when the masculine male proctor said he enjoyed the film, the participants scored the film lower than initially expected. The presence of a highly or moderately "masculine" male, though he made favorable comments in each condition, may have caused the participants to adhere more rigidly to socialized male gender roles and thus rate the movie lower than subjects in the atypically "masculine" proctor group, who did not feel the pressure to assert masculinity in their rating of *Pretty Woman*. (See McCreary et al., 1996.)

Certain irregularities in the study provoked questions that might be investigated in future research. Due to factors beyond the researcher's control, each condition had a different number of participants. The counterstereotypical condition, which had significant findings, had the smallest number of participants; as a result, those scores are subject to greater statistical variation due to strong individual opinion. However, one might also question whether the number of males present influences a subject's tendency to admit to a counterstereotypical opinion or value judgment. If the study were to be replicated to find for stereotype differences alone, it would be crucial for the number of participants in each condition to be the same. On the other hand, a separate study might use multiple viewing groups of varying individual sizes to determine the effect of group size in gender-stereotype-determined valuations.

Another issue to consider is the effect of the fictional nature of the film to which the male viewers were asked to react. A study reported in *Business Week* suggests that men are more willing to show empathy when they know the stories eliciting their emotional response are fictional. Jennifer Argo, one of the authors of the study, is quoted as saying that fictional works provide "an excuse to relax gender stereotypes" (as cited in Coplan, 2008, p. 17). This factor was not considered in the study reported here.

Discussion: DeGroot interprets data, draws conclusions, expresses concerns, and raises questions for further study.

Citations of six or more authors: First author plus *et al.*

References Heading (centered), new page; entries
alphabetized by author

Biernat, M. (2003). Toward a broader view of social stereotyping. *American Psychologist,*

↔ *58,* 1019–1027. doi:10.1037/0003-066X.58.12.1019
½"

Coplan, J. H. (2008, January 28). When it's all right for guys to cry. *Business Week,*

4068, 17. Retrieved from http://www.businessweek.com

Edwards, G. H. (1992). The structure and content of the male gender role stereotype:

An exploration of subtypes. *Sex Roles: A Journal of Research, 27,* 553–551.

Kunda, Z., & Thagard, P. (1996). Forming impressions from stereotypes, traits, and behav-

iors: A parallel-constraint-satisfaction theory. *Psychological Review, 103,* 284–308.

Mansfield, H. C. (2006). *Manliness.* New Haven, CT: Yale University Press.

McCreary, D. R., Wong, F. Y., Wiener, W., Carpenter, K. M., Engle, A., & Nelson, P. (1996).

The relationship between masculine gender role stress and psychological adjust-

ment: A question of construct validity? *Sex Roles: A Journal of Research, 34,*

507–516.

Milchan, A. (Producer), Reuther, S. (Producer), & Marshall, G. (Director). (1990). *Pretty*

woman [DVD]. USA: Touchstone Home Video.

Plummer, D. C. (2001). The quest for modern manhood: Masculine stereotypes, peer cul-

ture, and the social significance of homophobia. *Journal of Adolescence, 24,* 15–23.

Rudman, L. A., & Fairchild, K. (2004). Reactions to counterstereotypic behavior: The role

of backlash in cultural stereotype maintenance. *Journal of Personality and Social*

Psychology, 87, 157–176.

Journal article: Accessed through database, DOI included

Magazine article: Accessed through a website—URL of home page provided

Book: Scholarly press

Film: Medium in brackets

Journal article: PDF accessed through database, no DOI—page numbers included, no URL

Sontag, M. S., Peteu, M., & Lee, J. (1999). *Clothing in the self-system of adolescents: Relationships among values, proximity of clothing to self, clothing interest, anticipated outcomes and perceived quality of life.* Retrieved from Michigan State University Extension website: http://web1.msue.msu.edu/msue/imp/modrr/rr556098.html

Vescio, T. K., Snyder, M., & Butz, D. A. (2003). Power in stereotypically masculine domains: A social influence strategy X stereotype match model. *Journal of Personality and Social Psychology, 85,* 1062. doi:10.1037/0022-3514.85.6.1062

(a) (b) (c)

Figure 1. Male proctor in three conditions: (a) stereotypical, (b) counterstereotypical, and (c) control.

Photographs courtesy of Jane Carter

Research report on website: URL of report included; sponsor named in retrieval statement

Figure caption: Label *(Figure)* and number in italics; caption below illustration

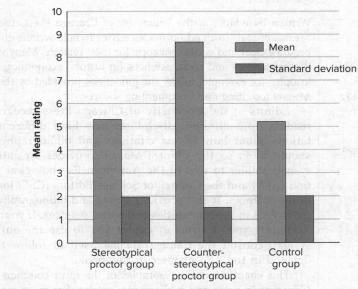

Figure 2. Tukey HSD post hoc test results for the three groups: Group with the stereotypical proctor, group with counterstereotypical proctor, and control group.

20 Documenting Sources: *Chicago* Style

> *More about*
> MLA style,
>   304–62 (ch. 18)
> APA style,
>   363–405 (ch. 19)
> CSE style,
>   435–49 (ch.21)

Written by editors at the University of Chicago Press, the *Chicago Manual of Style* (16th ed.) provides advice to help writers and editors produce clear and consistent copy for their readers. Many writers in the humanities and social sciences (in history, economics, and philosophy, for example) follow the guidelines provided by the *Chicago Manual* for citing and documenting sources.

Editors at the University of Chicago Press recognize that readers from different disciplines may have different expectations about how in-text citations and bibliography entries should look, so the *Chicago Manual* provides an author-date system similar to that of the American Psychological Association (APA) and the Council of Science Editors (CSE) for writers in the sciences. It also provides a note and bibliography system for writers in the humanities and social sciences. If your readers (including your instructor) expect you to use the author-date system, consult the *Chicago Manual* itself or follow the style detailed in the APA chapter in this book.

This chapter includes examples of the most common types of *Chicago*-style notes and bibliography entries. For more information or for examples of less common types of sources, consult the *Chicago Manual* itself. You can also subscribe to the *Chicago Manual* online.

Writing Responsibly | Citing and Documenting Sources

When you cite and document sources, you demonstrate how thoroughly you have researched your topic and how carefully you have thought about your sources, which encourages your audience to believe you are a credible researcher. In your citations and documentation you acknowledge any material from which you have quoted, paraphrased, summarized, or drawn information, and you join the conversation on your topic by adding your own interpretation. Accurate entries in the body of your project and bibliography allow your audience to find and read your sources so that they can evaluate your interpretation and learn more about the subject themselves. Accurate entries also demonstrate the care with which you have written your research project, which further reinforces your credibility, or ethos.

to AUDIENCE

20a Creating *Chicago*-Style Notes and Bibliography Entries

The note system offered by the *Chicago Manual* allows you to include full bibliographic information in a footnote or endnote or to use an abbreviated footnote or endnote with a bibliography. The University of Chicago Press recommends using abbreviated notes with a bibliography.

> **footnote** Note that appears at the bottom of the page

Examples of the *complete* form of notes and bibliography entries for different types of sources appear in the next section. An *abbreviated* note typically includes enough information for readers to recognize the work and find it in the bibliography. It usually includes the author's surname, a shortened version of the title that includes the title's keywords in the same order as they appear on the title page, and the page number you are citing. Here is an example of an abbreviated note and a bibliography entry for the same book:

> **endnote** Note that appears in a list of notes at the end of the project

NOTE
(ABBREVIATED)

1. Vancouver, *Voyage of Discovery*, 283.

BIBLIOGRAPHY

Vancouver, George. *A Voyage of Discovery* to the North Pacific Ocean and Round the World, 1791–1795. Edited by W. Kaye Lamb. London: Hakluyt Society, 1984.

A complete bibliographic note or bibliography entry includes three parts: the author's name, the title of the work, and the publication information (print, electronic, or both). The information you include in each of these parts will differ depending on the type of source you are citing. There are many models, but every variation cannot be covered, so be prepared to adapt a model to your special circumstances.

> Annotated visual of where to find author and publication information, 300–03 (Documentation Matters tutorial preceding ch. 18)

Tech — Creating Footnotes and Endnotes

Most word processing programs, including Microsoft Word and Google Docs, allow you to insert footnotes and endnotes easily. This automated system for inserting footnotes will automatically renumber all the notes in your project if you add or delete one. However, the software for managing notes may not provide many formatting options, so check with your instructor in advance to make sure the software's default format is acceptable.

> *More about*
> Formatting notes (*Chicago* style), 423
> Formatting bibliographies (*Chicago* style), 423

Quick Reference Examples of *Chicago*-Style Note and Bibliography Entries

Books—Printed and Electronic

In a printed book, the information you need to create a note and bibliography entry (with the exception of the page numbers) is on the title and copyright pages, at the beginning of the book. In an online or e-book, print and electronic publication information usually appears on the first few screens.

1. One author

a. Printed The basic note for a printed book looks like this:

> Ref. No. Author's first name Surname, *Title: Subtitle* (Place of Publication:
>
> Publisher, date of publication), page(s).

Here is an example of an actual note:

> 1. Richard Wrangham, *Catching Fire: How Cooking Made Us Human*
>
> (New York: Basic Books, 2011), 96-98.

The basic bibliography entry for a printed book looks like this:

> Author's surname, First Name. *Title: Subtitle*. Place of publication: Publisher,
>
> date of publication.

Here is an example of an actual bibliography entry:

> Wrangham, Richard. *Catching Fire: How Cooking Made Us Human*.
>
> New York: Basic Books, 2011.

The *Chicago Manual* allows for either full publishers' names (the name minus words like *Incorporated* or *Publishers*) or abbreviated versions (*Wiley* instead of *John Wiley & Sons,* for example). Be consistent within your research project. This chapter uses full names.

b. Database

> 2. W. E. B. Du Bois, *The Souls of Black Folk* (1903; Bartleby.com, 1999), chap. 1,
>
> www.bartleby.com/114/.

> Du Bois, W. E. B. *The Souls of Black Folk*. Reprint of the 1903 edition, Bartleby.com,
>
> 1999. www.bartleby.com/114/.

If the online book is *not* available in print or is not yet in final form and might change by the time your readers seek it out, provide your access date immediately before the DOI or URL. Separate the access date from the surrounding citation by commas in a note and by periods in a bibliography entry.

Chicago Note & Bibliography Entries

1. One author
2. Two or three authors
3. More than three authors

Tech **Guidelines for Formatting URLs**

In *Chicago* style, if a URL will not fit on a single line, break it after a colon (:) or a double slash (//), before or after an ampersand (&) or equals sign (=), and before a dot or other punctuation mark.

c. E-book

3. Charles C. Mann, *1491: New Revelations of the Americas before Columbus* (New York: Alfred A. Knopf, 2005), Adobe Reader e-book, chap. 3.

Mann, Charles C. *1491: New Revelations of the Americas before Columbus.* New York: Alfred A. Knopf, 2005. Adobe Reader e-book.

2. Two or three authors

4. David Gold and Catherine Hobbs, *Educating the New Southern Woman: Speech, Writing, and Race at the Public Women's Colleges, 1884–1945* (Carbondale, IL: Southern Illinois University Press, 2013).

5. William Rick Crandall, John A. Parnell, and John E. Spillan, *Crisis Management: Leading in the New Strategy Landscape* (Thousand Oaks, CA: Sage, 2012), 119.

Gold, David, and Catherine Hobbs. *Educating the New Southern Woman: Speech, Writing, and Race at the Public Women's Colleges, 1884–1945.* Carbondale, IL: Southern Illinois University Press, 2013.

Crandall, William Rick, John A. Parnell, and John E. Spillan. *Crisis Management: Leading in the New Strategy Landscape.* Thousand Oaks, CA: Sage, 2012.

> 1st author only listed surname first

3. More than three authors

6. Lawrence Niles et al., *Life Along the Delaware Bay: Cape May Gateway to a Million Shorebirds* (Piscataway, NJ: Rutgers University Press, 2012), 87.

Niles, Lawrence, Joanna Burger, Amanda Dey, and Jan Van der Kam. *Life Along the Delaware Bay: Cape May Gateway to a Million Shorebirds.* Piscataway, NJ: Rutgers University Press, 2012.

> 1st author plus *et al.* ("and others" in Latin) in note

> All authors in bibliography entry

4. Unnamed (anonymous) author If no author is listed, begin with the title.

7. *Terrorist Hunter: The Extraordinary Story of a Woman Who Went Undercover to Infiltrate the Radical Islamic Groups Operating in America* (New York: Ecco, 2003), 82.

Terrorist Hunter: The Extraordinary Story of a Woman Who Went Undercover to Infiltrate the Radical Islamic Groups Operating in America. New York: Ecco, 2003.

5. Two or more works by the same author Your note will be the same as for any book by one or more authors. In your bibliography, alphabetize the entries by the first important word in the title, and replace the author's name with three dashes in entries after the first.

> Howard, Philip K. *Life Without Lawyers: Restoring Responsibility in America*. New York:
>
> W. W. Norton, 2011.

> – – –. *Sacred Cows: How Dead Laws Drag Down Democracy*. New York: W. W. Norton,
>
> 2012.

Examples 1–3, 408

6. Group or corporate author

> group as author
> 8. Blackfoot Gallery Committee, *The Story of the Blackfoot People: Nitsitapiis-*
>
> *inni* (Richmond Hill, ON: Firefly Books, 2002), 15.

> group as author
> Blackfoot Gallery Committee. *The Story of the Blackfoot People: Nitsitapiisinni*.
>
> Richmond Hill, ON: Firefly Books, 2002.

7. Editor (no author)

> 9. R. K. Ashdowne, ed., *Dictionary of Medieval Latin from British Sources, fas-*
>
> *cicule XVII, Syr-Z* (New York: Oxford University Press, 2013), 22.

> Ashdowne, R. K, ed. *Dictionary of Medieval Latin from British Sources, fascicule XVII,*
>
> *Syr-Z*. New York: Oxford University Press, 2013.

NOTE When the abbreviation *ed.* appears after a name, it means *editor*, so for more than one editor, change the abbreviation from *ed.* to *eds.*

***Chicago* Note & Bibliography Entries**

3. More than three authors
4. Unnamed (anonymous) author
5. Two or more works by the same author
6. Group or corporate author
7. Editor (no author)
8. Author and editor or translator
9. Selection from an edited book or anthology

8. Author and editor or translator

10. John Locke, *The Second Treatise of Government*, ed. Thomas P. Peardon (Indianapolis: Oxford University Press, 1990), 124.

11. Adania Shibli, *We Are All Equally Far from Love*, trans. Paul Starkey (Northampton, MA: Interlink Books, 2012), 71.

Edited by, Translated by, in bibliography

Locke, John. *The Second Treatise of Government*. Edited by Thomas P. Peardon. Indianapolis: Oxford University Press, 1990.

Shibli, Adania. *We Are All Equally Far from Love*. Translated by Paul Starkey. Northampton, MA: Interlink Books, 2012.

NOTE When the abbreviation *ed.* appears before a name, it means *edited by*, so do not add an *-s* when there is more than one editor.

9. Selection from an edited book or anthology

selection author | selection title | title of book in which selection appears

12. Rebecca Arnold, "Fashion," in *Feminist Visual Culture*, ed. Fiona Carson and Claire Pajaczkowska (New York: Routledge, 2011), 208.

Arnold, Rebecca. "Fashion." In *Feminist Visual Culture*, edited by Fiona Carson and Claire Pajaczkowska, 207–22. New York: Routledge, 2011.

selection pgs.

10. Edition other than the first

13. Patricia S. Daniels, Stephen G. Hyslop, and Douglas Brinkley, eds., *National Geographic Almanac of World History*, 3rd ed. (National Geographic, 2014), 72.

Daniels, Patricia S., Stephen G. Hyslop, and Douglas Brinkley, eds. *National Geographic Almanac of World History*. 3rd ed. Washington, DC: National Geographic, 2014.

11. Introduction, preface, foreword, or afterword by a different writer

14. Sister Helen Prejean, introduction to *Lead Me On, Let Me Stand: A Clergyman's Story in White and Black,* by William H. Barnwell (Columbia, SC: University of South Carolina Press, 2015), 7.

Prejean, Sister Helen. Introduction to *Lead Me On, Let Me Stand: A Clergyman's Story in White and Black,* by William H. Barnwell, 3–12. Columbia, SC: University of South Carolina Press, 2015.

12. Entry in an encyclopedia or dictionary For a well-known reference work such as the *American Heritage Dictionary* or the *Encyclopedia Britannica,* a bibliography entry is not necessary.

a. Printed

15. *The American Heritage Dictionary,* 2nd college ed., s.v. "plagiarism."

b. Online Unless a "last updated" date appears on the site, include an access date before the URL.

16. *Dictionary.com,* s.v. "plagiarism," accessed July 14, 2016, http://dictionary .reference.com/browse/plagiarism.

13. Multivolume work

vol. title
17. Robert Caro, *The Years of Lyndon Johnson,* vol. 3, *Master of the Senate* (New York: Alfred A. Knopf, 2002), 4.

18. George Brown Tindall and David E. Shi, *America: A Narrative History,* 8th ed. (New York: W. W. Norton, 2003), 2:123.
vol. pg.

Caro, Robert. *The Years of Lyndon Johnson.* Vol. 3, *The Master of the Senate.* New York: Alfred A. Knopf, 2002.

Chicago Note & Bibliography Entries

10. Edition other than the first
11. Introduction, preface, foreword, or afterword by a different writer
12. Entry in an encyclopedia or dictionary
13. Multivolume work
14. Book in a series

s.v. Abbreviation of the Latin phrase *sub verbo,* "under the word"

Vols. published in different years with different titles

Vols. published in same year with same title

Tindall, George Brown, and David E. Shi. *America: A Narrative History.* 8th ed. 2 vols. New York: W. W. Norton, 2003.

14. Book in a series

                book title

19. Thomas Rickert, *Ambient Rhetoric: The Attunements of Rhetorical Being,*

          series title

Pittsburgh Series in Composition, Literacy, and Culture (Pittsburgh, PA: University of Pittsburgh Press, 2013), 121.

              book title

Rickert, Thomas. *Ambient Rhetoric: The Attunements of Rhetorical Being.*

          series title

Pittsburgh Series in Composition, Literacy, and Culture. Pittsburgh, PA: University of Pittsburgh Press, 2013.

15. Sacred text

     book lines   version

20. 1 Kings 3:23–26 (King James Version).

           verse

21. Qur'an 17:1–2.

Generally, sacred texts are not included in the bibliography.

16. Dissertation or thesis For an unpublished dissertation or thesis, place the title in quotation marks; titles of published dissertations or theses are italicized. Include the type of document (*PhD diss., MA thesis*), the university where it was submitted, and the date of submission.

22. Jessica Davis Powers, "Patrons, Houses and Viewers in Pompeii: Reconsidering the House of the Gilded Cupids" (PhD diss., University of Michigan, 2006), 43–57, ProQuest (AAI 3208535).

Powers, Jessica Davis. "Patrons, Houses and Viewers in Pompeii: Reconsidering the House of the Gilded Cupids." PhD diss., University of Michigan, 2006. ProQuest (AAI 3208535).

Annotated visual of where to find author, title, and publication information, 300–03 (Documentation Matters tutorial preceding ch. 18)

Periodicals—Printed and Electronic

A periodical is a publication issued at regular intervals—newspapers are generally published every day, magazines every week or month, and scholarly journals four times a year. For periodicals, include not only the title of the article (in quotation marks) but also the title of the periodical (in italics). The type of publication information you include depends on the type of periodical you are citing.

More about
Formatting author information:
Examples 1–6, 409–11

17. Article in a scholarly journal The information you need to create a note and bibliography entry for a printed journal article appears on the cover or title page of the journal and on the first and last page of the article. For articles downloaded from a database, the information appears on the screen listing the articles that fit your search terms, on the full record of the article, or on the first and last page of the file you download. For articles that appear in journals published solely online, you will find the publication information on the website's home page, in the journal's table of contents, or on the first page of the article.

a. Printed The basic note for an article in a printed journal looks like this:

> Ref. No. Author's first name and Surname, "Title of Article," *Title of Journal*
>
> Vol. no., issue no. (Year of publication): Pages.

Months (May) or seasons (Winter) may be included before the year of publication, but they are not required. If a journal is paginated by volume—for example, if issue 1 ends on page 175 and issue 2 begins on page 176—the issue number may be omitted. Here are examples of notes and bibliography entries of journals with and without issue numbers.

Paginated by Issue (Issue Number Included)

> 23. Bishupal Limbu, "Democracy, Perhaps: Collectivity, Kinship, and
> the Politics of Friendship," *Comparative Literature* 63, no. 1 (2011): 92.

(vol. no. issue no.)

> Limbu, Bishupal. "Democracy, Perhaps: Collectivity, Kinship, and the Politics of
> Friendship." *Comparative Literature* 63, no. 1 (2011): 92.

Paginated by Volume (No Issue Number)

> 24. Sarah Brown, "The Role of Elite Leadership in the Southern Defense
> of Segregation, 1954-1964," *Journal of Southern History* 77 (2011): 832.

(vol. no.)

Chicago Note & Bibliography Entries

15. Sacred text
16. Dissertation or thesis
17. Article in a scholarly journal
18. Article in a magazine
19. Article in a newspaper (signed)

HTML Hypertext markup language, the coding system used to create websites and web pages

PDF Portable document format, a method for sharing documents without losing formatting

DOI Digital object identifier, a permanent identifier given to electronic sources

Brown, Sarah. "The Role of Elite Leadership in the Southern Defense of Segregation, 1954–1964." *Journal of Southern History* 77 (2011): 827–64.

b. Accessed through a database Most researchers locate journal articles through subscription databases available through their college library. Frequently, articles indexed in such databases are also available in HTML or PDF format through the database. If the article you are citing is available in PDF format, include the page numbers you are citing in your note and the page range in your bibliography entry. If the article is available only in HTML format, add a subhead or paragraph number to your note if this will help readers locate the passage you are citing. To cite an article accessed through a subscription database, add the name of the database and reference number (if any) at the end of your entry, or include the URL if stable. More and more academic journals are also adding digital object identifiers (DOIs); if the article you are citing includes a DOI, add it in place of the database information.

25. Kevin P. Dwyer et al., "Team Crisis: School Psychologists and Nurses Working Together." *Psychology in the Schools* 52, no. 7 (2015): 707, doi: 10.1002/pits.21850. Wylie Online Library.

Dwyer, Kevin P., et al. "Team Crisis: School Psychologists and Nurses Working Together." *Psychology in the Schools* 52, no. 7 (2015): 702–713. doi: 10.1002/pits.21850.

c. Online Online journals may not provide page numbers. Provide a subheading or paragraph number (if the article provides them), and include the DOI (if there is one) or the URL for the article (if there is not).

26. Margaret F. Gibson, "Stressing Reproduction: Reading into Parents of Disabled Children." *Disability Studies Quarterly* 32, no. 1 (2012), http://www.dsq-sds.org/article/view/1654/3055.

Gibson, Margaret F. "Stressing Reproduction: Reading into Parents of Disabled Children." *Disability Studies Quarterly* 32, no. 1 (2012), http://www.dsq-sds.org/article/view/1654/3055.

18. Article in a magazine Omit volume and issue numbers, and replace the parentheses around the publication date (month and year or month, day, and year) with commas. Page numbers may be omitted.

a. Printed

27. Marian Smith Holmes, "The Freedom Riders," *Smithsonian*, February 2009, 72.

Holmes, Marian Smith. "The Freedom Riders." *Smithsonian*, February 2009, 70-75.

b. Accessed through a database

28. Lina Zeldovich, "Ancient Beer Recipes Lead to Modern Health Remedies," *Newsweek*, October 9, 2015. Access World News.

Zeldovich, Lina. "Ancient Beer Recipes Lead to Modern Health Remedies." *Newsweek*, October 9, 2015. Access World News.

c. Online

29. Alice Karekezi, "The Science of Warp," *Salon*, December 11, 2011, www.salon.com/2011/12/11/the_science_of_warp/.

Karekezi, Alice. "The Science of Warp." *Salon*, December 11, 2011. www.salon.com/2011/12/11/the_science_of_warp/.

19. Article in a newspaper (signed) Because page numbers may differ from edition to edition, use the edition name and section letter or number (if available) instead. A bibliography entry may be omitted.

a. Printed

If the city in which the newspaper is published is not identified on the newspaper's masthead, add it in parentheses; if it might be unfamiliar to readers, add the state, also.

30. Jim Kenneally, "When Brockton Was Home to a Marathon," *Enterprise* (Brockton, MA), April 20, 2006, sec. 1.

Kenneally, Jim. "When Brockton Was Home to a Marathon." *Enterprise* (Brockton, MA), April 20, 2006, sec. 1.

For well-known national newspapers (such as the *Christian Science Monitor,* *USA Today,* and the *Wall Street Journal*), no city or state is needed. If you are unsure whether the newspaper is well known, consult your instructor or a reference librarian.

b. Accessed through a database

31. John M. Broder, "Geography Is Dividing Democrats over Energy," *New York Times,* January 26, 2009, late edition, sec. A, LexisNexis Academic.

database

Broder, John M. "Geography Is Dividing Democrats over Energy." *New York Times,* January 26, 2009, late edition, sec. A. LexisNexis Academic.

c. Online

32. Victor Davis Hanson, "Oil-Rich America?" *Chicago Tribune,* December 8, 2011, www.chicagotribune.com/news/politics/sns-201112080900--tms--vdhansonctnvh-a20111208dec08,0,6557873.column

article URL

Hanson, Victor Davis. "Oil-Rich America?" *Chicago Tribune,* December 8, 2011. www .chicagotribune.com/news/politics/sns-201112080900--tms--vdhansonctnvh-a20111208dec08,0,6557873.column

20. Article or editorial in a newspaper (unsigned) When no author is named, place the newspaper's title in the author position in your bibliography entry. (*Chicago* style does not require a bibliography entry for unsigned newspaper articles or editorials, but your instructor might.)

21. Review

33. Anthony Tommasini, review of *Siegfried,* by Richard Wagner, conducted by Fabio Luisi, Metropolitan Opera, New York, *New York Times,* October 29, 2011, sec. C.

Tommasini, Anthony. Review of *Siegfried,* by Richard Wagner, conducted by Fabio Luisi, Metropolitan Opera, New York. *New York Times,* October 29, 2011, sec. C.

22. Letter to the editor Omit the letter's title, page numbers, and the edition name or number.

34. John A. Beck, letter to the editor, *Los Angeles Times,* March 16, 2010.

Beck, John A. Letter to the editor. *Los Angeles Times,* March 16, 2010.

Other Electronic Sources

Although it is usually easy to find citation information for books and articles in periodicals, websites can be a bit trickier. Most of the information you need will appear at the bottom or top of the web page or on the site's home page. Sometimes, however, you may need to look further. Click on links such as "About us" or "More information." Frequently, websites do not provide complete information, so provide as much information as you can. If no author is listed, place the site's sponsor in the "author" position. If key information is missing, include a phrase describing the site, in case the URL changes.

Annotated visual of where to find publication information, 300–03 (Documentation Matters tutorial preceding ch. 18)

23. Website The basic note for a website looks like this:

> Ref. No. Website Title, Author, Sponsoring Organization, last update or access date if last update not provided, URL.

However, website titles that are the same as book titles or other types of publications should follow the styling for that publication. Here is an example of an actual note for a website that has the same title as a book:

> 35. *Victorian England: An Introduction*, Christine Roth, University of Wisconsin-Oshkosh, Department of English, accessed April 2, 2016, www.english.uwosh.edu/roth/VictorianEngland.htm.

The bibliography entry for the note above looks like this:

> Roth, Christine. *Victorian England: An Introduction*. University of Wisconsin-Oshkosh, Department of English. Accessed April 2, 2016. www.english.uwosh.edu/roth/VictorianEngland.htm.

Include an access date only when the publication date or last update is not indicated. *Chicago* style does not require an entry in the bibliography for web content, but if your instructor does, follow the example above.

24. Web page or wiki article When referring to a specific page or article on a website or wiki, place that page's title in quotation marks. For a wiki article, begin with the article's title.

36. "Centennial Farm and Ranch Program," Montana History Wiki, Montana

Historical Society, last modified August 4, 2011, http://montanahistorywiki.pbworks

.com/w/page/21639590/Centennial%20Farm%20and%20Ranch%20Program.

Montana History Wiki, Montana Historical Society. "Centennial Farm and Ranch Pro-

gram." Last modified August 4, 2011. http://montanahistorywiki.pbworks.com/w/

page/21639590/Centennial%20Farm%20and%20Ranch%20Program.

25. Discussion list or blog posting A blog post need not be included in the bibliography.

26. CD-ROM If there is more than one version or edition of the CD-ROM, add that information after the title.

37. *History through Art: The 20th Century* (San Jose, CA: Fogware Publishing,

2000). CD-ROM, chap. 1.

History through Art: The 20th Century. San Jose, CA: Fogware Publishing, 2000. CD-ROM.

Audio and Visual Sources

The information you need to create notes and bibliography entries for most audio and visual sources appears on the cover, label, or program or in the credits at the end of a film or a television show. Begin with the author, director, conductor, or performer, or begin your citation with the name of the work, depending on what your project emphasizes. The *Chicago Manual* provides few models of audiovisual sources. Those below are based on the principles explained in *Chicago*.

27. Motion picture (film, video, DVD)

38. *Juno*, directed by Jason Reitman, written by Diablo Cody (2007; Los Angeles:

Fox Searchlight Home Entertainment, 2008), DVD.

Juno. Directed by Jason Reitman, written by Diablo Cody. 2007. Los Angeles: Fox

Searchlight Home Entertainment, 2008. DVD.

28. Music or other audio recording

39. Johannes Brahms, *Piano Concerto no. 1 in D minor, op. 15*, Berliner Philharmoniker, conducted by Claudio Abbado, Philips Classics Productions BMG D153907, 1986, compact disc.

Brahms, Johannes. *Piano Concerto no. 1 in D minor, op. 15*. Berliner Philharmoniker. Claudio Abbado (conductor). Philips Classics Productions BMG D153907, 1986, compact disc.

29. Podcast

40. Melvyn Bragg, host, "The Indian Mutiny," *In Our Time*, BBC Radio 4, podcast audio, February 18, 2010, www.bbc.co.uk/programmes/b00qprnj.

Bragg, Melvyn, host. "The Indian Mutiny." *In Our Time*, BBC Radio 4, February 18, 2010. Podcast audio. www.bbc.co.uk/programmes/b00qprnj.

30. Performance

41. Jay O. Sanders, *Titus Andronicus*, dir. Michael Sexton, Anspacher Theater, New York, November 29, 2011.

Sanders, Jay O. *Titus Andronicus*. Directed by Michael Sexton. Anspacher Theater, New York, November 29, 2011.

31. Work of art If a reproduction of the work appears in your project, identify the work in a figure caption. If you discuss the work but do not show it, cite it in your notes but do not provide an entry in your bibliography. If the reproduction is taken from a book, follow the model for a selection from an edited book or anthology.

42. Alexander Calder, *Two Acrobats*, 1929, wire sculpture, Menil Collection, Houston.

More about
Figure captions (*Chicago* style), 422–23

Example 9, 412

Miscellaneous Sources—Printed and Electronic

32. Government publication For documents published by the Government Printing Office (or GPO), including the publisher is optional. If you omit the publisher, change the colon after the location to a period.

33. Interview (published or broadcast)
a. Printed or broadcast

43. Barack Obama, interview by Maria Bartiromo, *Closing Bell*, CNBC, March 27, 2008.

Obama, Barack. Interview by Maria Bartiromo. *Closing Bell*, CNBC, March 27, 2008.

b. Online

44. Barack Obama, interview by Maria Bartiromo, *Closing Bell*, CNBC, March 27, 2008, www.cnbc.com/id/23832520.

Obama, Barack. Interview by Maria Bartiromo. *Closing Bell*. CNBC, March 27, 2008. www.cnbc.com/id/23832520.

34. Personal communication Unless your instructor requires it, no bibliography entry is needed for a personal communication.
a. Letter

45. Theresa Dunn, letter to the author, August 13, 2016.

b. Email

46. Chris M. Anson, email message to the author, November 11, 2014.

35. Indirect source If you do not have access to the original source, your note and bibliography entry should name both the original source and the source from which you borrowed the material.

20b Using *Chicago* Style for Tables and Figures

The *Chicago Manual* recommends that you number tables and figures in a separate sequence (*Table 1, Table 2, Figure 1, Figure 2*) both in the text and in the table title or figure caption. Tables and figures should be placed as close as possible after the text reference. For tables, provide a brief identifying title and place it above the table. For figures, provide a caption that includes any information about the figure that readers will need to identify it, such as the title of a work of art, the artist's name, the work's location, and a brief description. If the figure or table, or information used to create the figure or table, comes from another source, provide a source note. Source notes for tables generally appear below the table, while source information for figures appears at the end of the figure caption.

20c Formatting a *Chicago*-Style Research Project

More about
MLA-style format-
ting, 345–49
Formatting
college
projects, 101

The *Chicago Manual* provides detailed instructions about manuscript preparation for authors submitting their work for publication, but it does not offer
formatting instructions for college projects. Follow the formatting instructions provided in chapter 9 or chapter 18, or consult your instructor.

1. Format notes.

While acknowledging that not all scholars agree, Mann observes, "If Monte Verde is

correct, as most believe, people were thriving from Alaska to Chile while much of

northern Europe was still empty of mankind and its works."[8]

Mann, Charles C. 1491: New Revelations of the Americas Before Columbus (New York: Alfred A. Knopf, 2005) p. 173

The *Chicago Manual* recommends numbering bibliographic notes consecu-
tively throughout the project, using superscript (above-the-line) numbers.
Type the heading "Notes" at the top of a new page following the end of
the text, and type the notes below the heading. (You may need to insert a
page break if your word processor has automatically created endnotes on
the last page of your paper.)

2. Format the bibliography.

More about
Hanging indent,
345, 347, 393

To begin your list of works cited, type the heading "Bibliography," "References,"
or "Works Cited" at the top of a new page. (Ask your instructor which heading is preferred.) Entries should be formatted with a hanging indent: Position
the first line of each entry flush with the left margin, and indent subsequent
lines by half an inch. Entries should be alphabetized by the author's surname.

Writing
Responsibly — Of Deadlines and Paperclips

Instructors expect students to turn in thoughtful, carefully proofread, and neatly formatted papers on time—usually in class on the due date. They also expect writers to clip or staple the pages of the paper *before* submitting. Do justice to yourself by being fully prepared.

to SELF

Student Model **Research Project: *Chicago* Style**

The research project that follows was written by Sara Sweetwood for a history course at Pace University. Sweetwood fulfills her responsibilities to topic and audience by drawing on a variety of relevant and reliable sources to make her case. She fulfills her responsibility to the writers from whom she borrows information and ideas by citing them in abbreviated notes in the text and by providing a complete entry for each work in the list of works cited at the end of the project. She demonstrates her credibility as a researcher and a writer by providing evidence to support her claims and by revising, editing, and proofreading her project carefully.

½"

1"

Sara Sweetwood

English 108

Professor Anderson

December 15, 2016

Identifying information (double spaced)

If your instructor requires a title page, see the model on p. 397

Title (centered)   The Rise and Fall of Bound Feet in China

Descriptive title

Throughout history and across the world, every culture has promoted different standards or definitions of feminine beauty. In Japan, there was the geisha, a woman who perfected the art of performance and grace. In America, there were "sex-symbols," like Marilyn Monroe and her ubiquitous image of attractiveness and perfection during the mid-20th century. In China, the definition of beauty for a significant span of time, from the 10th to the 20th century, resided in the feet.[1] During this time, the Chinese bound young girls' feet so that they would not grow. These tiny feet were considered beautiful and erotic, and this practice was a mainstay in Chinese culture for around one thousand years, before it was finally abolished in the 20th century.

Thesis at end of first paragraph to guide reader

There is no definitive answer as to when foot binding began. Historians generally agree that the practice originated sometime during the Shang Dynasty, in power from about 1600 to 1046 B.C.[2] There are several different tales to explain where exactly the custom began. One such story says that a fox disguised itself as the Shang Empress and tried to hide its clubbed feet, inspiring the idea of the shape that bound feet take on.[3] Another theory says that the Shang Empress, who had misshapen feet, had requested that the practice become mandatory so that her deformed feet would become a model of beauty, and other women in the kingdom

Claim in topic sentence; supporting facts in balance of paragraph

1"

1"

425

strived to emulate her. An alternate version of this story suggests that women in China copied the Empress' deformity out of pity.[4] Some attribute the practice to Emperor Li Yu, who ruled from 961 to 976 B.C.[5] Li Yu, supposedly attracted to small feet, asked one of his concubines, named Yao Niang, to wrap her feet in bindings and perform a dance on the tips of her toes. She was a talented dancer and other members of the nobility began to wrap their feet as well in the hope that Li Yu would give them attention as he did to her.[6]

The practice stayed within rich women and the nobility until the early 17th century, when it eventually worked its way down the social ladder and soon "millions of Chinese women of all socioeconomic backgrounds" were binding their feet. (See Figure 1.) Because the process was lengthy and expensive, a typical lower class family would only bind the feet of their eldest daughter, while the younger ones would work on farms as laborers.[7] As Adele Fielde, a Baptist missionary who lived in China in the 1800s, said, "near the coast, even in the farmsteads and among the most indigent, everyone has bound feet. It is not [. . .] a sign of wealth, for [. . .] the poorest follow [the custom]. [. . .] Taking all of China together, probably nine-tenths of the women have bound feet."[8]

The practice probably became so widespread for a variety of reasons. First, the painful process forced the women to walk in a delicate manner, called the "lotus gait," that men found erotic and ladylike.[9] It also essentially handicapped the women, forcing them to rely on a maid's help to perform basic tasks and thus prevent infidelity and promote reliance on the husband.[10] "A woman who was kept physically restricted was, presumably, less likely to be mentally independent. Her very helplessness conveyed an elevated status to her husband and his family. Anyone who could afford a 'helpless' wife must be a successful man, regardless of his actual social or economic reality."[11] It is hypothesized that having bound feet became a status symbol because it proved that a family was not in need of a woman's labor, and could instead afford the lengthy process.[12]

Example 3

Foot binding often began as early as the age of four and as late as age twelve, though the average age to start the process was six. The practice was started so early in a girl's life because younger feet were softer, made up of pre-bone cartilage, and therefore were more easily breakable. Normally, the process commenced in the frigid wintertime temperatures when the feet were numb and less susceptible to pain, because the first few months were said to be the most excruciating.[13] The toes, save for the biggest, would be broken and then pressed to the bottom of the foot. The feet were then bound tightly with cotton wrappings in this position.[14] Both the feet and the bandages were routinely soaked in an herb and animal blood mixture that was believed to soften the feet. The girls were kept in these wrappings for varying, gradually increasing lengths of time. Young girls could be punished if they attempted to remove these bandages.[15] Gradually, the feet were forced into smaller and smaller pairs of shoes until the desired size was reached, which normally occurred after two years of binding.[16] One very important aspect of foot binding was the idyllic standard known as the "golden lotus," referring to a perfectly bound foot that measured three inches or less in length. Women strived to attain this measurement. A perfectly bound foot would "be shaped like the bud of a lotus flower—full and round at the heel and coming to a thin point at the front."[17] Women

Transition sentence

[Figure identified in caption]

Figure 1. For a thousand years in China, until the mid-20th century, many women of all classes had bound feet, conforming to an idealized standard of beauty.

who fulfilled the required dimensions to earn the title of having perfect feet were more desired by men.[18]

   The process of binding feet was also riddled with superstitions. There were **[Transition]** several dates commonly chosen for their relation to deities. Before beginning the process of foot binding, it was customary for mothers to consult a diviner or astrologer to determine the luckiest day to begin.[19] One was the twenty-fourth day of the eighth lunar month, the birthday of a goddess called the Little-footed Miss. Another date chosen was the nineteenth day of the second lunar month, the birthday of Kuan Yin, goddess of mercy. Another popular date in some areas of China was in the seventh lunar month, during the corn and hemp festival. It is hypothesized that people believed that beginning foot binding on this date was lucky because the foot would resemble the slender shape that the stalks of corn and hemp have.[20] Before binding the feet, the mother would place the tiny shoes meant for bound feet at the altar of these goddesses. She would light incense and candles, and offer fruits and dumplings, which the daughter would subsequently eat. It was believed that eating these dumplings would help her feet resemble the supple and small qualities of the food.[21]

This practice was not without health consequences for those subjected to it. Because the tight bindings and curled toes prevented proper blood flow, it was common for the toes to become necrotic. This could result in the loss of appendages, or in severe circumstances, gangrene, potentially leading to death. Toenails that were not trimmed could cut into the skin and cause infection, as bacteria was easily formed underneath the tight bandaging.[22] The process caused young girls excruciating pain, as it required repeatedly breaking and tightly binding the toes. It crippled young girls, and left them partially disabled for the remainder of their lives:

> The [process] permanently changed the feet so that later unbinding could not restore their natural form. Foot binding greatly inhibited the mobility of Chinese girls and women for the rest of their lives. It permanently stopped their running, slowed their walking, and reduced their balance. As they aged, many women could only walk with canes.[23]

Sister Ann Colette Wolf worked in China from 1946 to 1967 in a school established by missionaries called the Sisters of Providence. On encountering employees with bound feet, she wrote, "It was pitiful to see them walk. [. . .] Usually a person had to employ two women to do the work which one woman could have done if she had not been so crippled."[24]

A study conducted by historians examined the effects bound feet had on older women later in life.[25] The historians surveyed about 200 women aged seventy years

Transition sentence

Signal phrase

and older living in and around Beijing. The study found that women with bound feet were more likely to have fallen during the past year. They also had greater history of fractures, and were more likely to be unable to squat or stand from a chair unassisted. In the end, the historians concluded that, "over the centuries, foot binding produced severe lifelong disability for many millions of women. The deformities of foot binding linger on as a common cause of disability in elderly Chinese women."

After being a prominent part of Chinese culture for one thousand years, the abolition of foot binding was a lengthy process. It began in the 18th century with some influential Chinese writers and scholars, like Kung Tzu-chen and Li Ruzhen, calling for an end to the practice. Li Ruzhen said, "I thought that all women must have been unfilial, and their mothers bound their feet to protect them from the death penalty. I had no idea they were bound for beauty. If we cut off someone's nose to make it smaller, wouldn't that person be considered deformed?" [26] An increase in contact with foreigners brought with it an influx in the exchange of ideas. Westerners traveling to China protested against the practice. In the late 1890s, Chinese scholar Kang Yu Wei led the No Bind Feet Society, imploring fathers to prevent their sons from marrying bound footed women. Kang Yu Wei wrote a letter to the Empress Dowager in which he talked about how the foreigners photographed women with bound feet and dispersed it among themselves, condemning the practice as barbaric. [27]

> Transition sentence

Another step forward towards ending foot binding came in 1905, when the Empress Dowager Ci-xi put in place several reforms, including advocating that the practice be brought to an end, as it was cruel and damaging to the health of girls. [28]

> Transition sentence

In 1912, the Qing Dynasty fell and a new Nationalist government formed. The leader Sun Yat-sen amplified the pressure to end bound feet. Although some relented in the cities, the practice carried on in more rural areas. In 1928, the anti-foot binding agenda was enhanced by several new edicts that were put in place by the Nationalist government. The first called for all school textbooks to contain a chapter on the ban on the practice. Girls under the age of fifteen were ordered to cease binding their feet. Another incentive to end foot binding was the offering of monetary rewards for removed bindings, while families with bound footed girls were fined.[29] Although these reforms decreased the number of foot bindings, it was not until 1949 when the Chinese Communists came into power that foot binding was formally abolished. The practice, they said, resulted in the loss of otherwise healthy workers.[30] A huge challenge the new government faced was incorporating those with bound feet into the workforce. It remedied this by splitting up the type of work assigned. Those who were able bodied were assigned tasks like planting and harvesting in the fields, while those who were not as healthy were assigned less physical jobs like weeding plants and clearing out waste.[31]

With the government ban on foot binding still in effect today, the practice has come to a stop, and there is no reason to think it will ever return. Despite its prominence in China for a thousand years, foot binding eventually came to be viewed as cruel and unhealthy. Thus, a practice that once defined womanly beauty and dictated marriages and courtships is today just another footnote in Chinese history.

Conclusion: Provides brief summary and reiterates significance of cultural practice

Notes Heading (centered), new page

Short form of notes used with bibliography

Reference work: no entry in bibliography, full entry here; use "s.v.," sub verbo, "under the word" (Latin)

Many researchers consult Wikipedia for an introduction to their topic, but its information needs to be verified by more scholarly sources

1. Ebrey, *Cambridge Illustrated History of China*, 160–61.

2. *Wikipedia: The Free Encyclopedia*, s.v. "Shang Dynasty," Wikimedia Foundation, accessed December 9, 2014, http://en.wikipedia.org/wiki/Shang_Dynasty.

3. *H2G2*, s.v. "Chinese Foot Binding," BBC, n.d. accessed December 9, 2014, http://www.bbc.co.uk/dna/ptop/alabaster/A1155872#footnote2.

4. Ibid.

5. *Wikipedia: The Free Encyclopedia*, s.v. "Li Yu," Wikimedia Foundation, accessed December 9, 2014, http://en.wikipedia.org/wiki/Li_Yu_(Southern_Tang).

6. Jackson, *Splendid Slipper*, 12.

"Ibid." (abbreviation of *ibidem*, Latin for "in the same place") used when source cited in note immediately above

7. Ibid., 11.

8. Fielde, *Pagoda Shadows*.

9. Jackson, *Splendid Slippers*, 121.

10. Lee Yao, *Chinese Women*, 93–96.

11. Jackson, *Splendid Slippers*, 15.

12. Laurel Bossen et al., "Feet and Fabrication, 347–83.

13. Jackson, *Splendid Slippers*, 27.

14. Ibid., 35.

15. Lee Yao., 93–96.

16. Jackson, *Splendid Slippers*, 35.

17. Ibid., 27.

18. Ibid., 24.

19. Ibid., 31.

20. Ibid., 28.

21. Ibid., 31.

22. *H2G2*, "Chinese Foot Binding."

23. Bossen et al., "Feet and Fabrication," 348.

24. Wolf, *Sisters of Providence*.

25. Cummings, et. al., "Consequences of Foot Binding among Older Women in Beijing, China," 1677–79.

26. Jackson, *Splendid Slippers*, 140–43.

27. Ibid., 144–45.

28. Ibid., 152.

29. Ibid., 154.

30. Ibid., 157.

31. Snow, *Red Star Over China*.

Works Cited

Bossen, Laurel, et al. "Feet and Fabrication: Footbinding and Early Twentieth-Century Rural Women's Labor in Shaanxi." *Modern China* 37, no. 4 (2011): 347–83. *Academic Search Premier.*

"Chinese Foot Binding." *H2G2*. BBC, n.d. Accessed Dec. 9, 2016. http://www.bbc.co.uk/dna/ptop/alabaster/A1155872#footnote2.

Cummings, Steven R., Xu Ling, and Katie Stone. "Consequences of Foot Binding among Older Women in Beijing, China." *American Journal of Public Health* 87, no. 10 (1997): 1677–79. *Academic Search Premier.* Accessed Nov. 18, 2016.

Ebrey, Patricia Buckley. *Cambridge Illustrated History of China*, 2nd ed. New York: Cambridge University Press, 2010.

Fielde, Adele M. *Pagoda Shadows: Studies from Life in China*, 6th ed. Boston: W. G. Corthell, 1890.

Jackson, Beverley. *Splendid Slippers: A Thousand Years of an Erotic Tradition.* Berkeley: Ten Speed, 1997.

Lee Yao, Esther S. *Chinese Women: Past and Present.* Mesquite, TX: Ide House, 1983.

"Li Yu." *Wikipedia: The Free Encyclopedia*. Wikimedia Foundation. Accessed Dec. 9, 2016. http://en.wikipedia.org/wiki/Li_Yu_(Southern_Tang).

"Shang Dynasty." *Wikipedia: The Free Encyclopedia*. Wikimedia Foundation. Accessed Dec. 9, 2016. http://en.wikipedia.org/wiki/Shang_Dynasty.

Snow, Edgar. *Red Star Over China*. New York: Bantam, 1968.

Wolf, Sister Ann Colette. *Against All Odds: Sisters of Providence, Mission to the Chinese.* St.-Mary-of-the-Woods, Indiana: St. Mary's, 1990.

Sidebar labels:
- Entires arranged alphabetically
- Online article: Stable URL provided
- Journal article: Accessed through a database
- Book (printed): Scholarly press
- Book (printed): Popular press

Text Credits

p. 425: Courtesy of Sara Sweetwood.

21 Documenting Sources: CSE Style

Writers in the sciences customarily use formatting and documentation guidelines from *Scientific Style and Format: The CSE Manual for Authors, Editors, and Publishers* (7th ed.) published by the Council of Science Editors (CSE). CSE style requires that sources be cited briefly in the text and documented in a reference list at the end of the project. The goal of providing in-text citations and a list of references is to allow readers to locate and read the sources for themselves and to distinguish the writer's ideas from those borrowed from sources.

> *More about*
> MLA style,
>   304–62 (ch. 18)
> APA style,
>   363–405 (ch. 19)
> *Chicago* style,
>   406–34
>   (ch. 20)

21a Creating CSE-Style In-Text Citations

In-text citations, which appear in the body of your project, identify any material borrowed from a source, whether it is a quotation, paraphrase, summary, or idea. The CSE offers three formats for citing sources in the body of the project:

- Name-year
- Citation-sequence
- Citation-name

Writing Responsibly | Citing and Documenting Sources

When you cite and document sources, you acknowledge any material from which you have quoted, paraphrased, summarized, or drawn information, and you join the conversation on your topic by adding your own interpretation, data, methods, and results. Simultaneously, you give interested readers (including your instructor) a way to join the conversation. Accurate entries allow your audience to find and read your sources so that they can evaluate your research and learn more about the subject themselves. Accurate entries also demonstrate the care with which you have written your project, which reinforces your credibility, or ethos.

to AUDIENCE

The *name-year system* requires you to include the last name of the author and the year of publication in parentheses whenever the source is cited:

> Advances have clarified the role of betalains and carotenoids in determining
> author   date
> the color of flowers (Groteworld 2006).

If you use the author's name in your sentence, include just the year of publication in parentheses:

> author
> Christoffel (2007) argues that public health officers adopted the strategies
> date
> they did because they were facing a crisis.

The name-year system tells readers immediately who wrote the source and how current it is, which is particularly crucial in the sciences. This system involves many rules for creating in-text citations (for example, how to create in-text citations for several authors, with organizations as authors, and so on), which can make it difficult to apply the rules consistently.

The *citation-sequence* and *citation-name systems* use a superscript number (the same number for a source each time it is cited) to refer the reader to a list of references at the end of the project.

> Some testing of the River Invertebrate Prediction and Classification System (RIVPACS)
> had already been conducted[1]. Biologists in Great Britain then used environmental data
> to establish community type[2], and two studies developed predictive models for testing
> the effects of habitat-specific sampling[3,4]. These did not, however, account for the earlier
> RIVPACS research[1].

Place reference numbers before punctuation marks. When drawing information from multiple sources, include multiple citations, separated by commas (no space between commas and reference numbers).

Tech **Creating Superscript Numbers**

The footnoting function in your word processing program will not work for inserting reference numbers for the citation-sequence or citation-name systems because it will only insert the reference marks in sequence (*1, 2, 3, . . .*), whereas the CSE system requires that you use the same superscript number for a source each time you cite it. Instead, insert superscript numbers manually, without using your word processing program's footnote function, and type your list of references separately. (Use the Help function of your word processor to learn about inserting superscript numbers.)

When using the citation-sequence system, arrange the sources in your reference list in order of first mention in your research report and then number them. (The first work cited is number 1, the second work cited is number 2, and so on.) When using the citation-name system, alphabetize sources and then number them. (The first work alphabetically is number 1, the second work alphabetically is number 2, and so on.)

The citation-sequence and citation-name systems need no rules about how to form in-text citations, but they do require readers to turn to the reference list to see the name of the author and the source's date of publication. Since the word processor's footnoting system cannot be used, numbering (and renumbering) of notes must be done by hand. To avoid the confusion that can arise during revision and editing, consider using a simplified author-date system while drafting the research project and inserting the numbers for the citation-sequence or citation-name system in the final draft.

Check with your instructor about which system to use, and use it consistently. If your instructor does not have a preference, consider the advantages and drawbacks of each system before making your choice.

21b Preparing a CSE-Style Reference List

A research report or project in CSE style ends with a list of cited references. How you format those references depends on the type of source and the system you use.

Books—Printed and Electronic

In a printed book, you can find most or all of the information you need to create a reference list entry on the copyright and title pages at the beginning of the book. In an online or e-book, print and electronic publication information often appears at the top or bottom of the first page or is available through a link.

1. One author

a. **Printed** The basic format for a printed book looks like this:
Name-year system

> Author's surname First and Middle Initials. Date of publication. Title: subtitle. Place of publication: Publisher.

CSE Reference List Entries

1. One author
2. Two or more authors
3. Group or corporate author

Annotated visual of where to find author and publication information, 300–03 (Documentation Matters tutorial preceding ch. 18)

No punctuation between surname and initials and no period or space between initials

Citation-sequence and citation-name systems

Lines after the first align with the author's name, not the reference number.

Annotated visual of where to find author, title, and publication information, 300–03 (Documentation Matters tutorial preceding ch. 18)

Ref. No. Author's surname First and Middle Initials. Title: subtitle. Place of publication: Publisher; date of publication.

NOTE Book titles are neither italicized nor underlined in CSE style.

Here are examples of actual reference list entries:

Name-year system

Wedge, M. 2012. Pills are not for preschoolers: a drug-free approach for troubled kids. New York (NY): W. W. Norton.

Citation-sequence and citation-name systems

1. Wedge, M. Pills are not for preschoolers: a drug-free approach for troubled kids. New York (NY): W. W. Norton; 2012.

CSE Reference List Entries

1. One author
2. Two or more authors
3. Group or corporate author

b. Online

Name-year system

Stroup A. 1990. A company of scientists: botany, patronage, and community

at the seventeenth-century Parisian Royal Academy of Sciences [Internet].

print publication information · access date

Berkeley (CA): University of California Press. [cited 2016 Mar 2]. Available from:

URL (permalink)

http://ark.cdlib.org/ark:/13030/ft587006gh/.

Citation-sequence and citation-name systems

2. Stroup A. A company of scientists: botany, patronage, and community at the

seventeenth-century Parisian Royal Academy of Sciences [Internet]. Berkeley (CA):

University of California Press; 1990 [cited 2016 Mar 2]. Available from: http://

ark.cdlib.org/ark:/13030/ft587006gh/.

2. Two or more authors

Name-year system

Janzon L, Hallmen J. 2014. Bugs up close: a magnified look at the incredible world of

insects. New York (NY): Skyhorse.

Citation-sequence and citation-name systems

3. Janzon L, Hallmen J. Bugs up close: a magnified look at the incredible world of

insects. New York (NY): Skyhorse; 2014.

If the source has more than ten authors, list the first ten; after the tenth
author, insert the words *et al.*

3. Group or corporate author

Name-year system

Institute of Medicine Committee on the Use of Complementary and Alternative

Medicine by the American Public. 2005. Complementary and alternative medicine in

the United States. Washington (DC): National Academies Press.

CSE Reference
List Entries

1. One author
2. **Two or more authors**
3. **Group or corporate author**
4. Edited book
5. Selection from an edited book or conference proceedings

Period after citation
only if it concludes
in a forward slash

Follow the order of
authors on the title
page. No *and* before
last author.

Citation-sequence and citation-name systems

4. Institute of Medicine Committee on the Use of Complementary and Alternative Medicine by the American Public. Complementary and alternative medicine in the United States. Washington (DC): National Academies Press; 2005.

4. Edited book

Name-year system

Vogt T, Dhamen W, Binev P, editors. 2012. Modeling nanoscale imaging in electron microscopy. New York (NY): Springer.

Citation-sequence and citation-name systems

5. Vogt T, Dhamen W, Binev P, editors. Modeling nanoscale imaging in electron microscopy. New York (NY): Springer; 2012.

5. Selection from an edited book or conference proceedings

Name-year system

selection author   selection title
Berkenkotter C. 2000. Scientific writing and scientific thinking: writing the
                                                      book title
scientific habit of mind. In: Goggin MD, editor. Inventing a discipline: rhetoric
scholarship in honor of Richard E. Young. Urbana (IL): National Council of
                        selection pages
Teachers of English. p. 270–284.

Citation-sequence and citation-name systems

6. Berkenkotter C. Scientific writing and scientific thinking: writing the scientific habit of mind. In: Goggin MD, editor. Inventing a discipline: rhetoric scholarship in honor of Richard E. Young. Urbana (IL): National Council of Teachers of English; 2000. p. 270–284.

To cite a paper published in the proceedings of a conference, add the number and name of the conference, the date of the conference, and the location of the conference (separated by semicolons and ending with a period) after the title of the book and before the publication information.

presenter   title of presentation
Hazen RM. Mineral evolution, mineral ecology, and the coevolution of life and rocks.
                                                        date of   location of
                    name of conference   presentation   conference
American Society for Cell Biology Conference; 2014 Dec 6; Philadelphia (PA).

6. Dissertation For dissertations published by University Microfilms International (UMI), include the access number.

Name-year system

Song LZ. 2003. Relations between optimism, stress and health in Chinese and

American students [dissertation]. Tucson (AZ): University of Arizona.
access information   location   access no.
Available from: UMI, Ann Arbor, MI; AAI3107041.

Citation-sequence and citation-name systems

7. Song LZ. Relations between optimism, stress and health in Chinese and American

students [dissertation]. Tucson (AZ): University of Arizona; 2003. Available from:

UMI, Ann Arbor, MI; AAI3107041.

If the location of the college is not listed on the title page of the dissertation, place square brackets around this information: [Tucson (AZ)].

Periodicals—Printed and Electronic

The information needed to document a printed journal article is on the cover or table of contents of the journal and the first and last pages of the article. For articles downloaded from a database, the information you need appears on the screen listing the articles that fit your search terms, on the full record of the article, or on the first (and last) page of the file you download. For journal articles published online, the information you need appears on the website's home page, on that issue's web page, or on the first screen of the article.

7. Article in a scholarly journal

a. Printed The basic citation for an article in a scholarly journal looks like this:
Name-year system

Author's surname First and Middle Initials. Year of publication. Title: subtitle.

Abbreviated Journal Title. Vol. number(Issue number):page numbers.

CSE Reference
List Entries

4. Edited book
5. Selection from
   an edited
   book or con-
   ference pro-
   ceedings
6. **Dissertation**
7. **Article in a
   scholarly
   journal**
8. Article in a
   magazine
9. Article in a
   newspaper

More about
Formatting author
information:
Examples 1–5,
437–41

Annotated visual
of where to
find author and
publication infor-
mation, 300–03
(Documentation
Matters tutorial
preceding ch. 18)

Citation-sequence and citation-name systems

Ref. No. Author's surname First and Middle Initials. Title: subtitle. Abbreviated Journal Title. Year of publication; Vol. number(Issue number):page numbers.

Here is an actual citation of each type:

Name-year system

> Journal titles: Omit punctuation, articles (*an*, *the*), and prepositions (*of*, *on*, *in*), and abbreviate most words longer than 5 letters (except 1-word titles like *Science* and *Nature*).

Cox L. 2007. The community health center perspective. Behav Healthc. 27(3):20–21.

Citation-sequence and citation-name systems

8. Cox L. The community health center perspective. Behav Healthc. 2007:27(3):20–21.

> **DOI** Digital object identifier, a permanent identifier assigned to electronic articles

b. **Accessed through a database** Most researchers locate journal articles through subscription databases available through their college library. Frequently, articles indexed in such databases are available in HTML or PDF format through a link from the database. As yet, the CSE does not provide a model for an article accessed through an online database, but since most library databases are by subscription, readers will probably find the URL of the database's home page more useful than a direct link to the article itself. If a DOI is available, include it.

Name-year system

Yuan F, Mayer B. 2012. Chemical and isotopic evaluation of sulfur sources
and cycling in the Pecos River, New Mexico, USA. Chem Geol [Internet].
medium
access date *database*
[cited 2016 Aug 7];291(1–2):13–22. In: Science Direct. Available from:
URL (database home page) DOI
www.sciencedirect.com doi:10.1016/j.chemgeo.2011.11.014

> No period after URL or DOI

Citation-sequence and citation-name systems

9. Yuan F, Mayer B. Chemical and isotopic evaluation of sulfur sources and cycling in the Pecos River, New Mexico, USA. Chem Geol [Internet]. 2004 [cited 2016 Aug 7];291(1–2):13–22. Available from: www.sciencedirect.com doi:10.1016/ j.chemgeo.2011.11.014

CSE Reference List Entries

6. Dissertation
7. Article in a scholarly journal
8. Article in a magazine

c. Online Omit page numbers for online articles. When a subscription is not required to access the article, provide a direct permalink URL to the article; otherwise, provide the URL to the journal's home page. If a DOI is provided, include it.

Name-year system

Patten SB, Williams HVA, Lavorato DH, Eliasziw M. 2009. Allergies and major

depression: a longitudinal community study. Biopsychosoc Med [Internet].

URL (permalink)
[cited 2016 Feb 5];3(3). Available from: www.bpsmedicine.com/content/3/1/3

DOI
doi:10.1186/1751-0759-3-3

Citation-sequence and citation-name systems

10. Patten SB, Williams HVA, Lavorato DH, Eliasziw M. Allergies and major depres-

sion: a longitudinal community study. Biopsychosoc Med [Internet]. 2009

[cited 2016 Feb 5];3(3). Available from: www.bpsmedicine.com/content/3/1/3

doi:10.1186/1751-0759-3-3

8. Article in a magazine
a. Printed
Name-year system

Schulz K. 2015 Oct 19. Pond Scum. New Yorker. 40–45.

Citation-sequence and citation-name systems

11. Schulz K. Pond Scum. New Yorker. 2015 Oct 19; 40–45.

b. Accessed through a database
Name-year system

Schulz K. 2015 Oct 19 [cited 2016 Apr 23]. Pond Scum. New Yorker [Internet]: 138–149.

Available from: www.newsbank.com

Citation-sequence and citation-name systems

12. Schulz K. Pond Scum. New Yorker [Internet]. 2015 Oct 19 [cited 2016 Apr 23]:

138–149. Available from: www.newsbank.com

CSE Reference
List Entries

6. Dissertation
7. Article in a scholarly journal
8. Article in a magazine
9. Article in a newspaper
10. Website

No period after URL (unless it concludes with a forward slash) or DOI

c. Online
Name-year system

Coghlan A. 2007 May 16 [cited 2016 May 19]. Bipolar children—is the

US overdiagnosing? NewScientist.com [Internet]. Available from:
                    URL (permalink)
www.newscientist.com/channel/health/

mg19426043.900-bipolar-children--is-the-us-overdiagnosing.html/.

Citation-sequence and citation-name systems

13. Coghlan A. Bipolar children—is the US overdiagnosing? NewScientist.com [Inter-

    net] 2007 May 16 [cited 2016 May 19]. Available from: www.newscientist.com/

    channel/health/mg19426043.900-bipolar-children--is-the-us-overdiagnosing.html/.

9. Article in a newspaper
a. Printed
Name-year system

                                                    edition section 1st pg.
Stern J. 2015 Dec 5. How terror hardens us. New York Times (Late Ed.). Sun. Rev.:1

Citation-sequence and citation-name systems

14. Stern J. How terror hardens us. New York Times (Late Ed.). 2015 Dec 5; Sun.

    Rev.:1.

b. Accessed through a database
Name-year system

Stern J. 2015 Dec 5 [cited 2016 Feb 7]. How terror hardens us. New York Times

[Internet]. Sun. Rev.:1. Available from: www.lexisnexis.com

Citation-sequence and citation-name systems

15. Stern J. How terror hardens us. New York Times [Internet]. 2015 Dec 5 [cited 2016

    Feb 7]; Sun. Rev.:1. Available from: www.lexisnexis.com

c. Online

Name-year system

LaFee S. 2006 May 17. Light can hold fatal attraction for many nocturnal

animals. San Diego Union-Tribune [Internet]. [cited 2016 May 20]. [about
length
11 paragraphs]. Available from: www.signonsandiego.com/news/science/.

Citation-sequence and citation-name systems

16. LaFee S. Light can hold fatal attraction for many nocturnal animals. San Diego

Union-Tribune [Internet]. 2006 May 17 [cited 2016 May 20]. [about 11 paragraphs].

Available from: www.signonsandiego.com/news/science/.

> Include permalink
> URL if available;
> if not, use URL of
> home page.

Miscellaneous Sources—Printed and Electronic

The information needed to document a website or web page usually appears at the top or bottom of the home page or web page. You may also need to look for a link to a page labeled "About us" or "Contact us." Frequently, information needed for a complete reference list entry is missing, in which case provide as much information as you can.

10. Website

Name-year system

In the name-year system, a sample reference entry for a website looks like this:

Author. Title of website [Medium (Internet)]. Publication date [Access date]. Available

from: URL (home page)

Here is an example of an actual entry:

MIT news [Internet]. 2009 Feb 9 [cited 2016 Mar 10]. Available from: http://

web.mit.edu/newsoffice/index.html/.

The site has no author, so the reference list entry begins with the name of the site's sponsor.

> Annotated visual
> of where to find
> author, title, and
> publication infor-
> mation, 300–03
> (Documentation
> Matters tutorial
> preceding ch. 18)

CSE Reference
List Entries

7. Article in a
   scholarly jour-
   nal
8. Article in a
   magazine
9. **Article in a
   newspaper**
10. **Website**
11. Web page
12. Discussion list
    or blog post-
    ing

Citation-sequence and citation-name systems

When referencing an entire website, the only difference between the name-year system and the citation-sequence and citation-name systems is that the citation-sequence and citation-name entries add a reference number at the beginning of the entry.

11. Web page When documenting a web page or a document on a website, provide the URL for the web page, not the site's home page.

Name-year system

article author   article title
Schorow S. 2009 Feb 5. Aliens at sea: anthropologist Helmreich studies
                                                                website
researchers studying ocean microbes. MIT News [Internet]. [cited 2015 Mar 10].
                                      URL (web page)
Available from: http://web.mit.edu/newsoffice/2012/alien-ocean-0205.html

Citation-sequence and citation-name systems

17. Schorow S. Aliens at sea: anthropologist Helmreich studies researchers studying

ocean microbes. MIT News [Internet]. 2009 Feb 5 [cited 2015 Mar 10]. Available

from: http://web.mit.edu/newsoffice/2009/alien-ocean-0205.html

12. Discussion list or blog posting

Name-year system

                    date/time posted
Bolden C. 2015 Jul 17, 10:47 am [cited 2015 Aug 27]. Request for observations of
                              disc. list   medium
parasites in fisheries. In: FISH-SCI [Internet discussion list]. [Lulea (Sweden): National

Higher Research and Education Network]. [about 2 paragraphs]. Available from:

http://segate.sunet.se/cgi-bin/wa?A0=FISH-SCI

Citation-sequence and citation-name systems

18. Bolden C. Request for observations of parasites in fisheries. In: FISH-SCI [Internet

discussion list]. [Lulea (Sweden): National Higher Research and Education Net-

work]; 2015 Jul 17, 10:47 am [cited 2015 Aug 27]. [about 2 paragraphs]. Available

from: http://segate.sunet.se/cgi-bin/wa?A0=FISH-SCI

13. Email message

Name-year system

email author   date/time sent   subject line
Martin SP. 2012 Nov 18, 3:31 pm. Revised results [Email]. Message to:
email recipient   length
Lydia Jimenez [cited 2016 Nov 20]. [about 2 screens].

Citation-sequence and citation-name systems

19. Martin SP. Revised results [Email]. Message to: Lydia Jimenez. 2012 Nov 18, 3:31

    pm [cited 2016 Nov 20]. [about 2 screens].

14. Technical report or government document
If no author is listed, use the name of the governing nation and the government agency that produced the document, and include any identifying number.

Name-year system

Department of Health and Human Services (US). 1985 May. Women's health. Report

of the Public Health Service Task Force on Women's Health Issues. [publisher

unknown]. PHS:85-50206.

Citation-sequence and citation-name systems

20. Department of Health and Human Services (US). Women's health. Report of the

    Public Health Service Task Force on Women's Health Issues. [publisher unknown];

    1985 May. PHS:85-50206.

21c Formatting a CSE-Style Research Project

The CSE does not specify a format for the body of a college research report, but most scientific reports include the following sections:

- Abstract
- Introduction
- Methods
- Results
- Discussion
- References

More about
Writing an abstract, 394
Formatting college papers, 101
Formatting in APA style, 392–96

Ask your instructor for formatting guidelines, refer to the general formatting guidelines provided in chapter 9, or follow the formatting guidelines for APA style in chapter 19.

Start a new page for your reference list, and title it "References."

Name-year system List entries in alphabetical order by author's surname. If no author is listed, alphabetize by the first main word of the title (omitting articles such as *the, a,* and *an*). Do not number the entries.

Citation-sequence system Number your entries in order of their appearance in your project. Each work should appear in your reference list only once, even if it is cited more than once in your project. Double-check to make sure that the numbers in your reference list match the numbers in your text.

Citation-name system Alphabetize the entries in your reference list first (by the author's surname or the first main word of the title if no author is listed). Then number them. Each work should appear in your reference list only once, even if it is cited more than once in your project. Double-check to make sure that the numbers in your reference list match the numbers in your text.

Student Model **Research Project: CSE-Style Reference List**

The sample reference list on page 449 is taken from a laboratory report by Alicia Keefe, University of Maryland. Keefe fulfilled her responsibility to the writers from whom she borrowed information and ideas by supplying a complete citation for each source. She fulfilled her responsibility to her reader by formatting the entries using the name-year system in CSE style, in keeping with her reader's expectations.

Writing
Responsibly **Of Deadlines and Paperclips**

Instructors expect students to turn in thoughtful, carefully proofread, and neatly formatted projects on time—usually in class on the due date. They also expect writers to clip or staple the pages of the paper *before* the project is submitted. Do justice to yourself by being fully prepared.

to SELF

References

Web page: Date cited and URL of web page provided

FlyBase: phylogeny. 2015 May 13. FlyBase [Internet] [cited 2015 7 Dec]. Available from: http://flybase.org/wiki/FlyBase:Phylogeny

Journal article: Accessed through a database, no DOI; URL of database home page provided

Hoikkala A, Aspi J. 1993 [cited 2008 Apr 28]. Criteria of female mate choice in *Drosophila littoralis, D. montana,* and *D. ezoana.* Evolution [Internet]. 47(3):768–778. Available from: http://web.ebscohost.com

Journal article: Printed, title of journal abbreviated

Ives JD. 1921. Cross-over values in the fruit fly, *Drosophila ampelophila,* when the linked factors enter in different ways. Am Naturalist. 6:571–573.

Mader S. 2016. Lab manual. 12th ed. New York (NY): McGraw-Hill.

Journal article: Accessed through a database, with DOI

Marcillac F, Bousquet F, Alabouvette J, Savarit F, Ferveur JF. 2005 [cited 2016 Apr 28]. A mutation with major effects on *Drosophila melanogaster* sex pheromones. Genetics [Internet]. 171(4):1617–1628. Available from: http://web.ebscohost.com doi:10.1534/genetics.104.033159

Journal article: Printed, one-word journal title not abbreviated

Service PM. 1991. Laboratory evolution of longevity and reproductive fitness components in male fruit flies: mating ability. Evolution. 47:387–399.

Part Six

Genre
Matters
Writing in and beyond College

22 Writing in Literature and the Other Humanities

> *More about*
> Summarizing, 115,
> 257–60
> Annotating,
> 118–21
> Reading journal,
> 121–22
> Enjoying what
> you read,
> 115–16

© Darren Greenwood/Design Pics

There is rarely one right way to interpret or appreciate literature, art, music, or events in history. Instead, the texts studied in these humanities disciplines offer readers multiple doors to understanding. At first glance, these doors may seem confusing, but they actually offer rewarding opportunities to explore the many ways of being human.

22a Adopting the Approach of Literature and the Other Humanities

Whether focused solely on the text and the reader's experience of it or on its social, historical, or cultural contexts, writing in the humanities is an act of interpretation. Yet while those who study the humanities produce multiple meanings, each interpretation must be based on evidence from or about the text.

1. Read actively and reflectively.

Understanding works of literature and other texts in the humanities is not merely a matter of extracting information, but it does begin with reading to gain a basic understanding of the text. Begin by summarizing: What is the main point of the work? In literature, this is the *theme*. A summary will help you get to the heart of the matter, but keep in mind that literary analysis must do more than summarize what the text says.

Next, annotate or make notes about the work. Some of your notes may provide perspectives on the work that you can use later when writing. The notes in Figure 22.1 (p. 454), for example, show the beginnings of themes that Jewel Andrews explores in her analysis of Percy Bysshe Shelley's "Poetical Essay on the Existing State of Things."

Finally, allow yourself to enjoy what you are reading. If you make an effort to appreciate the language, note insights, or make connections to something in your own experience, you will get more out of your reading.

2. Analyze the text.

Understanding a historical event or work of literature, philosophy, or art involves analysis, dividing the work or event into its component parts to see how they work together.

Usually you will need to study the text again (and again) to identify the elements from which it is constructed and to determine how these parts work together. The Quick Reference box on page 455 lists some of the elements that a literary analysis should take into consideration.

3. Adopt a critical framework.

Coming to terms with a text requires more than comprehension and analysis. It also requires *interpretation* (determining what the elements *mean*), *synthesis* (connecting the text to what you already know and to other works you have read), and sometimes *critique* (evaluating the methods and effects of a work). You may compare two or more texts as an aid to understanding, or you may adopt a critical, theoretical approach to the work.

In introductory classes in literature and the other humanities, students are often expected to take a *formalist approach,* looking closely at the work itself (the primary source) to understand how it functions. Examples of other popular approaches are outlined in the Quick Reference box on page 456.

Student Model
Explication: "My View on a Long-Lost but Timeless Poem: Shelley's 'Poetical Essay on the Existing State of Things,'" Jewel Andrews, 466, 468–71

> *More about*
> Analysis, 124–26, 263–64, 271–73

> *More about*
> Person, 458–59, 648–49
> Level of diction, 19–20, 565–66
> Style, 520–94 (part 7, Style Matters)
> Figures of speech, 574–75

> *More about*
> Interpretation, 263–64, 263–64, 271–73
> Synthesis, 127–29, 263–64, 271–73
> Critique, 131–34, 263–64, 271–73

Writing Responsibly   Reading with Study Guides

SparkNotes and similar study guides, long a staple of college bookstores and now available online, may tempt struggling students to substitute the guide for the text itself. Do not succumb! You not only deprive yourself of a learning experience, but you may also find that the study guide leaves you unprepared for the sophisticated level of understanding your instructor expects. If you are having difficulty making sense of a text, discuss the work with classmates, read essays about or reviews of the work at your college library, watch a reading or a performance of the work, or seek advice from your instructor.

to SELF

Student Model Textual Analysis

Poetical Essay on the Existing State of Things
By Percy Bysshe Shelley

DESTRUCTION marks thee! o'er the blood-stain'd heath

Is faintly borne the stifled wail of death;

Millions to fight compell'd, to fight or die

In mangled heaps on War's red altar lie.

The sternly wise, the mildly good, have sped

To the unfruitful mansions of the dead.

Whilst fell Ambition o'er the wasted plain

Triumphant guides his car—the ensanguin'd rein

Glory directs; fierce brooding o'er the scene,

With hatred glance, with dire unbending mien,

Fell Despotism sits by the red glare

Of Discord's torch, kindling the flames of war.

For thee then does the Muse her sweetest lay

Pour 'mid the shrieks of war, 'mid dire dismay;

For thee does Fame's obstrep'rous clarion rise,

Does Praise's voice raise meanness to the skies.

Are we then sunk so deep in darkest gloom,

That selfish pride can virtue's garb assume?

Does real greatness in false splendour live?

When narrow views the futile mind deceive,

When thirst of wealth, or frantic rage for fame,

When legal murders swell the lists of pride;

When glory's views the titled idiot guide,

Then will oppression's iron influence show

The great man's comfort as the poor man's woe.

Handwritten margin notes:

Why "essay" and not "poem"?

Thought-provoking: "the sternly wise, the mildly good"

Lots of use of the word "red" (= blood)

Dramatic phrase! "Unfruitful mansions of the dead"

"car" probably means "chariot"?

Did regular people really talk like this in Shelley's time, or is he playing with words for rhythm and rhyme?

Abbreviates words, often by removing syllables. To keep a tight rhythm?

Lots of unnatural-sounding word order to make it rhyme.

"legal murders" and "titled idiot"—great phrasing!

FIGURE 22.1 **Notes from a close reading of the poem "Poetical Essay on the Existing State of Things," by Percy Bysshe Shelley**

Quick Reference — Elements of Literature

When writing about a work of literature, consider the following elements and ask yourself these questions:

Genre. Into what broad category, or *genre* (fiction, poetry, drama), does the work fit? Into what narrower category (mystery, sci-fi; sonnet, ode; comedy, tragedy) does the work belong? What expectations are set up by the genre, and how does the work adhere to or violate these expectations?

Plot. What happens? Does the plot unfold chronologically (from start to finish), or does the text use flashbacks or flash-forwards? Does the plot proceed as expected, or is there a surprise?

Setting. Where and when does the action occur? Is the setting identifiable? If not, what hints does the text give about the where and when? Are time and place consistent, or do elements from other times or places intrude?

Character. Who is the *protagonist*, or main character? Who are the supporting characters? How believable are the characters? Do they represent types or individuals?

Point of view. Who is telling the story—one of the characters or a separate narrator? What point of view does the narrator take—the first-person (*I*) or third-person (*she, he, it*)? Does the narrator have special insight into the characters or recount events as an outsider?

Language/style. What level of diction (formal, informal, colloquial, dialect) does the text use, and why? How are words put together? Does the text contain long, complex sentences or short, direct ones? Does the text contain figurative language (such as metaphor and simile), or is the writing more literal?

Theme. What is the main point of the story? If you were to tell the story as a fable, what would its moral be?

Symbol. Do any of the characters, events, or objects represent something more than their literal meaning?

Irony. Is there a contrast between what is said and what is meant, between what the characters know and what the reader knows?

Allusion. Does the work contain references to literary and cultural classics or sacred texts?

Before adopting a critical approach, consider the issues you have discussed in class or in other classes you are taking. A psychology class, for example, may provide a theory that will help you explain the behavior of a character; an economics class may help you understand the market forces affecting the plot; a women's studies class may provide methods of interpretation that will give you new perspectives on historical events.

22b Using the Resources of Literature and the Other Humanities

As you prepare to write about a text, ask your instructor whether you should consult outside sources. *Primary sources* for studying a literary work include the work itself; they may include the author's letters or email messages, diaries, interviews, annotated manuscripts, or performances (live or recorded).

Biographical approach. Focus on the author's life to understand the work. Does the work reflect the trajectory of the author's own life or perhaps depict a working out in literature of something the author was unable to work out in reality?

Deconstructionist approach. Focus on gaps, discontinuities, or inconsistencies in the text that reveal or challenge the assumptions of the dominant culture. What do these inconsistencies communicate that the author may not have intended?

Feminist approach. Focus on the power relations between men and women (or elements in the work that take on gender traits). Does the work reinforce traditional power relations or challenge them?

Marxist approach. Focus on the power relations among social classes (or among elements that take on class characteristics). Does the work reinforce the status quo or challenge it?

New historicist approach. Focus on the social-historical moment in which the work was created. How does the work reflect that historical moment?

Postcolonial approach. Focus on the power relations between colonizing and colonized peoples (or on elements in the work that reflect traditional power dynamics). Does the work reinforce or challenge those power relations?

Queer approach. Focus on the power relations between "normal" and "deviant." How differently can a text be read when the reader rejects this dichotomy?

Reader response approach. Focus not on the author's intentions or the text's meaning but on the experience of the individual reader. How does the individual reader construct meaning in the act of reading?

To write about Percy Bysshe Shelley's poem "Poetical Essay on the Existing State of Things," Jewel Andrews not only analyzed the poem but also explored the online exhibit "Shelley's Ghost: Reshaping the Image of a Literary Family," which has videos, podcasts, interactive media, and artifacts such as digital scans of historical documents and Shelley's original notebooks and manuscripts. Writers, academics, and civic leaders often visit college campuses; sitting in on a talk or even interviewing such people is an opportunity to include a primary source that will inform your research on a topic. Primary sources in the other humanities might include any of the following:

- In film studies, a classic film like *Citizen Kane* (1941) or a popular movie like *Spotlight* (2015); a director's annotated script; or a series of storyboards, comic-strip-like sketches showing the main characters, action, and shot sequences in a film

- In classics, a lyric poem by the ancient Greek poet Sappho; a history of ancient Rome by Livy (59 BCE–17 CE), or a vase depicting an important event in classical history

- In art history, a painting, sculpture, or other artistic production or a video of an artist at work

- In philosophy, a text like Plato's *Meno* or a lecture by a philosopher like Peter Singer

- In history, a historical document, such as the Mayflower Compact (1620), or court records detailing an event like the My Lai massacre during the Vietnam War

Secondary sources are works about the author, period, text, or critical framework you are using. They provide information about the primary source you are studying. Use secondary sources to develop and support, not to substitute for, your own interpretation. Shona Sequiera used the framework provided by the documentary *Ethnic Notions,* a secondary source, to assess the main character in Zora Neale Hurston's novel *Their Eyes Were Watching God* (1937), her primary source. You can find secondary sources by searching your library's catalog, specialized databases (such as the *MLA International Bibliography, Historical Abstracts,* the *Arts and Humanities Citation Index,* or the *Philosopher's Index*), the *Book Review Digest,* and the *Literary Criticism Index.*

22c Citing and Documenting Sources— MLA and *Chicago* Style

Whenever you borrow ideas or information or quote from a work, you must cite the source in the text and document it in a bibliography or list of works cited. While there are other style guides, most writers in literature and the other humanities use either the style detailed in the *MLA Handbook,* 8th edition, or in the *Chicago Manual of Style,* 16th edition. Ask your instructor which you should use.

22d Using the Language of Literature and the Other Humanities

Each discipline uses language distinctively, and your writing will be most effective when it follows conventions that are accepted in the discipline in which you are writing.

1. Use the specialized vocabulary of the discipline correctly.

Most academic disciplines in the humanities use specialized vocabulary. Learning that vocabulary will help you understand sources and communicate effectively with your audience. To master this new language, consult discipline-specific dictionaries and encyclopedias, such as *The Penguin Dictionary of Literary Terms and Literary Theory, The Columbia Dictionary of Modern Literary and Cultural Criticism,* or *The Oxford Encyclopedia of British Literature.* Consider the terms in context, and ask your instructor for help.

Student Model
Interpretative analysis: "Transcending Stereotypes in Hurston's *Their Eyes Were Watching God,*" Shona Sequiera, 462–66

> **More about**
> Finding information, 210–32 (ch. 13)

> **More about**
> In-text citation (MLA), 304–21
> Works-cited list (MLA), 321–44
> Notes and bibliography (*Chicago*), 407–21

> **More about**
> Finding subject-specific reference works, 212

2. Use past and present tense correctly.

More about
Tense, 672–78

Writers in the humanities, including literary studies, usually choose the present tense when writing about the work being studied (the events, characters, and setting) or the ideas of other scholars, and they use the present or past tense (as appropriate) when discussing actual events, such as the author's death or a historical or cultural event from the time that the work was published.

Uses present tense to discuss the work studied

Present Tense

These witches and ghosts are real, and often present, for Haun's characters, and "witch doctors" have busy practices fending them off. Dreams and visions are carefully noted and heeded, and the natural world is festooned with warning signs.

—Lisa Alther, "The Shadow Side of Appalachia: Mildred Haun's Haunting Fiction"

Uses past tense to discuss past events

Past Tense

Margaret Lindsey, defamed as a sorceress (incantatrix) by three men in 1435, successfully purged herself with the help of five women; her accusers were warned against making further slanders under pain of excommunication.

—Kathleen Kamerick, "Shaping Superstition in Late Medieval England"

3. Use first and third person correctly.

More about
Person, 478, 648–49

The use of the first person (*I, we*) or third person (*he, she, it, they, Elena, the conflict*) pronoun varies from one humanities discipline to another. In part, this reflects a difference in emphasis: Are writers emphasizing their arguments or the evidence on which they are based? In philosophy, the goal is often to advance one's own perspective:

First person (*I*)

I begin, in Section 1, by clarifying the kind of groups and the type of collective rights that I shall be concerned with.

—Steven Wall, "Collective Rights and Individual Autonomy"

In literary studies, the emphasis is on the work of literature, so writers use the third person whenever reasonable. Compare these two versions of a sentence from Jewel Andrews' essay on Shelley's poem "Poetical Essay on the Existing State of Things":

First Person	Third Person
When I first read the poem, I thought Shelley was writing about the brutality and tragedy of war in general, but a closer look made it clear to me he's taking aim at Britain's involvement in the Napoleonic Wars against the French.	A first reading of the poem suggests that he is writing about the brutality and tragedy of war in general, but a closer read . . . makes it clear he's taking aim at Britain's involvement in the Napoleonic Wars against the French.

The version in the third person shifts the emphasis from the writer to the poem and is thus less personal and more persuasive. (Notice also that it shifts to the present tense.)

4. Use the active voice.

In the humanities, writers typically use the active voice:

> **More about**
> Active versus
> passive voice,
> 525

ACTIVE	Janie's relationship with her third husband, Tea Cake, plays a key role in transforming her concept of racial identity.
PASSIVE	A key role in transforming her concept of racial identity was played by Janie's relationship with her third husband, Tea Cake.

Use of the active voice promotes a clear, concise style and specifies who did what to whom. Of course, some circumstances may require the passive voice, as when the "who" is unknown or when you want to emphasize the action rather than the actor.

5. Use the author's full name at first mention and surname only thereafter.

In writing about the works of others, provide the author's complete name ("Zora Neale Hurston") the first time it is mentioned; subsequently, use the author's surname ("Hurston") only, unless this will cause confusion. (When writing about the Brontë sisters, for example, you may need to specify whether you are discussing Charlotte or Emily Brontë.) You may use the first name when writing about a fictional character, but it is not customary to refer to an author by first name.

> **More about**
> Capitalizing titles,
> 838–39
> Quotation marks
> versus italics for
> titles, 813,
> 838–39,
> 842–44

6. Include the work's title in your title.

When writing about a work of literature or another text (a painting or film, for example), provide the title of the work in the title or subtitle of your project and again in the first paragraph of your text. Capitalize the title correctly and use italics or quotation marks as needed.

22e Writing about Fiction

> **More about**
Analyzing assign-
ments, 22–24,
196–98, 493

A common assignment in the humanities is the *interpretive analysis,* which calls on the writer to study one or more elements of a text; in literature, a writer might study a character or the setting; in philosophy, a writer might study the use of a particular word or concept (*freedom, free will*); in history, a writer might study the repercussions of a historical event. In some disciplines (such as literature, philosophy, or film), a writer might analyze a single primary source or compare one or more primary sources. Often (particularly in history and art history), students will be asked to draw on secondary as well as primary resources in addition to providing their own analysis.

Student Models

Interpretive
analysis: "Transcend-
ing Stereotypes in
Hurston's *Their Eyes
Were Watching God*,"
Shona Sequiera,
462–66
Explication: "My View
on a Long-Lost but
Timeless Poem:
Shelley's 'Poetical
Essay on the Existing
State of Things'"
Jewel Andrews, 466,
468–71

Another writing assignment that is common in literature and the per-forming arts is the *critique* or review: an assessment of a work of literature or art or of a performance (a play, concert, or film). Some disciplines, such as literature or philosophy, may call on students to *explicate* a text, or pro-vide a close reading (line by line or even word by word). Often, a close reading will focus on one or more of the elements of literature. (See the Quick Reference box on p. 455.)

Of course, many writing assignments in college will combine assign-ment types: To write an academic essay about a work of literature, follow the steps in the writing process discussed in part 1 (pp. 6–110) and the specific recommendations in the sections below.

Professional

Model

Review: "This 116-Year-
Old Russian Play
Pulses with 21st-
Century Urgency,
Jenny Lower,"
473–74

1. Devise a literary thesis.

Narrow your focus to an idea you can develop fully in the assigned length. To devise a topic in literature, ask yourself questions about the elements of the work:

- What are the central conflicts among or within characters?
- What aspects of the plot puzzled or surprised you, and why?
- How might the setting (time and place) have influenced the behavior of the characters?
- Did the writer use language in a distinctive (or difficult or obscure) way, and why?

- What images recurred or were especially powerful, and why?
- What other works did you think about as you were reading this one, and why?

Then answer one of your questions. Your answer can be your *working thesis*.

As you draft your paper, you should analyze or interpret (not merely summarize) the text, as these contrasting examples demonstrate:

SUMMARY THESIS	In this poem, Shelley invokes the suffering and tragedy of war.
INTERPRETIVE/ ANALYTICAL THESIS	In this poem, Shelley uses symbolism and rhythm to denounce the actions of his government and evoke the devastating toll of war.

To support the first thesis, the writer could merely report the poem's main point. To support the second thesis, however, the writer must analyze the poem's symbolism and rhythm and then use that analysis to explain her interpretation of the poem's central conflict.

2. Support your claims with evidence from the text.

As with any writing project, you can use idea-generating techniques like brain-storming, freewriting, and clustering to figure out what your thesis is and why you believe it. Then turn back to the text: What details from the work illustrate or support your reasons? These are the *evidence* your readers will need. Consider this passage from Jewel Andrews' essay:

> The 172-line "Poetical Essay" is full of the poet's outrage at the state of the world. A first reading of the poem suggests that he is writing about the brutality and tragedy of war in general, but a closer read plus research on Shelley and his writing makes it clear he's taking aim at Britain's involvement in the Napoleonic Wars against the French, and at the imprisonment of an Irish journalist critical of British military operations. Shelley sets the tone right away: "Millions to fight compell'd, to fight or die / In mangled heaps on War's red altar lie" (lines 3–4) and, in a takedown of the privileged ruling class into which he was born, he taunts: "When glory's views the titled idiot guide" (24). The lines "Ye cold advisers of yet colder kings, / To whose fell breast no passion virtue brings" (37–38) make it clear whose side he is on.

Andrews argues that Shelley uses powerful symbolism to depict the barbarity of war and the cold arrogance of the aristocracy, and she offers concrete evidence from the text—some quoted, some summarized—to support her claim. Note that Andrews does not merely drop the evidence from the poem into her essay but instead explains its relevance.

More about
Writing ethically, 6–12 (ch. 1), Writing Responsibly boxes (listed on the last pages facing inside back cover)
Planning, 13–33 (ch. 2)
Organizing and drafting, 34–51 (ch. 3)
Crafting and connecting paragraphs, 52–78 (ch. 4)
Drafting and revising visuals, 79–87 (ch. 5)
Revising, editing, proofreading, and formatting, 88–110 (ch. 6)

More about
Devising a thesis, 35–36

More about
Idea-generating techniques, 24–30

More about
Incorporating evidence, 45–47, 271–73

Topic sentence: States claim

Evidence: Uses quotations and summary from the poem and explains their relevance

3. Support your claims with evidence from outside the text.

Depending on your approach, you may also draw on evidence from outside the text. In the essay in the section that follows, Shona Sequiera draws her critical framework from a documentary film she watched in class. She also draws counterevidence from a secondary source, an essay in a scholarly collection.

Student Model Writing about Fiction: Interpretive Analysis

The essay that follows by Shona Sequiera, a student at Connecticut College, offers an interpretation of the main character in Zora Neale Hurston's novel *Their Eyes Were Watching God* (1937). In her essay, Sequiera rebuts a common criticism of Hurston's characters—that they are "folk," simple, colorful, but not fully human. Measuring the protagonist (or main character), Janie Crawford, against the analysis of caricatured black roles described in the documentary *Ethnic Notions*, Sequiera argues that Janie develops over the course of the novel into a fully developed character who escapes stereotype.

Shona Sequiera

Professor Flood

English 342

3 May 2016

Transcending Stereotypes in Hurston's
Their Eyes Were Watching God

Parodic images of African Americans permeated popular culture—art, film, and stage performance—from the 1820s through the 1960s, becoming deeply ingrained in the American psyche and shaping "the most gut level feelings about race" in the United States *(Ethnic Notions)*. These images form a damaging visual tapestry of white-constructed black identity. As an African American writer, Zora Neale Hurston carried the burden of telling stories *of* her people and *for* her people in a manner that both protested and counteracted false representations of them in mainstream culture. Although *Their Eyes Were Watching God* (1937) has been widely criticized for painting a caricatured picture of African American life (Spencer 113–14), Hurston's heroine, Janie, is ultimately able to transcend oppressive stereotypes and come into her own.

As presented in the novel, Janie Crawford is not a stereotype but a sexual, romantic, feeling woman who immerses herself in the "great fish-net" (193) of life. After her second husband Jody's death, Janie scrutinizes "her skin and features" (83) to find that "the young girl was gone but a handsome woman had taken her place" (83), a textual moment in which the heroine looks past her skin color and into the life experiences that molded and situated her within the framework of her

---

Title: Includes author's surname and title of novel

Names author, includes title of work in first ¶

Thesis statement

Topic sentence

Supporting evidence: Uses quotations from novel and explains relevance

Page reference for quote from *Their Eyes*

cultural community. Janie's setting free "the weight, the length, the glory" (83) of her "plentiful hair" (83) is a metaphorical rejection of the control Jody tried to impose upon her sexuality. While Janie may retain the self-assertiveness and independence with men of the mammy figure (*Ethnic Notions*), her physical beauty, lack of fulfillment in motherhood, and disdain for mundane domestic life separate her from that figure. Instead of a stereotypical character, Janie's taking "careful stock of herself" (83) allows her to move from under the control of men to a position of self-assertiveness and independence. By the novel's end, Janie comes to represent a positive image of black women who are not merely color-coded mammy figures (*Ethnic Notions*) but valuable contributors to and members of black culture.

> Evidence and interpretation: Refers to stereotype in *Ethnic Notions* and explains why stereotype does not apply

> Topic sentence

Like the stereotypical black comedian *Ethnic Notions* identifies as a common type and not unlike the stereotype of the black female sex worker that the scholar Jennifer Thorington Springer describes in her review of Austin Clarke's novel *The Polished Hoe*, Janie acts for other people's pleasure. After Jody's death she "starched and ironed her face, forming it into just what people wanted to see" (83). Unlike those figures, however, she does not appear to be content and yet crumbles with depression, humiliation, and self-hatred. She rejoices within—"She sent her face to Joe's funeral, and herself went rollicking with the springtime across the world" (88).

> Supporting evidence: Uses quotation as support and explains relevance

> Topic sentence

In particular, Janie's relationship with her third husband, Tea Cake, plays a key role in transforming her from a stereotype into a realistic black character. Over the course of the novel, Janie journeys from believing that she "wuz just like de rest" (9) of the white Washburn children to marrying the dark-complexioned Tea Cake, who teaches her to love the skin she lives in. Unlike Mrs. Turner, the mulatto who despises

> Supporting evidence: Uses quotation and summary, and explains relevance

her own blackness, Janie learns both to value skin color as an important component of herself and her culture and to look beyond external appearance to see that the life Tea Cake represents—a happy-go-lucky, romantic, and adventurous existence—is the one that most fulfills her.

Historically, African Americans have been called upon to be the vessels through which damaging white notions of blackness have been showcased (*Ethnic Notions*). Yet Janie Crawford transcends the stereotypical roles expected of her and proves that even though (or especially because) all three husbands are "gone from [her]" (83) upon her return to Eatonville, she values herself enough to move on with her life. Janie plays for neither a white nor a black audience but for herself. As a result, she defies white and black expectations of African American women and is able to experience the depths of love in a period when a black person must not love a thing too much (Morrison 45). In painting a romantic yet realistic portrait of Janie's joy *and* suffering, Hurston argues that the African American experience cannot be defined through distorted notions of color, but that it must be celebrated as a culture of living, fully human beings. Janie's journey toward constructing self-identity provided a model for the African American community, demonstrating how to change their notions of themselves and the ways in which they cater to the dictates of the dominant white culture. Unlike Ethel Waters, who laments in *Ethnic Notions* that "darkies never dream," Janie Crawford dares not only to dream, but to follow her dreams and defy societal guidelines that restrict people on the basis of race, class, and gender.

Conclusion: Restates thesis (in different words)

Shows importance of her analysis

Emphasizes contrast between analysis in *Ethnic Notions* and her own conclusions about Janie's character

Works Cited

Clarke, Austin. *The Polished Hoe*. Amistad, 2004.

Ethnic Notions. Directed by Marlon Riggs, KQED, 1986.

Hurston, Zora Neale. *Their Eyes Were Watching God*. HarperCollins, 2000.

Morrison, Toni. *Beloved*. Penguin, 1987.

Spencer, Stephen. "Racial Politics and the Literary Reception of Zora Neale Hurston's
    Their Eyes Were Watching God." *Multiethnic Literature and Canon Debates.*
    Edited by Mary Jo Bona and Irma Maini, State U of New York P, 2006, pp. 111–26.

Springer, Jennifer Thorington. "Constructing Radical Black Female Subjectivities:
    Survival Pimping in Austin Clarke's *The Polished Hoe.*" *Frontiers: A Journal of
    Women Studies*, vol. 36, no. 2, 2015, pp. 169–191. *Project Muse*, hdl.handle
    .net/1805/8986.

22f Writing about Poetry

While the shape of the poem on the page can be important, poetry is traditionally a spoken art form. When writing about poetry, start by reading the poem aloud or listening to the poet read the work. In addition to the issues that apply to writing about literature generally, pay special attention to the sound, structure, and language of the work. (For more information on writing about poetry, see the Quick Reference box on the next page.)

Student Model Writing about Poetry: Explication

The essay that begins on page 468 was written by Jewel Andrews. Andrews draws evidence from a close reading of the poem "Poetical Essay on the Existing State of Things" (see Figure 22.1) to support her claim that poet Percy Bysshe Shelley uses symbolism and rhythm to persuade readers to accept his view of war. To build her case, Andrews also draws on other primary sources, including videos, podcasts, and interactive media relating to the poet and artifacts and historical documents that belonged to Shelley.

Quick

Reference Writing about Poetry

When writing about a poem, consider the following elements and ask yourself these questions:

Sound

Rhythm. Is the rhythm part of the traditional form of the poem? If not, which words are stressed, and how is this relevant to the poem's meaning?

Rhyme. Is the rhyme scheme part of the traditional form of the poem? If not, what is the purpose of the rhyme scheme? If the poem does not rhyme, are there any other sounds linking words or lines in the poem?

Alliteration/Assonance/Consonance. Does the poem use alliteration (the repetition of a consonant sound at the beginning of a stressed syllable) to link lines or words within a line? Does the poem use assonance or consonance, the repetition of a vowel or consonant sound, to link words or lines in a line? What effects do these choices have on the reader or listener?

Structure

Verse form. Is the poem written in a traditional verse form (such as the sonnet or the limerick), or is the form open, or free? Does the verse form relate to the meaning of the poem?

Line length. Are the poem's lines of regular length, or do lengths vary from line to line or from stanza to stanza? Do sentences carry over from line to line, or does each line express a complete thought? If line lengths are irregular, does length emphasize or deemphasize a thought?

Stanzas. Are lines grouped into regular (or irregular) stanzas? If so, does the stanza convey a single unit of thought, or does an idea or sentence continue across stanzas?

Language

Imagery. What sensory "pictures" does the poem call to mind—the stifling warmth of a July day in the Deep South? The luxuriant springtime riot of mountaintop flowers? What is the relationship between the images the poem calls forth and the ideas it conveys?

Figurative language. Simile (a comparison using *like* or *as*—"My love is like an ice pick"), metaphor (a comparison that does not use *like* or *as*—"My love is an ice pick"), and a host of other figures of speech create images in the reader's mind. Can you identify any figures of speech in the poem and, if so, how do they affect meaning?

Connotation. Poets choose words for their connotative (implicit) as well as for their denotative (literal) meanings. Consider the emotional difference between the verbs *gripe* and *lament*. Both mean "to complain," but, oh, the difference between the two. Note the connotations of the words in the poem you are studying and how they help create the overall effect of the poem.

Repetition. Poets may choose to repeat an important word or phrase. If a word or phrase is repeated (as is the word *and* in "The Raven"), consider its significance. How does this repetition affect your understanding and experience of the poem?

The last stanza from Edgar Allan Poe's "The Raven" (lines 103–8) demonstrates the issues of sound, structure, and language:

And the ráven, never flítting, **still is sítting,**
    still **is sítting**
On the pállid bust of Pállas just above my
    chamber doór;
And his eyes´ have all the see´ming of a
    démon's that is drea´ming,
And the lámp-light o'er him strea´ming
    throws his **shádow on the floor´;**
And my soul´ from out that **shádow** that
    lies floa´ting **on the floor´**
        Shall be lifted—nevermore´!

Jewel Andrews

Professor Sewell

English 110

5 May 2016

My View on a Long-Lost but Timeless Poem:

Shelley's "Poetical Essay on the Existing State of Things"

Ask someone today to describe the work of nineteenth-century English poet Percy Bysshe Shelley and you might hear "sentimental" or, worse, "corny." To our twenty-first-century ears, his elaborate verse can sound overripe. But Shelley (1792–1822), one of the greatest Romantic poets of his or any era, was far from mushy: Born a wealthy aristocrat, his radical political and social views made him an outcast in his own country, and he fled to Italy with his wife, Mary Shelley (who later wrote *Frankenstein*). Shelley's political poetry expressed his passionate views on war, poverty, imperialism, and the failure of governments. In his "lost" poem "Poetical Essay on the Existing State of Things"—rediscovered in 2006 and made available to the public in 2015, roughly 200 years after he wrote it at age 18—Shelley uses symbolism and rhythm to denounce the actions of his government, ridicule those in power, and evoke the devastating toll of war.

The 172-line "Poetical Essay" is full of the poet's outrage at the state of the world. A first reading of the poem suggests that he is writing about the brutality and tragedy of war in general, but a closer read plus research on Shelley and his writing makes it clear he's taking aim at Britain's involvement in the Napoleonic Wars against the French, and at its imprisonment of an Irish journalist critical of British military operations (*The Economist*). Shelley sets the tone right away: "Millions to fight compell'd, to fight or die / In mangled heaps on War's red altar lie" (lines 3–4) and, in a takedown of the privileged ruling class into which he was born, he taunts: "When glory's views the titled idiot guide" (24). The lines "Ye cold advisers of yet colder kings, / To whose fell breast no passion virtue brings" (37–38) make it clear whose side he is on.

Uses quotation and summary as evidence, and explains relevance

Topic sentence

Shelley employs the color red throughout to symbolize blood and death: "War's red altar lie" (4), "Fell Despotism sits by the red glare" (11), and "To snatch at fame, to reap red murder's spoil" (43). Similarly, he uses words and phrases like "shrieks of war," "legal murders," and "tenfold grief" to bring to life fearful images of suffering and misery.

Topic sentence

As well as the blood and death symbolism, Shelley conjures up vivid pictures of social tyranny: "Then will oppression's iron influence show / The great man's comfort as the poor man's woe" (25–26) and "Must starving wretches torment, misery bear?" (48). The potent phrase "Oppression's iron influence" is paired with "great man's comfort" to depict the power and privilege of the ruling classes, while the "starving wretches" who must "bear" their "torment" and "misery" summon up the powerlessness of the poor and downtrodden.

Explains significance of symbol

Topic sentence (begins second half of essay)

In addition to symbolism, Shelley employs rhythm and rhyme to convey a sense of anger and urgency. When read aloud, the tight rhythmic pattern of the couplets is obvious. For example, lines 51–52 ("Yet shall the vices of the great pass on, / Vices as glaring as the noon-day sun") and 103–104 ("Though hot with gore from India's wasted plains, / Some Chief, in triumph, guides the tightened reins") have an almost chanting, marching cadence, a beat that reinforces the theme of the battlefield. The poet's reference to India indicates his strong anti-colonial feelings at a time when the British Empire's global reach was enormous. According to British poet Michael Rosen in an interview in *The Guardian*, Shelley "spends a good few lines on pointing out the oppression of British imperialism in

India," in lines like "The fainting Indian, on his native plains / Writhes to superior power's unnumbered pains" (145–146).

> Conclusion: Thesis restated, importance of poem's theme reiterated

Throughout the poem, Shelley uses powerful symbolism and rhythm to articulate his staunch political positions and disgust at the status quo. His words and phrasing are not always easy to understand—after all, he was writing two hundred years ago, when the use of inverted sentences (in which the verb comes before the subject) and archaic words like "meed" (which means "a deserved share or reward") was common. But reading and analyzing the poetry of Percy Bysshe Shelley is well worth the effort; beyond his eloquent phrasing and sharp use of symbolism and meter, this poem, and his other poetical poems such as "The Masque of Anarchy" and "Men of England," are as relevant today as they were when they were written. Let Shelley—who famously said in an essay called "A Defence of Poetry" that "poets are the unacknowledged legislators of the world"—have the last word: "Poetry is a sword of lightning, ever unsheathed, which consumes the scabbard that would contain it."

> Provides closure by circling back to poet

Notes

1. "Poetical Essay" was purchased by the University of Oxford's Bodleian Libraries, which has uploaded a digital copy that can be accessed through its website.

2. The online exhibition "Shelley's Ghost: Reshaping the Image of a Literary Family" is a partnership of the Bodleian Libraries and the New York Public Library.

Works Cited

Flood, Alison. "Lost Shelley Poem Execrating 'Rank Corruption' of Ruling Class Made Public." *The Guardian*, 10 Nov. 2015, www.theguardian.com/books/2015/nov/10/lost-shelley-poem-execrating-rruling-class-public-poetical-essay-on-the-existing-state-of-things.

"Out of the Attic: Fresh Light on the Young Revolutionary." *The Economist*, 14 Nov. 2015, p. 54.

Shelley, Percy Bysshe. "A Defence of Poetry" (1821). *Poetry Foundation*, 13 Oct. 2009. www.poetryfoundation.org/learning/essay/237844.

Works Consulted

Clark, Nick. "Percy Bysshe Shelley Lost Poem to Go Public at University of Oxford." *The Independent*, 10 Nov. 2015, www.independent.co.uk/arts-entertainment/art/news/poetical-essay-on-the-existing-state-of-things-lost-poem-by-percy-bysshe-shelley-to-go-on-display-a6729206.html.

Martyris, Nina. "How Percy Shelley Stirred His Politics into His Teacup." *NPR*, 4 Aug 2015, www.npr.org/sections/thesalt/2015/08/04/429363868/how-percy-shelley-stirred-his-politics-into-his-tea-cup.

Rich, Adrienne. "Legislators of the World." *The Guardian*, 18 Nov. 2006, www.theguardian.com/books/2006/nov/18/featuresreviews.guardianreview15.

"Unknown Shelley Poem Discovered." *BBC News*, 13 July 2006, news.bbc.co.uk/2/hi/entertainment/5177232.stm.

Typically not required, but if your instructor wishes to see works you consulted other than those cited in your project, follow this format.

22g Writing about Drama

More about
Elements of liter-
ature, 455

Like students of fiction, students of drama focus on character, plot, language, symbols, and the theme (or main point) of the work. Unlike fiction, plays are written to be acted. When writing about drama, you may be asked to go beyond the words on the page, to watch a performance of a play and to critique it in a review. When writing about a performance, offer an assessment not only of the actors' performances and the director's staging, but also of the set, costumes, props, lighting, and sound design, analyzing whether they helped to create a distinctive overall effect. Some issues to consider when critiquing a play are listed in the Quick Reference box below.

Professional Model Writing about Drama: Review of a Play

In the review that follows, Jenny Lower of the *LA Weekly* offers a supportive review of the play *Uncle Vanya*, focusing her attention on the ways in which the cast, director, costumes, props, and even the translation contribute to its success. She attends to the needs of her entire audience: For those new to the famous play, the title and introduction of Lower's review offer background information, and the body of her review provides plot summary. For Lower's more experienced theatergoing audience, she offers comparisons with other productions of the play. The model features the added interest of showing how summary can be woven into a review, rather than presented as a single block of information.

Quick Reference Writing about Drama

When writing about drama, consider the following elements and ask yourself these questions:

Actors' performances. How well did the actors depict the characters? Did they bring something more to the character than you had recognized on the printed page? Did they build on an unspoken motive, a lie, or omission from the dialogue?

Direction. How effective was the director in shaping the overall production? Were the design elements consistent with the script and performances? Were the pacing and mood of the performance appropriate?

Stage set. Were the stage sets realistic or abstract? Did they reinforce the setting (the place and time) of the play, or were they in contrast to the conventional setting? How effective were the stage sets in reinforcing the themes of the play?

Costumes. Were the costumes appropriate to the characters? Were they appropriate to the period in which the play was set, or were they in contrast to that period? How effective were the costumes in advancing the themes?

Props. What stage properties (props) were used, and what symbolic value might they have?

Lighting and sound design. How effective was the lighting in contributing to the mood of the play? Did music underscore scene changes or contribute to the mood? Was sound used to create appropriate atmospheric effects? How effective were lighting and sound design in reinforcing the themes of the play?

This 116–Year–Old Russian Play Pulses with 21st–Century Urgency

By Jenny Lower

© Karianne Flaathen

Linda Park is engrossing as the beautiful Yelena, who starts trouble in *Uncle Vanya* at Antaeus Theatre Company.

Boredom is contagious in Anton Chekhov's *Uncle Vanya,* now receiving an energetic revival at the Antaeus Company. The locus of the ennui is Yelena (Linda Park), the gorgeous, restless young wife of Serebryakov (Lawrence Pressman), an elderly professor who has retired to his family's provincial estate.

"You infected us all with your uselessness," complains Astrov (Jeffrey Nordling), a rugged country doctor who all but abandons his patients to bask in Yelena's beauty. He's a proto-environmentalist and a vegetarian, and one of two men infatuated with her.

In the hands of a less able cast and director, all this lethargy and squandered potential could have led to a production that engulfs the audience in torpor as well, as plenty of dismal Chekhovian stagings prove. But Robin Larsen's lively staging reveals the humor and urgency of this 116-year-old play. She is aided by playwright Annie Baker's contemporary translation, crafted from a literal Russian translation, which lends warmth and relevance to the language.

This Vanya resonates, in part thanks to Baker's work, with jarringly modern concerns.

Vanya (Don R. McManus) is the erstwhile brother-in-law of Yelena's husband, and the play's most pathetic figure. Unlike Astrov, Vanya causes no stirrings in Yelena's heart. After 25 years of working the estate like a peasant to finance the professor's life in the city, his proletarian admiration for the family scholar has hardened to contempt.

He has no wife, no children, and no intellectual legacy, despite mental power he claims could have allowed him to become "a Schopenhauer or a Dostoevsky." Then there's Vanya's niece and Serebryakov's daughter from his first marriage, Sonya (Rebekah Tripp), self-sufficient and practical, in love these six years with Astrov, who barely notices her.

Apart from Astrov's rants about the degradation of the Russian forests, we hear class turmoil in Vanya's disgust that Serebryakov has never raised his salary, and in his fury when the professor reveals his plan to sell the estate out from under Vanya and Sonya in order to purchase a vacation home in Finland. Where will they live?

Yet many of the play's key moments, serious though they are, tremble on the brink of hilarity.

When McManus (sharing the role with Arye Gross; all parts are partner–cast) finally locates the

Critique: A moment when the production almost spins out of control

Critique: Praise for the performance of one actor

Support: Partial plot summary

passion that has escaped Vanya for so long, he erupts in an enraged gesture so grandiose in its futility that the scene slips briefly into farce.

Park's Yelena exhibits operatic indifference, her self-absorption never more comically absolute than when Sonya suggests ways she might occupy herself. And poor Sonya's trust in her step-mother is so misplaced, it's difficult not to muster a pitying laugh when Yelena's offer to appraise the doctor's feelings for her step-daughter leads, as it must, to a declaration of love for herself.

But Larsen never allows these scenes to lose their poignancy.

McManus and Tripp are especially powerful in the climactic encounter, reeling from their separate heart-aches, as Serebryakov's plan to dismantle their life's work slowly worms into their consciousness.

There is heartbreak in the way Nordling's eyes follow Park in the final scene as she shrouds her hair with a scarf. Lynn Milgrim as the indulgent nurse Marina and Morlan Higgins, returning to the stage after a three-year absence as the pockmarked neighbor Waffles, lend a steadying presence. Higgins helps ease the transitions with wistful musical interludes strummed on his mandolin.

Critique: Praise for the director's control and actors' performance

Support: The effects of costuming

Background information about one of the actors

Support: The effects of a prop

Work Together

In groups of three or four, discuss the differences between the review above (pp. 473–74) and one of the student papers in this chapter (pp. 463–66, 468–71). How does the difference in purpose, audience, context, and genre affect the tone, the type of evidence provided, and the focus of the writing project?

Text Credits

p. 454: Percy Bysshe Shelley, *Poetical Essay on the Existing State of Things* (1811). **p. 458:** Alther, Lisa, "The Shadow Side of Appalachia: Mildred Haun's Haunting Fiction" *Appalachian Heritage* 36(2) Spring 2008, pp, 30–38. **p. 458:** Kamerick, Kathleen, "Shaping Superstition in Late Medieval England" *Magic, Ritual, and Witchcraft* 3(1) Summer 2008. **p. 458:** Wall, Steven, "Collective Rights and Individual Autonomy" *Ethics* 117(2) January 2007, pp. 234–264. **p. 463:** Shona Sequiera, Connecticut College. **p. 467:** Poe, Edgar Allan, "The Raven" (1845). **p. 468:** Courtesy of Laura Sewell. **p. 473:** Lower, Jenny, "This 116-Year-Old Russian Play Pulses with 21st-Century Urgency" *LA Weekly*, October 21, 2015. Copyright © 2015 by Jennifer Lower. Used with permission.

23 Writing in the Sciences and Social Sciences

© Anadolu Agency/Getty Images

A scientist—a biologist, nurse, or physicist, for example—looking at these women playing volleyball would focus on their heart or respiration rates, or on the velocity at which the ball is traveling, because scientists focus on the characteristics, systems, and processes of the natural world, whether of people, plants, or planets. A social scientist—an anthropologist, economist, or sociologist, for example—would focus on who they are and how they work together, because social scientists focus on the behavior of people, as individuals and in groups. What unites the sciences with the social sciences, though, is a reliance on *empirical* (experimental, observational) research.

23a Adopting the Approach of the Sciences and Social Sciences

The search for verifiable data anchors the writing produced by both scientists and social scientists. Writing is integral to the work of these disciplines because it is the basic tool for keeping records and sharing results. Researchers make their notebooks and reports useful to other researchers by doing the following:

- Explaining their methods clearly and carefully so that others can repeat the experiment

- Describing data accurately and thoroughly (including the data that *disprove* the hypothesis)

- Placing their findings in the context of research conducted by others
- Offering reasonable conclusions based on those data

23b Using the Research Methods of the Sciences and Social Sciences

More about
Observational
  studies, 231
Surveys, 231–32
Interviews,
  229–30

The research on which scientists base their claims is *primary:* They collect data by conducting tests—experiments, observational studies, and surveys, questionnaires, and interviews—to challenge their hypotheses. Scientists usually collect *quantitative* (numerical) data, while social scientists may collect quantitative or *qualitative* (descriptive) data.

Quantitative data, which might include the temperature at which a liquid vaporizes or the number of subjects who answer a question in the same way, can be gathered through experiments, surveys, questionnaires, and interviews. For quantitative data to be meaningful, it must be based on careful measurements and observations, and it must be gathered from a sample that is both representative of the group and large enough that unusual responses will not skew the results. Any scientist who conducts the same experiment should achieve the same results.

Qualitative (nonnumerical) data provide information about the experiences of individuals. This information may be drawn from interviews, observation, or both, and it often takes the form of a case study or ethnography. Qualitative data might include reports on the feeling a medication induces or descriptions of a subject's behavior. For qualitative research to be useful, the data must be based on a rich understanding of the phenomenon or issues being studied and must provide great detail. Qualitative

Writing Responsibly | Presenting Data Accurately

Writing in the *Quarterly Journal of Medicine*, editor and neurologist Christopher Martyn explains the importance of accurately representing research:

> Time, energy and public money are wasted when researchers follow false leads . . . [E]very time a case of fraud hits the headlines, the reputation of scientists and scientific research takes a knock. In

biomedical research, patients may even be harmed, if conclusions are drawn from fraudulent clinical studies (244).

When conducting an experiment, be especially careful to record data accurately. You are far more likely to receive a bad grade for falsifying data than for acknowledging that your experiment did not achieve the desired result.

to TOPIC

data must be organized carefully for the researcher to make sense of the information.

23c Citing and Documenting Sources—APA and CSE Style

Whenever you borrow ideas or information or quote from a work, you must cite the source. While there are a variety of style guides, many scientists use the style developed by the Council of Science Editors to document their sources, while social scientists often use the style devised by the American Psychological Association. Ask your instructor which you should use. All academic documentation styles require you both to cite sources in your text and to provide full bibliographic information in a reference list at the end of your project.

> *More about*
> APA style,
> 363–05 (ch. 19)
> CSE style,
> 435–49 (ch. 21)

23d Using the Language of the Sciences and Social Sciences

Since the goal of scientists and social scientists is to convey information, writers in these disciplines concentrate on making their language as clear and precise as possible. Your writing will be most effective when it follows conventions for writing that are accepted in the discipline in which you are writing.

> *More about*
> Figures of
> speech,
> 574–75
> Writing concisely,
> 520–28
> (ch. 26)

1. Learn the discipline's vocabulary.

Even at the introductory level, most writing in the sciences and social sciences requires that you learn some specialized terminology and use it with precision. You can learn vocabulary from the context or from the word parts (prefixes, roots, and suffixes) that form the term. The following resources can provide comprehensive explanations:

- Discipline-specific dictionaries and encyclopedias: Since each discipline will have its own terminology, search your library's catalog for appropriate reference sources using the words *dictionary* or *encyclopedia* and the name of the discipline (such as *sociology* or *biology*). Some discipline-specific reference works may be available via your library's website.

> *More about*
> Searching an
> online library
> catalog,
> 223–26

- Textbooks: Most textbooks in the sciences and social sciences set key terms in boldfaced or italic type and define them at first use. Check for an index or glossary at the back of the book or for a list of key terms in the margins or at the end of each chapter.

- Your instructors: Pay attention in lectures not just to what your instructors *say* but also to how they *use* words. Instructors may also define key terms or list them on slides, handouts, or the board.

The following excerpt from a student's report demonstrates both an understanding of and comfort with the specialized vocabulary of her discipline:

> The Mars Global Surveyor (MGS) magnetometer experiment was most useful due to its examination of magnetic properties present in Mars' crust. The most constructive portion was gained when the spacecraft altitude was below 200 km to as low as 101 km during the first ten minutes of periapsis (the period during which MGS was closest to the planet's surface).
>
> —Molly Patterson, Colgate University, Untitled report for Geology 105

2. Use the third person and passive voice to describe how research was conducted.

> *More about*
> Person, 458–59,
> 648–49
> Active versus
> passive voice,
> 459, 559–61

Scientists and social scientists write research reports so that other researchers can follow their procedures and produce an identical result. Since (in principle) the individual conducting the research is unimportant, researchers in the sciences typically use the third person and passive voice to describe how research was conducted:

> Third person

> Passive voice

> The materials consisted of two PsyScope computer programs run on Macintosh computers and a paper and pencil questionnaire. The participant was first assigned a room for experiment one (conditioning manipulation). The participant was then given the informed consent form, which was signed prior to the start of the experiment. The lights were turned off and the participant read the instruction. The experimenter asked if there were any questions.
>
> —Amy M. Ehret, Illinois State University, "Effects of Stigma on Approach and Avoidance Behaviors in Social Situations"

Some social scientists use the first person (*I, we*) when discussing observations they made as a participant or the conclusions they drew from their research. Social scientists typically avoid the passive voice when describing the actions of participants.

3. Use the past tense to discuss methods and present tense to discuss implications.

> *More about*
> Tense, 672–78

Scientists and social scientists use the past tense to discuss methods of data collection or the behavior of research participants, and they use the present tense to discuss the implications of their research. This is neatly demonstrated in the sentence below:

> Since this study included only middle-class Caucasians, it is not representative of the population as a whole.

—Robyn Worthington, Bristol Community College,
"Nature versus Nurture: Does Birth Order Shape Personality?"

Past tense

Present tense

23e Writing Assignments in the Sciences and Social Sciences

Common types of writing projects in the sciences and social sciences include the following:

- Literature review: In a literature review, writers summarize research on a specific topic, analyze and evaluate the sources and the research on which these studies were based, and synthesize sources to develop a thorough understanding of the topic.

- Research or laboratory notebook: In a research or laboratory notebook, writers record in precise detail (1) the materials (including sketches of setups if complex) in the order used; (2) a chronological list of the procedures followed; and (3) the results (raw data, clearly labeled and logically organized), including any graphs or calculations.

- Research or laboratory report: In a research or laboratory report, writers provide a detailed description of research, including methods, results, and discussion.

Unlike a humanities research project, a research or laboratory report in the sciences and social sciences usually follows a standard format:

Title page   The title page should include the following information:

- Title: Titles should accurately describe the project; titles should avoid playfulness or puns and should convey as briefly as possible the most important aspects of the report.

- Author's name

- Instructor's name and course number

- Date of submission

- Author notes

Student Model
Research report
"Nature versus
Nurture," Robyn
Worthington, 481–89

> **More about**
Summarizing, 115,
257–60
Analyzing,
124–26, 263–64,
271–73
Evaluating
sources,
233–46 (ch. 14)
Synthesizing,
127–29, 263–64,
271–73

> **More about**
Author notes,
391–92

Abstract A brief summary of the report, the *abstract* usually includes a one-sentence summary of the most important points in each section of the report. Abstracts are typically 150–250 words long.

Introduction The introduction provides necessary background, such as a brief review of other, closely related studies, indicates the purpose of conducting the research, and states the limits of what the research is intended to show.

Methods The methods section provides the following:

- Information about participants or subjects, including the number of participants and any relevant demographic information about them

- A description of the methods used to collect information (for example, face-to-face interview, online questionnaire, or telephone survey) or to conduct the experiment

- The equipment used (if any)

- The methods of recording data

The methods section must provide enough detail that others could repeat the study or experiment and achieve the same results.

More about
Matching graphic
to information,
80–83
Numbering
figures and
tables, 394–95
(APA)

Results The results section provides details of your outcomes. Information graphics are used to convey results succinctly.

Discussion The discussion section of the report offers readers an interpretation of the results, showing how the data collected support (or fail to support) the hypothesis. The discussion indicates the limitations of the data (what they do not indicate), and it relates the results to those of earlier researchers. (Do the data confirm, undermine, or extend earlier research?) The discussion concludes with an analysis of the implications of the research.

More about
Creating an
APA-style
reference list,
374–91
Creating a
CSE-style
reference list,
437–47

References The reference list includes secondary sources and begins on a new page, with the heading (the word *References*) centered at the top of the page.

Tables and figures Tables follow the reference list; figures follow tables. Each table or figure appears on a separate page.

Appendixes Appendixes include any figures, tables, photographs, or other materials that amplify but are not central to the discussion. Appendixes should be mentioned in the main body of the text so that readers know to consult them. Each appendix should include only one figure, set of data, and so on, but a report can include several appendixes. If more than one appendix is included, each should be assigned a letter (Appendix A, Appendix B, and so on). Arrange the appendixes in the order in which they are mentioned in the text, and give each appendix a succinct, descriptive title, such as "Appendix A: Background Questions."

Work **Together**

Read the research report on pages 482–89. Then in groups of three or four, discuss the differences between the research report and one of the student projects in the previous chapter (pp. 463–66, 468–71). How do the approach, language, and structure of the two writing projects differ?

Student Model   Research Report

The research report that follows describes a study on birth order and personality conducted by Robyn Worthington, a student at Bristol Community College. Worthington's study follows APA style.

Title page:
Includes title
that accurately
reflects research
topic

Nature versus Nurture: Does Birth Order Shape Personality?

Robyn Worthington

Dr. Mary Zahm

Psychology 52

December 17, 2016

Abstract

Abstract: Pro-
vides summary of
most important
points in each
section.

Psychological researchers agree that the personalities of siblings differ, but there is much disagreement about the reasons for the differences. Many variables have been studied, including age range, birth order, gender, and nonshared environmental factors. This study examines the extent to which birth order affects personality and attempts to show a correlation. A revised sample of 51 participants completed a Myers-Briggs Type Indicator Test. Results show a significant relationship between birth order and introversion/extraversion, but they do not support the hypothesis fully.

Introduction

Uses first person to emphasize personal observation

As the mother of three boys, I have been stunned by the differences in their personalities. Despite having the same parents and the same home environment, their personality differences are great. Researchers in psychology agree that siblings differ, but there is much disagreement about the reasons for the differences. Variables such as age range, birth order, gender, and nonshared environmental factors have been studied as possible causes. This study investigates a possible correlation between birth order and personality.

Shifts to third person

Introduction: Explains issues under consideration, offers brief review of related studies

Darwin's theory of evolution, specifically his principle of divergence, has been used as a possible explanation for the differences in sibling personality (Sulloway, 1996). Darwin theorized that "given enough time, species tend to evolve multiple forms that diverge in character, a process called adaptive radiation" (Sulloway, p. 85). In the nineteenth century, naturalist Charles Darwin observed that a species of finches living in isolation and competing for resources developed biological variations that made them successful competitors. "One might really fancy," he said in *The voyage of the Beagle* "that, from an original paucity of birds in this archipelago, one species had been taken and modified for different ends" (Darwin, 1909, p. 399). One factor in adaptive radiation is development in different environmental niches. According to Sulloway (1996), the family environment is not a single environment, but a collection of microenvironments. The oldest child comes into an (intact) family of two; the family environment the next child experiences includes two parents and a sibling with whom the second child must compete; the third child finds a family with two parents and two siblings with each of whom the third child must compete, and so on. In short, as each child is born, the family environment changes, including the way that the parents interact with each child and the way the children interact with each

Capitalizes Beagle because it is the proper name of a ship

other, and this difference in family environment can affect personality (Leman, 1985). By developing diverging personalities, younger siblings avoid competing with older, bigger, more experienced siblings on the same grounds (Sulloway, 1996).

> **Topic sentence**

Certain characteristics of personality have been associated with birth order. Oldest, or first borns, have been characterized as ambitious high achievers who are usually confident, organized, and conservative (Leman, 1985; Sulloway, 1996). Both Sulloway and Leman suggest that children born second tend to diverge as much as possible from the first born, taking on a totally different set of characteristics. They are noted as being more sociable, more cooperative, and more open to experience than their conservative older siblings, who have a tendency to relate strongly with their parents. Youngest children tend to be charming, affectionate, outgoing, and used to being the center of attention; they may also be spoiled and impatient (Leman, 1985).

> **Support:** Uses evidence from sources (Sulloway, Leman)

> **Topic sentence**

Gender, age range, and nonshared environment are also thought to be factors in personality differences in siblings. In a study of university psychology students, Tammy Mann (1993) predicted that nonshared environmental factors would account for personality differences more than other factors. However, the results showed that the family constellation variables of age, birth order, and gender may be more firmly associated with personality differences in siblings than the nonshared environment. In fact, 27% of the correlations between constellation variables and sibling personality differences were statistically significant (Mann, 1993).

> **Support:** Uses facts, statistics from source (Mann)

> **Counterevidence:** Shows differing opinions of other scientists, and explains why her research is nevertheless potentially useful

Not all empirical studies have successfully demonstrated the theory of birth order and personality that Sulloway draws from Darwin; some have produced negative findings (Roher, Egloff, & Schmukle, 2015). Additional testing, then, may help determine the usefulness of the theory.

Methods

This study used Darwin's theory of evolution as well as the theory proposed by Frank Sulloway concerning birth order and personality as models. The hypothesis to be tested is that birth order would account for the differences in personality among siblings. Birth order was defined as either oldest, middle, youngest, or only child. Personality was assessed by the Myers-Briggs Type Indicator (Briggs & Myers, 1980), in the categories of extraversion/introversion, sensing/intuition, thinking/feeling, and judging/perceiving.

The initial sample consisted of 70 randomly selected adolescents and adults from whom 55 surveys were returned. For statistical calculations, only-children were eliminated from the sample, as their number was too few. The revised sample consisted of 51 people ranging in age from 14 to 90 years of age. All were European American and considered themselves of middle-class backgrounds. Of the 51 subjects, 16 reported being an oldest sibling, 17 reported being a middle sibling, and 18 reported being a youngest sibling.

The Myers-Briggs Type Indicator Test was distributed to the participants along with a background questionnaire (Appendix) on which subjects supplied personal data, including birth order. The surveys were collected, scored, and labeled with four letters which corresponded to the participants' personality type:

E (extraversion) or I (introversion)

N (intuitive) or S (sensing)

F (feeling) or T (thinking)

J (judging) or P (perceiving)

Hypothesis

Defines key term

Methods: Description of participants, materials; explanation of how data were collected and analyzed

The information collected was statistically evaluated by establishing a null and an alternate hypothesis for each personality trait. The scores were placed in a contingency table, and the calculations were performed and evaluated using the chi-square test for goodness of fit.

Results

Results: Explains outcomes (with visual representation of results) and discloses shortcomings

A statistically significant relationship between birth order and personality traits was found in one of the four areas. Calculations revealed a significant relationship between extraversion/introversion at the .005 (0.5%) level of significance. Of the 16 oldest children, 14 preferred introversion, 10 out of 17 middle siblings showed a preference for extraversion, and 12 out of 18 youngest siblings showed a preference for extraversion. (See Figure 1.) In all other areas, the calculations fell short of a reliable level of significance. In the traits of sensing/intuition, thinking/feeling, and judging/perceiving, the test values were below 1, too low for even a .005 (0.5%) level of significance.

Discussion

Discussion: Interprets results

While this study was able to demonstrate a significant relationship between birth order and the traits of extraversion/introversion, the data collected do not support the hypothesis that birth order can account for the differences in other aspects of personality in siblings. The variables involved may be too difficult to assess using the statistical methods of this study. Other characteristics, such as gender and number or spacing of children, all influence the way that parents relate to their children and the way that siblings relate to each other, so these factors, too, are likely to affect personality. Other factors include genetics and nonshared environmental experiences such as playgroups and nursery school/day care, friends, teachers, and so forth—all of which may have an impact on personality.

With so many variables, assessing the causes of personality differences in siblings is extremely difficult. Based on the results of this study, I have concluded that personality development is not likely the result of any one factor but, instead, a combination of many. Further, since this study included only middle-class European Americans, it cannot be assumed to be representative of the population as a whole. Future research might include a cross-sectional study of various ethnic and socioeconomic groups as a better representation of the population. An interesting result of the study was that, when the personality traits were divided by gender, 24 out of 31 females demonstrated a preference for the trait of feeling to that of thinking. Future research might include a study of the effect of gender on personality differences or personality differences among siblings based on gender.

Conclusion: Summarizes findings, acknowledges shortcomings, suggests new avenues for research

References

Briggs, K. C., & Myers, I. B. (1980). *Myers-Briggs type indicator.* Palo Alto, CA: Consulting Psychologists Press.

Darwin, C. (1909). *The voyage of the Beagle.* P. F. Collier. Retrieved from https://play.google.com/books/reader?id=MDILAAAAIAAJ&printsec=frontcover&output=reader&hl=en&pg=GBS.PP1

Leman, K. (1985). *The birth order book.* Tappan, NJ: Revell.

Mann, T. L. (1993). A failure of nonshared environmental factors in predicting sibling personality differences. *Journal of Psychology, 127,* 79–86. Retrieved from http://www.heldref.org/pubs/jrl/about.html

Rohrer, J., Egloff, B., & Schmukle, S. (2015). Examining the effects of birth order on personality. *Proceedings of the National Academy of Sciences.* Retrieved from http://www.pnas.org/cgi/doi/10.1073/pnas.1506451112

Sulloway, F. J. (1996). *Born to rebel: Birth order, family dynamics, and creative lives.* New York, NY: Random House.

References: Provides full bibliographic information in APA style for all sources cited in report

Figure 1. Preference for extraversion/introversion among siblings.

Appendix: Background Questions

Date of birth: _____

Sex: M _____ F _____

How many siblings do you have? _____ (Brothers _____ Sisters _____)

What is your birth order? Oldest _____ Middle _____ Youngest _____ Only child _____

How many years separate you from the siblings who were born just before and/or

just after you? A brother _____ years older A sister _____ years older

  A brother _____ years younger A sister _____ years younger

As a young child, did you attend day care or nursery school? Yes _____ No _____

If yes, how old were you when you first attended? _____

How many years did you attend? _____

Text Credits

p. 476: Christopher, Martyn, "Fabrication, Flasification and Plagiarism" *Quarterly Journal of Medicine* 96(4) April 2003.
pp. 243–244. p. 482: Worthington, Robyn, Bristol Community College, "Nature versus Nurture: Does Birth Order Shape Personality?"

24 Preparing for and Taking an Essay Exam

© Alamy Images RF

Long before marathon runners cross the finish line, they get ready for the 26.2-mile race. They practice regularly, eat well, and learn the terrain ahead of time. They also use strategy, knowing how to pace themselves and when to turn up the heat. And they do not panic if someone else dashes ahead. Runners know that being prepared is crucial to running a good race.

Students who succeed on essay exams have many of these attributes. They prepare by reviewing their notes and answering practice questions, and they have a test-taking strategy that allows them to get to the finish line. All of this preparation—not cramming the night before—is what leads to a good grade.

24a Preparing for an Essay Exam

You begin to prepare for any college test by reading, taking notes, listening, and working on your assignments. An essay exam, however, requires some special preparation.

1. Take good notes and review them often.

Stay up-to-date on your reading assignments, and take good notes:

- Highlight and underline important terms and concepts, but do not overdo it—highlighting everything means you must reread everything.

- Write down your thoughts and questions, and connect what you are reading to other ideas or situations.

Tech Note-Taking Technologies

Experiment with a variety of note-taking technologies: index cards that can later be sorted, arranged, and labeled; a big notebook that's hard to lose; cloud tools like Google Docs or an app such as Evernote or OneNote for a hand-held device; a laptop on which you can type quickly. As you experiment, pay attention to the pros and cons of your note-taking technology. Recent research suggests you will comprehend and remember the most if you take notes by hand. Other research suggests that using a laptop or hand-held device in class can open you up to distractions such as Snapchat and Instagram. There is no such thing as multitasking; it's just switching quickly from one task to another, without your full attention being on any of them. If the laptop or device is within view of your classmates, you may be distracting them from class, too.

- Note any statements in the text that strike you as especially crucial or interesting—or that might show up on an essay exam.

- For complicated texts, write outlines or summaries that will help you figure out what is going on, keep track of the development of ideas, and recall the material later on.

- When taking notes in class, focus on the major points your instructor is making—do not try to write down every detail.

Keep all your notes in a reading journal. As you review them, focus on the most important ideas and information. Using a highlighter or a pen in a new color, take notes *on* your notes, marking the big topics or drawing connections among major ideas. Reviewing your notes regularly (not just the day before an exam) will help you learn important concepts and identify material you are likely to be asked about.

Study Groups An alternative to coming up with questions on your own is to work in small study groups. Each member could devise a question or an outline for the rest of the group, or members might work together to come up with questions and answers. Study groups work well when members share their ideas and learn from one another; they fail when some members rely too heavily on others to do their thinking for them. Group work can be a challenge when members do not share the same goals, experiences, or cultural or linguistic backgrounds. Before any project starts, be sure to discuss members' expectations.

2. Devise and answer practice questions.

After reviewing your notes, consider the terms and concepts that seem essential, and identify issues or patterns that have arisen repeatedly in readings and lectures. Then brainstorm questions based on these terms, concepts, issues, and patterns. As you brainstorm, be sure to include questions that you fear will be asked, as well as ones you hope will be on the exam. For each of the questions you develop, devise a brief outline and draft a practice answer.

3. Understand the rules for the exam.

Regardless of how you study, ask your instructor exactly what will be required and what will be allowed.

- Is use of a dictionary, thesaurus, or writer's handbook permitted during the exam? What about phones, tablets, or laptops?

- How many questions will there be? Will different questions be worth different numbers of points, or will all questions be equally weighted?

- Is partial credit available for partial answers or for an outline of an answer?

- Are sample questions and answers available?

24b Previewing the Exam

When you sit down to take an essay exam—or any test, for that matter—you may have the impulse to start writing immediately. It is a good idea, though, to take a few minutes to look over the exam, decide on a strategy, and make sure you understand the questions.

1. Read the exam, and develop a test-taking strategy.

The first step in writing a successful exam is to read the entire exam before writing anything. As you read, develop a strategy for taking the test:

- Determine how many points are assigned to each question, and set a time limit for answering each part. Give yourself more time for the questions that are worth more points: Finishing a 50-point question is more important than finishing a 10-pointer.

- Check off the questions that you find easy and can complete quickly. You may want to start with some of those.

Reference Common Verbs on Essay Exams

What Is the Question?	What Am I Supposed to Do?
1. **Analyze** the architectural style of Frank Lloyd Wright.	1. **Name** the elements of his style, and then **critically examine** those elements and the style as a whole.
2. **Compare and contrast** the major economic problems of the North and South during the Civil War.	2. Name the economic problems, and explain how they were **similar and different** in the North and South.
3. **Define** the terms *denotation* and *connotation*, and discuss these terms in regard to the word *brother*.	3. Give the **main characteristics** of the terms. **Show that you understand** the definitions by applying them to *brother*.
4. **Describe** how bees build a hive.	4. Create, in words, a **step-by-step** picture of what bees do.
5. **Evaluate** John F. Kennedy's performance as commander in chief during the Cuban Missile Crisis.	5. State what you think of Kennedy's performance, and give specific and concrete **evidence** for your opinion(s).
6. **Illustrate** the effects of global warming on mammals of the Arctic, including the walrus and the polar bear.	6. Give specific **examples** of the effects on the animals named and at least one additional animal.
7. **List** and **explain** the four main causes of an economic recession.	7. **Jot down** the causes and **tell clearly** how each results in a recession.
8. **Summarize** Carl Rogers's humanist approach to psychology.	8. Give the **main points** of his approach, and keep your answer **concise.**

- Leave yourself a little time to read through your answers to add or clarify information; to correct errors of spelling, usage, and grammar; and to rewrite illegible words.

2. Analyze the questions: What do they ask you to do?

When you read an exam question, it may be easier to identify the topic than to know what you are supposed to *do* with it. *Compare* is quite different from *define* or *summarize,* so pay close attention to the verbs and do what they tell you. (See the Quick Reference box above for sample question analyses.)

Be alert for two-part questions; make sure you answer both parts. Ask your instructor to clarify any question that is vague or confusing.

Asking for the answer (or even a hint) is inappropriate (and probably will not work), but asking your instructor to define an unfamiliar word (as long as it is not a key term) is perfectly reasonable.

> *More about*
> Analyzing the assignment, 22–24, 196–97
> Writing about literature, 452–74 (ch. 22)
> Writing in the sciences and social sciences, 475–89 (ch. 23)
> Comparison-contrast, 66–68
> Definition, 68–69
> Summarizing, 115, 257–60

24c Writing an Effective Answer

To structure an essay exam answer, follow the same rules that guide you when you write any other essay.

1. Respond to the question, provide support, organize logically, and review your work.

Writing an effective answer means answering the question you are asked, providing sufficient supporting evidence, and organizing your response clearly and logically, then reviewing your work. Use these tips for showing off what you have learned.

More about
Informal (scratch)
   outlines, 40–41
Thesis
   statements,
   34–37
Transitions, 60–61
Supporting your
   ideas, 45–47

- Write a thesis statement, one or two sentences that express your main point and that respond directly to the question.

- Outline the points you want to make. Jot down the evidence you will use.

- Draft your answer. Start with your thesis and use your outline to fill in your explanation of the thesis.

- Leave ample margins on each side of the page and several blank lines below each answer, in case you decide to add information later on.

- When you have finished your draft, reread it, correcting any problems with coherence, correctness, and legibility.

Writing Responsibly | Using Your Computer during an Essay Exam

Check with your instructor in advance of an essay exam to see whether you can write your exam on a laptop. The computer will allow you to present a readable copy: You can use cut-and-paste to revise and reorganize your answer and run a spell-check program to catch and correct the most obvious typos. It would be inappropriate—and unfair to your classmates—to do anything other than write, so avoid the temptation to consult online sources; only open your word processing program and leave your browser closed.

to OTHER WRITERS

Quick **Reference** What an Effective Answer Does—and Does Not Do

An effective answer . . .	An effective answer does not . . .
has a clear thesis that answers the question	answer the question you hoped would be asked
answers the question that was asked	stick in information on the topic that is unrelated to the question
provides ample and accurate supporting evidence	pad the answer by repeating what you have already said
answers the question parts in the order they were asked	make personal judgments that the question does not ask for
uses the method of development suggested by the question (such as analysis, comparison-contrast, definition)	

Student Model Effective Essay Exam Response

The sample answer on page 496 responds directly to the exam question by comparing The *Big Lebowski* and *The Big Sleep* and by including the core concept "film noir" in the answer. Notice that this writer fulfills his responsibility to his reader (and to himself) by demonstrating that he understands the issues discussed in class and can synthesize information from films he has seen to support his claims.

Essay Exam Question

Identify and compare/contrast the films from which the stills below are taken. Be sure to include in your discussion at least one of the core concepts we have discussed in class, such as genre, dialogue, film noir, and so on. (30 points)

Thesis: Big Lebowski is a variation on film noir, main difference is kind of hero

Thesis answers question

Though The Big Lebowski is generally considered a parody of film noir detective stories such as The Big Sleep, this 1998 cult classic might also be categorized as a contemporary variation on the style. As the still photos show, the differences are obvious: gonzo comedy aside, Lebowski chiefly differs in the nature and quality of its hero.

Core concept discussed in class

Emphasizes contrast between heroes

Instead of the occasionally superhuman wit and capability of Philip Marlowe, we have The Dude, called by the film's narrator "one of the laziest people on the planet Earth." However, though The Dude's ineptitude is largely played for laughs, much of the humor derives from discomfort and even dread; his insufficiency as a hero only heightens the sense of alienation.

Supports claims with details about heroes from these films

At the beginning of The Big Sleep, Marlowe is made to sit in an orchid hothouse, where he proceeds to grow more physically uncomfortable with every passing moment, but he is able to speak his client's language, anticipate his interests and needs, and ultimately earn the general's quiet admiration. The Dude, in contrast, is so out of his depth that he seems incapable of scoring a single point against anyone he meets. When The Dude finds himself in a shadow-drenched room, the viewer may not feel an immediate sense of dread, but it does seem clear that the protagonist has little hope of prevailing. In a particularly revealing scene, The Dude's "client" taunts him with the failure of his generation's ideals, and our hero has no real answer.

Conclusion compares/contrasts heroes

These two scenes reveal the core of the typical noir hero: the individual who loses, over and over again, and who is compelled to absorb these defeats and continue on, often with a diminished sense of self. The hero responds by creating a persona to act as surrogate for this loss—one as the hard-boiled detective (Marlowe), and the other as the hyper-passive Dude.

Returns to key concept and how these heroes display it

25

Professional and Civic Writing

by Amy Rupiper Taggart

© Burke/Triìo Productions/Photolibrary/ Getty Images

If you bought a bag of apples at the grocery store on Wednesday and discovered on Thursday that most of them were rotten, you would probably complain to the produce manager and ask for a refund. If this kind of thing happened often, you might write a letter to the store's owner. If you found something rotten in a government agency or corporation, you might write a letter to the editor to bring the problem to the attention of your community. If you found an issue that you could help resolve, you might offer a proposal for solving the problem and promote your program with a press release. Business writing, then, is more than memos or résumés and cover letters. It is something we all do, whether as employees or as citizens.

25a Using Business Letter Formats

Regardless of what you do after college, you will need to know how to write a good business letter. In company settings, letters are used to communicate with people outside the office—with customers, for example. While some professional communications may be sent by email (letters to the editor, for example, are frequently submitted electronically), more formal communications or communications that should remain private (such as notifying employees of a salary increase) are best relayed in printed form.

In your personal life, you may need to write a business letter to request information, thank someone, or comment on a product or service. The formality of the context can serve as a guide in determining whether email or a printed letter is more appropriate.

497

Whether sending letters by conventional mail or email, be considerate of your reader's time and present information courteously and concisely. These guidelines can help you write an effective business letter:

- **State your purpose in the first paragraph**. Readers in the workplace want to see at a glance what the letter is about.

- **Be clear and specific throughout the letter**. A vague, muddled, or repetitious letter may be ignored.

- **Keep your paragraphs short**. This will help your reader grasp your major points quickly.

- **Adopt a positive yet somewhat formal tone**. Make sure the tone fits the audience and purpose.

- **Reread and edit your letter**. Clarify your points, reduce wordiness, and correct all errors. Grammatical and typographical errors may severely diminish your credibility with your reader.

1. Use a standard letter format.

Whatever the purpose of your business letter, follow one of two standard formats:

Professional Models
Business Letters: Full
 block style, 501
 Modified block
 style, 506

1. **Full block style**. Align all text with the left-hand margin. This is the best choice when you are writing a letter on letterhead stationery.

2. **Modified block style**. Align the following elements just to the right of the center of the page: return address, date, closing, and signature. Align everything else with the left-hand margin.

In addition to using an appropriate letter style, follow these design guidelines:

- Use 8½ × 11–inch white or off-white paper. You may also use letterhead stationery, especially if you are communicating as a representative of a company or organization.

- Single-space your paragraphs and insert an extra line of space between them; do not indent paragraphs.

- Use a standard size (number 10) envelope, and fold the letter horizontally in thirds.

- Follow standard practice for addressing the envelope: addressee's full name, title, and address (with zip code) in the middle of the envelope; and your name and address in the upper left-hand corner. Use your computer's software to generate a neatly typed envelope or address label.

2. Include standard elements.

As you type your letter, incorporate the typical elements of a business letter:

Return address and date If you are using letterhead stationery with a pre-printed address, add just the date. Otherwise, include your full address. Spell out the names of months.

Inside address Give the name, title (if appropriate), and full address of the person to whom you are writing. Spell out words like *Street* or *Road*, but use the two-letter postal abbreviations for states.

Salutation In some instances, you may address a letter to a company or organization (*Dear Habitat for Humanity*) or to a job title (*Dear Shipping Department Manager*), but it is preferable to address your letter to an actual person, even if you have to contact the company to determine who that person is. Also, use appropriate titles (abbreviated before the name), such as *Mr., Ms., Dr., Gen., Prof.,* or *Rev.* Professional titles supersede gender-specific titles. For example, if you were writing to a female minister, you would address the letter to *Rev. Aldrich,* not *Ms. Aldrich.* If you have the person's name but do not know the gender, use the whole name: *Dear Pat Gonzalez.*

> *More about*
> Titles before and
> after names, 850
> Abbreviating
> titles, 849–50

Body Type each paragraph flush with the left margin and put a line of space between paragraphs. Do not use paragraph indention.

Closing and signature Using the formality of the letter as a guide, choose an appropriate closing phrase, such as *Sincerely, Yours truly,* or *Best regards.* Four lines (two double spaces) below the closing, type your full name, and sign in the space above.

Additional information Below your name, include other kinds of information, such as *Cc.* if you are sending a copy to someone in addition to the addressee or *Enc.* if you are enclosing items with the letter.

Sample business letter, block style The letter in full-block style on page 501 (Figure 25.1) is on letterhead stationery that includes the company's address and other contact information. If this letter had been written on plain paper, a return address would be needed directly above the date. Most items and all paragraphs are separated by two lines (one double space), but below the date and below the closing, four lines of space are required.

25b Writing Business Letters

The letters you write as an employee or in your personal life will have a variety of purposes. On Monday you may be a businessperson writing a letter of apology to a customer, and on Tuesday you might be a private citizen writing a letter of complaint. It is helpful, then, to look at some guidelines for writing different kinds of business letters.

1. Letters of complaint

When writing a letter of complaint, your challenge is to exercise restraint. Be reasonable and informed, and get to the point. Effective complaint letters do not cast the recipient of the letter in a negative light. When writing a letter of complaint, follow these four steps:

1. Describe the problem at the outset, and include details.
2. Explain the importance of the problem and why the recipient should be involved in the solution.
3. State your hopes for the solution to the problem.
4. If you have had positive experiences with the person or organization in the past, mention that; it will help your cause.

2. Letters of apology

In the workplace, you may receive letters from customers who are complaining about the service you offer or the product you provide. In a letter of apology (Figure 25.1), your goal is to fix or make up for the problem, reassure the customer that he or she is important, and restore the reputation of your company or organization.

Writing
Responsibly Letters to the Editor

When private citizens write a letter to the editor of a newspaper or magazine, they often feel strongly about something—a previous article in the publication, a political candidate, or a local problem. If you write such a letter, keep your emotions in check. Make your point, get your facts straight, assume a courteous tone, and avoid personal attacks against the publication or writer. Most publications now accept such letters via email; read your submission over carefully and adjust the tone before hitting send.

to AUDIENCE

Professional Model Business Letter: Apology

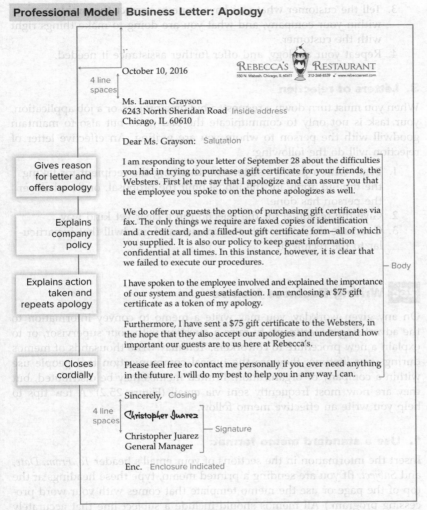

October 10, 2016

REBECCA'S RESTAURANT
550 N. Wabash, Chicago, IL 60611   312-268-8539 • www.rebeccasrest.com

Ms. Lauren Grayson
6243 North Sheridan Road Inside address
Chicago, IL 60610

Dear Ms. Grayson: Salutation

Gives reason for letter and offers apology

I am responding to your letter of September 28 about the difficulties you had in trying to purchase a gift certificate for your friends, the Websters. First let me say that I apologize and can assure you that the employee you spoke to on the phone apologizes as well.

Explains company policy

We do offer our guests the option of purchasing gift certificates via fax. The only things we require are faxed copies of identification and a credit card, and a filled-out gift certificate form—all of which you supplied. It is also our policy to keep guest information confidential at all times. In this instance, however, it is clear that we failed to execute our procedures.

— Body

Explains action taken and repeats apology

I have spoken to the employee involved and explained the importance of our system and guest satisfaction. I am enclosing a $75 gift certificate as a token of my apology.

Furthermore, I have sent a $75 gift certificate to the Websters, in the hope that they also accept our apologies and understand how important our guests are to us here at Rebecca's.

Closes cordially

Please feel free to contact me personally if you ever need anything in the future. I will do my best to help you in any way I can.

Sincerely, Closing

4 line spaces

Christopher Juarez
— Signature

Christopher Juarez
General Manager

Enc. Enclosure indicated

FIGURE 25.1 **Sample letter of apology (full block style)**

Follow these steps in writing a letter of apology:

1. State the problem in the first paragraph, and apologize for it.
2. Explain your company's policy (if appropriate), and admit that correct procedures were not followed.

3. Tell the customer what you have done to correct the problem within your company, and what you are doing to make things right with the customer.

4. Repeat your apology, and offer further assistance if needed.

3. Letters of rejection

When you must turn down a request, a bid on a project, or a job application, your task is not only to communicate the bad news but also to maintain goodwill with the person to whom you are writing. An effective letter of rejection will do the following:

1. Begin with a positive statement, thanking the recipient for taking the time to apply for the job, submit the proposal, or do whatever the person has done.

2. Give the reason(s) for the rejection in a clear yet kind way.

3. Conclude the letter with an expression of goodwill that is particular to the recipient.

Professional Model
Business memo
(email), 503

25c Writing Business Memos

On any given workday, you may write a memo to convey information to the advertising department, to raise a question with your supervisor, or to explain a new procedure to coworkers. You may write thousands of memos during your lifetime; they are the typical communication tool people use within a company or organization. Printed memos may be distributed, but they are now most frequently sent via email (Figure 25.2). A few tips to help you write an effective memo follow.

More about
Writing and
answering
email,
175–79, 504

1. Use a standard memo format.

Insert the information in the sections of your email's header *To, From, Date,* and *Subject.* (If you are sending a printed memo, type these headings at the top of the page or use the memo template that comes with your word processing program.) All memos should include a subject line that accurately summarizes the content of the message. If recipients are being copied, list them in the *Cc* line. Attachments to emailed memos usually appear in the header; for printed memos with attachments, add *Enc.* at the end of the message.

Professional Model Business Memo

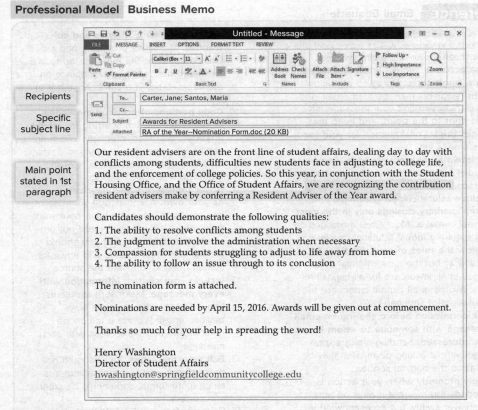

Our resident advisers are on the front line of student affairs, dealing day to day with conflicts among students, difficulties new students face in adjusting to college life, and the enforcement of college policies. So this year, in conjunction with the Student Housing Office, and the Office of Student Affairs, we are recognizing the contribution resident advisers make by conferring a Resident Adviser of the Year award.

Candidates should demonstrate the following qualities:
1. The ability to resolve conflicts among students
2. The judgment to involve the administration when necessary
3. Compassion for students struggling to adjust to life away from home
4. The ability to follow an issue through to its conclusion

The nomination form is attached.

Nominations are needed by April 15, 2016. Awards will be given out at commencement.

Thanks so much for your help in spreading the word!

Henry Washington
Director of Student Affairs
hwashington@springfieldcommunitycollege.edu

FIGURE 25.2 Sample memo (emailed)

2. Get right to the point.

Use a tone appropriate for your reader, but be clear, specific, and concise. In your first paragraph, name the issue the memo is addressing and explain briefly why you are writing. In subsequent paragraphs or in a list, add any necessary details. A numbered or bulleted list is particularly effective in memos because it helps readers "see" your points or questions clearly. Conclude on a positive note, and thank the recipient if appropriate.

25d Writing Job Application Letters

A letter of application (Figure 25.3) is essentially a sales letter: Your goal is to sell yourself to a prospective employer and to get an interview. To do

Quick

Reference Email Etiquette

Following email etiquette (or *netiquette*) can make you more effective in social as well as professional settings. Here are fifteen tips for writing effective email:

1. **Use accurate subject lines, and focus on a single topic.** Doing so will help your recipients manage their email, and it will help you find your message later.

2. **Get right to the point, and keep messages brief.** Consideration for your reader's time is key.

3. **Maintain an appropriate tone.** Remain cordial and avoid *flaming* (or launching a personal attack).

4. **Include salutations (or greetings) and complimentary closings only in the most formal contexts.** Most email messages do not require a formal salutation or closing.

5. **Follow the rules of capitalization.** Avoid writing all but the most informal messages in all lowercase (or all capital) letters. (Words in all capital letters are the equivalent of shouting.)

6. **Ask permission before sharing an email message with someone to whom it was not addressed.** Sending along a message without asking permission may be unfair to the original sender.

7. **Reply promptly when your action is needed.** You may not always be able to answer swiftly, but do acknowledge receipt of the message, and let the sender know when to expect a full reply.

8. **Avoid hitting "reply all" unless every recipient will be interested in the reply.** With the quantity of email circulating today, most recipients will appreciate *not* being included if the message is not directed toward them.

9. **Avoid "spamming" friends and colleagues.** Messages promising bad luck if you do not send the message on to five (or more) friends are commonplace on the Internet, but you can choose *not* to comply.

10. **Copy portions of previous messages, or reference the email string for clarity.** If readers will need information from an earlier message, either copy and paste a portion of the message or refer the reader to a specific message.

11. **Never represent someone else's words as your own.** Acknowledge your use of any words or ideas you have borrowed from others. Usually, you need not provide a formal citation, but you should include the writer's name and any information needed to locate the source.

12. **Include your contact information with every message.** Make sure recipients know how to contact you in ways besides email: Provide a telephone number and mailing address with each message.

13. **Edit your messages.** Email should not be confused with text messaging; it is much more formal and should be clear and correct.

14. **Pause before sending!** While the temptation to shoot off an angry message is sometimes great, avoid it. Treat the email recipient with courtesy, even when you are annoyed.

15. **Archive your messages.** If you are likely to need to refer to a message you have sent or received, either print it out or save an electronic copy.

so, your letter should be enthusiastic yet formal. Before you begin to write, learn something about the company or organization. You can then reveal a bit of your knowledge in your letter, which will show the recipient that you are serious about the job. Like other types of professional correspondence,

Writing
Responsibly — Personal Emails and IM at Work

When you send email on computers that are the property of a business or organization, the correspondence is considered the property of the organization and is subject to search should there be a suspicion of abuse. Therefore, write responsibly at work, and assume that your email (or instant messages) may be viewed by others.

to SELF

letters of application should follow some common guidelines concerning format and content:

> **More about**
> Conciseness,
>   520–28 (ch. 26)
> Flaming, 186
> Tone, 19–20, 138,
>   565, 570–72
> Capitalization,
>   835–41 (ch. 54)

- Use one of the two standard letter formats: block format (Figure 25.1) or modified block format (Figure 25.3), and limit the letter's length to a single page.

- Address the letter to a specific person, even if you have to phone the company to determine who that is.

- Start by mentioning the specific job you are applying for and how you learned about it.

- In the next paragraph or two, explain why you are applying for this job, and list your specific qualifications.

- Point out the items in your résumé that are a good "fit" for this job, but do not just repeat the résumé.

Conducting Global Business in the United States Here are a few tips that may help you get a job and be successful at it:

- *Take advantage of your language skills.* Because many corporations operate globally and have clients from diverse backgrounds, be sure to mention—on your résumé and in a job interview—any languages besides English in which you are fluent.

- *Do not include personal information (such as age, religion, marital status) or a photograph on your résumé.* It is not the custom in the United States to include personal information or a photograph with a job application, and US employers are legally barred from assessing job qualifications on the basis of these factors.

- *Be direct and concise in your business writing.* Although your culture of origin or your other writing experiences may suggest a more indirect approach, follow the advice in this chapter if you are writing to a US organization.

Student Model Job Application

7716 W. Birchwood Street
Chicago, IL 60648

July 1, 2016

Mr. Aaron Gieseke
Recruitment, Human Resources
Museum of Science and Industry
57th Street and Lake Shore Drive
Chicago, IL 60637

Dear Mr. Gieseke:

I am applying for the entry-level position of assistant to the curator, which you advertised in the June 30 issue of the *Chicago Tribune*. Since childhood, I have been delighted by the museum's extraordinary exhibits, from Colleen Moore's Fairy Castle to the walk-through heart and chick hatchery. I would welcome the opportunity to put my skills and knowledge to work at your renowned institution.

Two years ago, I was fortunate to take several in-depth courses in museum curatorship at James Cook University. With European curators as teachers, I came to understand the many facets of running a museum, including preserving artifacts and tapping sources of funding. I also learned about the myriad jobs that go on behind the scenes and decided that museum life was where I wanted to be in my professional life.

This decision was reinforced many times over while I was an intern at the Smithsonian last summer. I especially enjoyed working with researchers on new interactive exhibits and using my Spanish language skills with international visitors. Inasmuch as the Museum of Science and Industry was the first to initiate interactive exhibits and welcomes thousands of overseas travelers each year, I believe my qualifications are ideal for the job.

My résumé is enclosed. I would be delighted to meet with you for an interview at any time. You may phone me at (312) 555–5683 or email me at sonjaja1996@uic.edu. I look forward to hearing from you.

Sincerely,

Sonja Jacques

Sonja Jacques

Enc.

Annotations (right margin):

- Modified block style: Return address and date align right of center
- Addresses specific person formally
- Mentions specific job and shows familiarity with museum
- Highlights educational ties to job
- Links work experience to job and shows knowledge of museum
- Asks for interview and gives contact information
- Modified block style: Closing and signature align with return address

FIGURE 25.3 Sample job application letter (modified block style)

- Conclude by asking for an interview and providing information about how you may be reached.

- Edit and proofread your letter carefully: A job application letter must be well written and contain no errors.

Throughout the letter, you need to walk a fine line: Do not be too modest about your accomplishments, but do not exaggerate your qualifications, either.

25e Writing Résumés

A *résumé* is a brief document that summarizes your work and educational experience for a prospective employer. Like a job application letter, it is a tool for selling yourself and obtaining an interview. Thus, in drafting a résumé, keep your audience and purpose in mind: Who will read this résumé? What will they want to know? Especially for those new to the workforce, focus on the skills you have acquired from your work experience. For example, you might explain that you "maintained good customer relations" and "presented a positive corporate image" in your job at a fast-food restaurant. If you are changing careers—from computer programming to advertising, for example—revise your résumé accordingly.

> Sample résumés:
> Traditional, 508
> Scannable, 510

Tell the truth on your résumé, but cast the information in a positive light. Also think about what you have done that is appropriate for this particular job. You may have nearly forgotten the tutoring you did at your campus literacy center when you were a first-year student, but that experience is relevant if you are applying for a teaching position.

Quick Reference Designing a Print Résumé

- Leave plenty of white space; avoid a crowded look to make your résumé more readable.
- Use a slightly different design for your name and contact information to make your résumé more attractive and attention getting (Figure 25.4).
- Use a table format for other sections, aligning items on the left and setting off headings in boldface or capitals. You may want to use the résumé template that comes with your word processing software or add

other design elements. However, be careful not to overdesign the document—keep it simple and easy to read.
- Single-space all sections, and put an extra line of space between them.
- Proofread your résumé until you are sure the document has no grammatical or typographical errors.
- Use a standard font, such as Times New Roman, and print your résumé on 8½ × 11–inch white or off-white paper. Use black ink only.

Student Model Traditional Résumé

Name and contact information set off from rest of résumé

Education first, as typical for recent graduate

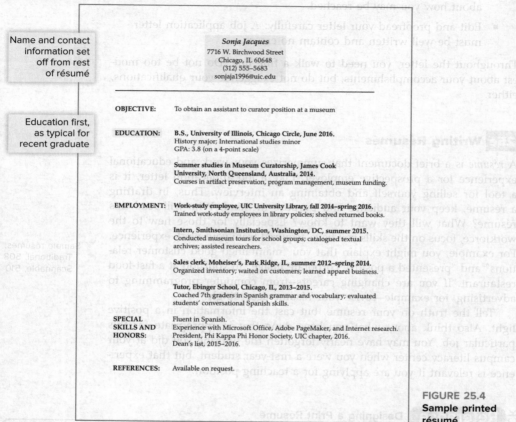

Sonja Jacques
7716 W. Birchwood Street
Chicago, IL 60648
(312) 555–5683
sonjaja1996@uic.edu

OBJECTIVE: To obtain an assistant to curator position at a museum

EDUCATION: **B.S., University of Illinois, Chicago Circle, June 2016.**
History major; International studies minor
GPA: 3.8 (on a 4-point scale)

Summer studies in Museum Curatorship, James Cook University, North Queensland, Australia, 2014.
Courses in artifact preservation, program management, museum funding.

EMPLOYMENT: **Work-study employee, UIC University Library, fall 2014–spring 2016.**
Trained work-study employees in library policies; shelved returned books.

Intern, Smithsonian Institution, Washington, DC, summer 2015.
Conducted museum tours for school groups; catalogued textual archives; assisted researchers.

Sales clerk, Moheiser's, Park Ridge, IL, summer 2012–spring 2014.
Organized inventory; waited on customers; learned apparel business.

Tutor, Ebinger School, Chicago, IL, 2013–2015.
Coached 7th graders in Spanish grammar and vocabulary; evaluated students' conversational Spanish skills.

SPECIAL SKILLS AND HONORS: Fluent in Spanish.
Experience with Microsoft Office, Adobe PageMaker, and Internet research.
President, Phi Kappa Phi Honor Society, UIC chapter, 2016.
Dean's list, 2015–2016.

REFERENCES: Available on request.

FIGURE 25.4
Sample printed résumé

1. Traditional print résumés

More about
Document design, 166–74 (ch. 9)

A résumé (Figure 25.4) arranges information in standard categories and a familiar sequence to make it easy for prospective employers to glean your qualifications quickly. This is not the place to demonstrate your flair for creative writing or flamboyant design. (The Quick Reference box on page 507 includes some basic guidelines for designing and formatting a print résumé.) Here are some tips to help you keep the content of your résumé on track:

- Arrange each section in reverse chronological order, with most recent job or degree first. If there are major gaps in your work history, or if you have changed careers, you may want to organize your résumé according to the skills that are particularly relevant to the job you are applying for. Keep in mind, however, that most employers prefer to read résumés in reverse chronological order.

- Use active verbs and parallel construction throughout. For example, if you use *managed* for the first verb, you might use *organized* and *researched* thereafter.

- Limit your résumé to one page unless your work experience is extensive. Most recent college graduates should write a one-page résumé.

More about
Active versus
passive voice,
559–61
Parallelism,
542–50 (ch. 28)

Most résumes include the following sections:

Contact information List your full name, mailing address, telephone number, and email address at the top of the résumé. If you have separate home and school addresses, give them both, but make it clear to the recipient (perhaps in your cover letter) how and when you can be contacted at each location.

Career objective Indicate the specific position you are applying for or your career objective. Instead of *position in publishing,* say *entry-level editorial position in children's publishing.*

More about
Portfolios,
106–110

Education List the degrees you hold (college and above), the institutions that granted them, the date you received them (or anticipate receiving them), and your major and minor. Mention any honors such as being on the dean's list, and include your grade-point average if it is high (say, 3.5 or above on a 4-point scale). Include certificates, such as teaching certification.

Employment history Give the names and addresses of employers, titles of jobs, primary duties, and dates of employment.

Skills, awards, or memberships List computer skills (such as proficiency in PageMaker, Excel, or Dreamweaver) and other skills that are relevant to the job, such as fluency in a foreign language. Include awards and memberships that are pertinent. For example, if you were applying for a job at a community organization, you would want to state that you served as a volunteer and on the board of directors of Big Brothers Big Sisters.

References Provide names, mailing addresses, phone numbers, and email addresses of three to six people who have agreed to serve as your references, or at the bottom of your résumé add *References available on request.* In either case, be sure to obtain permission to list someone as a reference in advance.

Student Model Scannable, Optimized Résumé

Sonja Jacques
7716 W. Birchwood Street
Chicago, IL 60648
(312) 555–5683
sonjaja1996@uic.edu

Keywords for employer's database search

SKILLS
Artifact preservation, museum funding, program management, personnel training, cataloging, customer service, Spanish language, Internet research, tutoring, MicroSoft Office, PageMaker

Headings set in all capitals, flush left, with no boldface, italics, or other design features

OBJECTIVE
Assistant to museum curator

EDUCATION
B.S. University of Illinois, Chicago Circle, June 2016.
History major; International studies minor
GPA: 3.8 (on a 4-point scale)

Summer studies in Museum Curatorship, James Cook University, North Queensland, Australia, 2014.

Nouns used instead of verbs (*trainer* not *trained*) throughout

EMPLOYMENT
Work-study employee, UIC University Library, fall 2014–spring 2016.
Trainer of work-study employees in library policies; shelver of returned books.

Intern, Smithsonian Institution, Washington, DC, summer 2015.
Conductor of museum tours for school groups; cataloguer of textual archives; assistant to researchers.

Sales clerk, Moheiser's, Park Ridge, IL, summer 2012–spring 2014.
Inventory organization; customer service; experience with apparel business.

Tutor, Ebinger School, Chicago, IL, 2013–2015.
Coach of 7th graders' Spanish grammar and vocabulary; evaluator of conversational Spanish skills.

HONORS
President, Phi Kappa Phi Honor Society, UIC chapter, 2011.
Dean's list, 2015–2016.

REFERENCES
Available on request

FIGURE 25.5
Sample scannable résumé

Writing
Responsibly Representing Yourself

When the job ad calls for a "claims adjuster" and you've done that work but with the title "claims specialist," feel free to list "claims adjuster" under your Skills section. But if you've just been an intern who's done errands for claims adjusters, don't list "claims adjuster" as a skill. A résumé that represents you falsely might get you a job—for a short while—and a reputation in the industry that you don't want to live with.

2. Scannable, optimized electronic résumés

Employers may request an electronic résumé (Figure 25.5)—one that is sent within the text of an email message or as an attachment—so they can scan it to include in a database. To meet this requirement, a traditional print résumé needs to be revised and redesigned:

- Position all copy flush with the left margin. Use only capitals to set off headings. Eliminate italics, boldface, and all other design or format features.

- Wherever possible, change your skills from verbs (*supervised*) to concise nouns (*supervisor of*). If you have the job description, try to use the keywords it mentions. (Employers frequently use keywords to screen out inappropriate applications.)

- Especially when they receive numerous applications, employers may use a pattern-recognition software that scans résumés to see who has the basic qualifications named in the job ad. It is advisable to modify your résumé for each job, "optimizing" it with a section located near the top of the résumé titled "Skills" that includes keywords matched to the job ad.

- Below your contact information, list keywords from your résumé, such as titles of positions you have held (*assistant*) or skills you possess (*Spanish*).

- When your résumé is complete, email it to yourself first, to make sure it is error-free and that the layout is readable.

NOTE Conventions for electronic or scannable résumés change over time and may vary from company to company. Check with your prospective employer to make sure your résumé fits the company's requirements.

Make It **Your Own**

Find an appealing job ad in a local newspaper or website, or find a posting in your school's job center. Then draft a résumé for the position following the recommendations in the section above.

Work **Together**

In groups of three or four, review each other's résumés. How could you rephrase the career objectives to tailor them more specifically to the job description? How might you revise the résumé to make it more appealing to the target audience?

25f Writing Reports and Proposals

As a student, you may have written reports about research you have conducted. You may have written proposals as well, perhaps suggesting to your college administration that campus parking be expanded. In this case, you would have done some research on parking problems to back up your suggestions. When you write as an employee or as a volunteer, reports and proposals have these same attributes: They provide information for a specific purpose, they usually involve research and analysis, and they may suggest some kind of change. Proposals, in particular, offer solutions for problems and seek funding for the project.

Reports and proposals may vary greatly in length, from a single page to more than a hundred pages. Long reports and proposals usually follow specific formats (which are dictated by the organization you are writing for), they include a table of contents, and they are divided into sections (with subheadings) such as the following:

- **Abstract, executive summary, or overview.** A one-paragraph summary of the entire report or proposal that highlights its purpose, major findings, and conclusions or recommended actions

- **Introduction or statement of the problem.** A discussion of the topic or problem that explains succinctly what is at issue and why it is important

- **Research methods and results.** A clear description of how you gathered information and what you discovered from your research (if appropriate, use graphs or tables to bolster your written explanation)

- **Conclusion or proposed solution.** A discussion of the relevance of your report or of the specific solution you are proposing (for a proposal, be sure to help readers see that your solution is preferable to other possible solutions and that it is feasible in terms of financing, staffing, or other potential roadblocks)

> *More about*
Choosing the
  appropriate
  information
  graphic, 80–83
Revising informa-
  tion graphics,
  84–87
Persuasive argu-
  ments, 136–39
Tone, 19–20, 138,
  565, 570–72

(The cover and first page of the executive summary of a report on school crime and safety appear in Figure 25.6 on the next page.)

As you draft a report or proposal, maintain an objective tone, and include only relevant and reliable information. Keep your purpose and audience in mind. It is not unusual for reports and proposals to be read by many different people (such as managers, sales representatives, and accountants). When this is the case, think about their various concerns and the questions they will want answered. For example, if you are proposing that the sales staff have larger, more expensive cars, how will you justify the extra cost to the financial experts?

FIGURE 25.6 **Sample report**

25g Writing Press Releases

Press, or *media, releases,* like the one shown in Figure 25.7, are brief articles that announce events to newspapers, magazines, and online media outlets. If you work in the advertising or marketing department of an organization, part of your job might be writing press releases. Similarly, you could write them as a volunteer for a local charity or sporting club. Whatever organization they are written for, press releases follow a standard format because reporters and editors need to read them quickly and decide whether or not to use the information they contain. Here are some guidelines to follow when drafting a press release:

- Use your organization's letterhead, if possible, and include all pertinent contact information (address, phone number, email address, website URL, and so on).

- At the top of the first page, type *For Immediate Release* and the date.

- Include an article title in bold or capital letters.

- To enable editors to cut your release for length easily, put the most important information up front and less important details toward the end.

- Use an objective tone, and make sure the content is factual and newsworthy.

Professional Model Press Release

march of dimes®
march for babies®

FOR IMMEDIATE RELEASE JAN. 16, 2016

For more information contact:
(Karin Roseland 701-235-5530)

March of Dimes Foundation

Karin Roseland
State Director

North Dakota Chapter
1350 Page Dr. #102
Fargo, ND 58103
Telephone 701-235-5530
Fax 701-235-8725
EMAIL kroseland@marchofdimes.com

marchforbabies.com

> *Uses letterhead*
>
> *"For immediate release" and date at top of first page*

Family Teams Key to March for Babies
Premier March of Dimes Fundraising Event

> *Article title in bold*

Fargo ND, January 16, 2016—The 2016 March of Dimes March for Babies will take place on April 18, 2016 at 8:00 a.m. at Scheels Arena. Formerly known as WalkAmerica, March for Babies is the March of Dimes' largest fundraising event that benefits all babies—those born healthy as well as those who need help to survive and thrive. The event has been renamed to make a clear connection to what the March of Dimes is all about—the health of babies.

> *Most important information in first paragraph*

Family Teams are made up of friends and family members who want to honor their own children or children they know—babies born prematurely or with a birth defect; babies who didn't survive; or healthy, full-term babies. Family Teams help remind everyone of the urgency of the mission of the March of Dimes. More than 20,000 Family Teams participated nationwide in 2015, raising over $100 million.

"We love to walk each year as a Family Team," said Jenny Smith, team captain. "Our first years, we participated because our neighbor's daughter was born premature. Now we walk to celebrate our own children—each born full-term and healthy. We know how fortunate we are."

"We hope many new Family Teams will be inspired to join us this year with the common goal of helping the March of Dimes improve baby health by preventing premature birth, birth defects and infant mortality," says Stacy Jacobs, Family Team committee member.

"It's easy to join or start a family team," added Jacobs. "Just visit marchforbabies.org or call toll-free 1-800-525-9255 to sign up or to donate to help babies be born healthy."

In 2016, national March for Babies sponsors are CIGNA, United Airlines, Famous Footwear, FedEx, nesting.com, and Kmart, the March of Dimes' number one corporate partner which has raised more than $100 million for babies. Additional national sponsorship is provided by Discovery Health, Mead Johnson Nutritionals, Outdoor services and Ther-Rx.

"In this community, we are proud also to be sponsored by U.S. Bank, BCBS, Loaf & Jug, and many other partners," Jacob said.

#   #   #

About March of Dimes
The March of Dimes is the leading nonprofit organization for pregnancy and baby health. With chapters nationwide and its premier event, March for Babies, the March of Dimes works to improve the health of babies. For the latest resources and information, visit marchofdimes.com

FIGURE 25.7 Sample press release

Make It **Your Own**

Draft a press release announcing a student activity on campus (real or imagined). Make sure to include the most important information in the first paragraph and to provide information that is newsworthy.

Work **Together**

Exchange press releases with a classmate, and take turns role-playing the position of editor of a local newspaper. Would you publish your partner's press release? Why or why not?

Student Model   Business News Article

Brigham Young University student Mallory Reese wrote the following project for a business-writing class. Her assignment was to write a short article on a business-related topic, suitable for a company newsletter or industry magazine. Because the content of Reese's text was informational, it was well suited to being presented brochure-style.

Text Credits

p. 514: "Family Teams Key to March for Babies," March of Dimes, North Dakota Chapter, January 1, 2016. Reprinted with the permission of Karin Roseland, State Director, March of Dimes North Dakota Chapter. p. 516: Courtesy of Mallory Reese.

RIDE THE WAVE

HOW ADVENTUROUS FEMALE MILLENNIALS WILL CHANGE THE OUTDOOR INDUSTRY

by Mallory Reese

Good surfers know that in order to ride a wave, they need to see the wave before it appears, and catch the wave before it breaks. Within the outdoor industry, the women's market stands as an avenue with a large potential for growth. Current trends suggest a wave of young, adventurous females moving into decision-making roles could dramatically change the outdoor industry.

RISE OF THE SHE-VENTURERS

Although men still outnumber women in participation in outdoor recreation, in recent years, overall female participation has seen a steady increase. From 2009–2014, women's participation grew by 3%. But, what is more compelling is an analysis of the millennial generation. Females aged 19–24 now far outnumber their male counterparts by 18% and are the fastest-growing sector of outdoor enthusiasts. In the next five years, these women will become decision makers in their households; they will enter the workforce, they will control the majority of family purchases, and they will be responsible for raising the next generation of outdoor enthusiasts.

Market Power
In the US, women decide **85%** of consumer purchases. This amounts to **$7 trillion** spent annually.

Unfortunately, many outdoor companies rely on the simple and ineffective "shrink it and pink it" approach—a strategy where products and services are only superficially adapted for a woman's needs. If the outdoor industry hopes to "catch the wave" of millennial women, it needs to adapt now.

To remain competitive, outdoor companies need to design better products and engage female customers in unique ways. And, if the industry wants to accelerate growth, it needs to hire more women.

"NO MORE BARBIE GEAR"

Attracting women consumers starts with product design. The market for women's clothing and equipment has grown immensely—from 2002 to 2004 sales for women's-specific clothing and equipment jumped by 60%. In comparison men's and unisex clothing grew by a mere 4%.

Designing products for women is a balancing act.

FIGURE 1 **Examples of the "shrink it and pink it" approach.**

Women consumers present a unique challenge because they want products to be both functional and fashionable. To best meet the needs of female consumers, designers should keep in mind two principles. First, functionality stems from making changes that fit a woman's body. For example, Tubbs Snowshoes saw a 300% increase in its women's market after making two simple changes: (1) modifying bindings to better fit women's boots and (2) changing the frame shape to allow for women's shorter strides.

Second, "fashionable" does not always equate to more feminine prints or colors. Companies like Lululemon have excelled in the women's market because of a focus on more relevant modifications including flattering clothing cuts, high-quality fabrics, and attention to detail (stitching, fasteners, and zippers). These elements make Lululemon's products appropriate for both an early morning workout or a night out on the town.

Companies that skillfully combine fashion with functionality will acquire a loyal following of female customers.

GIRLS' DAY OUT

Meeting the needs of female consumers doesn't end with product design. Companies can engage female customers by providing opportunities for women to use the products they sell.

The Outdoor Industry Foundation found that one of the key barriers to women's participation in the outdoors was inexperience. Thirty-four percent of women felt they didn't have the know-how needed for outdoor activities. To help women feel confident participating in the outdoors, companies like REI and L.L. Bean offer "Women's-Only Adventures." Their events include courses in stand-up paddleboarding, fly fishing, rock climbing, mountain biking, and shotgun sports.

These programs help women learn valuable skills and meet inspiring mentors. But, more

© Ingram Publishing/SuperStock

FIGURE 2 **Women's-only adventures build confidence and brand equity**

importantly, the events help build brand equity and develop a base of loyal female customers.

HIRE MORE WOMEN

Ultimately, to make lasting changes, companies will benefit from hiring more female professionals. Women working in the outdoor industry can provide the insight necessary to reach the powerful sector of women consumers.

In an article published in *SGB Weekly* (an outdoor retail journal), president of Burton Snowboards Donna Burton Carpenter highlighted the lack of women leaders in the outdoor industry. She remarked, "90 percent of the resumes we get are from men. Even at Roxy [a female-specific outdoor apparel company], the president and the VP of marketing and sales are all men. Columbia's entire senior management team is men. As an industry, we are pretty male-dominated."

How Big Is the Outdoor Industry? It generates **$646 billion** in annual sales—nearly double what Americans spent on gasoline, household utilities, and pharmaceuticals in 2010.

Yet multiple studies show that companies with more women in leadership positions have superior financial performance. Catalyst, a nonprofit organization that promotes women and business, studied 353 Fortune 500 companies over 5 years. Companies with the most women in senior management positions had a 35% higher return on equity. Researchers from Carnegie Mellon and MIT studying teamwork had similar findings—the highest-performing groups were also those with the most women.

The outdoor industry is moving in the right direction. In 2013, a team of female manufacturing engineering students at Brigham Young University designed a line of women's-specific outdoor lighting products for Black Diamond, which specializes in rock climbing and backcountry ski gear. Bryan Howell, the professor directing the project, explained that Black Diamond is a traditionally "testosterone-driven" company. Howell said the "estrogenized" designs showed the innovation, quality, and creativity that come when products are designed for women, by women.

More recently, in January of 2015, the CEOs of 14 outdoor retailers including REI, Backcountry.com, and Patagonia signed a pledge to "accelerate women's leadership in their companies." The pledge was accompanied with a $1.5 million grant from REI to the Outdoor Industries Women's Coalition to carry out pledge objectives.

RIDE THE WAVE

The steps companies take now to prepare for the flood of female consumers could determine whether outdoor companies "ride the wave" or get sucked into the surf. Improving women's-specific product designs and developing unique approaches to engaging female consumers will help companies get ahead of the tide. Hiring more female professionals will further solidify industry efforts to suceed in the outdoor women's market.

For further reading:

"The Bottom Line: Connecting Corporate Performance and Gender Diversity." *Catalyst*, 2004, BMO Financial Group, www.catalyst.org.

Brown, Meaghen, and Axie Navas. "No More Barbie Gear." *Outside*, 13 Mar. 13 2015, www.outsideonline.com.

"CEOs Sign OIWC Pledge to Advance Women's Leadership in the Outdoor Industry." News release, 23 Jan., 2015, *REI Co-Op*, www.newsroom.rei.com.

Gallagher, Alisha. "Industrial Design Students Light the Future for Female Adventurers." BYU News Release, 10 Apr. 2013, www.news.byu.edu.

"Getting Women Active." *The Outdoor Industry Foundation*, www.outdoorfoundation.org.

Griffin, Cara. "Don't Stop Now." *SGB*, Mar. 2015, Business Source Premier.

Johnson, Lisa. "Beyond Pink Thinking." *Outdoor Industry Special Edition*, www.outdoorfoundation.org.

"Outdoor Participation Report 2009–2014." *The Outdoor Industry Foundation*, www.outdoorfoundation.org.

"Outdoor Participation Report 2014." *The Outdoor Industry Foundation*, www.outdoorfoundation.org.

"The Outdoor Recreation Economy." *Outdoor Industry Association*, 2012, www.outdoorindustry.org.

Woolley, Anita, et al. "Why Some Teams Are Smarter than Others." *The New York Times*, 16 Jan. 2015, www.nytimes.com.

Yu, Daniela, et al. "Unleashing the Power of the Purse." *Gallup Business Journal*, 17 Oct. 2014, www.gallup.com/businessjournal.

ACTION TIP
To join other leaders in the outdoor industry in furthering women's leadership, visit: www.oiwc.org/page/pledge

Part Seven

Style
Matters

Writing Engagingly

26 Writing Concisely

© Tim Clayton/Contributor/Corbis Sport

Young children just learning to play soccer tend to swarm around the ball, each one duplicating the effort of the others, so that they move the ball toward the goal uncertainly. With practice and time, however, players learn to work together efficiently to control the ball. Every player counts; none wastefully duplicates the work of another.

Wordy writing is like young children's soccer: The point gets made haltingly if at all. Sentences crowded with unnecessary words compel readers to separate what matters from what does not. *Concise* writing, in contrast, is like the play of a practiced team: Each point is made forcefully and without duplication of effort.

Every word counts. Consider this example:

WORDY	The fact is that there is only one thing that should make us experience the emotion of fear and that is to all intents and purposes the emotion of fear itself.
CONCISE	The only thing we have to fear is fear itself.

—Franklin Delano Roosevelt, first inaugural address

> *More about*
> Sentence length and variety, 552–55

Writing Responsibly

Conciseness versus the Too-Short Paper

Effective writing should be concise but not necessarily brief. Concise writing provides readers with all the information they need without distractions, but it does not skimp on essential detail. It may take a long sentence to express a complex thought. Do not shortchange your readers—or your ideas—by omitting necessary detail.

to AUDIENCE

The first sentence is crowded with wordy expressions (*the fact is*), redundancies (*the emotion of fear*), and roundabout constructions (*there is only one thing*). The second, concise and direct, helped rally Americans to confront the Great Depression.

Quick Reference   **Strategies for Writing Concisely**

- Cut wordy expressions. (521)
- Cut ineffective or unnecessary repetition. (523)
- Revise roundabout constructions. (524)
- Consolidate phrases, clauses, and sentences. (526)

Most of us write inadvertently wordy first drafts. As you revise, look for opportunities to tighten your prose. The Quick Reference box above offers some strategies.

26a   Eliminating Wordy Expressions

First-draft writing sometimes contains common but wordy expressions that pad and clutter sentences. As you revise, prune these away.

Conciseness What one culture considers wordy, another may consider elegant. Not only culture but also context affects what readers expect: In literary contexts and even in some personal writing, US readers sometimes appreciate rich, expansive sentences. In academic contexts, however, US readers usually prefer writing that is concise and to the point.

1. Empty phrases

Some wordy expressions, like *to all intents and purposes, in fact, the fact is,* and *in the process of,* carry no information, and you can delete them.

▶ My roommate was ~~in the process of~~ applying for the job, but ~~in fact~~ it had already been filled.

Similarly, intensifiers—modifiers like *absolutely, actually, definitely, really,* and *totally*—may add little meaning to the words they modify.

▶ The tourists were ~~absolutely~~ thrilled. None of them had ~~actually~~ seen a polar bear before.

Phrases built around words like *aspect, character, kind, manner,* and *type* are also often mere filler.

▶ They ~~are the kind of people who~~ have always ~~behaved in a generous manner.~~ *been generous.*

2. Roundabout expressions

Some wordy expressions say in many words what is better said with one.

Wordy Expression	Concise Alternative
at the present time	*now* (or delete entirely)
at that point in time	*then* (or delete entirely)
until such time as	*until*
at all times	*always*
at no time	*never*
most of the time	*usually*
in this day and age	*today*
due to the fact that	*because*
in spite of the fact that	*although, even though*
has the ability to	*can*
in the event that	*if*
in the neighborhood of	*around*

▶ ~~Due to the fact that~~ the housing market is ~~weak at this point in time,~~
   Because   *weak,*

   many homeowners are waiting to sell until ~~such time as~~ conditions

   improve.

3. Redundant expressions

Some wordy expressions are **redundant,** stringing together two or more
words that convey the same meaning.

Wordy Expression	Concise Alternative
blue in color	*blue*
in close proximity	*close*
each and every	*each* (or *every*)
end result	*result*
few/many in number	*few/many*
final outcome	*outcome*
past history	*history*
plans for the future/	*plans*
* future plans*	
repeat again	*repeat*
round in shape	*round*
sum total	*total*

> **Tech**   **Style Checkers and Wordiness**
>
> Although they might occasionally flag an inappropriate roundabout construction, computer style checkers are generally unreliable judges of wordiness. Rely on readers—yourself, your instructor, writing center tutors, your friends—to help you determine what is and is not acceptable.

▸ The candidate's mistakes during the campaign were ~~few in number~~ ^{few,} but they cost her the election, and she plans ~~for the future~~ never to repeat them ~~again~~.

26b Eliminating Ineffective or Unnecessary Repetition

Ineffective or unnecessary repetition can dull your prose and tire your readers.

1. Repetition and redundancy

As you revise your writing, look for words repeated unnecessarily, whether exactly or in varied form.

DRAFT	Biographer Robert Caro's informative overview provides particularly revealing information about the Johnson administration.
REVISION	Biographer Robert Caro's informative overview is particularly revealing about the Johnson administration.

Redundancy, another form of unnecessary repetition, is not restricted to the kind of stock phrases listed in the previous section; it happens whenever one expression duplicates the meaning of another.

▸ The portrait is ~~a likeness~~ of Gertrude Stein.

A portrait *is* a likeness of a particular person.

2. Elliptical constructions

Sometimes grammatically necessary words can be omitted from a sentence when the context makes their meaning and function clear, and you can take advantage of such *elliptical constructions* to tighten your prose.

▸ On Friday mornings Ghazala does assigned readings, and on Friday ~~afternoons she does~~ research. ^{afternoons,}

> **EXERCISE 26.1 Eliminating wordy expressions and unnecessary repetition**

Edit the following sentences to eliminate wordy expressions and unnecessary repetition.

> **EXAMPLE**
>
> *begin with Harry's discovery*
> The ~~beginning of the~~ Harry Potter books ~~starts when Harry discovers the fact~~
> ~~that he has magical abilities.~~

1. When the seventh and final book of J. K. Rowling's popular series of books about Harry Potter, called *Harry Potter and the Deathly Hallows,* was released, people everywhere all over the world lined up outside bookstores to buy a copy due to the fact that the series is so popular and this was the last book in the series.

2. Those people who read carefully and know about such things can find references in the Harry Potter series to other writers who wrote before Rowling, such as the writers Dante and George Orwell.

3. In spite of the fact that Rowling's work has the ability to impress many people and is popular, the critic Harold Bloom complained that Rowling's style is very repetitive and also complained that she used too many clichés that she did not need to use in order to tell her story.

4. Others have complained about contradictions in the books that are small but really annoying to readers, such as the fact that in spite of all of the amazing spells everyone can make, no one makes a spell to get rid of Eloise's acne.

26c Avoiding Indirect Constructions

Certain sentence patterns tend toward wordiness and indirection. These include *expletive constructions,* sentences in the *passive voice,* and sentences built around weak verbs.

> **More about**
> Expletive
> constructions,
> 735–36

1. Sentences that begin with *There are..., It is...*

Expletive constructions are sentences that begin with expressions like *there are, there is,* or *it is.* (Do not confuse *expletive* in this sense with its other sense of *swear word* or *curse*.) Revising to eliminate expletives will often make a sentence more direct and concise.

DRAFT   There are several measures that institutions can take to curb plagiarism.

REVISION   Institutions can take several measures to curb plagiarism.

2. Passive voice

In an active-voice sentence, the subject performs the action of the verb. In a passive-voice sentence, the subject receives the action.

More about
Passive versus
active voice,
559–61,
680–83

        subj.   verb
ACTIVE   Jared photographed the bear.

            subj.   verb
PASSIVE   The bear was photographed by Jared.

Rewriting to use the active voice usually makes sentences more concise and direct.

DRAFT   A motion was proposed by the committee chair that the vote be delayed until the cost of the program could be accurately determined by the finance subcommittee.

REVISION   The committee chair proposed to delay the vote until the finance subcommittee could accurately determine the program's cost.

3. Sentences built around nouns derived from verbs

If the sentence is built around a weak verb such as *is, are, were,* or *was* (all forms of the verb *to be*), sometimes replacing the verb can produce a more concise and vivid result.

            noun   verb
DRAFT   The destruction of the town by the tornado was complete.

                    verb
REVISION   The tornado destroyed the town.

> **EXERCISE 26.2 Eliminating indirect constructions**

Edit the following sentences to eliminate roundabout constructions.

EXAMPLE

Sleep deprivation
~~It is sleep deprivation that~~ is a serious problem for many college students.
                 ^

1. In college, it is students who must plan their schedules and extracurricular activities carefully so they get enough sleep.

2. There are several sleep-related consequences that college students face if they do not manage their time.

3. Schoolwork is more difficult for students who are sleep deprived.

4. The reduction in the ability to concentrate as a result of inadequate sleep is serious.

5. Illness is also more frequent for sleep-deprived college students due to the fact that lack of sleep depletes the immune system.

26d Consolidating Phrases, Clauses, and Sentences

> **clause** A word group with a subject and a predicate
> **phrase** A group of related words that lacks a subject, predicate, or both

You can often make your writing more concise by reducing *clauses* to *phrases* and clauses or phrases to single words.

DRAFT   Scientists cite glaciers, which have been retreating, and the polar ice caps, which have been shrinking, as evidence of global climate change.

REVISION   Scientists cite retreating glaciers and shrinking polar ice caps as evidence of global climate change.

Sometimes you can also combine two or more sentences into one more concise, effective sentence.

DRAFT   Scientists note that glaciers have been retreating and the polar ice caps have been shrinking. Most of them now agree that these phenomena are evidence of global climate change.

REVISION   Most scientists now agree that retreating glaciers and the shrinking polar ice caps are evidence of global climate change.

➔ EXERCISE 26.3 Combining sentences for conciseness

Reduce clauses to phrases and phrases to words as appropriate to combine each of the following passages into a single concise sentence.

EXAMPLE

Scientists in the United States have been analyzing the results of studies that connect obesity and sleep deprivation. Scientists in the United Kingdom have also been analyzing data about sleep and obesity.

Scientists in the United States and the United Kingdom have been studying the connection between obesity and sleep deprivation.

1. Some scientists conclude from their data that lack of sleep can be the cause of weight gain. Other scientists conclude from the same data that obesity and related health problems are more likely to cause lack of sleep.

2. Scientists in the United Kingdom and scientists in the United States worked together on one study, and they found as a result of their research that there is a relationship between sleep and hormones that control appetite. In that study they compared two groups of people. In one group were people who sleep for less than five hours a night. In the other group were people who sleep for more than eight hours a night.

3. The study found that people who sleep for less than five hours a night have 15 percent more of the hormone ghrelin, which increases appetite. The study found that people who sleep for less than five hours a night also have 15 percent less of the hormone leptin, which suppresses appetite.

4. Another study was reported by Swiss scientists. They studied 496 people between twenty-seven and forty years of age. The study lasted for thirteen years. The study found that twenty-seven-year-olds who slept for only a "short duration" were much more likely to be obese than forty-year-olds who got the same amount of sleep. This study found that the connection between sleep and obesity started to diminish after age thirty-four.

➔ **EXERCISE 26.4 Editing for conciseness**

Use the strategies described in this chapter to make the following passage concise and direct.

> It is a fact that citizen, or amateur, scientists have the ability to contribute to the work of professional scientists. They can be of use in many different scientific fields of endeavor. For example, in the area of biology, citizen scientists can report the observations that they make. They have the ability to report observations about bird migration, seasonal change, and other factors that they can view in the vicinity of their own backyards. The widespread, detailed data provided by amateurs can help scientists bring their studies to completion.
>
> In the area of astronomy, discoveries that are very significant have been made by amateurs. These include the very first sightings of many comets. They also include important observations of variable stars. Variable stars are stars that change in brightness over time. There are organizations and even awards for amateur astronomers. This shows how important their work is.

Make It **Your Own**

Reread a piece of your writing, ideally a recent or current project, and look for sentences that could be made more concise. If you find any, make a note of the problem and how you could fix it, then add this to your list of areas to consider as you revise your prose.

Work **Together**

Working with two or three classmates, read a piece of each other's writing and identify where and how your classmates' sentences could be made more concise. Compare your results with those of the others in the group. What did each of you see that others did not? Write a few sentences reflecting on how this collaborative activity might help you revise your own work in the future.

Text Credit

p.520: Franklin Delano Roosevelt, First Inaugural Address, March 4, 1933.

27 Using Coordination and Subordination

© Randy Duchaine/Alamy Stock Photo

Look up as you enter the East Wing of the National Gallery of Art in Washington, DC, and a dramatic sight confronts you. Hanging from the skylight over the building's large atrium is a giant sculpture by Alexander Calder—a 920-pound, 76-foot-long mobile made of multicolored metal rods and plates—that despite its size and weight sweeps gracefully overhead. Calder achieved this elegant effect by carefully coordinating elements of equal weight, balancing heavy elements with a series of lighter subordinate elements that descend in a branching cascade from the cable that secures the mobile to the ceiling. The subordinated and coordinated elements combine to convey Calder's visual message.

Writers can similarly use coordination and subordination to craft sentences that best convey their intended meaning. *Coordination* establishes the equal weight or importance of two or more sentence elements.

equal weight

▶ We entered the museum, and a dramatic sight confronted us.

equal weight

▶ The mobile is made of rods and plates.

Tech Style Checkers and Coordination and Subordination

Using coordination and subordination requires you to figure out the logical relationships among the ideas you want to express and to decide on their relative importance, so that you can make these relationships clear to your audience. A computer style checker cannot do that for you.

Subordination establishes the supporting or modifying role of one or more sentence elements.

|——————————— main idea ———————————|| ———— modifying subordinate
▶ Heavy elements balance lighter elements that descend in a branching

idea ————————————————— ||—————— modifying subordinate idea ————————|
cascade from the cable that secures the mobile to the ceiling.

27a Coordinating Terms, Phrases, and Clauses

Coordination can link or contrast two or more equally important terms, *phrases*, or *clauses*.

> **phrase** A group of related words that lacks a subject, a predicate, or both
> **clause** A word group with a subject and predicate. An *independent clause* can stand alone as a sentence; a *subordinate clause* cannot.

1. Terms and phrases

To coordinate terms and phrases requires either a coordinating conjunction (such as *and, but, for, nor, or, so,* or *yet*) or a correlative conjunction (such as *both…and, either…or,* or *neither…nor*). Usually no punctuation separates two coordinated words or phrases.

> **More about**
> Coordinating and correlative conjunctions, 611–12

▶ Both Steven Spielberg and George Romero attended the New York Film Academy.

▶ London's Theatre Royal in Drury Lane has staged performances by the Shakespearean actor Edmund Kean and by the Monty Python comedy troupe.

Commas usually separate more than two terms or phrases in a coordinated series.

▶ From John Webster's point of view in 1612, the greatest playwright might have been George Chapman, William Shakespeare, or Ben Jonson.

2. Independent clauses

> **More about**
> Punctuating coordinated independent clauses, 639–47

To coordinate two independent clauses, use a comma and a coordinating conjunction, a semicolon, or a semicolon and a conjunctive adverb such as *for example, however, in addition,* or *therefore.*

▶ Today we consider Shakespeare to be the greatest English playwright, but his contemporaries regarded him as just one among many.

▶ Adele's debut CD was a huge success; it sold millions of copies.

▶ The play received glowing reviews and won a Tony award; however, it closed after only a short run.

27b Coordinating Effectively

Coordinating elements in a sentence gives them equal importance or weight. How you coordinate those elements shows your readers the relationship among them.

1. Conjunctions and their meaning

Conjunctions differ in meaning, and some can have more than one meaning depending on context (see the Quick Reference box on the next page).

A conjunction whose meaning does not match the relationship between coordinated elements might confuse readers and obscure the writer's point. In the following sentence, for example, changing *and* to *but* reveals what the writer intended to emphasize: the contrast between Einstein's youth and his accomplishments.

▶ Einstein was still young, ~~and~~ *but* he had revolutionized physics.

2. Independent clauses joined with a semicolon

Use a semicolon to join two independent clauses that have a logical connection to each other. The second clause can contrast with the first, provide an example of it, or give a reason for it.

> *More about*
> Semicolons,
> 796–802

CONTRAST	During the polar winter, the sun never rises; during the polar summer, it never sets.
EXAMPLE	The movie was a financial success; it set a record for opening-day box office receipts.
EXPLANATION	She wanted to be sure to have the assignment done for tomorrow; Spanish is her favorite class.

Reference — Conjunctions and Their Meaning

Meaning	Conjunctions	Examples
addition	*and, both...and*	*Both* advances in ship design *and* the introduction of the magnetic compass helped make possible the European voyages of discovery.
sequence	*and*	The lawyer turned *and* faced the jury.
cause and effect	*so, for,* (sometimes) *and*	The housing market has softened, *so* sellers have had to lower their prices.
choice	*or, whether...or, either...or, nor, neither...nor*	Tournament games can be played on neutral courts *or* home courts.
		Neither ESPN *nor* any other network wants to show empty arenas.
contrast	*but, yet*	The police raided the house, *but* the suspect had fled.
		The poll indicates support for the law *yet* doubt about its chance for passage.
	not just...but, not only...but also	*Not just* the NCAA *but* the teams and fans should have a voice in the decision. [In addition to contrasting the coordinated elements, these conjunctions emphasize one over the other, suggesting that the first is commonplace and expected, the second new and noteworthy.]

When you join clauses with a semicolon and a conjunctive adverb, the conjunctive adverb specifies the relationship.

▸ During the polar winter, the sun never rises; in contrast, during the polar summer, it never sets.

3. Inappropriate coordination

Coordination is inappropriate when it combines elements that are not of equivalent importance or weight. The following sentence, for example, puts an incidental fact—Einstein's year of birth—on an equal footing with a statement about his early accomplishments. The revision subordinates the minor information in a modifying phrase.

INAPPROPRIATE COORDINATION	Albert Einstein was born in 1879, and by 1905 he had published four important scientific papers.
REVISED	Albert Einstein, born in 1879, had published four important scientific papers by 1905.

4. Excessive coordination

In everyday speech, people often coordinate long strings of sentences with *and* and other conjunctions. What is acceptable in speech, however, quickly becomes tedious, even confusing, in writing. As you edit, look for such *excessive coordination.*

EXCESSIVE COORDINATION	Steven Spielberg graduated from Saratoga High School, in Saratoga, California, in 1965, and he applied to the University of Southern California's film school three times, but he was rejected each time, so he finally decided to attend California State University at Long Beach, and while he was at Cal State he started an unpaid internship at Universal Studios, and an executive was impressed by his talent, so in 1969 he was allowed to direct a television episode there, and by 1975 he was directing films like *Jaws*, and that was his first big hit as a movie director, so perhaps in the end he was lucky to have been rejected by USC.
REVISED	Steven Spielberg, who graduated in 1965 from Saratoga High School in Saratoga, California, applied to the University of Southern California's film school three times and was rejected each time. Finally, he decided to attend California State University at Long Beach. While he was at Cal State, he started an unpaid internship at Universal Studios. An executive there was impressed by his talent, so in 1969 he was allowed to direct a television episode there. By 1975, he was directing films like *Jaws*, his first big hit as a movie director. Perhaps, in the end, he was lucky to have been rejected by USC.

> **EXERCISE 27.1 Eliminating inappropriate and excessive coordination**

Edit the following sentences to eliminate excessive or inappropriate coordination.

EXAMPLE

Your parents probably encouraged you to start the day with a good
                    breakfast, and   *right. The*
breakfast, ~~so~~ now a five-year study suggests they were ~~right, but the~~
              ^   ^
study found that the more likely adolescents are to eat breakfast, the less

likely they are to be overweight.

1. The study was conducted in the public schools of the Minneapolis–St. Paul area, and researchers found that there was a direct relationship between eating breakfast and body mass index (BMI), yet the more often an adolescent had breakfast, the lower was his or her BMI.

2. The adolescents studied were an average of fifteen years old at the start of the study, and those who ate breakfast consumed more carbohydrates and fiber, received fewer calories from fat, so got more exercise.

3. The relationship between breakfast eating and BMI was consistent throughout the study's entire five years, but the researchers controlled for age, sex, race, socioeconomic status, smoking, and concerns about diet and weight.

4. The study only observed an association between breakfast-eating habits and body mass, yet it did not prove a causal relationship, and nevertheless, one of the authors said that the research provided some useful guidance for healthy eating.

5. He noted that eating a healthy breakfast would encourage healthy eating for the rest of the day, yet it might help to lessen the urge for fast food or vending-machine food, and parents could also contribute, he added, by setting a good example and having a good breakfast themselves.

27c Identifying Important Ideas and Supporting Information with Subordination

Unlike coordination, which links equal ideas, subordination indicates which part of the sentence contains your important ideas, and which parts contain supporting examples, explanations, and details. Putting information in a subordinate structure de-emphasizes it, showing that it is supporting material rather than major claims.

> ⊢————— main idea —————⊣ ⊢————— main idea —————⊣
> ▶ The evidence is conclusive; my client is innocent.
>
> Coordination gives each idea equal weight.

> ⊢————— subordinated idea —————⊣ ⊢——— main idea ———⊣
> ■ As the evidence proves conclusively, my client is innocent.
>
> The emphasis is on the client.

> ⊢————— main idea —————⊣ ⊢——— subordinated idea ———⊣
> ▶ The evidence proves conclusively that my client is innocent.
>
> The emphasis is on the evidence.

Subordination can also clarify the logical relationship among a series of ideas. The revised version of the following passage clarifies the chronological relationship among the facts listed in the draft, and it emphasizes the most significant fact—that comic books did not become widely popular until 1938.

DRAFT   The first comic books appeared in the early 1920s. Nearly four decades earlier, comic strips had begun appearing in the major newspapers. Comic books did not gain widespread popularity until June 1938. Writer Jerry Siegel and artist Joe Shuster debuted their character Superman in June 1938.

REVISED   Although comic books first appeared in the 1920s, which was nearly four decades after comic strips had begun to appear in the major newspapers, they did not gain widespread popularity until June 1938, when writer Jerry Siegel and artist Joe Shuster debuted their character Superman.

1. Subordinating techniques

To subordinate information within a sentence, put it in a subordinate clause, reduce it to a modifying phrase or word, or include it in an appositive.

■ **Subordinate clause.** Subordinate clauses begin with a *subordinating* word, usually either a subordinating conjunction (such as *after, although, because, before, that,* or *when*) or a relative pronoun (such as *that, what, which, who,* or *whose*).

> *. whose reign was from 1473 to 1458 BCE.*
> ▶ Hatshepsut was one of only a few women to rule ancient Egypt.
>   ^
> ~~Her reign was from 1473 to 1458 BCE.~~

> **More about**
> Subordinating
> conjunctions
> and relative
> pronouns,
> 622–24, 630–3

Quick

Reference Subordination and Punctuation

In most cases, a comma follows a subordinate structure that begins an independent clause.

> After the 1965 Newport festival, fans complained about Dylan's switch from acoustic to electric guitar.

A subordinate structure that interrupts or ends an independent clause may or may not be set off with punctuation, depending on whether the information in it is **essential** (restrictive) or **nonessential** (nonrestrictive). A structure is essential if it specifically identifies the word or words it modifies. No punctuation

sets off interrupting or concluding restrictive structures.

> Athletes who win Olympic gold medals often earn money by endorsing products.

A structure is nonessential if the meaning or identity of the word or words it modifies is clear without it. A comma or other punctuation usually sets off interrupting or concluding nonessential structures. (See pp. 787–89.)

> Michael Phelps, the most decorated Olympian of all time, is a published author.

- **Modifying phrase or word.**

  Enticed by months of clever advance marketing, millions
  ▶ ~~Millions~~ of people bought the new multimedia smartphone within
     days of its release. ~~They had been enticed by months of clever advance marketing.~~

- **Appositive.**

  , *a giant mobile made of multicolored metal rods and plates,*
  ▶ The sculpture sweeps gracefully overhead. ~~It is a giant mobile made of multicolored metal rods and plates.~~

> **appositive** A noun or noun phrase that renames a preceding noun or noun phrase

2. Choosing a subordinating term

Understanding the meaning of subordinating terms is essential to using subordination effectively (see the Quick Reference box on the next page).

Use a subordinating term whose meaning matches the relationship you intend to convey between a subordinate element and the element it modifies. The following sentence uses a term referring to cause in a context that calls for a term referring to purpose. Revising requires either changing the term or rewording the clause.

DRAFT He ran for mayor because he could bring the town's budget under control.

Reference Subordinating Terms and Their Meaning

Meaning	Conjunctions	Examples
time	*after, as, before, since, until, when, whenever, while*	Comics grew in popularity *after* Superman appeared in 1938.
place	*where, wherever*	Home is *where* the hearth is.
cause or effect	*as, because, since, so that*	*Because* of the water main break, traffic came to a standstill.
condition	*even if, if, provided that, since, unless*	*If* you finish the job today, you can take a vacation day tomorrow.
purpose	*in order that, so that, that*	She finished the job quickly *so that* she could have a day off.
identification	*that, when, where, which, who*	Svetlana Alexievich is the author *who* won the Nobel Prize for literature in 2015.
contrast or comparison	*as, although, as if, even though, though, whereas*	*Although* Einstein was still a young man, he had revolutionized physics.

REVISED   He ran for mayor so that he could bring the town's budget under control.

             or

      He ran for mayor because he wanted to bring the town's budget under control.

Be particularly careful with the subordinating conjunctions *as* and *since*, which can refer ambiguously to both cause and time.

DRAFT   As she was applying the last coat of varnish, Leena declared the restoration complete.

REVISED   While she was applying the last coat of varnish, Leena declared the restoration complete.

             or

      Because she was applying the last coat of varnish, Leena declared the restoration complete.

3. Avoiding illogical subordination

State key ideas in an independent clause, and put illustrations, examples, explanations, and details in subordinate structures. Illogically subordinating a main idea to a supporting idea can confuse readers. The following sentence subordinates the idea of Einstein's accomplishments to the idea of his youth, illogically implying that he was young in spite of his accomplishments rather than accomplished in spite of his youth.

ILLOGICAL SUBORDINATION	Einstein was still young, although he had revolutionized physics.
REVISED	Although he was still young, Einstein had revolutionized physics.

4. Avoiding excessive subordination

Excessive subordination—stringing together too many subordinate structures—can make a sentence hard to read. The string of subordinate structures in the following sentence leaves readers unsure by the end where they began. The revision into two sentences clarifies the information the writer wants to convey.

EXCESSIVE SUBORDINATION	San Francisco, although generally an ideal habitat for peregrine falcons, is not entirely so, as became clear recently when rescuers had to remove falcon eggs from a nest on the Bay Bridge, despite the parents' protests, because once hatched, the fledglings would probably have drowned while learning to fly.
REVISED	San Francisco, although generally an ideal habitat for peregrine falcons, is not entirely so. Rescuers had to remove falcon eggs from a nest on the Bay Bridge recently, despite the parents' protests, because once hatched, the fledglings would probably have drowned while learning to fly.

> **EXERCISE 27.2 Eliminating excessive or illogical subordination**

Edit the following passage to eliminate excessive or illogical subordination.

An increasing number of high school seniors, although possessing excellent grades and good prospects for gaining admittance into the colleges of their choice, are opting for another alternative called a "gap year," which involves spending the year after graduating from high school doing something other than going to college. One recent graduate said she worked so hard in high school that she felt as if she had been continually running a marathon, without enough time for her three college-level physics courses, her clarinet practice, her band competitions, and her volunteer work, all of which often left her exhausted at the end of the day. She was accepted at several colleges, although she spent her gap year teaching English in Japan. This woman, who felt so pressured by her high school schedule that she chose to postpone college, has plenty of company, which includes a young man working on a farm in Costa Rica, a man who cares for injured sled dogs in Canada, a woman who builds guitars in England, and a woman who studies ballet in New York City, all activities that, according to the man in Costa Rica, "give you a break from being a student so you can reclaim the person inside." Even if many young people feel that their gap year gives them a refreshing, stimulating, and maturing change, they are delaying their start at college.

27d Using Coordination and Subordination Together

Used together, coordination and subordination can add grace and variety to your writing and help readers identify the points you want to emphasize. In this passage from a paper on Shakespeare's views on war in his play *Henry V*, student Jonathan Adler holds readers' interest and guides them to his concluding point by using both coordination and subordination in sentences of varied length.

More about
Variety and emphasis, 551–61

Instead of glorifying war, Shakespeare shows us in *Henry V* that war is costly and that it has consequences. For his own security, however, Shakespeare had to disguise these views about war; speaking out against the government during his time was a risky thing to do. This need for disguise is where his dark comedy or satire comes in. In comedy and satire he can hide his anti-war sentiments while at the same time expressing them and mocking the entire process of going to war.

—Jonathan Adler, Syracuse University

Coordination and Subordination Mastery of subordination is considered a sign of sophistication in American academic writing, but this is not true of all languages or cultures. If academic style in your native language or your style in other contexts favors coordination over subordination, you may need to make a conscious effort to use more subordinated structures in your writing. If your style favors subordination over coordination, you may have a tendency to oversubordinate your sentences in academic English. Your goal should be to strike a balance between both coordination and subordination.

EXERCISE 27.3 Combining sentences with coordination and subordination

Use coordination and subordination to combine sentences in the following passages in the way that seems most effective to you. Try to vary the coordination and subordination techniques you use.

1. Every holiday season, some people complain about the need to exchange gifts. Many are annoyed by the crowds, the expense, the materialism, and the overall stress of finding and buying suitable presents.

2. There are people who even refuse to take part in gift giving during the holidays. Some psychologists say that these people may be passing up an important opportunity to bond with their family and friends.

3. People's gift lists indicate who is important and unimportant in their lives, researchers note. A partner can use gift giving to show interest, strengthen a relationship, or even signal that the connection should end.

4. A recent study examined gift giving by pet owners. Researchers heard from owners why they gave their pets gifts. Owners said they wanted to make the pets happy. They also wanted to improve their pets' care and make them feel more comfortable.

5. Especially noteworthy is that the pets cannot return the gifts they receive. The act of giving itself makes the pet owners feel good. Simply knowing they are taking care of their pets gives them pleasure.

→ **EXERCISE 27.4 Using coordination and subordination correctly**

Edit the following passage to correct any errors in the use of coordination and subordination.

It is a task almost everyone does twice a day for just about their entire lives, yet not many people do it well, for tooth brushing is supposed to take more time than nearly anyone wants to spend on it, and we usually do not do it properly. The American Dental Association is the country's foremost authority on dental hygiene, and it tells us to brush each tooth to the gum line. Although most people are too impatient to brush as long as they should, the entire process ought to take two minutes. While people have been using a form of the standard toothbrush, with bristles attached to a six-inch-long handle, for more than 5,000 years, the task has always been the same, which is to remove the left over bits of food from our last meal, but we brush for too short a time, and we also commonly brush too hard, no matter what our dentists tell us, even though brushing too hard can cause serious harm to teeth and gums, and this damage can be expensive to repair. People's ineptitude at brushing has inspired an entire industry of toothbrush devices that are elaborate technological wonders that do the brushing for us provided that we reposition the electric toothbrushes when they beep, and we passively wait for them to do their job. Most tooth-brushing devices are made by well-known companies, and they all claim that their products are superior at cleaning teeth. Nevertheless, there are few well-controlled studies showing one brush to be better than any other. Whereas most dental experts agree that using a standard toothbrush thoroughly and gently will remove plaque from teeth as well as an electronic gadget will, an expensive tooth-cleaning machine does have one advantage, which is that people are more likely to use it than the ordinary toothbrush they get from their dentist for free.

⌐ Make It **Your Own**

Reread a piece of your writing, ideally a recent or current project, and identify coordinate and subordinate structures. Look for any that need to be revised. If you find any, make a note in the margins of the paper identifying which section of this chapter explains the revision and add this to your list of areas to consider as you revise your prose.

Text Credit

p. 539: Jonathan Adler, Syracuse University.

28 Using Parallelism

Piero di Cosimo (Florentine, 1462–1521), Portraits of Giuliano and Francesco Giamberti da Sangallo, 1482–1485

© Rijksmuseum, Amsterdam

These 15th century portraits by Piero di Cosimo have two nearly matching, or parallel, parts. Each half of the diptych consists of similar—but not identical—features: paintings of two men, dark Florentine costumes, and idealized Italian landscapes in the background. The portraits are the same size, identically framed. Within this structure, however, the images differ: the faces, hair, clothing, caps, and background are all unique, and the men look at each other rather than in the same direction. Still, there are enough parallels in the composition that the portraits of the father-and-son architects Giuliano and Francesco Giamberti da Sangallo work as a pair, together suggesting the stature and humanity of the two subjects.

The artist uses visual parallelism to convey his subjects' connectedness despite their individuality. Similarly, writers use grammatical *parallelism*—the expression of equally important ideas in similar grammatical form—to increase the clarity of their writing and to emphasize important points. Abraham Lincoln, for example, deployed parallelism to powerful effect as he urged his fellow citizens to persevere in the Civil War in this closing passage from the Gettysburg Address:

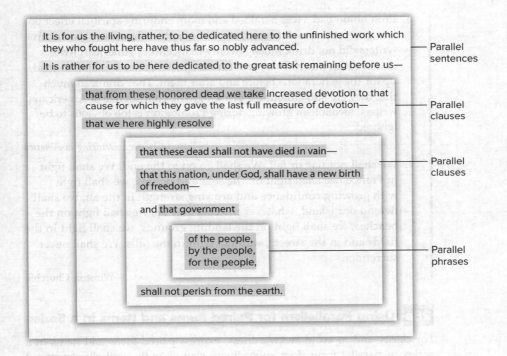

It is for us the living, rather, to be dedicated here to the unfinished work which they who fought here have thus far so nobly advanced. — Parallel sentences

It is rather for us to be here dedicated to the great task remaining before us—

that from these honored dead we take increased devotion to that cause for which they gave the last full measure of devotion— — Parallel clauses

that we here highly resolve

that these dead shall not have died in vain— — Parallel clauses

that this nation, under God, shall have a new birth of freedom—

and that government

of the people, — Parallel phrases
by the people,
for the people,

shall not perish from the earth.

> **EXERCISE 28.1 Identifying parallelism**

Identify and describe the parallel structures in the following passages.

1. It was the best of times, it was the worst of times, it was the age of wisdom, it was the age of foolishness, it was the epoch of belief, it was the epoch of incredulity, it was the season of Light, it was the season of Darkness, it was the spring of hope, it was the winter of despair, we had everything before us, we had nothing before us, we were all going direct to heaven, we were all going direct the other way—in short, the period was so far like the present period, that some of its noisiest authorities insisted on its being received, for good or for evil, in the superlative degree of comparison only.

   —Charles Dickens, *A Tale of Two Cities*

2. Those who see quickly, will resolve quickly and act quickly.

   —Jane Austen, *Mansfield Park*

3. Prohibition had a less heralded and more enduring spiritual effect on two generations of American writers. Nineteenth-century American writers did not drink much. Twenty-first-century American writers do not drink much. Twentieth-century writers after Prohibition made up for the generations before and after them. They drank so much that they are still famous for drinking. The coincidence of American writers' alcoholism growing during Prohibition is too obvious to be ignored.

—Susan Cheever, *Drinking in America*

4. We shall not flag or fail. We shall go on to the end. We shall fight in France, we shall fight on the seas and oceans, we shall fight with growing confidence and growing strength in the air, we shall defend our island, whatever the cost may be, we shall fight on the beaches, we shall fight on the landing grounds, we shall fight in the fields and in the streets, we shall fight in the hills. We shall never surrender.

—Winston Churchill

28a Using Parallelism for Paired Items and Items in a Series

For clarity and to avoid awkwardness, express paired ideas and items in a series in parallel form. Join subordinate clauses with similarly structured clauses, join phrases with similarly structured phrases, and join individual terms with other terms of the same form.

1. Items paired with a conjunction such as *and* or *but*

> *More about*
> Coordinating
> conjunctions,
> 611–12

Coordinating conjunctions include *and, but, for, nor, or, so,* and *yet.*

▶ Girls learn at a young age to be passive and ~~that they should be~~ deferential.

The original uses *and* to pair an infinitive phrase (*to be passive*) with a subordinate clause (*that they should be deferential*); the revision uses *and* to join a pair of adjectives (*passive* and *deferential*).

▶ The course always covers the twentieth century through World War II
   also touches
but sometimes ~~touching~~ on the beginning of the Cold War ~~is possible also~~.

In the revision, the verbs *covers* and *touches on* are in parallel form.

Deceptive Parallelism Parallel structure is found in most languages, so the concept will probably not be unfamiliar to you. Use caution, however, to ensure that items that seem parallel are all grammatically equivalent. For example, in "He spoke only positively and friendly about his previous professor," *positively* and *friendly* appear parallel, but *positively* is an adverb whereas *friendly* is an adjective. To be parallel, the sentence requires restating along these lines: "He had only positive and friendly things to say about his previous professor."

2. Items paired with correlative conjunctions

Conjunctions such as *both . . . and, either . . . or, neither . . . nor,* and *not only . . . but also* are **correlative conjunctions.** They come in pairs, and they link ideas of equal importance. Readers expect items linked by a correlative conjunction to be parallel. To be parallel, however, the items linked by the correlative conjunctions must have the same grammatical form.

More about Coordinating conjunctions, 611–12

FAULTY PARALLELISM	The defense attorney not only convinced the jury that her client had no motive for committing the crime, but also was nowhere near the scene of the crime when it occurred.

This suggests that the defense attorney, not her client, was nowhere near the crime scene.

STILL FAULTY	The defense attorney convinced the jury not only that her client had no motive for committing the crime, but also was nowhere near the scene of the crime when it occurred.

A clause beginning with *that* follows *not only,* so a clause beginning with *that* should follow *but also.*

REVISED	The defense attorney convinced the jury not only that her client had no motive for committing the crime, but also that he was nowhere near the scene of the crime when it occurred.

3. Items in a series

Like paired items, three or more equivalent items in a series should be in parallel form.

FAULTY PARALLELISM	The detectives secured the crime scene, examined it for clues, and the witnesses were then called in for questioning.
REVISED	The detectives secured the crime scene, examined it for clues, and then called in the witnesses for questioning.

Tech Parallelism and Computer Style Checkers

A computer's style checker cannot identify ideas that merit parallel treatment in an otherwise grammatical sentence.

> **More about**
Clear compari-
sons, 702–05
Including function
words, 728–29

28b Maintaining Parallelism in Comparisons

When you compare two items with *than* or *as,* the items should be in the same grammatical form.

> ▶ Getting into debt is unfortunately much easier than ~~to get~~ *getting* out of it.

28c Including Function Words to Maintain Parallelism

Words such as articles (*a, an, the*), conjunctions, and prepositions indicate the relationships among other words in a sentence. They should be included or repeated as needed in linked items for clarity and grammar as well as for parallelism.

> ▶ The trail leads over high mountain passes and *through* dense forests.

Trails lead *over* passes but *through* forests.

> ### EXERCISE 28.2 Correcting parallelism errors

Correct any errors in parallelism in the following sentences.

EXAMPLE

This spot offers a good view not only of herons but ~~you can~~ also ~~see~~ *of* egrets.

1. Many types of wading birds, some rare, are attracted to this island to rest during migration, to feed, and they nest here as well.

2. Perhaps surprisingly, this habitat is located not in a national park or wildlife refuge but it is found in the middle of New York harbor.

3. However, until ten or fifteen years ago, the area was inhospitable to wildlife because it was missing one crucial factor: not food or shelter but the presence of clean water.

4. Starting with the Clean Water Act of 1972 and accelerating within the last fifteen years with state legislation, regional planning, and as more federal funds were appropriated, the water in the harbor has become hospitable to wildlife.

5. Today, more than 2,000 pairs of shorebirds, including not only several species of herons, snowy egrets, but also great egrets, and glossy ibis nest on the different islands.

Writing
Responsibly   Using Parallelism to Clarify Relationships among Ideas

An important component of the writing process is figuring out the *relationships* among your ideas and making those relationships clear to your readers. As you revise, ask yourself questions like these: What is the cause and what is the effect? What items are truly a part of the group and what items are not? Which ideas are important and which ideas provide supporting information?

Using parallelism can help you emphasize for your reader that certain ideas are of equal impor-

tance. (Coordination and subordination, discussed in the previous chapter, can also help you emphasize that ideas or information are of equal or unequal importance.)

Experimenting with some of the techniques you are learning in this chapter, and in other chapters in this part, can lead to new insights about your topic.

to AUDIENCE

28d Maintaining Parallelism for Items in Lists and Outlines

Each item in a list or an outline should be in the same grammatical form as the others.

1. Items in a list

Whenever you have a list of three or more items, those items should be in the same grammatical form. The following list is difficult to read in its draft form because the first and third items begin with independent clauses, whereas the other three begin with a noun followed by a bit of commentary. The revision puts them all in the noun followed by commentary form.

DRAFT LIST

Among the top ten most healthful foods, these are my favorites:

1. <u>Avocados are delicious unadorned.</u> I also enjoy them sliced in half with the hole filled with a mixture of olive oil and lime juice.

2. <u>I like nuts because they are so portable.</u>

3. <u>Berries.</u> All of them are delicious, except blackberries.

4. <u>Yogurt.</u> I avoid the kind with fruit on the bottom.

5. <u>Garlic.</u> I like it, but it doesn't like me.

REVISED

Among the top ten most healthful foods, these are my favorites:

1. <u>Avocados.</u> They are delicious unadorned. I also enjoy them sliced in half with the hole filled with a mixture of olive oil and lime juice.

2. <u>Nuts.</u> I like them because they are so portable.

3. <u>Berries.</u> All of them are delicious, except blackberries.

4. <u>Yogurt.</u> I avoid the kind with fruit on the bottom.

5. <u>Garlic.</u> I like it, but it doesn't like me.

2. Items in outlines

Maintain parallelism in outlines and headings by keeping all items at the same level in the same form. In the original version of the following outline, three of the top-level headings—I, II, and IV—are noun phrases whereas III is a question. Likewise, under heading I, the first subheading begins with a noun whereas the second and third are *gerund* phrases, and under heading IV, the last item is an independent clause. Revising the outline so that the headings are parallel makes it easier to understand.

gerund The *-ing* form of a verb used as a noun

DRAFT OUTLINE	REVISED OUTLINE
I. Types of literary fraud	I. Types of literary fraud
A. Plagiarism	A. Plagiarism
B. Forging documents	B. Forgery
C. Misrepresenting the facts	C. Misrepresentation
II. Examples of literary fraud	II. Examples of literary fraud
A. Kaavya Viswanathan	A. Kaavya Viswanathan
B. Clifford Irving	B. Clifford Irving
C. James Frey	C. James Frey
III. Why do people commit literary fraud?	III. Motives for literary fraud
A. Financial gain	A. Financial gain
B. Personal glory	B. Personal glory
C. Insecurity	C. Insecurity
D. Weak writing skills	D. Weak writing skills
E. Busy schedule	E. Busy schedule
IV. Problems with literary fraud	IV. Problems with literary fraud
A. Copyright infringement	A. Copyright infringement
B. Breach of faith	B. Breach of faith
C. Readers take actions based on erroneous assumptions	C. Reader actions based on erroneous assumptions

> **EXERCISE 28.3 Parallelism in lists**

Correct the parallelism errors in the following list.

Favorite Leisure Activities

1. Reading, especially contemporary novels
2. I really enjoy going to the movies with my friends.
3. To hike in the woods and to camp out
4. On the weekends, I enjoy online role-playing game marathons
5. Listening to classic rock and folk music

28e Using Parallelism to Create Emphasis

Placing ideas in parallel form highlights their differences and similarities.

> All the images are copies of the same original, the same size, and ~~they have equal space between them~~ within a grid of rows and columns.

all are ^

all are equally spaced ^

More about Parallelism and emphasis, 558–59

As the passage from Lincoln's Gettysburg address at the beginning of this chapter illustrates, parallelism can be a forceful tool for emphasizing important ideas. John F. Kennedy provides another example in his famous Inaugural Address. Notice how the president's parallelisms generate an almost musical cadence that drives us toward his concluding point.

> Let every nation know, whether it wishes us well or ill, that we shall pay any price, bear any burden, meet any hardship, support any friend, oppose any foe to assure the survival and the success of liberty.
>
> —John F. Kennedy

> **EXERCISE 28.4 Parallelism and emphasis**

Use parallelism to combine and emphasize the ideas in the following groups of sentences.

EXAMPLE

The ancestor of the modern horse evolved in North America
                                              ago,
about 4 million years ago. ~~It~~ spread to Eurasia over the Bering land
bridge, and then   ^
~~bridge. Horses~~ became extinct in North America at the end of the last
    ^
Ice Age about 12,000 years ago.

1. Scientists have long debated where and when the horse was domesticated. They have also debated where and when dogs and the pig were domesticated. The time and place of the domestication of other animals, such as cattle, sheep, and goats, is much clearer.

2. Dogs were domesticated before horses. Cattle were domesticated before horses. Goats were domesticated before horses. Pigs were domesticated before horses. Sheep were domesticated before horses.

3. Scientists now believe that horses were domesticated about 6,000 years ago in Central Asia. This conclusion is based on DNA evidence. It is also based on evidence obtained from archaeological remains. It is also based on studies of contemporary nomadic peoples whose lifestyles may resemble those of the people who first domesticated the horse.

4. All the evidence about horse domestication points to a complicated process. This process went on over a long time. This process occurred at many different places. This process was further complicated by climate changes during the last Ice Age, which altered the wild horses' habitat and forced them to migrate north.

Make It **Your Own**

Reread three pieces of your recent writing and identify examples of parallelism. Look for faulty parallelism, and if you find any, make a note in the margins of the paper identifying which section of this chapter explains the revision. Add this to your list of areas to consider as you revise your prose.

Text Credits

p. 543: Abraham Lincoln, The Gettysburg Address, November 19, 1863. **p. 543:** Dickens, Charles, *A Tale of Two Cities* (1859). **p. 543:** Austen, Jane, *Mansfield Park* (1814). **p. 544:** Cheever, Susan, *Drinking in America: Our Secret History.* Copyright © 2015 by Susan Cheever. Twelve/Hachette Book Group. **p. 544:** Winston Churchill, speech to House of Commons, 4 June 1940. Copyright © Winston S. Churchill. Reproduced with permission of Curtis Brown Ltd., London, on behalf of The Estate of Winston S. Churchill. **p. 549:** John F. Kennedy, Inaugural Address, January 20, 1961.

IN THIS CHAPTER

a. Varying sentence length, structure, 552

b. Varying sentence openings, 553

c. Creating emphasis with rhythm, 555

d. Creating emphasis with punctuation, 557

e. Using questions, commands, exclamations, 558

f. Using strategic repetition, 558

g. Choosing emphatic verbs, 559

h. Choosing active or passive voice, 559

© Burstein Collection/Corbis

In this painting, *At the Opera*, artist Mary Cassatt captures our interest with a variety of visual elements, among them the large figure of the woman in the foreground; the more sketchily rendered figures in the background; the curving form of the balconies; the bright points of red and white; and the contrasting large, dark areas. Cassatt also structures the painting to emphasize certain elements over others and to direct our attention to a story unfolding within the scene. Our eyes go first to the woman in the foreground; then we follow her gaze through her opera glasses and let the curve of the balcony railing draw our attention to the upper left, where a male figure also is looking through opera glasses—not toward the stage, however, but at the woman in the foreground.

Writers also use variety and emphasis to capture and hold their readers' attention and to direct those readers to the subtleties of the story being told. Speakers use intonation, tone of voice, and timing to avoid monotony and emphasize or de-emphasize particular words or phrases. Writers use variety and emphasis to help readers "hear" the words of the text in their mind's ear.

Quick Reference — Achieving Variety and Emphasis

- Vary sentence length and structure. (552)
- Vary sentence openings. (553)
- Use rhythm strategically. (555)
- Choose appropriate punctuation. (557)
- Introduce questions, commands, and exclamations when appropriate. (558)
- Use strategic repetition. (558)
- Choose emphatic verbs and favor the active voice. (559)

simple sentence One independent clause and no subordinate clauses

compound sentence Two or more independent clauses and no subordinate clauses

complex sentence One independent clause with at least one subordinate clause

compound-complex sentence Two or more independent clauses with one or more subordinate clauses

29a Varying Sentence Length and Structure

Confronting readers with page after page of sentences of uniform length—long, short, or in between—can tire them and make it hard for them to pick out important details. To hold readers' attention and direct it to the points you want to emphasize, vary the length of your sentences and include a mix of sentence structures: *simple, compound, complex,* and *compound-complex.*

Short sentences deliver information concisely and dramatically. They are most emphatic, however, when they are mixed with longer sentences. In the following passage, too many short sentences in a row create a choppy effect, leaving the reader with the impression that each point is equally important. The revision combines most of the short sentences into longer sentences that clarify the relationship among the ideas the writer wants to convey. The writer's main point is now dramatically isolated in the one short sentence that remains.

DRAFT The whole planet is at risk. We need to put a stop to the wild spread of this disease. The key is education. First, we should educate those living with the virus. Then we should let them educate the world. They can help us win this war against HIV. They can help other people understand that everyone is vulnerable.

REVISION With the whole planet at risk, we need to put a stop to the wild spread of this disease. The key is education. First, we should educate those living with the virus; then we should let them educate the world. They can help us win this war against HIV by helping other people understand that everyone is vulnerable.

→ **EXERCISE 29.1 Editing for varied sentence length and structure**

Revise the paragraph to create a more coherent result with a mix of sentence lengths and types.

In Central America and Mexico 3,000 years ago, people played a ballgame. It was called *Tlatchtil* in Náhuatl, which was their language. It used solid rubber balls; they weighed about 6 lbs. They kept the ball in motion by hitting it with their hips. It was played in elaborate stone ballcourts with rings on the sides. The team that got the ball through the ring won. There is some evidence of ballgames ending in sacrifice of players to the gods. We don't know whether the winners or the losers died. Other evidence suggests the game was played to settle conflicts and avoid war.

29b **Varying Sentence Openings**

In the default structure of an English sentence, the subject comes first, then the verb, and then the direct object if there is one. Reflecting this structure, most sentences start with the subject. However, a long string of subject-first sentences can make your text monotonous. Use modifying clauses and phrases to vary your sentence openings and to emphasize important information.

Adverbs and adverbial phrases and clauses   Where you place an *adverb*, and the phrases and clauses that function as adverbs, affects the rhythm of a sentence and the information it emphasizes.

adverb A word that modifies a verb, adjective, other adverb, or entire phrase or clause and that specifies how, where, when, and to what extent or degree

ADVERBIAL SUBORDINATE CLAUSE

Stocks can be a risky investment because they can lose value.

Because they can lose value, stocks can be a risky investment.

Stocks, because they can lose value, can be a risky investment.

ADVERBIAL PREPOSITIONAL PHRASES

We were in the same lab for physics class last semester.

Last semester, we were in the same lab for physics class.

For physics class, we were in the same lab last semester.

> *More about* Sentence structure, 613–27

NOTE Moving an adverb can sometimes alter the meaning of a sentence. Consider these two examples:

- ▸ The test was surprisingly hard.
- ▸ Surprisingly, the test was hard.

In the first, *surprisingly* modifies *hard*, suggesting that the writer found the test harder than expected; in the second, *surprisingly* modifies the whole clause that follows it, suggesting that the writer expected the test to be easy.

Adjectival phrases   The placement of *adjectives* and most adjectival phrases and clauses is less flexible than the placement of adverbs. However, participles and *participial phrases*, which act as adjectives, can often come at the beginning of a sentence as well as after the terms they modify.

adjective A word that modifies a noun or pronoun with descriptive or limiting information
participial phrase A phrase in which the present or past participle acts as an adjective

- ▸ New York City's subway system, flooded by torrential rains, shut down at the height of the morning rush hour.
- ▸ Flooded by torrential rains, New York City's subway system shut down at the height of the morning rush hour.

An adjective phrase that functions as a *subject complement* can also sometimes be repositioned at the beginning of a sentence.

▶ The Mariana Trench is almost seven miles deep, making it the lowest place on the surface of the earth.

▶ Almost seven miles deep, the Mariana Trench is the lowest place on the surface of the earth.

More about Placement of adjectives, 697–705

Appositives and absolute phrases   An *appositive* is a noun or noun phrase that renames another noun or noun phrase. Because they designate the same thing, the appositive and the original term can switch positions.

▶ The governor, New York's highest official, ordered an investigation into the subway system's failure.

▶ New York's highest official, the governor, ordered an investigation into the subway system's failure.

An *absolute phrase,* consisting of a noun or pronoun with a participle, modifies an entire independent clause. It can often fall either before or after the clause it modifies.

▶ The task finally completed, the workers headed for the parking lot.

▶ The workers headed for the parking lot, the task finally completed.

More about Transitional expressions, 60–61

Transitional expressions   A *transitional expression* relates the information in one sentence to material that precedes or follows. Its placement affects the emphasis that falls on other parts of the sentence. The second passage below, for example, calls more attention to Superman's distinctiveness than the first does.

▶ Most comic book characters from the 1930s quickly fell into obscurity. However, Superman was not one of them.

▶ Most comic book characters from the 1930s quickly fell into obscurity. Superman, however, was not one of them.

▶ **EXERCISE 29.2 Varying sentence openings**

Revise the following sentences to begin with something other than the subject.

EXAMPLE
Soaring in search of food, ravens
~~Ravens~~ patrol the misty blue sky high above the valley, ~~soaring in search of food~~.

1. The Canaan Valley, one of the highest valleys east of the Mississippi, was designated a National Natural Landmark in 1974.

2. This ecosystem, with its many species of plants and animals, is an example of northern forest.

3. It seems out of place, located here in West Virginia.

4. The valley is more than 3,000 feet deep and enjoys cool summers and snowy winters.

5. The valley is likely to remain wild and natural for many years to come because it is protected by federal and state governments.

29c Creating Emphasis with Rhythm

Sentences, like music, have rhythm, and within that rhythm, some beats get more stress than others. Readers readily notice the beginning of a sentence, where they usually find the subject, and they notice the end, where everything wraps up. Take advantage of readers' habits by slotting important or striking information into those positions. In the following example, the writer changed the subject of the sentence from *ready availability* to the more significant *free news* and moved *financial ruin* to the end, dramatically underscoring the seriousness of the challenge newspapers face.

DRAFT   The ready availability of free news on the Internet threatens financial ruin for traditional newspapers.

REVISED   Free news, readily available on the Internet, threatens traditional newspapers with financial ruin.

A common way to organize information in longer sentences is with a cumulative or loose structure. A *cumulative sentence* begins with the subject and verb of an independent clause and accumulates additional information in subsequent modifying phrases and clauses.

> That's the news from Lake Wobegon, where all the women are strong, all the men are good-looking, and all the children are above average.
>
> —Garrison Keillor, tag line from the radio show *A Prairie Home Companion*

A *periodic sentence*, in contrast, reserves the independent clause for the end, preceded by modifying details. The effect is to build suspense that highlights key information when it finally arrives.

> Through the center of town, up the strip, past the housing developments and shopping malls, street lights giving way to the thin streaming illumination of the

headlights, trees crowding the asphalt in a black unbroken wall: that was the way to Greasy Lake.

—T. Coraghessan Boyle, "Greasy Lake"

An *interrupted periodic sentence* begins with the subject of the independent clause but leaves the conclusion of the clause to the end, separating the two parts with modifying details. In the following example, the subject of the sentence is highlighted in yellow, and the predicate is highlighted in blue.

> The archaeologist Howard Carter, peering through the small opening to the main chamber of Tutankhamen's tomb at treasures hidden from view for more than three millennia, when asked what he saw, replied "wonderful things."

An *inversion* is a sentence in which, contrary to normal English word order, the verb precedes the subject. Inverted sentences call attention to themselves. Used sparingly, they can help you emphasize a point or create a sense of dramatic tension.

> verb   subj.
> ▸ Into the middle of town rode the stranger.

Developing an Ear for Sentence Variety Many of the sentence structures that add variety to written English are uncommon in conversation and as a result may not come naturally to you even if you are fluent in conversational English. To develop an ear for sentence variety in your academic writing, try going through this chapter and imitating some of the structures it describes with examples of your own. Ask an instructor or another skilled writer of English to check your work to see if you have produced effective sentences.

▸ **EXERCISE 29.3 Cumulative and periodic sentences**

Combine the sentences in each of the following passages into a single cumulative sentence. Then combine them again, this time into a periodic sentence.

CUMULATIVE SENTENCE

                                                            , which
Mosses generally live in shady areas. ~~These areas~~ are more likely to be
        and therefore reduce
                    ∧
damp. ~~This reduces~~ the risk of the moss drying out.

PERIODIC SENTENCE

Because mosses need to avoid drying out and shady areas tend to be
~~Mosses generally live in shady areas. These areas are more likely to be~~
damp, mosses generally live in shady areas.
~~damp. This reduces the risk of the moss drying out.~~

1. Moss is often killed by gardeners. It can inhibit the growth of small plants. It absorbs water through its leaves, preventing the water and fertilizer from reaching the roots of plants around it.

2. Moss is important in Japanese temple gardens. Some believe it to be calming. It is also used in bonsai gardening. The moss is believed to add a sense of age.

3. Water run-off from roofs fills sewers and is a problem in many cities. Modern sustainable buildings often have green roofs. Moss is a common plant for green roofs. It is light in weight. It does not have deep roots. It absorbs water.

29d Creating Emphasis with Punctuation

One way to draw your readers' attention to significant material is to place it at the end of a sentence after a colon or dash.

> **More about**
> Colons, 828–30
> Dashes, 824–26

▶ According to photographer William Klein, the advertising campaign for fashion designer John Galliano wasn't just influenced by Klein's visual techniques—it stole them.

▶ The judge had two words for Galliano's use of Klein's signature visual style: copyright infringement.

You can also draw attention to nonessential phrases or clauses within an independent clause when you set them off with dashes instead of commas.

> **More about**
> Essential and nonessential modifiers, 787–89

▶ The judge had two words—copyright infringement—for Galliano's use of Klein's signature visual style.

The punctuation between two independent clauses can affect the way readers perceive the relationship between them. A dash (as we have just seen) or a period creates a more emphatic separation than a semicolon or a comma and coordinating conjunction.

> **More about**
> Periods, 820–21
> Semicolons, 796–802
> Commas, 778–95

▶ The jury convicted the defendants. The judge sentenced them to life.

▶ The jury convicted the defendants; the judge sentenced them to life.

▶ The jury convicted the defendants, and the judge sentenced them to life.

29e Using Questions, Commands, and Exclamations

More about
Sentence categories, 625–27

Most sentences are *declarative*: They make a statement—declare something—about their subjects. Other types of sentences include questions, commands, and exclamations. When used sparingly, these can add variety to prose and draw attention to important ideas. Overused, they sound gimmicky or childish.

Questions in academic writing tend to be *rhetorical*; they are meant to call attention to an issue, not to elicit an answer.

> [F]or all our focus on happiness it is by no means clear that we are happier as a result. Might we not even say that our contemporary concern is something of an inauspicious sign, belying a deep anxiety and doubt about the object of our pursuit? Does the fact that we worry so much about being happy suggest that we are not?
>
> —Darrin M. McMahon, "The Pursuit of Happiness in Perspective"

More about
Person, 458–59

Commands are a type of second-person sentence: The subject of a command, even when unstated, is always *you*. The second person is best reserved for addressing the reader directly, and commands, in particular, are useful for describing a process or conveying advice.

> When in doubt tell the truth.
>
> —Mark Twain, *Following the Equator*

Exclamations are emphatic statements or expressions of strong emotion. Interjections are exclamatory words that stand alone within a sentence. Both are usually punctuated with exclamation marks, and both are rare in academic writing.

> The one fact that I would cry from every housetop is this: the Good Life is waiting for us—here and now!
>
> —B. F. Skinner, *Walden II*

29f Using Strategic Repetition

Redundancy and other forms of unnecessary repetition clutter writing and distract readers. Repetition is sometimes necessary, however, for clarity and to maintain parallelism.

Writers can also use repetition strategically for emphasis, calling attention to important ideas. Repetition for emphasis works especially well within parallel structures, as in this sentence from a student project.

Some children are never told that they are adopted, never given the opportunity to search for their biological parents.

—Jessica Toro, Syracuse University

More about
Parallelism,
542–50

Toro could have used *or* instead of the second *never,* but the repetition dramatically underscores her concern about the consequences of a particular policy toward adopted children.

29g Creating Emphasis with Emphatic Verbs

Verbs that describe an action directly are often more emphatic than verbs like *be, have,* or *cause* that combine with nouns or adjectives to describe an action indirectly.

► Many economists ~~have a belief~~ that higher gasoline taxes would *believe* be ~~beneficial to~~ the economy in the long run. The increased costs *benefit* would ~~have a stimulating effect on~~ research into alternate energy *stimulate* sources and eventually ~~cause a reduction~~ in both carbon emissions *reduce* and our dependence on oil.

29h Choosing the Active or Passive Voice

In an active-voice sentence, the subject performs the action of the verb; in a passive-voice sentence, the subject receives the action of the verb. Active-voice sentences are usually more emphatic, direct, and concise than their passive voice counterparts.

More about
Voice in verbs,
665, 680–83
Passive voice
and wordiness,
524–26

ACTIVE VOICE: EMPHATIC

Rising oil prices stimulate research into alternate energy sources.

PASSIVE VOICE: UNEMPHATIC

Research into alternate energy sources is stimulated by rising oil prices.

However, if you want to emphasize the recipient of an action over the performer, or agent, of the action, the passive voice can be an appropriate choice. In this famous sentence from his address to the nation on December 8, 1941, for example, President Franklin Delano Roosevelt used the passive voice to focus on the United States as the victim of the attack on Pearl Harbor.

> ▸ Yesterday, December 7th, 1941—a date which will live in infamy— the United States of America was suddenly and deliberately attacked by naval and air forces of the Empire of Japan.

Because it can allow the agent to remain unidentified, the passive voice can also be an appropriate choice when the identity of the agent is unknown or unimportant.

> ▸ According to the coroner, the victim had been murdered between 3 and 4 in the morning.
>
> The identity of the murderer is unknown.

> ▸ *The Second Sex*, a major work in feminist philosophy, was first published back in 1949.
>
> The focus is on the date of publication, not the specific identity of the author.

Similarly, in science writing, the passive voice allows the description of procedures without constant reference to the individuals who carried them out.

> ▪ The effects of human activities on seagrasses were studied at Sandy Neck and Centerville beaches from 31 March 2014 to 30 March 2016.

Writing Responsibly | Voice and Responsibility

Because the passive voice allows the agent of an action to remain unnamed, it lends itself to misuse by people avoiding responsibility for their own or others' mistakes and misdeeds. Consider, for example, the classic dodge of the cornered politician or bureaucrat: "Mistakes were made."

Be on the lookout for this evasive use of the passive voice in your own writing and the writing of others. It is a usage that comes all too readily to hand when we need to convey unflattering or damaging information about ourselves or those we represent.

to TOPIC

▸ **EXERCISE 29.4 Emphatic verbs, active verbs**

Revise each of the following sentences, replacing indirect expressions with emphatic verbs and, when appropriate, changing verbs from passive to active voice.

EXAMPLE

> *believe that the founders of Plymouth Colony advocated*

Many people ~~have a belief that Plymouth Colony was founded by advocates of~~
                                                                  ∧

religious freedom.

1. The Pilgrims, as they came to be called, experienced persecution in England and made a decision to move to Holland.

2. In Holland, however, many members of the congregation found it a struggle to find employment and experienced economic suffering.

3. In addition, parents found the influence of Dutch language and culture on their children a source of worry and a threat to the group's survival.

4. Therefore, in 1619, a decision was made by the Pilgrims' leaders to move the entire group to the New World.

5. Although the Pilgrims wanted freedom to worship as they pleased, it was not assumed by them that religious freedom was desirable for all.

6. Rather, they were of the opinion that there was one proper way to worship and that proper way was the one observed by them.

Make It **Your Own**

Reread three pieces of your recent writing and edit them for variety and emphasis using the strategies covered in this chapter. If you find many sentences needing revision, add this to your list of areas to consider as you revise your prose.

Work **Together**

Working in a small group, review three examples of different types of writing—such as an advertisement, informational text, and a short story—and analyze the authors' use of the strategies covered in this chapter. What did each of you see that others did not? Write a few sentences reflecting on how this collaborative activity might help you revise your own work in the future.

Text Credits

p. 555: Keillor, Garrison, A Prairie Home Companion. **p. 555:** Boyle, T. Coraghessan, "Greasy Lake" *Greasy Lake and Other Stories*, copyright © 1979, 1981, 1982, 1983, 1984, 1985 by T. Coraghessan Boyle. (Penguin Books, 1986). **p. 558:** McMahon, Darrin M., "The Pursuit of Happiness in Perspective" *Cato Unbound*, April 8, 2007. **p. 558:** Mark Twain, *Following the Equator* (1897). **p. 558:** Skinner, B. F., *Walden II*, copyright © 1948, 1976 by B. F. Skinner. (Hackett Publishing Co., 2005). **p. 559:** Jessica Toro, Syracuse University.

30 Choosing Appropriate Language

IN THIS CHAPTER

a. Using language in context, 562

b. Avoiding biased, hurtful language, 566

Mick Stevens The New Yorker Collection/The Cartoon Bank

"We have only jobs here, Mr. Sanderson, not 'gigs.'"

During a job interview, both the applicant and the interviewer need to dress appropriately, behave appropriately, and use language appropriately. Neither would be likely to show up in a bathing suit, jump up and down on a couch, use language that might offend the other, or, like the applicant in this cartoon, refer to the position casually as a "gig." Such issues of appropriateness apply to your writing as well. In every document you write, use language that is appropriate to the context and avoids bias.

30a Using Language in Context

We all adjust our language to suit our audience and purpose. No form of the language is intrinsically better or more correct than another, but certain forms have become standard for addressing a broad audience in an academic setting or in the workplace. In this context, using appropriate language usually means the following:

- Avoiding nonstandard dialects
- Avoiding regionalisms, colloquialisms, and slang

- Avoiding overly technical terminology (jargon and neologisms)
- Adopting a straightforward tone, one that is neither overly informal nor pompously inflated

1. Nonstandard dialects

A *dialect* is a variant of a language with its own distinctive pronunciation, vocabulary, and grammar. A linguist once quipped that the only difference between the standard form of a language and its other dialects is that the standard form has an army and a navy. The standard form, in other words, became standard because it is the dialect of the elite and powerful.

Nonstandard dialects of English are not "bad" English, as many mistakenly believe. If you speak a dialect like Appalachian English or African American Vernacular English and you are addressing an audience of peers from your community, then your home dialect *is* appropriate. If you are addressing a broader audience or writing in an academic or workplace context, however, the dialect known as Standard American English, or Edited English, is usually the appropriate choice.

> *More about*
> The grammar
> of Standard
> American
> English, 602–27

2. Regionalisms, colloquialisms, and slang

Regionalisms are expressions that are characteristic of particular areas. Saying the car "needs washed" is acceptable in Pittsburgh but not in Boston. The expression "I might could do it" might be acceptable in Pikeville, Kentucky, but not in Des Moines, Iowa. Regionalisms can be appropriate in conversation or informal writing but are usually out of place in formal academic writing.

> *be able to*
> ▸ Many scientists believe that we might ~~could~~ slow global warming if
>
> we can reduce carbon emissions.

Colloquialisms are informal expressions common in speech but usually out of place in formal writing.

> *children*
> ▸ An R rating designates a movie that is not appropriate for ~~kids~~
>
> *an adult.*
> under 17 who are not accompanied by a ~~grown up~~.

Used judiciously, however, the occasional colloquialism can add verve to your writing.

> ▸ The musicians were only kids, none of them more than ten years old, but they played like seasoned professionals.

Writing
Responsibly | **Avoiding Online Shortcuts**

Users of text messaging, instant messaging, and social networking sites have developed a host of acronyms and abbreviations—like *BTW* for "by the way" and *IMO* for "in my opinion"—that save typing time and space on the tiny screens of mobile phones. With the possible exception of informal email, these expressions are almost never appropriate in other contexts, particularly not in academic or business writing. The same applies to emoticons and emojis like :-) and 👍 as well as other shortcuts such as writing entirely in lowercase without punctuation, as in *i saw her this am.*

to SELF

Slang is the extremely informal, inventive, often colorful (and sometimes off-color) vocabulary of a particular group. In general, slang is inappropriate in formal writing, but as with colloquial language, when used sparingly and judiciously, it can enliven a sentence and help emphasize an important point.

3. Neologisms and jargon

The world changes. Technology advances, new cultural trends emerge, and new research alters our understanding of ourselves and gives rise to new fields of study. As these changes occur, people necessarily invent new words and expressions—*neologisms.* Some neologisms gain wide currency and establish themselves as acceptable vocabulary for formal writing. Other neologisms, however, soon disappear or never move from informal to formal usage. When you consider using a neologism, ask yourself whether a more familiar synonym might serve as well. If the neologism is necessary but you are not sure your audience will be familiar with it, define it.

> ▶ Some instructors use wikis as tools for teaching collaborative writing.
> *, websites that allow a group of users to create and edit content collectively,*

The term *jargon* refers to the specialized vocabulary of a particular profession or discipline. Doctors speak of *adenomas* and *electroencephalograms.* Automobile mechanics speak of *camber angles* and *ring-and-pinion gears.* Lawyers speak of *effluxions of time* and *words of procreation.* English professors speak of *discursive historicity* and *terministic screens.* For an audience of specialists, this kind of insider vocabulary can efficiently communicate concepts that might otherwise take several sentences, even paragraphs, to explain. If you are addressing other specialists, jargon may be appropriate. If you are addressing a general audience, however, it is usually inappropriate. In most cases, avoid it. When a specialized term is needed, define it.

when their lease expired.

▸ The tenants lost the apartment ~~due to the effluxion of time on~~
   ^
   ~~their lease.~~

4. Appropriate formality

When you speak or write to close friends and intimates from your own
age group, your language will probably—and appropriately—be relaxed and
informal, sprinkled with dialect, slang, and colloquial expressions. Writing
for most college courses or in the workplace, however, requires a formal
tone and clear, straightforward language free of slang and colloquialisms.
Clear and straightforward, however, should not mean simpleminded or condescending. Use challenging vocabulary if it aptly expresses your meaning,
but do not try to impress your readers by inflating your writing with fancy
words mined from a thesaurus.

> *More about*
> Using a thesaurus,
> 582

INAPPROPRIATELY INFORMAL	Tarantino is always ripping scenes from earlier flicks to use in his own.
POMPOUS	It is a characteristic stylistic mannerism of the auteur Quentin Tarantino to allusively amalgamate scenic quotations from the repertory of his cinematic forebears in his own oeuvre.
APPROPRIATE	In his movies, the director Quentin Tarantino routinely alludes to scenes from earlier movies.

> **EXERCISE 30.1 Editing for language in context**

Edit the following passage to establish appropriate formality for a college paper and to eliminate inappropriate regionalisms, colloquialisms,
slang, and jargon.

There are many reasons why folks are now trying essentially to effect a
truncation of their consumption of meat. Some believe that having less
meat will make them healthier. Some are desirous of losing weight by cutting their intake of fat. Some are doing it merely to be copycats. Regardless
of the motivation, nutrition experts say that reducing meat consumption is
not rocket science and can be effectuated by following some simple steps.

To begin with, chill out about getting enough protein. Plants supply protein too, and some, such as spinach and lentils, proffer greater quantities
of protein per calorie than a cheeseburger does. Per capita, Americans
currently scarf up about a half pound of meat per day. The biggest bump
in the road can be cooking more meat than you need, so start buying less

meat than you usually do. When you have less meat on hand, you'll eat less of it. Have a go at planning meals with meat on the side of the plate instead of smack dab in the middle. Ramp up the amount of vegetables you buy, and dig up recipes for yummy vegetable dishes. Promulgate some rules for yourself; for example, you may want to have meatless breakfasts and lunches, and then eat whatever you like for dinners. Buckle down on this, and you'll soon find that meat plays a smaller role in your meals.

30b Avoiding Biased or Hurtful Language

> *More about*
> Stereotyping,
> 140–43, 159–60

Biased language unfairly or offensively characterizes a particular group and, by extension, its individual members. It can be as blatant as a hatefully uttered racial, ethnic, or sexual slur, but it can also be subtle and unintentional, as in thoughtless stereotyping or an inappropriately applied label.

A **stereotype** is a simplified, uncritical, and often negative generalization about an entire group of people: *Blondes are ditzy; athletes are weak students; lawyers are unscrupulous; politicians are dishonest.* Even when they seem positive, stereotypes lump people together in ways that offensively ignore their individuality. In an article in the *New York Times,* for example, Chinese American writer Vivian S. Toy remembers among her "painful experiences of being different" that a college adviser once recommended that she switch her major to biology "since Chinese are better suited for the sciences."

We label people whenever we call attention to a particular characteristic about them. *Labeling* is appropriate when it is relevant.

▶ Laura Grimm was the first female athletic director in the Western Pennsylvania Interscholastic Athletic League.

Labeling is inappropriate, and usually offensive, when it is irrelevant.

▶ Muhammad Ali, an African American, was a famous boxer.

To appreciate how irrelevant the label "African American" is in that last sentence, consider the following:

▶ Babe Ruth, a man, was a famous baseball player.

1. Gender bias

English has no pronouns that designate an individual person without also designating that person's gender (*she, he, her, him, hers, his, herself, himself*). This lack creates problems when a writer uses the singular to refer generically to a whole class of people or to people in general.

▶ The sensible student is careful what [*he? she?*] posts about [*himself? herself?*] on social networking sites such as Instagram or Twitter.

Until about the 1970s, the conventional solution to this problem was to use the masculine pronoun as the generic pronoun. In other words, depending on context, *he* referred either to a particular male human or to "he or she," a generic human of either gender. On the other hand, *she* always meant "female," never "she or he." Similarly, the terms *man* and *mankind* could refer generically to humanity as a whole, but *woman* and *womankind* only to women. Since the 1970s, writers have been replacing this usage—together with other vocabulary that reinforces gender stereotypes—with gender-neutral alternatives.

***Avoid generic* he**   One way to avoid the generic *he*—and often the most graceful way—is to switch from singular to plural.

> ~~The sensible student~~ is careful what ~~he posts~~ about ~~himself~~ on
> Sensible students are   they post   themselves
> social networking sites such as Instagram or Twitter.

Another alternative is to use *he or she* (or *she or he*).

▶ The sensible student is careful what he or she posts on social networking sites.

Be sparing with this option, however; used many times in quick succession, it becomes awkward.

AWKWARD   The sensible student is careful what he or she posts about himself or herself on the social networking sites he or she frequents.

> *More about*
Pronoun-
antecedent
agreement,
658–63

NOTE The use of *they* as a generic pronoun for singular antecedents is common in speech, and publications such as *The Washington Post* have endorsed it. Many readers consider this usage ungrammatical, however; when in doubt, avoid it.

> ▸ ~~The sensible student is~~ *Sensible students are* careful what they post about themselves.

***Avoid generic* man** Replace terms like *man, men,* and *mankind* used to represent all human beings with gender-neutral equivalents such as *humanity, humankind,* or *humans.*

> ▸ ~~Man is the only animal~~ *Humans are the only animals* to have ventured into space.

Replace occupational names that have the term *man* in them with gender-neutral alternatives.

> ▸ ~~Congressmen~~ *Members of Congress* have excellent health insurance.

Avoid gender stereotypes and inappropriate gender labeling Some occupations with gender-neutral names are stereotypically associated with either men or women. Avoid perpetuating those stereotypes with inappropriate gender labeling.

> ▸ Nursing is an ancient, honorable profession. ~~Women~~ *People* who choose it can expect a rewarding career.

> ▸ ~~Women~~ *Job seekers* with children may want to apply to companies that offer flexible hours to working ~~mothers~~ *parents.*

> ▸ ~~Ladies~~ *Women* and men will be evaluated according to the same criteria.

2. Cultural labels

Use cultural labels with care. Racial and ethnic labels are appropriate only when race or ethnicity is relevant to the topic under discussion. The same is true for references to disabilities, sexual orientation, or other personal characteristics. When you do use labels, avoid terms that may give offense; instead, call people what they want to be called. When referring to a transgender person, use whichever pronoun that person prefers. And be aware that terms date. A label that used to be acceptable may take on negative connotations over time. People from Asia are *Asians,* not *Orientals* (a term many find disparaging). *Native American* and *American Indian* (or just *Indian*), on the other hand, are generally acceptable to the people they designate. The term *African American* is now widely accepted as a designation for Americans of African descent. The words *gay* and *lesbian* are preferable to *homosexual.* Best in all cases is to be as specific as context permits. If what you mean is *Vietnamese,* or *Japanese,* or *Inuit,* or *Lakota,* or *Catalan,* or *Sicilian,* then use those terms, not the more general *Asian,* or *Native American,* or *European.*

31 Choosing Effective Words

IN THIS CHAPTER

a. Finding the right word, 570

b. Choosing compelling words and figures, 572

c. Mastering idioms, 576

d. Avoiding clichés, 577

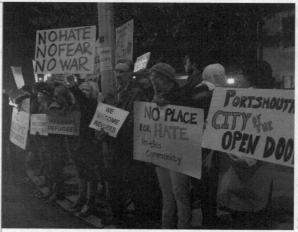

© Darren McCollester/Getty Images News

In the late 1960s, antiwar demonstrations were in the news regularly, accompanied by images of young protestors. Their arguments in their speeches were complex, variously based in ethics, humanitarianism, politics, and self-preservation. Their chants and protest signs, however, were simple: "End the war." In addition to the literal meaning of that sentence, it carried emotional associations, as well; "end the war" also means "stop the killing." Today's protests are no less political or emotional. They continue to prove that, whether in the streets or on the page, language matters.

31a Diction: Finding the Right Word

Diction, or the choice of words to best convey an idea, requires attention to both literal meaning and emotional associations. The literal meaning of a word, its dictionary definition, is its *denotation.* When you use a word, be sure its denotation matches your intended meaning. Be particularly careful, for example, not to misuse words that are similar in pronunciation or spelling.

> **More about**
> Commonly confused words, 587, G14–G19

Tech **Word Choice and Grammar and Style Checkers**

> The grammar and style checkers in most word processing programs offer only marginal help with effective word choice. They often cannot distinguish an incorrectly used word from a correctly used one—affect from effect, for example—nor can they differentiate the emotional associations of words whose literal meaning is similar.

▶ Calling someone a Scrooge ~~eludes~~ *alludes* to a Charles Dickens story about

a selfish man.

   To *elude* is to evade or escape; to *allude* is to make an indirect reference.

▶ The psychology of perception includes the study of optical ~~allusions~~ *illusions*.

   An *allusion* is an indirect reference; an illusion is a mistaken

perception.

Be careful, too, with words that differ in meaning even though they are otherwise closely related.

▶ Many people owe their lives to the ~~heroics~~ *heroism* of volunteer firefighters.

   Heroics are melodramatic, excessive acts; *heroism* is courageous, potentially self-sacrificing behavior.

▶ **EXERCISE 31.1 Denotation**

Consult a dictionary, style guide, the Quick Reference box on p. 574, or the Glossary of Usage at the end of this book as needed to find and correct any misused words in the following sentences.

EXAMPLE

The reporter tried but failed to ~~illicit~~ *elicit* a comment about climate change from

the candidate.

1. Most scientists now except human activity as a cause of global warming.

2. Melting glaciers and rising sea levels are often sited as affects of global warming.

3. People in coastal areas may have trouble adopting to rising sea levels.

4. Another eminent result of global warming may be the breakup of ice shelves in Antarctica.

5. The strength of any one hurricane, however, cannot feasibly be attributed to global warming.

The secondary meanings of a word—the psychological or emotional associations it evokes—are its **connotations.** The word *walk,* for example, has many synonyms, including *amble, saunter, stride,* and *march.* Each of these, however, has distinctive connotations, as their effect in the following sentence suggests:

The candidate ~~walked~~ (ambled / sauntered / walked / strode / marched) to the podium to address her supporters.

The verb *walk* in this context is emotionally neutral, but the others all have connotations that suggest something about the candidate's state of mind. *Amble* suggests a relaxed aimlessness, whereas *saunter* suggests a jaunty self-confidence. *Stride* and *march* both suggest purposefulness, but *march,* with its military associations, also carries a hint of aggressiveness.

A word's connotations can also vary from reader to reader. To some people, for example, the word *wilderness* evokes a place of great danger; to others, a place of excitement; and to still others, a treasure to be preserved.

→ **EXERCISE 31.2 Word choice and tone**

Using a blog search engine such as Technorati or Google Blog Search, find two blogs on the same general topic (the environment or politics, for example). What is the tone of each? How do the writers' word choices create that tone? Discuss the denotations and connotations of five words in each blog that help set its tone. Explain which of the two blogs you find more appealing, and why.

31b Choosing Compelling Words and Figures

Some words are general, some specific, and others fall between:

← more general		more specific →
consume	eat	devour
fruit	apple	Granny Smith
mountain	California peak	Mt. Whitney

In addition, some words are concrete, designating things or qualities that can be seen, heard, felt, smelled, or touched; and others are abstract, designating concepts like *justice, capitalism,* or *democracy.*

Writing
Responsibly | Word Choice and Credibility

The denotation and connotation of the words you choose can powerfully influence the tone of your writing, the effect you have on your readers, and what your readers conclude about you. Highly charged vocabulary, as in the following examples, might lead readers to question the writer's reliability:

> Hippie tree huggers are threatening the jobs of thousands of hardworking loggers.

> Conscientious activists are trying to protect endangered forests from rapacious, tree-murdering logging companies.

In academic writing, you will enhance your credibility if you describe conflicting positions in even-toned language:

> Environmentalists discuss their conflict with the logging industry in terms of the threat industry practices pose to a critical resource; the logging companies, contending that they are responsible forest stewards, describe the conflict in terms of their contribution to local economies.

Once you have looked at the issue fairly, nothing prevents you from then supporting one of these positions and challenging the other.

to AUDIENCE

1. Compelling words

Bring your writing to life by combining general and abstract language with the specific and concrete. Use general and abstract language to frame broad issues, and specific, concrete language to capture readers' attention and help them see things through your eyes. Using general language without specifics leaves readers to fill in the blanks on their own, and using specific language without the general and abstract leaves readers wondering what the point is.

The first of the two following descriptions of the Badwater ultramarathon lacks specific language that can tell us how long the race is, why it is challenging, or exactly where it takes place. The second fills in those details with concrete words—like "hottest spot in America," "stinking water hole," "135 miles," "Death Valley," "piney oasis," "8,300 feet up the side of Mt. Whitney," and "asphalt and road gravel." With these specifics, the writer David Ferrell evokes the challenges of the race without recourse to the abstract word *challenging.*

GENERAL AND ABSTRACT	Badwater is a long, physically challenging race over a partially paved course that begins in a geological depression and ends partway up a mountain.
CONCRETE AND SPECIFIC	Badwater is a madman's march, a footrace through the summer heat of the hottest spot in America. It extends 135 miles from a stinking water hole on the floor of Death Valley to a piney oasis 8,300 feet up the side of Mt. Whitney. The course is nothing but asphalt and road gravel. Feet and knees and

shins ache like they are being whacked with tire irons. Faces turn into shrink-wrap.

—David Ferrell, "Far Beyond a Mere Marathon"

Quick Reference Figures of Speech

Figure and Definition	Examples
simile: An explicit comparison between two unlike things, usually expressed with *like* or *as*	Feet and knees and shins ache like they are being whacked with tire irons. —*David Ferrell* Only final exams, like the last lap of a long race, lay between the members of the senior class and their diplomas.
metaphor: An implied comparison between unlike things stated without *like, as,* or other comparative expressions	Faces turn into shrink-wrap. —*David Ferrell* After crossing the finish line of their last exams, seniors looked forward to that moment on the victory stand when the president of the college would bestow a diploma on them.
analogy: An extended simile or metaphor, often comparing something familiar to something unfamiliar. Well-constructed analogies can be particularly effective for explaining difficult concepts.	What that means [that the universe is expanding] is that we're not at the center of the universe, after all; instead, we're like a single raisin in a vast lump of dough that is rising in an oven where all the other raisins are moving away from each other, faster and faster as the oven gets hotter and hotter. —*David Perlman, "At 12 Billion Years Old, Universe Still Growing Fast"*
personification: The attribution of human qualities to nonhuman creatures, objects, ideas, or phenomena	The plague that rampaged through Europe in the fourteenth century selected its victims indiscriminately, murdering rich and poor in equal proportion.
hyperbole: Deliberate exaggeration for emphasis	That little restaurant on Main Street makes the best pizza on the planet.
understatement: The deliberate use of less forceful language than a subject warrants	The report of my death was an exaggeration. —*Mark Twain, clearly alive and well, responding to an obituary about him in a London paper*
irony: The use of language to suggest the opposite of its literal meaning or to express an incongruity between what is expected and what occurs	I come to bury Caesar, not to praise him. —*Mark Antony, in Shakespeare's play* Julius Caesar, *in a speech that praises the murdered leader effusively*

2. Figures of speech

In the example above, notice how Ferrell, in addition to providing concrete specifics, also uses striking comparisons and juxtapositions to paint a vivid picture of the rigors of the race and to suggest the mind-set required to compete in it. He calls the race "a madman's march," for example, and conjures up a beating with a tire iron and an image of a shrink-wrapped face to convey the physical punishment contestants endure. These are examples of *figurative language,* or *figures of speech,* the imaginative use of language to convey meaning in ways that reach beyond the literal meaning of the words involved.

Among the most common figures of speech are similes and metaphors. A *simile* is an explicit comparison between two unlike things, usually expressed with *like* or *as:* "Feet and knees and shins ache like they are being whacked with tire irons." A *metaphor* is an implied comparison between two unlike things stated without *like, as,* or other comparative expressions: "Faces turn into shrink-wrap." (A list of common figures of speech appears in the Quick Reference box on p. 574.)

→ **EXERCISE 31.3 Compelling words and figures**

Use your imagination—and additional sentences, if need be—to flesh out the following sentences with concrete, specific words and figurative language where appropriate. If you use figures of speech, make a note identifying each and explaining how it is used.

EXAMPLE

The party last night was fun because we played games and I met some people I like.

Last night's party at Jan's house was hopping until about 3 a.m., but I didn't notice the time rushing by because we played an absorbing role-playing game in which each of us tried to capture all of the others without being captured. I also met Brad, who shares my interest in composing music, and Mia, with whom I talked about anime for an hour.

(Comment: "Time rushing by" is a metaphor that is used to emphasize how quickly the evening passed.)

1. Alexandra's apartment is rather small and plain.

2. Next year, I will study abroad at the place I've always dreamed of visiting.

3. This meal was delicious and surprisingly healthful.

4. The movie was not for squeamish people.

5. I know the exact features I want in a car.

3. Inappropriate figures of speech and mixed metaphors

Used judiciously, figures of speech can spice up your writing. Used in the wrong context or piled inconsistently one on the other in *mixed metaphors,* they can be jarring, even silly. The original simile in the following example incongruously invokes the image of a pole vaulter, an athlete who goes mostly up and down, to describe a speeding train, which travels mostly horizontally. The revision, comparing the train to a race horse, is more apt.

> ▶ The new high-speed train, like a champion ~~pole vaulter,~~ ^{thoroughbred,} made it from Boston to Washington in record time.

Mixed metaphors—which combine multiple, conflicting images for the same concept—confuse readers.

MIXED METAPHOR	Confronted with the tsunami of data available on the Internet, researchers, like travelers caught in a blinding desert sandstorm, may have trouble finding the nuggets of valuable information buried in a mountain of otherwise worthless ore.

The sentence above, seeking to emphasize the challenges of online research, invokes tsunamis, sandstorms, mountains, and mining.

REVISED	As they mine the mountain of data available on the Internet, researchers may have trouble identifying the nuggets of valuable information buried with the otherwise worthless ore they dig up.

The revision elaborates a single metaphor that compares finding useful information online to mining for precious minerals.

31c Mastering Idioms

Idioms are expressions whose meaning does not depend on the meanings of the words that compose them. Each idiom is a unified package of meaning with its own denotations and connotations. The following sentence, for example, would make no sense if you tried to interpret it based on the literal meaning of the words *call, on,* and *carpet:*

> ▶ The directors called the CEO on the carpet for the company's poor sales in 2016.

Of course, the expression *call on the carpet* has nothing to do with calls or carpets. It is an idiom that, understood as a whole, means *to reprimand* or *scold.*

Most dictionaries list idiomatic uses of particular words. The entry for the word *call* in the *Merriam-Webster Online Dictionary,* for example, provides definitions for the idioms *call for, call forth, call into question, call it a day,* and *call it quits,* among others. For more detailed information on the history and meaning of particular idioms, consult a specialized dictionary such as the *American Heritage Dictionary of Idioms.*

> *More about*
> Specialized
> dictionaries,
> 580–82

Idioms, Prepositions, and Phrasal Verbs Because idioms can be understood only as a whole, you have to learn them as a whole, just as you would any unfamiliar word. Pay particular attention to the way prepositions combine with other words in idiomatic ways. A *phrasal verb,* for example, is a combination of a verb with one or more prepositions that has a different meaning than the verb alone.

> *More about*
> Prepositions,
> 769–76
> Phrasal verbs,
> 752–54

Raisa *saw* the flat tire on her car. [She looked at it.]

Raisa *saw to* the flat tire on her car. [She had it repaired.]

31d Avoiding Clichés

A *cliché* is a figure of speech, idiom, or other expression that has grown stale from overuse (see the Quick Reference box on the next page for some examples). Clichés come quickly to mind because they express common wit and wisdom in widely recognized phrases. For the same reason, they provide an easy substitute for fresh thought and expression. They may help you frame a subject in the early drafts of a paper, but they can also make your writing sound trite and unimaginative. You should edit them out as you revise your work. As the following example indicates, writing that is loaded with clichés is often also loaded with mixed metaphors.

CLICHÉ LADEN	As the campaign pulled into the home stretch and the cold hard fact of the increasingly nip-and-tuck polls sank in, the candidates threw their promises to stay on their best behavior to the wind and wallowed in the mire of down-and-dirty attack ads.
REVISED	As Election Day neared and the polls showed the race tightening, the candidates abandoned their promises of civility and released a barrage of unscrupulous attack ads.

Quick

Reference   Dodging Deadly Clichés

When you encounter clichés like these in your writing, delete them or replace them with fresher images of your own.

best thing since sliced bread	hit the nail on the head	smart as a whip
beyond a shadow of a doubt	a hundred and one percent	straight and narrow
cold, hard fact	in the prime of life	think outside the box
cool as a cucumber	just desserts	throw [something] to the wind
down and dirty	nip and tuck	tried and true
down the home stretch	no way, shape, or form	wallow in the mire
easier said than done	on their best behavior	without a moment's hesitation
face the music	one foot out the door	zero tolerance
faster than greased lightning	plain as the nose on your face	
green with envy	slow as molasses	

What Is the Difference between an Idiom and a Cliché? The only thing that separates an idiom from a cliché is the frequency with which it is used. If you are a native English speaker, be alert to idioms that appear often in popular sources and in conversation, and try to avoid those in academic and professional writing. If you are not a native English speaker, you may not recognize an idiom as a cliché if you have not encountered it often in your reading. If you have questions about clichés and idioms, ask your instructor or consult a dictionary of idioms, such as *McGraw-Hill's Dictionary of American Idioms and Phrasal Verbs* or the *Longman American Idioms Dictionary*.

EXERCISE 31.4 Avoiding clichés and mixed metaphors

Edit the following sentences to eliminate clichés and mixed metaphors.

EXAMPLE

Mayor Wyndham has been reelected regularly because people feel

that she is ~~tried and true~~ and does not do anything unexpected.
                reliable

1. Her new proposal hit the town council like a ton of bricks.
2. She wanted to have the county reroute the main road to the capital smack dab through town, forcing traffic to run a gauntlet through our commercial center.

3. Store owners, who have recently seen their sales sink like a stone, thought the plan hit the nail on the head and were happy as clams.

4. However, most townspeople flooded the mayor's office with an avalanche of angry calls and emails opposing the proposal.

5. Opponents insisted that in no way, shape, or form would they take to a proposal that threatened the peace and quiet that had attracted them to the town in the first place.

Make It **Your Own**

Review one of your recent writing projects and identify any passages that include misused words, words with an inappropriate connotation, or words that are overly general or abstract. If you find many areas needing revision, add this to your list of areas to consider as you revise your prose.

Text Credits

pp. 573–574: Ferrell, David, "Far Beyond a Mere Marathon," *Los Angeles Times,* August 23, 1997. **p. 574:** Ferrell, David, "Far Beyond a Mere Marathon," *Los Angeles Times,* August 23, 1997. **p. 574:** Ferrell, David, "Far Beyond a Mere Marathon," *Los Angeles Times,* August 23, 1997. **p. 574:** Perlman, David, "At 12 Billion Years Old, Universe Still Growing Fast" *SFGate* May 26, 1999. **p. 574:** Mark Twain, in a letter to Frank E. Bliss, November 4, 1897. **p. 574:** William Shakespeare, *Julius Caesar* (1599).

32 Using the Dictionary and Spelling Correctly

A DICTIONARY

OF THE

ENGLISH LANGUAGE:

© *Private Collection/The Bridgeman Art Library International*

Samuel Johnson's *Dictionary of the English Language* (1755), although not the first ever published, established many of the conventions still found in dictionaries today. Johnson identified a core vocabulary of some 43,500 words; labeled each word's part of speech; briefly traced its origins; provided a concise, elegant (and sometimes humorous) definition of the word in all its senses; and accompanied each definition with an illustrative quotation. Johnson hoped to define and fix a standard of proper spelling and usage, but his dictionary, like those that have followed it, also reflects the state of the language in the time and place in which it was created.

32a Choosing a Dictionary

Dictionaries today come in a variety of forms, both printed and electronic, large and small, general purpose and specialized.

Abridged dictionaries Sometimes referred to as "desk dictionaries," these handy volumes contain information on approximately 200,000 words. Examples include *The American Heritage College Dictionary, Merriam-Webster's Collegiate Dictionary,* the *Random House Webster's College Dictionary,* and *Webster's New World College Dictionary. The American Heritage College Dictionary* is available online at *Yahoo! Education. Merriam-Webster's Collegiate Dictionary* is available online as the *Merriam-Webster Online Dictionary.* Most word processing programs also include a built-in dictionary with many features of an abridged dictionary.

Unabridged dictionaries Unabridged dictionaries contain detailed entries for most words in the English language, some half a million words in total. The most comprehensive unabridged dictionary is the twenty-volume *Oxford English Dictionary* (known as the *OED*). Others include *Random House Webster's Unabridged Dictionary* and *Webster's Third New International Dictionary, Unabridged.*

Both the *OED* and *Webster's Third New International* are available online for a fee. You should be able to find an unabridged dictionary in the reference section of any library, however, and many libraries provide access to online versions.

 Dictionaries for Second-Language Learners In addition to translation dictionaries and standard abridged and unabridged dictionaries, you may also want to consult an all-English dictionary tailored for the second-language learner, such as *Heinle's Newbury House Dictionary of American English,* the *Longman Dictionary of American English,* or the *Oxford Dictionary of American English.* To understand American slang and idioms, consult a dictionary such as *McGraw-Hill's Dictionary of American Slang and Colloquial Expressions.* Since slang and idioms change rapidly, you should also consult native-speaking peers.

Specialized dictionaries Specialized dictionaries focus on a particular aspect of English vocabulary.

- Dictionaries of usage provide guidance about the use of particular words or phrases. Examples include *The American Heritage Book of English Usage* (available online at Bartleby.com) and *Right, Wrong, and Risky: A Dictionary of Today's American English Usage. The New Fowler's Modern English Usage* provides guidance on British as well as American usage.

- Subject-specific dictionaries explain the specialized terminology of particular fields and professions. Examples include *The Dictionary of Anthropology, Black's Law Dictionary,* and *A Dictionary of Business and Management.* For links to subject-specific dictionaries and glossaries available online, try Glossarist and YourDictionary.com.

> *More about*
> Subject-specific
> dictionaries,
> 210–14

- Thesauruses and synonym dictionaries provide lists of words that are equivalent to or that overlap in meaning with one another (***synonyms***), as well as words that have contrasting meanings (***antonyms***). They can help you find just the right word for a particular context or an alternative to a word you have been

> *More about*
> Denotation and
> connotation,
> 19–20, 570–72

Writing
Responsibly | Choose Accurate Synonyms

When you consult a thesaurus, be sure you check both the meanings (*denotations*) and the associations (*connotations*) of the words you find there. A carelessly chosen synonym can distort the information you intend to convey. Suppose, for example, that you wanted to replace *intimidate* in the sentence "The professor's brilliance intim-idated her students." Looking in a thesaurus, you might find both *overawe* and *bludgeon* listed as synonyms. *Overawe* is an appropriate substitute, probably more precisely reflecting the effect of the professor on her students than *intimidate*. *Bludgeon*, in contrast, inaccurately conjures visions of a bloody crime scene.

to TOPIC

overusing. Examples include *Merriam-Webster's Dictionary of Syn-onyms* and *The New American Roget's College Thesaurus*. Note also that most word processing programs have a built-in thesaurus.

> **EXERCISE 32.1 Using a thesaurus**

Look up one of the following words in a thesaurus. Choose three synonyms for that word and write a separate sentence for the original word and for each synonym that accurately reflects both its meaning and connotation.

make	problem	funny
talent	strange	fight

32b Using a Dictionary

Figure 32.1 shows the entry for the word *respect* in the *Merriam-Webster Online Dictionary*, the online counterpart to the eleventh edition of *Merriam-Webster's Collegiate Dictionary*. Although most online and printed abridged dictionaries present the same kinds of information, each has its own format and system of abbreviations.

> **More about**
> Hyphenation,
> 858–63

> **More about**
> Regular and
> irregular verbs,
> 666–67
> Regular and
> irregular plurals,
> 591–93

Spelling, word division, and pronunciation Entries begin with the word cor-rectly spelled followed by acceptable variant spellings, if any. Dots show the division of the word into syllables, indicating where to put a hyphen if you must break the word between lines of text. Next, the pronunciation of the word is given. The print version has a key to pronunciation symbols; the online version has a link to this key, but it also gives the pronunciation in an audio link.

First entry (as noun)

Pronunciation with audio link

Definitions and links to related online entries

Idioms with links to related online entries

Usage examples

Etymology and date of earliest use

Synonyms and antonyms

By permission. From *Merriam-Webster's Collegiate® Dictionary, 11th Edition ©2016 by Merriam-Webster, Inc. (www.Merriam-Webster.com).*

FIGURE 32.1 The entry for *respect* in the *Merriam-Webster Online Dictionary*

Grammatical functions and forms Labels indicate the part of speech and other grammatical aspects of a word. Most dictionaries specify the forms of irregular verbs (*draw, drew, drawn*) but not of regular verbs like *respect*, and they provide irregular plurals (*woman, women*) but not regular plurals (*dogs*). The entry shown in Figure 32.1 includes a definition of the plural form *respects* because it has a usage that does not apply to the singular form.

> **More about**
> Idiomatic expres-
> sions, 576–77

Definitions and examples If a word has more than one definition, each is numbered, and any additional distinctions within a definition are labeled with a letter. Several definitions in the entry for *respect* as a noun include examples of the word used in context. At the end of the entry are the definitions of several idiomatic expressions that include *respect*.

> **More about**
> Usage in "A
> Glossary of
> Usage,"
> G14–G19

Synonyms and usage Most dictionaries list synonyms for the entry word; in online dictionaries, clicking on a synonym will take you to the full entry for that word. Usage labels offer guidance on how to use a word appropriately.

EXERCISE 32.2 Using a dictionary

Look up the following words in a dictionary. Write down any alternate spellings, mark its division into syllables, and underline the stressed syllable.

permanent	develop	approximate
addition	opportunity	component

32c Avoiding Common Spelling Problems

For most people, spelling does not come easily. Even voracious readers and expert writers need to review common spelling problems, such as spelling from pronunciation, confusing homonyms, and confusing different forms of the same word.

 Using a Bilingual Dictionary as an Aid to English Spelling If your first language has, like Spanish, a more phonetic spelling system than English has, a bilingual or translation dictionary can help you find the spelling of English words. For example, if you think *physician* begins with the letter *f*, you will have a hard time finding the correct spelling in an English dictionary, but if you look up *médico* in a Spanish-English dictionary, you will immediately find the proper spelling.

1. The unreliability of pronunciation

The word *Wednesday* is pronounced without the first *d* and the second *e* ("Wensday"). The letters *ow* in *sow* are pronounced as in *cow* when *sow* is used as a noun meaning "female pig." When *sow* is used as a verb meaning "to plant seeds," however, the letters *ow* are pronounced like the *ew* in *sew*. As these examples indicate, you cannot rely on the way a word sounds to guide you to its correct spelling.

2. Homonyms and other problematic words

Many spelling errors result from confusion over homonyms and near-homonyms like those in the Quick Reference box on page 587.

- *Homonyms* are groups of words that sound exactly alike but have different spellings and meanings, such as *to/too/two* and *cite/sight/site*.
- *Near-homonyms* are groups of words such as *personal/personnel* and *conscience/conscious* that are close but not the same in pronunciation. Near-homonyms also include groups such as *breath/breathe* and *advice/advise* that are different forms of the same word.

There is no easy formula for mastering these words. If any of them give you trouble, try to memorize their spellings and meanings, and always check for them as you proofread your writing.

> *More about*
> Confusing words
> and phrases
> in "A Glossary
> of Usage,"
> G14–G19

Use American Rather Than British Spelling Multilingual writers who began their study of English outside the United States may be accustomed to British spelling, which is often different from American, as the following list shows. Some writers striving for formality mistakenly believe that British spellings are preferable. If you are writing for a US audience, be sure to follow American style. When in doubt, consult an American dictionary, which will give the preferred American spelling before any alternates.

American	British
airplane	aeroplane
labor/mold	labour/mould
theater	theatre
check	cheque
counseled	counselled
defense	defence
plagiarize	plagiarise
program	programme
color	colour

→ **EXERCISE 32.3 Using homonyms and near-homonyms**

In each of the following sentences, underline the correct word from among the choices in parentheses.

EXAMPLE

In a popular cooking show, contestants (our, <u>are</u>) asked to (device, <u>devise</u>) each (<u>course</u>, coarse) of a meal in less (then, <u>than</u>) thirty minutes.

1. Each contestant must use the ingredients in a basket (to, too, two) produce a (grate, great) dish with his or her own (personnel, personal) (flair, flare).

2. (It's, Its) often the (forth, fourth) ingredient that (presents, presence) problems in the (dessert, desert) course.

3. The judges (compliment, complement) each chef's ability to (elicit, illicit) the full flavor of each ingredient, explain where the meal is (week, weak), and offer (advise, advice) about (where, were) each chef can improve.

4. They (our, are) very (fair, fare) and follow (their, they're, there) (conscience, conscious), but at the end of each round (its, it's) not always clear (which, witch) chef will be "chopped."

32d Remembering Spelling Rules

Mastering a few key rules—and noting their exceptions—can improve the accuracy of your spelling.

Writing Responsibly | Spelling Errors

A misspelled word is not an important issue when you are texting friends, but in other situations it may signal that you are careless about details. If you misspell *accountant* in a job-application letter to a financial firm, for example, the recipient may wonder how accurate you are about numbers. If you misspell a name, people may interpret it as a sign of indifference or disrespect.

to SELF

Quick Reference — Some Homonyms and Near-Homonyms

accept (to take willingly)
except (to exclude)

advice (counsel)
advise (to offer counsel)

affect (to influence; feeling)
effect (to cause; a result)

all ready (fully prepared)
already (by this time)

allude (to mention indirectly)
elude (to avoid)

allusion (an indirect reference)
illusion (a deceptive or false perception)

altar (a raised structure for religious ritual)
alter (to change)

are (form of be)
our (relating to us)

ascent (upward advance)
assent (to concur)

bare (unclothed; to make known)
bear (an animal; to support)

board (a piece of wood; to get on a vehicle)
bored (uninterested)

brake (stopping mechanism)
break (to wreck; a pause)

capital (seat of government)
capitol (building for the legislature)

cite (to acknowledge a source)
sight (something to see)
site (a place)

complement (to complete)
compliment (an admiring remark)

conscience (moral awareness)
conscious (awake, mindful)

council (a governing or advisory group)
counsel (advice; to advise)

descent (downward movement)
dissent (disagreement)

desert (desolate area; to abandon)
dessert (a meal's last course)

device (a contrivance)
devise (to contrive)

discreet (prudent, unpretentious)
discrete (distinct)

elicit (to bring out)
illicit (illegal)

eminent (highly regarded)
imminent (about to happen)
immanent (inherent)

fair (attractive; impartial)
fare (a price for transportation)

forth (forward)
fourth (following third)

gorilla (a great ape)
guerrilla (a fighter in unconventional warfare)

grate (to grind or irritate)
great (large or superior)

hear (to perceive sound)
here (at this place)

hole (an opening)
whole (complete)

incidence (rate of occurrence)
incidents (occurrences)

its (possessive of it)
it's (it is or it has)

lead (a metal; to go ahead of)
led (past tense of lead)

meat (edible animal flesh)
meet (to encounter)

passed (past tense of pass)
past (before the present)

patience (calm persistence)
patients (people under medical care)

peace (tranquility)
piece (a part)

personal (private; individual)
personnel (employees)

plain (not complicated)
plane (aircraft; carpenter's tool)

presence (being in attendance)
presents (gifts)

principal (most significant; chief)
principle (rule or tenet)

rain (precipitation)
reign (monarch's period of rule)
rein (strap used to control an animal; to restrain)

raise (to lift)
raze (to demolish)

respectfully (with respect)
respectively (in the order given)

right (correct; opposite of left)
rite (ceremony or ritual)
wright (one who fashions a thing)
write (to form words on a surface)

road (street)
rode (past tense of ride)

stationary (immobile)
stationery (writing paper)

than (compared to)
then (at that time; therefore)

their (possessive of they)
there (in that place)
they're (they are)

to (toward)
too (also)
two (number after one)

waist (midriff; narrow part)
waste (garbage; to squander)

weak (not strong)
week (seven days)

wear (to have on)
where (in what direction or place)
were (past tense of be)

weather (condition of the atmosphere)
whether (word that introduces choices or alternatives)

which (what one)
witch (sorcerer)

who's (who is or who has)
whose (possessive of who)

your (possessive of you)
you're (you are)

1. The *ie/ei* rule

The traditional rule—"*i* before *e* except after *c* or when sounded like *ay* as in *neighbor* and *weigh*"—will help you spell words like *believe, receive,* and *sleigh* correctly.

I BEFORE *E*	diesel, piece, pier, retrieve, shield, siege
E BEFORE *I* AFTER *C*	ceiling, conceit, conceive, deceit, perceive, receipt
EI SOUNDS LIKE *AY*	beige, deign, eighteen, reindeer, sleigh, veil

Some exceptions: *feisty, forfeit, heifer, height, heir, neither, protein, sovereign, seize, their, weird*

> **EXERCISE 32.4 Spelling *ie* and *ei* words**
>
> Correct any misspellings in the following sentences.
>
> **EXAMPLE**
>
> When Angie ~~recieved~~ *received* the ~~reciept~~ *receipt* for her rental deposit, she knew she had reached a milestone in her life.
>
> 1. It was her first apartment, and the cielings were eighteen feet high!
>
> 2. With that hieght, she could retreive her tall sculpture from her parents' backyard and install it in her apartment.
>
> 3. Of course, creating such an oversized sculpture had been a conciet, but she had always beleived that art should have no boundaries.
>
> 4. Now that fiesty conviction in the form of a huge peice of biege metal would take palpable shape in the very first home of her own.

2. Prefixes

Prefixes attach to the beginning of a root word to modify its meaning. Prefixes have no effect on the spelling of the rest of the word, even if the last letter of the prefix and the first letter of the root word are the same. For example, *re-* combines with *wind* to form *rewind, dis-* combines with *inherit* to form *disinherit,* and *mis-* combines with *statement* to form *misstatement.* In some cases, however, a hyphen separates a prefix from the rest of the word, as in *anti-inflammatory.*

> **More about**
> Prefixes and hyphenation, 859–60

3. Suffixes

Suffixes attach to the end of a root word to change its meaning and grammatical form. The suffix *-ly,* for example, changes the adjective *sweet* to the adverb *sweetly.* Unlike prefixes, suffixes often affect the spelling of the preceding root.

More about
Suffixes and
  hyphenation,
  859–60

Words that end with a silent e   In most instances, drop the silent *e* if the suffix starts with a vowel:

observe → observant   response → responsible   revoke → revoked

Retain the silent *e* if the suffix starts with a consonant:

hope → hopeful   love → lovely   polite → politeness

Some exceptions: *advantageous, argument, duly, enforceable, judgment, serviceable*

Words that end with y   For most words that end with a consonant and *y,* change the *y* to an *i* when you add a suffix:

apology → apologize   deny → denies

heavy → heavier   merry → merriment

Retain the *y* if the suffix is *-ing,* if a vowel precedes the *y,* or if the word ending in *y* is a proper name:

spy → spying   play → playful   McCoy → McCoys

Suffixes -cede, -ceed, *and* -sede   To avoid confusing these three suffixes, remember these facts:

1. *Supersede* is the only English word that ends in *-sede.*
2. *Exceed, proceed,* and *succeed* are the only words that end in *-ceed.*
3. All other similar words use the suffix *-cede: accede, concede, precede, secede.*

Suffixes -ally *versus* -ly *and* -efy *versus* -ify   When a word ends in *ic,* use the suffix *-ally.* In all other instances, use *-ly:*

basic → basically   magic → magically

brisk → briskly   confident → confidently

Only four words use the suffix *-efy: liquefy, putrefy, rarefy, stupefy.* All other such words use the suffix *-ify: beautify, certify, justify, purify.*

Words that end with a consonant Do not double a final consonant if the suffix begins with a consonant (*commitment, fearless, kinship, poorly*). For suffixes that begin with a vowel, follow these guidelines:

- **One-syllable root words.** Double the final consonant if only one vowel precedes it:

  bit → bi**tt**en   chat → cha**tt**y   skip → ski**pp**ing

  For other one-syllable words, do not double the consonant:

  chart → char**t**ed   droop → droo**p**ing   speak → spea**k**er

- **Multisyllable words.** Double the final consonant if only one vowel precedes the final consonant and if the final syllable of the root is accented in the new word containing the suffix:

  admit → ad**mitt**ance   concur → con**curr**ent

  control → con**troll**ed

For multisyllable words that do not meet these criteria, do not double the final consonant:

  devil → de**vil**ish   parallel → paral**lel**ism

  erupt → eru**pt**ed   proclaim → proclai**m**ing

In *devilish* and *parallelism,* the accent is on the first syllable of the root word; the final *t* in *erupt* is preceded by a consonant; and the final *m* in *proclaim* is preceded by two vowels.

 EXERCISE 32.5 Adding suffixes

Correct any misspelled words in the following list, and circle those that are spelled correctly.

changeable	truly	beginning	tragicly
deploing	argueable	replys	running
supercede	regreted	optimally	angrily
principally	soly	sponsorred	

More about
Capitalization,
835–41

Tech **Use Spelling Checkers Cautiously**

Most of today's word processing programs correct some misspelled words while you type, identify other words that may be misspelled, and let you run a manual spelling check whenever you wish. Although these features are helpful, you cannot depend on them alone to guarantee error-free spelling.

- Spelling checkers do not differentiate homonyms and commonly confused words, such as *descent, dissent* or *too, two.* If you type a correctly spelled word that happens not to be correct for the context, a spelling checker will not mark it wrong.

- If you misspell a word, a spelling checker may suggest replacing it with the wrong word. For example, if you type *retify* for *rectify,* the checker's first recommendation might be *ratify,* which is clearly the wrong word.

- A spelling checker will alert you to many situations in which you need to capitalize, but it will not alert you to the unnecessary use of capitals, as in *Shakespeare is an Important British writer.*

Spelling checkers, then, are a useful tool but not a replacement for a dictionary and careful proofreading.

32e Forming Plurals

Most English nouns form the plural by adding the suffix -s or -es. Some nouns, however, like *child* (plural *children*) and *man* (plural *men*), have irregular forms, and some compound nouns form the plural on a word that is not the last one in the compound.

1. Regular plurals

- To form the plural of most English nouns, add an -s.

  letter → letters   shoe → shoes   Erickson → the Ericksons

- To form the plural of nouns that end with s, sh, ch, x, or z, add -es.

  miss → misses   dish → dishes   latch → latches

  box → boxes   fez → fezzes   Davis → the Davises

- To form the plural of some nouns that end with f or fe, change the f to a v and add -s or -es.

  loaf → loaves   scarf → scarves   thief → thieves

  knife → knives   wife → wives

- However, words that end in *ff* or *ffe* and some words that end in *f* or *fe* form the plural just with the addition of an *-s*.

  bluff → bluffs   giraffe → giraffes

  chief → chiefs   safe → safes

- To form the plural of nouns that end with *o*, add *-s* if the *o* is preceded by a vowel or if the word is a proper noun.

  duo → duos   ratio → ratios   video → videos

  Add *-es* if the *o* is preceded by a consonant.

  echo → echoes   potato → potatoes   veto → vetoes

  Some exceptions: *autos, ponchos, sopranos, tacos*

- To form the plural of words that end with *y*, add *-s* if the *y* is preceded by a vowel or if the word is a proper noun.

  decoy → decoys   essay → essays   Hagarty → the Hagartys

  Change the *y* to *i* and add *-es* if the *y* is preceded by a consonant.

  berry → berries   enemy → enemies   family → families

2. Irregular plurals

The only way to learn irregular plurals is to memorize them. Many nouns have irregular plurals that have survived from earlier forms of English.

  woman → women   child → children   deer → deer

  foot → feet   ox → oxen   sheep → sheep

  mouse → mice

Other nouns with irregular plurals were borrowed into English from languages such as Greek, Latin, and French and retain the plural form of the original language.

  analysis → analyses   criterion → criteria   phenomenon → phenomena

  alumna → alumnae   medium → media   tableau → tableaux

  alumnus → alumni   nucleus → nuclei

For many such words, a regularized plural form is acceptable as an alternative to the irregular form: *index, indices/indexes; fungus, fungi/funguses*

3. Plurals of compound nouns

To form the plural of compound nouns composed of separate or hyphenated words, add -*s* or -*es* to the main noun in the compound.

brigadier generals   chiefs of staff   runners-up

If there is no main noun, add -*s* or -*es* at the end: *singer-songwriters*.
For compounds that are spelled as one word, add -*s* or -*es* at the end.

keyboards   spaceships   touchdowns

An exception: *passersby*

→ EXERCISE 32.6 Forming plurals

Write the plural form of each of the following singular nouns.

buzz	rally	half	ploy
mother-in-law	domino	study	tooth
handcuff	moose	studio	goose
spoof	person	tomato	

32f Improving Your Day-to-Day Spelling

Writers who have mastered all the rules in this chapter may still occasionally misspell some words. Here are a few tips for further reducing misspellings in your work:

- If you tend to misspell the same word or types of words repeatedly, keep track of them in a vocabulary log and check for them specifically when you proofread.

- Use a dictionary often, and keep one handy next to your computer.

- Remember that pronunciation may lead you astray in your spelling. Although you may say "goverment," do not forget that *govern* is the root word, so the word is spelled *government*, with an *n*.

- Use a spelling checker with caution (see the Tech box on p. 591), and proofread carefully.

Make It **Your Own**

With the spelling checker on, type this sentence into a blank word processing document:

> Fore score and seven yours ago, are fathers brought fourth on this continence anew nation, conceived in liberty and dedicated to the preposition that awl men our created equal.

Now compare the sentence to the first sentence of Abraham Lincoln's Gettysburg Address:

> Four score and seven years ago, our fathers brought forth on this continent a new nation, conceived in liberty and dedicated to the proposition that all men are created equal.

How many errors did your spelling checker catch? Introduce two or more similar errors into other famous passages (or into passages from a textbook or a newspaper or magazine article), and see how dependably the spelling checker catches them. For famous quotations, consult a printed collection like *Bartlett's Familiar Quotations, The Yale Book of Quotations,* or *The Oxford Dictionary of Quotations.* Or consult an online source like The Quotations Page <quotationspage.com> or the quotations sections of The Other Pages <theotherpages.org /quote.html>.

Work **Together**

With a classmate, exchange printouts (double-spaced) of the sentences with the errors you introduced in the Make It Your Own exercise above. Correct the sentences by hand; then check your work against the original sources.

Text Credits

p. 583: Screenshot: "respect" from www.merriam-webster.com/dictionary. Copyright © Merriam-Webster, Incorporated. Used with permission.

Grammar
Matters

Writing with Clarity

Recognizing and Correcting Fragments (628–38)

A fragment is an incomplete sentence punctuated as if it were complete.

frag   The system of American higher ~~education. It is~~ founded on principles of

            education is
           ^

honesty and academic integrity.

     Reducing the incidence of plagiarism among college students will be difficult,

     however, without
     ~~however. Without~~ an understanding of its causes that goes beyond simplistic explanations.
     ^

Maintaining Subject-Verb Agreement (648–58)

A verb and its subject agree when they match each other in person (first, second, or third) and number (singular or plural).

sv agr   For this reason, nearly everyone invested in this system—students, instructors, and

            recognizes
     administrators—~~recognize~~ that plagiarism cannot be tolerated.
         ^

---

                have
     That plagiarism and related misconduct ~~has~~ become all too common is beyond dispute.
                ^

Maintaining Pronoun-Antecedent Agreement (658–63)

A pronoun agrees with its antecedent (the word the pronoun replaces) when they match each other in person (first, second, or third), number (singular or plural), and gender (masculine, feminine, or neuter).

            students are
pn ag   In this myth, the ~~student is~~ too apathetic and slothful to finish their assignments on their
            ^

     own; instead, they cheat.

     Such students may treat the attainment of impressive marks as a necessity and will betray

                they revere   *their*
     the very academic system ~~he or she reveres~~ in order to sustain ~~his or her~~ average.
                ^   ^

Recognizing and Correcting Fused (Run-On) Sentences (639–47)

In a fused (or run-on) sentence, one independent clause incorrectly follows another with no punctuation or joining words between them.

fs   Practices among higher education students are not much ~~better according to~~ *better. According to* research by Donald

L. McCabe, a professor at Rutgers University who has done extensive work on cheating, 38% of

college students admitted to committing forms of plagiarism in the previous year (Rimer 7).

Recognizing and Correcting Comma Splices (639–47)

In a comma splice, two independent clauses are incorrectly joined by a comma alone, without a coordinating conjunction such as *and* or *but*.

cs   It is late at night, *and* a student sits staring at a computer.

Using Irregular Verb Forms Correctly (664–83)

Regular verbs form the past tense and past participle by adding *-ed* to the base form; irregular verbs do not.

vb   A paper is due the following morning, and research needs to be done, notes need to be ~~took~~ *taken*,

and, in the end, an essay needs to be ~~wrote~~ *written* and edited.

Avoiding Unclear Pronoun Reference (692–96)

Pronoun reference is clear when readers can effortlessly identify a pronoun's antecedent (the word the pronoun replaces).

ref   Undeniably, some ~~of it~~ *plagiarism* occurs because students find ~~it~~ *plagiarizing* easier than simply doing the work required.

The argument that laziness is ~~its main cause, however, is~~ *the main cause of plagiarism, however, is* at best incomplete and seems,

moreover, to be fed by unfair stereotypes of ~~them~~ *students* as bored by academic rigor, more interested

in video games or social media than the hard work of learning.

Draft of student project with sentence problems

Why Students Cheat:
The Complexities and Oversimplifications of Plagiarism (Draft 1)

frag

sv agr

The system of American higher education. It is founded on principles of honesty and academic integrity. For this reason, nearly everyone invested in this system—students, instructors, and administrators—recognize that plagiarism cannot be tolerated. People also agree that a lot of plagiarism is occurring. Reducing the incidence of plagiarism among college students will be difficult, however. Without an understanding of its causes that goes beyond simplistic explanations.

frag

sv agr

That plagiarism and related misconduct has become all too common is beyond dispute. A survey published in *Who's Who among American High School Students* (reported by Newberger) indicated that 15 percent of top-ranked high schoolers plagiarize. Practices among higher education students are not much better according to research by Donald L. McCabe, a professor at Rutgers University who has done extensive work on cheating, 70% of college students "copied almost word for word from a source and submitted as their own work" (41). A 2006 study by Hand, Conway, and Moran showed that plagiarism was common among the 411 students who participated in their research.

fs

There is a commonly held myth about how most plagiarism occurs. It is late at night, a student sits staring at a computer. A paper is due the following morning, and research needs to be done, notes need to be took, and, in the end, an essay needs to be wrote and edited. The student, overwhelmed, succumbs to the temptations of plagiarism—"cutting and pasting" from sources, downloading an essay from the Internet, or simply buying a paper from another student. In this myth, the student is too apathetic and slothful to finish their assignments on their own; instead, they cheat.

cs

vb

pn agr

Undeniably, some of it occurs because students find it easier than simply doing the work required. The argument that laziness is its main cause, however, is at best incomplete and seems, moreover, to be fed by unfair stereotypes of them as bored by academic rigor, more interested in video games or social media than the hard work of learning.

ref

ref

ref

In fact, some plagiarism grows from the opposite of these characteristics. High-achieving students, for example, fear what a bad grade will do to their otherwise stellar GPA. Such students may treat the attainment of impressive marks as a necessity and will betray the very academic system he or she reveres in order to sustain his or her average.

pn agr

For the final draft of this project, see pp. 151–56. For editing and proofreading symbols and abbreviations, see inside back cover.

Avoiding Confusing Shifts in Tense and Voice (706–13)

Shifts from one tense to another or from the active to the passive voice are confusing when they occur for no clear reason.

shift Students who view writing papers as hoops they must jump through to graduate, for
         are   *download*
instance, ~~were~~ more likely simply to ~~have downloaded~~ a paper from an online "paper
         ^   ^
mill" than to write one themselves.

_____

Students draw a distinction between their interests and their academic assignments,
         they rationalize plagiarism
and ~~plagiarism is rationalized by them~~ as a way to escape an "unfair" academic obligation.
         ^

Avoiding Incomplete Constructions (728–31)

A phrase or clause is incomplete if it is missing any words required for idiomatic and grammatical clarity.

                                                                              to
inc Websites such as *essaytown.com*, which will write a paper to order, cater students like
                                                                      ^
these, who consider at least some aspects of academia essentially useless.

Avoiding Mixed Constructions (723–27)

A mixed construction is a sentence with parts that do not fit together grammatically or logically.

         students who recognize
mix Even ~~recognizing~~ the importance of citation may not know how to cite their sources
         ^
correctly.

Distinguishing Adjectives and Adverbs (697–705)

Adjectives modify nouns or pronouns; adverbs modify verbs, adjectives, other adverbs, and entire phrases and clauses.

                              the rapid movement of
ad The Internet is a place of free exchange and information ~~movement rapidly~~ from
                                                              ^
computer to computer.

Draft of student project with sentence problems

shift Other students plagiarize more from lack of interest in a particular course than general idleness. Students who view writing papers as hoops they must jump through to graduate, for instance, were more likely simply to have downloaded a paper from an online "paper mill" than to write one themselves. For them, a college writing class is something to be endured rather than an opportunity for learning.

shift Students draw a distinction between their interests and their academic assignments, and plagiarism is rationalized by them as a way to escape an "unfair" academic obligation. Websites such as *essaytown.com*, which will write a paper to **inc** order, cater students like these, who consider at least some aspects of academia essentially useless.

Many other instances of plagiarism are committed by students whom it turns **case** out have honest intentions but are ignorant of citation methods. Michael Gunn, a British student, copied quotations from Internet sources in numerous papers over several years and was shocked to learn that this qualified as plagiarism (Baty). **mix** Even recognizing the importance of citation may not know how to cite their sources correctly. A student who omits the source of a paraphrase in a paper would probably be surprised to learn that him or her is often considered as guilty of plagiarism as the **case** student who downloads an essay.

The Internet has compounded confusion with regard to citation. The Internet is a **ad** place of free exchange and information movement rapidly from computer to computer. In this environment, ownership and citation become hazy. As John Leland, a reporter for *The New York Times*, writes, "Culture's heat now lies with the ability to cut, paste, clip, sample, quote, recycle, customize, and re-circulate." Many students, for example **mm** by highlighting it, copying it, and pasting it into a word processing document, find it easy and "natural" to take text from an online source. Having trouble keeping track **dm** of everything they have read, however, the chances increase of students accidentally plagiarizing by forgetting to cite a copied text. So, too, does the likelihood of "patchwriting," the substitution of synonyms or the shuffling of sentences in a borrowed text without putting the information fully into the writer's own words (Howard 233). Finally, some students will also be tempted to commit intentional plagiarism, choosing to leave a block of copied text uncited.

For the final draft of this project, see pp. 151–56. For editing and proofreading symbols and abbreviations, see inside back cover.

He, She, Who or *Him, Her, Whom*? Matching Pronoun Case to Function (686–92)

A case problem occurs when the form of a pronoun—subjective, objective, or possessive—does not correspond to its grammatical role in a sentence.

case   Many other instances of plagiarism are committed by students ~~whom it turns out~~ have honest
                                                    who, it turns out,

intentions but are ignorant of citation methods.

A student who omits the source of a paraphrase in a paper would probably be surprised to learn
          he or she
that ~~him or her~~ is often considered as guilty of plagiarism as the student who downloads an essay.

Avoiding Misplaced Modifiers (714–19)

A misplaced modifier is an ambiguously, confusingly, or disruptively placed modifying word, phrase, or clause.

        find it easy and "natural" to take text from an online source—for
mm   Many students—for example by highlighting it, copying it, and pasting it into a word processing

document—~~find it easy and "natural" to take text from an online source.~~

Avoiding Dangling Modifiers (719–22)

A dangling modifier does not clearly modify the subject or any other part of a sentence, leaving it to the reader to infer the intended meaning.

        Because students can have
dm   ~~Having~~ trouble keeping track of everything they have read, however,

                       that they will plagiarize accidentally
the chances increase ~~of students' accidentally plagiarizing~~ by

forgetting to cite a copied text.

601

33 Understanding Grammar

©Purestock/SuperStock

The rules of baseball, which give the game meaning and structure, have become second nature to proficient players. Most of these rules are inflexible: A player who ran around the bases carrying the ball would not be playing baseball. Some rules vary, however: In the American League but not in the National League, teams can designate another player to bat instead of the pitcher.

Languages, too, have rules—*grammars*—that structure words so they can convey meaning. Just as baseball players have internalized the rules of the game, so have we all internalized the grammar of our native language. Most rules of grammar are inflexible. Any English speaker, for example, would recognize a statement like *throw Maria ball the base first to* as ungrammatical. Some aspects of grammar, however, can vary over time, from region to region, and from group to group.

The form of English that is accepted today in academic settings and in the workplace in the United States is known as **Standard American English.** Although it is not better or more correct than other varieties, Standard American English is what readers expect to encounter in academic and business writing in the United States. This chapter reviews the rules of Standard American English grammar, and the chapters that follow it in part 8 focus on particular aspects of grammar and usage that many writers find troublesome.

> **More about**
> Common sentence
>   problems,
>   596–601
>   (*Grammar
>   Matters* tutorial
>   preceding this
>   chapter)

Writing Responsibly — Why Grammar Matters

Sometimes a writer uses non-standard grammar as a way of drawing attention to issues of culture and power, or as a way of asserting the legitimacy of non-standard dialects. In most cases, though, writers have a responsibility to use language their readers regard as grammatically correct. A shared standard of grammar eases communication and demonstrates your respect for your readers.

to AUDIENCE

PARTS OF SPEECH

The term *parts of speech* refers to the functions words play in a sentence. English has eight parts of speech:

- nouns
- pronouns
- verbs
- adjectives

- adverbs
- prepositions
- conjunctions
- interjections

The same word can have more than one function, depending on the context in which it appears.

▶ Many students work to help pay for college. [*Work* is a verb.]
▶ Mastering calculus requires hard work. [*Work* is a noun.]

33a Nouns

Nouns name ideas (*justice*), things (*chair*), qualities (*neatness*), actions (*judgment*), people (*Albert Einstein*), and places (*Tokyo*). They fall into a variety of overlapping categories:

- *Proper nouns* name specific places, people, or things and are usually capitalized: *Nairobi, Hudson Bay, Hillary Rodham Clinton,* the *Taj Mahal.* All other nouns are *common nouns,* which name members of a class or group: *turtle, sophomore, skyscraper.*

- *Collective nouns* name a collection that can function as a single unit: *committee, administration, family.*

- *Concrete nouns* name things that can be seen, touched, heard, smelled, or tasted: *planet, liquid, symphony, skunk, pepper.* **Abstract nouns** name qualities or ideas that cannot be perceived by the senses: *mercy, fear.*

- *Countable* (or *count*) *nouns* name things or ideas that can be counted. They can be either *singular* or *plural:* *cat/cats, assignment/assignments, idea/ideas.*

- *Uncountable* (or *noncount*) *nouns* name ideas or things that cannot be counted and do not have a plural form: *homework, knowledge, pollution.*

> **More about**
> Count and non-count nouns,
> 744–45,
> 749–50

Reference   The Parts of Speech

Parts of Speech	Functions	Examples
Nouns	name ideas, things, qualities, actions, people, and places	Sarah usually drives her blue car to work, but, alas, it needs expensive repairs.
Pronouns	rename or take the place of nouns or noun phrases	Sarah usually drives her blue car to work, but, alas, it needs expensive repairs.
Verbs	express action, occurrence, or state of being	Sarah usually drives her blue car to work, but, alas, it needs expensive repairs.
Adjectives	modify nouns or pronouns with descriptive or limiting information, answering questions such as *What kind? Which one?* or *How many?*	Sarah usually drives her blue car to work, but, alas, it needs expensive repairs.
Adverbs	modify verbs, adjectives, and other adverbs as well as entire phrases and clauses, answering such questions as *How? Where? When?* and *To what extent or degree?*	Sarah usually drives her blue car to work, but, alas, it needs expensive repairs.
Prepositions	relate nouns or pronouns to other words in a sentence in terms of time, space, cause, and other attributes	Sarah usually drives her blue car to work, but, alas, it needs expensive repairs.
Conjunctions	join words, phrases, and clauses to other words, phrases, or clauses and specify the way the joined elements relate to each other	Sarah usually drives her blue car to work, but, alas, it needs expensive repairs.
Interjections	express strong feeling but otherwise serve no grammatical function	Sarah usually drives her blue car to work, but, alas, it needs expensive repairs.

Countable and Noncountable Nouns In many languages the classification of nouns as count or noncount affects the way they combine with articles (*a, an, the*) and other determiners (*my, your, some, many, this, these*). Awareness of the effect of this aspect of nouns on sentence grammar will help you avoid errors.

More about
Noun plurals,
591–92

Most nouns form the plural with the addition of a final *-s* or *-es*: *book/books, beach/beaches, country/countries*. A few have irregular plurals: *woman/women,* *life/lives, mouse/mice.* For some nouns, the singular and the plural forms are the same: *deer/deer, fish/fish.*

Nouns indicate possession with a final *s* sound, marked in writing with an apostrophe: *Rosa's idea, the students' plan.*

> **More about**
> Apostrophes and possession,
> 803–7

33b Pronouns

Pronouns rename or take the place of nouns or *noun phrases.* The noun that a pronoun replaces is called its *antecedent.* The Quick Reference box on page 606 summarizes the types of pronouns and their functions.

> **noun phrase** A noun and its modifiers

> **More about**
> Pronouns,
> 657–63,
> 684–96

→ **EXERCISE 33.1 Identifying nouns and pronouns**

Circle the nouns and underline the pronouns in the following sentences.

EXAMPLE

On his (way) to pick up his (aunt) at the (airport,) (Bradley) found himself stuck in (traffic)

1. Making the situation even worse, the driver behind him kept honking his horn.

2. Bradley felt his car shake a bit and realized that the driver behind him had bumped his rear fender slightly while pulling out to change lanes.

3. The other driver was out of sight by the time Bradley reminded himself to get the car's license number.

4. He arrived at the airport a few minutes late, saw that his car's fender was unharmed, scanned the monitor for information about incoming flights, and learned that many, including his aunt's, were an hour behind schedule.

33c Verbs

Verbs express action (*The quarterback throws a pass*), occurrence (*The play happened in the second half*), or state of being (*The fans are happy*). Verbs also carry information about time (tense), as well as person, number, voice, and mood.

> **More about**
> Verb forms,
> 664–71

Two kinds of verbs combine to make up a *verb phrase: main verbs* and *helping* (or *auxiliary*) *verbs.* Main verbs carry the principal meaning of a verb phrase. Almost all verb constructions other than the present and past

Quick Reference Pronouns and Their Functions

Type and Function	Forms	Examples
Personal pronouns take the place of specific nouns or noun phrases.	**Singular:** *I, me, you, he, him, she, her, it* **Plural:** *we, us, you, they, them*	Yue bought the tickets for Adam, and she gave them to him before the concert.
Possessive pronouns are personal pronouns that indicate possession.	**Singular:** *my, mine, your, yours, his, her, hers, its* **Plural:** *our, ours, your, yours, their, theirs*	Adam gave one of the tickets to his roommate.
Reflexive pronouns refer back to the subject of a sentence.	**Singular:** *myself, yourself, himself, herself, itself, oneself* **Plural:** *ourselves, yourselves, themselves*	Laetitia reminded herself to return the books to the library.
Intensive pronouns rename and emphasize their antecedents.	Same as reflexive pronouns	Dr. Collins herself performed the operation.
Demonstrative pronouns rename and point to nouns or noun phrases. They can function as adjectives as well as nouns.	**Singular:** *this, that* **Plural:** *these, those*	Yameng visited the Forbidden City. That was his favorite place in China. That place was his favorite.
Relative pronouns introduce subordinate clauses that describe the pronoun's antecedent.	*who, whom, whoever, whomever, what, whose, whatever, whichever, that, which*	I. M. Pei is the architect who designed the East Wing of the National Gallery.
Interrogative pronouns introduce questions.	*who, whoever, whom, whomever, what, whatever, which, whichever, whose*	Who designed the East Wing of the National Gallery?
Indefinite pronouns do not refer to specific people or things.	**Singular:** *anybody, anyone, anything, each, either, everybody, everyone, everything, much, neither, nobody, no one, nothing, one, somebody, someone, something* **Singular or plural:** *all, any, more, most, some* **Plural:** *both, few, many, several*	Everybody talks about the weather, but nobody does anything about it. —Attributed to Mark Twain
Reciprocal pronouns refer to the individual parts of a plural antecedent.	*each other, one another*	The candidates debated one another many times before the primary.

tense, however, require a combination of one or more helping verbs with a form of the main verb. Some helping verbs (forms of *be, have,* and *do*) also function as main verbs. Others, called *modal verbs* (*can, could, may, might, must, shall, should, will, would,* and *ought to*), function only as helping verbs.

Modal Auxiliaries Modal auxiliaries can pose special problems for multilingual students because other languages use very different grammatical strategies to express intention, possibility, or expectation. For more on their meaning and use, see pages 758–61.

Helping verbs always precede the main verb in a verb phrase.

|— verb phrase —|
main
verb
▶ The player   **hit**   a long home run.

helping   main
verbs   verb
▶ The home run **may have broken** a distance record.

helping   main
verbs   verb
▶ The children **have been playing** for two hours.

NOTE Do not confuse *verbals* with complete verbs. Verbals are verb forms functioning as nouns, adjectives, or adverbs, not as verbs within a predicate.

> *More about*
> Verbals, 620–21,
> 629

▶ The potters *fired* the vessels in their kiln. [*Fired* is a verb.]

▶ The *fired* clay is rock hard. [*Fired* is a verbal, in this case an adjective modifying *clay.*]

▶ EXERCISE 33.2 Identifying verb phrases

Underline the verb phrases in the following sentences, and circle the main verb in each. Note that some sentences may have more than one verb phrase.

1. Rennie has been to the zoo more often this year than ever before.

2. Her twin nieces began walking recently, and since then their favorite activity has been going to the zoo with Aunt Rennie.

3. This spring the twins were excited about the newly arrived pandas.

4. By the time Rennie and the twins finally got to the zoo, the pandas had become accustomed to visitors and chewed calmly on some bamboo.

33d Adjectives

More about
Adjectives,
698–706

Adjectives modify nouns or pronouns with descriptive or limiting information. They answer questions such as *What kind? Which one?* or *How many?*

	adj. noun
WHAT KIND?	a warm day
WHICH ONE?	the next speaker
HOW MANY?	twelve roses

Adjectives most commonly fall before nouns in a noun phrase and after *linking verbs* as *subject complements*.

linking verb A verb
that conveys a state
of being linking a
subject to its com-
plement
subject complement
An adjective, pro-
noun, or noun phrase
that follows a linking
verb and describes
or refers to the sen-
tence subject

> adj.   noun   adj.   noun
> ▶ The young musicians played a rousing concert.

> pro- link.   adj.
> ▶ They were enthusiastic.
> noun verb

More about
Comparative
adjectives,
702–3

Many adjectives change form to express comparison: *young, younger, youngest; enthusiastic, more/less enthusiastic, most/least enthusiastic.*

Possessive, demonstrative, and indefinite pronouns that function as adjectives—as well as the articles *a, an,* and *the*—are known as *determiners* because they specify or quantify the nouns they modify. Determiners always precede other adjectives in a noun phrase. Some, like *all* and *both,* also precede any other determiners.

> det. adj. noun   det. noun   dets.   adj. noun
> ▶ The new gym is in that building with all those solar panels on
> det. noun
> the roof.

The Ordering of Adjectives The ordering of adjectives in noun phrases and the use of articles and other determiners in English can be challenging for multilingual writers. English sentences tend to place adjectives before nouns, while adjective placement in other languages varies, and some languages do not use articles at all. For more on these topics, see pages 763 and 744–51.

33e Adverbs

Adverbs modify verbs, adjectives, and other adverbs, as well as entire phrases and clauses. They answer such questions as *How? Where? When?* and *To what extent or degree?*

More about
Adverbs,
697–705

HOW?	adverb ⎯⎯⎯⎯⎯⎯⎯⎯⎯⎯ verb adv. Embarrassingly, my cell phone rang loudly. The adverb *loudly* modifies the verb *rang*. The adverb *embarrassingly* modifies the whole sentence.
WHEN?	adv. adj. Dinner is finally ready. The adverb *finally* modifies the adjective *ready*.
WHERE? **EXTENT?**	verb adv. adv. Stop right there! The adverb *right* modifies the adverb *there*, which modifies the verb *stop*.

Like adjectives, many adverbs change form to express comparison: *far, farther, farthest; frequently, more/less frequently, most/least frequently.*

A *conjunctive adverb* is a transitional expression that can link one independent clause to another. The conjunctive adverb modifies the second clause and specifies its relationship to the first. A period or semicolon, not a comma, should separate independent clauses linked with a conjunctive adverb.

More about
Comparative
adverbs, 702–3

▶ Writers have several options for joining independent clauses; a comma alone, however, is not one of them.

Quick Reference   Common Conjunctive Adverbs

accordingly	however	otherwise
also	indeed	similarly
anyway	instead	specifically
as a result	likewise	still
besides	meanwhile	subsequently
certainly	moreover	suddenly
finally	nevertheless	then
for example	next	therefore
furthermore	nonetheless	thus
hence	now	

More about
Adjective and
  adverb phrases,
  620, 717–18
Adjective and
  adverb clauses,
  623–24

NOTE In addition to individual words, whole phrases and clauses can function as adjectives and adverbs within sentences.

EXERCISE 33.3 Identifying adjectives and adverbs

Underline the adjectives and circle the adverbs in the following sentences.

1. Grace had always liked to have a tidy bedroom.

2. She decided to ask Maritza gently if they could have a little chat about neatness.

3. The two were good friends as well as roommates, so they agreeably worked out a compromise.

4. They split their small room into equal halves, and each cleaned her half as thoroughly as she wished.

33f Prepositions

Prepositions relate nouns or pronouns to other words in a sentence in terms of time, space, cause, and other attributes.

▶ The lecture begins at noon in the auditorium.

As the Quick Reference box on the next page indicates, prepositions can consist of more than one word.

EXERCISE 33.4 Identifying prepositions

Underline the prepositions in each of the following sentences.

1. Many people drink coffee despite worrying about the health risks.

2. Over the last twenty years, research has shown that coffee is safe in moderation, and it may even offer some health benefits.

3. According to some studies, regular coffee drinkers have a lower incidence of type 2 diabetes than people who do not drink coffee.

4. However, because the main ingredient in coffee is caffeine, a mildly addictive stimulant, excessive use is not recommended.

Reference   Common One-Word and Multiword Prepositions

about	at	far from	near	past
above	because of	for	near to	since
according to	before	from	next to	through
across	behind	in	of	to
after	below	in addition to	off	toward
against	beneath	in case of	on	under
ahead of	beside	in front of	on account of	underneath
along	between	in place of	on behalf of	until
among	by	in spite of	on top of	up
around	by means of	inside	onto	upon
as far as	close to	inside of	out of	with
as to	down	instead of	outside	within
as well as	during	into	outside of	without
aside from	except	like	over	

33g Conjunctions

Conjunctions join words, phrases, and clauses to other words, phrases, or clauses and specify the way the joined elements relate to each other.

- *Coordinating conjunctions* (*and, but, or, for, nor, yet,* and *so*) join grammatically equivalent elements, giving them each equal significance.

  ▸ Ingenious and energetic entrepreneurs can generate effective but inexpensive publicity. [The conjunction *and* pairs two adjectives; the conjunction *but* contrasts two adjectives.]

- *Correlative conjunctions* are pairs of terms that, like coordinating conjunctions, join grammatically equivalent elements. Common correlative conjunctions include *either ... or, neither ... nor, both ... and, not only ... but also,* and *whether ... or.*

  ▸ Fred Thompson has been both an actor and a presidential candidate.

- *Subordinating conjunctions* link subordinate clauses to the independent clauses they modify.

  ▸ The party could not begin until the guest of honor had arrived.

> **More about**
> Independent and subordinate clauses, 622–25

Quick Reference — **Common Subordinating Conjunctions**

after	before	since	when
although	even if	so that	where
as	even though	though	while
as if	if	unless	
because	once	until	

→ **EXERCISE 33.5 Identifying conjunctions**

Underline the conjunctions in the following sentences, and label the type of conjunction (coordinating, correlative, or subordinating) each is.

1. Photography was Randall's hobby, so he volunteered to take photos at the community service club's fund-raising car wash.

2. He said he would send the story and photos not only to the local newspaper but also to the school's TV station.

3. After the car wash, Randall had to decide whether to download the photos to his computer or ask to use his friend Amita's computer, which was faster and had more memory than his.

4. Although he decided to ask Amita, he ended up using his own computer anyway because hers needed repairs.

5. In the end, once he had followed up his photo story submission with phone calls, both the newspaper and TV station decided to run the story.

33h Interjections

Interjections are words like *alas, bah, oh, ouch,* and *ugh* that express strong feeling—of regret, contempt, surprise, pain, or disgust, for example—but otherwise serve no grammatical function.

▸ Ugh! That's the worst coffee I ever tasted.

▸ "Bah," said Scrooge.

—Charles Dickens, *A Christmas Carol* (1843)

SENTENCE STRUCTURE

All sentences have two basic parts: a subject and a predicate. The *subject* is the thing the sentence is about. The *predicate* states something about the subject.

▶ Digital technology transformed the music industry.

Sentences fall into one of four functional categories:

- *Declarative sentences* (the most common type) make a statement.

  ▶ Digital technology transformed the music industry.

- *Imperative sentences* give a command.

  ▶ Join the digital bandwagon to survive in today's competitive media marketplace.

- *Interrogative sentences* ask a question.

  ▶ Will digital technology make printed books obsolete?

- *Exclamatory sentences* express strong or sudden emotion.

  ▶ How I hate updating apps on my phone!

33i Subjects

The *simple subject* of a sentence is a noun or pronoun. The *complete subject* consists of the simple subject plus any modifying words or phrases.

|— complete subject —|
               simple
               subject

▶ *Two robotic <u>vehicles</u>* began exploring Mars in January 2004.

A *compound subject* contains two or more simple subjects joined by a conjunction.

|———————————— compound subject ————————————|
                ss   conj   ss

▶ *The six-wheeled, solar-powered <u>Spirit</u> and the identical <u>Opportunity</u>* landed within three weeks of each other.

In imperative sentences (commands), the subject, *you*, is unstated.

▶ [<u>You</u>] Learn about space exploration at www.nasa.gov.

Quick

Reference Finding the Subject

The complete subject of a sentence is the answer to the question "Who or what did the action or was in the state defined by the verb?"

├— complete subject —┤ verb

▶ Two robotic vehicles landed safely on Mars in January 2004.

What landed on Mars in January 2004? Two robotic vehicles did. The subject is *two robotic vehicles.*

├——————— complete subject ———————┤ verb

▶ The scientists and engineers who designed the rovers cheered.

Who cheered? The scientists and engineers who designed the rovers did. The subject is *the scientists and engineers who designed the rovers.*

The subject usually precedes the verb, but it is not always the first element in a sentence. In the following sentence, for example, the phrase *in July 2007* modifies the rest of the sentence but is not part of the subject.

├— subject —┤ verb

▶ In July 2007, Martian dust storms restricted the activity of the rovers.

In interrogative sentences (questions), the subject falls between a helping verb and the main verb or, if the main verb is a form of *be,* after the verb.

helping main
verb ├—subject—┤ verb

▶ Did the rovers find evidence of water on Mars?

verb ├——— subject ———┤

▶ Were *Spirit* and *Opportunity* more durable than expected?

More about
Word order and emphasis,
556–57

Writers occasionally invert normal word order and place the subject after the verb for emphasis.

verb ├——— subject ———┤

▶ Out of the swirling dust emerged the hardy Mars rover.

The subject also follows the verb in sentences that begin with *there* followed by a form of *be.* In these **expletive constructions,** the word *there* functions as a placeholder for the delayed subject.

v ├— subject —┤

▶ There are two vehicles roaming the surface of Mars.

English Word Order In English, word order is less flexible than in many other languages, and the position of a word often affects its grammatical function and meaning. English sentences tend to place subjects before verbs and verbs before their objects. English readers expect this order, so using other word orders can cause confusion.

More about English word order, 735–42

33j Predicates

The *simple predicate* of a sentence is the main verb and any helping verbs. The *complete predicate* is the simple predicate together with any objects, complements, and modifiers.

      ⊢――― complete predicate ―――⊣
      simple
      pred.

▸ Polynesian mariners *settled the Hawaiian Islands.*

      ⊢―――――――― complete predicate ――――――――⊣
      simple pred.

▸ The first settlers *may have arrived as early as the fourth century CE.*

A *compound predicate* is a complete predicate with two or more simple predicates joined by a conjunction.

      ⊢―――――――――――――――――――――― complete
      simple pred.

▸ Polynesian mariners *navigated thousands of miles of open ocean* and

   predicate ―――――――――⊣
   sp

settled the islands of the South Pacific.

➔ EXERCISE 33.6 Identifying subjects and predicates

For each of the following sentences, underline and label the simple subject and simple predicate; then circle and label the complete subject and complete predicate.

1. Carlynn had never gone on a camping trip before.

2. Everyone else was diligently working to set up the campsite.

3. Carlynn's cousin Marilupe handed Carlynn a hatchet and told her to find some dead wood for the campfire.

4. Later, an exhausted Carlynn and a still energetic Sara stacked the wood and assembled some large rocks in a circle.

5. Then Marilupe amazed Carlynn as well as everyone else by demonstrating how to start a fire without matches.

33k Verb Types and Sentence Patterns

There are three kinds of verb, *intransitive, linking,* and *transitive,* and they combine with other elements in the predicate in five basic sentence patterns.

1. Subject → intransitive verb

Intransitive verbs require no object and can stand alone as the only element in a predicate. They are often modified, however, by adverbs and adverbial phrases and clauses.

▶ The volcano *erupted*.

▶ The volcano *erupted* suddenly in a powerful blast of ash and steam.

Quick

Reference Five Sentence Patterns

1. subject → intransitive verb

   s   iv
   ▶ The lights dimmed.

2. subject → linking verb → subject complement

      s   lv   sc
   ▶ The audience fell silent.

3. subject → transitive verb → direct object

      s   tv   do
   ▶ The orchestra played the overture.

4. subject → transitive verb → indirect object → direct object

      s   tv   io   do
   ▶ The show gave the audience a thrill.

5. subject → transitive verb → direct object → object complement

      s   tv   do   oc
   ▶ The applause made the actors happy.

2. Subject → linking verb → subject complement

A *subject complement* is an adjective, pronoun, or noun phrase that describes or refers to the subject of a sentence. A *linking verb* connects the subject to its complement. Linking verbs express states of being rather than actions. The verb *be*, when used as a main verb, is always a linking verb. Other verbs that can function as linking verbs include *appear, become, fall, feel, grow, look, make, prove, remain, seem, smell, sound,* and *taste.*

```
                        link.
|— subj. —|            vb.    |— subj. comp. —|
```
▸ The Oscar   is   a coveted award.

▸ The patient   felt   better.

3. Subject → transitive verb → direct object

Transitive verbs have two *voices*: active and passive. *Transitive verbs* in the *active voice* require a *direct object*—a pronoun or noun phrase that receives the action of the verb.

> *More about*
> Voice in verbs,
> 680–83
> Voice and
> style choices,
> 560–62

```
                          active
|———— subject ————|    trans. vb.    |——— do ———|
```
▸ The undersea volcano   created   a new island.

The *passive voice* reverses the role of the subject, making it the recipient of the action of the verb. An active-voice sentence can usually be transformed into a passive-voice sentence of the same meaning. The subject of the passive-voice version is the direct object of the active-voice version.

```
                         passive
|—— subject ——|        trans. verb
```
▸ A new island   *was created*   by the undersea volcano.

In the passive voice, the agent of the action can be left unstated.

▸ A new island *was created*.

NOTE Many verbs can be either transitive or intransitive.

```
                              |——— do ———|
```
TRANSITIVE   My sister *won* the Scrabble game.

INTRANSITIVE   My sister always *wins*.

When in doubt about the usage of a verb, check a dictionary.

4. Subject → transitive verb → indirect object → direct object

Some transitive verbs can take an *indirect object* as well as a direct object. The indirect object, which precedes the direct object, identifies the beneficiary of the action of the verb.

⊢——— s ———⊣	⊢— tv —⊣	⊢—— io ——⊣	⊢——————— do ———————⊣
▸ Juan	lent	Ileana	his notes.
▸ The donor	bought	the library	a new computer center.

Often, the indirect object can also be stated as a prepositional phrase that begins with *to* or *for* and follows the direct object.

    ▸ Juan lent his notes *to Ileana.*

    ▸ The donor bought a new computer center *for the library.*

    Verbs that can take an indirect object include *ask, bring, buy, call, find, get, give, hand, leave, lend, offer, pass, pay, promise, read, send, show, teach, tell, throw,* and *write.*

> **More about**
> Indirect objects,
> 738–40

Indirect Objects The use of indirect objects is highly idiomatic in English. The verbs that take them are similar to others that do not. Likewise, in some situations an indirect object before the direct object is interchangeable with a prepositional phrase after it, but in others only one or the other is acceptable. Learning how to use indirect objects effectively, then, requires exposure to a broad variety of English-language situations and texts.

5. Subject → transitive verb → direct object → object complement

An *object complement* is an adjective or noun phrase that follows the direct object and describes the condition of the object or a change that the subject has caused it to undergo.

⊢——— s ———⊣	⊢—— tv ——⊣	⊢——— do ———⊣	⊢——— oc ———⊣
▸ The fans	considered	the umpire's call	mistaken.
▸ The manager	named	David Ortiz	designated hitter.

→ EXERCISE 33.7 Identifying objects and complements

In the following sentences, underline the objects and complements. Then write DO above each direct object, IO above each indirect object, SC above each subject complement, and OC above each object complement.

1. Before he died, my grandfather wrote my mother a long letter.

2. It is actually a family history in letter form.

3. In it, my grandfather describes his own parents' arduous journey from their homeland to their new home in America.

4. The story makes me grateful for their courage.

331 Phrases

A *phrase* is a group of related words that lacks a subject, a predicate, or both. Phrases function in various ways within sentences, but cannot function as sentences by themselves. A phrase by itself is a *fragment,* not a sentence.

> **fragment** An incomplete sentence punctuated as if it were complete

1. Noun phrases

A *noun phrase* consists of a noun together with any modifiers. Noun phrases function as subjects, objects, and complements within sentences.

|———— noun phrase/subject ————|
▶ *Sam's mouth-watering apple pie* emerged piping hot from the oven.

|———— noun phrase/direct object ———|
▶ The guests devoured *Sam's mouth-watering apple pie.*

|———— noun phrase/subj. comp. ———|
▶ The high point of the meal was *Sam's mouth-watering apple pie.*

An *appositive phrase* is a noun or noun phrase that renames a noun or noun phrase and is grammatically equivalent to it.

|———— appositive ————|
▶ The high point of the meal, *Sam's mouth-watering apple pie,* emerged piping hot from the oven.

2. Verb phrases

A *verb phrase* consists of a main verb and all its helping verbs. Verb phrases function as the simple predicates of sentences and clauses.

|———— verb phrase ————|

▸ By Election Day, the candidates *will have been campaigning* for almost two years.

3. Prepositional phrases

A *prepositional phrase* is a preposition followed by the *object of the preposition:* a pronoun or noun and its modifiers. Prepositional phrases function as adjectives and adverbs.

▸ The train arrives in an hour. [The prepositional phrase *in an hour* functions as an adverb modifying the verb *arrives.*]

▸ She recommended the book about Einstein. [The prepositional phrase *about Einstein* functions as an adjective modifying the noun *book.*]

→ EXERCISE 33.8 Identifying prepositional phrases

In the following sentences, underline each prepositional phrase, write above it the type (adjective or adverb), and circle the words it modifies.

1. Roger said he was a little nervous before he stepped into the canoe.

2. Miguel told Roger to sit in the front of the canoe.

3. Miguel, who had been on many canoe trips before, expertly steered from the canoe's back seat.

4. The trip down the river was enjoyable for both Roger and Miguel.

4. Verbal phrases

Verbals are verb forms that function as nouns, adjectives, or adverbs. Although they may have objects and complements, verbals lack the information about tense, person, and number required of a complete verb.

A *verbal phrase* consists of a verbal and any modifiers, objects, or complements. There are three kinds of verbal phrases: gerund phrases, infinitive phrases, and participial phrases.

Gerunds   A *gerund* is the present participle (or *-ing* form) of a verb used as a noun; and like nouns, gerunds and gerund phrases can function as subjects, objects, and complements.

|——— gerund phrase/subject ———|
▶ *Increasing automobile fuel efficiency* will reduce carbon emissions.

|——— gerund phrase/dir. obj. ———|
▶ The mayor recommends *improving the city's mass transit system.*

Infinitives   An *infinitive* is the *to* form of the verb (*to decide, to eat, to study*). Infinitives and infinitive phrases can function as adjectives and adverbs as well as nouns.

|– noun phrase/subj. comp. –|
▶ The goal of the law is *to increase fuel efficiency.*

|——— adjective phrase ———|
▶ Congress passed a law *to increase fuel efficiency.*

|——— adverb phrase ———|
▶ *To reduce traffic congestion,* the city improved its mass transit system.

Infinitive versus Gerund after the Verb   Some verbs can be followed by a gerund but not an infinitive, others by an infinitive but not a gerund, and still others by either a gerund or an infinitive. Lists of verbs and what can follow them do exist, but learning specific examples is a matter of experience with a broad variety of English-language situations and texts.

❯ *More about*
Infinitive versus gerund after verbs, 756–57

Participial phrases   In a *participial phrase* the present participle or past participle of a verb acts as an adjective. The present participle ends in *-ing*. The past participle of regular verbs ends in *-ed,* but some verbs have irregular past participles.

❯ *More about*
Irregular past participles, 667–69

▶ *Surveying the disheveled apartment,* Grace wondered whether it would be possible to room with Maritza.

▶ *Deeply concerned,* she asked, "How long have you lived alone?"

> **EXERCISE 33.9 Identifying verbal phrases**

In the following sentences, underline each verbal phrase. Then write above it the type (gerund, infinitive, or participial).

1. Seeking economic opportunity or freedom from political or religious repression, millions of immigrants came to the United States between the end of the Civil War and the early 1920s.

2. Many of the newcomers intended to return to their homelands.

3. Most immigrants during this period came from southern and eastern Europe, replacing the Irish and German immigrants who had pre-dominated before the Civil War.

4. Leaving home and settling in a new environment must have been difficult.

5. Not always welcomed in their new communities, immigrants often settled together in ethnic enclaves.

5. Absolute phrases

Absolute phrases modify entire sentences rather than particular words within sentences. They usually consist of a pronoun or noun phrase followed by a participle. Set off by commas, they can often fall flexibly before, after, or within the rest of the sentence.

▶ *All our quarrels forgotten,* we sat before the fire and talked quietly.

When the participle in an absolute phrase is a form of *be,* it is often omitted as understood.

▶ *Her interview [having been] successful,* she was offered the job on the spot.

33m Independent and Subordinate Clauses

A *clause* is a word group with a subject and a predicate. An *independent* (or *main*) *clause* can stand alone as a sentence.

|——— independent clause ———|
▶ Sam's pie won first prize.

A *subordinate* (or *dependent*) clause is a clause within a clause.

|————————— independent clause —————————|
                                    |——— sub. clause ———|

▶ Sam baked the pie that won first prize.

That is, a subordinate clause functions inside an independent clause (or another subordinate clause) as a noun, adjective, or adverb but cannot stand alone as a sentence. A subordinate clause by itself is a *fragment*. A subordinating word—either a *subordinating conjunction* (see the Quick Reference box on p. 612) or a *relative pronoun* (see the Quick Reference box on p. 606)—usually signals the beginning of a subordinate clause.

More about
Subordinate
 clause frag-
 ments, 635–36
Punctuating
 subordinate
 clauses,
 781–83, 787–89

1. Adjective clauses

Like adjectives, *adjective clauses* (also called *relative clauses*) modify nouns or pronouns. They usually begin with a relative pronoun that immediately follows the word the clause modifies and refers back to it.

                     s   v   do

▶ Sam baked the pie *that* won first prize.

                s   v   do

▶ The donor *who paid for the library's new computer center* is a recent graduate.

In both of these examples, the relative pronoun is the subject of the subordinate clause, and the clause follows normal word order, with the subject before the verb. When the relative pronoun is the direct object, however, it still comes at the beginning of the clause, reversing normal word order.

                  do   s   v

▶ The candidate *whom* *we supported* lost the election.

More about
Who versus
 whom, 691–92

Adjective clauses can also begin with the subordinating conjunctions *when* and *where*.

▶ Tupelo, Mississippi, is the town *where Elvis Presley was born.*

It is sometimes acceptable to omit the relative pronoun that introduces an adjective clause when the meaning of the clause is clear without it.

▶ The candidate [*whom*] *we supported* lost the election.

2. Adverb clauses

More about
The meaning of subordinating conjunctions, 537

Adverb clauses usually begin with a subordinating conjunction, which specifies the relation of the clause to the term it modifies. Like adverbs, adverb clauses can modify verbs, adjectives, and adverbs as well as whole phrases and clauses.

▶ The baby boom began *as World War II ended.*

The adverb clause modifies the verb *began.*

▶ The economy grew faster *than many Americans thought it would.*

The adverb clause modifies the adverb *faster.*

▶ The 1950s were an affluent decade, *although the general prosperity did not extend to all.*

The adverb clause modifies the preceding independent clause.

3. Noun clauses

Noun clauses do not modify other parts of a sentence but instead replace noun phrases as subjects, objects, or complements within an independent clause. Noun clauses can begin with a relative pronoun as well as with certain subordinating conjunctions, including *how, if, when, whenever, where, wherever, whether,* and *why.*

— subject —
▶ *Whoever crosses the finish line first* wins the race.

— subject comp. —
▶ Home is *where the heart is.*

— direct object —
▶ The evidence proves *that the defendant is not guilty.*

➜ EXERCISE 33.10 Identifying subordinate clauses

In the following passage, underline the subordinate clauses. Then write above each clause its function (noun, adverbial, or adjectival).

> Spring break is a time when most students want just to take it easy and have fun. Martin usually did just that, although he sometimes thought he should spend the time more productively. However, he never could figure out how he could turn this desire to be useful into reality. Then he saw a story in the school newspaper about the community service club's spring break project, which was to help build a home for someone in need. He decided that this was his opportunity to do something different. That he had to pay for the trip himself required Martin to spend many hours working to raise the funds. He washed cars, shoveled snow, babysat, walked dogs, and did other errands for his neighbors over the winter until he had the $600 that he needed. The bus took Martin and the other participants to the home site, which was four hundred miles from the school. The days at the construction site started earlier than the students usually liked to get up, but they all found it exciting to learn how to build a house. The construction had progressed substantially by the end of the spring break week. Martin and his fellow student home builders returned feeling as though they had used their week off doing something useful.

33n Sentence Types

Sentences fall into four types depending on the combination of independent and subordinate clauses they contain. Including a mix of types in your writing and choosing the appropriate type for the information you intend to convey can help you hold your readers' attention and emphasize important points.

> **More about**
> Sentence variety,
> 552–57

1. Simple sentences

A *simple sentence* has only one independent clause and no subordinate clauses.

|————————— independent clause —————————|
▶ Lance Armstrong won the Tour de France seven times.

A simple sentence need not be short or even uncomplicated. A sentence with a compound subject, a compound predicate, or both is still a simple sentence as long as it has a single complete subject, a single complete predicate, and no subordinate clauses.

> ▸ ┌──────────────────────────────────── independent
> Lance Armstrong and Miguel Indurain each won the Tour de
> clause ────────────────────────────────────┘
> France and dominated professional cycling.

2. Compound sentences

More about
Avoiding comma
splices and
fused sentences, 639–47
(ch. 35)

A *compound sentence* has two or more independent clauses but no subordinate clauses. A comma and a coordinating conjunction, a semicolon, or a semicolon and a conjunctive adverb usually join the clauses in a compound sentence.

> ▸ ┌──────────────── independent clause ────────────────┐
> Lance Armstrong won the Tour de France seven times, and
> ┌──────────────── independent clause ────────────────┐
> in 2002, *Sports Illustrated* named him Sportsman of the Year.

> ▸ ┌─────────── independent clause ───────────┐ ┌───── independent
> Armstrong's seven wins were in consecutive years; two other cyclists
> clause ─────────────────────────────────────┘
> had previously won in five consecutive years.

3. Complex sentences

A *complex sentence* consists of a single independent clause with at least one subordinate clause.

> ▸ ┌─────── subordinate clause ───────┐┌─────── independent clause ───────
> After an investigation found him involved in doping, Armstrong
> ─────────────────────────────────┐
> was stripped of his titles.

> ▸ ┌── independent
> ┌─────────── subordinate clause ───────────┐
> The Tour de France, which is the world's longest cycling race, covers
> clause ───────────────────────────────────┘
> nearly 2,000 miles in 22 days.

4. Compound-complex sentences

A *compound-complex sentence* has two or more independent clauses with one or more subordinate clauses.

▶ The Tour has long been plagued by allegations of doping among
|———————————————— independent clause ————————————————|

contestants, but the 2007 race, which saw three riders disqualified for
|————————| |———————————————————————————independent
|————————————————subordinate

doping-related offenses, was particularly scandal ridden.
clause ——|
clause ———————————————————|

➤ **EXERCISE 33.11 Identifying sentence types**

Next to each of the following sentences, write the type of sentence it is: simple, compound, complex, or compound-complex.

1. Lindsay practices her breathing exercises every day with her husband, Larry, who coaches her enthusiastically.

2. Lindsay and Larry attend weekly childbirth classes, meet other expectant parents, learn about the stages of labor, and practice massage and relaxation techniques.

3. One couple, although friendly to Lindsay and Larry, often interrupt the instructor, so Larry is sometimes annoyed by them.

4. Lindsay and Larry will be first-time parents, but they are learning important information by attending the classes.

5. As they learn more, Lindsay and Larry gain confidence as prospective parents; however, the childbirth video made them nervous at first.

Make It **Your Own**

Write down five sentences from a reading assignment or from a newspaper article. Identify the independent and dependent clauses in each sentence, and label each sentence as simple, compound, complex, or compound-complex.

Work **Together**

Exchange your sentences and your analysis of them with those of another student, and check each other's work. Consult your professor if you disagree about any sentences.

34

Avoiding Sentence Fragments

© Nikolay Tzolov/Getty Images

An open drawbridge is not a complete bridge; it is two bridge fragments, neither of which, by itself, will get travelers all the way across a river. Similarly, a sentence *fragment* is not a complete sentence. It may begin with a capital letter and end with a period (or a question mark or an exclamation point), but it lacks all the elements of a complete sentence. It takes readers only partway through the writer's thought, leaving them searching for the missing pieces. Although writers may use them intentionally in certain contexts, fragments are almost always out of place in academic and business writing.

> **subject** A noun or pronoun that names the topic of a sentence
> **complete verb** A main verb together with any helping verbs needed to indicate tense, voice, and mood

34a Recognizing Fragments

A sentence must have at least one *independent clause,* which is a group of related words that has a *complete verb* and a *subject* but does not start with a subordinating term such as *although, because, who,* or *that.* A word group punctuated like a sentence that does not satisfy these conditions is a fragment, not a sentence.

> **More about**
> Verbs, 664–83
> (ch. 37)

1. No verb

A *complete verb* consists of a main verb together with any helping verbs needed to express tense, mood, and voice. If a word group

Reference   **Identifying Fragments**

To determine whether a word group is a fragment or a sentence, ask yourself these questions:

1. **Does it have a complete verb?** If the answer is no, it is a fragment.
2. **Does it have a subject?** If the answer is no, it is a fragment.
3. **Does it begin with a subordinating word but otherwise stand alone?** If the answer is yes, it is a fragment.

lacks a complete verb, it is a *phrase,* and if that phrase is punctuated as a sentence, it is a phrase fragment.

FRAGMENT (NO VERB)   Her beautiful new sports car.

SENTENCE   Her beautiful new sports car was smashed beyond repair.
subj. complete verb

Verbals are words that look like verbs—they are derived from verbs—but they lack the information about tense required of a complete verb. Instead, they function as nouns, adjectives, or adverbs. Verbals can include past participles (the *-ed* form in most verbs), present participles (the *-ing* form), and infinitives (the *to* form). Verbal phrases, by themselves, are fragments, not sentences.

> *More about*
> Verbals,
> 620–21, 629

FRAGMENT   An inspired teacher making a difference in her students' lives.
verbal   verbal

SENTENCE   An inspired teacher, she is making a difference in her students' lives.
verbal   subj. verb

2. No subject

The subject of a sentence is the answer to the question "Who or what did the action defined by the verb?" If a word group lacks a subject, it is a phrase. If the phrase is punctuated like a sentence, it is a phrase fragment.

FRAGMENT   Serves no purpose.
verb

SENTENCE   The breadmaker in my cupboard serves no purpose.
subject   verb

More about
Imperatives, 678

Imperatives (*commands*) look like they do not have a subject. Actually their subject is understood to be *you*, and they are sentences, *not* fragments.

	verb
IMPERATIVE SENTENCE	Come here right now!

Including a Stated Subject Unlike in most other languages, all sentences in formal English except commands always require an explicitly stated subject. See chapter 43, "Understanding English Word Order and Sentence Structure."

More about
Subordinate
clauses,
623–26

3. Begins with a subordinating term

A subordinate clause and an independent clause both have a subject and verb, but a subordinate clause begins with a subordinating term, either a subordinating conjunction or a relative pronoun (see the Quick Reference box on the next page). The subordinating term links the subordinate clause to another clause, where it functions as a noun, adjective, or adverb. A subordinate clause cannot stand alone as a sentence, and if it is punctuated like a sentence, it is a subordinate clause fragment.

	subordinator
FRAGMENT	When the drawbridge closes.

		subordinator
SENTENCE	We will cross the river	when the drawbridge closes.

	subordinator
FRAGMENT	Which made driving hazardous.

		subordinator
SENTENCE	The storm left a foot of snow,	which made driving hazardous.

Be careful to distinguish between relative pronouns used to introduce a subordinate clause and the same words used as interrogative pronouns to introduce questions. Questions beginning this way are complete sentences.

	relative pronoun
FRAGMENT	Who will be attending.

	interrogative pronoun
SENTENCE	Who will be attending?

Quick

Reference   Subordinating Terms

Subordinating Conjunctions

after	*before*	*since*	*unless*	*whereas*
although	*even if*	*so that*	*until*	*while*
as	*even though*	*than*	*when*	*why*
as if	*if*	*that*	*whenever*	
because	*once*	*though*	*where*	

Relative Pronouns

that	*who*	*whom*	*whose*	*which*
what	*whoever*	*whomever*	*whatever*	*whichever*

> **EXERCISE 34.1 Identifying fragments**

Identify each of the following word groups as a sentence or a fragment; then further label each fragment as a phrase fragment or a subordinate clause fragment.

> *More about*
> Different types of
> pronouns, 606

EXAMPLE

Which have women heads of state. *[fragment, subordinate clause]*

1. In 2006, Michelle Bachelet became the first female president of Chile.

2. Who would have predicted such a turn of events just a few years earlier?

3. Not many observers at the time.

4. Because Chile was for many years a bastion of gender conservatism.

5. Electing Bachelet changed all that.

6. The voters went to the polls.

7. With an open mind.

8. The people of Chile were excited.

9. Waving flags and banners, honking horns, blowing whistles, and chanting slogans.

10. Which is a promising sign for the future.

34b Correcting Fragments

Once you have identified a fragment, you have two options for correcting it:

1. Connect the fragment to a related independent clause.

   ▶ The first mission to Pluto was launched in 2006. ~~Arrived~~ *and arrived* in 2015.

   ▶ Archaeologists sift through the dust slowly. ~~Looking~~ *, looking* for personal belongings buried with the deceased.

2. Convert the fragment into an independent clause.

   ▶ The first mission to Pluto was launched in 2006. ~~Arrived~~ *It arrived* in 2015.

   ▶ Archaeologists sift through the dust slowly. ~~Looking~~ *; they are looking* for personal belongings buried with the deceased.

These options apply to both phrase fragments and subordinate clause fragments. Either option can fix a fragment; deciding on the best one is a stylistic choice that depends on the context in which the fragment occurs.

Writing Responsibly　Sentence Fragments and Context

Although writers sometimes use them deliberately in certain contexts (see 34c), for a variety of reasons you should avoid sentence fragments in your academic or business writing. One is that fragments can create ambiguities, as in the following example:

▶ Our small town has seen many changes. Some long-time stores went out of business. Because the new mall opened. There are now more options for family entertainment.

Did the new mall put stores out of business, provide new entertainment options, or both? To clarify this ambiguity, the writer would need to attach the fragment to the preceding sentence or the following sentence, or rewrite these sentences in some other way.

Another reason to avoid fragments is that readers may interpret them as the result of carelessness or a lack of competence, which would undermine your efforts to present yourself authoritatively.

to TOPIC

| **Tech** | **Grammar Checkers and Sentence Fragments** |

The grammar checkers in word process-ing programs may miss some fragments and, in some cases, may incorrectly flag imperatives as fragments. Although your grammar checker can help you, you will still need to edit your prose carefully for fragments.

1. Phrase fragments

Phrase fragments lack a subject, a complete verb, or both. As you edit your writing, watch for fragments based on certain kinds of phrases in particular. These include prepositional phrases, verbal phrases, appositive phrases, the separate parts of compound predicates, and items in lists and examples.

Prepositional phrases   A *prepositional phrase* consists of a preposition (such as *as, at, for, from, in addition to, to,* or *until*) followed by a pronoun or noun and its modifiers. You can usually correct a prepositional phrase fragment by attaching it to an adjacent sentence.

> The Kenyon College women won the NCAA Division III title
>
> ~~again that year. For~~ *for* the seventeenth consecutive year.

> *More about*
> Prepositions and prepositional phrases, 610–11, 621, 769–76

Verbal phrases   Although verbals are derived from verbs, **verbal phrases** can function as adjectives, adverbs, or nouns within a sentence but not as sen-tences on their own. In the following example, *stranding* is a verbal.

> *gas, stranding*
> The car had run out of ~~gas. Stranding~~ us in the middle of nowhere.

Appositive phrases   An *appositive phrase* is a noun or **noun phrase** that renames a preceding noun or noun phrase and is grammatically equivalent to it. Appositives become fragments when they are separated by a period from the phrases they rename.

> *meal, Sam's*
> The diners eagerly awaited the culmination of the ~~meal. Sam's~~
>
> mouth-watering apple pie.

> *More about*
> Appositives, 619

> **noun phrase** A noun together with any modifiers

Compound predicates   A *compound predicate* consists of two or more com-plete verbs, together with their objects and modifiers, that are joined by a coordinating conjunction (such as *or, and,* or *but*) and that share the same

> *More about*
> Compound predi-cates, 615

subject. A fragment results when the last part of a compound predicate is punctuated as a separate sentence.

> ▸ By the end of May, the band members hated each other. ~~But~~ *but* still
>
> had six weeks left to tour.

More about
Punctuation for
lists, 825, 829

Lists and examples Lists become fragments when they are separated from the sentence to which they belong. To correct list fragments, link them to the sentence by rephrasing the passage or replacing the period with a colon or a dash.

FRAGMENT   Three authors are most commonly associated with the Beat movement. Allen Ginsberg, Jack Kerouac, and William Burroughs.

REVISED   Three authors are most commonly associated with the Beat movement: Allen Ginsberg, Jack Kerouac, and William Burroughs.

or

The three authors most commonly associated with the Beat movement are Allen Ginsberg, Jack Kerouac, and William Burroughs.

Examples or explanations that begin with transitional words such as *for example, in contrast,* and *in addition* can be sentences; they are fragments, however, if they are punctuated like a sentence but lack a subject or a complete verb, or otherwise consist of only a subordinate clause. In the following example, the writer corrected a phrase fragment by rephrasing and attaching it to the preceding sentence.

> ▸ People today have access to many sources of news and ~~opinion. For~~ *opinion, including, for*
>
> example, the Internet and cable television as well as broadcast tele-
>
> vision and print newspapers and magazines.

The writer of the next example corrected a subordinate clause fragment by deleting the subordinating word *that,* which turns the fragment into a sentence.

> ▸ Certain facts underscore the rapid growth of the Internet. For
>
> *example,*
> ~~example that~~ web browsers did not become widely available until
>
> the mid-1990s.

→ **EXERCISE 34.2 Correcting sentence fragments**

Correct each sentence fragment below and write at the end what kind of fragment it is (prepositional phrase, verbal phrase, appositive phrase, compound predicate, list or example).

EXAMPLE

The most unforgettable character I know is my ~~grandfather. Jacob~~ Black.

grandfather, Jacob

∧

[appositive phrase]

1. Even though he was only five feet four inches tall, he was a championship boxer. During high school.

2. Boxing was what many young men pursued. Back in the 1940s.

3. Later, he joined the army. Becoming a first sergeant in the quartermaster corps.

4. He was responsible for setting up army camps in Korea. Also for supervising supplies, cooking, and recreation.

5. He must have been a pretty tough guy in those days. Not the warm and loving grandpa I knew later on.

2. Subordinate clause fragments

A subordinate clause has a subject and a verb but begins with a subordinating word or phrase—a subordinating conjunction or a relative pronoun—and cannot stand alone as a sentence. When you correct a subordinate clause fragment, be sure to consider the relationships among the ideas you are expressing before deciding whether to transform the subordinate clause into an independent clause or to connect it to a related independent clause. Subordinating conjunctions, for example, specify the relationship between the information in a subordinate clause and the clause it modifies. If that relationship is important, you will probably want to correct the fragment by connecting it to the independent clause to which it relates.

> *More about*
> Subordination
> and subordi-
> nating conjunc-
> tions, 534–40

▶ Twitter continues to gain popularity as a source of information. ~~Because~~

because

∧

it can publish late-breaking news as soon as it occurs.

The correction retains the subordinating conjunction *because* and with it important information about the cause-and-effect relationship between the two parts of the sentence. That information would have been obscured if the writer had simply deleted the subordinating conjunction to change the fragment into a separate sentence: *They can publish late-breaking news as soon as it occurs.*

In other cases, revising a subordinate clause fragment into a separate sentence by deleting the subordinating word can produce a clearer, less awkward result than would attaching it to another sentence.

> ▶ Horses and camels have something in common. ~~That the~~ The ancestors
>
>   of both originated in the western hemisphere and migrated to the
>
>   eastern hemisphere.

More about
Punctuating
subordinate
clauses and
other subordi-
nate structures,
537, 787–89

A subordinate clause that begins with a subordinating conjunction is usually set off by a comma if it comes at the beginning of a sentence but not if it comes at the end. The punctuation of a subordinate clause that begins with a relative pronoun depends on whether the clause is *essential* (it specifically identifies the word or words it modifies) or *nonessential* (the identity of the word or words it modifies is clear without it).

→ EXERCISE 34.3 Correcting subordinate clause fragments

Correct each fragment below and write at the end whether the fragment begins with a subordinating conjunction or a relative pronoun.

EXAMPLE

Northern Florida is dotted with natural ~~springs. That~~ springs that are direct outlets of a huge aquifer, or groundwater source. *[relative pronoun]*

1. The springs discharge millions of gallons of cool, clean, fresh water each day. Because the aquifer is very close to the surface.

2. The area contains many rivers, lakes, and ponds. That are fed from the springs.

3. Although the area still seems rural and remote. The water attracts many vacationers.

4. For many years people came to visit area tourist attractions. That included "mermaid" shows and glass-bottom boat rides.

5. Today, however, the region has gained a reputation for ecotourism. Because it abounds with state parks, water trails, and campgrounds.

34c Using Intentional Fragments Effectively and Judiciously

Writers sometimes use fragments not in error but intentionally for emphasis or to reflect how people actually speak. Exclamations and the answers to questions often fall into this category.

▸ Another loss! Ouch!

▸ What caused this disaster? The collapse of our running game.

Intentional fragments are also common in advertising copy, and many writers use them for effect when the context makes their full meaning clear.

▸ All science. No fiction.

—Toyota advertisement

▸ Man is the only animal that blushes. Or needs to.

—Mark Twain, *Following the Equator*

Consider your writing situation, your context and genre, and especially your audience before deciding to use a sentence fragment deliberately. If your purpose is careful reporting or analysis, you should probably avoid the intentional sentence fragment because it can create ambiguity (see the Writing Responsibly box on p. 632). In academic or business writing, where clarity of expression is highly prized, fragments are frowned upon and can undermine your authority. On the other hand, if your purpose is expressive or you are writing in an informal context or genre (for example, in a blog or for a fanzine), the occasional intentional fragment can be highly effective.

➔ EXERCISE 34.4 Correcting sentence fragments

Identify and correct any sentence fragments in the following paragraph.

> On January 2, miners of the morning shift reported for work. As usual beginning the descent to the coal seam deep underground. Not all had descended into the mine when the explosion happened. There were two crews. One still aboveground. The explosion occurred at 6:31 a.m. Causing a power outage throughout the mine. Which filled with smoke. And deadly carbon monoxide. A mine rescue team was called. But not until 8:04 a.m. Because it took the mine supervisors that long to ascertain what had happened. Meanwhile, the trapped miners had only a limited supply of oxygen. Distraught families gathered aboveground waiting for news. At last a shout rang out. "Alive!" A collective sigh of relief and thanksgiving was audible. As family members waited to see their loved ones once again.

Make It **Your Own**

Reread three texts you have written recently or a draft you are working on and look for sentence fragments. If you find any, make a note of what kind they are and correct them; then add this to your list of areas to consider as you revise your prose.

Work **Together**

Exchange texts and analyze your classmate's writing for sentence fragments. Underline any you find and make a note of what kind they are. Compare your results with those of the others in the group. What did each of you see that others did not? Were some types of fragments easier to find than others? If so, make a note of any you had difficulty finding and add them to your revision checklist.

35 Avoiding Comma Splices and Fused Sentences

IN THIS CHAPTER

a. Correctly joining independent clauses, 639

b. Identifying comma splices and fused sentences, 640

c. Recognizing when comma splices and fused sentences occur, 641

d. Correcting comma splices and fused sentences, 643

> *More about*
> Clauses, 622–25

> *More about*
> Coordination, 529–41

© Krista Kennedy

How things are joined together is important, whether those "things" are pipes or sentences. If they are not correctly connected, they work poorly or not at all. A blowtorch is a good tool for reconnecting leaky pipes; correct punctuation is a good tool for repairing the comma splices and run-ons in "leaky" sentences. If clauses are incorrectly joined with a comma alone (a *comma splice*), the comma is too weak to show the connection between the two thoughts. If the clauses crash into one another with no separating punctuation (a *fused*, or *run-on, sentence*), readers will not know where one thought ends and the other begins.

35a Correctly Joining Independent Clauses

An *independent clause* can stand on its own as a sentence. Related independent clauses can follow one another as separate sentences, each ending in a period.

> |———————————— independent clause ————————————| |—
> ▶ The blues singer Alberta Hunter retired in the 1950s. She
> |————————— independent clause —————————|
> made a successful comeback in the 1970s.

Alternatively, you can join (or *coordinate*) independent clauses in a compound sentence with a variety of coupling mechanisms that let readers know one clause is ending and another beginning. Of these, two are the most common:

- A comma and a coordinating conjunction (*and, but, or, nor, for, so, yet*)

▶ The blues singer Alberta Hunter retired in the 1950s, but she made a successful comeback in the 1970s.

- A semicolon

▶ The blues singer Alberta Hunter retired in the 1950s; she made a successful comeback in the 1970s.

You can also use a colon or a dash between independent clauses when the first clause introduces the second or the second elaborates on the first. (The colon is usually more appropriate in formal writing.)

▶ The blues singer Alberta Hunter retired in the 1950s: she made a successful comeback in the 1970s.

35b Identifying Incorrectly Joined Independent Clauses: Comma Splices and Fused Sentences

When a writer improperly joins two independent clauses with a comma alone, the result is a *comma splice.*

|—————— independent clause ——————|

COMMA SPLICE Ronald Reagan was originally an actor, he turned

|— independent clause —|
to politics in the 1960s.

When a writer runs two independent clauses together with no punctuation between them, the result is a *fused sentence* (also called a *run-on sentence*).

|—————— independent clause ——————| |——

FUSED Politics and acting have something in common they
SENTENCE

|—————— independent clause ——————|
both require an affinity for public performance.

Writing
Responsibly Clarifying Boundaries

Comma splices and fused sentences obscure the boundaries between linked ideas. If you leave them uncorrected in your writing, you burden readers with a task that should be yours: to identify where one idea ends and another begins and to specify how those ideas relate to each other.

to AUDIENCE

Quick Reference   Identifying Comma Splices and Fused Sentences

When two independent clauses are joined by	The result is
A comma and coordinating conjunction	**Not** a comma splice or fused sentence
A semicolon	**Not** a comma splice or fused sentence
A colon or dash	**Not** a comma splice or fused sentence
A comma alone	A **comma splice—revise**
No punctuation at all	A **fused sentence—revise**

35c Recognizing When Comma Splices and Fused Sentences Tend to Occur

To avoid comma splices and fused sentences in your own work, pay attention to situations in which they are particularly likely to occur:

1. When the second clause begins with a conjunctive adverb (such as *for example, however,* or *therefore*) or other transitional expression

   COMMA SPLICE   The blues singer Alberta Hunter retired in the 1950s, however, she made a successful comeback in the 1970s.

   REVISED   The blues singer Alberta Hunter retired in the 1950s; however, she made a successful comeback in the 1970s.

2. When the grammatical subject of the second clause is a pronoun whose antecedent is the subject of the first clause

   COMMA SPLICE   Ronald Reagan was originally an actor, he turned to politics in the 1960s.

   REVISED   Ronald Reagan was originally an actor, but he turned to politics in the 1960s.

Tech   Comma Splices, Fused Sentences, and Grammar Checkers

Grammar checkers in word processing programs do not reliably identify comma splices or fused sentences. They catch some, but they miss many more.

3. When the first clause introduces the second or the second explains or elaborates on the first

FUSED SENTENCE	Politics and acting have something in common they both require a willingness to perform in public.
REVISED	Politics and acting have something in common: They both require a willingness to perform in public.

4. When one clause is positive and the other negative

COMMA SPLICE	We were not upset that the exam was postponed, we were relieved.
REVISED	We were not upset that the exam was postponed; we were relieved.

→ **EXERCISE 35.1 Identifying comma splices and fused sentences**

In each of the following sentences, underline the independent clauses. Then write CS after each comma splice, write FS after each fused sentence, and circle the numbers of sentences that are correct as is.

EXAMPLE

This is our dog her name is Dusty. *[FS]*

1. Dusty is a mutt, she is not a purebred dog.
2. Some people think she is a German shepherd others just ask what kind of dog she is.
3. I always say she is just a dog.
4. Dogs like Dusty are called a variety of names, mongrel is probably the most common.

Writing
Responsibly | Is a Comma Splice Ever Acceptable?

Comma splices often show up in compound sentences composed of two short, snappy independent clauses in parallel form, particularly when one is advertising:

Buy one, get one free.

It can appear, too, in the work of experienced writers, who may use it deliberately because they feel a period, semicolon, or comma and coordinating conjunction would be too disruptive a separation in sentences like these:

You're not a man, you're a machine.

—George Bernard Shaw,
Arms and the Man

Go ahead, make my day.

—Joseph C. Stinson, screenplay to
Sudden Impact

However, this usage looks like an error and will confuse readers, and thus it is best avoided in academic writing.

to AUDIENCE

5. Mutt and mixed-breed are other common names that are used for these dogs.

6. Mixed-breed dogs have fewer genetic disorders than do purebred dogs the inbreeding of purebreds has created genetic problems.

7. For example, German shepherds often have hip problems, collies often have eye diseases.

8. One type of mixed-breed is the crossbreed, a deliberate cross between two purebred strains.

9. As for Dusty, she certainly looks like a German shepherd she also looks like a Norwegian elkhound.

10. To me, she is the world's greatest dog, I love her very much.

35d Correcting Comma Splices and Fused Sentences

The Quick Reference box on this page lists five strategies for correcting comma splices and fused sentences. The strategy you choose should depend on the logical relationship between the clauses and the meaning you intend to convey.

1. Separate sentences

Correcting a comma splice or fused sentence by dividing the independent clauses into separate sentences makes sense when one or both of the clauses are long or when the two clauses do not have a close logical relationship.

> ▶ My friends and I began our long-anticipated trip to Peru in early July we
>
> <small>. We</small>
>
> arrived in Lima on Saturday morning and flew to Cuzco that same day.

Quick Reference

Ways to Correct Comma Splices and Fused Sentences

1. Use a period to divide the clauses into separate sentences. (643)
2. Join the clauses correctly with a comma and coordinating conjunction. (644)
3. Join the clauses correctly with a semicolon. (644)
4. Join the clauses, if appropriate, with a colon or dash. (644)
5. Change one independent clause into a subordinate clause or modifying phrase. (645)

Use a period also when the second clause is a new sentence that continues a quotation that begins in the first clause.

▶ "We must not be enemies," Abraham Lincoln implored the South in

his first inaugural address, "Though passion may have strained, it

must not break our bonds of affection."

2. Coordinating conjunction

More about
The meaning of coordinating conjunctions, 531–32

When you join independent clauses with a comma and a coordinating conjunction (*and, but, or, nor, for, so,* or *yet*), choose the conjunction that best fits the logical relationship between the clauses.

▶ We needed to adjust to the altitude before we began hiking in the

, so
Andes we spent three days sightseeing in Cuzco.

3. Semicolon

More about
Coordinating with a semicolon, 531–32, 797–98

Join two independent clauses with a semicolon when they have a clear logical relationship, either of contrast, example, or explanation.

▶ Most languages spoken in Europe belong to the Indo-European

;
language family, a few, such as Basque, Finnish, and Hungarian,

do not.

Using a semicolon in combination with a conjunctive adverb or other transitional expression can clarify the relationship between the clauses.

▶ Most languages spoken in Europe belong to the Indo-European

; however,
language family, Basque, Finnish, and Hungarian are exceptions.

4. Colon or dash

More about
Punctuating for emphasis, 557
Colons, 828–30
Dashes, 824–26

You can use a colon or, less commonly, a dash to join independent clauses when the first clause introduces the second or the second explains or elaborates on the first. This usage can create a more emphatic separation between the clauses than would a semicolon.

▶ The message is clear, smoking kills.

▶ Don't get kicked out of school, learn to study effectively.

5. Subordinate clause and modifying phrase

You can correct a comma splice or fused sentence by turning one of the independent clauses into a subordinate clause or by reducing the information in it to a modifying phrase. Note, however, that putting information in subordinate clauses and phrases usually de-emphasizes it in relation to the information in the independent clause it modifies.

> *More about*
> Subordination
> and emphasis,
> 534–39

COMMA SPLICE	Spanish, like French and Italian, is a Romance language, it derives from Latin, the language of the Romans.
REVISED: SUBORDINATE CLAUSE	Spanish, like French and Italian, is a Romance language |——————— subordinate clause ———————| because it derives from Latin, the language of the Romans.
REVISED: MODIFYING PHRASE	|——————— modifying phrase ———————| Spanish, a Romance language like French and Italian, derives from Latin, the language of the Romans.

> ➤ **EXERCISE 35.2 Correcting comma splices and fused sentences**
>
> Choose one of the methods described above to correct each comma splice or fused sentence. Circle the numbers of any sentences that are correct as is.
>
>   **EXAMPLE:**
>
>   Disaster films are almost as old as film itself the first was made in 1901.
>
>   1. Obviously, disasters are natural subjects for films they are dramatic and visually interesting.
>   2. Early disaster movies focused on natural events such as fires, floods, and earthquakes, later ones showed human-made tragedies.
>   3. The first modern disaster movies were made in the 1950s, they focused on airplane crashes.

4. The golden age of disaster movies was probably the 1970s, the most popular of all was *Airport,* released in 1970.

5. It was followed by numerous sequels as well as by other hugely successful examples of the genre, such as *The Towering Inferno.*

6. Since that time, the summer blockbuster has remained everyone's idea of a good time it usually includes enough romance and drama, as well as special effects, to please everyone.

7. The genre even spawned its own subgenre, the disaster spoof, represented by the hits *Airplane* and *Airplane II.*

8. With the increasing sophistication of computerized special effects in the 1990s disaster films enjoyed a huge revival they had flagged in popularity in the 1980s.

9. However, real disasters like the attack on the World Trade Center may have changed all that how much fun is it to see a film like *Snowpiercer*?

10. Other disaster films that refer to real events, such as *The Day After Tomorrow,* which focused on the effects of global warming, have been successful only time will tell whether the genre will survive.

→ **EXERCISE 35.3 Correcting comma splices and fused sentences**

Revise the following passage to correct any comma splices or fused sentences.

Opera is an art form that combines music, lyrics, and dialog, so is musical comedy, however. Then what is the difference between them? Perhaps it is their origins opera arose in the seventeenth century primarily in Italy as an attempt to revive classical Greek drama. Musical comedy arose in the United States in the twentieth century out of vaudeville and other plotless musical shows such as burlesque and reviews. Regardless, there is a great deal of overlap between the two forms today although the famous composer and lyricist Stephen Sondheim says that if something is performed in an opera house, it is an opera, but if it is performed in a theater, it is a musical comedy, today many works are performed in both places.

Make It **Your Own**

Choose a text you have recently written or are writing. On one page of that text, underline each independent clause and check each sentence to be sure it does not include fused sentences or comma splices; if it does, revise the sentences accordingly and add this to your revision checklist.

Work **Together**

Exhange your revised pages with a classmate and double-check each other's work. Where do you have differences of opinion? Review this chapter to resolve any differences.

Text Credits

p. 642: Shaw, George Bernard, *Arms and the Man* (1894). **p. 642:** Stinson, Joseph C. (screenplay), *Sudden Impact* (Warner Bros. 1983).

36 Maintaining Agreement

© Chad Baker/Stone/Getty Images

In many languages, the grammatical form of some words in a sentence must match the form of other words. When the forms match, the reader can easily understand the sentence; when they do not, the effect can be like trying to force a square peg into a round hole, leaving the reader distracted or confused. In English, subjects and verbs require this kind of matchup, or *agreement,* as do pronouns and the words to which they refer.

SUBJECT-VERB AGREEMENT

A verb and its subject have to agree, or match each other, in person and number. *Person* refers to the form of a word that indicates whether it corresponds to the speaker or writer (*I, we*), the person addressed (*you*), or the people or things spoken or written about (*he, she, it, they, Alice, milkshakes*). *Number* refers to the form of a word that indicates whether it is singular, referring to one thing (*a student*), or plural, referring to more than one (*two students*).

36a Understanding How Subjects and Verbs Agree

With just a few exceptions, it is only in the present tense that verbs change form to indicate person and number. Even in the

---

Tech Grammar Checkers and Subject-Verb Agreement

Grammar checkers in word processing programs can alert you to many subject-verb agreement problems, but they can also miss errors and can flag some constructions as errors that are not. Make your own informed judgment about any changes the computer might recommend.

present tense, they have only two forms. One form, which ends in *-s*, is for third-person singular subjects; the other is for all other subjects.

> **More about**
> The forms of regular and irregular verbs, 664–83

	Singular subject	verb	Plural subject	verb
First Person	I	vote	we	vote
Second Person	you	vote	you	vote
Third Person	he, she, it, the student	votes	they, the students	vote

Most nouns form the plural with the addition of an *-s* (*dog, dogs*) or *-es* (*coach, coaches*).

In other words, an *-s* on a noun makes the noun plural; an *-s* on a present-tense verb makes the verb singular.

> **More about**
> Regular and irregular plural nouns, 591–93

	Noun	Verb
Singular	The dog	barks
Plural	The dogs	bark

NOTE Nouns with irregular plurals include *woman* (plural *women*), *foot* (plural *feet*), *child* (plural *children*), and phenomenon (plural *phenomena*).

> **verb phrase** A *main verb* together with any *auxiliary*, or *helping, verbs.* The main verb carries the principal meaning of the phrase; the auxiliaries provide information about tense, voice, and mood.

1. Agreement with *be* and with helping verbs

Unlike any other English verb, *be* has three present-tense forms (*am, are, is*) and two past-tense forms (*was, were*). In **verb phrases** that begin with a form of *be, have,* or *do* as a helping verb, the subject agrees with the helping verb.

	|— subject —|	|— verb phrase —|
SINGULAR	The *price* of oil	*has* been fluctuating.
PLURAL	Commodity *prices*	*have* been fluctuating.
SINGULAR	The *price*	*was* fluctuating.
PLURAL	*Prices*	*were* fluctuating.

> **More about**
> Forms of *be, have,* and *do,* 667–70

The modal auxiliaries—*can, could, may, might, must, shall, should, will, would,* and *ought to*—have only a single form; they do not take an *-s* ending for third-person singular subjects.

> **More about**
> Modal auxiliaries, 656–58

	|- subject -|	|- verb phrase -|
SINGULAR	The *price*	*can* change.
PLURAL	*Prices*	*can* change.

Writing
Responsibly | **Dialect Variation in Subject-Verb Agreement**

The rules of subject-verb agreement are not the same in all dialects of English. In various communities in the English-speaking world, you might hear people say things like *"The cats is hungry," "We was at the store," "That coat needs washed,"* or *"She be walking to school."* In the contexts in which they occur, these variations are not mistakes; they reflect rules that are different from those of Standard American English. Still, the subject-verb agreement rules of Standard American English are what most readers in the United States expect to encounter.

to AUDIENCE

2. Subject-verb agreement pitfalls

> **More about**
> Identifying sen-
> tence subjects,
> 613–15

The basic rules of subject-verb agreement may be clear, but writers (and speakers) nonetheless often trip over them. As the Quick Reference box on the next page indicates, these errors usually involve problems identifying the subject of a sentence and determining whether it is singular or plural.

36b Ignoring Words That Intervene between the Subject and the Verb

In English, the subject of a sentence is usually near the verb. As a result, writers sometimes mistakenly treat words that fall between the subject and the verb as if they were the subject. The writer of the following sentence mistook the singular noun phrase *Order of the Phoenix* for the true subject, the plural noun *members*. The revision corrects the agreement error.

FAULTY   The members of the Order of the Phoenix is dedicated to thwarting Voldemort.

REVISED   The members of the Order of the Phoenix are dedicated to thwarting Voldemort.

NOTE When a singular subject is followed by a phrase that begins with *as well as, in addition to, together with,* or some similar expression, the verb is singular, not plural.

▶ Harry Potter, together with the other members of the Order of the
   is
   Phoenix, are determined to thwart Voldemort.

Quick

Reference   Avoiding Subject-Verb Agreement Pitfalls

1. Ignore words that intervene between the subject and the verb. (650)
2. Distinguish plural from singular compound subjects. (651)
3. Distinguish singular from plural indefinite pronouns. (653)
4. Understand collective noun subjects. (653)
5. Find agreement when the subject is a measurement, a number, or the word *number*. (654)
6. Recognize that some nouns that end in -s are singular. (655)
7. Treat titles, words as words, and gerund phrases as singular. (655)
8. Match the number of a relative pronoun subject (*who, which, that*) to its antecedent. (656)
9. Match the verb to the subject when the subject follows the verb. (656)
10. Match a linking verb with its subject, not its subject complement. (657)

36c Distinguishing Plural from Singular Compound Subjects

A *compound subject* consists of two or more subjects joined by a *conjunction* (*Jack and Jill, one or another*).

> **conjunction** Part of speech that joins words, phrases, or clauses to other words, phrases, or clauses and specifies the way the joined elements relate to each other

1. Compounds joined by *and* or *both ... and*

Most compound subjects joined by *and* or *both ... and* are plural.

▶ Twitter *and* Instagram *are* two popular social networking websites.

▶ *Both* Twitter *and* Instagram *allow* users to post links to photos and videos.

A compound subject joined by *and* is singular, however, if the items in the compound refer to the same person or thing.

▶ The winner *and* next president *is* the candidate with the most electoral votes.

A compound subject joined by *and* is also singular if it begins with *each* or *every*.

▶ *Each* paper *and* exam *contributes* to your final grade.

However, if it is followed by *each*, a compound joined by *and* is plural.

▶ The research paper *and* the final exam *each* *contribute* 25 percent toward your final grade.

2. Compounds joined by *or, nor, either . . . or, neither . . . nor*

When a compound subject is joined by *or, nor, either . . . or,* or *neither . . . nor,* the verb agrees with the part of the compound that is closest to the verb.

▶ *Neither* the coach *nor* the players *were* worried by the other team's early lead.

The second part of the compound is plural, so the verb is plural.

Applying this rule can produce an awkward result when the first item in a compound is plural and the second is singular. Reversing the order often resolves the problem.

AWKWARD	*Neither* the players *nor* the coach *is* happy about last night's loss.
REVISED	*Neither* the coach *nor* the players *are* happy about last night's loss.

Sometimes the result is so awkward that the only solution is to reword the sentence. This happens particularly when the subject includes the pronouns *I, we,* or *you* and the verb is a form of *be.*

AWKWARD	*Neither* Carla *nor* I *am leaving* until the job is finished.
REVISED	Carla *and* I *are not leaving* until the job is finished.
	or
	Neither Carla *nor* I *will leave* until the job is finished.

→ **EXERCISE 36.1 Making subjects and verbs agree**

Underline the subject in each of the following sentences, and then circle the verb that agrees with it.

EXAMPLE

Mr. Jefferson's computer, as well as its programs, (is)/ are) out of date.

1. The members of the panel (agrees/agree) that he needs a new computer.
2. Many students today (has/have) their own very fast computers.
3. Both Ms. Lopez and Mr. Handler (is/are) installing new software on their computers.
4. Mr. Jefferson's old computer (prevents/prevent) him from using that software.
5. His new computer and software (is/are) scheduled to arrive next week.

36d Distinguishing Singular and Plural Indefinite Pronouns

Indefinite pronouns (see the Quick Reference box below) refer to unknown or unspecified people, quantities, or things. Most indefinite pronouns always take a singular verb.

▸ *Everybody talks* about the weather, but *nobody does* anything about it.

—Attributed to Mark Twain

Some indefinite pronouns (*both, few, many, others, several*) always take a plural verb.

▸ *Many* of us *make* New Year's resolutions, but *few* of us *keep* them.

Some indefinite pronouns (*all, any, more, most, some*) are either singular or plural, depending on context.

▸ *Some* of these questions *are* hard.

▸ *Some* of this test *is* hard.

In the first sentence, *some* takes a plural verb because it refers to the plural noun *questions;* in the second sentence, *some* takes a singular verb because it refers to the singular noun *test.*

36e Understanding Collective Noun Subjects

A *collective noun* designates a collection, or group, of individuals: *audience, chorus, committee, faculty, family, government.* In US English, a collective noun is singular when it refers to the group acting as a whole.

▸ The *faculty is* revising the general education requirements.

The group acts as a whole.

Quick Reference   **Common Indefinite Pronouns**

Always singular: *another, anybody, anyone, anything, each, either, everybody, everyone, everything, much, neither, nobody, no one, nothing, one, somebody, someone, something*

Always plural: *both, few, many, others, several*

Variable: *all, any, more, most, some*

A collective noun is plural when it refers to the members of the group acting individually.

▶ The *faculty are* unable to agree on the new requirements.

The individual members of the group disagree among themselves.

If this usage sounds odd to you, however, you can reword the sentence with a clearly plural subject.

▶ The *members* of the faculty *are* unable to agree on the new requirements.

36f Finding Agreement When the Subject Is a Measurement, a Number, or the Word *Number*

Numbers, fractions, and units of measure take a singular verb when they refer to an undifferentiated mass or quantity.

▶ Over *three billion barrels* of gasoline *was* consumed in the United States in 2014.

▶ *One-third* of the applicant pool *is* fully qualified for the job.

▶ *Seven thousand dollars is* too high a price for that car.

Numbers, fractions, and units of measure take a plural verb when they refer to a collection of individual people or things.

▶ That year, *more than 600,000 immigrants became* naturalized citizens of the United States.

▶ *About a third* of the applicants with a college education *are* fully qualified for the job.

▶ *More than 300 applications* for the job *were* filed with the employment service.

The word *number* is plural when it appears with *a* but singular when it appears with *the*.

▶ *A number* of voters *are* in favor of the transportation bond.

▶ *The number* of voters in favor of the transportation bond *is* low.

36g Recognizing Nouns That Are Singular Even Though They End in -s

Some nouns that end in *-s* are singular. Examples include diseases like *diabetes* and *measles*.

▶ *Measles is* a contagious disease.

Words like *economics, mathematics,* and *physics* are singular when they refer to an entire field of study or body of knowledge.

▶ *Economics is* a popular major at many schools.

They are plural, however, when they refer to a set of individual traits related to the field of study.

▶ *The economics* of the music industry *are* changing rapidly.

36h Treating Titles, Words as Words, and Gerund Phrases as Singular

The titles of books, articles, movies, and other works; the names of companies and institutions; the names of countries; and words treated as words are all singular even if they are plural in form.

▶ *Harry Potter and the Order of the Phoenix was* the fifth book in J. K. Rowling's popular series.

▶ *The Centers for Disease Control and Prevention helps* protect the nation's health.

▶ *The United States is* one of the world's largest food exporters.

▸ *Fungi is* one of two acceptable plural forms of the word *fungus;*

funguses is the other.

Gerunds and gerund phrases are also always singular.

- *Conducting excavations is* just one part of an archaeologist's job.

> **gerund** The present participle (-*ing* form) of a verb used as a noun

36i Matching a Relative Pronoun (*Who, Which,* or *That*) to Its Antecedent When the Pronoun Is the Subject of a Subordinate Clause

> **More about**
> Pronouns and their antecedents, 658–63, 692–96

A relative pronoun (*who, which,* or *that*) that functions as the subject of a subordinate clause is singular if its **antecedent** (the word it refers to) is singular, but it is plural if its antecedent is plural.

▸ People *who live* in glass houses should not throw stones.

▸ The cactus is a plant *that thrives* in a hot, dry environment.

Be careful with antecedent phrases that include the expressions *one of* or *only one of. One of* usually signals a plural antecedent; *only one of* signals a singular antecedent.

▸ Barack Obama is *one of several presidents* of the United States *who were elected* to two terms.

Several presidents were elected to two terms, and one of them was Obama. The pronoun *who* refers to the plural noun *presidents.*

▸ Franklin D. Roosevelt is *the only one* of those presidents *who was elected* to more than two terms.

Only one president, Roosevelt, was elected to more than two terms. The pronoun *who* refers to that particular one and is singular.

36j Finding Agreement When the Subject Follows the Verb

> **More about**
> Inverted word order, 556

If you reverse normal order and put the subject after the verb for emphasis or dramatic effect, be sure the verb agrees with the actual subject, not a different word that precedes the verb.

▸ Onto the tennis court *stride* the defending champion and her challenger.

The subject is the plural compound *the defending champion and her challenger,* not the singular term *tennis court.*

The subject also follows the verb in sentences that begin with *there* followed by a form of *be* (*there is, there are, there was, there were*).

           There are

▸ ~~There's~~ more people registered to vote than actually vote on

Election Day.

The subject, *people,* is plural, so the verb should be plural.

36k Matching a Linking Verb with Its Subject, Not Its Subject Complement

A *linking verb* (such as *was* or *were*) connects the subject of a sentence to a *subject complement,* which describes or refers to the subject. When either the subject or the subject complement is singular but the other is plural, make sure the verb agrees with the subject.

> *More about*
> Linking verbs and
> subject comple-
> ments, 617

                                 was

▸ One influential voting bloc in the election ~~were~~ young voters.

The subject is the singular noun *bloc,* not the plural noun *voters.*

➤ EXERCISE 36.2 Making subjects and verbs agree

Underline the subject in each of the following sentences and circle the verb. If the verb agrees with the subject, do nothing else. If the subject and verb do not agree, write the correct form of the verb above the error.

EXAMPLE

           sounds

The traffic ⟨sound⟩ very loud.

1. The number of vehicles using Reynolds Road have nearly doubled in a year.

2. Mr. Ojiba is the only one of the Town Council members who agrees with the proposal to install traffic-slowing speed bumps in the road.

3. A significant number of residents is opposed to installing traffic lights.

4. There was no other solution proposed to the Council.

5. The road provides a much more direct route into the city.

6. Everyone want there to be a solution to this problem.

PRONOUN-ANTECEDENT AGREEMENT

Pronouns rename or take the place of nouns, noun phrases, or other pronouns. The word or phrase that a pronoun replaces is its *antecedent.* Pronouns and their antecedents must agree in person (first, second, or third), number (singular or plural), and gender (neuter, feminine, or masculine). The antecedent usually appears before the pronoun but sometimes follows it. The two pronouns in the following example have the same antecedent—*Emma*—which follows the first pronoun and precedes the second.

▶ In _her_ haste, *Emma* shut down the computer without saving _her_ work.

 A Possessive Pronoun Agrees with Its Antecedent, Not the Word It Modifies In English, a possessive pronoun (such as *his, hers,* or *its*) agrees with its antecedent, not the word it modifies. In the following example, *father* is the antecedent, so the pronoun should be masculine.

> his
▶ The father beamed joyfully at ~~her~~ newborn daughter.
      ^

As with subject-verb agreement, the basic rule of pronoun-antecedent agreement—match the pronoun to its antecedent in person, number, and gender—is uncomplicated. However, writers often find themselves uncertain how to apply the rule in certain situations, as the Quick Reference box on the next page summarizes.

Tech	**Grammar Checkers and Pronoun-Antecedent Agreement**

Grammar checkers in word processing programs cannot identify pronoun-antecedent agreement errors.

361 Matching Pronouns with Indefinite Pronoun and Generic Noun Antecedents

Antecedents that are singular but have a plural sense are among the most common sources of pronoun-antecedent confusion. These include the following:

> *More about*
> Singular and plural indefinite pronouns, 653

▶ *Indefinite pronouns* such as *each, everybody,* and *everyone* that are singular even though they refer to groups.

▶ *Generic nouns*—that is, singular nouns used to designate a whole class of people or things rather than a specific individual. In this sentence, for example—*The* <u>aspiring doctor</u> *faces years of rigorous training*—the expression *aspiring doctor* generically designates all would-be doctors.

1. Singular indefinite pronoun or generic noun antecedents

A pronoun with a singular indefinite pronoun or generic noun antecedent should be singular. Do not let the plural sense of the antecedent distract you.

> ▶ The dog is a domesticated animal, unlike ~~their~~ cousins the wolf
>
>   *its*
>
>   and coyote.

The antecedent is the singular generic noun *dog,* so the pronoun should be singular too.

   This rule creates a problem, however, when the indefinite antecedent refers to both women and men. Correct agreement requires a singular pronoun, but using *he* as a substitute for either *man* or *woman* results in gender bias.

> *More about*
> Avoiding gender bias, 567–68

GRAMMATICALLY CORRECT BUT GENDER-BIASED AGREEMENT

In past downturns *the affluent consumer* continued to spend, but now even *he* is cutting back.

Quick | **Reference**   **Avoiding Pronoun-Antecedent Agreement Pitfalls**

1. Match pronouns with indefinite pronoun and generic noun antecedents. (659)
2. Match pronouns with collective noun antecedents. (661)
3. Match pronouns with compound antecedents. (662)

Writers often try to avoid this conflict with a gender-neutral plural pronoun such as *they,* resulting in faulty pronoun-antecedent agreement.

UNBIASED BUT GRAMMATICALLY INCORRECT AGREEMENT

In past downturns, *the affluent consumer* continued to spend, but now even *they* are cutting back.

This usage is common in everyday speech, but it is inappropriate for formal writing (although, as the Writing Responsibly box on the next page suggests, some language experts now think differently).

You can avoid both gender bias and faulty agreement by rephrasing according to one of these strategies:

1. Make both the antecedent and the pronoun plural.

   ▸ In past downturns, ~~the affluent consumer~~ *affluent consumers* continued to spend, but now even ~~he is~~ *they are* cutting back.

2. Rephrase the sentence without the pronoun.

   ▸ ~~In past downturns, the~~ *Even the* affluent consumer *, who* continued to spend ~~but now even he~~ *in past downturns,* is *now* cutting back.

3. Use *he or she* or the appropriate variant (for example, *him or her* or *her or him*), but sparingly.

   ▸ In past downturns, the affluent consumer continued to spend, but even he is *she or* now cutting back.

Quick Reference

Three Strategies for Avoiding Gender Bias with Indefinite Antecedents

1. Make both the antecedent and the pronoun plural.
2. Rephrase the sentence without the pronoun.
3. Use *he or she, she or he,* or the appropriate variant (for example, *him or her* or *her or him*), but sparingly.

Writing
Responsibly / Using a Plural Pronoun with a Singular Antecedent

The use of a plural pronoun with singular indefinite antecedents is common in everyday speech, and many language experts now maintain that it should be acceptable in formal writing, too. It is a usage, after all, that some of the finest writers in the English language have seen fit to employ:

God send everyone their heart's desire!
—Shakespeare, *Much Ado About Nothing*, 3.4

Everybody who comes to Southampton finds it either their duty or pleasure to call upon us... .
—Jane Austen, from a letter

Nonetheless, many readers still find the usage grating, so it is best to avoid it when you are writing for a general audience in an academic or business context.

to AUDIENCE

CAUTION Avoid overusing the phrases *he or she* and *his or her*. They can make your text sound stuffy and strained.

2. Plural or variable indefinite pronoun antecedents

Although most indefinite pronouns are singular, some (*both, few, many, others, several*) are always plural.

▶ *Both* of the candidates released *their* income tax returns.

Others (*all, any, more, most, some*) are singular or plural depending on the context.

▶ When the teacher surprised the *students* with a pop quiz, she discovered that *most* had not been doing *their* homework.

▶ Although some of the river's *water* is diverted for irrigation, *most* still makes *its* way to the sea.

36m Matching Pronouns with Collective Noun Antecedents

Collective nouns (for example, *audience, chorus, committee, faculty, family, government*) are singular when they refer to a group acting as a whole.

▶ *My family* traces *its* roots to West Africa.

Collective nouns are plural when they refer to the members of a group acting individually.

▸ *The billionaire's family* fought over *their* inheritance.

36n Matching Pronouns with Compound Antecedents

Compound antecedents joined by *and* are usually plural and take a plural pronoun.

▸ Back in 2012, *Clinton and Obama* were the leading candidates for *their* party's nomination.

Pronouns with compound antecedents joined by *or, nor, either… or,* or *neither… nor* agree with the nearest antecedent. To avoid awkwardness when one of the antecedents is plural and the other singular, put the plural antecedent second.

Neither the coach nor the players worried that *their* team might lose.

When the antecedents differ in gender or person, however, the results of the "nearest antecedent" rule can be so awkward that the only solution is to reword the sentence:

AWKWARD	It was clear after the New Hampshire primary that either Barack Obama or Hillary Clinton would find herself the Democratic Party's nominee for president.
REVISED	It was clear after the New Hampshire primary that either Barack Obama or Hillary Clinton would be the Democratic Party's nominee for president.

→ EXERCISE 36.3 Editing for pronoun-antecedent agreement

Edit the following sentences to correct errors in pronoun-antecedent agreement and avoid gender bias.

EXAMPLE

their
Zoe and her parents felt as though something was missing from ~~her~~ family.

1. Nearly every home in their neighborhood had their own dog, cat, or other type of pet.

2. That is why the Conyer family was slowly walking through the animal shelter, looking over every animal as Zoe, Robert, and their parents passed his cage.

3. Some of the dogs they passed barked frantically, but others just lay idly in his or her cages.

4. Then Robert pointed to a puppy enthusiastically pawing at their cage and whining to attract the family's attention.

5. That's when they found Molly, a cheerful, agreeable, and gentle dog who immediately immersed itself in the life of the Conyer family.

> ## Make It **Your Own**
>
> Reread several papers that you have recently written and note where you handled agreement issues well. If you see areas in need of revision, edit them and add this issue to your revision checklist.

Text Credits

p. 661: William Shakespeare, *Much Ado About Nothing* (1612). **p. 661:** Jane Austen, letter to Cassandra Austen, October 1, 1808.

37 Using Verbs

© Comstock/Getty Images RF

Verbs are the driving force in a sentence. They specify the action (*Sylvia <u>won</u> the race*), occurrence (*She <u>became</u> a runner in high school*), or state of being (*She <u>was</u> tired after the track meet*) that affects the subject. Verbs also provide information about time (*tense*), the identity of the subject (*person* and *number*), whether the subject is acting or being acted on (*voice*), and the attitude or manner of the writer or speaker (*mood*) (see the Quick Reference box on the next page).

VERB FORMS

37a Understanding the Basic Forms of Verbs

With the exception of the verb *be,* all verbs have five forms: base, *-s* form, past tense, past participle, and present participle.

	Base Form	*-s* Form	Past Tense	Past Participle	Present Participle
Regular Verb	campaign	campaigns	campaigned	campaigned	campaigning
Irregular Verb	choose	chooses	chose	chosen	choosing

Quick

Reference   What Information Do Verbs Reveal?

Verbs provide information about tense, person and number, voice, and mood.

- **Tense.** When does the action occur? In the **present** (laugh/laughs), **past** (laughed), or **future** (will laugh)?
- **Person.** Does the verb form tell you that the subject is speaking (I laugh), spoken to (You should laugh), or spoken about (He laughs)?
- **Number.** Are the subject and its accompanying verb **singular** (He laughs) or **plural** (They laugh)?

- **Mood.** Is the verb **indicative**, stating or questioning something about the subject (He laughs)? Is it **imperative**, giving a command (Douse the coach!)? Is it **subjunctive**, expressing a possibility (If the coach were doused again, she might lose patience with her players)?
- **Voice.** Is the verb **active**, with the subject performing the action (He laughs), or **passive**, with the subject being acted upon (The coach is doused with water by her players)?

- The *base form* is what you find when you look up a verb in the dictionary. Use it with a plural noun or the pronouns *I, we, you,* or *they* to express a present or habitual action, occurrence, or state of being.

  ▶ Presidential candidates *campaign* every four years.

  ▶ I usually *choose* candidates based on their policies.

- The *-s form* is the base form plus *-s* or *-es.* Use it with a singular noun or a singular pronoun (*he, she, it*) to express present or habitual action, occurrence, or state of being.

  ▶ My favorite senator always *campaigns* in our town.

  ▶ She *chooses* positive messages instead of negative ones.

> **More about**
> Verb tenses,
> 672–79
> Voice, 680–83

- The past-tense form of regular verbs such as *campaign* is the base form plus *-d* or *-ed;* the past-tense forms of irregular verbs such as *choose* vary. Use the past tense with singular or plural subjects to express past action, occurrence, or state of being.

  ▶ The mayor *campaigned* downtown yesterday.

  ▶ Some people *chose* to protest his appearance.

- The past participle is the same as the past tense in most verbs but varies in some irregular verbs. Use the past participle in combination with forms of *have* to form the perfect tenses and with forms of *be* to form the passive voice.

  ▶ The candidate *has <u>campaigned</u>* nonstop.

  ▶ Our town *was <u>chosen</u>* by the candidate for his last campaign stop.

- The present participle of all verbs, regular and irregular, is formed by adding *-ing* to the base form. Use the present participle with forms of *be* to form the progressive tenses.

  ▶ Senator Brown *is campaigning* here today.

  ▶ They *have been choosing* a running mate.

More about
Verb forms as
  modifiers,
  620–22

verbal A verb form that functions as a noun, adjective, or adverb

NOTE Past and present participles sometimes function as *verbals*, not verbs. Past participles, for example, can sometimes be modifiers (*an educated public*), and present participles can be modifiers (*her opening statement*) or nouns (*campaigning is exhausting*).

37b Using Regular and Irregular Verb Forms Correctly

The vast majority of English verbs are *regular*, meaning that their past-tense and past-participle forms end in *-d* or *-ed*:

Base	Past Tense	Past Participle
climb	climb**ed**	climb**ed**
analyze	analyz**ed**	analyz**ed**
copy	cop**ied**	cop**ied**

However, about two hundred English verbs are *irregular*, with past-tense and past-participle forms that do not follow one set pattern:

Base	Past Tense	Past Participle
build	built	built
eat	ate	eaten
see	saw	seen

The forms of irregular verbs can easily be confused.

▶ My wool shirt ~~shrunk~~ *shrank* when I washed it in hot water.

Tech　**Grammar Checkers and Verb Problems**

Grammar checkers in word processing programs will spot some errors that involve irregular or missing verbs, verb endings, and the subjunctive mood, but they will miss other errors and may suggest incorrect solutions. You must look for verb errors yourself and carefully evaluate any suggestions from a grammar checker.

If you are unsure whether a verb is regular or irregular or what form you should use in a particular situation, consult a dictionary or the Quick Reference box on page 668. In the dictionary, you will find any irregular forms listed in the entry for the base form of a verb.

→ **EXERCISE 37.1 Choosing the correct irregular verb**

In the following sentences, fill in the blank with the correct form of the word in parentheses.

EXAMPLE

The *Titanic* ___sank___ (sink) after it ___struck___ (strike) an iceberg.

1. Today, ships with special hulls _____ (cut) through new ice to _____ (take) tourists to _____ (see) Antarctica.

2. One photographer on an arctic cruise _____ (say) she _____ (take) a photograph of Gentoo penguins that _____ (have) bright orange beaks.

3. She _____ (write) in her journal that she _____ (see) their big tails _____ (swing) from side-to-side as they walked.

4. When a naturalist _____ (tell) them these birds may _____ (become) extinct because the temperature has _____ (rise), reducing the _____ (freeze) area where they live, she _____ (feel) very sad.

37c Combining Main Verbs with Helping Verbs to Form Complete Verbs

Almost all verb constructions other than the present and past tenses require the combination of a *main verb* with one or more *helping verbs* (or *auxiliary verbs*) in a *verb phrase.* The most common helping verbs are *be, have,* and *do,* all three of which can also function as main verbs (*they are hungry; she had lunch; they did the dishes*). *Be,* unlike any other English verb, has eight forms.

FORMS OF BE

Base		*be*
Present Tense	I	*am*
	we, you, they	*are*
	he, she, it	*is*
Past Tense	I, he, she, it	*was*
	we, you, they	*were*
Past Participle		*been*
Present Participle		*being*

Quick Reference — Common Irregular Verbs

Base Form	Past Tense	Past Participle	Base Form	Past Tense	Past Participle
arise	arose	arisen	leave	left	left
be	was/were	been	lend	lent	lent
bear	bore	borne, born	let	let	let
beat	beat	beaten	lie (recline)†	lay	lain
become	became	become	lose	lost	lost
begin	began	begun	make	made	made
bid	bid	bid	mean	meant	meant
bite	bit	bitten, bit	pay	paid	paid
blow	blew	blown	prove	proved	proved, proven
break	broke	broken	quit	quit	quit
bring	brought	brought	read	read	read
build	built	built	ride	rode	ridden
burst	burst	burst	ring	rang	rung
buy	bought	bought	rise	rose	risen
catch	caught	caught	run	ran	run
choose	chose	chosen	say	said	said
come	came	come	see	saw	seen
cost	cost	cost	send	sent	sent
cut	cut	cut	set	set	set
dig	dug	dug	shake	shook	shaken
dive	dived, dove	dived	shoot	shot	shot
do	did	done	shrink	shrank	shrunk
draw	drew	drawn	sing	sang	sung
drink	drank	drunk	sink	sank	sunk
drive	drove	driven	sit	sat	sat
eat	ate	eaten	sleep	slept	slept
fall	fell	fallen	slide	slid	slid
feel	felt	felt	speak	spoke	spoken
fight	fought	fought	spend	spent	spent
find	found	found	spread	spread	spread
flee	fled	fled	spring	sprang, sprung	sprung
fly	flew	flown			
forget	forgot	forgotten, forgot	stand	stood	stood
freeze	froze	frozen	steal	stole	stolen
get	got	gotten, got	strike	struck	struck, stricken
give	gave	given	swim	swam	swum
go	went	gone	swing	swung	swung
grow	grew	grown	take	took	taken
hang (suspend)*	hung	hung	teach	taught	taught
have	had	had	tear	tore	torn
hear	heard	heard	tell	told	told
hold	held	held	think	thought	thought
hide	hid	hidden	throw	threw	thrown
hit	hit	hit	wake	woke, waked	waked, woken
keep	kept	kept	wear	wore	worn
know	knew	known	win	won	won
lay	laid	laid	wind	wound	wound
lead	led	led	write	wrote	written

*Hang is regular—hang, hanged, hanged—when used to mean "kill by hanging."
†Lie is regular—lie, lied, lied—when used to mean "to be untruthful."

FORMS OF *HAVE* AND *DO*

Present Tense (Base and -s Form)	I, you, we, they	*have*	*do*
	he, she, it	*has*	*does*
Past Tense		*had*	*did*
Past Participle		*had*	*done*
Present Participle		*having*	*doing*

The *modal verbs—can, could, may, might, must, shall, should, will, would,* and *ought to*—function only as helping verbs. Modals indicate ability, intention, permission, possibility, desire, and suggestion. They do not change form to indicate number or tense.

Modal Verbs English modal verbs have a range of meanings and unusual grammatical characteristics that you may find challenging. For example, they do not change form to indicate number or tense:

> *More about*
> Modals, 758–60

▶ In a close election, one or two votes ~~cans~~ make a difference.
            can
            ∧

The main verb carries the principal meaning of the verb phrase; the helping verbs, if any, carry information about tense and voice. A *complete verb* is a verb phrase with all the elements needed to determine tense, voice, and mood. Main verbs can stand alone as complete verbs only in their present-tense and past-tense forms.

> ⊢— complete verb —⊣
> main verb

▶ The candidates   campaigned   until Election Day.

Main verbs in other forms (past or present participles) require helping verbs.

> ⊢— complete verb —⊣
> helping
> verbs   main verb

▶ The candidates   have been campaigning   for almost two years.

Sometimes in informal speech you can drop needed helping verbs, and some dialects allow certain constructions as complete verbs that Standard English does not allow. Helping verbs can sometimes be contracted (*they've voted already, we'll register tomorrow*) but in formal writing should never be omitted entirely.

                    have
▶ The candidates been campaigning for almost two years.
                    ∧

CAUTION Do not use *of* for *have* in a verb phrase with a modal. When you use informal contractions like *could've* or *might've* in speech, remember that they mean *could have* and *might have*.

37d Including -s or -es, -d or -ed Endings When Required

> **More about**
> Subject-verb
> agreement,
> 648–58

Sometimes when speaking informally, you can omit the verb endings *-s, -es, -d,* or *-ed* or blend the sound of an ending inaudibly with the initial sound of the following word. Some dialects do not always require these endings. In formal writing, include them, or not, as standard usage requires.

> says   supposed   need
> ▶ My dad s̶a̶y̶ I am s̶u̶p̶p̶o̶s̶e̶ to mow the lawn. I also n̶e̶e̶d̶s̶ to trim the
>   ^   ^   ^

> moved   used
> hedges. Before he m̶o̶v̶e̶ to Phoenix, my brother u̶s̶e̶ to do the mowing.
>   ^   ^

> **More about**
> Phrasal verbs,
> 752–54

Phrasal Verbs Phrasal verbs, such as *ask out* and *give in,* combine a verb with one or more prepositions or adverbs known as particles. The verb and particle combination of a phrasal verb has a distinct meaning, one that is different from the stand-alone words that form it. Because phrasal verbs are idiomatic, native English speakers are usually comfortable using them spontaneously. But that does not mean they can explain why one "gets on" a plane but "gets in" a boat.

> **EXERCISE 37.2 Correcting verb endings**

In the following sentences, correct any verbs that have the wrong or missing verb endings *-s, -es, -d,* or *-ed.*

EXAMPLE

> mixed
> In our first year of college, many of us m̶i̶x̶ studying with partying, but not
>   ^
> does
> one of us d̶o̶ that now.
>   ^

1. Tonight, Eyal and Aaron wants to see the movie, but Franco and I are determine to get our papers finish before we goes out.

2. I use to do my work at the last minute, so I never revise my papers.

3. Last semester I declare my major, so now I am concern about my grades.

4. My roommate say she go to the Writing Center, and they have always helps her.

5. I schedule an appointment for next week, before we go to the party.

37e Distinguishing *Rise* from *Raise*, *Sit* from *Set*, *Lie* from *Lay*

The forms of *rise* and *raise*, *sit* and *set*, and *lie* and *lay* are easily confused. One verb in each pair (*rise, sit,* and *lie*) is **intransitive,** meaning that it does not take a direct object. The other verb in each pair (*raise, set,* and *lay*) is **transitive,** meaning that it does take a direct object (underlined in the following examples).

> *More about*
> Transitive and
> intransitive
> verbs, 616–19

- *Rise* means "to move or stand up." *Raise* means "to cause something (the direct object) to rise."

  ▶ The plane *rises* into the air. The pilot *raises* the landing gear.

- *Sit* means "to be seated." *Set* means "to place or put something (the direct object) on a surface."

  ▶ The passengers in coach *sit* in cramped seats. The attendants *set* drinks on their trays.

- *Lie* means "to recline." *Lay* means "to place or put something (the direct object) on a surface."

  ▶ The passengers in first class *lie* in fully reclining seats. During the landing, the pilot *lays* the plane gently on the runway.

Quick Reference   Distinguishing *Rise* from *Raise*, *Sit* from *Set*, and *Lie* from *Lay*

Base Form	-s Form	Past Tense	Past Participle	Present Participle
rise (to get up)	rises	rose	risen	rising
raise (to lift)	raises	raised	raised	raising
sit (to be seated)	sits	sat	sat	sitting
set (to place)	sets	set	set	setting
lie (to recline)	lies	lay	lain	lying
lay (to place)	lays	laid	laid	laying

A further difficulty with *lie* and *lay* is their confusing overlap of forms: The past tense of *lie* is *lay,* whereas the past tense of *lay* is *laid.* Changing the previous example to the past tense illustrates the issue.

> ▸ The passengers in first class ~~laid~~ in fully reclining seats. During the
>   ^{*lay*}
>   landing, the pilot ~~lay~~ the plane gently on the runway.
>   _{*laid*}

> ▸ **EXERCISE 37.3 Using *rise/raise*, *sit/set*, and *lie/lay* correctly**

In the following paragraph, correct any errors involving *rise/raise, sit/set,* and *lie/lay.*

> Senna began her daily exercise routine as soon as she raised from bed. She seldom laid in bed long after her alarm went off. She usually set the alarm to go off at 4:30 a.m. Most of her neighbors were still laying in their beds when she was rising barbells over her head. Each time she rose a weight, she held it up for several seconds, then gently sat it down. She would also set on the floor and later lay down flat for some stretching exercises. After these warm-ups, Senna went out for a run and watched the sun raise over the lake. As she ran, she tried not to rise her knees too high, and she never let her arms lay idly at her side. Home again from her run, she would sometimes lay down again for a few minutes before beginning her workday.

TENSE

37f Understanding Which Verb Tense to Use

Verb *tenses* provide information about the time in which an action or event occurs—past, present, or future—about whether or not the action is ongoing or completed, and about the time of one action relative to another.

1. Simple tenses

Use the *simple present tense* for current or habitual actions or events and to state general truths. Accompanied by a reference to a future event, the simple present can also indicate a future occurrence (also see *section 37h*).

CURRENT ACTION	Hernando *opens* the door to his classroom.
HABITUAL ACTION	He *enjoys* teaching second-graders.
GENERAL TRUTH	Earth *is* the third planet from the sun.
FUTURE OCCURRENCE	Winter *ends* in two weeks.

Use the *simple past tense* for completed actions or occurrences.

▶ The bell *rang.* Hernando *asked* his students to be quiet.

Use the *simple future tense* for actions that have not yet occurred.

▶ He *will give* them a spelling test this afternoon.

2. Perfect tenses

The perfect tenses generally indicate the completion of an action before a particular time. Use the *present perfect tense* for an action that started in the past but is now completed or for an action that started in the past but is ongoing.

COMPLETED ACTION   I *have read* all the Harry Potter books.

ONGOING ACTION   I *have read* books all my life.

Use the *past perfect tense* for actions completed by a specific time in the past or before another past action.

▶ Because the students *had studied* hard for their test, they knew most of the spelling words.

   The studying—*had studied* (past perfect)—came before the know-ing—*knew* (simple past).

Use the *future perfect tense* for an action that will be completed by a definite time in the future.

▶ By the time the semester ends, Hernando's students *will have improved* their spelling grades.

3. Progressive tenses

The progressive tenses indicate ongoing action. Use the *present progressive tense* for an action that is ongoing in the present.

▶ Matilda *is learning* Spanish.

Use the *past progressive tense* for an action that was ongoing in the past.

▶ Last night, Yue *was practicing* for her recital.

Reference **An Overview of Verb Tenses and Their Forms**

Simple Tenses

Simple present	base or *-s* form	I *learn* something new every day.
Simple past	past tense form	I *learned* Spanish many years ago.
Simple future	*will* + base form	I *will learn* to ski next winter.

Perfect Tenses

Present perfect	*has/have* + past participle	I *have learned* to water ski already.
Past perfect	*had* + past participle	I *had learned* to water ski by the time I was nine.
Future perfect	*will have* + past participle	I *will have learned* how to skydive by September.

Progressive Tenses

Present progressive	*am/is/are* + present participle	I *am learning* about Japanese food.
Past progressive	*was/were* + present participle	I *was learning* to make sushi yesterday.
Future progressive	*will be* + present participle	I *will be learning* new skills next week.
Present perfect progressive	*have/has been* + present participle	I *have been cooking* seriously since I was a teenager.
Past perfect progressive	*had been* + present participle	I *had been preparing* simple dishes even before then.
Future perfect progressive	*will have been* + present participle	I *will have been enjoying* this hobby for two decades by the end of the year.

Use the *future progressive tense* for an ongoing action that will occur in the future.

▶ Elena *will be working* as a publishing company intern next summer.

Use the *present perfect progressive tense* for an ongoing action that began in the past.

▶ Hernando *has been working* on his master's degree in education since 2015.

Use the *past perfect progressive tense* for an ongoing past action that is now completed.

▶ Until this semester, he *had been taking* education courses at night.

Use the *future perfect progressive tense* for an ongoing action that will be finished at a definite time in the future.

▶ By the end of August, Hernando *will have been studying* education for more than six years.

Do Not Use the Progressive Tenses with All Verbs Certain verbs, typically those that convey a mental process or a state of being, are not used in the progressive tenses. Examples include *appreciate, belong, contain, envy, fear, know, like, need, owe, own, remember, resemble, seem,* and *want*.

>   seems   owed
▶ She ~~is seeming~~ angry with her boyfriend. He ~~was owing~~ her an apology.
>   ∧   ∧

37g Following Conventions for the Use of the Present Tense

The present tense is conventionally used for describing works of art, for describing events in literary works, and for stating scientific facts.

>   bring   is
▶ In the series *Sylvia Plath: Girl Detective*, producers Mike Simses and Kate Simses ~~brought~~ us a cheerful character who ~~was~~ not at all
>   ∧   ∧
depressed.

>   has
▶ Watson and Crick discovered that DNA ~~had~~ a double helix structure.
>   ∧

Although the discovery was in the past, it remains true.

In general, use the present tense to introduce a quotation, paraphrase, or summary.

>   notes,
▶ As Harriet Lerner ~~noted,~~ "Anger is neither legitimate nor illegitimate,
>   ∧

meaningful nor pointless. Anger simply is."

More about
APA documen-
tation style,
363–64

EXCEPTION The APA documentation style calls for the use of the past tense or the past perfect tense for reporting findings or introducing cited material.

> Chodoff (2002) ~~claims~~ that in their efforts to put a diagnostic label
> ^claimed^
> on "all varieties and vagaries of human feelings," psychiatrists ~~risk~~
> ^risked^
> medicalizing "the human condition itself."

More about
Inappropriate
shifts in tense,
706–7

37h Using Tense Sequence to Clarify Time Relationships

When a sentence contains two separate actions, readers need a clear idea of the time relationship between them, which writers communicate by their choice of tenses, or **sequence of tenses.** Change verb tenses when there is reason to do so, but do not shift tenses unnecessarily.

In a sentence with two past actions, for example, use the simple past tense for both verbs if the actions occurred simultaneously.

> When he *arrived* at the station, the train *departed.*

He arrived and the train departed at the same time.

If the actions happened at different times, use the past perfect tense for the action that occurred first.

> By the time he *arrived* at the station, the train *had departed.*

The train departed before he arrived.

1. Infinitives and tense sequence

An *infinitive* consists of *to* followed by the base form of the verb (*to listen, to go*). Use this form, the *present infinitive,* for an action that occurs after or simultaneously with the action of the main verb.

> Ivan is known to be a good student.

The knowing and the being happen together.

> Everyone expects Ivan to ace the exam.

The expectation is about Ivan's future performance on the exam.

Use the *perfect infinitive—to have* and the past participle (*to have listened, to have gone*)—for an action that happened before the action of the main verb.

▸ Ivan is said to have studied all weekend.

 The studying took place before the talk about it.

2. Participles and tense sequence

Use the present participle (*listening, going*) to express action that happens simultaneously with the action of the main verb, regardless of the tense of the main verb.

▸ *Handing* her son Robbie a cup of coffee, Mona offered him some brownies.

Use the past participle (*listened, gone*) or the present perfect participle (*having listened, having gone*) to express action that happens before the action of the main verb.

▸ *Discouraged* by her daughter's aloofness, Mona asked her son to help.

 Mona was discouraged before she asked.

▸ *Having mediated* their disagreements for years, Robbie refused to intervene.

 Robbie mediated before he refused.

➜ **EXERCISE 37.4** Editing for verb tense and verb tense sequence

In the following paragraph, correct any errors in verb tense and revise sentences if necessary to achieve appropriate verb tense sequence.

EXAMPLE

Having worked

~~Working~~ on many knitted items in the past, I realized I ~~will~~ like to earn a living as
 ^   *would* ^

a knitter.

By the end of this year, I have been knitting for over fifteen years. I was a knitter for as long as I can remember. My mother told me that, when I was about five, she has begun teaching me how to knit. All through my childhood I had always knitted whenever I had sat down to watch television. Once, when my dad had driven us from Memphis to Denver for a vacation, I knitted practically the entire way. By the time we will have arrived in Denver, I knitted most of a sweater for my brother. While I was in high school, I was starting a knitting club. At first, there were only two or three people in the club, but gradually we had recruited several new members, and it was getting to be a lot of fun. Recently, I begun knitting scarves, hats, mittens, and other items to sell on a crafts website. I believe that sometime in the future I will have been making a good living from my knitting.

MOOD

37i Understanding Verb Mood

The *mood* of a verb indicates whether a speaker or writer views what is said as a fact, a command, or a possibility. Most English sentences are in the *indicative mood,* which states facts or opinions and asks questions.

- ▶ Our research papers *are* due tomorrow morning.
- ▶ *Did* you *say* the deadline had changed?

The *imperative mood* issues commands, gives instructions, or makes requests. The subject of an imperative sentence (*you*) is usually left unstated.

- ▶ *Hand in* your papers by Friday afternoon.
- ▶ *Turn* left at the third stoplight.
- ▶ Please *pass* the salt.

The *subjunctive mood* expresses possibility (or impossibility), as in hypothetical situations, conditions known to be untrue, wishes, suggestions, and requirements.

- ▶ If I *were* finished, I could go to bed.
- ▶ The doctor suggests that he *get* more exercise.

37j Using the Subjunctive Mood Correctly

The subjunctive has three tenses: present, past, and past perfect. The present subjunctive is always the base form of the verb, regardless of the person or number of the subject: *Ramon asks that his teacher <u>give</u>* (not *gives*) *him an*

Writing Responsibly | Using the Subjunctive in Formal Writing

Because the subjunctive has been fading from everyday usage, the indicative may seem more acceptable to you. Most readers, however, still expect to find the subjunctive used in formal writing.

> *were*
> ▶ I wish that I ~~was~~ finished.
>   ^

to AUDIENCE

extension. The past subjunctive of *be* is *were: I wish I were* (not *was*) *finished.* For all other verbs, the past subjunctive is identical to the past tense. Similarly, the past perfect subjunctive is identical to the past perfect indicative.

The subjunctive has been fading from everyday usage, and as a result, the indicative (*I wish I was finished*) may seem an acceptable alternative to you. Most readers, however, expect to find the subjunctive used appropriately (*I wish I were finished*) in formal writing.

Clauses with verbs in the subjunctive are always subordinate clauses. They include ***conditional clauses*** that begin with *if, as if,* or *as though* and describe a condition known to be untrue. Conditional clauses put forward a set of circumstances and modify a main clause that states what follows from those circumstances.

▶ If I *were* taller, I would try out for basketball.

▶ The candidate acts as though he *were* already the winner.

If the main clause includes a modal auxiliary such as *would, could,* or *should,* do not use a similar construction instead of the subjunctive in the *if* clause.

were
▶ If I ~~would have been~~ taller, I would try out for basketball.
         ^

Verbs in the main clause that express a wish, request, recommendation, or demand also trigger the subjunctive in the subordinate clause.

were
▶ The hikers wished their campground ~~was~~ not so far away.
                                      ^

fix
▶ Citizens are demanding that the government ~~fixes~~ the economy.
                                              ^

▸ Senators have requested that the president ~~is~~ more responsive to the
                                                         be
                                                         ^
  middle class.

▸ Alicia's adviser recommended that she ~~takes~~ calculus.
                                                  take
                                                  ^

→ **EXERCISE 37.5 Using the subjunctive mood correctly**

In each of the following sentences, circle the correct verb form.

EXAMPLE

If Cally (was /(were)) a morning person, she would be more alert for her 8:00 a.m.
classes.

1. The professor requests that students (be/are) in their chairs at the
   beginning of class.

2. He reacts to tardiness as if it (was/were) a personal insult.

3. One student's adviser recommended that she (get/gets) more sleep
   and breakfast.

4. If this class (were/was) part of her major, she would be more inclined
   to do so.

5. She just wishes the semester (were/was) over.

VOICE

37k Understanding Voice

The term *voice* refers to the role of the subject in a sentence. Only transitive
verbs—verbs that take a direct object—can be in the passive voice. In the
active voice, the subject is the actor and the direct object is acted upon.

ACTIVE

David hit the ball out of the park.

David is the subject, and *the ball* is the direct object.

In the *passive voice,* the subject is acted upon. To change an active-voice
sentence into the passive voice, make the direct object the subject, combine
the appropriate form of *be* with the past participle of the main verb, and
identify the actor in a phrase beginning with *by.*

PASSIVE

The ball was hit out of the park by David.

The passive voice also permits you to leave the actor unidentified.

PASSIVE (AGENT UNIDENTIFIED)

The ball was hit out of the park.

To change the passive voice to active, make the subject into the direct object and the actor into the subject, and change the verb from the passive form to its active form.

> ▸ David's ~~baseball career was enhanced by his~~ generosity off
>   *enhanced his baseball career.*
>   the field./
>   ∧

If the passive-voice sentence leaves the actor unidentified, you will need to supply one.

>   *Americans elected the*
> ▸ ~~The~~ country's first African American president ~~was elected~~ in 2008.
>   ∧

371 Choosing between the Active and Passive Voice

The active voice is usually preferable to the passive voice because it is the livelier and more direct of the two. The passive voice, in contrast, can deaden prose and obscure a writer's point.

More about
Style and voice,
535–37

In certain situations, however, the passive voice can be the appropriate choice:

- When the recipient of an action is more important than the actor or the identity of the actor is unimportant

  ▸ The song "Glory" was given the award for Best Original Song by the Academy of Motion Pictures Arts and Sciences.

  The writer wants to focus on the song, not on who gave the award.

- In reports of scientific procedures
  ▶ Five hundred patients *were treated* with Cytoxan over a six-month period.
  The purpose of a scientific report is to describe what happened, not to focus on the scientists who conducted the research.

- When the actor is unknown or cannot be identified
  ▶ Our home *was burglarized* while we were on vacation.

→ EXERCISE 37.6 Changing passive voice to active

Revise each of the following sentences, changing the passive voice to the active voice.

EXAMPLE

Passive: The stage directions for the play were adapted by the director.

Active: *The director adapted the stage directions for the play.*

1. The costumes and props had been designed in order to increase the play's grandeur.

2. Taylor's performance was made more compelling than it otherwise would have been by the brilliant staging of the scene.

3. Because the play's scenes were rehearsed by the actors every day, excitement about the play spread across the campus.

4. Folding chairs were brought by the maintenance crew so the unexpected attendees on opening night could sit.

→ EXERCISE 37.7 Revising verbs

In the following paragraph, correct any verb errors.

My trip back to Chicago from San Francisco start out just fine. It was a beautiful afternoon, the plane boarding went fairly quickly, and the flight left right on schedule. I lied back in my seat for a nice nap when the pilot announced that there was some rough weather ahead, but it should not have affected our flight's arrival time. I heard this type of announcement once before on what turned out to be a horrible flight, so I should of start worrying right then. I was thinking that if I were to check the weather that morning, my flight might have been changed and I might have avoided this. We soon heard that the storm got so serious that all airports in the Chicago area will have been shut down and we will be landing in Topeka, Kansas, instead. It was evening by the time we had gotten our luggage at Topeka's airport, where we learned that all hotels had already been booked. I end up renting a car and I drive all night. It was rainy and windy when I arrive in Chicago, but most of the storm passed by then.

Make It **Your Own**

Write a paragraph about a true or fictional event that did not go according to plan. Write what you or the protaganist expected to happen, why things went wrong, how it turned out, and, finally, what might have been done differently.

Work **Together**

Exchange your paragraph with a classmate and circle each other's verbs. If you see any that need to be revised, underline them and in the margin write the pages in this chapter that discuss the issue. When you have both finished, review the recommended revisions and write a brief reflection about how they might make your paragraph easier to understand. If you found this difficult, add verbs to your revision checklist.

38

Understanding Pronoun Case and Reference

© Suzi Pratt/FilmMagic/Getty Images

When you play an online multiplayer game like World of Warcraft, Dota 2, or Halo, you may be interacting with dozens of other players who could be located almost anywhere in the world. Neither you nor they are physically present in the game. Instead, you all have virtual stand-ins—avatars—to represent you. Your avatar acts on your orders and may even change form—from human to animal or student to soldier, for example—depending on the way in which you want it to function in a particular environment.

Like avatars, pronouns are stand-ins. They represent other words—their *antecedents*—from one place to another in speech or writing. Also like avatars, they sometimes change form depending on the role you want them to play within a sentence.

PRONOUN CASE

Nouns, and the pronouns that represent them, can play various roles within a sentence. They can be subjects:

> **More about**
> Subjects and objects, 613–19

	subject	
NOUN	**The Steelers**	lost.
PRONOUN	**They**	lost.

They can be objects (including direct objects, indirect objects, and objects of prepositions):

	subject		direct object
NOUN	The Bears	beat	**the Steelers.**
PRONOUN	We	beat	**them.**

They can indicate possession:

	possessive		possessive	
NOUN	**Chicago's**	team	beat	**Pittsburgh's**	team.
PRONOUN	**Our**	team	beat	**their**	team.

> **More about**
> Indicating possession with apostrophes, 803–9

The term *case* refers to the different forms a noun or pronoun takes— *subjective, objective,* or *possessive*—depending on which of these roles it serves. Nouns do not change much—they have the same form as subjects that they do as objects, and they indicate possession with an *s* sound that is marked in writing with an apostrophe (*Chicago's team*). In contrast, most *personal pronouns* and some *relative* and *interrogative pronouns* are shape shifters—they have distinct forms for many of their roles.

> **personal pronouns**
> Pronouns that take the place of nouns or noun phrases
> **relative pronouns**
> Pronouns that introduce subordinate clauses that describe the pronoun's antecedent
> **interrogative pronouns** Pronouns that introduce questions

		Subjective Case	Objective Case	Possessive Case
Personal Pronouns				
Singular	1st person	*I*	*me*	*my, mine*
	2nd person	*you*	*you*	*your, yours*
	3rd person	*he*	*him*	*his*
		she	*her*	*her, hers*
		it	*it*	*its*
Plural	1st person	*we*	*us*	*our, ours*
	2nd person	*you*	*you*	*your, yours*
	3rd person	*they*	*them*	*their, theirs*
Case-Variant Relative and		*who*	*whom*	*whose*
Interrogative Pronouns		*whoever*	*whomever*	

Some case errors are easy to detect because they sound wrong to native speakers of English.

▸ Hermione is one of Harry's best friends, and ~~her~~ often gives ~~he~~ sound advice.

she / him

In many situations, however, the ear is an unreliable guide to proper case usage.

38a Using the Subjective Case for Subject Complements

A pronoun that functions as a *subject complement* following a form of *be* used as a main verb should be in the subjective case, not the objective case.

> Asked who spilled the milk, my sister confessed that the guilty one
>   she.
> was ~~her.~~
>   ^

subject complement
An adjective, pronoun, or noun phrase that follows a linking verb and describes or refers to the sentence subject

If this usage sounds overly formal, try reversing the subject and subject complement.

>   she was
> Asked who spilled the milk, my sister confessed that the guilty
>   one.   ^
> ~~one was her.~~
>   ^

38b *She and I* or *Her and Me*? Keeping Track of Case in Compounds

Pronouns that are part of compound subjects or subject complements should be in the subjective case.

> compound subject
> ┌─────────────────┐
> |
>   I
> My friends and ~~me~~ chat online while we play computer games.
>   ^

Pronouns that are part of compound objects should be in the objective case.

> compound dir. obj.
> ┌──────────────────────┐
>   me
> My parents call my brothers and ~~I~~ every weekend.
>   ^

Pronouns that are part of compound possessives should be in the possessive case.

> compound possessive
> ┌──────────────────────┐
>   my
> My father often gets ~~me~~ and my brother's names confused.
>   ^

Quick Reference   Editing for Case in Compounds

To determine the correct case of a pronoun in a compound, isolate the pronoun from the rest of the compound; then read the result aloud to yourself. If the pronoun sounds wrong, replace it with the one that sounds right.

Faulty	[My friends and] me chat online while we play computer games.
Revised	My friends and I chat online while we play computer games.

Me chat online is clearly wrong. Replacing the objective pronoun *me* with the subjective pronoun *I* corrects the problem.

Faulty	My parents call [my siblings and] I every weekend.
Revised	My parents call my siblings and me every weekend.

My parents call I is clearly wrong. Replacing the subjective pronoun *I* with the objective pronoun *me* corrects the problem.

Faulty	My father often gets me [and my brother's] names confused.
Revised	My father often gets my and my brother's names confused.

My father gets me names confused is clearly wrong. Replacing the objective pronoun *me* with the possessive pronoun *my* corrects the problem.

→ **EXERCISE 38.1 Pronoun case in subject complements and compounds**

Circle the correct pronoun from each pair in parentheses.

EXAMPLE

When we were about twelve, Sofia and (I)/ me) were intensely interested in rocketry.

1. Actually it was (she/her) who first joined the rocketry club, and then she got me involved.

2. We got so good at building and launching model rockets that other kids would call (she or I/her or me) whenever they had problems.

3. As we got older and our interests changed, (she and I/her and me) gradually lost our fascination with rocketry.

4. Now that I'm in college, one of (me/my) and my roommate's favorite pastimes has become rocketry.

38c Keeping Track of Pronoun Case in Appositives

> **appositive phrase**
> A noun or noun phrase that renames a preceding noun or noun phrase and is grammatically equivalent to it

The case of a pronoun in an *appositive phrase* should reflect the function of the phrase the appositive renames. If the original phrase is a subject or subject complement, as in the first of the following examples, the pronoun should be in the subjective case; if it is an object, as in the second example, the pronoun should be in the objective case.

> ▸ The two most talented actors in our school, Valentino and her, always
>
> get the best roles in school productions.

(correction: *she*, above *her*)

> ▸ The director always wants the best artists, she and I, to work on
>
> the scenery.

(corrections: *her* above *she*, *me* above *I*)

38d Deciding between *We* and *Us* before Nouns

In expressions that combine *we* or *us* with a noun, use *we* with nouns that function as subjects or subject complements and *us* with nouns that function as objects. To decide which is which, say the sentence to yourself with the pronoun alone.

> ▸ Us gamers live vicariously in the game world through our avatars.

(correction: *We* above *Us*)

> *Us live vicariously* is clearly wrong. The subjective pronoun *we* should replace the objective pronoun *us.*

> ▸ Our avatars act vicariously in the game world on behalf of we gamers.

(correction: *us* above *we*)

> *Avatars act on behalf of we* is clearly wrong. The objective pronoun *us* should replace the subjective pronoun *we.*

➔ **EXERCISE 38.2 Pronoun case in appositives and before nouns**

Circle the correct pronoun or pronouns from each pair in parentheses.

EXAMPLE

As spring break approached, it became clear that both of us, (Owen and I)/ Owen and me), had no ride home.

1. As a result, (we/us) non–car owners started asking all of our friends how they got home in this situation.

2. Everyone took pity on the two stranded guys, (Owen and I/Owen and me), but nobody was able to offer us a ride.

3. Eventually, someone told (we/us) that (we/us) simply had to take the bus from our small college town to the train station in the state capital.

4. This way, the two seemingly abandoned non–car owners, (Owen and I/Owen and me), became informed and even empowered commuters.

38e Using the Objective Case Both before and after an Infinitive

Both the subject and object of an *infinitive* should be in the objective case.

> I asked *her* to recommend *me* for the job.
> Both *her*, the subject of the infinitive *to recommend,* and *me*, its direct object, are in the objective case.

> **infinitive** The *to* form of a verb (*to decide, to eat, to study*)

38f Deciding on Pronoun Case with the *–ing* Form of a Verb

In most cases, use the possessive form of a noun or pronoun with a *gerund* (the present participle, or *-ing* form of a verb used as a noun).

> **More about**
> Gerunds, 621

> Professor Nolan, I appreciate ~~you~~ taking time to advise me on
>
> your
>
> my résumé.

Use the objective form of a noun or pronoun, however, when the *-ing* word functions as a modifier rather than a noun.

PRONOUN IS THE MODIFIER	Margo is a Jordan Spieth fan. She admires *his playing*.
PRONOUN IS MODIFIED	Margo saw *him playing* at the U.S. Open.

38g Clarifying Pronoun Case in Comparisons with *Than* or *As*

In comparisons with *than* or *as,* the choice of pronoun case can sometimes result in two otherwise identical sentences with significantly different meanings.

> ▸ Amy likes her new car more than I.

> ▸ Amy likes her new car more than me.

In the first sentence, the subjective case (*I*) signals a comparison between Amy's and the writer's fondness for Amy's car (she thinks better of it than the writer does). In the second sentence, the objective case (*me*) signals a comparison between Amy's fondness for her car and her fondness for the writer (she thinks better of her car than of the writer). To avoid confusing readers in situations like this, identify which pronoun your meaning requires by supplying any words needed to make the comparisons explicit.

> ▸ Amy likes her new car more than I *do.*

> ▸ Amy likes her new car more than *she likes* me.

> **EXERCISE 38.3** Pronoun case with infinitives, gerunds, and comparisons

Circle the correct pronoun from each pair in parentheses.

> **EXAMPLE**
>
> My uncle has put an enormous amount of time into (him / his) gardening.

1. When he was very young, his mother taught (he/him) to help (she/her) in their backyard garden.
2. Now that he has his own backyard, it turns out that he loves gardening even more than (she/her).
3. While I certainly like to watch (him/his) gardening, I don't enjoy doing it myself.
4. Even before I could walk and talk, it was obvious that I didn't like gardening as much as (he/him).
5. I must admit, though, that I allowed (he/him) to show (I/me) how to care for a few of his fruit trees.

38h Using *Who, Whom, Whoever,* and *Whomever*

The pronouns *who, whom, whoever,* and *whomever* have two jobs. As *relative pronouns* they introduce *subordinate clauses.* As *interrogative pronouns* they introduce questions.

> **subordinate clause**
> A word group with a subject and predicate that cannot stand alone as a sentence but instead functions within a sentence as a noun, adjective, or adverb

■ Use *who* or *whoever* for the subject of a subordinate clause or question.

┝────── subordinate clause ──────┥
subj.

▶ Tiger Woods, *who* began playing as a toddler, dominated golf in his early adulthood.

┝────── question ──────┥
subj.

▶ *Who* began playing golf as a toddler?

■ Use *whom* or *whomever* for the object of a subordinate clause or question. Notice, however, that contrary to normal word order, in which direct objects follow verbs, *whom* and *whomever* usually come at the beginning of a clause or question.

┝────── subordinate clause ──────┥
dir. obj.

▶ Woods, *whom* many golf fans still admired, fell out of the list of top golfers after his back surgery.

┝────── question ──────┥
dir. obj.

▶ *Whom* do many golf fans admire?

■ The case of a relative pronoun is determined by its role in a clause, not the role of the clause in the sentence. The relative pronoun in the following example is the subject of its clause and so should be in the subjective case—*whoever*—even though the clause as a whole is the object of the preposition *to.*

Writing **Responsibly**   Case and Tone

Many people now ignore the distinction between *who* and *whom,* using only *who.* In academic and business writing, however, many readers will assume that you do not understand correct usage if you use *who* when *whom* is called for. So, even if *whom* and *whomever* sound inappropriately formal, even old-fashioned, to your ear, consider what your reader's expectations are and adjust your usage accordingly.

to AUDIENCE

▶ In professional golf, the winner's prize goes to ~~whomever~~ _{whoever} completes the course in the fewest strokes.

■ Match the pronoun to its verb, not to the verb of an intervening clause. In the following example, the pronoun should be the subjective case *who* because it is the subject of *was,* not the object of *know.*

▶ Thomas Edison, ~~whom~~ _{who} many people know was the inventor of the lightbulb, was also the inventor of the phonograph.

▶ **EXERCISE 38.4 Distinguishing *who, whom, whoever, whomever***
Circle the correct pronoun from each pair in parentheses.

EXAMPLE

Ayrton, (who / whom) grew up in southern California, was visiting New York City for the first time.

1. It was the middle of winter, and taxis seemed to stop for (whoever/whomever) stood furthest into the street, but not for him.

2. (Whoever/Whomever) would have guessed that when Ayrton slipped on some ice and fell on his back, everybody on the street would surround him and reach down to help him up?

3. These were not the uncaring people (who/whom) he had assumed New Yorkers were.

4. He was soon back on his feet thanks to a tough-looking old man (who/whom) Ayrton invited to join him for a coffee.

CLEAR PRONOUN REFERENCE

Pronoun reference involves the clarity of the relationship between a pronoun and its antecedent. With clear pronoun reference, readers can easily identify the antecedent of a pronoun.

▶ Mario talked to his sister Roberta about her career plans.
The pronoun *his* clearly refers to Mario; the pronoun *her* clearly refers to Mario's sister.

Pronoun reference is unclear when readers cannot be certain what a pronoun's antecedent is.

▸ Mario talked to Paul about his career plans.
  Did Mario and Paul talk about Mario's career plans or Paul's? Without more information, readers will be uncertain.

38i Avoiding Ambiguous Reference

The reference of a pronoun is ambiguous when it has two or more equally plausible antecedents.

▸ Mario talked to Paul about his career plans.

One way to resolve ambiguous reference is to replace the pronoun with the appropriate noun.

▸ Mario talked to Paul about Paul's career plans.

To avoid repeating the noun, rephrase the sentence in a way that eliminates the ambiguity.

▸ Paul talked about his career plans with Mario.
  The position of the pronoun *his* associates the plans clearly and unambiguously with Paul, not Mario.

38j Avoiding Confusingly Broad Reference with *It, This, That,* and *Which*

When pronouns such as *it, this, that,* and *which* refer broadly to an entire clause, sentence, or series of sentences, readers may be uncertain about what specific information the pronouns cover.

- Who owns Antarctica? Several countries—including Argentina, Australia, Chile, France, New Zealand, Norway, the United Kingdom, and the United States—all claim or reserve the right to claim all or part

  These competing claims make the question of ownership
  of the continent. ~~This makes it~~ difficult to answer.
  ∧

The revision specifies what information the writer meant by *this* and *it*.

38k Avoiding Implied Reference

A pronoun should have a clearly identifiable antecedent, not an unstated, or implied, antecedent. In the following example, the only word that could serve grammatically as the antecedent to *they* is *stories,* but stories are not places. The writer's intended antecedent is implied in the adjective *small-town,* as the revision makes clear.

DRAFT	From her stories of her small-town childhood, they seem like great places to grow up.
REVISED	Her stories of her childhood make small towns seem like great places to grow up.

Similarly, in the next example, the antecedent to *he—Einstein—*is implied, confusingly, in the possessive form *Einstein's.*

▸ According to Einstein's theory of relativity, ~~he showed that~~ mass and energy are interchangeable.

38l Reserving *You* for Directly Addressing the Reader

In formal writing, reserve the pronoun *you* (and the implied *you* of commands) to address the reader directly, as in "you, the reader." Do not use *you* as a substitute for indefinite words such as *anybody, everybody,* or *people.*

▸ Before computers and the Internet, ~~you~~ got ~~your~~ news mostly from

  people their

newspapers, radio, and television.

38m Avoiding the Indefinite Use of *They* and *It*

In formal writing, the pronouns *they* and *it* need specific antecedents. Avoid using these pronouns to refer to unspecified people or things.

▸ At Hogwarts School of Witchcraft and Wizardry, ~~they~~ use owls, not

  students

email, for sending messages.

▸ ~~In~~ The beginning of the chapter~~,~~ ~~it~~ compares pronouns to computer-
game avatars.

38n Designating People with *Who, Whom,* and *Whose,* Not *That* and *Which*

When you are speaking, you are as likely to use *that* as you are to use *who* or *whom* to refer to people. In formal writing, however, you should usually use only *who* and *whom* to refer to people.

▸ According to his website, people ~~that~~ ^{who} have special needs will be served by the Jordan Spieth Charitable Fund.

Use *that* and *which* for animals and things.

▸ The stray cats ~~who~~ ^{that} live in the alley sometimes howl at night.

For pets and other named animals, however, *who* or *whom* is often more appropriate than *that* or *which.*

▸ Our cat Juniper, ~~which~~ ^{who} is now twelve years old, is still healthy and spry.

The possessive pronoun *whose* is also best reserved for people but can apply to animals and things when avoiding it requires the awkward use of the phrase *of which.*

▸ The polar bear is an animal ~~the~~ habitat ~~of which~~ ^{whose} is threatened by global warming.

→ EXERCISE 38.5 Editing for pronoun reference

Edit the following passage to eliminate problems with pronoun reference.

Everyone who knew Colin identified him as someone that loved music. When you wanted to know about a band's background, you would ask Colin, who had made a life's work of studying the histories of musicians and composers. When Sydnee Sandford, a popular host on his college's radio station, interviewed Colin about the 1960s rock musicians that she was featuring on her show, he became instantly famous on campus. That is what started it. A week later, the radio station manager told Colin that they would like to know if he wanted his own radio program. It appealed to him, but he also understood that he was a person that was quite shy and uncomfortable with public speaking. Based on his past experiences at speaking before audiences, they caused him to avoid giving her an answer. Sensing his obvious discomfort, she pointed out that she herself was also shy and had long been terrified of public speaking. She said that her answer was that you would discuss on your show and interview others about what interested you the most. Colin remembered how easy it was to talk on her show because he enjoyed the topic.

Colin's show aired at 3 to 4 a.m., and the only person the taste of which in music he used as a guide was himself. Soon he attracted a huge listenership on campus.

Make It **Your Own**

Write a true or fictional paragraph about giving someone a birthday present. Consider writing about deciding what to give, how you found the present, and how the recipient reacted. Use at least six different pronouns, with at least one from each of the three pronoun cases: subjective, objective, and possessive.

Work **Together**

Exchange your paragraph with a classmate and circle each other's pronouns. If you see any that need to be revised, underline them, and in the margin write the pages in this chapter that discuss the issue. When you have both finished, review the recommended revisions and write a brief reflection about how they might make your paragraph easier to understand. If you found this difficult, add pronouns to your revision checklist.

39 Using Adjectives and Adverbs

IN THIS CHAPTER

a. Differentiating adjectives and adverbs, 697

b. Using adjectives as subject complements, 698

c. Choosing *bad* or *badly*, *good* or *well*, 699

d. Using negatives correctly, 701

e. Avoiding nouns as adjectives, 701

f. Using comparative forms, 702

> *More about*
> The characteristics of English adjectives, 762–64

©Jumpstart Studios/Getty Images RF

The clothing, jewelry, and hairstyles we choose—our modifiers—send a message to others about how we want them to perceive us. A flamboyant dress, a tattoo, eye-catching jewelry, and flowing hair send one impression; a tailored business suit sends another. Similarly, we send readers a message about how we want our words to be understood by our choice of adjectives and adverbs to modify them.

39a Differentiating Adjectives and Adverbs

Adjectives modify (or describe) nouns and pronouns, answering questions such as *What kind? Which one?* or *How many? Adverbs* modify verbs, adjectives, other adverbs, and entire phrases, clauses, and sentences; they answer questions such as *How? Where?* or *When?*

Although many adverbs end in the suffix *-ly*, many do not (*later, often, quite, seldom*), and dozens of adjectives do (*elderly, lowly, scholarly*). The only reliable way to distinguish an adjective from an adverb is not from its form but from its function (see the Quick Reference box on p. 698).

 English Adjectives Do Not Have Plural Forms In English, adjectives do not change form to agree with the words they modify.

good
Traditions can provide ~~goods~~ foundations for innovation.
      ^

> **Quick**

Reference The Functions of Adjectives and Adverbs

Adjectives modify:

Nouns	*sunny* day
Pronouns	someone *responsible*

Adverbs modify:

Verbs	spoke *forcefully*
Adjectives	*painfully* loud
Adverbs	*very* cautiously
Phrases	*finally* over the finish line
Clauses and sentences	*Eventually,* the story ended.

39b Using Adjectives, Not Adverbs, as Subject Complements after Linking Verbs

Linking verbs express a state of being rather than an action or occurrence. They link the subject to a *subject complement,* which describes or refers to the subject. In other words, the subject complement modifies the subject, not the verb; it can be an adjective or a noun, but not an adverb.

The verb *be,* when used as a main verb, is always a linking verb.

▶ The *solution* is <u>simple</u>.

The adjective *simple* modifies the subject, *solution.*

> **More about**
> Linking verbs and subject complements, 617

Other verbs, such as *appear, become, feel, look, prove, sound,* and *taste,* may function as linking verbs in one context and action verbs in another. A word following one of these verbs should be an adjective if it modifies the subject and an adverb if it modifies the verb.

▶ *Maria* looked <u>anxious</u> to the dentist.

Looked is a linking verb and the adjective *anxious* is a subject complement that describes Maria's state of mind as the dentist perceived it.

▶ Maria *looked* <u>anxiously</u> at the dentist.

Looked is an action verb modified by the adverb *anxiously,* which describes the manner in which Maria performed the action of looking.

39c Choosing *Bad* or *Badly, Good* or *Well*

In casual speech, we commonly mingle adjectives and adverbs. In writing, however, adjectives are used to modify nouns and pronouns, and adverbs are used to modify verbs, adjectives, or other adverbs. Do not confuse *bad* with *badly, good* with *well,* or *real* with *really.* Use the adjective form of these pairs for subject complements. Include *-ly* endings when needed, and use an adjective, not an adverb, to modify a direct object.

> **Tech** **Grammar Checkers and Adjective-Adverb Problems**
>
> Grammar checkers in word processing programs catch some adjective and adverb errors but miss many others. A grammar checker, for example, missed errors such as *The Patriots played bad, the boat rocked gentle,* and *Tomás looked well in his tuxedo.*

- *Bad* is an adjective; *badly* is an adverb.

    ▸ The Patriots played ~~bad~~ *badly* in the fourth quarter.

    Badly modifies the action verb *played.*

    ▸ The quarterback feels ~~badly~~ *bad* about the loss.

    Feels is a linking verb; *bad* modifies *quarterback.*

- The word *good* is an adjective, and *well* is its adverb counterpart. *Well* is an adjective, however, when it is used to mean "healthy."

    ▸ Leah did ~~good~~ *well* on her final exams.

    The adverb *well* modifies the verb *did.*

    ▸ Tomás looks ~~well~~ *good* in his tuxedo.

    Looks is a linking verb; the adjective *good* modifies *Tomás.*

    ▸ After a late-night graduation party, Leah is not feeling ~~good~~ *well.*

    Well is used as an adjective because it refers to health.

- Do not confuse the adjective *real* with the adverb *really.*

    ▸ The actors are ~~real~~ *really* enthusiastic about tonight's performance.

> **More about**
> Conciseness,
> 520–28
> (ch. 26)

NOTE Intensifiers like *really* often add little or no meaning to a sentence and can usually be dropped in the interest of conciseness.

- Do not confuse adverbs that end in -ly with their adjective counterparts that do not.

  > gently
  ▶ You should play ~~gentle~~ with small children.

  The adverb *gently* modifies the verb *play*.

More about
Direct objects
and object
modifiers,
616–19, 737–39

object complement
An adjective or noun
phrase that follows
the direct object
and describes the
condition of the
object or a change
the subject has
caused it to undergo

- Never use an adverb to modify a direct object. When a modifier
  follows a direct object, ask yourself, "What word is being modified?" If the answer is "the verb," then the modifier should be an
  adverb, but if the answer is "the direct object," then the modifier
  is an **object complement** and should be an adjective or noun.

  ▶ The divorce left *Kayla cautious* about future relationships.

  The adjective *cautious* modifies the direct object *Kayla*.

  ▶ She *conducted* herself *cautiously* with potential new friends.

  The adverb *cautiously* modifies the verb *conducted,* not the direct object
  herself.

→ **EXERCISE 39.1 Correcting common adjective-adverb problems**

Revise the following sentences to correct any adjective or adverb errors.

EXAMPLE

> really
Most people are ~~real~~ surprised to learn that Bennett and Raul are

> good
roommates and even ~~well~~ friends.

1. Raul takes unusual good care of his clothes and dresses fashionable.

2. Bennett feels indifferently about clothes and dresses real sloppy.

3. Of course, Raul always keeps his side of their room awful messily.

4. Bennett, on the other hand, puts absolute everything careful in its
   proper place.

5. Despite these stark differences, the two of them get along real good.

39d Using Negatives Correctly

In a sentence with a *double negative,* two negative modifiers describe the same word. Because one negative cancels the other, the message becomes positive. In Standard American English, double negatives can be acceptable, but only to emphasize a positive meaning. The sentence *It is <u>not unlikely</u> that the attorney will be disbarred,* for example, means that the attorney's disbarment is likely. Although some dialects allow the use of double (and more) negatives to emphasize a negative meaning, and many people use them that way in casual speech, you should avoid them in formal writing. Remember that the negative word *not* is part of contractions such as *couldn't* and *shouldn't* and that words like *barely, hardly,* and *scarcely* have a negative meaning.

▶ Students ~~shouldn't~~ never park in a faculty-only lot.
    should

▶ I ~~can't~~ hardly argue with facts like those.
    can

39e Avoiding Long Strings of Nouns Used as Adjectives

One noun can often function as an adjective to modify another: *government worker, traffic violation, college course.* Multiple nouns strung together this way, however, can be cumbersome and confusing.

CONFUSING   The *teacher education policy report* will be available tomorrow.

REVISED   The *policy report on teacher education* will be available tomorrow.

Order of Adjectives in a Series When more than one adjective modifies a noun, the adjectives usually need to follow a specific order:

▶ a ~~European~~ stunning racehorse
    European

Charts like the one on page 763 may help you learn what that order is, but to follow that order reliably, you will need consistent exposure to a broad range of English-language situations and texts. For guidance on ordering multiple adjectives, see page 763.

39f Using Comparative and Superlative Adjectives and Adverbs

Most adjectives and adverbs have three forms for indicating the relative degree of the quality or manner they specify: positive, comparative, and superlative. The *positive form* is the base form—the form you find when you look the word up in the dictionary.

POSITIVE   Daryl is *tall.*

The *comparative form* indicates a relatively greater or lesser degree of a quality.

COMPARATIVE   Daryl is *taller* than Ivan.

The *superlative form* indicates the greatest or least degree of a quality.

SUPERLATIVE   Daryl is the *tallest* player on the team.

Regular adjectives and adverbs form the comparative and superlative with either the suffixes *-er* and *-est* or the addition of the words *more* and *most* or *less* and *least.* A few adjectives and adverbs have irregular comparative and superlative forms (see the Quick Reference box on the next page). If you are not sure whether to use *-er/-est* or *more/most* for a particular adjective or adverb, look it up in a dictionary. If the entry shows *-er* and *-est* forms, use them. If no such forms are listed, use *more* or *most.*

1. Comparative or superlative

Use the comparative form to compare two things, the superlative to compare three or more.

> ▸ Between John Oliver and Margaret Cho, I think Cho is the ~~funniest.~~
>
>   *funnier.*

> ▸ Of all comedians ever, I think Wanda Sykes is the ~~funnier.~~
>
>   *funniest.*

2. Redundant comparisons

Do not combine the comparative words *more/most* with adjectives or adverbs that are already in comparative form with an *-er* or *-est* ending.

> ▸ Trains in Europe and Japan are ~~more~~ faster than trains in the United States.

Quick

Reference   Forming Comparatives and Superlatives

Regular Forms

	Positive	Comparative	Superlative
Adjectives	*bold*	*bolder/less bold*	*boldest/least bold*
	helpful	*more/less helpful*	*most/least helpful*
Adverbs	*far*	*farther*	*farthest*
	realistically	*more/less realistically*	*most/least realistically*

Irregular Forms

	Positive	Comparative	Superlative
Adjectives	*bad*	*worse*	*worst*
	good	*better*	*best*
	little	*less* (quantity)/*littler* (size)	*least* (quantity)/*littlest* (size)
	many	*more*	*most*
	much	*more*	*most*
	some	*more*	*most*
Adverbs	*badly*	*worse*	*worst*
	well	*better*	*best*

3. Complete comparisons

Make sure your comparisons are logical and that readers have all the information they need to understand what is being compared to what.

More about
Complete
comparisons,
729–32

▶ The nurses' test scores were higher ̸ *than those of the pre-med students.*
⌃

The original makes us ask, "Higher than what?" The addition clarifies the comparison.

4. Absolute terms

Expressions like *more unique* or *most perfect* are common in everyday speech, but if you think about them, they make no sense. *Unique, perfect,* and other words such as *equal, essential, final, full, impossible, infinite,* and *unanimous* are absolutes, and absolutes are beyond compare. If something is unique, it is by definition one of a kind. If something is perfect, it cannot be improved upon. In formal writing, then, avoid using absolute terms comparatively.

▶ Last night's performance of the play was the ~~most perfect~~ *best* yet.

> ### EXERCISE 39.2 Revising errors with comparatives and superlatives

In the following sentences, correct any errors with the comparative or superlative forms of adjectives and adverbs.

EXAMPLE

Cameron is more ~~frugaller~~ *frugal* than even I am and may be the most

~~frugallest~~ *frugal* person I know.

1. Cameron's apartment is the most coldest of anyone's.

2. He must have the lower fuel bill in our area although his house is probably not more energy efficient.

3. Cameron feels that it is most essential for him to spend the smaller amount of money he can on anything.

4. According to him, people are more unhappy when they spend more.

5. I don't know whether I feel most admiration or disgust for Cameron's frugality, but I admit I have learned from him more useful pointers on saving money.

> ### EXERCISE 39.3 Revising for problems with adjectives and adverbs

In the following paragraphs, correct any errors in adjective or adverb usage.

It was her last year of college, and Gillian was finding life to be extreme exhilarating and real overwhelming at the same time. She had worked hardest in the previously three years to complete her required courses so that this year she could be more selective about the courses she took. That is why, although she was a chemistry major, she was taking several courses that scarcely had nothing to do with chemistry. She was furthering her study of Russian and was doing a lot of translating between Russian and English, which was terrible stressful at times. Her opera course was a purely delight, and she also loved studying European history from 1500 to 1789, although that required an immense amount of reading.

She was also enjoying her extracurricular activities, but she couldn't barely fit them all into her demanding schedule. Playing flute in the wind ensemble was fun, especially since she was the more accomplished musician in the group. However, playing in the band for the musical was bad taxing because the score was highly intricate.

Make It **Your Own**

Write a paragraph describing what you would have in your dream house if you were fabulously rich. Use at least six adjectives and six adverbs in your descriptions of your house's features, making at least two of the adjectives or adverbs comparative or superlative.

Work **Together**

Exchange your paragraph with a classmate and circle each other's adjectives and adverbs. If you see any that need to be revised, underline them and in the margin write the pages in this chapter that discuss the issue. When you have both finished, review the recommended revisions and write a brief reflection about what effect they would have on your paragraph. If you found this difficult, add adjectives and adverbs to your revision checklist.

40 Avoiding Confusing Shifts

IN THIS CHAPTER

a. Avoiding shifts in tense, 706

b. Avoiding shifts in mood and voice, 707

c. Avoiding shifts in person and number, 709

d. Avoiding shifts in direct and indirect discourse, 711

> **More about**
> Verb tenses, 672–78

© Matthew J. Lee/The Boston Globe via Getty Images

When NASCAR drivers round the curves or head into the straightaway, they need to shift gears, but an expert driver shifts only when doing so will provide a clear advantage. Similarly, good writers try not to jar their readers with unnecessary shifts in style or grammar.

40a Avoiding Awkward Shifts in Tense

Verb tenses place events in a sentence in time. Sentences with more than one verb may require a shift in tense from one to another if the verbs refer to events that occur at different times.

▶ Yesterday *was* snowy, and today *is* cloudy and cold, but according to the weather report, the weekend *will be* warm and sunny.

The sentence contrasts past, present, and future weather conditions.

Readers can be confused, however, by shifts in tense that do not correspond to shifts in time. Avoid such inappropriate shifts, particularly when you are telling a story or describing a sequence of events.

▶ The guide waited until we had all reached the top of the pass;
then she ~~leads~~ *led* the way down to the river and ~~makes~~ *made*
sure everybody ~~is~~ *was* safe in camp.

Convention dictates the use of the present tense for writing about literary events and characters as well as about films, plays, and other similar works.

> In *Madame Defarge*, the principal villain of *A Tale of Two Cities*,
>   *depicts*
> Charles Dickens ~~depicted~~ the cruel ironies of the French Revolution.
>   ^

40b Avoiding Awkward Shifts in Mood and Voice

Two other characteristics of verbs are mood and voice; as with tense, shifts in mood and voice should help make clear what the writer intends to convey.

> **Tech**   **Catching Confusing Shifts**
>
> The grammar and style checkers in word processing programs are unreliable at differentiating appropriate and confusing shifts. One style checker, for example, had no objection to this absurd statement: "Yesterday it will rain; tomorrow it snowed two feet." On the other hand, the same style checker flags every occurrence of the passive voice, regardless of whether it is appropriate to the passage in which it appears.

1. Shifts in mood

English verbs have three moods: indicative, imperative, and subjunctive. Most sentences are consistently in the indicative mood, which is used to state or question facts and beliefs. You may, however, inadvertently shift inappropriately between the imperative mood—used for commands, directions, and entreaties—and the indicative mood when explaining a process or giving directions.

> Dig a narrow hole about six inches deep, place the tulip bulb firmly at the bottom of the hole, and then ~~you can~~ fill the hole with dirt.

The subjunctive mood is used in certain situations to express a wish or demand or to make a statement contrary to fact. Although many of us often replace it with the indicative in everyday speech, readers expect to encounter it in formal writing.

More about
Mood, 678–80

>   *were*
> If the presidential primary ~~was~~ held earlier in the year, our state's
>   ^
> voters would have a greater voice in the outcome of the race.

2. Shifts in voice

Avoid shifting needlessly between the active voice, in which the subject performs the action of the verb (*I wrote the paper*) and the passive voice, in which the subject receives the action (*The paper was written by me*). As

More about
Voice, 559–61,
680–83

originally written, the following passage started out in the active voice (*British consumed, Italians favored*) but then shifted to the passive voice for no reason:

> ► During the eighteenth century, the British consumed most of their
> carbohydrates in the form of processed sugar. The Italians favored
>   *the French preferred*
> pasta, whereas sourdough bread ~~was preferred by the French~~.
>   ∧   ∧

→ **EXERCISE 40.1 Correcting verb shifts in tense, mood, and voice**
Correct the following sentences to make the verbs consistent in tense, mood, and voice. Check for shifts both within and between sentences. If a sentence needs no revision, circle its number.

EXAMPLE

                                                            relaxed
After she mowed the lawn and pulled some weeds, Kris relaxes on the
                                                         was ∧
porch watching the hummingbirds until supper is ready.
                                                   ∧

1. As most birdwatchers know, hummingbirds can do many things that other birds could not do.

2. With their wings being beaten an astonishing fifty times a second or more, hummingbirds sometimes fly as fast as sixty miles per hour.

3. Because hummingbirds expend so much energy, they needed to eat often, usually every twenty minutes.

4. With the highest metabolic rate of any animal, they burn energy faster than tigers, elephants, and all other birds.

5. Hummingbirds' most amazing feature, though, is their ability to fly in any direction—including upside down—something no other bird was capable of doing.

6. When birdwatchers study hummingbirds up close, the uniqueness of the species can be fully appreciated.

7. In addition, get a good view of the birds' long bills and stunning iridescent feathers.

8. Given hummingbirds' constant need for food, which they obtain from nectar and flowers, one would expect to have found them only in warm climates.

9. However, if birdwatchers are able to travel around the country, they would discover some species in chilly locales, such as the Rocky Mountains and Alaska.

10. Many hummingbirds migrate to warmer areas during winter months, but they returned to cooler areas in the spring and summer.

40c Avoiding Awkward Shifts in Person and Number

Person refers to the identity of the subject of a sentence and the point of view of the writer. In the first person (*I, we*), the writer and subject are the same. In the second person (*you*), the reader and subject are the same. In the third person (*he, she, it, they, Marie Curie, electrons*), the subject is the writer's topic of discussion, what the writer is informing the reader about. *Number* refers to the quantity (singular or plural) of a noun or pronoun.

> More about
> Person and num-
> ber, 648–50

1. Shifts in person

Many situations require a shift in person. You might be telling a story in the first person, for example, but you will almost certainly have to relate some parts of it in the third person.

▸ We approached the spooky old house with trepidation. The front door creaked open. We stepped inside.

Arbitrary shifts in person, in contrast, are distracting to readers. The writer of the following passage, for example, began in the first person but shifted jarringly to the second person. The revision establishes a consistent first-person point of view.

▸ When I get together with my friends in the tech club, we usually

discuss the latest apps. ~~You~~ tend to forget, though, that a
        ^*We*

garden spade and a ballpoint pen are also technological tools and

that thousands of nonelectronic items become part of ~~your~~
                                                  ^*our*

technological world every year.

Most academic writing is in the third person. The second person, including commands, is best reserved for addressing readers directly, telling them how to do something or giving them advice. (You have probably noticed that this handbook often addresses you, the reader, in just this way.) Be consistent, however, and avoid shifting arbitrarily between second and third person.

▶ To train your dog properly, ~~people~~ need plenty of time, patience,
  $\overset{you}{\wedge}$
and dog biscuits. You should start with simple commands like "sit"

and "stay."

2. Shifts in number

More about
Avoiding gender
bias, 567–68,
659–61

Most inappropriate shifts in number are errors in agreement between a pronoun and its antecedent and are often the result of a writer's desire to avoid gender bias. These kinds of errors arise most commonly when the antecedent is a singular generic noun (*person, doctor*) or indefinite pronoun (*anyone, everyone*).

FAULTY   When a <u>person</u> witnesses a crime, <u>they</u> should report it to
          the police.

The antecedent of the plural pronoun *they* is the singular generic noun *person*.

Several options are available for revising such shifts. One is to use the plural throughout. Another is to replace the plural pronoun with *he or she* (although this expression becomes tedious when overused). A third is to rephrase the sentence to avoid the problem entirely.

REVISED: When people witness a crime, they should
PLURAL THROUGHOUT   report it to the police.

REVISED: When a person witnesses a crime, he or she
HE OR SHE   should report it to the police.

REVISED: Anybody who witnesses a crime should report
REPHRASED   it to the police.

Look, too, for illogical shifts in number between two related nouns. As originally written, for example, the following sentence suggests that the passengers shared a single computer.

▶ All passengers had to open their ~~computer~~ for a security inspection.
  $\overset{computers}{\wedge}$

➤ **EXERCISE 40.2 Correcting shifts in person and number**

Correct the following sentences so that they are consistent in person and number.

> **EXAMPLE**
>   *historians*
> Although a ~~historian~~ may understand past migrations, they do not have all
>   ^
> the answers to current urban expansions.

1. During the nineteenth century, miners, merchants, and entrepreneurs flocked to the thriving river town of Galena, Illinois, to seek your fortune.

2. Galena was indeed "the west" in those days because you could not yet find any major cities west of the Mississippi River.

3. A Galenian can boast that their city, once the lead-mining capital of the world, was also home to Ulysses S. Grant and nine Civil War generals.

4. A Galenian is also likely to be proud of their town's renowned collection of original nineteenth-century architecture.

5. The mines are long closed, and the river resembles a meandering stream, but Galena remains a historic treasure where a visitor can step into yesterday, escape their busy life, and you can relax.

40d Avoiding Awkward Shifts in Direct and Indirect Quotations and Questions

Direct quotations reproduce someone's exact words and must always be enclosed in quotation marks: *My roommate announced, "The party will start at 8 p.m."* *Indirect quotations* report what someone has said but not in that person's exact words: *My roommate announced that the party would start at 8 p.m.*

Abrupt shifts between direct and indirect quotations, like the one in the following example, are awkward and confusing. Both of the revised versions are clearer and easier to follow than the original. In this instance, however, direct quotation is the best choice because Berra's own words express his humor most effectively.

> **More about**
> Punctuating
>   direct and
>   indirect quota-
>   tions, 810–13,
>   815–19
> Quoting sources,
>   260–62,
>   327–47
> Direct sources,
>   296–97

AWKWARD SHIFT	Yogi Berra said that you should go to other people's funerals or "otherwise, they won't come to yours."
REVISED: DIRECT QUOTATION	As Yogi Berra said, "You should always go to other people's funerals. Otherwise, they won't come to yours."
REVISED: INDIRECT QUOTATION	Yogi Berra said that you should go to other people's funerals because, otherwise, they won't come to yours.

> **More about**
> Punctuating direct and indirect questions, 821–22

Abrupt shifts between direct and indirect questions are confusing. A **direct question** is stated in question (interrogative) form and ends with a question mark: *When does the library open?* An **indirect question** reports a question in declarative form and ends with a period: *I wonder when the library opens.*

AWKWARD SHIFT	The author asks how much longer can the world depend on fossil fuels and whether alternative sources of energy will be ready in time.
REVISED: DIRECT QUESTION	The author asks two questions: How much longer can the world depend on fossil fuels, and will alternative sources of energy be ready in time?
REVISED: INDIRECT QUESTION	The author asks how much longer the world can depend on fossil fuels and whether alternative sources of energy will be ready in time.

> **EXERCISE 40.3 Revising confusing shifts**

Revise the following passage to eliminate confusing shifts.

In a taste test described in *The New York Times,* a cross section of the country's population sampled thousands of products in several locations, and store brands were given high marks by the testers. When the testers tried both national and store brands for such products as cereal, cream, pizza, and chicken nuggets, the researchers determine that the store brands were preferred over national brands by testers. While the testers did favor some national-brand products, such as chicken nuggets, cheese pizza, chocolate ice cream, and potatoes au gratin, the testers overwhelmingly prefer store-brand raisin bran. Store-brand frozen broccoli and chocolate chip cookies were also winners.

Although store brands have achieved a near equality with national brands in the minds of many consumers, shoppers are still careful in their choices. A shopper might ask, why shouldn't I buy a store brand if it tastes as good as a name brand? But if you find the store brand isn't good enough, you wouldn't buy it even if it was a lot cheaper.

Make It **Your Own**

Write a five- or six-sentence paragraph describing your favorite vacation, real or imaginary. Include in your paragraph as many types of awkward shifts in tense, mood, voice, person, and number as you can. You may include shifts both within and between sentences. Label this paragraph "Version A." Then rewrite your paragraph, eliminating the awkward shifts. Label this "Version B."

Work **Together**

Exchange Version A with a classmate and edit each other's paragraph to eliminate the unnecessary shifts. Compare your corrections with your classmate's Version B. Discuss and resolve any differences. If you found this difficult, add it to your revision checklist.

Text Credits

p. 712: Berra, Yogi, *When You Come to a Fork in the Road, Take It.* Hyperion, 2002, p. 163.

41 Avoiding Misplaced and Dangling Modifiers

Library of Congress, Prints & Photographs Division

Since 1886 the Statue of Liberty has dominated New York harbor, holding aloft a torch in the hand of her outstretched right arm. In 1876, however, while work on the rest of the statue continued in France, the arm and torch stood incongruously at the Philadelphia Centennial Exhibition, displayed there, and later in New York's Madison Square Park, to help raise funds for the construction of the statue's pedestal. This photograph of the display may strike you as strange because this huge piece of sculpture does not belong in a park; it is supposed to be attached appropriately to the rest of the statue. Similarly, when you misplace modifiers in your sentences, you may inadvertently confuse or surprise your readers.

MISPLACED MODIFIERS

A modifying word, phrase, or clause is misplaced if readers have to puzzle out what it modifies or if they stumble over it while trying to get from one part of a sentence to the next. Look for such *misplaced modifiers* as you revise your drafts.

Tech Misplaced Modifiers and Grammar and Style Checkers

The grammar and style checkers in word processing programs usually cannot tell what a modifier is supposed to modify, so they rarely flag those that are misplaced confusingly far from their intended targets or that seem ambiguously to modify more than one term. They do flag most split infinitives and some other disruptive modifiers.

41a Avoiding Confusing or Ambiguous Placement

Place modifiers so that they clearly refer to the words you intend them to modify and only those words.

1. Modifiers confusingly separated from the words they modify

We tend to associate modifiers with the words closest to them. A modifier positioned far from its intended target might appear to modify some other part of the sentence instead—and might confuse or amuse your readers.

▶ The couple moved to a bigger apartment after their first child *because they needed more space*

was born ~~because they needed more space.~~

The couple's need for space did not cause the birth of their child.

▶ For more than four years, the two rovers had been exploring *that landed in January 2004*

the surface of Mars ~~that landed in January 2004.~~

The rovers landed, not the surface of Mars.

> ### EXERCISE **41.1** Correcting confusingly placed modifiers

Revise the following sentences so that all modifiers are clearly and logically positioned.

EXAMPLE

Mr. Doyle walked down Main Street to Town Hall, the building that housed all the town's administrative offices, with determination.

Mr. Doyle walked with determination down Main Street to Town Hall, the building that housed all the town's administrative offices.

1. Because it was a quiet, peaceful, and relaxing town, he knew that a lot of people had chosen to move there, and he knew that like him they didn't like the changes.

2. So he had decided to go to Town Hall and formally protest the installation of a traffic light on Reynolds Road in the main intersection of town, dressed in his finest suit.

3. He went straight to the main desk, walking through the large, ornate doors of the building.

4. He was there to protest the proposed traffic light, he told the receptionist, which was a direct threat to the town's long-standing harmony and tranquility.

5. The receptionist said that after holding several public meetings on the issue, he was very sorry but the Town Council had already voted for the traffic light.

2. Squinting modifiers

A *squinting modifier* confuses readers by appearing to modify both what precedes it and what follows it.

DRAFT   People who study hard usually will get the best grades.

The sentence is ambiguous: Do people who make a practice of studying hard get the best grades, or do the best grades usually (but not always) go to people who study hard? The following revisions show that the sentence can be clarified in two different ways:

REVISION   People who usually study hard will get the best grades.

REVISION   People who study hard will usually get the best grades.

3. Ambiguous limiting modifiers

Limiting modifiers include qualifying words such as *almost, even, exactly, hardly, just, merely, only, scarcely,* and *simply.* Always place these words in front of the words you intend to modify. Do not place them in front of a verb unless they modify the verb. Otherwise, you risk ambiguity.

In the following example, the ambiguous placement of the limiter *just* leaves the reader with a variety of possible interpretations. If *just* is understood to modify *offers,* the sentence makes the unlikely suggestion that the only class the math department offers is Calculus III at night on Thursdays. The revisions provide three equally likely alternative readings.

AMBIGUOUS   The math department just offers Calculus III at night
                 on Thursdays.

REVISED   At night on Thursdays, the math department offers just Calculus III. [That is the only math course you can take on Thursday nights.]

REVISED   On Thursdays, the math department offers Calculus III just at night. [That is the only time you can take the class on Thursdays.]

REVISED   The math department offers Calculus III at night just on Thursdays. [That is the only day you can take the class at night.]

41b Avoiding Disruptive Placement

A modifier is disruptive when it awkwardly breaks the flow among grammatically connected parts of a sentence.

1. Separation of subject from verb or verb from object

Long adverbial phrases and clauses tend to be disruptive when they fall between subjects and verbs (as in the first example below), within verb phrases (as in the second example), or between verbs and their objects (as in the third example).

▶ *True Blood, well after its last episode aired in August 2014,* continued
   well after its last episode aired in August 2014.
to elicit admiring commentary and analysis.
                                          ∧

If it maintains a large following, the
▶ The show might, if it maintains a large following, dominate
  ∧
streaming video for years to come.

▶ The show often jarringly contrasts, leaving the viewer torn between

desire and revulsion, the physical attractiveness of vampires with
, leaving the viewer torn between desire and revulsion.
their violent nature.
                     ∧

An adjective phrase or clause that modifies the subject of a sentence is not usually disruptive when it falls between subject and verb. On the contrary, it would likely be misplaced in any other location.

▸ The two Mars rovers, *which both landed in January 2004*, were designed to last only 90 days.

2. Split infinitives

An infinitive consists of *to* and the base form of a verb (*to share, to jump, to remember*). An infinitive splits when a modifier is inserted between the *to* and the verb. Grammarians have traditionally considered infinitives to be indivisible units and split infinitives to be improper. Although many authorities now consider them acceptable, split infinitives can be awkward and often should be revised, particularly in formal writing.

▸ Grant's strategy was *to ~~relentlessly~~ attack* Lee's army despite the
relentlessly

heavy losses the Union army suffered as a result.

Sometimes, however, a modifier is less awkward when splitting an infinitive than in any other spot in a sentence. If the adverb *relentlessly* were placed anywhere else in the following sentence, for example, it would not clearly and unambiguously modify only the word *attack*. Placed before the infinitive or at the end of the sentence, it could be understood to modify *urged*; placed after the infinitive, it could be understood to modify *retreating*.

▸ Lincoln urged his generals to *relentlessly* attack retreating enemy forces.

Writing
Responsibly | **Misplaced Modifiers in the Real World**

Misplaced modifiers can sometimes cause real distress. A confusing instruction like the one below from the website of the Federal Emergency Management Agency (FEMA) might bewilder a homeowner struggling to recover from a natural disaster.

> You will need your social security number, current and pre-disaster address, phone numbers, type of insurance coverage, total household annual income, and a routing and account number from your bank *if you want to have disaster assistance funds transferred directly into your bank account.* [Emphasis added.]

As written, this suggests that an applicant for relief needs all of the listed items in order to have disaster assistance deposited directly into a bank account. Here is what the writer probably meant to say:

> You will need your social security number, current and pre-disaster address, phone numbers, type of insurance coverage, total household annual income, and, *if you want to have disaster assistance funds transferred directly into your bank account,* a routing and account number from your bank.

to TOPIC

→ EXERCISE 41.2 Correcting disruptive modifiers

In the following sentences, move any disruptive modifiers, and revise any awkward split infinitives.

EXAMPLE

ever since she'd bought it.

Amber's laptop, ~~ever since she'd bought it,~~ had worked flawlessly.

1. Over the last week, however, she had been, mainly with the keyboard, having problems with it.

2. Often, when she hit the *r* key, she would see an *x* on her screen, and hitting, even when tapping gently and carefully, the *o* key gave her a *b* on the screen.

3. The technical support specialist with whom she spoke finally, after talking Amber through several troubleshooting routines, instructed her to mail the computer to a repair facility.

4. She worried that the repair process, leaving her to indefinitely rely on her library's computers, would take a long time.

5. When the repaired computer, two weeks later, arrived in the mail, Amber discovered that the repair staff had considerately replaced not only the laptop's keyboard, but its motherboard as well, and the computer worked better than ever.

DANGLING MODIFIERS

Consider the following sentence:

▶ While paddling the canoe toward shore, our poodle swam alongside.

Who or what is paddling the canoe? Surely not the poodle, yet that is what the sentence seems, absurdly, to suggest. The problem here is that the phrase *while paddling the canoe toward shore* does not actually modify the subject, *poodle,* or anything else in the sentence. It dangles, unattached, leaving it to the reader to infer the existence of some unnamed human paddler. Correcting this *dangling modifier* requires either making the paddler the subject of the sentence (as in the first revision below) or identifying the paddler in the modifier (as in the second revision).

▸ While paddling the canoe toward shore, our poodle ~~swam~~ alongside.

I saw ... *swimming*

▸ While ~~paddling~~ the canoe toward shore, our poodle swam alongside.

I paddled

41c Identifying Dangling Modifiers

Dangling modifiers have the following characteristics:

> **verbal** Verb form that functions as a noun, adjective, or adverb

> **More about**
> Phrases and clauses,
> 619–625

- They are most often phrases that include a **verbal** (a gerund, infinitive, or participle) that has an implied but unstated actor.
- They occur most often at the beginnings of sentences.
- They appear to modify the subject of the sentence, so readers expect the implied actor and the subject to be the same.
- They dangle because the implied actor and the actual subject of the sentence are different.

DANGLING INFINITIVE PHRASE

To learn about new products, the company's sales meeting occurs annually in August. [Meetings do not learn.]

DANGLING PARTICIPIAL PHRASE

Hoping to boost morale, an attractive resort hotel is usually selected for the meeting. [Resorts cannot hope.]

DANGLING PREPOSITIONAL PHRASE WITH GERUND OBJECT

After traveling all day, the hotel's hot tub looked inviting to the arriving sales reps. [The sales reps traveled, not the hot tub.]

41d Correcting Dangling Modifiers

Simply moving a dangling modifier will not correct it.

DANGLING   To learn more about new products, the company's sales meeting

occurs annually in August.

STILL   The company's sales meeting occurs annually in August to learn
DANGLING
more about new products.

To correct a dangling modifier, first determine the identity of the modifier's unstated actor. You then have two options:

1. Rephrase to make the implied actor the subject of the sentence

2. Rephrase to include the implied actor in the modifier

Use the approach that works best given the purpose of the sentence in your draft.

MAKING THE IMPLIED ACTOR THE SUBJECT

sales reps attend   annual
To learn about new products, the company's sales meeting ~~occurs~~

~~annually~~ in August.

management usually selects
Hoping to boost morale, an attractive resort hotel ~~is usually selected~~ for

the meeting.

In both these cases, the implied actor—*sales reps* in the first, *management* in the second—was missing entirely from the original sentence.

INCLUDING THE IMPLIED ACTOR IN THE MODIFIER

As the sales reps arrived after   *them.*
~~After~~ traveling all day, the hotel's hot tub looked inviting to ~~the arriving~~

~~sales reps.~~

In this case, the implied actor, *sales reps,* appeared in the original sentence but needed to be repositioned.

> **EXERCISE 41.3 Correcting dangling modifiers**

Revise the following sentences to eliminate dangling modifiers.

EXAMPLE

As soon as Derek stepped aboard,
~~On stepping aboard,~~ the boat began to roll back and forth.
⌃

1. To avoid seasickness in the bobbing boat, focusing on the distant shoreline was a great help.

2. Having little hope of actually catching anything, expectations for success were low.

3. Having dropped his line into the water, a tug indicated that he had a bite.

4. Reeling in the fish, everyone cheered because the first-timer had made the first catch.

5. Catching a few more fish and not getting seasick, the trip was clearly a success.

Make It **Your Own**

Reread several papers that you have recently written and note where you handled modifiers well. Circle any confusingly placed, ambiguous, disruptive, or dangling modifiers and edit them using the information in this chapter. If you found several, add this issue to your revision checklist.

42 Avoiding Mixed and Incomplete Constructions

IN THIS CHAPTER

MIXED CONSTRUCTIONS

a. Correcting mixed constructions, 723

b. Correcting mismatched subjects, predicates, 725

INCOMPLETE CONSTRUCTIONS

c. Using essential words, 728

d. Avoiding incomplete comparisons, 729

M.C. Escher, Waterfall, 1961.

This disorienting image by artist M. C. Escher shows an impossible building, a mixed construction with a water channel that appears to flow horizontally but somehow ends up two stories higher than it begins, with the water cascading back to its source. As you edit your writing, look for sentences that similarly start in one direction but turn disorientingly in another, leaving readers unsure where you have taken them. Look, too, for sentences that omit words readers need to grasp fully your intended meaning.

MIXED CONSTRUCTIONS

When a sentence begins one way and then takes an unexpected turn—in grammar or logic—the result is a *mixed construction.* To find and correct mixed constructions in your drafts, keep your eye on the way your sentences begin, and make sure every predicate has a grammatically and logically appropriate subject.

42a Recognizing and Correcting Grammatically Mixed Constructions

Grammatically mixed constructions can occur when a writer treats an introductory phrase or clause that cannot function as the subject of a sentence as if it were the subject. The following example starts with a long prepositional phrase (underlined) that the writer mistakenly uses as the subject of the sentence. A prepositional phrase, although it can modify the subject or other parts of a sentence, cannot be the subject. The result is a *sentence fragment,* not a sentence.

> **sentence fragment**
> An incomplete sentence punctuated as if it were complete

723

MIXED	As a justification by American leaders for dropping atomic bombs on Hiroshima and Nagasaki maintained that doing so persuaded the Japanese to surrender without the need for an invasion that might have cost hundreds of thousands of casualties.

Fixing a sentence like this requires identifying a grammatical subject and isolating it from the introductory phrase. Here is one possible revision (with the subject underlined):

REVISED	As a justification for dropping atomic bombs on Hiroshima and Nagasaki, American leaders maintained that doing so persuaded the Japanese to surrender without the need for an invasion that might have cost hundreds of thousands of casualties.

Here is a more concise alternative that eliminates the introductory phrase altogether:

REVISED	American leaders maintained that dropping atomic bombs on Hiroshima and Nagasaki persuaded the Japanese to surrender without the need for an invasion that might have cost hundreds of thousands of casualties.

> **More about**
> Clauses, 623–25
> Relating ideas
> with subordina-
> tion, 534–40

In the next example, the writer follows a subordinate clause (*Because the bombings had devastating effects*) with the verb *provoked*, which has no subject. The editing changes the first part of the sentence into a noun phrase subject for *provoked*.

>   *The devastating effects of the bombings*
> ▸ ~~Because the bombings had devastating effects~~ provoked intense
>   ^
>
> debate over the morality of the military decision.

Mixed constructions also occur when a writer treats a modifying phrase or clause as if it were the predicate of a sentence. Look for this kind of mixed construction, especially in sentences that begin with the phrase *the fact that*. The following example begins with a subject, *the fact*, followed by a long adjective *that* clause that modifies the subject but cannot at the same time be the predicate of the sentence.

> **subject comple-**
> **ment** An adjective,
> pronoun, noun, or
> noun phrase that
> follows a linking
> verb and refers to
> the subject of the
> sentence

MIXED	The fact that Hiroshima and Nagasaki, which were devastated by the bomb, are once again thriving cities.

One way to revise this sentence is to add the verb *is*, making the *that* clause into a **subject complement.**

REVISED	The fact is that Hiroshima and Nagasaki, which were devastated by the bomb, are once again thriving cities.

> **More about**
> Eliminating wordy
> expressions,
> 521–23

Better yet is simply to eliminate the phrase *the fact that*, a wordy expression that adds no information to the sentence.

REVISED   Hiroshima and Nagasaki, which were devastated by the bomb, are once again thriving cities.

When drafting a project, you may find yourself not only mixing constructions but also confusingly mixing up several ideas in the effort to get your thoughts down. Clarifying snarls like these may require you to pull the ideas apart and sort them into separate sentences.

MIXED   While the first atomic bomb had been successfully tested by scientists of the Manhattan Project on July 16, 1945, at Alamogordo, New Mexico, then less than one month later an American plane, after years of intensive research, dropped the bomb that destroyed Hiroshima on August 6.

REVISED   After years of intensive research, scientists of the Manhattan Project successfully tested the first atomic bomb on July 16, 1945, at Alamogordo, New Mexico. On August 6, less than one month later, an American plane dropped the bomb that destroyed Hiroshima.

42b Recognizing and Correcting Mismatched Subjects and Predicates

The error of *faulty predication* occurs when a subject and predicate are mismatched—when they do not fit together logically. For example, the original subject of the following sentence, *recommendation*, does not work with the verb *insisted*. Recommendations cannot insist; doctors can.

>   *doctor*
> ▶ The ~~doctor's recommendation~~ insisted that Joe visit a chiropractor
>   ^
>
> immediately.

Many instances of faulty predication involve a mismatch between the subject and subject complement in sentences in which the verb is a form of *be* or other *linking verb.*

> **linking verb** A verb that connects a subject to a subject complement

MISMATCHED   Only <u>students</u> who are absent because of illness or a

family emergency will be <u>grounds</u> for a makeup exam.

REVISED   Only students who are absent because of illness or a family emergency will be permitted to take a makeup exam.

Two forms of expression involving the verb *be* that have become commonplace in everyday speech are examples of faulty predication and should be avoided in formal writing. These are the use of *is where* or *is when* in definitions and the use of *the reason is . . . because* in explanations.

1. *Is where, is when*

Using the expressions *is when* and *is where* creates illogical definitions if the terms defined do not involve a place (*where*) or a time (*when*).

> ▸ A tornado is ~~where~~ *a violent storm in which* high winds swirl around in a funnel-shaped cloud.
>
> A tornado is a storm, not a place.

> ▸ A friend is ~~when~~ *who* someone cares about you and has fun with you.
>
> A friend is a person, not a time.

The expressions result in grammatical mismatches, too, because *where* and *when* introduce adverb clauses, which cannot function as subject complements.

2. *The reason . . . is because*

Explanations using the expression *the reason . . . is because* are similarly mismatched both logically (*the reason* and *because* are redundant) and grammatically (*because* introduces an adverb clause, which cannot function as a subject complement). The following example shows two simple ways to fix this kind of faulty predication—by changing the subject of the sentence or by substituting *that* for *because*.

> ▸ ~~The reason~~ I wrote this paper ~~is~~ because my instructor required it.
> ▸ The reason I wrote this paper is ~~because~~ *that* my instructor required it.

Obligatory Words and Unacceptable Repetitions in English Unlike some languages, formal written English requires a stated subject in all sentences except commands.

> ▸ ~~Rained~~ *It rained* all day yesterday.

More about
Including a stated subject and eliminating redundant subject and object pronouns, 734–37

On the other hand, formal written English does not permit the use of a pronoun to emphasize an already stated subject or direct object.

▶ Maria, ~~she~~ forgot to take her umbrella.

_____

→ EXERCISE 42.1 Correcting mixed constructions

Revise the following sentences to eliminate mixed constructions. Some sentences may be revised in more than one way.

EXAMPLE

While discouraging human athletes from using chemicals to improve

performance ~~ignores~~ *, we ignore* the reality that animals use any chemicals they can
                    ^

to gain an advantage.

1. Because a hedgehog needs to avoid predators gnaws on the skin of poisonous toads.

2. The reason the hedgehog does this is because it gets the toad's toxin and then spread it over its body, making itself immune to enemies.

3. As male cardinals and house finches eat as many berries as they can in the fall unconcerned with the low nutritional value of the food.

4. Eating the berries is where the birds obtain carotenoids, the red and orange pigments that make their feathers so colorful in the spring.

5. The fact that the male *Cosmosoma myrodora* moth, which also collects steroid toxins to help attract the opposite sex.

6. The male moth's drive to lap up toxin from the leaves of certain vines stores a supply of the toxin in pouches on his abdomen.

7. When the male moth's abdominal pouches get large and heavy attracting female moths.

8. During their mating is when the male's pouches burst and spread the steroid toxins all over the female.

9. The fact is that this is how the female *Cosmosoma myrodora* moth becomes inedible to spiders.

10. By denying human athletes the use of steroids is unfair when animals use the chemicals to such great advantage?

INCOMPLETE CONSTRUCTIONS

As you draft sentences, you may unintentionally leave out grammatically or logically essential words. Sometimes these omissions result in sentence fragments. Often, however, they create seemingly minor but nonetheless distracting grammatical or idiomatic bumps. As you proofread and edit your drafts, be especially alert for such missing words in compound and other constructions and in comparisons.

42c Adding Essential Words to Compound and Other Constructions

> *More about*
> Writing concisely,
> 520–28
> (ch. 26)

In compound constructions, the omission of *nonessential* repetitions can often help tighten prose.

> ▸ Investigators wondered about the causes of the fire and [about] who might have been involved. They questioned six officials and then [they] arrested two.

> **elliptical construc-**
> **tion** A construction
> in which otherwise
> grammatically nec-
> essary words can
> be omitted because
> their meaning is
> understood from the
> surrounding context

Such *elliptical constructions* work, however, only when the stated words in one part of a compound match the omitted words in other parts. When grammar or idiom requires different words—different verb forms, different prepositions, or different articles, for example—those words should be included.

> ▸ The candidate claimed that she always had and always would ^supported^ support universal health care coverage.

The word *supported* is needed because *had support* would be ungrammatical.

> ▸ On the campaign trail and ^in^ debates, her opponent for the nomination insisted that his plan was better than hers.

In this situation, the word *debates* requires the preposition *in*, not *on*.

> ▸ A yearning for change, ^an^ unsettled economy, and ^the^ character of the candidates themselves combined to sustain high voter turnout during the primary season.

The word *unsettled* requires a different form of the indefinite article (*a, an*) than *yearning,* and in this situation the word *character* requires the definite article (*the*) rather than the indefinite article.

Occasionally, you may need to repeat a modifier for clarity.

▶ The candidates asked their loyal backers and opponents to support

the winner, whoever that might be.

> *their*

The repeated *their* makes clear that the adjective *loyal* applies only to *backers* and not to *opponents.*

Although you can often omit the word *that* without obscuring the meaning of a subordinate clause, sometimes you need to include it to avoid confusion.

> *that*

■ I know Sheila, who is a sympathetic person, will not be terribly

upset about the stains on the silk shirt ~~that~~ I borrowed from her.

In the original, without the first *that,* *Sheila* could be understood as the object of *know* rather than the subject of the long subordinate clause that follows. On the other hand, the *that* at the end of the sentence can be eliminated because no such ambiguity affects the subject (*I*) of the clause it introduces.

42d Avoiding Incomplete or Ambiguous Comparisons

Comparisons show how two items are alike or different. For comparisons to be clear, the items they juxtapose must be logically equivalent. The original version of the following sentence confusingly compares a group of people, children, to a process, growing up. The editing makes the two sides of the comparison equivalent.

> **More about**
> Comparisons,
> 702–3

▶ Children who grow up on farms are more active than ~~growing up in~~

big cities.

> *those who grow up in*

To be complete, comparisons must fully specify what is being compared to what.

▶ Lemon eucalyptus is better at deterring ticks.

> *than tea tree oil*

Be careful how you use the terms *any* and *any other* when you compare one item to others that belong to the same category.

▸ Mount Everest is higher than any mountain in the world.
  ^ other

> Mount Everest is a mountain in the world, so without the modifier *other,* the sentence suggests that Mount Everest is higher than itself.

▸ Aconcagua, the highest mountain in South America, is higher than any ~~other~~ mountain in North America.

> The sentence compares a mountain in South America to mountains in North America, not to other mountains in South America.

Be sure, also, to include any information you need to avoid ambiguity in your comparisons. In its draft form, the following comparison has two possible interpretations, as the revisions make clear.

DRAFT	Scientists are better informed about the face of Mars than the lower mantle of Earth's layers.
REVISED	Scientists are better informed about the face of Mars than <u>they are about</u> the lower mantle of Earth's layers.
REVISED	Scientists are better informed about the face of Mars than <u>about</u> the lower mantle of Earth's layers.

▸ Stephen King's horror stories are scary as Edgar Allan Poe's.
  as
  ^

▸ **EXERCISE 42.2 Correcting incomplete constructions**

Revise the following sentences to eliminate incomplete constructions. Some sentences may be revised in more than one way.

EXAMPLE

traveling by

Traveling by airplane was once more convenient than train.
  ^

1. Yuko understood, from what she heard on the news, air travel had become more difficult in recent years.

2. The airline Yuko chose for her trip to Los Angeles had a more reliable on-time record than any air carrier.

3. She thought she had been careful about her flight planning as she possibly could have been.

4. Unfortunately, she could not have planned for a sudden severe storm during her flight, resulting disruptions in the country's air travel system, and unexpected landing of her flight at Albuquerque, New Mexico, at midnight.

5. She learned that the plane would need repairs and the airline unable to continue the flight to Los Angeles for days.

6. Yuko knew Helen, who sat next to her on the plane, was willing to rent a car and drive the rest of the way to Los Angeles.

7. After an all-night drive, an exhausted Yuko concluded that, whenever available, train travel would be better.

Make It **Your Own**

Reread several papers that you have recently written and note where you handled sentence constructions well. If you see examples of mixed or incomplete constructions, or ambiguous comparisons, edit them and add this issue to your revision checklist.

Part Nine

Language
Matters
Guidance for Multilingual Writers

43 Understanding English Word Order and Sentence Structure

by Ted E. Johnston and M. E. Sokolik

> *More about*
> Sentence types, 613
> Word order in questions, 739–40

> **clause** A word group with a subject and a predicate. An *independent clause* can stand alone as a sentence; a *subordinate clause* cannot.

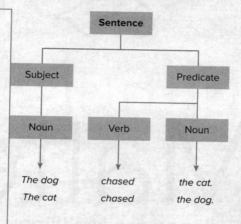

English is a word-order language, which means that the position of a word in a sentence often determines its grammatical function. As a result, *The dog chased the cat* means something different from *The cat chased the dog.* This chapter describes and explains word order and related aspects of English sentence structure.

43a Observing Normal Word Order

In declarative sentences (as opposed to questions or commands), normal word order is subject-verb-object (or S-V-O). That is, the subject comes first, then the verb, and then the direct object, if there is one, or any other words that make up the predicate.

                                               v   ?   ?

FAULTY WORD ORDER   Chased the cat the dog.

                                                s   v   o

NORMAL WORD ORDER   The dog chased the cat.

43b Including a Stated Subject

Except for commands, English sentences and *clauses* require a subject to be stated, even if the identity of the subject is clear from a previous sentence or clause. In the following example, the pronoun *he*, referring to the subject of the first sentence, can serve as the subject of both clauses of the second sentence.

▶ Nico has a hard life for a ten-year-old. ~~Is~~ just a boy, but is expected

   to work like a man.

Similarly, a subordinate clause requires a stated subject even if its subject is a pronoun or another noun phrase that obviously refers to the same entity as the subject of the clause that precedes it.

|— sub. clause —|
she
▶ Lucy asked for directions because was lost.

In commands, the subject is unstated but is understood to be "you."

▶ [you] Leave now!

43c Managing *There* and *It* Constructions

Expletives are words that are empty of content; that is, they do not refer to anything. In English, the words *there* and *it* are often used as expletives.

In *there* constructions, *there* precedes a form of *to be. There*, however, is not the subject. The subject follows the verb, and the verb is either singular or plural, depending on the subject. The expletive *it*, on the other hand, is always the singular subject of its clause. *It* constructions are often used to indicate an environmental condition or some aspect of time. The verb in expletive *it* constructions is often a form of *be*, but other verbs can be used, especially those related to process (for example, *start, continue, end*). The expletives *there* and *it* cannot be omitted from such clauses, even though they do not refer to anything.

There are
▶ ~~Are~~ not enough reasons to support your argument.

there
▶ Waiter, I am not pleased that is a fly in my soup.

it   *it*
▶ When was almost 3:00 p.m., started hailing really hard.

In a similar construction, the pronoun *it* is not empty, but refers to content that follows the verb. In the following sentence, for example, *it* refers to *to drive during a snowstorm.* In either case, empty or meaningful, *it* is the subject and cannot be omitted.

▶ ~~Is~~ dangerous to drive during a snowstorm.
  ^It is

43d Eliminating Redundant Subject and Object Pronouns

Although English requires a stated subject in all clauses except commands, the use of a pronoun to reemphasize an already stated subject is not acceptable in writing, even though such constructions often occur in informal speech.

▶ Rosalinda, ~~she~~ left early for the airport.
  subj.   redundant subject

Similarly, when *which* or *that* begins a clause and serves as the clause's subject or direct object, do not also add *it* to serve as the subject or direct object. In the following sentences, for example, both *which* and *it* refer redundantly to the movie *The Big Short*; to correct the sentences requires eliminating one or the other pronoun.

▶ Last night I saw *The Big Short*, which ~~it~~ impressed me very much.
  subj.   redundant subject

or

▶ Last night I saw *The Big Short*; ~~which~~ it impressed me very much.

▶ I liked *The Big Short*, which many of my friends liked ~~it~~ too.
  dir. obj.   redundant object

or

▶ I liked *The Big Short*; ~~which~~ many of my friends liked it too.

> **EXERCISE 43.1 Using normal word order and including a subject**

In the following sentences, correct word-order errors involving subjects or omissions of *it* or *there*.

EXAMPLE

It was
~~Was~~ obvious the students hadn't studied for the test.
∧

1. Without a doubt, is nothing more breathtaking than seeing a double rainbow after a storm.

2. I am excited by this letter, which I received it late yesterday.

3. Was still too early to plant the tomatoes, so died all of them.

4. We read that are several new dance clubs opening this weekend.

5. We left the office because was after five o'clock.

6. Don't you think is a little silly to argue about who is the better cook?

7. My aunt and uncle, they are both working in California as computer programmers.

8. Is completely impossible to dislike that professor!

9. This is an uplifting story because has such an optimistic ending.

10. I read a controversial article that it claims North and South America were settled much earlier than previously thought.

43e Structuring Sentences with Direct Objects, Indirect Objects, and Object Complements

Direct objects, indirect objects, and object complements can follow a transitive verb.

1. Direct and indirect objects

A *direct object* receives or carries the action of a transitive verb. Certain transitive verbs—such as *ask, find, give, order, send, show, teach, tell,* and *write*—can also take an *indirect object,* which names the recipient of the direct object. The indirect object falls between the verb and the direct object.

> **More about**
> Direct and indirect objects,
> 616–18

>   s   v   io   do
> ▸ She sent Michiko a book on Scandinavian cuisine.

Alternatively, the recipient of the direct object can be identified in a phrase beginning with a preposition, usually *to,* that follows the direct object.

▸ She sent a book on Scandinavian cuisine to Michiko.

<small>s   v   do   io</small>

When the direct object is a personal pronoun, the verb must be followed by a prepositional phrase, not an indirect object.

▸ She sent ~~Michiko~~ it ⌃ *to Michiko*

Several common verbs do not take indirect objects even though the actions they refer to are similar to those of verbs that do. These verbs include *answer, carry, change, close, complete, deliver, describe, explain, keep, mention, open, propose, put, recommend, repair* (or *fix* when it means *repair*), and *say.* With these verbs, the function of the indirect object can be performed only by a prepositional phrase beginning with *to* (or sometimes *for*) that follows the direct object.

▸ The doctor explained ~~my father~~ the dangers of secondhand smoke ⌃ *to my father*

▸ The professor opened ~~us~~ the door to understanding ⌃ *for us*

2. Object complements

An *object complement* follows a direct object and describes a condition of the object or a change in the object that the subject has caused the object to undergo.

▸ Some workers here make my job impossible.

<small>do   obj. comp.</small>

Placing an object complement before the direct object will either make a sentence ungrammatical or change its meaning. The following sentence, as originally written, was ungrammatical.

▸ The players have just elected ~~their team captain~~ Paul ⌃ *their team captain.*

The following sentences, in contrast, are both grammatical but have different meanings.

▸ We need to keep all the <u>happy</u> workers.

▸ We need to keep all the workers <u>happy</u>.

The first sentence, with the adjective *happy* before the direct object, recommends retaining the workers who are already happy, but not necessarily those who are not. The second, with *happy* in the object complement position after the direct object, recommends taking action to make sure that not one of the workers feels unhappy.

→ EXERCISE **43.2** Using objects and object complements

Correct any errors related to indirect objects or object complements in the following sentences. Next to sentences with an error, write IO if the problem is related to indirect objects and OC if it is related to object complements. Mark any correct sentences OK.

EXAMPLE

We want the ~~closed~~ door, please.   closed,   OC

1. We painted the yellow walls because yellow is a cheerful color.

2. She sent me a very informative email.

3. I consider his inappropriate remarks and refuse to respond to them.

4. The owner described me the house in great detail.

5. The president appointed me his new assistant.

6. Frank has a build very muscular.

7. I had an extra blanket, so I gave a homeless man it.

8. We ordered the carpet baby blue, not the beige one.

9. The last treatment did to the patient more harm than good.

10. The teacher explained the students the assignment one more time.

43f Observing Word-Order Patterns in Questions

In questions, unlike declarative statements, a verb nearly always precedes the subject.

- To form a question with one-word forms of the verb *be*, simply invert subject and verb.

        s   v   v   s

The grapes are ripe.   Are the grapes ripe?

- In all other cases, a question requires a helping verb as well as a main verb. The subject goes after the first helping verb in a verb phrase and before the rest of the verb phrase.

   s   hv mv   hv   s   mv

They have left for New York.   Have they left for New York?

     s   hv mv   hv   s   mv

The children can go with us.   Can the children go with us?

     s   hv   hv   mv   hv   s   hv   mv

The painters should have finished. Should the painters have finished?

- To form a question with one-word verbs other than forms of *be*, use the appropriate form of *do* as the helper.

    s   v   hv   s   mv

The prisoner escaped.   Did the prisoner escape?

- Questions that begin with question words like *what, who,* and *why* normally follow the same word order as other questions.

        hv   s   mv

What is the engineer saying about the project?

- If the question word is the subject, however, the question follows subject-before-verb word order.

    s   v   do

Who is saying these things about the project?

43g Observing Inverted Word Order When Certain Conjunctions or Adverbs Begin a Clause

When they appear at the beginning of a sentence or clause, certain adverbs, adverb phrases, correlative conjunctions (such as *neither . . . nor* and *not only . . . but also*), and the conjunction *nor* by itself require inverted word order similar to that used in questions.

the parents   they
▶ *Neither* ~~the parents~~ have called the principal, *nor* ~~they~~ have informed
   ∧
the school board.
                           do
▶ The twins don't bowl, *nor* they play tennis.
                              ∧

Negating or limiting adverbs such as *rarely, seldom, no sooner,* and *no longer* also require inverted word order when they start a sentence or clause. Such sentences have a formal tone.

the dancers
▶ *Seldom* ~~the dancers~~ have had the opportunity to perform in public.
                  ∧

Moving the adverb to the interior of the sentence cancels the inversion.

▶ The dancers have *seldom* had the opportunity to perform in public.

Usually, this less formal, noninverted version of such sentences is preferable to the inverted version.

> *More about*
> Adverbs,
> 697–705,
> 764–68

▶ **EXERCISE 43.3 Working with word-order inversions**

In the following sentences, correct any word-order errors related to inversions. Mark any correct sentences OK.

EXAMPLE

   do   do
Neither we want to go the party, nor we want to help pay for it.
   ∧   ∧

1. Neither he takes classes at the university, nor he works.

2. Jossette has been working on her research project?

3. When Chen bought his new computer?

4. We rarely went to dinner with friends.

5. Rarely it rains in the desert.

6. Goes she often to parties?

7. Couldn't Fatima have done something sooner about the error?

8. Why smoking should be banned in bars?

9. Not only she works hard, but she also studies hard.

10. Mark neither reads French nor speaks it.

Make It **Your Own**

In an issue of a newsmagazine such as *Time,* the *Economist, U.S. News and World Report,* or the *Week,* find two examples each of sentences with indirect objects, object complements, and inversions involving "not only," "neither/nor," or some other initial adverb or adverbial phrase. Copy the sentences and underline the components in each sentence identifying the feature. Write two examples of your own for each type of sentence patterned on the examples you found.

Work **Together**

In small groups, check the examples group members wrote in the Make It Your Own activity above. Does everyone agree with the results? Why or why not? Ask your instructor if you are uncertain about any of the examples.

44 Using Nouns and Noun Determiners
by Ted E. Johnston and M. E. Sokolik

IN THIS CHAPTER

a. Understanding different types of nouns, 743

b. Using nouns with articles and other determiners, 744

> **More about**
> Types of nouns,
> 603–5

> **More about**
> Forming noun
> plurals, 591–94

"What can I say? I was an English major."

© J.C. Duffy/The New Yorker Collection/The Cartoon Bank

English nouns rarely appear by themselves. Most of the time they are paired with words such as *a, an, the, my, that, each, one, ten, several, more, less,* and *fewer.* These words are known as *determiners* because they help us figure out—or determine—how a noun works and what it means when we encounter it in a sentence. As this cartoon suggests, learning to use nouns and determiners appropriately can sometimes challenge native speakers as much as it does multilingual students.

44a Understanding Different Types of Nouns

To use a noun correctly, you need to know whether it is a *proper noun* or a *common noun*, and, if it is a common noun, whether it is *count* or *noncount*. A **common noun** identifies a general category and is usually not capitalized: *woman, era, bridge, corporation, mountain, war*. A **proper noun** identifies someone or something specific and is usually capitalized: *Hillary Clinton, Middle Ages, Golden Gate Bridge, Burger King, Himalayas, World War II*.

Count nouns name discrete, countable things. **Noncount nouns** (also called **noncountable nouns** or **mass nouns**) usually name entities made of a continuous substance or of small, indistinguishable particles, or they refer to a general quality. A *drop*, a *grain*, and a *suggestion*, for example, are count nouns, but *water, sand,* and *advice* are noncount nouns.

- Count nouns can be singular (*drop*) or plural (*drops*). Most noncount nouns are singular, even those that end in *-s,* and thus should be matched with singular verbs. Noncount nouns cannot be preceded by a number or any other term that would imply countability (such as *a, an, several, another,* or *many*), nor can they be made plural if they are singular.

> helps
> ▸ Aerobics ~~help~~ me to relax.
>   ^

Here are some examples of contrasting count and noncount nouns:

Count	Noncount
car/cars	traffic
dollar/dollars	money
noodle/noodles	spaghetti
pebble/pebbles	gravel
spoon/spoons	silverware

- Many nouns can be noncount in one context and count in another.

  ▸ While speaking of *love* [noncount], my grandmother recalled the three *loves* [count] of her life.

  In the opening phrase, *love* is an abstraction. In the main clause, *loves* refers to the people the grandmother has loved.

- All languages have count and noncount nouns, but a noun that is count in one language may be noncount in another.

44b Using Nouns with Articles (*a, an, the*) and Other Determiners

The *articles a, an,* and *the* are the most common determiners. Other determiners include possessives (*my, your, Ivan's*), numbers (*one, five, a hundred*), and other words that quantify (*some, many, a few*) or specify (*this, those*).

1. Articles with common nouns

The main function of the *indefinite articles, a* and *an,* is to introduce nouns that are new to the reader. The *definite article, the,* usually precedes nouns that have already been introduced or whose identity is known or clear from the context. Noncount nouns and plural count nouns also sometimes appear with no article (or the *zero article*).

Quick Reference   Some Common Noncount Nouns

Although there is no hard-and-fast way to distinguish noncount from count nouns, most noncount nouns do fall into a few general categories.

Abstractions and Emotions	advice, courage, happiness, hate, jealousy, information, knowledge, love, luck, maturity, patriotism, warmth
Mass Substances	air, blood, dirt, gasoline, glue, sand, shampoo, water
Food Items	beef, bread, corn, flour, gravy, pork, rice, salt, sugar
Collections of Related Items	cash, clothing, equipment, furniture, graffiti, information, jewelry, luggage, mail, traffic
Games and Other Activities	aerobics, baseball, checkers, homework, news, Pilates, poker, pool, soccer, tennis, volleyball
Weather-Related Phenomena	cold, drizzle, frost, hail, heat, humidity, lightning, rain, sleet, snow, sunshine, thunder
Diseases	arthritis, chicken pox, diabetes, influenza, measles
Fields of Study	botany, chemistry, mathematics, physics, sociology

- Use *a* before a consonant sound (*a cat*) and *an* before a vowel sound (*an elephant*). Do not be misled by written vowels that are pronounced as consonants (*a European tour*) or written consonants that are pronounced as vowels (*an hour early*). Be especially careful with words that begin with *h* (a hot stove, an honorary degree) and *u* (a uniform, an upheaval).

- Use *a* or *an* only with singular count nouns. A singular count noun *must* be preceded by an article or some other determiner even if other modifiers come between the determiner and the noun.

  ▸ A friend of mine bought an antique car on eBay.

- Never use *a* or *an* with a noncount noun.

  ▸ A ~~good~~ advice is hard to find.
    Good

- Use *a* or *an* when you first introduce a singular count noun if the specific identity of the noun is not yet known to the reader or is not otherwise clear from the context. Use *the* for subsequent references to the same noun.

▸ A friend of mine bought an antique car on eBay. She restored the car and sold it for a tidy profit. The profit came in handy when she took a vacation.

The is appropriate for *car* in the second sentence because it refers to the same car introduced in the first sentence. The word *profit* in the second sentence takes *a* because it is making its first appearance there. The third sentence continues the process.

■ Use *the* with both count and noncount nouns whose specific identity has been previously established or is clear from the context.

▸ We admired the antique car that my friend bought on eBay.

The modifying clause *that my friend bought on eBay* identifies a specific car.

▸ She sold it for a tidy profit and used the money for a vacation.

The context clearly identifies the money with the profit.

▸ My friend is traveling around the world for three months.

The noun *world* logically refers to the planet we live on—not, say, Mars or Venus.

More about
Superlatives,
702–4

▸ Vicky is the fastest runner on her team.

The superlative *fastest* refers specifically to one person.

■ No article is used to introduce noncount nouns or plural count nouns used generically—that is, to make generalizations.

▸ Good advice is hard to find.
▸ Good teachers can change lives.

■ Both the definite and indefinite articles can introduce singular nouns used generically. Sometimes either is appropriate:

▸ The good teacher can change lives.
▸ A good teacher can change lives.

Sometimes the generic meaning is clear with only one or the other:

▸ Thomas Alva Edison invented a lightbulb.
                                    ^
                                   the

2. Articles with proper nouns

Proper nouns in English almost never occur with the indefinite article (*a, an*), and most occur with no article:

▶ Ruby grew up in Lima, Peru, but now lives in Wichita, Kansas.

There are many exceptions, however:

- Certain place names always occur with *the: the* Bronx, *the* Philippines, *the* Northeast, *the* Pacific Ocean.

- The names of ships (including airships) conventionally occur with *the: the* Queen Mary, *the* Challenger.

- Many product names can be used with *a* or *the* or sometimes both: *the* Cheerios, *an/the* iPhone, *a/the* Toyota.

- Many multiword proper nouns occur with *the: the* United States, *the* Brooklyn Bridge, *the* Department of State, *the* War of 1812. Others do not, however. The city of Chicago, for example, is home to both *the* Wrigley Building (with article) and *Wrigley Field* (no article).

- Most plural proper nouns occur with *the: the* Bartons, *the* Chicago Cubs.

➤ EXERCISE 44.1 Using articles correctly

Insert *a, an, the*, or no article as appropriate in the blanks in the following paragraph.

I feel ___¹ anger whenever I see ___² poor child suffering from ___³ hunger. In ___⁴ United States, we believe that ___⁵ children need ___⁶ good breakfast every morning to do well in ___⁷ school, so schools provide ___⁸ breakfast for them. I realize that ___⁹ economic situation is often worse in ___¹⁰ other countries than here, but even here, there is more hunger than ___¹¹ people realize. ___¹² hungriest children are found in ___¹³ rural areas of our country. ___¹⁴ boy I once knew told me that many nights he went to bed hungry after working in ___¹⁵ fields. ___¹⁶ boy later moved to ___¹⁷ nearby city and his family was able to get ___¹⁸ assistance from ___¹⁹ various charitable organizations.

3. Nouns and other determiners

More about
Order of
adjectives,
762–63

As with articles, the use of other determiners with nouns depends on the kind of noun in question, particularly whether it is singular or plural, count or noncount. In all cases, determiners precede any other adjectives that modify a noun.

Possessive nouns or pronouns Use possessive nouns (*Julio's*) and possessive pronouns (*my, our, your, his, her, its, their, whose*) with any count or noncount noun.

sing. count	plural count	noncount
Ann's book	*Ann's* books	*Ann's* information
her book	*her* books	*her* information

This, that, these, those The demonstrative pronouns *this, that, these,* and *those* specify, or single out, particular instances of a noun. Use *this* and *that* only with noncount nouns and singular count nouns. Use *these* and *those* only with plural count nouns.

sing. count	plural count	noncount
this book	—	*this* information
that book	—	*that* information
—	*these* books	—
—	*those* books	—

Quantifying words or phrases Use numbers only with count nouns: *one shirt, two shirts.* See the Quick Reference box on the next page for a list of other quantifying words and how they work with different kinds of nouns in most contexts.

Few *versus* a few *and* little *versus* a little The determiners *few* and *a few* (for count nouns) and *little* and *a little* (for noncount nouns) all indicate a small quantity, but they have significant differences in meaning. *Few* means a negligible amount, whereas *a few* means a small but significant number. Likewise, *little* means *almost none,* whereas *a little* means *some.*

▶ Rhoda has *few* good friends.

  She is almost friendless.

▶ Rhoda has *a few* good friends.

  She has significant companionship.

Quick Reference   Matching Nouns with Quantifying Words and Phrases

Quantifying Word or Phrase	Singular Count Nouns	Plural Count Nouns	Noncount Nouns	Examples
any, no	✓	✓	✓	You can read <u>any</u> book on the list.
				Have you read <u>any</u> books this summer?
				Do you have <u>any</u> information about the reading list?
another, each, every, either, neither	✓	no	no	I read <u>another</u> book last week.
the other	✓	✓	✓	<u>The other</u> book is a murder mystery.
				I haven't finished <u>the other</u> books on the reading list.
				<u>The other</u> information is the most reliable.
a couple of, a number of, both, few, a few, fewer, fewest, many, several	no	✓	no	The professor assigned <u>fewer</u> books last term.
a lot of, lots of, all, enough, more, most, other, some	no	✓	✓	<u>Some</u> books are inspiring.
				<u>Some</u> information is unreliable.
little, a little, much, a great deal of, less, least	no	no	✓	I need <u>a little</u> information about the course requirements.

▶ Pete provided *little* help before the party.

   He didn't do his share.

▶ Pete gave me *a little* help after everyone left.

   He made himself useful.

Indicating extent or amount with noncount nouns Because a noncount noun is always singular, do not make it plural or add a determiner that implies a plural form. For example, do not use a determiner such as *a large number of, many,* or *several* immediately before a noncount noun. Instead, use a determiner such as *a great deal of, less, little, much,* or *some*—or revise the sentence another way.

some
▶ The city is doing researches on the proposal.

The modifier *some* is appropriate for the noncount noun *research* because it does not imply plurality.

loaves of
▶ Gina bought two breads at the store.

In the edited version, *two* modifies the count noun *loaves*.

incidents of violence
▶ We do not have many violences in our neighborhood.

great deal
▶ A large number of information is available on your topic.

A large number of, which suggests plurality, cannot be used with *information,* a noncount noun.

EXERCISE 44.2 Editing for noun and determiner usage

Correct any errors resulting from the improper use of nouns and determiners in the following passage.

A great deal of students showed up at the class party this past weekend. Everyone seemed to have fairly good time despite few major problems that I am now being blamed for. However, whenever we plan this kinds of events in future, we need much more people to help. So little people actually helped that I essentially had to do all work on my own. Therefore, I refuse to take a blame for all things that went wrong. Everyone should be aware that other person (who will remain nameless) who had agreed to help me organize event didn't do his share of job. He was supposed to coordinate the individuals who had volunteered to set up and decorate hall and then to remind others who had indicated that they would provide necessary items not to forget to do so. Because he didn't call anyone, that tasks never got done, but I did best I could by myself. Not surprisingly, biggest problem we had was that there were not enough supplies. For example, we had less sodas than we needed, so some guests had to drink lot of water because it was so hot that evening. Another examples was that we didn't have as many ice as we needed, and there weren't enough plastic glasses or napkins. I had to send someone out to buy much of this items using my own moneys.

Make It **Your Own**

Write five sentences with plural references using noncount nouns from five of the categories in the Quick Reference box on page 745. For example, you might write, "The recipe calls for *five cups of flour.*" Next, referring to the Quick Reference box on page 749, write three sentences with count nouns and three with noncount nouns using different quantifiers. For example, you might write, "I read *a couple of* science fiction *novels* over spring break."

Work **Together**

In small groups, exchange your work on the exercise above. Discuss your differences, and consult your instructor if you need help arriving at a consensus.

45 Managing English Verbs
by Ted E. Johnston and M. E. Sokolik

© Howard Berman/The Image Bank/Getty Images

Verbs can express an action or occurrence (*The dog jumps for the Frisbee*) or indicate a state of being (*The dog is frisky*). In many languages, verbs can have several forms. For example, they may change to indicate the identity of a subject or object or the time frame in which an event happens. English verbs, in contrast, have only a few forms, but these combine with other words to accomplish the same functions.

45a Using Phrasal Verbs

Phrasal verbs—sometimes called *multiword verbs*—consist of a verb and one or two *particles.* The particle takes the form of a preposition or adverb, and it combines with the verb to create a new verb with a new meaning. For example, the verb *throw* means to project something through the air. The phrasal verb *throw out* consists of the verb *throw* and the particle *out*; it means to dispose of something.

▶ Segundo threw out his old notebook.
  phrasal vb. ——particle
  verb

▶ Segundo threw his old notebook on his bed.

The meaning of a verb-and-particle combination differs from the meaning of the same words in a verb-and-preposition combination. The phrasal verb *look up*, for example, means to consult

More about
Verbs and verb phrases, 620, 649, 664–72

or find something in a reference work, which is different from the meaning of *look* followed by a phrase that happens to begin with the preposition *up*.

PHRASAL VERB	phrasal vb. Svetlana looked up the word in the dictionary.
VERB WITH PREPOSITIONS	verb prep. Svetlana looked up the steep trail and began to hike.

A transitive phrasal verb is *separable* if its direct object can fall either between the verb and the particle (separating them) or after the particle.

▶ She looked up the address online.
      dir. obj.

▶ She looked the address up online.
      dir. obj.

Quick Reference Some Common Phrasal Verbs and Their Meanings

SEPARABLE		INSEPARABLE	
ask out	invite for a date	*add up to*	total
calm down	make calm, become calm	*barge in on*	interrupt unannounced
give up	surrender	*call on*	visit, or ask for a response directly
hand in	submit		
hand out	distribute	*come across*	find accidentally
		drop in	visit unannounced
look up	find something in a reference work	*get out of*	evade an obligation, exit
put back	return to original position	*give in*	surrender
put down	criticize meanly; suppress	*grow up*	mature
		hint at	suggest
take back	return; retract	*look down on*	disdain
take off	remove	*look up to*	admire
take on	assume responsibility for	*put up with*	tolerate
		run into	encounter; collide
take up	begin a hobby or activity	*stand in for*	substitute for
throw out	dispose of	*turn up*	show up, arrive

If the direct object of a separable phrasal verb is a pronoun, it must come between the verb and the particle.

> *it in.*
> I decided to hand ~~in it.~~
> ^

A phrasal verb is *inseparable* if no words can fall between the verb and the particle.

FAULTY	I came an old photo across in the drawer.
REVISED	I came across an old photo in the drawer.

The meaning of a phrasal verb changes when the particle changes (see the Quick Reference box on page 753). The phrasal verb *take on*, for example, means "to assume responsibility for."

▶ She **took on** the editing of the newsletter.

The phrasal verb *take back*, in contrast, means "to return" or "to retract."

▶ She **took** all her overdue books **back** to the library.

→ EXERCISE 45.1 Using phrasal verbs correctly

Put a check by the sentences that use verbs and phrasal verbs incorrectly, and then revise those sentences so they are correct.

EXAMPLE

> *him*
> After the accident, the EMT calmed down ~~him.~~   ✓
> ^

1. I hear that Lisa is sick. Who is going to stand in for her?
2. I cannot find my glasses. Have you come them across?
3. The instructor handed the assignment out yesterday.
4. Is there any way for us to get this assignment out of?
5. If you do not understand a word, look up it.
6. That jacket looks too warm. Why don't you take off it?
7. Will you take these back to the store?
8. I ran an old friend into at the movie theater.

45b Using Gerunds and Infinitives after Verbs and Prepositions

A *gerund* is the *-ing* form of a verb used as a noun (*listening, eating*). An *infinitive* is the base form of a verb preceded by *to* (*to listen, to eat*).

1. Gerunds and infinitives after verbs

- Only gerunds can follow some verbs, and only infinitives can follow others.

  - The committee recommended ~~to submit~~ *submitting* the proposal for a vote.

  - Rosa Parks refused ~~sitting~~ *to sit* in the back of the bus.

- Some verbs can be followed by either gerunds or infinitives. For some of these verbs, the choice of gerund or infinitive has little effect on meaning, but for a few the difference is significant.

SAME MEANING	The economy *continued* to grow.
	The economy *continued* growing.

DIFFERENT MEANINGS	Juan *remembered* to email his paper to his professor. [He didn't forget to do it.]
	Juan *remembered* emailing his paper to his professor. [He recalled having done it already.]

- Some verbs that can be followed by an infinitive can also be followed by an infinitive after an intervening noun or pronoun.

  - Yue *wanted* to study the violin.

  - Yue's parents *wanted* her to study the violin.

- Certain verbs, however, take an infinitive only after an object noun or pronoun.

  - The candidate *urged* citizens to vote on Election Day.

A few verbs (for example, *feel, have, hear, let, look at,* and *see*) require an *unmarked infinitive*—the base verb alone, without *to*—after an intervening noun or pronoun.

> Paolo let his children ~~to go~~ to the movies.
> *go*

> Jen heard a dog ~~to bark~~ late at night.
> *bark*

2. Gerunds after prepositions

Only a gerund, not an infinitive, can be the object of a preposition.

> The article is about ~~to travel~~ in South America.
> *traveling*

Quick Reference   Gerund or Infinitive after Selected Verbs

Some verbs that can be directly followed by a gerund but not an infinitive

admit	discuss	imagine	practice	risk
avoid	enjoy	mind	quit	suggest
consider	escape	miss	recall	tolerate
deny	finish	postpone	resist	understand

Some verbs that can be directly followed by an infinitive but not a gerund

agree	claim	hope	offer	refuse
appear	decide	manage	plan	wait
ask	expect	mean	pretend	want
beg	have	need	promise	wish

Some verbs that can be directly followed by a gerund or an infinitive with little effect on meaning

begin	hate	love	start
continue	like	prefer	

Some verbs for which choice of gerund or infinitive affects meaning

forget	remember	stop	try

Some verbs that take an infinitive only after an intervening noun or pronoun

advise	command	force	persuade	tell
allow	convince	instruct	remind	urge
cause	encourage	order	require	warn

45c Using Participles as Adjectives

Both the present participle and the past participle of a verb can function as adjectives, but they convey different meanings, especially if the base verb refers to an emotion or state of mind such as anger or boredom. The *present participle* (or *-ing* form) usually describes the cause or agent of a state of affairs. The *past participle* (the *-ed* form in regular verbs) usually describes the result of the state of affairs.

> **More about**
> Regular and
> irregular verb
> forms, 664–72,
> 668

State of Affairs	Cause	Result
verb	adj.	adj.
Physics class bored me today.	The class was bor*ing*.	I was bor*ed*.
verb	adj.	adj.
Dr. Sung's lecture interested me.	The lecture was interest*ing*.	I was interest*ed*.

> **EXERCISE 45.2** Using gerunds, infinitives, and participial adjectives

Use the verbs in parentheses to correctly complete each sentence. The first one is done as an example. Some may have more than one correct solution.

1. That movie was really *boring* (bore). I fell asleep after twenty minutes.

2. Juan was _____ (astonish) to see a rare bird in his backyard.

3. Martine advised Hugo _____ (see) the museum exhibit. Our father begged us not ____ (drive) there in the icy weather.

4. We had to postpone ____ (give) our parents an anniversary party because my mother had to work Saturday.

5. We enjoy ____ (cook) for our friends.

6. The customer inquired about ____ (purchase) a new microwave oven.

7. Nikolai admitted _____ (borrow) his roommate's computer without ____ (ask).

8. Mike continued _____ (watch) TV during dinner.

9. The sergeant commanded the advancing troops _____ (march) up the hill.

More about
Verb forms,
664–68
Subject-verb
agreement,
648–58

45d Using Helping Verbs for Verb Formation

Most English verb constructions, other than the present and past tenses, consist of a main verb with one or more helping (auxiliary) verbs. The main verb carries the principal meaning, and the helping verbs carry information about time, mood, and voice. There are two kinds of helping verbs: simple and modal.

- The simple helping verbs—*have, do,* and *be*—also function as main verbs, and like other main verbs, they change form to indicate person and tense.

- The modal helping verbs—including *can, could, may, might, must, ought to, shall, should, will,* and *would*—carry information about attributes of the main verb such as ability, intention, permission, possibility, desire, and suggestion (see the Quick Reference box on the next page). Unlike the simple auxiliaries, the modal auxiliaries do not change form to indicate number or tense.

  ▸ All the contestants at the Olympics can swim fast, but Michael

    can

    Phelps ~~cans~~ swim faster than any of the others.

  ▸ William should work all day today, and he ~~shoulded work~~

    should have worked

    yesterday too.

NOTE When you hear such contractions as *should've* or *could've* in speech (or similar contractions with other modals), remember that the contracted word is *have* (*should have, could have*), not *of*.

- In a verb phrase, auxiliaries almost always precede the main verb, and modals precede any other auxiliaries.

  auxiliaries   main verb
  modal simple
  ▸ In June, Chen will have been living in Seattle for ten years.

- When forming verbs, include needed auxiliaries.

  is
  ▸ Demetrio taking six courses this semester.

  have
  ▸ My grandparents been visiting Scotland every year.

Quick **Reference**   Modals and Meaning

Modals	Meaning	Examples
can, could	Used to indicate ability, possibility, and willingness and to request or grant permission	Sam <u>can</u> paint wonderful watercolors. [ability] You <u>can</u> leave class early today. [grant permission] <u>Could</u> we meet at the library? [request permission] I'm so hungry I <u>could</u> eat a horse. [possibility] I <u>could</u> work your shift if you need me to. [willingness]
may, might	Used to request and grant permission and to offer suggestions. For requests, *might* has a more hesitant and polite connotation than *may,* but they are otherwise usually interchangeable.	<u>May</u> I see the comments you wrote? [request permission] <u>Might</u> I borrow your car this afternoon? [more polite request for permission] It <u>may/might</u> rain this afternoon. [possibility] You <u>may/might</u> want to bring an umbrella. [suggestion]
must	Expresses necessity, prohibition (in the negative), and logical probability	Passengers <u>must</u> pass through airport security before boarding. [necessity] Passengers <u>must not</u> leave their seats while the seatbelt sign is illuminated. [prohibition] We <u>must</u> be on our final approach. [logical probability]
shall, should, ought to	*Should* and *ought to* express advisability and expectation, usually interchangeably. *Shall* expresses intention as well as advisability, but in American English it usually appears only in questions.	<u>Shall/Should</u> we eat in or go out for dinner tonight? [advisability] We <u>should/ought to</u> eat out less to save money. [advisability] The <u>pizza should/ought to</u> arrive in 20 minutes or so. [expectation]
will, would	*Will* expresses intention, willingness, and expectation. *Would* expresses intention, willingness, typical or repeated action, and logical assumption, and it is also used for polite requests.	I <u>will</u> finish the laundry if you want. [willingness] I <u>will</u> apply to graduate school next year. [intention] The bus <u>will</u> arrive soon. [expectation] <u>Would</u> you mind opening the window? [request] Amalia decided she <u>would</u> apply to graduate school. [intention] When preparing dinner, he <u>would</u> always clean up as he cooked. [repeated action] That alarm you're hearing <u>would</u> be the monthly test of the emergency system. [logical probability]

- In general, never follow a modal with another modal, and always follow a modal with the base form of a simple auxiliary or main verb.

be able to
▸ Tomás should ~~can~~ finish his calculus homework before the
⌃
movie starts.

▸ Yuki must ~~to~~ take three more courses to graduate.

➤ EXERCISE 45.3 Using modal auxiliaries

The following email message has six errors in the use of modals and auxiliaries. Edit the message to correct these errors. The first error has been found for you.

Hi, Mario,

am
I hope everything is going well. I writing to ask you a favor. We want to
⌃
organize an auction for the baseball team. If you might could contribute a little time, that would to be great! We need someone who cans contact potential donors, assign starting bids for items, and mail out publicity. We think we might raise as much as $10,000 for team uniforms if we can get enough volunteers. I really hope you will to help us out. Do you think you come on Saturday for a short meeting?

Thanks in advance!

Bill

⌐ Make It **Your Own**

Review a recent piece of writing you completed for one of your classes. Print a new copy and circle all the verbs, gerunds, infinitives, and participial adjectives. Note any that you find confusing or that were marked by your instructor as incorrectly used. Make notes about their correct use by consulting this book, your instructor, or your college writing center.

Work **Together**

The use of modals affects how polite (or impolite) a piece of writing is considered to be. Working with a partner, consider the following pairs of sentences. Decide which in each pair is more polite, and discuss why. Does it depend on your audience? Be prepared to discuss your conclusions with your class.

1. a. Can you open the window?
   b. Would you mind opening the window?

2. a. Might I have a bite of your cake? It looks delicious.
   b. Could I have a bite of your cake?

3. a. Can I get a letter of recommendation from you?
   b. May I ask you to write me a letter of recommendation?

46

Managing Adjectives and Adverbs
by Ted E. Johnston and M. E. Sokolik

© Dream Pictures/ Getty Images

Just as a coat of paint can change our perception of the surface it covers, adjectives and adverbs color our understanding of the words they modify. *Adjectives* modify nouns and pronouns. *Adverbs* modify verbs, adjectives, other adverbs, and entire phrases, clauses, and sentences. This chapter will help you use adjectives and adverbs correctly and place them appropriately in your sentences.

46a Placing Adjectives in the Proper Order

> *More about*
> Articles and other determiners, 744–50
> Cumulative versus coordinate adjectives, 785–86

- Most English adjectives have only one form, regardless of whether the noun they modify is singular or plural.

  ▶ Serena wants a <u>white</u> dress, but many of these <u>white</u> dresses are not to her liking.

- English adjectives usually come before a noun (*Serena has a white dress*) or after a *linking verb* (*Serena's dress is white*).

- When multiple adjectives cumulatively modify the same noun, the kind of information they convey determines their proper order (see the Quick Reference box on the next page).

> **linking verbs** *Be* and other verbs that express a state of being rather than an action and connect a subject to its subject complement

NOTE More than three adjectives in a sequence can be awkward. Instead, vary your sentences to distribute the adjectives without confusing your readers.

Quick

Reference Putting Cumulative Adjectives in Standard Order

Article or Other Determiner	Overall Evaluation or Opinion	Size	Shape or Other Intrinsic Aspect	Age	Color	Essence: Nationality, Material, or Purpose	Noun
two		big			red	rubber	balls
an	exciting			new		mystery	novel
my		tiny	helpless	newborn			kitten
those	funny			old	black-and-white		sitcoms
the	delicious		round			French	pastry

46b Choosing the Correct Prepositions with Adjectives

On a particular day, you might be excited *by* a lecture, mad *at* a friend, or happy *about* the election in Pakistan. As these phrases reveal, you need to be careful when combining adjectives and prepositions. When in doubt, consult a dictionary to make sure you are using the proper idiom. The editing in the following paragraph gives additional examples of correct idiomatic usage:

> More about Prepositions, 769–76

Ally is delighted ~~in~~ her midterm grades. She had been nervous ~~of~~ flunking
       (with)   (about)

biochemistry. Ally is grateful ~~at~~ her instructors. When she struggled,
                               (to)

they were not disappointed ~~at~~ her, and they were proud ~~about~~ her when
                          (in)   (of)

she succeeded. She is dedicated ~~with~~ completing her nursing degree.
                                (to)

➔ EXERCISE 46.1 Using adjectives correctly

Correct problems with adjective order or prepositions used after adjectives in the following sentences. (The Quick Reference box above will help you with some of these.) If a sentence has no problems, circle its number.

EXAMPLE

                new
The ~~new~~ ridiculous parking regulations are hurting students financially.

1. In our old cozy kitchen, we had a blue round table.

2. The professor gave a historical lengthy overview World War II.

3. The mayor is devoted for eliminating gang violence in our city.

4. There used to be a beige big leather sofa in the waiting room.

5. The lawyer's final pathetic defense of his client was embarrassing.

6. Everyone should be alarmed with global warming.

7. My economical new hybrid car helps me cope with the price of gas.

8. The witness said he saw a green old van leave the scene of the crime.

9. That gray-haired wise doctor still maintains a practice private.

10. The residents are worried from the possibility of another hurricane.

46c Placing Adverbs Correctly

- An adverb cannot be located between a verb and its object.

  > Susan plays ~~beautifully~~ the piano~~.~~ _beautifully_

  In this sentence, *beautifully* fits correctly only at the end, after *piano*, the direct object.

- Many adverbs, primarily those related to time (such as *often* and *frequently*), may be placed either before the subject or verb or after the direct object.

  > *Recently,* Susan learned ~~recently~~ a new concerto.

  > Susan *recently* learned ~~recently~~ a new concerto.

  > Susan learned ~~recently~~ a new concerto *recently.*

- When a main verb has no helping verbs, the adverb should precede it. When the main verb has helping verbs, the adverb should usually be placed between the first helper and the main verb.

  > Carla <u>carelessly</u> *wasted* gas by leaving the motor running.

▶ Carla ~~carelessly~~ *has been wasting* gas by leaving the motor running.
   _{carelessly}

Some adverbs (but not all) can be placed between the second helper and the main verb.

▶ Carla ~~carelessly~~ has been wasting gas by leaving the motor running.
   _{carelessly}

- In most instances, place an adverb first if it modifies the entire sentence.

   ▶ <u>Surprisingly,</u> she has decided to change her major to psychology.

- When certain negative adverbs or adverb phrases begin a sentence, they require a change in the standard subject-verb order. Included in this group are *not only, at no time, never, rarely,* and *seldom.*

   ▶ Seldom I ~~have~~ been so proud of my brother.
      _{have}

> *More about*
> Inverted word
> order when
> certain negative
> adverbs start
> a sentence,
> 740–41

▶ **EXERCISE 46.2 Putting adverbs in the right place**

Correct any adverb placement problems in the following sentences. Circle the number of any sentences that are already correct.

EXAMPLE

The doctor gave me ~~unintentionally~~ the wrong information.
_{unintentionally}

1. The children played fast and furiously the game and then fell instantly asleep.

2. Sam is doing well in math now that he is doing diligently the homework.

3. Seldom does the manager promote new employees so quickly.

4. We should consider always the suggestions of our employees rather than implementing suddenly changes.

5. Not only Tom works on Saturday, but also on Sunday.

6. Little Ralph has sadly never learned to read.

7. The judge soon should make his decision.

8. Do you really think that Ivan treats Martha unfairly?

46d Dealing with Confusing Adverbs

Certain English adverbs seem similar but actually have significantly different connotations and functions. Often-confused words include *too* with *so*, *too* with *either*, *not* with *no*, *hard* with *hardly*, and *such* with *so*.

1. *Too* and *so*

To give an adjective a negative or more negative meaning, use *too* in most instances. To intensify any adjective, use *so* or *very* or a similar adverb.

▶ The professor realized her first test had been ~~so~~ difficult
  <small>too</small>

  and was surprised to find us still ~~too~~ excited about the class.
  <small>so</small>

2. *Too* and *either*

When following up a statement about one subject's action with a statement about another subject's doing likewise, use *either* after a verb that is grammatically negative (as with *not* or *never* or *won't* or *hasn't*), and use *too* after a verb that is grammatically positive. Remember that unless verbs such as *avoided* or *refused* are used with a negative adverb (such as *not*), they are grammatically positive, even though by themselves they have negative meanings.

▶ Floyd <u>didn't join</u> the fraternity, and I <u>didn't, either.</u>
  Neither one joined.

▶ Floyd <u>joined</u> the fraternity, and I <u>did, too.</u>
  Both joined.

▶ Floyd <u>refused to join</u>, and I <u>did, too.</u>
  Neither one joined.

▶ Floyd <u>didn't refuse to join</u>, and I <u>didn't, either.</u>
  Both were willing to join.

3. *Not* and *no*

Because *no* is an adjective, it can only modify a noun. The adverb *not*, however, can modify an adjective, a verb, or another adverb. The expression *not a (an)* can replace the adjective *no* in front of a noun.

not   not   no (or: not a)
- Keith is ~~no~~ friendly. Because he will ~~no~~ talk to me, he is ~~not~~ friend
  of mine.

4. *Hard* and *hardly*

The word *hard* can be either an adjective or an adverb. As an adverb, it means *intensely* or *with great effort*. The adverb *hardly* means *just a little* or *almost not at all*.

- Juan got an *A* after he studied <u>hard</u> for the exam. Laura got a *D* because she <u>hardly</u> looked at her notes.

5. *Such* and *so*

Such a (an), *such*, or *so* can emphasize a type or a quality. Use *such a (an)* before an adjective that precedes a concrete noun: *She is <u>such a</u> wise person.* Use <u>such</u> by itself directly in front of an abstract noun: *<u>Such</u> wisdom is rare.* To intensify any freestanding adjective, as in the case of a subject complement, use *so*: *She is <u>so</u> wise.*

→ EXERCISE 46.3 **Correcting easily confused adverbs**

Correct any adverb errors in the following sentences, and circle the number of those sentences that have no errors.

> **EXAMPLE**
>
> either.
> Jack didn't go to the party, and I didn't, ~~too~~.

1. We worked hardly on this project, and all we got was a C.
2. We don't feel guilty about this decision, and you shouldn't, too.
3. The waiters here are so slow; we may never get our food.
4. Mark is not millionaire, but he is so generous person.
5. I really admire that she helps her elderly parents too much.
6. We have come so far to give up now.

Make It **Your Own**

Review a text that you were assigned to read in one of your classes, and find examples of cumulative adjectives used before a noun. Look for strings of two, three, or more adjectives not separated from one another by commas, being sure to include any noun determiners. Use the Quick Reference box on page 763 to account for the order in which the adjectives appear. Do any examples violate the usual order?

Work **Together**

Join with several other students and compare the examples of cumulative adjectives you analyzed in the exercise above. Consult your instructor if your group disagrees about the analysis of any of the examples.

47 Using Prepositions
by Ted E. Johnston and M. E. Sokolik

© Jeff Ward

Prepositions are words that specify a relationship between other words or phrases. They are seemingly insignificant words (*for, at, with, under, over*) that serve an important function. Like the thin line that indicates where sky ends and water begins, they provide important information about relationships between other words and phrases: "The mayor worked *against* the proposal"; "the laptop is *inside* my backpack."

To help you learn to use prepositions correctly, this chapter explains how to identify prepositions (*section 47a*), how to determine the function they serve (*47b*), and how to use them correctly (*47c* and *d*).

47a Recognizing Prepositions

Although there are fewer than one hundred single-word prepositions in use in English, many additional multiword prepositions function in similar ways. The Quick Reference box on the next page lists some of the most common of both.

→ EXERCISE 47.1 Recognizing prepositions

Identify the prepositional phrases in the following sentences. Underline the prepositional phrase, and circle each preposition.

> **EXAMPLE**
>
> A small air carrier might assume responsibility (for) the freight (from) the customer.

1. The Dehkhoda Institute, which is devoted to the teaching of Farsi, was founded in 1945.

769

Quick Reference — Common Single-Word and Multiword Prepositions

Single-Word Prepositions

about	beneath	like	to
above	beside	near	toward
across	between	of	under
after	by	off	underneath
against	down	on	until
along	during	onto	up
among	except	out	upon
around	for	outside	with
at	from	over	within
before	in	past	without
behind	inside	since	
below	into	through	

Multiword Prepositions

according to	by means of	in front of	on account of
ahead of	close to	in place of	on behalf of
as far as	due to	in spite of	on top of
as to	far from	inside of	out of
as well as	in accordance with	instead of	outside of
aside from	in addition to	near to	
because of	in case of	next to	

2. The black-backed jackal is an African canine with a foxlike appearance.

3. The first cricket test match was played in 1877 between Australia and England.

4. In November, snow fell on the coast, which is rare so early in the season.

5. The citywide depression lasted for two centuries, through famine and war, until the 1990s.

47b The Functions of Prepositions

Every preposition has multiple possible functions depending on the context in which it occurs. As a result, it is often easier to understand prepositions in terms of their function than to try to memorize what each one means.

The most basic use for a preposition is to indicate *location.* Other important functions are to indicate *time,* to indicate *condition* or *degree,* to specify *cause* or *reason,* and to designate *possession, attribute,* or *origin.*

Reference   Identifying Functions of Prepositions

Common functions of prepositions include the following:

1. To indicate *location* (771)
2. To indicate *time* (771)
3. To indicate *condition* or *degree* (772)
4. To specify *cause* or *reason* (772)
5. To designate *possession, attribute,* or *origin* (773)

1. Location

The most basic prepositions for indicating the location of things are *at, on,* and *in.*

- *At* specifies a general point of orientation.

  ▶ Meet me at the station.

- *On* specifies contact between two things.

  ▶ The book is on the table.
  ▶ The clipboard hangs on the wall.

- *In* specifies that one thing is contained within another.

  ▶ The solution is in the beaker.
  ▶ Liz is in San Francisco.

NOTE Many locations operate like *surfaces* or *containers.* Generally, use *in* for locations that seem like containers and *on* for locations that seem like surfaces.

CONTAINER   He sat in his car. [**Not:** *He sat on his car,* which would mean he was on top of it.]

SURFACE   He sat on the bus. [Buses, trains, and airplanes are usually considered surfaces because people can walk around on them.]

CONTAINER   We walked in the hallway.

SURFACE   We walked on the sidewalk.

2. Time

The most common prepositions for relating things to a moment in or period of time are *at, in, on,* and *by.*

- *At* designates a particular point in time.

  ▶ Let's meet at 4:00.
  ▶ The party ended at midnight.

- *In* can designate either a future time or a particular period.

  ▶ I'll leave in 10 minutes.
  ▶ We'll finish the job in April.

- *On* designates a particular day or date.
  - ▸ His birthday is on Friday.
  - ▸ Her birthday is on the twelfth.

- *By* indicates *no later than*.
  - ▸ Turn in your essay by 3:00 p.m.
  - ▸ They decided to leave by 5:00 a.m. to avoid rush hour.

3. Condition/Degree

Prepositions of condition or degree indicate the state of the object. Some common prepositions in this category are *of, on, in, about,* and *around.*

- *In* or *on* can specify a condition. These uses are often idiomatic.
  - ▸ The house is on fire.
  - ▸ She is on vacation.
  - ▸ Charlie is not in trouble.
  - ▸ Darlene left her desk in perfect order.

- *Of* is used in phrases indicating fractions or portions.
  - ▸ Three of the books are required for the course.
  - ▸ One of those coats is mine.

- *Around* or *about* can indicate approximation.
  - ▸ That book costs around twenty dollars.
  - ▸ I walked about ten miles.

4. Cause/Reason

Prepositions showing cause include *from, of, for,* and *because of.*

- *From* indicates cause or explains a condition.
  - ▸ We were wet from the rain.
  - ▸ We were tired from walking all day.

- *For* often indicates a cause and answers the question *Why?*
  - ▸ Oregon is famous for its forests.
  - ▸ He got an award for selling more cars than anyone else.

- *Of* and *because of* both show a reason.
  - ▸ The patient died of pneumonia.
  - ▸ I sneezed because of my cold.

5. Possession/Attribute/Origin

The most common prepositions showing possession, attribute, or origin are *of, from,* and *with.*

- Possession is typically shown with *of.*
  - ▶ That song is one of Wilco's.
  - ▶ The composer of the song is Jay Bennett.

- An attribute can be indicated by *with.*
  - ▶ He was a man with real talent.
  - ▶ He is the one with the red beard.

- *From* can show origin.
  - ▶ Bennet was from Illinois.
  - ▶ The CD came from a website.

NOTE Indicating possession with *of* instead of *'s* or *s'* is often awkward.

| AWKWARD | the bike of Bob |
| PREFERRED | Bob's bike |

→ **EXERCISE 47.2 Determining the function of a preposition**

Write in the function of the underlined preposition in the space to the right of each sentence. Choose from *Location, Time, Condition/Degree, Cause/Reason,* or *Possession/Attribute/Origin.*

EXAMPLE

She bought the car <u>with</u> greater fuel efficiency. <u>attribute</u>

1. The construction will be completed <u>in</u> 2012. _____

2. In 1946, Margolin moved <u>to</u> Lebanon. _____

3. Bellatrix is described as a tall woman <u>with</u> pale skin. _____

4. Let's meet <u>at</u> the library to study tonight. _____

5. We were dying <u>of</u> thirst. _____

6. He's having a birthday party <u>in</u> July. _____

7. Hearing loss is estimated to begin <u>at</u> age 30. _____

8. There are no students <u>from</u> Japan here. _____

47c Using Prepositions Correctly

Certain verbs or nouns will suggest the use of particular prepositions. It may help to memorize these phrases:

- *give* something *to* someone
- *take* something *from* someone
- *sell* something *to* someone
- *buy* something *from* someone
- *lend* something *to* someone
- *borrow* something *from* someone
- get *married* or *engaged to* someone
- *fill* something *with* something
- *shout to* someone (in greeting)
- *shout at* someone (in anger)

> **More about**
> Passive voice,
> 525, 680–83
> Direct and
> indirect objects,
> 617–18, 737–39

In addition, some prepositions serve a particular grammatical function. For example, in passive constructions, the preposition *by* identifies who or what did something.

- The car was repaired by Pat.

Similarly, indirect objects, when placed after rather than before a direct object, are usually preceded by *to*:

- Theo gave the present to his father.

EXERCISE 47.3 Using prepositions correctly

Insert the correct preposition into the blanks below. In some cases, more than one preposition may be acceptable.

EXAMPLE

He came _from_ a small village _in_ the middle _of_ the country.

1. Our sense ____ identity—____ who we are and what we have done—is tied ____ our memories.

2. *The Big Knife* is a 1955 film directed and produced ____ Robert Aldrich and based ____ the play ____ Clifford Odets.

3. Ronald and Reginald Kray were identical twin brothers and the foremost organized crime leaders ___ London ___ the 1950s and 1960s.

4. The original manuscripts ___ Oscar Wilde today are found ___ many collections, but ___ far the largest collection is found ___ the William Andrews Clark Memorial Library ___ UCLA.

5. Tortell is a Catalan pastry stuffed ___ marzipan, which ___ some special occasions is topped ___ glazed fruit. It is traditionally eaten ___ January 6.

47d Necessary and Unnecessary Prepositions

Unfortunately, there is no rule of grammar to tell when a preposition is needed. Consider these examples:

▸ I like to listen music.
         to

▸ She was looking the book.
         at

Similarly, there is no rule to tell when one is not needed:

▸ In one block from the school, there is a coffee shop.
   One

▸ We were discussing about climate change in class.

To make things more complicated, sometimes a phrase is acceptable with or without a preposition.

▸ I've lived here for six years.
▸ I've lived here six years.

One strategy for mastering these usages, some of them idiomatic, is to notice in your reading when you encounter unfamiliar constructions involving prepositions. Some students keep a grammar log or other notebook to help them remember these constructions.

→ EXERCISE 47.4 **Distinguishing between necessary and unnecessary prepositions**

Correct the following passage for preposition usage. Cross out any prepositions that are not needed, insert any that are missing, and leave unchanged any that are correctly used. There are thirteen preposition errors in the passage, not including the one in the example.

EXAMPLE

by

Flip the Frog is an animated cartoon character created an American

∧

cartoonist, Ub Iwerks, who also helped with to create another famous

character—Mickey Mouse.

Flip starred a series cartoons distributed by MGM from 1930 to 1933. Apart Flip, the series had many other characters, including Flip's dog and a mule named of Orace.

Flip's first appearance was in a cartoon called by *Night.* Iwerks animated this short feature while working his friend Walt Disney in 1930. After a number disagreements between them, Iwerks left Disney and went on to accept an offer to open a cartoon studio his own a salary of $300 a week. Disney at the time couldn't match with this offer. The first cartoon series Iwerks was expected to create featured on a character called Tony the Frog, but Iwerks didn't like the name and had it changed Flip.

Make It **Your Own**

In a paper you have recently written or are now writing, look for preposition errors. How many do you find? What functions of these prepositions do you recognize (location, time, etc.)? How would you fix the errors?

Work **Together**

For a paper you have recently written or are now writing, exchange texts with a classmate and analyze your classmate's writing for prepositional errors. How many do you find? How would you correct them? (If your partner is a native speaker of English, you may find very few errors. If this is the case, note any preposition usages that are unfamiliar to you and discuss their meaning with your partner.) Be prepared to discuss what you gained from this exercise.

Part Ten

Detail Matters

Punctuation and Mechanics

@

©Tetra images/Getty Images RF

48 Using Commas

©Exactostock/SuperStock

Commas function as dividers within—but not between—sentences: Think of each sentence as a room. If the periods are walls between these rooms, then the commas are screens used to make subdivisions within a room. As a screen might set off a dressing area from a larger bedroom, so a comma sets off information inside the main sentence. As a screen might divide a large room into work spaces, so commas mark divisions between independent clauses. Problems with commas can be caused not only by omitting them but also by inserting them where they are *not* needed: Imagine having a screen in your kitchen between your stove and refrigerator.

The rules for comma placement are fairly straightforward. A list of the rules writers use most often appears in the Quick Reference box on the next page.

Writing Responsibly | Commas and Clarity

Like Alice in Wonderland, most of us aim to say what we mean and mean what we say. But incorrect use of commas can have us saying something we do *not* mean (or meaning something we do not say). Consider this example, with and without commas:

This sentence . . .	means . . .
Writing to my mother is a terrible chore.	I find writing to my mother a real pain!
Writing, to my mother, is a terrible chore.	My mother finds writing a real pain!

You have a responsibility to your reader to look carefully at your use of commas when editing a document; ask yourself, "Do I mean what I say and say what I mean?" If the answer is no, correct your use of commas.

to AUDIENCE

Quick Reference   Common Comma Do's and Don'ts

Do use a comma . . .

. . . to separate independent clauses joined by a coordinating conjunction. (780)

                                  coord.
          independent clause   conj.   independent clause

▶ Hip-hop music was born in the 1970s, but it continues to flourish.

. . . to set off introductory elements from an independent clause. (781)

             subordinate clause   independent clause

▶ Although it was born in New York City, rap has become popular around the world.

. . . to separate three or more items in a series. (784)

                     ①   ②

▶ Some early hip-hop artists include Afrika Bambaataa, Grandmaster Flash,

   ③
Run DMC, and LL Cool J.

. . . to separate coordinate (but not cumulative) adjectives. (785)

                     coordinate adjectives

▶ Hip-hop soon grew to have a huge, enthusiastic audience outside the New York club scene.

. . . to set off nonessential elements. (787)

                   nonessential clause

▶ Afrika Bambaataa, who adopted the name of a Zulu chieftain, formed Zulu Nation to attract kids toward hip-hop and away from gangs.

Do not use a comma . . .

. . . following a coordinating or subordinating conjunction. (780, 781)

▶ Run DMC was popular enough to be featured on the game Guitar Hero,
   sub. conj.
although, the songs the group played are by the band Aerosmith.

. . . to separate paired elements. (780)

▶ Even scholars are writing about hip-hop music, and culture.

. . . to separate independent clauses not joined by a coordinating conjunction. (780)

▶ LL Cool J's 1985 *Radio* was perhaps the first mainstream rap hit, it went platinum within five months.

. . . preceding the first item or following the last item in a series. (784)

                            ①   ②   ③

▶ Hip-hop has also merged with musical styles such as, hip house, nu soul, reggaetón,
   ④
and merenrap, to create exciting sounds.

. . . between a subject and its verb or a verb and its object or complement. (793)

   subj   verb   direct obj.

▶ LL Cool J, had, eight platinum records in a row.

48a Using Commas in Compound Sentences

Reference The Seven Coordinating Conjunctions

and	but	or	nor
for	so	yet	

In a *compound sentence* a comma and *coordinating conjunction* work together: The comma marks the break between the two *independent clauses,* and the coordinating conjunction joins them into a single sentence. When a coordinating conjunction combines two independent clauses, place a comma *before* it (not *after* it):

compound sentence
Two or more independent clauses linked by a comma and a coordinating conjunction or a semicolon

> independent clause   coord. conj.   independent clause
> ▶ My heart is in San Francisco, but my body is in New York.

NOTE Unless readers will be confused, the comma can be omitted when the two independent clauses are very short:

> ▶ I sing in Italian but I speak only English.

independent clause
A word group that includes a subject and a predicate that can stand alone as a sentence

Do not use a comma before the conjunction if both parts cannot stand on their own as sentences:

> independent clause   verb phrase
> ▶ My accountant left the country, and took my bank balance
>
> with him.

More about
Comma splices,
  639–47 (ch. 35)
Semicolons,
  796–802
  (ch. 49)

Paired items should not be separated by a comma:

> pairs
> ▶ Both my purse, and my bank account are empty.

When the clauses are long and already punctuated with commas, readers might find the sentence clearer if you replace the comma before the coordinating conjunction with a semicolon:

> ▶ Comic books are gradually becoming more respectable as works of serious fiction, with graphic novels such as *Maus* and *Watchmen* earning tremendous critical acclaim, yet some people still refuse to take them seriously.

NOTE Without a coordinating conjunction, a comma between two independent clauses creates a *comma splice.*

> **EXERCISE 48.1 Correcting commas in compound sentences**

Correct the sentences below by adding or deleting commas. (Some may already be correct.)

EXAMPLE

The dollar has dropped against the euro,so tourists have flocked
⌃
to the United States to shop.

1. The US dollar continues to be weak against both the euro, and the pound.

2. The yen remains strong against the US dollar but it fell against the Australian dollar as markets opened this morning.

3. The yen, and the yuan are strengthening.

4. The currencies of Latin America continue to be weak relative to the euro, but they are holding their own against the US dollar.

5. Japanese, and American travelers who visit Europe this summer will feel the pinch, but Australian, and Chinese visitors should find Europe a bargain.

48b Using a Comma after Introductory Elements

A word, phrase, or subordinate clause introducing an independent clause is usually followed by a comma. There are two exceptions:

- Exception 1: Do not insert a comma after the introductory element in an inverted sentence, where an introductory word group immediately precedes the verb

  introductory word group   verb
  ▸ Into the deep, dark jungle marched Dr. Livingston.

- Exception 2: Do not insert a comma after an introductory word group that acts as the subject of the sentence

  subject   verb
  ▸ Exploring deep, dark jungles is what he does.

When the introductory element is very brief, some writers omit the comma. If readers might be confused, even for a moment, include it:

▸ Before eating,the missionaries said grace.
⌃

subordinate clause
A word group that lacks a subject or predicate or that begins with a subordinating word or phrase; a word group that cannot stand alone as a sentence

phrase A group of related words that lacks a subject, predicate, or both; it cannot stand alone as a sentence, but it can function *in* a sentence as a noun, a verb, or a modifier

More about
Participial
phrases, 621
Prepositional
phrases, 620
Absolute phrases,
622

1. Insert a comma after introductory clauses.

When a *subordinate,* or dependent, clause introduces an independent clause, place a comma between the two.

> subordinate clause
▸ Although Banksy remained an elusive figure, his popularity continued to grow.

> subordinate clause
▸ Because his theories addressed the Great Depression, John Maynard Keynes became the most influential economist of the 1930s.

2. Insert a comma after introductory phrases.

Insert a comma following an introductory *phrase* to signal the start of the main clause:

> participial phrase
▸ Lacking Mozart's natural abilities, Salieri formed an obsessive hatred for his rival.

> prepositional phrase
▸ In an unguarded moment, the politician muttered an unprintable phrase into the live microphone.

> absolute phrase
▸ A vegetarian for many years, he suddenly craved bacon.

▸ EXERCISE 48.2 Inserting commas after introductory elements

Supply a comma as needed after introductory elements in the sentences below. (You will not need to add a comma in every sentence.)

EXAMPLE

With infection rates continuing to rise,developing nations in
                                        ∧
southern Africa and around the world face shrinking populations.

1. After the advent of the AIDS epidemic around 1990 the rate of population growth in southern Africa decreased substantially.

2. According to UNAIDS.org more than 36 million people had died of the disease by 2012.

3. In fact life expectancies in Zimbabwe fell by twenty-six years as a result of what is now a pandemic.

4. In 2012 35.3 million people were reported to be living with HIV.

5. Developing countries like Haiti and Cambodia sadly are experiencing AIDS-related drops in population growth rates.

48c Using Commas to Set Off Conjunctive Adverbs and Most Transitional Phrases

Transitional expressions and *conjunctive adverbs* are usually set off by commas.

> transition
> ► The basking shark, in fact, consumes only zooplankton and small fish.

> conjunctive adverb
> It may end up as dinner for an orca or tiger shark, however.

When the transitional expression or conjunctive adverb is used to link independent clauses, place a semicolon before it.

> conjunctive adverb
> ► The whale shark is the largest fish in today's oceans; nevertheless, it presents no threat to humans.

> **transitional expressions** Words and phrases that show the relationship between sentences

> **conjunctive adverb** A transitional expression that can link one independent clause to another; it modifies the second clause and specifies its relationship to the first

48d Inserting Commas to Set Off Interjections, Contrasting Information, Expressions of Direct Address, Parenthetical and Conversational Expressions, and Tag Questions

> interjection
> ► Wow, that wind farm is gorgeous!

> interjection
> ► Some people, sadly, think the industrial look of a wind farm is ugly.

> contrasting information
> ► The current energy situation requires us to revise, not cling to, traditional notions of beauty.

direct address

▶ Professor Kinneyꞈ how much do you know about offshore wind farming?

parenthetical

▶ The first US offshore wind farmꞈ it turns outꞈ was on Nantucket Sound.

conversational
   expression

▶ Noꞈ it isn't a single-handed solution to our energy problems.

tag

▶ Wind farms will nevertheless make a big contributionꞈ won't they?

48e Using Commas to Separate Items in a Series

Place a comma between items in a series of three or more.

▶ Our new house will feature solar panelsꞈ a hilltop windmillꞈ and rainwater conversion.

Some writers omit the comma before the coordinating conjunction (*and* in this example) in a series, but readers may find the final comma helpful in distinguishing paired and unpaired elements. The managing editor of the *Chicago Manual of Style* likes to quote this hypothetical dedication, which highlights the potential problems that can be caused by omitting the serial comma:

▶ I dedicate this book to my parents, Mother Teresa and the Pope.

 To Use or Not to Use the Serial Comma English-speaking nations may share a common language, but their rules for using it sometimes differ. British writers have more or less dispensed with the serial comma (except to avoid confusion), while Americans (except for journalists) continue to use it. When writing for a US audience, use the serial comma.

▶ *More about*
Using semicolons
in a series, 799

When the items in the series are long or contain internal commas, substituting semicolons for commas can make the sentence easier to read:

▶ Phillis Wheatley was born in Senegal in 1753,⁄ was sold into slavery

to a Boston, Massachusetts, family,⁄ studied Greek, Latin, and English,⁄

and became the first published African American writer.

→ **EXERCISE 48.3 Inserting commas in conjunctive adverbs, transitional phrases, interrupting words and phrases, and items in a series**

Supply commas as needed in the sentences below. (You will not need to add a comma in every sentence.)

EXAMPLE

My goodness,did I have a horrible cold last week!
            ⌄

1. I originally thought my sneezing was due to an allergy; however my doctor pointed out the difference between symptoms from an allergy and a cold.

2. A telltale sign for example is how quickly the symptoms develop.

3. Allergy symptoms start immediately, but cold symptoms, on the other hand, take a day or longer to develop and gradually worsen.

4. Allergies nearly always cause itchiness in the eyes nose and throat, while a cold usually does not.

5. My obvious cold symptoms according to my doctor were fever aches and chest congestion.

48f Using Commas to Separate Coordinate, Not Cumulative, Adjectives

Coordinate adjectives each modify the noun or pronoun they precede and are of equal weight; *cumulative adjectives,* on the other hand, modify not only the noun or pronoun they precede but also the next adjective in the series. Hence, the order of coordinate adjectives does not matter, but the order of cumulative adjectives does.

Consider the example below:

                                        coordinate adjectives
                                        ┌──────────────┐
▶ The girl struggled to hide her brooding͵ moody nature from the
  ┌──────────────┐
  coordinate adjectives

sympathetic͵ insightful child psychologist she visited weekly.
┌──────────────┐
        cumulative adjectives

More about
Adjective order,
762–63

While you could reverse *brooding* and *moody* or *insightful* and *sympathetic*, you could not reverse *insightful* and *child*: A *child insightful psychologist* does not make sense.

Quick Reference　Testing for Coordinate and Cumulative Adjectives

To determine whether two or more adjectives should be separated by a comma, try these two tests:

1. **Place the word *and* between the two adjectives.** If the phrase still makes sense, then the adjectives are coordinate, and you should put a comma between them:

   Yes: sexy and exciting boyfriend
   No: enormous and shoulder bag

2. **Reverse the order.** If the meaning remains the same no matter what order they appear in, then the adjectives are coordinate, and you should insert a comma between them:

   Yes: sexy, exciting boyfriend = exciting, sexy boyfriend
   No: enormous shoulder bag ≠ shoulder enormous bag

→ EXERCISE 48.4 Using commas with coordinate and cumulative adjectives

Add commas as needed in the sentences below.

EXAMPLE

How likely is it that a curious,adventurous sixth grader will take up

smoking?

1. As part of a revealing study, researchers interviewed 1,195 sixth graders and then spoke to them several times over the next four years.

2. The study suggested that two characteristics indicate a heightened identifiable risk level for becoming a smoker.

3. The clearest key indication for future smoking is that it is easy to get cigarettes.

4. The other demonstrated major characteristic is that young people tend to become smokers if they have friends who smoke.

5. Furthermore, combining these two characteristics is a strong indicative risk factor.

48g Using Commas to Set Off Nonessential Appositives, Phrases, and Clauses

Words, phrases, or clauses that add information to a sentence but do not identify the person, place, or thing being described are *nonessential* (or *nonrestrictive*) *elements* and are set off by commas from the rest of the sentence. Elements that identify the person, place, or thing being described are *essential* (or *restrictive*) and are *not* set off by commas. Consider the following sentence:

> essential   nonessential
> ▶ My coworker Philip, whom I had never seen without a tie, arrived at the office this morning wearing a toga.

> **More about**
> Essential and
> nonessential
> elements, 636

Philip picks out one coworker from among the rest, so that element is essential. The nonessential clause—*whom I had never seen without a tie*—provides important information about Philip, but it does not identify him from among the writer's colleagues, so it is nonessential.

Compare the sentence above to this sentence:

>   nonessential
> ▶ My coworker, Philip, showed up at work this morning wearing yoga pants.

In this sentence, *Philip* is set off by commas, suggesting that the writer has only one colleague, so identifying him by name is not essential.

1. Use commas with nonessential appositives.

An *appositive* renames a preceding noun phrase. When it identifies, or specifies, the noun phrase, it is essential and is not set off by commas:

> noun phrase   appositive
> ▶ The Roman emperor Claudius suffered from an ailment that caused him to limp and to stammer uncontrollably.

> **appositive** A noun
> or noun phrase that
> renames the noun,
> pronoun, or noun
> phrase that pre-
> cedes it

In this case, *Claudius* distinguishes this Roman emperor from all the other Roman emperors, so it is essential and should not be set off by commas.

When the appositive adds information but does not identify, it is nonessential and is set off by commas.

>   nonessential
> noun phrase   appositive
> ▶ The fourth Roman Emperor, Claudius, suffered from an ailment that caused him to limp and to stammer uncontrollably.

Because there was only one *fourth Roman emperor*, the name *Claudius* is nonessential.

2. Use commas with nonessential phrases.

A phrase that acts as an adjective, modifying a noun, pronoun, or noun phrase, can also be essential or nonessential: If it identifies what it is describing, then it is essential and should *not* be set off by commas; if it does not identify, then it is nonessential and *should* be set off by commas.

- noun   nonessential phrase
  The girl, asked by her father to behave, said, "I am being haive."
- noun   essential phrase
  The girl asked by her father to behave is my niece.

3. Use commas with nonessential clauses.

A subordinate (or dependent) clause can also act as an adjective, modifying a noun, pronoun, or noun phrase. When it identifies the noun, pronoun, or noun phrase, it is essential and is *not* set off by commas; when it does not, it is nonessential and *is* set off by commas.

Adverb clauses The placement of an adverb clause indicates whether it is essential or nonessential: If it appears at the beginning of the sentence, it is generally nonessential and set off by a comma; if it appears in the middle of the sentence, it is generally essential and is not set off by commas:

- nonessential adv. clause
  Because he found the politics required to win an Academy Award
  noun
  demeaning, George C. Scott refused to accept an Oscar for his performance in the movie *Patton*.
- noun
  George C. Scott refused to accept an Academy Award for his
  essential adv. clause
  performance in the movie *Patton* because he found the politics required to win an Oscar demeaning.

That clauses versus which clauses Subordinate clauses beginning with the word *that* are always essential and thus never set off by commas.

- essential clause
  Produce that has been genetically modified differs from its non–GM counterpart by a human-made alteration to its DNA.

The word *which*, on the other hand, is used today to introduce both essential and nonessential clauses:

nonessential clause

▶ Genetically modified produce, which is sold in grocery stores throughout the United States, is still looked on with suspicion by many consumers.

NOTE Some writers (and instructors), especially in the United States, believe *which* should be used exclusively with nonessential clauses.

➔ EXERCISE 48.5 Using commas with appositives, phrases, and clauses

Correct the errors in the following sentences by inserting or deleting commas as necessary.

EXAMPLE

Lyme disease,a bacterial infection,was named for the town in
            ∧   ∧
Connecticut where it was first identified.

1. The malady, Lyme disease, is transmitted by deer ticks.

2. A person can become infected by deer ticks, that wait among tall grass for someone or something to latch onto.

3. When someone gets Lyme disease he or she will sometimes develop a reddish rash that looks like a spreading bull's-eye.

4. Lyme disease is difficult to diagnose because many people, who have it, do not remember getting bitten by a tick.

5. There is a good protective measure completely covering the arms and legs whenever walking in tall grass that can help a person avoid deer ticks and the Lyme disease that they carry.

48h Using Commas with Quotations

In most cases, separate a *direct quotation* from a *signal phrase* with a comma:

signal phrase

▶ After learning that he had been appointed poet laureate, Charles Simic exclaimed, "I'm almost frightened to get out of bed—too much good luck in one week."

direct quotation The exact words someone has used; direct quotations must be placed in quotation marks to avoid plagiarism

signal phrase A noun or pronoun plus an appropriate verb identifying the writer from whom you are borrowing words or ideas

Exceptions

- When the quotation begins the sentence and ends with a question mark or exclamation point, no comma should be added.

  ▸ "When shall we three meet again, in thunder, lightning, or in rain?"⟨⟩asks the first witch in Shakespeare's *Macbeth*.

- When the quotation is integrated into your own sentence, omit the comma:

  ▸ Friar Lawrence warns Romeo that⟨⟩"these violent delights have violent ends."

- When the signal phrase is incorporated into a complete sentence that makes sense without the quotation, use a colon before the quotation:

  ▸ Hamlet exits the graveyard scene with a veiled threat⟨:⟩ "The cat will mew, and dog will have his day."

Indirect quotations should not be set off by commas.

- ▸ New poet laureate Charles Simic confessed that⟨/⟩ having so much good luck worried him.

> **indirect quotation**
> A quotation that has been paraphrased (put into the writer's own words), instead of taken word-for-word from the source

48i Using Commas with Numbers, Names and Titles, Place Names and Addresses, and Dates

Numbers, names and titles, place names and addresses, and dates are each punctuated according to specialized conventions, some of which vary from one community or discipline to another.

1. In numbers

> *More about*
> Numbers, 854–57 (ch. 57)

The following conventions are standard in most American English usage:

- In four-digit numbers, using a comma to mark divisions of hundreds is optional, except with years, when no comma should be included:

  ▸ The company paid $9⟨⟩347 for those supplies in 2016.
  ▸ The company paid $9⟨,⟩347 for those supplies in 2016.

- In five-digit numbers, a comma is used to mark divisions of hundreds.

  ▸ Workers have filed 93⟨,⟩471 unemployment claims since January.

2. Between personal names and titles

Use a comma to separate a personal name from a title that follows it:

■ Send the request to Janet Woodcock, director of the Center for Drug Evaluation and Research.

Use no comma when a title precedes the name or when the "title" consists of roman numerals:

▸ Send the request to Doctor Janet Woodcock.

▸ My son will be named Albert Farnsworth IV.

The titles Jr. and Sr. may appear with or without commas:

▸ Ken Griffey, Jr., appears in the *Simpsons* episode "Homer at the Bat."

▸ Ken Griffey Jr. appears in the *Simpsons* episode "Homer at the Bat."

3. In place names and addresses

Use a comma to separate names of cities from states, provinces, regions, or countries:

▸ Boston, Massachusetts, was the birthplace of Benjamin Franklin. Famous as an American patriot, Franklin also lived for several years in London, England, and Paris, France. He died at age eighty-four in Philadelphia, Pennsylvania.

Do *not* place a comma between the name of a state and the zip code:

▸ The Franklin Institute, founded to honor Benjamin Franklin, is located at 222 North 20th Street, Philadelphia, Pennsylvania 19103.

4. In dates

Use commas to set off dates in which the day follows the month and when dates include the time of day or the day of the week:

▸ I will never forget that my son was born at 5:17 a.m., Tuesday, March 17, 2009.

No comma is needed in dates when only the month and year are used or when the day *precedes* the month:

▸ My niece was born in February()2015.

▸ Her exact birth date is 13 February 2015.

> **EXERCISE 48.6 Using commas with numbers, names, places, and dates**

In the following sentences, add commas as necessary to mark numbers, names and titles, place names and addresses, and dates. (Not all sentences will need correction.)

EXAMPLE

The board of directors met on Tuesday, June 5, 2016, at 3:00 p.m., in
                                        ^   ^   ^

the institute's new offices in Swansea, Massachusetts.
                                            ^

1. Yvonne Gesinghaus, MD, disagrees with the board's decision.
2. According to Dr. Gesinghaus "We should spend the $10500 on research, not on a party in San Antonio Texas."
3. Nevertheless, she requests that we send an invitation to William Green Sr. 217 Adamson Parkway Seattle WA 90107.
4. His invitation must go out by 7 October 2016.
5. The next meeting of the board of directors has been rescheduled to Monday January 10 2017.
6. The finance officer told Dr. Gesinghaus that, the meeting on Monday will start promptly at 5 p.m.
7. Also, please change your records to reflect her new job title: Yvonne Gesinghaus Director of Research and Development.
8. The foundation she now works for is located in a suburb of Fall River Massachusetts.
9. The new director's annual salary will be $165000.
10. The increase will take effect in January 2018.

48j Using Commas to Avoid Ambiguity

A comma can separate ideas that might otherwise be misinterpreted, and it can mark places where words have been deleted.

1. To separate ideas

When two ideas could be misread as a single unit, add a comma to separate
the two:

▸ My friends who can afford to,take taxis frequently.

2. To replace omitted words and avoid repetition

Replace a repeated word with a comma after its first use:

▸ I vacationed in the Adirondacks, my brother,~~vacationed~~ in British
Columbia.

48k Avoiding Commas between Subjects and Verbs, Verbs and Objects

A single comma should not separate a subject from its verb or a verb from
its object unless another rule calls for it:

▸ The Senate finance committee/ is the focus of much attention.
  subject   *verb*

▸ The committee must explain/ its decision to a nervous public.
                   verb   *object*

➤ EXERCISE 48.7 Using commas to resolve ambiguity

Correct the following sentences by inserting or deleting commas as
necessary. (Not all sentences will need correction.)

EXAMPLE

The members who want to,contribute their time to painting the club's
meeting hall.

1. Fiona is painting a wall, and Helen the baseboards.

2. Those who can stay and keep painting through the second shift.

3. Although most members never help, those who do devote a great deal
   of their spare time to it.

4. The members who do enjoy a sense of satisfaction that they have made a difference.

5. Jason worked ten hours this week, Alika eight, and Jesse fifteen.

→ **EXERCISE 48.8 Avoiding unnecessary commas**

Delete any unnecessary commas from the following sentences.

EXAMPLE

Current treatments for multiple myeloma include/ chemotherapy, radiation, and stem-cell transplantation, but/ other treatments are under development.

1. In April 2007, researchers at the Mayo Clinic, discovered that a by-product of wood mold, chaetocin, kills multiple, myeloma, cells more effectively than current treatments, such as thalidomide, or stem-cell transplantation.

2. The doctor, who led the study told reporters, that the team had found chaetocin to cause myeloma cell, death in mice and, that it had also provided new avenues for research.

3. This cancer of the bone marrow cells, is currently incurable, but this new research on chaetocin holds, promise for a cure.

4. Chaetocin kills myeloma cells in mice by, accumulating in the cancer cells, slowing the growth of myeloma cells, and causing biological changes in cancer cells that led to, their death.

5. Dr. Bible, who led the team of researchers, noted that treatments are still several years off, but expects that his team's discovery will help patients in the future.

→ **EXERCISE 48.9 Using commas correctly**

Add or delete commas as needed in the paragraph below.

EXAMPLE

Americans,instead of losing their spirit of creativity,seem to be
　　　　^　　　　　　　　　　　　　　　　　　　^

getting more inventive/ than ever.

The United States Patent Office, was so overwhelmed that it had a back-log of 700000 applications and its average review time was thirty-one months. In an attempt to deal with the flood of applications the office proposed new rules. The new rules made inventors provide more infor-mation; in addition the agency would also allow expanded public review of applications. What's more and this may be of greater concern to inventors the office began approving a smaller percentage of applications. In 2007 it approved approximately 50 percent of applications which was down from 72 percent in 2000. To improve the chances of approval inventors, need to be sure that their inventions are both new, and useful. The description of an invention whether it is simple, or highly complex should also be understandable, and written clearly. At the turn of the twenty-first century American inventiveness was not only thriving but it was also more competitive than ever before.

Make It **Your Own**

Review your use of commas in a recent writing project of two or more pages. Add commas where needed and cross through unnecessary ones. Then analyze the impact these changes would have on your reader. (Refer to the sections in this chapter as needed.)

Work **Together**

Exchange your work on Exercise 48.9 with a partner. Check your classmate's use of commas. Did he or she make any errors? If so, refer to sections in this chapter to help you explain the effect these errors had on you as a reader. (Be specific.)

Text Credits

p. 789: Simic, Charles, quoted in "Simic Reflects on Poet Laureate Honor" NPR Weekend Edition Sunday, August 5, 2007. **p. 790:** Shakespeare, William, *Macbeth* (1605). **p. 790:** Shakespeare, William, *Romeo and Juliet* (1594). **p. 790:** Shakespeare, William, *Hamlet* (1600).

49 Using Semicolons

'I think Lassie is trying to tell us something, ma.'

© Gerard Whyman/CartoonStock

Although there are other uses of the semicolon, its main function is to link two independent clauses into a single sentence. The comma and a coordinating conjunction also play this role, so what makes the semicolon useful? It is the signal the semicolon sends to the reader; it tells the reader that the clause that follows will specify consequences, restate meaning, or introduce a contrast.

A list of the most important rules for using semicolons appears in the Quick Reference box on the next page.

Writing Responsibly | Sending a Signal with Semicolons

Writers who do not understand the role of the semicolon may use it to connect independent clauses randomly, and this can lead readers to see a connection between ideas that the writer did not intend or cannot explain. Consider this sentence: *Angelina is working in New York; Brad has a headache.* The semicolon here suggests that there is a logical relationship between the two clauses, that one is the cause or effect of the other, when in fact the two may reflect mere coincidence. Avoid conveying more than you meant; use the semicolon with care.

to TOPIC

Quick

Reference Common Semicolon Do's and Don'ts

Do use a semicolon . . .

. . . to link two closely related independent clauses when the second clause specifies the consequence of the first, restates its meaning, or introduces a contrast. (797)

▶ In 1911, Italian nationalist Vincenzo Peruggia stole the *Mona Lisa* from the Louvre in France; he believed fervently that da Vinci's painting should be displayed in Italy.

. . . when a conjunctive adverb or transitional phrase links them. (798)

▶ Peruggia was arrested while trying to sell the painting to a Florence art gallery; however, his mission was not entirely in vain.

. . . to distinguish items in a series with internal commas. (799)

▶ Before arresting Peruggia, authorities questioned Guillaume Apollinaire, a French poet; Pablo Picasso, a Spanish painter and founder of cubism; and various Louvre employees.

. . . to repair a comma splice. (799)

▶ Before the *Mona Lisa* was restored to Paris, it was exhibited in museums across Italy; as a result, Peruggia was hailed as a national hero and served only a brief prison term.

Do not use a semicolon . . .

. . . to link an independent clause to anything except another, related independent clause. (798)

    independent clause   phrase

▶ During his trial, Peruggia leapt to his feet; raging at the prosecutor, the judge, and

even his own lawyer.

    independent clause   subordinate clause

▶ Peruggia claimed he was motivated only by patriotism; even though he had demanded

a "reward" of half a million lire.

. . . to introduce a list. (799)

▶ Despite an outcry, the *Mona Lisa* was returned to France after visiting the

                    list

following Italian cities; Naples, Rome, Florence, Venice, and Milan.

49a Using a Semicolon to Link Independent Clauses

When two *independent clauses* are closely related and parallel, a semicolon emphasizes their relationship.

|——————————— independent clause 1 ———————————|
▶ Adjusting to life in a new country does not come easily;

|—— independent clause 2 ——|
I learned that firsthand.

> **independent (or main) clause** A word group that contains a subject and a main verb and that does not begin with a subordinating conjunction, relative pronoun, or relative adverb

More about
Parallelism,
542–50 (ch. 28)
Commas, 778–95
(ch. 48)
End punctuation,
820–23 (ch. 52)
Dashes, 824–26
Colons, 828–30
Coordinating con-
junctions
(list), 780

A semicolon replaces a comma and coordinating conjunction:

coord. conj.

▸ Summer traffic to Jones Beach can be slow, so you might want to take the train instead.

▸ Summer traffic to Jones Beach can be slow; you might want to take the train instead.

A semicolon is often used when the second clause emphasizes the consequences of the first, restates the first, or offers a contrast with the first:

emphasizes consequences

▸ My mother's taste is always changing; just when I think I know what she likes, she proves me wrong.

restates

▸ When the French arrived, this area was very different from what it has become; Detroit was once a deep forest.

contrasts

▸ People think of Franklin Delano Roosevelt as the architect of the New Deal; he actually designed buildings, too.

Do not use a semicolon to link a phrase or a subordinate clause to an independent clause:

phrase

▸ That Harry Potter film proved successful; grossing $22 million in

the first night.

49b Using a Semicolon before a Conjunctive Adverb or Transitional Phrase Linking Two Independent Clauses

More about
Conjunctive
adverbs (list),
609
Transitional words
and phrases
(list), 62

When a conjunctive adverb (such as *therefore, however,* and *furthermore*) or a transitional phrase such as *on the other hand* or *for example* comes between two independent clauses, precede it with a semicolon (and follow it with a comma).

▸ *Shakespeare in Love* introduced the playwright to a new generation

semi. + conj. adv. + comma

of moviegoers; moreover, it was an entertaining film.

When the conjunctive adverb or transitional phrase is placed within one of the independent clauses rather than between them, retain the semicolon between the clauses and insert a comma before and after the conjunctive adverb or transitional phrase:

▸ Film is a popular form of entertainment(;) it can be(,) in addition(,) a means of exploring literature's classic themes in contemporary contexts.

49c Using a Semicolon to Mark a Series with Internal Commas

Ordinarily, commas are used to mark items in a series:

▸ You can create an off-grid home by building with straw bales(,) using solar power(,) and generating additional energy with windmills on the property.

However, when the items are especially long or complex or when an item in the series has internal punctuation, use semicolons.

▸ The architectural firm of Hanover, Harvey, and Witkins recommends creating an off-grid home by building with straw bales(;) packing them tightly(,) which makes them flame-resistant(;) utilizing solar power(;) and generating additional energy through windmills on the property.

Do not use a semicolon to introduce a list.

▸ I used the following in my "green" home; straw bales, solar panels, and water-conserving fixtures.
⌄

49d Repairing a Comma Splice

One way to repair a *comma splice* is to replace the comma between the two independent clauses with a semicolon.

comma splice Two independent clauses joined by a comma alone

▸ Reporters Without Borders fights restrictions placed on journalists,
⌄
the group also raises awareness about this increasingly important issue.

Sometimes a comma splice occurs because a comma is placed before a conjunctive adverb or transitional phrase that links two independent clauses. To correct it, replace the comma with a semicolon:

> Most people don't think of babies as prospective employees/ however,
>
> in Hollywood infants can become working actors at fifteen days old.

49e Avoiding Overuse

More about
Sentence variety,
551–55

complex sentence
One or more subordinate clauses linked to an independent clause

Use semicolons sparingly to avoid suggesting that everything in the passage is of equal importance. Overusing semicolons can also be a sign that you need to vary your sentence structures. You can turn some independent clauses into phrases or create *complex sentences* by turning some of your independent clauses into subordinate clauses.

DRAFT

According to *The Los Angeles Times*, the earliest known gunshot victim in the Americas died in 1536; archaeological exploration in Peru has uncovered a pierced skull. The Inca warrior was shot by Spanish conquistadors. Historical records verify that a battle took place at the location in which the skull was found; the battle is now known as the "siege of Lima." As many as 72 victims' remains have been found; most were not shot; most were bludgeoned to death.

Combines independent clauses 2 and 3; clause 3 becomes a subordinate clause introduced by the relative pronoun *who*.

Combines independent clauses 4 and 5; clause 5 becomes a phrase.

REVISION

According to *The Los Angeles Times*, the earliest known gunshot victim in the Americas died in 1536. Archaeological exploration in Peru has uncovered the pierced skull of an Inca warrior who was shot by Spanish conquistadors. Historical records verify that the skull was found at the site of a battle now known as the "siege of Lima." As many as 72 victims'

—————— phrase ——————

remains have been found. Most were not shot but were instead bludgeoned

to death.

> Combines indepen-
> dent clauses 7 and
> 8; clause 8 becomes
> a phrase.

→ EXERCISE 49.1 Correcting the use of semicolons

Add or delete semicolons or replace them with a different punctuation mark to correct or improve the sentences below. (Some sentences may be correct.)

EXAMPLE

About 10 percent of Americans are dyslexic/ they have a learning disability that causes them to have difficulty with written language, particularly reading and spelling.

1. Very few corporate managers are dyslexic; and this is understandable, since corporate management requires strong reading and writing skills.

2. Their disability does seem to exclude dyslexics from participating in this major business sector, however, according to a recent study, dyslexics are well represented as entrepreneurs or small-business owners.

3. About 35 percent of the entrepreneurs surveyed identified themselves as dyslexic apparently, it is common for dyslexics to develop important strengths precisely because of their weakness.

4. The study concluded that dyslexics were more likely than nondyslexics to be willing to delegate authority, to be especially adept at key business skills, such as oral communication and problem solving, and to be owners of two or more businesses.

5. Researchers noted that dyslexics' willingness to delegate authority gives them a specific advantage over nondyslexic entrepreneurs; the ability to focus on what they do best.

EXERCISE 49.2 Using semicolons correctly

Add or delete semicolons or replace them with a different punctuation mark to correct or improve the paragraph below.

EXAMPLE

Many elderly people worry that they may lose certain mental abilities,

such as memory; recently, researchers have uncovered some potentially

useful methods of maintaining mental sharpness.

In general, the idea is for the aging to get plenty of mental and physical stimulation just as physical exercise strengthens muscles, mental exercise strengthens the brain. The brain needs novelty; new challenges; and continued stresses to maintain or increase its strength, this type of stimulation creates new nerve cells and connections between them. It is common for some cells of an elderly person's brain to deteriorate, however; the newly developed brain tissue may compensate for the lost brain cells. So those who knit should try ever more complicated patterns, those who like listening to opera should try to learn the libretto, and those who like crossword puzzles should try new kinds of puzzles; such as Sudoku and double crostics. Also important for keeping mentally sharp is to pursue stimulating activities with other people, these can include taking classes; playing bridge; or participating in a reading group.

Make It **Your Own**

Review your use of semicolons in a recent writing project of two or more pages. Add semicolons where needed and cross through unnecessary ones. Then analyze the impact these changes would have on your reader. (Refer to the sections in this chapter as needed.)

Work **Together**

Exchange Exercise 49.2 with a partner. Check your classmate's use of semicolons. Did he or she make any errors? If so, refer to sections in this chapter to help you explain the effect these errors had on you as a reader. (Be specific.)

50 Using Apostrophes

© Nick Pope/Dorling Kindersley/Getty Images

Apostrophes, like pins, replace something that is missing: Pins replace stitches; apostrophes replace letters in contractions (*can't, ma'am*). Apostrophes also make nouns and indefinite pronouns possessive (*Edward's* or *somebody's horse*). Centuries ago, English speakers indicated possession with a pronoun (*Edward his horse*), so, in fact, today's possessive form (*Edward's horse*) is also an age-old contraction. A list of the most important rules for using apostrophes appears in the Quick Reference box on the next page.

50a Using Apostrophes to Indicate Possession

In English, you can indicate possession (ownership) in nouns and indefinite pronouns by using the preposition *of:*

> noun
> ► Many admired the commitment (of) the volunteers. But the
> indef. pron.
> involvement (of) everybody is needed to make real progress.

Writing Responsibly | Contractions in Formal Writing

Contractions and other abbreviations provide useful shortcuts in speech and informal writing, and they are finding their way into more formal academic and business writing. They are still not fully accepted, however. To determine whether contractions will be acceptable to your readers or will undermine your authoritative tone, check with your instructor, look for contractions in academic journals in your field, or consult reports or business letters written by other company employees. If you are in any doubt, spell the words out.

to SELF

Reference   Common Apostrophe Do's and Don'ts

Quick

Do use an apostrophe . . .

. . . **to indicate possession** (with singular and plural nouns and indefinite pronouns) (803)

▶ The book's cover promised "a thrilling read," but we were skeptical.

▶ Everyone's taste is different.

▶ Most books' covers are beautifully designed.

▶ She borrowed Socrates' book, not Jess's.

. . . **to form a contraction or abbreviate a year** (807)

▶ Didn't you forget your anniversary last year?

▶ You only got married in '08!

Do not use an apostrophe . . .

. . . **with possessive pronouns, especially *its*** (805)

▶ Now that they've played their CD, I want to play our's.

▶ Sadly, it's sales are lagging.

. . . **with plurals** (805)

▶ I've got load's of song's in my brain just itching to get out.

. . . **with dates, letters, and numbers** (807)

▶ The members of her club were born in the 1970's.

. . . **with verbs ending in *-s*** (806)

▶ My mom still hope's to sell downloads to members of her book club.

You can also do so by adding an apostrophe, with or without an *-s*:

> noun   indef. pron.
▶ Many admired the students' commitment. But everybody's involvement is needed to make real progress.

noun A word that names ideas, things, qualities, actions, people, and places

1. With singular nouns and indefinite pronouns (but not personal pronouns)

Singular *nouns* and *indefinite pronouns* add an apostrophe and an *-s* to indicate possession:

▶ The factory's smokestacks belched thick, black smoke.

▶ No one's health was unaffected.

indefinite pronouns Pronouns that do not refer to specific people or things, such as *all, anybody, either, everybody, few, many, either, no one, someone*

> **Tech** **Apostrophes and Spelling or Grammar Checkers**
>
> Be wary of apostrophe-related "errors" identified by your device's spelling or grammar checker. These programs usually do a good job of automatically inserting apostrophes in contractions such as *don't*, but too often they erroneously change *its* to *it's*, and they do not automatically insert apostrophes for possessive proper nouns such as *Matthew's*. Pay attention to the program's suggestions, but always double-check them for accuracy.

Even for most singular nouns that already end in *-s*, add an *-'s*:

▶ Dolores(s) asthma was particularly aggravated.

Add an apostrophe alone to a singular noun or pronoun only when adding an *-'s* would make the word difficult to pronounce:

▶ Socrates(') pneumonia became so serious he had to be hospitalized.

Personal pronouns are *never* made possessive by adding an apostrophe. Be sure to use the possessive form, *not* a contraction.

▶ We regret that ~~you're~~ *your* new power plant will have to close, but ~~they're~~ *their* health is more important.

Be especially careful with *its:*

- *It's* (*it is*) is a contraction like *don't* (*do not*) and *can't* (*cannot*).
- *Its* is a *possessive pronoun* like *his* and *hers*.

If you tend to confuse *it's* and *its*, remember that the contraction *always* takes an apostrophe, but the personal pronoun *never* does:

▶ Buca di Beppo is celebrated for its lasagna, so it's a good idea to call ahead for reservations.

> **personal pronouns**
> Pronouns that replace specific nouns or noun phrases, such as *I, me, he, him, she, her, it, we, us, you, they, them*

> **possessive pronouns**
> Pronouns that indicate ownership, such as *my, his, yours, mine,* and *theirs*

2. With plural nouns

To make plural nouns possessive, first form the plural and then the possessive. When the plural form ends in *-s*, just add an apostrophe; when it does not end in *-s*, add an apostrophe and *-s*.

Singular	Plural	Possessive
lady	ladies	ladies'
person	people	people's

> ▸ By midnight, the ladies'⟨⟩ maids were exhausted.

> ▸ I'm often amazed by people⟨s⟩ consideration for the well-being of others.

This rule applies to family names that end in *-s*, too: Make the name plural and then possessive.

Williamses'
> ▸ The ~~William~~'s parties always ended at dawn.
          ^

NOTE Just because a word ends with an *-s* does not mean that it needs an apostrophe. Delete apostrophes from plural nouns and singular verbs:

noun (plu.)   verb (sing.)
> ▸ Your dog/s bark wildly, but my cat remain/s placid.

3. To indicate joint or individual ownership or possession

First, decide whether the apostrophe indicates *joint* or *individual ownership*. When the nouns share possession, make only the last noun possessive:

> ▸ Giorgione and Titian⟨'s⟩ painting *Portrait of a Venetian Gentleman* (c. 1510) is on view at the National Gallery of Art in Washington, DC.

> Giorgione and Titian painted the portrait collaboratively.

When the nouns each possess the same object, quality, or event, make each noun possessive:

> ▸ Giorgione's and Titian's paintings of Venus are important milestones in the art of the High Renaissance.

> Each produced paintings of Venus that are important milestones.

4. With compound nouns

While number (singular or plural) is usually attached to the core noun in a compound noun, the possessive is attached to the last noun:

core (plural)
> ▸ Jeremiah is driving his <u>sisters</u>-in-law crazy.

> Jeremiah has more than one sister-in-law, and he is driving them all crazy. Attach number to the core noun, *sister*.

last
▶ Jeremiah is driving his sister-in-law's car.

Jeremiah is using the car belonging to his sister-in-law; attach possession to the last noun, *law*.

core (plural) last
▶ Jeremiah has his sisters-in-law's unwavering support.

Jeremiah has more than one sister-in-law, and he has their unwavering support; attach the plural to the core noun (*sisters*) and possession to the last noun (*law's*).

50b Using Apostrophes in Contractions and Abbreviated Years

An apostrophe can stand in place of missing letters or numbers in a contraction or in an abbreviated year.

▶	I am	I'm	▶ Cannot	Can't
▶	He is, she is	He's, she's	▶ Could not	Couldn't
			Would not	Wouldn't
▶	It is/has	It's	▶ Let us	Let's
▶	They are	They're	▶ Who is	Who's
▶	You are	You're	▶ 2012	'12

50c Moving Away from Using Apostrophes to Form Plurals of Abbreviations, Dates, Numbers, and Words or Letters Used as Words

Only a few years ago, *-'s* was a common way of creating the plural for abbreviations, dates, and words or characters used as words. These practices are now in flux, but using apostrophes for this purpose seems to be falling out of fashion. Unless the style guide you use instructs otherwise, do not use apostrophes to form these plurals.

▶ My brother has stayed in more YMCA/s than anyone else I know.

▶ Van Gogh's paintings were first exhibited in the late 1880/s.

▶ Now he minds the *p*/s and *q*/s of students in composition classes.

▶ His students give him 5/s on his evaluations.

NOTE The Modern Language Association (MLA) still recommends the use of an apostrophe with the plurals of letters:

Now he minds the *p*'s and *q*'s of students in composition classes.

Use an apostrophe to form a plural letter if its absence might cause confusion.

may be misread as is

CONFUSING   You've dotted your *ts* and crossed your *is*.

CLEAR   You've dotted your *t*'s and crossed your *i*'s.

→ **EXERCISE 50.1 Correcting apostrophes**

Supply or delete apostrophes as appropriate. (Some sentences may be correct.)

EXAMPLE

The sopranos voice crack*'*s whenever she thinks about PhD*'*s in
          ^
musicology assessing her performance.

1. It was one of her biggest crowd's since her heyday in the 1990's.

2. Many of the audience member's were fans who gave the performance 10's.

3. The auditorium resounded with they're *bravo*'s and *more*'s.

4. Personally, I think singer's who can't hit the high notes should issue IOU's with each performance.

5. This singer's high *C*'s are always flat, and she deserve's *F* 's for how she manage's the tempo of her concerts.

6. My two sisters and brothers-in-laws applause was among the most enthusiastic of the entire audience.

7. At our' dinner after the concert, my sister's were in agreement over their appreciation of the soprano, and Suzie's and Amber's praise for the soprano was fervent and wholehearted.

8. I didn't want to hurt Suzies and Ambers feelings, so I kept my criticisms about the soprano to myself ' during dinner.

9. On the way to our's car I tugged my husband Marks arms and I told him how shocked I was at my sisters's not noticing the soprano's lack of professionalism.

10. Mark smiled and said, "Your wise to let you're sisters' savor the performance, but I think you should be honest but tactful at next weeks concert when we sit in the Jones' special box at the opera house."

→ EXERCISE **50.2** Using apostrophes correctly

In the following paragraph, add or delete apostrophes as necessary.

One of Adam Smiths contributions to modern economic's is the distinction between use value and exchange value. Writing in the 1700's, Smith defined *use value* as the ability to satisfy peoples wants. In Smiths analysis, *exchange value* is the amount of good's or service's that people are willing to pay for something. His economics can help us understand our's. Smiths pointing out the difference between use value and exchange value can help contemporary economist's understand that value doesnt just derive from price. Jeremy Reiss essay clearly reflects this understanding.

Make It **Your Own**

Review your use of apostrophes in a recent writing project of two or more pages. Add apostrophes where needed and cross through unnecessary ones. Then analyze the impact these changes would have on your reader. (Refer to the sections in this chapter as needed.)

Work **Together**

Exchange Exercise 50.2 with a partner. Check your classmate's use of apostrophes. Did he or she make any errors? If so, refer to sections in this chapter to help you explain the effect these errors had on you as a reader. (Be specific.)

51 Using Quotation Marks

© 2003 Mark Stivers. 11/19/03. www.markstivers.com. Reproduced by permission.

Indicating who said what is an important use of quotation marks. When we fail to indicate that words were spoken or written by others—whether accidentally or on purpose—we open ourselves up to charges of plagiarism. Misusing quotation marks can also confuse or annoy your readers. (Think how much better the couple in the cartoon would get along if the man would learn to use quotation marks correctly!) Learning when to use—and when *not* to use—quotation marks is an important part of a writer's responsibilities. A list of the most important rules for using quotation marks appears in the Quick Reference box on the next page.

51a Setting Off Direct Quotations

Double quotation marks (" ") indicate the beginning and end of direct quotations (someone's exact words, whether written or spoken):

▶ Of grappling with the unknown, Albert Einstein wrote this: "The most beautiful thing we can experience is the mysterious. It is the source of all true art and all science."

Single quotation marks (' ') indicate quotations within quotations:

▶ Barbara Jordan, the first black woman to represent a southern state in Congress, felt that when the Constitution was written she "was not included in that 'We, the people.'"

Quick Reference   Common Quotation Mark Do's and Don'ts

Do use quotation marks . . .

. . . to set off direct quotations. 810

▶ Eisenhower once said that "who wants to be president is either an egomaniac or crazy."

. . . to indicate irony (use sparingly). 814

▶ After an unsuccessful stint as president of Columbia University, Eisenhower let himself be "persuaded" to run for the US presidency.

. . . to refer to words as words. 813

▶ "Popular" is an adjective often attached to Eisenhower's presidency.

(Italics are also widely used for this purpose.)

Do *not* use quotation marks . . .

. . . to set off indirect quotations (paraphrases). 812

▶ Eisenhower once said that "lunatics or narcissists are the only people who would desire the presidency."

. . . for emphasis. 814

▶ Eisenhower was a five-star general and "Supreme" Commander of Allied forces in Europe during World War II.

. . . with slang or clichés. 815

▶ "Snafus" occur regularly in the army, but Eisenhower generally avoided them through careful planning.

In formal contexts, consider recasting to avoid slang. Clichés are rarely appropriate; rewrite to avoid them.

Quotation Marks in American English Use of quotation marks varies from place to place and culture to culture. In contemporary American English, double quotation marks signal a quotation, and single quotation marks signal a quotation within a quotation:

▶ John complained, "For the third time this month, Mary said, 'I need a few bucks to tide me over till payday.' And it's only June 15!"

British usage is the opposite:

▶ John complained, 'For the third time this month, Mary said, "I need a few bucks to tide me over till payday." And it's only June 15'

Writing Responsibly   Using Quotations Fairly

You have a responsibility to your reader and other writers to supply quotation marks whenever you borrow language from a source. Omitting quotation marks when needed can undermine your reputation as a writer to be trusted.

to OTHER WRITERS

> *More about*
> Plagiarism,
> 247–64
> Patchwriting,
> 253–57

More about
Paraphrasing,
253–57

Indirect quotations, which paraphrase someone's words, do *not* use quotation marks:

▶ Albert Einstein said that "the unknown inspires scientists as well as artists."

▶ Barbara Jordan felt that "she was excluded by the founding fathers when they drafted the US Constitution."

1. In dialog

When quoting dialog, start a new paragraph each time the speaker changes, and put all spoken words in quotation marks:

▶ "Have you brought women here before?" He smiled and kept chewing, so I said, "Do you always use the same tricks?"

▶ "What tricks?" He looked at me like he didn't understand.

—Leslie Marmon Silko, "Yellow Woman"

If one speaker continues for more than a paragraph, use quotation marks at the beginning of each paragraph, but omit closing quotation marks until the end of the speech.

Generally, introduce
block quotations
with a complete
sentence plus a
colon.

In block quotations,
use double quo-
tation marks for
quotations within a
quotation.

More about
Formatting block
quotations, 308,
346–47
(MLA style), 392
(APA style)

2. With long quotations

For lengthy quotations, omit quotation marks, and indent quotations in a block from the left margin:

▶ Lucio Guerrero examines how local Goths feel about their lifestyle's mass-market appeal:

For some, that suburbanization of Goth may be what saves the sub-culture. "If someone who identifies as Goth doesn't have easy access to the fashion or accouterments that they feel drawn to, but they do have access to a store like Hot Topic, then it's a positive thing," said Scary Lady Sarah, a local DJ and supporter of Chicago's Goth community.

—Lucio Guerrero, "Like a GOTH," *Chicago Sun-Times*

3. With quotations from poetry

When quoting one to three lines of poetry, use quotation marks and run the lines into your text. Indicate the end of each line by inserting a slash, with a space on each side:

Student Model
"My View on a Long-Lost but Timeless Poem: Shelley's 'Poetical Essay on the Exiting State of Things,'" 466, 468–71

▶ Shelley sets the tone right away. The violence in lines 3–4 ("Millions to fight compell'd, to fight or die / In mangled heaps on War's red altar lie") is a clear criticism of the ruling class into which he was born.

When quoting four or more lines, omit quotation marks, set the poetry as a block, and retain the original line breaks:

▶ Shakespeare's "Sonnet 147" begins with evocative imagery:

> My love is as a fever, longing still
> For that which longer nurseth the disease,
> Feeding on that which doth preserve the ill,
> Th' uncertain sickly appetite to please. (lines 1–4)

51b Indicating Titles of Short Works

Most American style guides suggest placing titles of short works in quotation marks and titles of long works in italics:

More about
Italicizing titles of longer works, 842–43

▶ Lahiri's short story "Year's End" appeared in the collection *Unaccustomed Earth*.

▶ "Front Lines," a poem by Gary Snyder, is from his book *No Nature*.

▶ Ben Brantley's review of *Romeo and Juliet*, "Rash and Unadvis'd Seeks Same," ran in *The New York Times*.

▶ *Outlander* is my guilty pleasure; "The Wedding" is my favorite episode.

▶ The podcast "Of Two Minds, One Consciousness" from the *Scientific American* website uses results from split-brain studies to explore thought.

More about
Citing and documenting sources, 304–62 (MLA style, ch. 18), 363–405 (APA style, ch. 19), 406–34 (*Chicago* style, ch. 20), 435–49 (CSE style, ch. 21)

▶ "Good for You," from Selena Gomez's album *Revival*, reached the top of the Billboard charts.

In APA, CSE, and *The Chicago Manual of Style* parenthetical style, omit quotation marks from the titles of short works in bibliographic entries.

51c Indicating Words Used in a Special Sense

Quotation marks can call attention to words used in a special sense. When talking *about* a word, enclose it in quotation marks to avoid confusion:

▶ Many people confuse "lay" and "lie."

Italics can also be used for this purpose.

To signal that you are using a word ironically or sarcastically, place it in quotation marks:

> ▸ I didn't know that the Indian "problem" on the plains began in the 1860s. . . .

—James Welch, Killing Custer

Use quotation marks sparingly for indicating irony. Overuse can annoy readers. Your words should usually be able to convey irony on their own.

Set a term to be defined in italics and the definition in quotation marks:

> ▸ Many writers don't realize that *e.g.* stands for "for example" in Latin.

51d Misusing Quotation Marks

It is important to use quotation marks where needed; it is also important to omit them where they are not needed.

> **More about**
> Using italics for
> emphasis, 845

1. *Not* for emphasis

> ▸ Beyoncé's debut album was *"*amazing,*"* hitting no. 1 on *Billboard* in its first week.

Let your words and the rhythms of your sentences create emphasis. On the rare occasion when something more is needed, use *italics,* not quotation marks.

2. *Not* with slang

If slang is acceptable in the context, use it without the apology that quotation marks represent; if it is not (as in business or academic writing), choose a more appropriate word or phrase:

> ▸ "Writing's on the Wall" won the Academy Award for best original
> besting
> song in 2016, "~~beating out~~" several strong contenders.

3. *Not* with clichés

Clichés are rarely appropriate; instead of attempting to justify them with quotation marks, revise the sentence to avoid them altogether:

drinks were served.

▶ I left the party before ~~the "sun was over the yardarm."~~
∧

51e Punctuating Quotations

Whether punctuation appears before or after the closing quotation mark depends on the punctuation mark.

1. With periods and commas

In American English, commas and periods go *inside* the closing quotation mark, except when a citation follows the quotation:

▶ "Sacred cows," said the sixties radical Abbie Hoffman, "make the tastiest hamburger."

▶ According to sixties radical Abbie Hoffman, "sacred cows make the tastiest hamburger" (qtd. in Albert 43).

Commas and Periods with Quotation Marks In Britain, as well as in many other countries that use the roman alphabet, commas and periods follow the closing quotation mark. Since American punctuation rules require that commas and periods come before the closing quotation mark, be sure to adjust your usage to meet US readers' expectations.

2. With question marks, exclamation points, and dashes

Question marks, exclamation points, and dashes go *inside* the closing quotation mark when they are part of the quotation:

▶ In Megan Mayhew Bergman's short story "The Seige at Whale Cay," Marlene asks, "You like girls with guns, don't you, Joe?"

They go *outside* the closing quotation mark when they are not:

▶ Why does Robert Duvall's character in *Apocalypse Now* (1979) say "I love the smell of napalm in the morning"? He explains that "it smells like victory"!

More about
Periods, 820–21
Commas, 778–95
(ch. 48)
Question marks,
821–22
Exclamation
points, 822–23
Dashes, 824–26

More about
Citing indirect
sources,
296–97; 316–17
(MLA), 373
(APA)

3. With colons and semicolons

Colons and semicolons go outside the closing quotation mark:

▶ "I was not going to ask for mercy;" so wrote Cheryl Strayed in *Wild*.

▶ "Lions and tigers and bears": These are the only problems Dorothy doesn't encounter on her yellow-brick road to self-knowledge.

51f Altering Quotations with Ellipses and Square Brackets

Original: "Sometimes driven behind the origin is the rhythm, and the rhythm, as it comes out, causes the rest of the poem to follow. Rhythm is, in a very real sense, primary."

To fit a quotation into your own sentence, you may alter the wording (but not the meaning) by adding, changing, or deleting words. You have a responsibility, though, to alert your readers to your changes: Enclose additions or changes in brackets, and replace deleted words with ellipses:

changed letter in brackets

▶ In an interview, the poet Gary Snyder explained that "[s]ometimes driven behind the origin is the rhythm . . . Rhythm is, in a very real sense, primary."

deletion marked by ellipses

Remember, too, it is unethical to distort the meaning of the original text by altering a quotation or taking a quotation out of context.

NOTE In MLA style, if you must change a capital to a lowercase letter (or vice versa), place brackets around the letter to alert readers to the change.

More about
Altering quotations fairly, 817, 828, 831

51g Introducing and Identifying Quotations

More about
Clauses, 622–25

Use a colon to introduce a quotation if the clause preceding the quotation could stand on its own as a sentence and could make sense without the quotation:

▶ Darwin's own words clarify the issue: "It is not the strongest of the species that survive . . . but the ones most responsive to change."

Use a comma with signal phrases such as "Darwin said" or "she wrote":

More about
Using signal phrases, 277–79, 304–6, 363–65

signal phrase

▶ Charles Darwin said, "It is not the strongest of the species that survive. . . but the ones most responsive to change."

Use no punctuation if the quotation is needed to complete the sentence (as when the word *that* precedes it), and do not capitalize the first word in the quotation:

▶ Darwin asserts that "[i]t is not the strongest of species that survive . . . but the ones most responsive to change."

If a signal phrase interrupts the quotation, insert a comma before the closing quotation mark and after the signal phrase:

signal phrase

▶ "It is not the strongest of species that survive," Darwin asserts, ". . . but the ones most responsive to change."

→ **EXERCISE 51.1 Correcting problems with quotation marks and other punctuation**

Edit the sentences below as needed to correct problems with quotation marks and other punctuation.

EXAMPLE

our
Ashley said that "~~Our~~ library research would go a lot faster if we did

together," ,"Why not?"
it ~~together",~~ and I said ~~why not.~~

1. On our way to the library, I said You're right. Some sources just aren't available online.

2. In fact, didn't Professor Fass say "Only one-third of your sources may be online?" asked Ashley.

3. "Yes," I said, but that depends on what the word online means; "I pointed to a copy of *The New York Times* that I found lying on a table."

4. Opening it to an article titled Resisting the Rush to a World of No Cash, I said that "I found this in the library, but why can't I get it online and simply pretend that I got it from the periodicals room"?

5. Ashley smiled and said What you call "pretending" is what some might call cheating.

6. In any case, she added, "I don't think I could find this copy of Michael Chabon's short story The Little Knife online, and she pointed out that at the library she could also thumb through the magazine in which it originally appeared for more information."

7. "I actually knew you were right," I said, because I needed to go to the library to do this: I was looking through the "Oxford English Dictionary" for the derivation of the word turncoat.

8. Then I noted that "in my paper on Vidkun Quisling, I'd like to go beyond the standard definition of turncoat: One who traitorously switches allegiance".

9. Ashley asked Can you work into your paper the quote from the *Godfather* trilogy, "Keep your friends close, but your enemies closer?"

10. As I searched the library's catalog, I said that "I'd try, but I thought I'd find so much useful material in the library that I might not be able to fit it in."

EXERCISE 51.2 Correcting errors with quotation marks

Edit the passage below to correct problems with quotation marks and other punctuation.

EXAMPLE

Ross said that "he came across this quote attributed to Albert

Einstein": Only two things are infinite, the universe and the stupidity

of people, and I'm not so sure about the universe."

These, said Ross, are from the collection of references I found during research but did not use. He showed us a copy of a book by Abbie Hoffman titled, "*Steal This Book*," noting that 'it is hard to find even in libraries because many people followed the title's advice.' Then he said, I was researching what people sell when I opened a copy of the newspaper "*The Rock Ridge Record*" to the want ads in the back". He pointed to a want ad that offered the following. Used tombstone: Perfect for someone named Hancock Arnold Henry Field. One only. Then Ross continued, 'Here is one of several quotes I've collected by Woody Allen': "Why does man kill? He kills for food. And not only food: frequently there must be a beverage." Ross added that "Woody Allen also wrote one of his favorite short stories," which was titled, Notes from the Overfed: After reading Dostoevsky and the new "*Weight Watchers*" magazine on the same plane trip. "Finally", said Ross, "for an English essay, I found this play on the word "strip" by Groucho Marx: If you want to see a comic strip, you should see me in the shower."

Make It **Your Own**

Review your use of quotation marks in a recent writing project of two or more pages. Add quotation marks where needed and cross through unnecessary ones. Then analyze the impact these changes would have on your reader. (Refer to the sections in this chapter as needed.)

Work **Together**

Exchange Exercise 51.2 with a partner. Check your classmate's use of quotation marks. Did he or she make any errors? If so, refer to sections in this chapter to help you explain the effect these errors had on you as a reader. (Be specific.)

Text Credits

p. 810: © 2003 Stivers. November 20, 2003 www.markstivers.com. **p. 812:** Silko, Leslie Marmon, "Yellow Woman" from *Storyteller*, copyright © 1981 by Leslie Marmon Silko (New York: Seaver Books, 1981). **p. 812:** Guerrero, Lucio, "Like a GOTH," *The Chicago Sun-Times*, September 16, 2005. **p. 813:** Percy Bysshe Shelley, *Poetical Essay on the Existing State of Things* (1811). **p. 813:** William Shakespeare, "Sonnet 147: My Love Is as a Fever Longing Still." **p. 814:** Welch, James, with Paul Stekler, *Killing Custer: The Battle of Little Bighorn and the Fate of the Plains Indians*, copyright © 1994 by James Welch and Paul Stekler (New York: W. W. Norton, 1994). **p. 815:** Hoffman, Abbie, quoted in *The New York Times*, April 20, 1989. **p. 815:** Bergman, Megan Mayhew, "The Seige at Whale Cay," *The Kenyon Review* Fall 2014, Volume XXXVI, Number 4. **p. 816:** Strayed, Cheryl, *Wild: From Lost to Found on the Pacific Crest Trail* (New York: Alfred A. Knopf, 2013). **p. 816:** My View from the Sidelines: Gary Snyder's 'Front Lines'. **p. 816:** Darwin, Charles, *On the Origin of the Species* (London: John Murray, 1859).

52

Using End Punctuation
Periods, Question Marks, and Exclamation Points

Imagine that each of the people in these photographs has just uttered the words "you're here." Just by looking at their faces, can you guess who was perplexed, thrilled, or neutral? In face-to-face encounters, sight and sound play a huge role in how we interpret tone and meaning, but in a written text, we depend on words and punctuation—especially the punctuation ending the sentence—to signal mood. Think of the question mark as a raised eyebrow, the exclamation point as wide eyes and an open mouth, and the period as the neutral expression we usually wear.

52a Using Periods to End Statements and Mild Commands

Periods mark the end of most sentences, including statements (or *declarative sentences*), *indirect* (or reported) *questions,* and mild commands:

STATEMENT	Our library has survived a flood and two fires.
MILD COMMAND/ INSTRUCTION	Please urge the council to situate the new library building on higher ground.
INDIRECT QUESTION	She wondered whether the water had ever risen so fast before.

Periods are also used with some, but not all, abbreviations.

More about Using periods with abbreviations, 848

52b Using Question Marks to End Direct (Not Indirect) Questions

Most writers do not need a handbook to tell them to use a question mark to end a *direct question:*

- When did Uzbekistan declare its independence?
- Did you know that the median age in Uzbekistan is only 23.2 years?

Use a period, not a question mark, to punctuate *indirect* questions, that is, questions that are reported, not asked directly:

- Dr. Wilson asked why the median age in Uzbekistan is so low.

Use a period, not a question mark, in requests phrased as questions:

- Would you please find out the life expectancy in Uzbekistan.

Writing Responsibly   Question Marks and Exclamation Points

In an email to a friend, you might use a series of question marks or exclamation points to convey surprise or lend emphasis:

- Isn't it about time Joey got rid of the soul patch???!

But such techniques are not appropriate in more formal contexts, such as an email to an instructor:

- I look forward to studying American history with you next term.!!!!

Overusing exclamation points or other punctuation may undermine your credibility with readers. Your responsibility to yourself as an authoritative writer is to use restraint.

to SELF

A question mark in parentheses can also suggest doubt about a date, number, or word.

▶ Life expectancy at birth in Uzbekistan is 67 (?).

You may also punctuate a series of questions with question marks, even when they are part of the same sentence:

Note that capital letters are optional if each question is not a complete sentence.

▶ Do you know what Uzbekistan's primary crop is? what language the majority speaks? what countries surround this landlocked nation?

52c Using Exclamation Points with Strong Commands or to Express Excitement or Surprise

Tech   Using Exclamation Points in Email Messages

Because warmth can be difficult to convey in email, writers sometimes use an exclamation point to soften the tone. Compare:

▶ We look forward to seeing you next week.

▶ We look forward to seeing you next week!

Use exclamation points sparingly; otherwise they lose their effectiveness.

When giving an emphatic command or expressing sudden excitement or surprise, use an exclamation point to end the sentence:

▶ Don't go there!

▶ "Mom is coming!"

The same sentence, when ended with a period, conveys much less urgency:

▶ Don't go there.

▶ "Mom is coming."

 EXERCISE 52.1 Using end punctuation
Write six sentences modeled on the examples above that use periods, question marks, and exclamation points appropriately. The context for this exercise is academic.

 EXERCISE 52.2 Editing end punctuation
Insert end punctuation—periods, question marks, and exclamation points—as needed. If multiple end punctuation is appropriate, explain why you chose the punctuation mark you did.

EXAMPLE

"Could you repeat the question?" That's the most common response law
                                    ∧
professor David Cole gets when he calls on disengaged students during

class at Georgetown University.
                              ∧

The laptop—the favorite in-class tool for college and university students across the country—is coming unplugged When used responsibly—for taking notes or quickly accessing research—a laptop provides valuable educational support But when used irresponsibly—for watching YouTube, surfing the Web, emailing, IM-ing, playing games, checking sports scores, and shopping for shoes instead of engaging in class—laptops become the scourge of professors, some of whom are now banning them, especially in law schools
. . . Herzog banned all laptops from his classes for a day, and was so "stunned by how much better the class was," that he has vowed to make the embargo permanent in the fall

—Kathy McManus, "Class Action: Laptops Not Allowed,"
Responsibility Project

Make It **Your Own**

Review your use of end punctuation in a recent writing project of two or more pages. Add end punctuation where needed and cross through unnecessary ones. Then analyze the impact these changes would have on your reader. (Refer to the sections in this chapter as needed.)

Work **Together**

Exchange Exercise 52.2 with a classmate. Check your partner's use of end punctuation. Did he or she make any errors? If so, refer to sections in this chapter to help you explain the effect these errors had on you as a reader. (Be specific.)

Text Credit

p. 823: Mcmanus, Kathy, "Class Action: Laptops Not Allowed." Responsibility Project by Liberty Mutual.

53

Using Other Punctuation

Dashes, Parentheses, Brackets, Colons, Ellipses, and Slashes

© Walter McBride/WireImage/Getty Images

Writers thinking about punctuation typically focus on the comma, the semicolon, the period, and maybe the quotation mark—the star players on the punctuation stage. But dashes, parentheses, brackets, colons, ellipses, and slashes also play key roles. Think of these other marks as the supporting players of punctuation: While you may call on them in only a limited number of situations, when needed, there is no better punctuation mark for the job. The Quick Reference box on the next page summarizes how these punctuation marks are used.

53a Using Dashes

Dashes can be used singly, when the information to be set off falls at the end of the sentence, or in pairs, when it falls in the middle. They are used to lend emphasis and to mark examples, explanations, and appositives:

▶ In almost every era of Western culture, women's clothing has been decidedly restrictive and uncomfortable—and the garments of the mid–nineteenth century are a prime example.

example

▶ To be fashionable, women had to wear clothing that hampered their mobility—cumbersome petticoats and long dresses dragged in puddles and snagged on stairways, turning even a short walk into a navigational challenge.

explanation

Quick

Reference **What These Punctuation Marks Do**

> **Dashes** lend emphasis and set off examples, explanations, appositives, contrasts, definitions, series items, interruptions, and shifts.
>
> **Parentheses** set off information of lesser importance.
>
> **Brackets** set off a writer's insertions in a quoted passage or replace parentheses within parentheses.
>
> **Colons** link introductory independent clauses to examples, explanations, appositives; they introduce lists (when the introductory clause does *not* include the words *including, like,* or *such as*); and they introduce quotations (when the introductory clause can stand on its own and make sense without the quotation).
>
> **Ellipses** indicate an omission or a delay for dramatic effect.
>
> **Slashes** divide lines of poetry, fractions, and URLs. In formal writing, slashes are not used to separate alternatives (*and/or, he/she*) or parts of dates (*10/23/09*).

appositive

▶ In the 1870s another torture device—the bustle—

was introduced.

Dashes also emphasize contrasts, definitions, and items in a list:

▶ The bustle, which emphasized a woman's backside,

contrast

was considered erotic in its day—but from a modern

perspective, it is quite modest.

▶ For both daytime and evening wear, women were strapped into

definition

corsets—close-fitting undergarments that laced tightly around the torso.

list

▶ The trappings of mid-nineteenth-century dress—six petticoats, a long

hem, a bulky bustle, and a tight corset—guaranteed women's

discomfort.

Dashes can also be used to indicate a break in thought, speech, or tone:

▶ Women's dress today ranges from the prim to the promiscuous—

break (in tone)

anything goes!

Tech **Typing a Dash**

The built-in keyboards on many phones and tablets do not have a single key for dashes, but you can type two hyphens (--) to represent the dash.

> *More about*
> Apostrophes,
> 803–9 (ch. 50)

CAUTION If you use dashes more than once or twice over several pages, consider replacing one or more with commas: As with antibiotics, overuse of dashes undermines their effectiveness.

53b Using Parentheses

Use parentheses to set off supplementary information (such as examples, dates, abbreviations, or citations) to avoid distracting readers from the main point. Parentheses also enclose letters or numbers delineating items in a list.

▸ The English word for a trifling flaw or offense (*peccadillo*) [example] comes from the Spanish word for a small sin, but many other borrowings from Spanish (*barbecue, chocolate, hammock, potato, tomato*) [examples] actually originated in languages of the peoples whom the Spanish conquered in the Caribbean, Mexico, and South America.

▸ In 1991, the Spanish government founded the Instituto Cervantes (IC), [abbrev.] named for Miguel de Cervantes (1547–1616), [dates] the author of *Don Quixote* (1605, 1615). [dates]

> Unless a complete sentence is enclosed, punctuation goes outside closing parenthesis.

Writing Responsibly   Dashes, Parentheses, or Commas?

Responsible writers remain alert to the tone their punctuation conveys. Compare these three versions of the same sentence and consider the effect the punctuation has on you as a reader:

- Echinacea is reputed—despite many scientists' skepticism—to prevent and relieve colds.
- Echinacea is reputed (despite many scientists' skepticism) to prevent and relieve colds.
- Echinacea is reputed, despite many scientists' skepticism, to prevent and relieve colds.

The dashes lend emphasis—sometimes even a touch of drama—to the material they enclose, while the parentheses downplay that material. The comma is the most neutral mark. Select the punctuation mark best suited to the effect you want your words to have on your readers.

to AUDIENCE

▸ The goals of the IC are (1) to promote the study of Spanish worldwide, (2) to improve the methods of teaching Spanish as a second language, and (3) to advance understanding of Spanish and Latin American cultures.

▸ The proverb "Make hay while the sun shines" first appeared in *Don Quixote* (vol. 1, ch. 11).

➔ **EXERCISE 53.1 Choosing between dashes and parentheses**

Edit the sentences below to add dashes or parentheses as needed. If either is possible, explain why you chose one over the other.

EXAMPLE

Getting old does not necessarily mean getting frail spending decades in pain, being stooped over, and having to use a walker for many people are now in good mental and physical health well into their nineties.

I used dashes here to emphasize the description of "getting frail."

1. People over 85 constitute the fastest-growing segment of our population, and by 2050 researchers project that a substantial number of Americans 800,000 will be over 100 years old.

2. Many studies predicting the length of people's lives indicate that about 35 percent of the factors are determined by genes that we cannot control which leaves about 65 percent that we may be able to influence.

3. One particular long-term study it tracked elderly men for 25 years pointed out that the men who lived to at least age 90 were primarily the ones who did not smoke; prevented diabetes, obesity, and high blood pressure; and exercised regularly.

4. A key indicator for many of the "young-elderly" 70-year-olds is eating healthily limiting calories, saturated fat, and sugar as well as getting high-quality protein and whole grains with plenty of fiber.

5. In addition, several long-term studies have shown that exercise for both women and men is the strongest predictor of healthy longevity.

More about
Altering quota-
tions with
ellipses and
brackets, 816

Capital replaced to
fit quotation into
writer's sentence.

Gutenberg's replaces
his in source for
clarity.

Freshwater added
to explain an
antiquated meaning
of "sweet."

Writer uses *[sic]* to
point out subject-
verb agreement
error (*are* should
be *is*).

53c Using Brackets

Square brackets have two primary uses—to indicate additions or changes to a quotation and to replace parentheses within parentheses:

▸ Ramo and Burke explain that "[i]n 1456, when the first Bible rolled off [Gutenberg's] press, there were fewer than 30,000 books in Europe."

▸ Only four years after Gutenberg printed his first book, the Spanish explorer Vincente Yanez Pinzón reached the mouth of the Amazon, which he called Río Santa María de la Mar Dulce ("River St. Mary of the Sweet [Freshwater] Sea").

Square brackets are also used to enclose the Latin word *sic*, which means *thus* or *so*. It is inserted into a quotation following an error to make clear that it was the original writer, not the person using the quotation, who made the mistake:

▸ The most compelling review noted that "each of these blockbusters are [sic] flawed in a different, and interesting, way."

NOTE The Modern Language Association (MLA) and the Council of Science Editors (CSE) do not recommend underlining or italicizing *sic*; *The Chicago Manual of Style* and the American Psychological Association (APA), on the other hand, do recommend setting this Latin word in italics.

53d Using Colons

More about
Independent
clauses, 622–25,
639–41

A colon is usually used after an independent (or main) clause to introduce and call attention to what follows. Colons are also used to separate titles from subtitles and in other conventional ways.

Writing Responsibly | Using [sic]

Use *[sic]* cautiously: Calling attention to an error simply to point out another writer's mistake can make you look impolite or even condescending and might undermine your reputation (or ethos) as a respectful writer. When you come across a simple typographical error in a passage you want to quote (the writer typed *teh* instead of *the*, for example), either paraphrase or simply correct the error.

to SELF

1. To introduce an example, explanation, appositive, or list

Use a colon following an independent (or main) clause to introduce an example, an explanation, an appositive, or a list:

examples

▸ Cervantes was unlucky: At the battle of Lepanto, he lost the use of his left hand, and on the return journey, he was captured by Algerian pirates.

▸ Writing *Don Quixote* gave its impoverished author something more

appositive

than just satisfaction: the opportunity to make some money.

▸ A number of important writers died on April 23: Rupert Brooke,

list

William Wordsworth, Miguel de Cervantes, and William Shakespeare.

A dash can substitute for a colon in these cases, but a colon is more appropriate in formal writing.

Colons are also used to introduce a list that is preceded by the phrases *as follows* or *the following*:

list

▸ The following writers all died on April 23: Rupert Brooke, William Wordsworth, Miguel de Cervantes, and William Shakespeare.

Do not introduce a list with a colon when the introductory clause concludes with *like, such as,* or *including*:

▸ A number of important writers all died on April 23, including: / Rupert Brooke, William Wordsworth, Miguel de Cervantes, and William Shakespeare.

> **More about**
> Using commas
> in quotations,
> 789–90

2. To introduce a quotation

Use a colon to introduce a quotation only when it is preceded by an independent clause that would make sense without it, but not when the quotation is introduced by a signal phrase such as *she said* or *Hughes asks*.

ind. clause makes sense without quotation

COLON   In 1918, William Strunk, Jr., gave writers a piece of time-

less advice: "Omit needless words."

signal phrase needs quotation to make sense

COMMA   In 1918, William Strunk, Jr., said, "Omit needless words."

3. Other conventional uses

- Between title and subtitle and between publication date and page numbers (for periodicals) and location and publisher (for books) in bibliographic citations for some documentation styles:

More about
MLA style,
    304–62
    (ch. 18)
APA style,
    364–405 (ch. 19)
Chicago style,
    406–34 (ch. 20)
CSE style, 435–49
    (ch. 21)

          title   subtitle
DelRosso, Jeana. "De-tangling Motherhood: Adoption Narratives in Disney's *Tangled*."

The Journal of Popular Culture.

                    title   subtitle   publisher
Satrapi, Marjane. *Persepolis 2: The Story of a Return*. Pantheon, 2004.

- Following the salutation and following *cc* in formal business correspondence:

  ▶ Dear Professor Howard:

  ▶ cc: Caroline Richardson

More about
Business letter
    formats,
    497–502

- Between chapter and verse in scripture; between hours, minutes, and seconds; in ratios:

  ▶ Song of Solomon 3:1–11

  ▶ 4:30 p.m.

  ▶ Women outnumber men in college 2:1.

4. Common mistakes with colons

- Do not insert a colon between a verb and its complement or object.

                        verb   object
  ▶ Young readers awaited: the next volume in Stephenie

  Meyer's vampire love saga.

- Do not insert a colon between a preposition and its object.

                                prep.   object
  ▶ *Vogue* announced a return to: hippie-style clothing.

> **EXERCISE 53.2 Using colons in a sentence**
> Write two sentences using colons, one to introduce an example or explanation and the other to introduce an appositive, list, or quotation. (See the section above for examples.)

53e Using Ellipses

Ellipses are sets of three periods, or *ellipsis points,* with a space between each. They are most often used to replace words removed from quotations, but they are also sometimes used to create a dramatic pause or to suggest that the writer is unable or unwilling to say something.

1. To indicate deletions from quotations

Although it is not acceptable to alter the meaning of a quotation, writers can and do omit words from quotations as needed to delete irrelevant information or to make a quotation fit into their own sentence. The ellipses alert readers that a change has been made:

> comma + ellipses
>
> ▸ *Don Quixote* begins like a fable: "In a village of La Mancha, ... there
>
> comma + ellipses
>
> lived not long since one of those gentlemen that keep a lance, ... a
>
> comma + ellipses   period + ellipses
>
> lean hack, ... and an old greyhound for coursing, ..."

> Use four dots—a period plus the ellipses—if a deletion occurs at the end of the sentence.

With a parenthetical citation, insert the ellipses before the closing quotation marks and the period after the citation.

> ellipses + close quote
>
> ▸ "They will have it his surname was Quixada ..." (1).
>
> citation + period

When only a few words are quoted or when the quotation begins with a lowercase letter, it is obvious that words have been omitted from the quotation, so no ellipses are needed:

> ▸ That Don Quixote keeps "a lean hack" suggests that he is no romantic hero, but instead minor, rather poor, country gentry.

NOTE If you are quoting a complete sentence, no ellipses are needed to indicate that the sentence comes from within a longer passage.

> ▸ *More about*
> Altering quotations,
> 285–87, 816, 828

Writing
Responsibly Altering Quotations

Exercise care when changing quotations: Never make a change that might distort the original or that might mislead readers, and always use ellipses and brackets to indicate an alteration.

to OTHER WRITERS

2. To indicate the omission of a line (or lines) of poetry

Use not a single ellipsis mark (three dots) but a whole line of dots to replace one or more missing lines of poetry:

► One of the most famous lines in Robert Frost's poem "Mending Wall" is "Good fences make good neighbors," but the speaker's meaning is lost when this line is taken out of context:

> There where it is we do not need the wall:
>
> ....
>
> My apple trees will never get across
> And eat the cones under his pines, I tell him.
> He only says, "Good fences make good neighbors." (lines 23–27)

3. To indicate a dramatic pause or interruption in dialog

An ellipsis can indicate an incomplete thought, a dramatic pause, or an interruption in speech:

► The disgruntled writer muttered, "The only word to describe my editor is ... unprintable."

> ## EXERCISE 53.3 Using brackets and ellipses with quotations

More about
Signal phrases,
277–85, 304–9,
363–65

Write a paragraph in which you quote a passage from another text, marking deletions with ellipses and enclosing additions in brackets. Your paragraph must include at least one addition and two deletions. Be sure to identify the quoted passage by using a signal phrase and parenthetical page number.

53f Using Slashes

The slash (or *virgule*) is used to mark the ends of lines in poetry when the poetry is run into a sentence:

► *Don Quixote* opens with some "commendatory verses" that warn the writer "Whoso indites frivolities, / Will but by simpletons be sought" (lines 62–63).

Slashes are also used in fractions and URLs:

► 1/2   1/3   3/4

► www.unh.edu/writing/cwc/handouts/

In informal contexts, the slash is sometimes used to indicate that either term is applicable:

▶ I've got so many courses this semester that I decided to take Spanish pass/fail.

In more formal contexts (such as academic or business writing), replace the slash with the word *or*, or rewrite the sentence:

DRAFT   An effective writer revises his/her work.

BETTER   An effective writer revises his or her work.

BEST   Effective writers revise their work.

Slashes are also used in dates, but only in informal or technical contexts or in tables where space is at a premium.

TECHNICAL OR INFORMAL   6/26/16

FORMAL   June 26, 2016 or 26 June 2016

→ **EXERCISE 53.4** Editing dashes, parentheses, brackets, colons, ellipses, and slashes

In the following paragraph, add or delete dashes, parentheses, brackets, colons, ellipses, and slashes as necessary.

American poet Anne Bradstreet 1612-1672 wrote many poems (expressing her religious devotion). She was a friend of Anne Hutchinson, who also wrote and spoke [on religious matters]. The American Puritans—of Bradstreet and Hutchinson's time—were unforgiving on religious matters [and banished Hutchinson for her beliefs]. It is not surprising, then, that Bradstreet's religious poetry expresses simple piety, as in the closing lines to the poem "Here Follow Several Occasional Meditations" "I'll serve Him here whilst I shall live And love Him to eternity." It is unsurprising, too, given the censorship exercised upon writers of the time, that she was reluctant to publish her poems. Today's readers may consider her excessively modest or timid about announcing herself as an author, but we must take her historical context into account . . . if we are to read her work—fairly.

Make It **Your Own**

Review your use of dashes, parentheses, brackets, colons, ellipses, and slashes in a recent writing project of two or more pages. Add punctuation marks where needed and cross through unnecessary ones. Then analyze the impact these changes would have on your reader. (Refer to the sections in this chapter as needed.)

Work **Together**

Exchange Exercise 53.4 with a classmate. Check your partner's use of punctuation. Did he or she make any errors? If so, refer to sections in this chapter to help you explain the effect these errors had on you as a reader. (Be specific.)

Text Credits

p. 827: de Cervantes Saavedra, Miguel, *The Ingenious Gentleman Don Quixote of La Mancha*, Volume 1, Chapter 11, translated by John Ormsby (Smith, Elder & Co., 1885). p. 829: Strunk Jr., William, *The Elements of Style* (New York: Harcourt Brace and Company, 1920). p. 831: de Cervantes Saavedra, Miguel, *The Ingenious Gentleman Don Quixote of La Mancha*, Volume 1, translated by John Ormsby (Smith, Elder & Co., 1885). p. 832: Frost, Robert, "Mending Wall." from *North of Boston* (1914). p. 832: de Cervantes Saavedra, Miguel, *The Ingenious Gentleman Don Quixote of La Mancha*, Volume 1, translated by John Ormsby (Smith, Elder & Co., 1885) p. 95. p. 833: Bradstreet, Anne, "Here Follow Several Occasional Meditations," *The Works of Anne Bradstreet in Prose and Verse*, edited by John Harvard Ellis (Charlestown: A. E. Cutter, 1867).

54 Capitalizing

© emicristea/123RF.com

Like a spire soaring over surrounding rooftops, a capital letter beckons the reader, calling attention to the word it adorns. But just as architecture varies from place to place, so the rules of capitalization vary from language to language.

In English, capital letters are used to call the reader's attention in a variety of contexts. The Quick Reference box on page 836 outlines the most important rules of capitalization in English. For cases not covered here, or when you are not sure, consult a dictionary. Your readers will think better of you if you avoid overcapitalizing.

Capitalization English capitalization can be confusing to people for whom English is a foreign language. In Spanish, French, and German, the first-person singular pronoun is lowercase (*yo, je, ich*), but in English it is capitalized (*I*), although the other personal pronouns (*she, he, it, they*) are not. In Spanish and French, the names of months and days of the week are lowercased, but not in English. In German, all nouns are capitalized, but in English only proper nouns are. Languages such as Arabic and Korean have no capital letters at all. Proofread your work carefully to adhere to the conventions of capitalization in the language in which you are writing, referring to this chapter and a good college dictionary as needed.

54a Capitalizing the First Word of a Sentence

Capitalize the first letter of the first word of every sentence:

Reference Common Capitalization Do's and Don'ts

Do capitalize . . .

. . . the first word of a sentence. (835)

▶ The day broke gray and dull. —Somerset Maugham, *Of Human Bondage*

. . . proper nouns and proper adjectives. (837)

▶ Aunt Julia, Beijing, Dad (used as a name), Band-Aid, Shakespearean, Texan

. . . the first, last, and important words in titles and subtitles. (838)

▶ *Avengers: Age of Ultron*

. . . the first-person pronoun *I*. (839)

▶ I think; therefore, I am. —René Descartes

. . . abbreviations and acronyms. (840)

▶ Eng. Dept., UCLA, NYPD

Do not capitalize . . .

. . . common nouns. (838)

▶ dog, cat, aunt, city, my dad, bandage

. . . compass directions. (838)

▶ north, south, northwest, southeast

. . . seasons or academic years and terms. (838)

▶ spring, freshman, intersession

▶ In response to Franklin Roosevelt's long tenure, the US Congress passed an amendment limiting a president to two terms.

This rule applies even to sentences in parentheses, unless they are incorporated into another sentence:

> **More about**
> Parentheses,
> 826–27

▶ His vice president, Harry S. Truman, decided not to run for reelection, although the amendment did not apply to him. (The sitting president was exempted.)

▶ Although the amendment did not apply to him (the sitting president was exempted), Truman decided not to run for reelection.

Capitalize the first word of a sentence you are quoting, even when it is incorporated into your own sentence:

> ▶ In response to a question about the amendment, President Eisenhower said, "By and large, the United States ought to be able to choose for its president anybody that it wants, regardless of the number of terms he has served."

Do not capitalize the first word when you are quoting only a phrase:

phrase

> ▶ President Eisenhower's "faith in the long-term common sense of the American people" made him feel the amendment was unnecessary.

When interrupting a quoted sentence, do not capitalize the first word of the second part:

> ▶ "By and large," Eisenhower said, "the United States ought to be able to choose for its president anybody that it wants, regardless of the number of terms he has served."

NOTE In MLA style, if you must change a capital to a lowercase letter (or vice versa) to incorporate a quotation into your sentence, place brackets around the letter to alert readers to the change.

> *More about*
> Brackets, 828
> Altering
> quotations,
> 816, 828,
> 831–32

If a colon links two *independent clauses,* capitalizing the first word following the colon is optional, but be consistent:

> ▶ Before Franklin Roosevelt, no US president had held office for more than two terms: That precedent was broken with Roosevelt's third inauguration.

or

> ▶ Before Franklin Roosevelt, no US president had held office for more than two terms: that precedent was broken with Roosevelt's third inauguration.

> **independent (or main) clause** A word group that contains a subject and a main verb and that does not begin with a subordinating conjunction, relative pronoun, or relative adverb

54b Capitalizing Proper Nouns and Proper Adjectives

Capitalize the first letter of *proper nouns* (the names of specific people, places, and things) and the adjectives derived from them. Do not capitalize common nouns (names for general groups of people, places, and things). The Quick Reference guide on page 838 provides examples of words in each group.

Quick

Reference Capitalize Proper Nouns and Proper Adjectives, but Not Common Nouns

Proper Nouns and Proper Adjectives	**Common Nouns**
ACADEMIC DEPARTMENTS AND DISCIPLINES	
Political Science Department, Linguistics 101	political science, linguistics
PEOPLE	
Senator Bob Corker, Mom (used as a name), Dickensian	the senator, my mother, novelistic
PLACES, COMPASS DIRECTIONS	
Yosemite National Park, Neptune, the Northwest	the park, that planet, northwest, midwestern
TIME PERIODS AND HOLIDAYS	
Tuesday, June, Memorial Day	a weekday, this summer, spring break
HISTORICAL EVENTS, PERIODS, AND DOCUMENTS	
Korean War, Roaring Twenties, the Emancipation Proclamation	the war, the twenties, the proclamation
ORGANIZATIONS, OFFICES, COMPANIES	
National Wildlife Federation, General Accounting Office, National Broadcasting Corporation	a conservation group, the legislative branch, the network, the corporation
TRADE NAMES	
Coke, Kleenex, Google	a soda, a tissue, a Web search
NATIONS, ETHNIC GROUPS, RACES, AND LANGUAGES	
Pakistan, Pakistani, African American, Caucasian, Swahili	her country, his nationality, their language
RELIGIONS, RELIGIOUS DOCUMENTS, AND RELIGIOUS TERMS	
Buddhism, Jewish, Vedas, Bible, Allah, God	your religion, a religious group, a sacred text, biblical, the deity
TRANSPORTATION	
Greyhound, Amtrak, U.S.S. *Constitution*	a bus, the train, this battleship

54c Capitalizing Titles and Subtitles

In general, capitalize the first and last words of titles and subtitles, as well as any other important words: nouns (*Pride, Persuasion*), verbs (*Is, Ran*), pronouns (*It, Their*), adjectives (*Green, Starry*), and adverbs (*Slow, Extremely*). Do not capitalize prepositions (*in, at, to, by*), coordinating conjunctions (*and, but, for, nor, or, so, yet*), *to* in infinitive verbs, or articles (*a, an, the*) unless they begin or end the title or subtitle or are part of the title of a periodical (*The New Yorker, The New York Times*).

Go Set a Watchman: A Novel

"Uptown Funk" (song)

"In the Basement of the Ivory Tower" (article)

The Dark Knight (movie)

Pokémon XD: Gale of Darkness (game)

Flying Popcorn (software)

NOTE Style guides may recommend different capitalization for titles and subtitles in reference lists and bibliographies. Check the style guide you are using and follow the rules described there.

More about
MLA style,
   304–62
   (ch. 18)
APA style,
   364–405 (ch. 19)
Chicago style,
   406–34
   (ch. 20)
CSE style,
   435–49 (ch. 21)

54d Capitalizing the First-Person Pronoun *I* and the Interjection *O*

In all formal contexts, capitalize the first-person singular pronoun *I*:

▸ I wish I could meet myself in twenty years.

Although rarely used in contemporary prose, the interjection *O* should always be capitalized:

▸ Awake, O north wind, and come, O south wind! —Song of Solomon 4.16

However, the word *oh* should be capitalized only when it begins a sentence:

▸ "Oh literature, oh the glorious art, how it preys upon the marrow in our bones." —D. H. Lawrence

Writing Responsibly   Capitalizing in Email and IM

In general, the rules of capitalization are the same online as they are in print. But while in print a writer may sometimes type a word in all capital letters for emphasis, in email or other online contexts, words typed in all capital letters are interpreted as shouting. When formatting is available, use italics (or boldface type) for emphasis in online writing; when such formatting is unavailable, place an asterisk before and after the word you want to emphasize. Also, although omitting capital letters in email and instant messages may be acceptable in informal contexts, to maintain a professional tone you should follow the rules of capitalization when texting or emailing in business or academic settings.

to SELF

More about
Abbreviations,
848–53
(ch. 56)

acronym Word
formed from the first
letter of each major
word in a name

54e Capitalizing Abbreviations and Acronyms

Abbreviations of proper nouns should be capitalized, and acronyms should
be typed in all capital letters:

| ABBREVIATIONS | U. of Mich., Anthro. Dept. |
| ACRONYMS | RADAR, NASA, OPEC |

EXERCISE 54.1 Correcting capitalization

The following sentences have been typed entirely in lowercase letters.
Supply correct capitalization.

EXAMPLE

When I
~~when i~~ moved into my first apartment this ~~september,~~ i quickly
          September I

                                    I   *Stop   Shop*
realized that i had to watch my pennies at ~~stop~~ and ~~shop~~.

1. when i went shopping with my friend jason, he called me a dumb
   shopper.

2. my cart was filled with products with names like kellogg's, maxwell
   house, and tide, but his cart had mostly store brands.

3. i told him that my mom would ask me, "why do you always have to
   have levi's? aren't the sears jeans just as good?" now that it was my
   own money, i understood.

4. on monday, i saw jason in the english class we have together, and
   as we opened up our books to a short story titled "king of the bingo
   game," i whispered to him, "thanks to you i saved fifteen dollars at
   the supermarket yesterday."

5. as we walked out of tyler hall and headed west to our history class, he
   said, "you'll have more money to spend on fashion if you spend less
   on detergent and ketchup."

Make It **Your Own**

Review your use of abbreviations and acronyms in a recent writing project of two or more pages. Add abbreviations and acronyms where needed and cross through unnecessary ones. Then analyze the impact these changes would have on your reader. (Refer to the sections in this chapter as needed.)

Work **Together**

The rules of capitalization have not always been in place for writers of English. In groups of two or three, revise the passage below to follow today's rules of capitalization in English. Refer to this chapter or to a good dictionary to settle any disputes.

> I do here in the Name of all the Learned and Polite Persons of the Nation, complain to your Lordship, as First Minister, that our Language is extremely imperfect; that its daily Improvements are by no means in proportion to its daily Corruptions; and the Pretenders to polish and refine it, have chiefly multiplied Abuses and Absurdities; and, that in many Instances, it offends against every Part of Grammar.
>
> —Jonathan Swift, *Proposal for Correcting, Improving, and Ascertaining the English Tongue* (1712)

Text Credits

p. 837: Dwight D. Eisenhower, News Conference, Washington, D.C., October 5, 1956. *Public Papers of the United States Presidents: Dwight D. Eisenhower* p. 862. **p. 839:** Song of Solomon 4.16, NET Bible®, copyright © 1996–2006 by Biblical Studies Press, LLC. **p. 839:** Lawrence, D. H., letter of June 10, 1912 to Walter De La Mare, *The Letters of D. H. Lawrence, Volume 1,* edited by James T. Boulton (Cambridge University Press, 1979). **p. 841:** Swift, Jonathan, *A Proposal for Correcting, Improving, and Ascertaining the English Tongue* (1712).

55 Italics and Underlining

IN THIS CHAPTER

a. Titles of longer works, 842

b. Emphasis, 844

c. Names of vehicles, 844

d. Words, letters, and numbers used as words, 844

e. Unfamiliar non-English words, 845

f. Hyperlinks, 845

© George Marks/Hulton Archive/Getty Images

Before the computer, writers typed on typewriters and used underlining to emphasize words; set off the titles of longer works; distinguish words, letters, and numbers used as words; set off unfamiliar non-English words; and call out the names of ships, airplanes, spacecraft, and other vehicles. Now writers type on computers and use italics for these purposes. The Quick Reference box on the next page outlines the most important rules for using italics and underlining.

> *More about*
> Using quotation marks with titles of shorter works, 813

55a Italicizing Titles of Longer Works

Use italics (or underlining) for titles of longer works, such as books, periodicals (magazines, journals, and newspapers), films, CDs, television series, and websites; use quotation marks for shorter works, such as stories, articles, songs, television episodes, and web pages:

▸ Annie Proulx's collection *Close Range: Wyoming Stories* includes the story "Brokeback Mountain," which originally appeared in *The New Yorker* magazine. Kenneth Turan, critic for *The Los Angeles Times,* called the 2005 film *Brokeback Mountain* "groundbreaking," and Roger Ebert of *The Chicago Sun-Times* gave it two thumbs up. The *Brokeback Mountain* soundtrack includes songs like "He Was a Friend of Mine" by Willie Nelson and "The Devil's Right Hand" by Steve Earle.

Quick Reference | **Common Italics Do's and Don'ts**

Do use italics . . .

. . . with titles of longer works. (842)

▶ We will be discussing the novel *Wuthering Heights* for the next two weeks. By the way, the novel's main character has nothing to do with the comic strip *Heathcliff.*

. . . for emphasis. (844)

▶ I ask you *not* to read beyond the first chapter until we have discussed it in class.

(Use italics for emphasis sparingly in academic prose.)

. . . with words, letters, and numbers used as words. (844)

▶ You will notice that several of the characters' names begin with the letter *h;* this can be confusing.

Do not use italics . . .

. . . with titles of short works. (842)

"Girl"

▶ Jamaica Kincaid's story ~~*Girl*~~ is only one page long.
                                    ∧

. . . with historical documents and religious works. (843)

Declaration of Independence   Bible

▶ The ~~*Declaration of Independence*~~ and the ~~*Bible*~~ take pride of
                              ∧   ∧

place on my grandmother's bookshelf.

. . . with links to websites and web pages (underline if a hyperlink). (845)

▶ If you do not want to buy the book that was discussed in Salon.com, you can download it from Project Gutenberg <u>www.gutenberg.org/etext/768</u>.

In addition, stand-alone items like court cases and works of art (paintings and sculptures) are italicized:

▶ *Bowers v. Hardwick*

▶ *Mona Lisa*

▶ *The Bronco Buster*

In contrast, the titles of major historical documents and religious works are not italicized:

▶ Magna Carta, Mayflower Compact, Kyoto Protocol

▶ Bible, Qur'an, Vedas

Writing Responsibly

Using Italics for Emphasis

When using italics for emphasis, consider your reader. Sometimes italics can help convey the writer's feelings, but will readers be interested? In a personal context, the use of italics in the sentence below might be acceptable:

▶ Should *I* call *him*, or should I wait for *him* to call *me*?

But such emphasis on the writer's emotions is usually inappropriate in a business or academic context.

to AUDIENCE

55b Italicizing for Emphasis

Italics are sometimes used for emphasis:

▶ Rowling wants readers to *identify* with Harry, not merely to *sympathize* with him.

In the sentence above, the italics heighten attention to the contrast. To be effective, use italics sparingly for emphasis. Using italics haphazardly or overusing them can annoy or even confuse readers:

▶ He wanted *readers* to know *his* characters, not *merely* to observe them.

55c Italicizing Names of Vehicles

The names of individual trains, ships, aircraft , and spacecraft are all italicized:

Titanic, Spirit of St. Louis, Challenger

However, vehicles referred to by company, brand, or model names are not:

Corvette, Boeing 747

55d Italicizing Words, Letters, or Numbers Used as Words

When referring to words, letters, or numbers used as words, set them off from the rest of the sentence with italics:

▶ My chemistry instructor used the word *interesting* to describe the results I got on my last lab. He told me to be more careful next time, to dot all my *i*'s and cross all my *t*'s.

55e Italicizing Unfamiliar Non-English Words and Latin Genus and Species

More about
Plurals of letters,
807–8

English is an opportunistic language; when encountering new things or ideas, English speakers often adopt words already used in other languages. The word *raccoon,* for example, comes from Algonquian and the word *sushi* from Japanese. Once they are fully absorbed, they are typed with no special formatting. Until then, borrowings should be italicized:

▶ The review provides a good example of *diegesis* in that it describes the film without making a judgment about it.

To determine whether a non-English word warrants italics, check your dictionary: Words familiar enough to be found in a college dictionary should not be set in italics.

Latin genus and species names are also set in italics:

▶ *Acer saccharum* are the Latin genus and species for the sugar maple.

55f Underlining Hyperlinks

In recent years, underlining has taken on a new, specialized meaning: It is used (along with color) to indicate hyperlinks in both printed and online documents (Figure 55.1). Because many documents today will ultimately appear online, writers are increasingly reserving underlining for hyperlinks and using italics for all the other purposes outlined in this chapter.

> **EXERCISE 55.1 Correcting underlining and italics**

Cross through any words or phrases that should not be italicized or underlined, and circle any words or phrases that should be.

EXAMPLE

The 1960s television show ⟨Hogan's Heroes⟩ depicted ~~*Nazism*~~ as a joke, and the show ⟨F Troop⟩ falsified the relationship between ~~*Native Americans*~~ and the military.

1. In a review of the book "Hot, Flat, and Crowded," by Thomas Friedman, David Victor reminds readers that the Soviet Union's 1957 launch of the spacecraft Sputnik galvanized the United States's space program and calls Friedman's book "a plea for a new Sputnik moment."

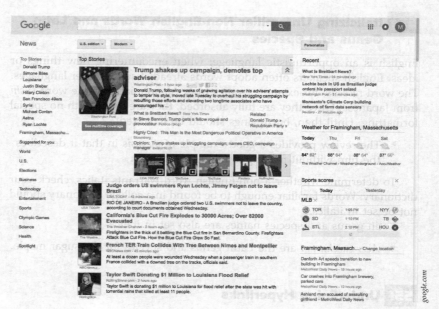

FIGURE 55.1
Hyperlinks The hyperlinks on many web pages (including the Google News page shown here) are set in bright-blue type to set them off from the surrounding text; they are often underlined as well or show underlining when a cursor rolls over the link.

google.com

2. The film The Matrix makes references to Plato's *Cave Allegory* from the book "The Republic" and is indebted to <u>Buddhist</u> philosophy in that it considers the world *maya,* or illusion, a concept expressed in the <u>Buddhist</u> religious works the *Tripitaka.*

3. Thomas Jefferson's motto while writing the Declaration of Independence might have been "novus ordo seclorum," a new order of the ages, for with that document a new nation was born.

4. In 1992, Vice President Dan Quayle mistakenly told a sixth grader that the student had spelled the word potato incorrectly and that the word should not end with an o but with an additional e.

5. Articles on these and other topics appear online in <u>Wikipedia</u>, www.wikipedia.org, but remember that Wikipedia is often more *comprehensive* than *reliable.*

→ EXERCISE 55.2 Adding italics and underlining

Underline any words in the passage below that should be set in italics or underlined, and add quotation marks where needed.

A study reported in the journal Archives of General Psychiatry linked the father's age with the likelihood that his children will develop bipolar disorder. The study, called Advancing Paternal Age and Bipolar Disorder by Emma M. Frans et al., looked for a link between paternal, not maternal, age, although a slight correlation with maternal age was also found. The suspected cause is a type of random mutation among sperm cells called de novo mutations. An article called Advancing Paternal Age and Autism, published two years ago, also found a link between the likelihood of having an autistic child and paternal age. Both articles can be found at the Archives of General Psychiatry website: http://archpsyc.ama-assn.org/.

Make It **Your Own**

Review your use of italics and underlining in a recent writing project of two or more pages. Add italics and underlining where needed and cross through unnecessary ones. Then analyze the impact these changes would have on your reader. (Refer to the sections in this chapter as needed.)

Work **Together**

Exchange Exercise 55.2 with a partner. Check your classmate's use of italics and underlining. Did your partner make any errors? If so, explain the effect these errors had on you as a reader. (Be specific.)

56 Using Abbreviations

When you see this familiar symbol, you know at a glance that the object it adorns was made from recycled materials. When they are familiar to the audience, icons like this one communicate information briefly and quickly. Abbreviations accomplish a similar goal in writing: They convey information rapidly, but they work only when readers know what they stand for.

While used frequently in business, scientific, and technical contexts, abbreviations are used sparingly in writing in the humanities and for a general audience, except in tables (where space is at a premium) and in bibliographic citations.

When you do abbreviate, use a period with a person's initials and with most abbreviations that end in lowercase letters:

> ▶ J. K. Rowling   Perry Mason, Esq.   St. John

> ▶ St.   Blvd.   Ave.

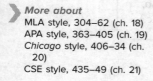

More about
MLA style, 304–62 (ch. 18)
APA style, 363–405 (ch. 19)
Chicago style, 406–34 (ch. 20)
CSE style, 435–49 (ch. 21)

Use a period after each letter with abbreviations of more than one word:

> ▶ i.e.   e.g.   a.m.   p.m.

Most abbreviations made up of all capital letters no longer use periods:

> ▶ BS   MA   DVD   UN

The Quick Reference box on the next page outlines the most important rules for using abbreviations.

Quick

Reference   Common Abbreviation Do's and Don'ts

Do use abbreviations . . .

. . . of titles before or after names. (850)

▶ Dr. Neil deGrasse Tyson *or* Neil deGrasse Tyson, PhD

. . . when they are familiar to readers. (850)

▶ The role of the CIA has changed dramatically since 2001.

. . . with specific numerals and dates. (851)

▶ My class on ancient Rome meets at 8:30 a.m. to study the period from 509 BCE to 476 CE. The book for that class costs $87.50.

. . . in names of businesses when they are part of the official name. (852)

▶ Warner Bros. Entertainment, Inc.   Spindletop Oil & Gas Co.

Do *not* use abbreviations . . .

. . . of titles not used with a proper name. (850)

    doctor   *colonel*

▶ My ~~dr.~~ is married to a ~~col.~~ in the Marines.

. . . of popular online terms in formal prose. (851)

Too much information

▶ ~~TMI~~ with very little focus makes this work a data parade without a point.

. . . of names, words, courses, parts of books, states and countries, days and months, holidays, and units of measurement in formal prose. (851)

    brothers   William   Joseph

▶ My ~~bros.~~ ~~Wm.~~ and ~~Jos.~~, even though they are both now over

    feet   *morning   Christmas*

six ~~ft.~~ tall, still love waking up early in the ~~a.m.~~ on ~~Xmas~~.

. . . of Latin terms. (852)

(Replace with English equivalents in prose.)

                         for example

▶ Leafy green vegetables, ~~e.g.,~~ arugula, kale, and spinach, can reduce the risk of heart disease.

56a　Abbreviating Titles before and after Names

▸ Mr. Mike Moore   Christopher Aviles, PhD

▸ Ms. Aoife Shaughnessy   Namazi Hamid, DDS

▸ Dr. Jonnelle Price   Robert Min, MD

▸ Rev. Jane Genung   Frederick C. Copelston, SJ

In most cases, avoid abbreviating titles when they are not used with a proper name:

                     professor
▸ I'm hoping my English ~~prof.~~ will write me a letter of recommendation.

Academic degrees are an exception:

▸ My auto mechanic comes from a highly educated family: His father has an MS, his mother has an MLS, and his sister has a PhD.

Never use a title both before and after a name: Change *Dr. Hazel L. Cunningham, PhD* to either *Dr. Hazel L. Cunningham* or *Hazel L. Cunningham, PhD*.

56b　Using Familiar Abbreviations: Acronyms and Initialisms

Acronyms and *initialisms* are abbreviations made of all capital letters formed from the first letters of a series of words. Acronyms are pronounced as words (*AIDS, CARE, NASA, NATO, OPEC*), while initialisms are pronounced as a series of letters (*DNA, HBO, JFK, USA*). Familiar acronyms and initialisms are acceptable in any context:

- Myanmar democracy advocate Aung San Suu Kyi met with a number of UN dignitaries during her trip to New York last month.

However, if the abbreviation is likely to be unfamiliar to readers, spell out the term on first use and follow it with the abbreviation in parentheses. Subsequently, just use the abbreviation:

- The International Olympic Committee (IOC) failed to take action following the arrest of two elderly Chinese women who had applied for permission to protest in the designated protest areas during the Beijing Olympics. A spokesperson claimed that the IOC has no control over the protest areas.

Writing Responsibly — Using Online Abbreviations Appropriately

A new breed of initialism has emerged in online discourse. Here are some examples:

BFN (bye for now)	OIC (oh, I see!)
IDK (I don't know)	OTOH (on the other hand)
IMO (in my opinion)	ROTFL (rolling on the floor laughing)
LOL (laughing out loud)	TMI (too much information!)
FWIW (for what it's worth)	TBH (to be honest)

The irreverence of some of these initialisms corresponds with the casual tone of online discourse. Use them in text messages or on informal networking sites, but avoid them in college and professional writing, including emails. While they might establish your online savvy or serve as a handy shorthand, they might also annoy readers in more formal contexts, undermining your ethos (credibility).

to SELF

> *More about*
> Ethos, 145–46

56c Using Abbreviations with Specific Years (BC, BCE, AD, CE), Hours (a.m., p.m.), Numbers (no.), Dollars ($)

▶ The emperor Augustus ruled Rome from 27 BCE until his death in 14 CE.

▶ The Roman historian Titus Livius (known as Livy) lived from 59 BC until AD 17.

▶ I didn't get home until 11:45 p.m. because the no. 27 bus was so late.

▶ I owe my sister $27.32, and she won't let me forget it.

> AD precedes the number; BC, BCE, and CE follow the number.

NOTE The abbreviations BCE (for *before the common era*) and CE (for *common era*) are now generally preferred over BC (*before Christ*) and AD (*anno domini*, "the year of the Lord" in Latin).

56d Avoiding Abbreviations of Names, Words, Courses, Parts of Books, States and Countries, Days and Months, Holidays, and Units of Measurement in Prose

       France,   Christmas   January

▶ In ~~Fr.,~~ people receive gifts not on ~~Xmas~~ but on ~~Jan.~~ 6.

       Monday   Psychology

▶ On ~~Mon.~~ mornings, ~~Psych.~~ 121 meets in a tiny classroom: It is only

feet
ten ~~ft.~~ wide.
       ^

English   *Elizabeth*
▸ My ~~Eng.~~ teacher, ~~Eliz.~~ Santos, recommends that we always read the
       ^   ^
introduction
~~intro.~~ first.
    ^

An exception is the names of businesses, when the abbreviation is part of the official name:

incorporated   *and*
▸ Dun & Bradstreet, Inc., was ~~inc.~~ in New York ~~&~~ is still located there.
                               ^   ^

56e Replacing Latin Abbreviations with English Equivalents in Formal Prose

Latin abbreviations, like those below, are generally avoided in formal writing (except in bibliographies).

▸ e.g.   for example   ▸ cf.   compare
▸ i.e.   in other words   ▸ et al.   and others
▸ etc.   and so forth   ▸ N.B.   note especially

NOTE Both *etc.* and *and so forth* are best avoided in formal prose. Instead, include all the items or precede a partial list with *such as* or *for example*. Follow *e.g.* and *i.e.* with a comma if you use them in tables or parenthetical material. Common Latin abbreviations are not italicized or underlined.

→ EXERCISE **56.1** Correcting abbreviations

Correct the use of abbreviations in the following sentences, which were written for an academic reader in the humanities.

EXAMPLE

spring   *Astronomy*   *History Astronomy*
This ~~spr.~~ I am taking ~~Astro.~~ 121, the ~~Hist.~~ of ~~Astro.~~
     ^   ^   ^   ^

1. My prof. (Dr. Wm. Irvine, PhD.) assigned a fascinating book on Ptolemy (83–168 A.D.), a Gr. astron. and astrol. who lived in Egypt.

2. Ptol. wrote his great treatise on astron., the *Almagest,* in 147 A.D.

3. In addition to the *Almagest,* Ptol. wrote other works, e.g., *Tetrabiblios, Harmonics,* and *Optics,* that are important in their fields.

4. The National Aeronautics and Space Administration has a good website, and one of its pages mentions Ptol.'s model for predicting eclipses, but it says he developed it in about BC 150, which I think is a mistake.

5. The final for this class is scheduled for Jan. 5, after Xmas, so I'm hoping Santa will bring me a copy of the *Almagest,* trans. by GJ Toomer.

6. I would buy a copy of it for myself but, OMG, it costs over 67.50 dollars.

7. To understand Ptol. more fully, I read ch. 2 from Seilik's book, which explains Ptol.'s geocentric model of the universe.

8. Cf. that with Evans's discussion in ch. 1 of *The Hist. and Pract. of Ancient Astro.*

9. I would major in astro. except that all the classes are held in a bldg. on a noisy blvd.

10. Instead, I will major in accounting, get a job with Ernst & Young or Kraft Bros., and study astro. on the side.

Make It **Your Own**

Rewrite a recent text message to avoid abbreviations. Then write a paragraph explaining how this change affects the tone of the message. (If you do not have such a text message, write one using at least two of the abbreviations in the Writing Responsibly box on p. 851.)

Work **Together**

In groups of two or three, craft a text message using as many abbreviations and initialisms as you can. Then trade messages with another group and translate.

57 Using Numbers

© GLG3/Getty Images

Are we "number one" or "#1"? It depends on the context. At a football game, while dressed in your team's colors, you would probably use the numeral: The context is informal and, besides, the word *one* might not fit as well on the giant hand! But just as you would not attend a job interview with your face painted blue and yellow, in many formal contexts spelling out the number is more appropriate.

Rules for deciding whether to use numerals or to spell out numbers vary widely according to context. In business and the news, single-digit numbers are usually spelled out, while numerals are used for numbers over ten. In the humanities, numbers that can be written in one or two words are usually spelled out, while numerals are used for larger numbers. In the sciences, numerals are customarily used for all numbers. The best practice is to choose a style that will make sense to your audience, and then be consistent in its use. The rules that follow are appropriate to an academic audience in the humanities.

> **More about**
> Appropriate language, 562–69 (ch. 30)
> Ethos, 145–46

Writing Responsibly | Ethos and Convention

Using numbers and symbols in conventional ways does not normally affect meaning. Yet conventional usage is important, especially in formal contexts like school or the workplace, because it lends support to your ethos, or credibility. As a marker of appropriateness, it can subtly affect the way your audience perceives you and how seriously they take what you have to say.

to SELF

854

57a Spelling Out Numbers When They Can Be Expressed in One or Two Words

Spell out numbers under a hundred and round numbers—numbers that can be expressed in one or two words:

▶ Satchel Paige pitched sixty-four scoreless innings and won twenty-one games in a row.

If your text uses a combination of numbers—some that can be expressed in one or two words and others that cannot—use numerals throughout for consistency's sake:

2,000

▶ Satchel Paige pitched an estimated ~~two thousand~~ baseball games
                                        ∧
during his career. At his first game, 78,383 fans were in attendance, and at his first game as a starter, 72,434 spectators looked on.

Avoid beginning a sentence with numerals. Instead, spell out the number or revise your sentence:

Seventy-eight thousand

▶ ~~78,000~~ people attended Satchel Paige's first game as a pitcher.
    ∧

▶ Satchel Paige's first game as a pitcher drew 78,000 fans.

Numbers over a million are often best expressed as a combination of words and numerals:

▶ Over 10 million fans attended Negro League baseball games in 1930.

57b Following Conventions for Dates, Times, Addresses, Specific Amounts of Money and Other Quantitative Information, and Divisions of Literary Works

- **Dates:** May 4, 2017   the fourth of May   429 BCE   1066 CE   AD 1066

- **Times, years:** 4:15 p.m.   seven o'clock   1990s   the nineties   1999–2017   from 1999 to 2017

- **Phone numbers, addresses:** (800) 555-5789
  26 Peachtree Lane   221 W. 34th Street
  Atlanta, GA 30303   New York, NY 10001

- **Exact sums of money:** $10.95 $579.89 $24 million
- **Decimals and fractions:** half   ½   three-quarters   ¾   4⅝   3.95

NOTE MLA style generally recommends using the percent symbol (%) with numerals. The *Chicago Manual* recommends using the word *percent* with numerals in writing for the humanities and the symbol % with numerals in writing for the sciences.

- **Scores, statistics, and percentages:** 5 to 4   42–28
  13.3 percent (or 13.3%)   3 out of 10
- **Measurements:** 55 mph   90–100 rpm   135 pounds   5 feet
  9 liters   41°F
- **Divisions of books, plays, poems:** part 3   book 7   chapter 15
  page 419 or p. 419   act 1   scene 3   lines 4–19

Punctuating Numbers in American English Conventions for punctuating numbers differ across cultures. In many European countries, for instance, commas separate whole numbers from decimal fractions, where periods mark divisions of thousands. In the United States, the convention is reversed:

▶ 2,541   94.7

→ **EXERCISE 57.1 Correcting numbers: Spelling out numbers or
   using numerals**

Revise the following sentences according to the rules for using numerals or spelling out numbers discussed above.

EXAMPLE

                 6:30
At about ~~six thirty~~ a.m., the planet Venus is visible low on the horizon;
thirty
  ∧
~~30~~ minutes before that, you can also see Jupiter.
  ∧

1. 1965 saw the first probe reach Mars; it took 22 close-up pictures of the planet and 2 pictures of its moons.

2. The *Mars Pathfinder* was launched on December four, nineteen ninety-six and landed seven months later, on July four, nineteen ninety-seven.

3. *Pathfinder* collected over 16,000 images and conducted 20 tests of the soil.

4. In all, *Pathfinder* collected over two billion bits of data.

5. Mars has a mountain that is seventy-eight thousand feet tall and a canyon that is six to seven times as deep as the Grand Canyon.

6. A Martian day is forty-five minutes longer than an Earth day.

7. Mars is about fifty percent smaller in diameter than Earth: Its diameter is about 4,200 miles, whereas Earth's is about eight thousand miles.

8. Venus, the 6th largest planet, is roughly the size of Earth, at about seven thousand seven hundred miles in diameter.

9. The 2nd closest planet to the sun, its surface can heat up to 900 degrees F.

10. I love to study the night sky, but living at 253 6th Avenue, New York, NY, I can see it only when I travel.

Make It **Your Own**

Review your use of numerals in a recent writing project of two or more pages. Add numerals where needed and cross through unnecessary ones. Then analyze the impact these changes would have on your reader. (Refer to the sections in this chapter as needed.)

Work **Together**

Read the student project in chapter 19 (pp. 397–405). In groups of two or three, discuss whether Heather DeGroot has followed the rules for using numbers laid out in this chapter. What effect does context have on following the rules? What effect would changing her treatment of numbers have on her intended audience?

58 Using Hyphens

More about
Using a dictionary, 582–84

© McGraw-Hill Education

Just as glue can hold pieces of paper, plastic, wood, and glass together, hyphens can bind pieces of a word into a single whole. They join parts of a compound adjective or number, link some prefixes and suffixes to the root word, connect numbers in a fraction, and link word parts that split at the end of a line.

Keep in mind, though, that while some words, like *cross-purposes* or *cross-examination,* use a hyphen, not all compounds need that glue: Some are so closely bound by usage that they have become a single unit (*crosscurrent*), while others are linked merely by placement (*crosshairs*). Consult a dictionary to determine how the parts of a compound should be connected, and if a compound word is not in the dictionary, follow the rules below.

58a Using Hyphens to Form Compounds

1. Hyphenate compound adjectives before the noun but not after.

Hyphenate compound modifiers when they precede the noun but not when they follow it:

noun

▶ The well-intentioned efforts by the International Olympic
  ∧
  Committee (IOC) to allow peaceful protests were blocked by the Chinese government.

Writing
Responsibly Hyphenating with Readers in Mind

Correct hyphenation can make reading easier for your audience, but over-hyphenating may drive readers crazy. When editing your paper, check a dictionary to make sure not only that all compounds are hyphenated correctly but also that you have not added hyphens where they are not needed. Keep a particularly close eye on phrasal (or multiword) verbs and subject complements, which do not need hyphens:

phrasal verb

▶ The police knocked on our door after Fred turned up the volume on the stereo.

subject complement

▶ Fred's new jacket is black and white.

to AUDIENCE

> *More about*
> Phrasal verbs,
> 752–54
> Subject comple-
> ments, 617

noun

▶ The efforts of the IOC to allow peaceful protests were well-intentioned but ill-conceived.

When an adverb ending in *-ly* is part of a compound adjective, no hyphen is necessary:

▶ In China, politically-sensitive websites were blocked by the government.

When two or more parallel compound adjectives share the same base word, avoid repetition by putting a space after the first hyphen and stating the base word only once:

Class- and race-based analyses of *To Kill a Mockingbird* show that Harper Lee was not completely able to rise above her social background.

2. Use a hyphen to link certain prefixes and suffixes to the root word.

In general, hyphens are not needed to attach prefixes and suffixes to the root word:

*de*compress   *pre*test   *re*define   *sub*category

But the prefixes *all-*, *ex-*, and *self-* and the suffix *-elect* are always attached to the root word with a hyphen:

▶ *all*-star   *ex*-boyfriend   *self*-absorbed   president-*elect*

When *all, elect, self,* and even *ex* (a word in Latin, meaning *from*) are freestanding words, they do not need a hyphen:

- ▸ *all* the participants in the game
- ▸ to *elect* the candidates
- ▸ her sense of *self*
- ▸ an *ex* officio member

In most cases, to avoid double or triple letter combinations, add a hyphen:

- ▸ *anti*-inflationary   *multi*-institutional   *re*-education   ball-*like*
- ▸ Exceptions: override   cooperate

If the prefix will be attached to a numeral or to a root that begins with a capital letter, insert a hyphen:

- ▸ post-1914   pre-1945   anti-Semite   un-American

Finally, if the prefix-plus-root combination could be misread as another word, add a hyphen to avoid confusion:

- ▸ He finally recovered from a bout of the flu.
- ▸ We re-covered the sofa with a floral fabric.

3. Use a hyphen in compound numbers under one hundred, between scores (in sports), and between numbers (to replace *from . . . to*).

Numbers over twenty and under one hundred are hyphenated when written out:

- ▸ Workaholics would work twenty-four hours a day, seven days a week, fifty-two weeks a year if their bodies would cooperate.

In sports scores, use a hyphen between numbers instead of *to.*

- ▸ The Vikings lost to the Bengals 23-17.

A hyphen can replace the words *from* and *to* with dates:

- ▸ The years from 1919 to 1938 offered a brief respite between the two world wars.

or

▶ The years 1919-1938 offered a brief respite between the two world wars.

But do not combine methods:

▶ from 1919/1938   or   ~~from~~ 1919-1938

to

58b Using Hyphens to Break Words at the Ends of Lines

Word processing programs generally "wrap" text (that is, they move a too-long word at the end of a line to the beginning of the next line). Still, you may occasionally need to break words manually. If you do, follow these rules:

syllable breaks

re·spon·si·bil·i·ty (ri spon'sə bil'i tē), *n., pl.* **-ties.** 1. the state, fact, or quality of being responsible. 2. an instance of being responsible: *The responsibility for this mess is yours!* 3. a particular burden of obligation upon one who is responsible: *the responsibilities of authority.* 4. a person or thing for which one is responsible.

FIGURE 58.1
Syllable breaks in the dictionary
Dictionaries indicate syllabification by placing dots between syllables.

- Break words between syllables. (Check your dictionary for syllable breaks, such as those shown in Figure 58.1.)

  ▶ CIA operatives in the Middle East have found it impossible to ~~infiltr~~ ~~ate~~ al Qaeda.

  infil-
  trate

- Break compound words between parts or after hyphens.

  ▶ Washington, DC's long-standing handgun ban was ~~overturn~~ ~~ed~~ in 2008 by the Supreme Court.

  over-
  turned

- Do not break one-syllable words or contractions.

  ▶ To determine surface area, multiply the ~~wid~~ ~~th~~ of a room by its length.

  width

- Break words so that at least two letters remain at the end of a line and at least three letters move down to the beginning of the next line.

  ▶ Increases in the cost of gas and food have ~~reduc~~ ~~ed~~ discretionary spending.

  re-
  duced

Tech **Breaking URLs and Email Addresses**

Most word processing programs offer automatic hyphenation of words. However, you must break URLs or email addresses manually. If you are following MLA or CSE style guidelines, break URLs only after a slash. If you are following *Chicago Manual* guidelines, break a URL or email address before a period or other punctuation, or after the @ symbol, a single or double slash, or a colon. Do *not* insert a hyphen.

> ## EXERCISE 58.1 Adding and deleting hyphens

Add and delete hyphens as needed in the following sentences. (You may consult a dictionary.)

EXAMPLE

The Deadhead phenomenon began in the mid-1960s, when the
                                                        ^

Grateful Dead became active in the Haight-Ashbury music scene.
                                                ^

1. In 1971, a long time friend of the Grateful Dead took on a self assigned project to put together a mailing list to keep fans informed of upcoming shows.
2. Clearly, there were more than just fifty or seventy five people on this list, because city to city caravans of tie dye wearing Deadheads soon sprang up.
3. Their long distance travel was motivated by changes night to night in the songs the musicians played.
4. Shows sold out for the long lived and well loved band, and a true blue community of Deadheads was created.
5. Although the band is now defunct, well and long proven loyalty is still highly-visible in thruway rest stops, where large groups of slack jawed fans, exhausted from concerts by Grateful Dead spinoff bands like RatDog and Phil Lesh and Friends, still congregate.

> ## EXERCISE 58.2 Correcting hyphens

Using a dictionary, correct the passage below, adding and deleting hyphens or revising as needed:

Attention Deficit Hyperactivity Disorder (ADHD) was first described in a children's book called "The Story of Fidgety Philip" (1845), written for the author's three year old son. Today, the National Institute of Mental Health estimates that from 3-5 percent of children have ADHD. But diagnosis is difficult because loss of self control and attention is common. To be diagnosed, children must have difficulties in two or more of the following areas: school-, social-, community-, home-, or playground-behavior. Other causes of inattention or hyperactivity include middle-ear infections that cause hearing loss, seizure disorders, and learning disabilities. Baby-sitters and class-room teachers frequently notice problems and recommend testing, but well-qualified and highly-experienced clinicians are best able to diagnose the disorder and recommend treatment.

Make It **Your Own**

Review your use of hyphens in a recent writing project of two or more pages. Add hyphens where needed and cross through unnecessary ones. Then analyze the impact these changes would have on your reader. (Refer to the sections in this chapter as needed.)

Work **Together**

Exchange Exercise 58.2 with a classmate. Check your partner's use of hyphens. Did he or she make any errors? If so, explain the effect these errors had on you as a reader. (Be specific.)

Glossary of Key Terms

A

ableism (185, 193)   The practice of treating disabled people as inferior to non-disabled people.

absolute phrase (554, 622)   A phrase consisting of a noun or pronoun followed by a participle (the *-ing* or *-ed* form of a verb) that modifies an entire clause or sentence: *Our spirits rising, we began our vacation.*

abstract (113, 218, 447)   Overview of a text, including a summary of its main claims and most important supporting points.

abstract noun (603)   See *noun.*

acronym (385, 840, 850)   An abbreviation formed from the first letters of a series of words and pronounced as a word (*AIDS, NASA*). Compare *initialism.*

active voice (525, 617, 680)   See *voice.*

adjective (553, 608, 697, 762)   A word that modifies a noun or pronoun with descriptive or limiting information, answering questions such as *what kind, which one,* or *how many: a happy camper, the tall building.*

adjective clause (623)   A subordinate clause, usually beginning with a relative pronoun (such as *who, whom, which,* or *that*), that modifies a noun or pronoun: *Sam baked the pie that won first prize.* Adjective clauses can also begin with the subordinating conjunctions *when* and *where.*

adverb (553, 609–10, 697, 762)   A word that modifies a verb, adjective, other adverb, or entire phrase or clause, answering questions such as *how? where? when?* and *to what extent or degree? The door opened abruptly.*

adverb clause (623, 788)   A subordinate clause, usually introduced by a subordinating conjunction such as *although, because,* or *until,* that functions as an adverb within a sentence: *I walk to work because I need the exercise.*

agreement (648–93)   The matching of form between one word and another.

Verbs must agree with, or match, their subjects in person and number (subject-verb agreement), and pronouns must agree in person, number, and gender with their antecedents (pronoun-antecedent agreement). See also *antecedent, gender, number, person.*

alignment (166)   Arrangement in a straight line (vertical, horizontal, or diagonal) of elements on a page or screen to create connections among parts and ideas.

alternating pattern of organization (66)   A method of organizing a comparison-contrast paragraph or essay by discussing each common or divergent trait of both items before moving on to the next trait. See also *block pattern of organization.*

analogy (574)   An extended comparison of something familiar with something unfamiliar. (See also *figurative language, simile, metaphor.*) An analogy becomes a false analogy (150) when the items being compared have no significant shared traits.

analysis (68, 124–26, 197)   The process of dividing an entity, concept, or text into its component parts to study its meaning and function. Analysis is central to critical reading and is a common strategy for developing paragraphs and essays in academic writing. Also called *classification, division.*

annotated bibliography (207–09)   A bibliography that includes not only retrieval information for each source but also information about the source, such as its content, its relevance to the writer's project, or the writer's evaluation of it.

annotation (118, 121)   The process of taking notes on a text, including writing down definitions, identifying key concepts, highlighting unfamiliar vocabulary and words that reveal tone, and making connections or noting personal responses.

antecedent (605, 658, 684)   The noun or noun phrase to which a pronoun

refers. In the sentence *The pitcher caught the ball and threw it to first base,* the noun *ball* is the antecedent to the pronoun *it.*

antonyms (581)   Words with opposite meanings—for example, *good* and *bad.* Compare *synonyms.*

APA style (363–405)   The citation and documentation style of the American Psychological Association, used frequently in the social sciences.

appeals (144–46)   Efforts to engage the reader. Emotional appeals (**pathos**) engage the reader's feelings; intellectual appeals (**logos**) engage the reader's rational faculties; ethical appeals (**ethos**) engage the reader's sense of fairness and respect for good character.

appositive (554, 619, 633, 688)   A noun or noun phrase that renames a preceding noun or noun phrase and is grammatically equivalent to it: *Miguel, my roommate, avoids early morning classes.*

arguable claim (136–63)   A claim on which reasonable people might hold differing opinions and that can be supported by evidence.

argument (11, 136)   An attempt to persuade others to accept your opinion by providing logical supporting evidence. See also *persuasive argument, purpose.*

article (744–51)   The words *a, an,* and *the. A* and *an* are **indefinite articles;** *the* is a **definite article.** The **zero article** refers to nouns that appear with no article.

asynchronous media (186)   Communication media such as email and discussion lists that allow users to participate at their own convenience. Compare *synchronous media;* see also *discussion list.*

audience (13–22, 90, 167, 188)   The intended readers for a written text or listeners for a presentation.

authority (130, 160)   An expert on a topic. An authority becomes a false authority when the person from whom the writer draws evidence is not truly an expert on the topic.

B

bar graph (80, 81)   An information graphic that compares data in two or more categories using bars of different heights or lengths.

belief (140–41)   A conviction based on values.

biased or hurtful language (119, 565)   Language that unfairly or offensively characterizes a group and, by extension, the individual members of that group.

bibliographic notes (345)   Notes that add information or point readers to other sources on the topic.

bibliography (214–17)   A list of works cited in a text, with full retrieval information (usually including author, title, publisher, date of publication, and type of publication) for each entry. Bibliographies are usually constructed following a style sheet such as MLA or APA. In *Chicago* style, the word bibliography is used for the end-of-project source list; in APA, it is called a reference list; and in MLA, it is called list of works cited.

block pattern of organization (67)   A method of organizing a paragraph or text by discussing all the significant traits of one item (such as a source, event, or theory) before moving on to discuss all the traits of another item. See also *alternating method.*

block quotations (308)   Exact quotations of longer than four lines (MLA style) or forty words (APA style) in which quotation marks are omitted and the quotation is indented as a block from the left margin of the text.

block-style letter (499)   A format for business letters in which all text is flush with the left margin and a line space is inserted before paragraphs. In **modified block style**, all text begins flush left except for the return address, date, closing, and signature.

blog (or **weblog**) (180, 336, 321)   An online journal that chronicles thoughts, opinions, and information often on a single topic. See also *asynchronous media.*

body (38–39, 189)   The portion of a text or presentation that develops and supports the thesis.

Boolean operator (221–22)   The terms *and, not,* and *or* used in databases and search engines for refining keyword searches.

brainstorming or listing (26)   A technique for generating ideas by listing all the ideas that come to you during a fixed amount of time; brainstorming can also take place in groups.

breadcrumb trail (or **click trail**) (181)   The sequence of links followed while navigating pages on a website.

C

case (685–92)   The form of a noun or pronoun that corresponds to its grammatical role in a sentence. Many pronouns have three cases: **subjective** (for example, *I, we, he, she, they, who*), **objective** (for example, *me, us, him, her, them, whom*), and **possessive** (for example, *mine, ours, his, hers, theirs, whose*). Nouns change form only to indicate possession.

cause and effect (68)   A method of paragraph or essay development that explains why something happened or what its consequences were or will be.

Chicago **style** (205)   The citation and documentation style recommended in the *Chicago Manual of Style,* used frequently in the humanities.

chronological organization (40)   A pattern of organization in which events are discussed in the order in which they occurred; chronological organization is used when telling a story (narrative) or explaining a process (process analysis).

citation (275, 304, 363)   The acknowledgment of sources in the body of a research project, usually tagged to a bibliography, works-cited list, or reference list. See also *in-text citation, parenthetical citation, signal phrase.*

citation-name system (436–37)   In CSE style, a system of acknowledgment for research projects that provides a superscript number in the text and a list of references, numbered in alphabetical order (usually by author's surname) at the end of the project.

citation-sequence system (436–37)   In CSE style, a system of acknowledgment for research projects that provides a superscript number in the text and a list of references, numbered in order of appearance, at the end of the project.

claim (36, 37, 136, 140, 141)   An assertion that is supported by evidence. A *claim of fact* asserts a verifiable piece of information; it can be a central claim in an informative text but not in an argumentative text. A *claim of causation* asserts the causes or effects of a problem; a *claim of policy* asserts how best to resolve a problem or what is the best course of action to take; a *claim of judgment or value* asserts that one's personal beliefs or convictions should be embraced. Claims of causation, policy, and value are all appropriate central claims in argumentative texts.

classical model (157)   A model for organizing an argument composed of five parts: introduction, background, evidence, counterclaims and counterevidence, and conclusion. Compare *Rogerian* and *Toulmin models.*

classification See *analysis.*

clause (526–28, 535–38, 622–25, 734)   A word group with a subject and a predicate. An **independent clause** can stand on its own as a sentence. A **subordinate** (or **dependent**) **clause** functions within a sentence as a noun, adjective, or adverb but cannot stand as a sentence on its own. See also *sentence.*

cliché (556–77)   A figure of speech, idiom, or other expression that has grown stale from overuse. See also *figurative language, idiom.*

click trail see *Breadcrumb Trail.*

climactic organization (40)   A pattern of organization that orders supporting paragraphs from least to most engaging or compelling.

clustering or mapping (27–28)   An idea-generating technique for organizing, developing, or discovering connections among ideas by writing a topic in the center of the page, adding related topics and subtopics around the central topic, and connecting them to show relationships.

coauthorship (51)   Two or more writers working together to research, brainstorm, compose, revise, or edit a text.

coherence, coherent (43, 52, 58)   The quality of a text in which sentences and paragraphs are organized logically and clearly so that readers can move from idea to idea without having to puzzle out the relationships among parts.

collaborative learning (31–33, 51) A process by which classmates or colleagues enhance understanding by studying together and reviewing one another's writing.

collective noun (653) See *noun.*

colloquialism (563) An informal expression common in speech but usually out of place in formal writing.

comma splice (639–46, 780, 799) The incorrect joining of two independent clauses with a comma alone—without a coordinating conjunction.

common knowledge (250) General information that is available from a number of different sources and that is considered factual and incontestable. Common knowledge does not require documentation.

common noun (743) See *noun.*

commonplace book (25) A written record (quotations, summaries, paraphrases) of the ideas of others and your own reactions to those ideas, preserved in a notebook or online document.

comparative form (702–05) See *comparison of adjectives and adverbs.*

comparison and contrast (66) A pattern of paragraph or essay development in which the writer points out the similarities and differences among items. See also *alternating method, block method.*

comparison of adjectives and adverbs (702–04) The form of an adjective or adverb that indicates the relative degree of the quality or manner it specifies. The **positive form** is the base form of the adjective (for example, *brave*) or adverb (for example, *bravely*). The **comparative form** indicates a relatively greater or lesser degree (*braver, more bravely*). The **superlative form** indicates the greatest or least degree (*bravest, most bravely*).

complement (616–17) See *subject complement, object complement.*

complete predicate (615) See *predicate.*

complete subject (613) See *subject.*

complete verb (628–29) A main verb together with any helping verbs needed to express tense, mood, and voice.

complex sentence (552, 626, 800) See *sentence.*

compound-complex sentence (552, 626) See *sentence.*

compound predicate (633–34) See *predicate.*

compound sentence (552, 626, 780) See *sentence.*

compound subject (580, 651) See *subject.*

conciseness (520) The statement of something in the fewest and most effective words needed for clarity and full understanding.

conclusion (39, 113, 189) The closing paragraph or section in a text. An effective conclusion provides readers with a sense of closure.

concrete noun (603) See *noun.*

conditional clause (679–80) A subordinate clause that begins with *if* and describes a set of circumstances (*conditions*) and that modifies an independent clause that describes what follows from those circumstances.

conjunction (611, 651) A word that joins a word, phrase, or clause to other words, phrases, or clauses and specifies the way the joined elements relate to one another. **Coordinating conjunctions** (*and, but, or, for, nor, yet,* and *so*) join grammatically equivalent elements, giving them each equal significance: *Jack and Jill went up the hill.* **Correlative conjunctions** are pairs of terms (such as *either … or, neither … nor,* and *both … and*) that join grammatically equivalent elements: *Both Jack and Jill fell down.* **Subordinating conjunctions** link subordinate clauses to the clauses they modify. *After Jack and Jill went up the hill, they both fell down.*

conjunctive adverb (609, 783) A transitional expression (such as *for example, however,* and *therefore*) that can relate one independent clause to a preceding independent clause.

connected (52) See *transition.*

connotation (19, 93, 572) The emotional resonance of a word. Compare *denotation.*

container (326, 331, 335, 338) When documenting a source, if it is part of a larger whole, in MLA style that whole—that host—is called a ***container***, and it is part of the entry in the list of works cited.

content notes (335) Footnotes or endnotes that clarify or justify a point in your text or that acknowledge the contributions of others in the preparation of your project.

context (13, 21, 32, 168, 187) The social, rhetorical, and historical setting in which a text is produced or read. The context in which Lincoln's Gettysburg Address was produced is different from the context in which it may be read today, but both are important for fully understanding the text.

contrast (166) In design, differences that call attention to and highlight one element among others.

coordinate adjectives (785) Two or more adjectives that separately and equally modify the noun they precede. Coordinate adjectives should be separated by a comma: *an innovative, exciting vocal group.*

coordinating conjunction (780) See *conjunction.*

coordination (529–34) The joining of elements of equal weight or importance in a sentence. See also *subordination.*

correlative conjunction (545) See *conjunction.*

counterevidence (137, 147–48) Evidence that undermines or contradicts your claim.

count noun (or **countable noun**) (743) See *noun.*

critical reading and thinking (112–35) A careful, systematic approach to a text or idea, going below the surface to uncover meaning and draw conclusions. Critical reading and thinking begins with reading actively; it requires analysis, interpretation, synthesis, and critique.

critique (129–35, 453, 460) An evaluation based on evidence accumulated through careful reading, analysis, interpretation, and synthesis. It may be positive, negative, or a bit of both.

CSE style (205) The citation and documentation style recommended in *Scientific Style and Format: The CSE Manual for Authors, Editors, and Publishers,* used frequently in the sciences.

cumulative adjectives (785) Two or more adjectives that modify not only the noun or pronoun they precede but also the next adjective in the series. Cumulative adjectives should not be separated by commas: *A great American rock band.*

cumulative sentence (555)   A sentence that begins with the subject and verb of an independent clause and accumulates additional information in subsequent modifying phrases and clauses: *The mountaineers set off, anticipating the view from the peak but wary of the dangers they faced to get there.*

D

dangling modifier (719–22)   A word, phrase, or clause that erroneously does not actually modify the subject or anything else in a sentence, leaving it to the reader to infer the intended meaning. In the sentence *As your parent, you should put on a sweater when it is cold,* the phrase *as your parent* dangles; it appears illogically to modify the subject, *you,* but actually refers to the speaker, as in *As your parent, I recommend that you put on a sweater when it is cold.*

database (220–23, 330)   A collection of data, now usually available in digital form. In research, databases provide citations to articles in academic journals, magazines, and newspapers.

declarative sentence (558)   See *sentence.*

deductive reasoning (137–39)   A form of reasoning that moves from a general principle to a specific case to draw a conclusion; if the premises are true, the conclusion must be true. Compare *inductive reasoning;* see also *syllogism.*

definite article (744)   See *article.*

definition (68–69, 119, 317)   An explanation of the meaning of a word or concept made by including it in a larger class and then providing the characteristics that distinguish it from other members of that class: In the definition *People are reasoning animals, people* is the term to be defined, *animals* is the larger class to which people belong, and *reasoning* is the trait that distinguishes people from other animals. Also, a pattern of paragraph or essay development in which the writer explains the special meaning of a term by explaining what the term includes and excludes.

degree (702–04)   See *comparison of adjectives and adverbs.*

demonstrative pronouns (605)   The pronouns *this, that, these,* and *those* used as nouns or adjectives to rename and point to nouns or noun phrases: *These are interesting times we live in.*

denotation (93, 570)   The literal meaning of a word; its dictionary definition. Compare *connotation.*

dependent clause (622)   A subordinate clause. See *clause.*

description (65)   A pattern of paragraph or essay development that draws on specific, concrete details to depict a scene or object in terms of the senses: seeing, hearing, smelling, touching, tasting.

determiner (608, 743)   An article (*a, an,* or *the*) or a possessive, demonstrative, or indefinite pronoun that functions as an adjective to specify or quantify the noun it modifies: *a cat, some cats, that cat, her cat.*

development (45–47, 65, 69, 271–73)   The depth at which a topic or idea is explored.

dialect (563)   A language variety with its own distinctive pronunciation, vocabulary, and grammar.

diction (570)   The choice of words that will best convey an idea.

direct object (617, 737)   See *object.*

direct question (712)   A sentence that asks a question and ends with a question mark. Compare *indirect question.*

direct quotation (683, 759)   A copy of the exact words that someone has written or spoken, enclosed in quotation marks or, for longer quotations, indented as a block. Compare *indirect quotation.*

direct source (711)   A text that you are yourself reading (as contrasted to a source *quoted in* a text you are reading).

discussion (394, 447, 429)   In APA and CSE style, the last section of a research project; the Discussion section provides the writer's opinion of the implications of the research.

discussion list (182–83)   An electronic mailing list that enables a group of people to participate in email conversations on a specific topic. See also *asynchronous media.*

division (68, 123–26, 197)   See *analysis.*

documentation (304, 363)   Information in a bibliography, reference list, or list of works cited that allows readers to locate a source cited in the text. See also *citation.*

document design (166–73)   The arranging and formatting of text elements on a page or screen using proximity (nearness), alignment, repetition, and contrast to indicate their relative importance and their relation to each other.

DOI (204, 416, 423)   Digital object identifier, a permanent identifier assigned to electronic publications.

domain (240–42)   The ending of the main portion of a URL; the most common domains are *.com* (commercial), *.edu* (educational), *.gov* (governmental), and *.net* (network).

double-entry reading journal (122–24)   An online or printed journal with one column for passages from sources (quotations, summaries, or paraphrases) and another column for the writer's response to the passage.

doublespeak (566)   Euphemisms that are deliberately deceptive, used to obscure bad news or sanitize an ugly truth.

drafting (44–46, 271–73)   The stage of the writing process in which the writer puts ideas on paper in complete sentences and paragraphs.

E

editing (94–96)   The stage of the writing process in which the writer fine-tunes the draft by correcting words and sentences and revises them to enhance clarity and power.

ellipses (831–32)   A set of three periods, or *ellipsis points,* with a space between each. Ellipses are used to replace words deleted from quotations; they are also sometimes used to create a dramatic pause or to suggest that the writer is unable or unwilling to say something.

elliptical construction (523, 728)   A construction in which grammatically necessary words can be omitted as understood because their meaning and function are otherwise clear from the context: *The movie [that] we saw last night is excellent.*

endnote (407)   A note that appears in a list at the end of the project.

entertaining text (14)   See *purpose.*

essential (or **restrictive**) **element** (636, 788)   A word, phrase, or clause that provides essential information about the word or words it modifies. Essential elements are not set off by commas: *The train that she is on has been delayed.* See also *nonessential element.*

et al. (310, 369)   Abbreviation of the Latin phrase *et alia,* "and others."

ethos (144)   See *appeals.*

euphemism (566)   An inoffensive word or expression used in place of one that might be offensive or emotionally painful.

evaluation (233–48)   In research, assessment of sources to determine their relevance and reliability.

evidence (90)   The facts, examples, statistics, expert opinions, and other information writers use to support their claims.

excessive coordination (533–34)   The joining of tediously long strings of independent clauses with *and* and other conjunctions.

excessive subordination (538–39)   The stringing together of too many subordinate structures.

exclamatory sentence (613)   See *sentence.*

exemplification (66)   A pattern of paragraph or essay development that explains by example or illustration.

expletive construction (524, 614, 735)   A kind of inverted construction in which *there* or *it* precedes a form of the verb *to be* and the subject follows the verb: *There are seven days in a week.*

explicate (460)   To read a text closely, analyzing it line by line or even word by word; explications of a text are common in literary analysis.

exploratory argument (136)   An argument in which the author considers a wide range of evidence before arriving at the most plausible position; in exploratory arguments, the thesis is often offered at the conclusion of the text. See also *argument, persuasive argument, purpose.*

expository report (140)   See *informative report.*

expressive text (14)   See *purpose.*

F

fact (140)   A piece of information that can be verified.

fallacy (119, 159)   A mistake in reasoning.

familiar to unfamiliar (40)   A method of organization that begins with material that is known by the audience and moves toward material that the audience will not know.

faulty predication (725–27)   A logical or grammatical mismatch between subject and predicate.

field research (229–32)   The gathering of research data in person rather than from sources. Field research includes interviews, observational studies, and surveys. See also *primary source.*

figurative language or **figures of speech** (575–76)   The imaginative use of language to convey meaning in ways that reach beyond the literal meaning of the words involved. See *analogy, hyperbole, irony, metaphor, personification, simile, understatement.*

flaming (186)   Writing a scathing, often ad hominem, response to someone with whom the writer disagrees, usually in email or on Internet forums.

focused freewriting (26)   See *freewriting.*

font (169–70)   Typeface; fonts may be serif (such as Times Roman) or sans serif (such as Arial), may be set in boldface, italics, or underlining, and may be in a larger or smaller size (the most common sizes are 10 point and 12 point).

footer (345)   Material (most often a page number, sometimes accompanied by title or author's name) appearing at the bottom of every page of a text.

footnote (407)   A note that appears at the bottom of the page.

formal outline (41–42)   See *outline.*

formalist approach (453)   An approach to literature and art that focuses on the work itself rather than on the author's life or other theoretical approaches.

format (101–05)   The look of a document created by choice of font and color and use of white space, lists, headings, and visuals. See also *layout.*

fragment (619, 628)   An incomplete sentence punctuated as if it were complete, beginning with a capital letter and ending with a period, question mark, or exclamation point.

freewriting (26–27)   An idea-generating technique that requires writing nonstop for a fixed period of time (often ten to fifteen minutes); in *focused freewriting,* the writer writes nonstop about a specific topic or idea.

function word (546)   A word that indicates the relationship among other words in a sentence. Examples include **articles, conjunctions,** and **prepositions.**

funnel introduction (70–72)   An essay introduction that begins with broad statements and narrows in focus to conclude with the thesis statement. See also *introduction.*

fused sentence or **run-on sentence** (639–47)   A sentence in which one independent clause improperly follows another with no punctuation or joining words between them.

future perfect progressive tense (675)   See *tense.*

future perfect tense (673)   See *tense.*

future progressive tense (674)   See *tense.*

future tense (673–75)   See *tense.*

G

gender (657)   The classification of nouns and pronouns as feminine (*woman, mother, she*), masculine (*man, father, he*), or neuter (*table, book, it, they*).

gender bias (567)   Stereotyping people according to their gender.

general to specific (40)   A method of organization that begins with a general statement (the **thesis statement** or **topic sentence**) and proceeds to provide specific supporting evidence.

generalization (159)   A broad statement. If not supported by specific details, a generalization becomes a hasty generalization (jumping to conclusions) or a sweeping generalization (application of a claim to all cases when it applies only to a few).

generic noun (658)   A noun used to designate a whole class of people or things rather than a specific individual or individuals: *the average child.*

genre (13, 20–22, 168, 187)   A category or type of writing; in literature, genres include poetry, fiction, and drama; in college writing, genres may include analytical essays, case studies, or observational reports.

gerund (548, 620, 656, 689, 755)   The present participle of a verb (the *-ing* form) used as a noun: *Walking is good exercise.*

grammar (602)   The rules of a language that structure words so they can convey meaning.

grounds (144)   In an argument, the evidence that supports the claim. See *Toulmin model.*

H

header (345–46)   Material (most often a page number, sometimes accompanied by title or author's name) appearing at the top of every page of a text.

heading (173–74)   A brief caption describing or labeling a section of text.

helping verb or auxiliary verb (605, 607, 667–70)   A verb that combines with a main verb to provide information about tense, voice, mood, and manner. Helping verbs include forms of *be, have,* and *do* and the modal verbs *can, could, may, might, must, shall, should, will, would,* and *ought to.*

home page (107, 179, 181)   On a website, the page designed to introduce visitors to the site.

homonyms (583, 587)   Words that sound exactly alike but have different spellings and meanings: *their, there, they're.*

HTML (218, 407)   Hypertext Markup Language, a coding system used to format texts for the web.

hyperbole (574)   Deliberate exaggeration for emphasis: *That restaurant makes the best pizza in the universe.* See *figurative language.*

hyperlink (181)   A navigation tool that allows users to jump from place to place on a web page or from web page to web page; hyperlinks (or links) appear as highlighted words or images on a web page.

hypertext (180)   An online text that provides links to other online files, texts, images, audio files, and video files, allowing readers to jump to other related sites rather than reading *linearly.*

hypothesis (199-200, 228, 231)   A proposed answer to a research question that is subject to testing and modification during the research process.

I

idea journal (24–25)   An online or printed record of your thoughts that you can draw on to develop or explore a topic.

idiom (576)   A customary expression whose meaning cannot be determined from the literal meaning of the words that compose it: *They struggled to make ends meet.*

imperative (630, 678)   See *mood, sentence.*

indefinite article (744-51)   See *article.*

indefinite pronoun (653, 658, 804)   A pronoun such as *anybody, anyone, somebody, some,* or *several* that does not refer to a specific person or thing.

independent clause (622, 626, 639, 780, 797, 837)   See *clause.*

indicative (678)   See *mood.*

indirect object (618, 737)   See *object.*

indirect question (712)   A sentence that reports a question and ends with a period: My teacher asked us *if we texted each other even when we're in the same room.* Compare *direct question.*

indirect quotation (711, 790)   A sentence that uses paraphrase or summary to report what someone has said rather than quoting word-for-word. Indirect quotations need to be cited but should not be marked with quotation marks or block indenting. Compare *direct quotation.*

indirect source (296–97, 316-17, 372, 422)   If you read a text that quotes or uses ideas from another source, that other source is for you an "indirect source": You are not reading that other source yourself but are reading about its ideas. If you want to use that material from the indirect source, you should acknowledge the indirect source as well as the source that was talking about it.

inductive reasoning (137)   A form of reasoning that draws conclusions based on specific examples or facts. Compare *deductive reasoning.*

infinitive (621, 676, 689, 755–56)   A verbal formed by combining *to* with the base form of the verb (*to decide, to eat, to study*). Infinitives can function as adjectives and adverbs as well as nouns. See *verbal.*

informal (scratch) outline (40)   See *outline.*

information graphics (80–83)   Graphics that convey and depict relationships among data; information graphics include tables, bar graphs, line graphs, and pie charts.

informational note (391–92, 397)   In APA style, a note that occurs on the first page of a text to identify the author, provide contact information, and acknowledge support and conflicts of interest; student projects usually omit informational, or author, notes.

informative (or **expository**) **report** (14, 36, 140)   A text in which the main purpose is to explain a concept or report information. See also *purpose.*

initialism (850)   Abbreviation formed from the first letters of a series of words and pronounced as letters (*DNA, HBO*). Compare *acronym.*

inseparable (755)   A transitive phrasal verb whose direct object can fall only after the particle, not before it.

intensive pronoun (606)   A pronoun that renames and emphasizes its antecedent: *Dr. Collins herself performed the operation.*

interjection (612)   Words like *alas* and *ugh* that express strong feeling but otherwise serve no grammatical function.

interpret, interpretation (123–27, 453)   Explain the meaning or significance of a text, artwork, or event.

interpretive analysis (459–61)   An in-depth interpretation of the meaning or significance of literary texts, cultural works, political events, and so on.

interrogative pronoun (685, 691)   A pronoun such as *who, whom, whose, what,* or *which* used to introduce a question: *What did she say?*

interrogative sentence (613)   See *sentence.*

interesting (52)   Paragraphs and essays that make the audience want to continue reading.

in-text citation (276, 304, 363, 435)   A citation that appears in the body of the research project. See also *parenthetical citation, signal phrase.*

intransitive verb (616, 671–72)   A verb that does not require a direct object: *The child smiled.*

introduction (39, 69, 113, 189, 447) The opening paragraph or section of a text. An effective introduction should identify your topic and your stance toward the topic, establish your purpose, and engage your readers. See also *funnel introduction.*

invention techniques (24–29) Prewriting strategies that help you generate and explore ideas. See *brainstorming, freewriting.*

inversion (556) An inversion is a sentence in which, contrary to normal English word order, the verb precedes the subject, usually to emphasize the point being made.

inverted-funnel conclusion (71) A conclusion that begins with a restatement of the thesis (in different words) and broadens out to discuss implications, next steps, or possible solutions. See also *conclusion.*

irony (574) The use of language to suggest the opposite of its literal meaning or to express an incongruity between what is expected and what occurs. See *figurative language.*

irregular verb (666–67) A verb that does not form the past tense or past participle by adding *-ed* to the base form.

J

jargon (564) The specialized vocabulary of a particular profession or discipline; inappropriately technical language.

journal (122–24) A place to record observations and ideas in writing. Also, a periodical that publishes scholarly articles. See also *periodical.*

journalists' questions (plus two) (28–29) Questions that ask *who, what, where, when, why,* and *how* to help you explore a topic. In college writing, also ask yourself about the significance of your topic (*Is it important?*) and its consequences (*What are its effects?*).

K

keyword (214–15) (a) A term entered into an Internet search engine, online database, or library catalog to find sources of information. (b) A word or phrase in a text that highlights or is essential to the message of the text.

L

labeling (566) Applying a word or phrase to describe an entire group, such as *autistic, Cub Scout,* or *Asian American.* When the label does not apply to all group members, or when it unfairly characterizes the group, it contributes to **stereotyping.**

layout (169) The visual arrangement of text and images using proximity (nearness), alignment, repetition, and contrast. See also *format.*

level of diction (19) The choice of words to convey a tone (formal or informal) appropriate to the audience. See *tone, connotation.*

linear text (180) A document, such as a novel or magazine article, that is arranged so that readers begin at page 1 and read through to the end. Compare *hypertext.*

line graphs (81, 83) A type of information graphic that uses lines and points on a graph to show changes over time.

link (181, 205, 243) See *hyperlink.*

linking verb (580, 589, 629, 670, 697) A verb that expresses a state of being rather than an action and connects the subject to its subject complement. The verb *be,* when used as a main verb, is always a linking verb. *They are excited.* See also *subject complement.*

logical fallacy (159–63) See *fallacy.*

logical organization (40) The arrangement of a sentence, paragraph, or entire text in a way that will seem sensible to readers, that will not confuse or puzzle them.

logos (144, 145) See *appeals.*

lurk (241) Read online discussions without contributing.

M

main verb (605, 667–70) The part of a verb phrase that carries its principal meaning. See *verb phrase.*

mechanics (835–63) Conventions controlling capitalization, italics, abbreviation, numbers, and hyphenation.

menu (108, 180) A list of the main sections of a website.

metaphor (574, 575) An implied comparison between unlike things stated without *like, as,* or other comparative expressions: *Her mind buzzed with original ideas.* See *figurative language, simile.*

metasearch engine (215–16) Internet search engines that return the top search results from several search engines at once, with duplicate entries deleted.

methods (231, 394, 447) In APA and CSE style, the section of a research project that explains the research methods and describes any research participants (such as people interviewed) or data collected.

misplaced modifier (714–19) An ambiguously, confusingly, or disruptively placed modifying word, phrase, or clause.

mixed construction (723–27) A sentence with parts that do not fit together grammatically or logically.

mixed metaphor (576) A combination of multiple conflicting figures of speech for the same concept. See *figurative language.*

MLA style (275–87) The citation and documentation style of the Modern Language Association, used frequently in literature and languages.

modal verb (607, 669) See *helping verb.*

modified block-style letter (498) See *block-style letter.*

modifier (553–55) A word, phrase, or clause that functions as an adjective or adverb to qualify or describe another word, phrase, or clause.

mood (665, 668–69) The form of a verb that indicates how the writer or speaker views what is written or said. The **indicative mood** states facts or opinions and asks questions: *I finished my paper.* The **imperative mood** issues commands, gives instructions, or makes requests: *Hand in your papers by Friday.* The **subjunctive mood** expresses possibility, as in hypothetical situations or wishes: *If I were finished, I could go to bed.*

N

name-year system (436–37) In CSE style, a system of acknowledgment for research projects that includes the last name of the author and the year of publication in parentheses in the text; is accompanied by an alphabetical list of references at the end of the project.

narration (65)   A pattern of paragraph or essay development that tells a story, usually in chronological (time) order. See also *chronological organization*.

near-homonyms (585, 587)   Words that are close but not the same in pronunciation (*moral, morale*) or are different forms of the same word (*breath, breathe*).

neologism (564)   A newly coined word or expression.

netiquette (504)   A word composed of parts of the words *Internet* and *etiquette* that refers to conventions of politeness in online contexts.

noncount noun (or **uncountable** or **mass noun**) (743)   See *noun*.

nonessential (or **nonrestrictive**) **element** (636, 728, 787)   A modifying word, phrase, or clause that adds information to the element it modifies but does not identify it. Commas should set off nonessential elements from the rest of the sentence. *My grandfather, who recently retired, worked for the same company for forty-five years.*

noun (603–05)   A word that names an idea (*justice*), thing (*chair*), quality (*neatness*), action (*judgment*), person (*Albert Einstein*), or place (*Tokyo*). Proper nouns name specific places, people, or things and are usually capitalized: *Nairobi, Hillary Rodham Clinton*. Common nouns name members of a class or group: *turtle, skyscraper*. Collective nouns name a collection that can function as a single unit: *committee, family*. Concrete nouns name things that can be seen, touched, heard, smelled, or tasted: *planet, symphony, skunk*. Abstract nouns name qualities or ideas that cannot be perceived by the senses: *mercy, fear*. Count (or countable) nouns name countable things and can be either singular or plural: *cat/cats, idea/ideas*. Noncount (or uncountable or mass) nouns **name ideas or things that cannot be counted and do not have a plural form:** *knowledge, pollution*.

noun clause (624)   A subordinate clause that functions as a noun. See *clause*.

noun phrase (605, 619, 633)   A noun and its modifiers.

number (648, 665, 709)   The form of a word that indicates whether it is singular, referring to one thing (*a student*), or plural, referring to more than one (*two students*).

O

object (617–19, 737–39)   A noun or pronoun (or a noun phrase or noun clause) that receives or benefits from the action of a transitive verb or that follows a preposition. A **direct object** receives the action of the verb: *My friend wrote a letter*. An **indirect object** benefits from the action of the verb: *My friend wrote me a letter*. The **object of a preposition** usually follows a preposition to form a prepositional phrase. *She sent the letter by mail*.

object complement (618, 738)   An adjective or noun phrase that follows the direct object and describes the condition of the object or a change that the subject has caused it to undergo: *The candidate declared his opponent incompetent*.

objective case (684–92)   See *case*.

objectivity (140–43, 235)   A text is objective when it makes reasonable claims supported by logical evidence; recognizes alternative perspectives; and treats those alternatives respectfully.

object of a preposition (620)   See *object*.

opinion (140)   The most plausible answer for now, based on an evaluation of the available facts. Opinions are subject to revision in light of new evidence and are often the basis of argumentation.

organization (90, 176)   Arranging the parts of a sentence, paragraph, or essay so that readers can most readily understand and appreciate it.

outline (40)   A method of classifying information into main points, supporting points, and specific details. An **informal** (or **scratch**) **outline** arranges ideas in order of presentation; a **formal outline** uses roman and arabic numerals, upper- and lowercase letters, and indentions to classify information into main points, supporting points, and specific details; a **sentence outline** writes out main points, supporting points, and specific details in

complete sentences; a **topic outline** uses words and phrases to indicate the ideas to be discussed.

P

paragraph (53–58)   A group of sentences that focus on a single topic or example, often organized around a *topic sentence*.

parallelism (542–48)   In writing, the expression of equivalent ideas in equivalent grammatical structures. In an outline, the use of the same pattern or form for headings at each level.

paraphrase (114, 250, 253–57)   The statement of the ideas of others in one's own words and sentence structures.

parenthetical citation (276, 305, 307, 365)   A citation to a source that appears in parentheses in the body of a research paper. Compare *signal phrase*; see also *in-text citation*.

participial phrase (553, 621)   A phrase in which the present or past participle of a verb acts as an adjective: *the writing assignment, the written word*.

participles (621–22, 664–66)   Forms of a verb that combine with helping verbs to form certain tenses and that, as verbals, can function as adjectives. The **present participle** is the *-ing* form of the verb. The **past participle** is the *-ed* form in regular verbs (the same as the past tense) but takes various forms in irregular verbs. See *participial phrase, tense, verbal*.

particle (752–54)   A preposition or adverb that combines with a verb to create a new verb with a meaning that differs from the verb's meaning on its own—for example, *throw away* versus *throw*.

parts of speech (603)   The categories in which words can be classified according to the role they play in a sentence. English has eight parts of speech: *noun, pronoun, verb, adjective, adverb, preposition, conjunction,* and *interjection*.

passive voice (524–25, 680)   See *voice*.

past participle (757)   See *participle*.

past perfect progressive tense (675)   See *tense*.

past perfect tense (673)   See *tense*.

past progressive tense (672–78) See *tense.*

past tense (672–78) See *tense.*

patchwriting (107, 248) A faulty paraphrase that relies too heavily on the language or sentence structure of the source text. Patchwritten texts may replace some terms from the source passage with synonyms, add or delete a few words, or alter the sentence structure slightly, but they do not put the passage fully into fresh words and sentences. At some colleges and universities, *patchwriting* is considered plagiarism.

pathos (146) See *appeals.*

patterns of development (65–69) See *analysis, cause and effect, comparison and contrast, definition, description, exemplification, narration,* and *process analysis.*

PDF (portable document format) (183, 218, 416) A file format developed by Adobe that allows documents to be opened in different systems without altering their formatting.

peer revising (96–98) A revising strategy in which the writer solicits feedback on a text from classmates, colleagues, or friends. See also *revising.*

perfect progressive tense (672–78) See *tense.*

perfect tenses (672–78) See *tense.*

periodical (218) A publication, such as a magazine, newspaper, or scholarly journal, that is issued at regular intervals—daily, weekly, monthly, quarterly. See also *journal.*

periodic sentence (555–57) A sentence that reserves the independent clause for the end, building suspense that highlights key information when it finally arrives.

person (648, 665, 709) The form of a word that indicates whether it corresponds to the speaker or writer (*I, we*), the person addressed (*you*), or the people or things spoken or written about (*he, she, it, they, Marta, milkshakes*).

persona (11, 93) The personality of the writer as reflected in tone and style.

personal pronoun (685, 805) The pronouns *I, me, you, he, him, she, her, it, we, us, they, them,* which take the place of specific nouns or noun phrases.

personal statement (108) In a portfolio, the writer's description of the contents and explanation for the choice and arrangement of selections. See also *portfolio.*

personification (574) The attribution of human qualities to nonhuman creatures, objects, ideas, or phenomena: *The tornado swallowed the house.* See *figurative language.*

persuasive argument (15, 37, 128) An argument that advocates for a claim. The writer's purpose is to convince readers to agree with or at least to respect a position on a debatable issue. See also *argument, exploratory argument, purpose.*

phrasal verb (670, 752–54) A verb combined with one or two particles that together create a new verb with a meaning different from that of the original verb alone. See *particle.*

phrase (528–30, 619–23, 629, 782) A group of related words that lacks a subject, predicate, or both. A phrase cannot stand alone as a sentence, but it can function *in* a sentence as a noun, a verb, or a modifier.

pie chart (80–81) An information graphic that depicts the relationship of the parts to the whole; its sections must add up to 100 percent.

plagiarism (203, 248–57) Presenting a work or a portion of a work of any kind—a paper, a photograph, a speech, a web page—by someone else as if it were one's own.

plain text (177) A computer text format that does not allow for styling such as boldface and italics.

plural (648–50) Referring to more than one thing. See *number.*

point of view (455) The perspective of the narrator in a work of literature.

portfolio (106–08) A printed or online collection of a writer's work. A portfolio may contain the writer's best work, a range of types of writing (a proposal, a report, a set of instructions), or a collection of texts from a single project (prewriting, outline, first draft, revised draft). A portfolio usually also includes a table of contents and a personal statement. See also *personal statement.*

positive form (702–05) See *comparison of adjectives and adverbs.*

possessive case (684–72) See *case.*

possessive pronoun (805) The pronouns *my, mine, your, yours, his, hers, its, our, ours, your, yours, their,* and *theirs,* which indicate possession.

predicate (615–16) The part of a sentence or clause that states (*predicates*) something about the subject. The **simple predicate** consists of a main verb together with any helping verbs: *Marta is writing her parents a long email.* The **complete predicate** consists of the simple predicate together with any objects, complements, and modifiers: *Marta is writing her parents a long email.* A **compound predicate** is a complete predicate with two or more simple predicates joined with a conjunction: *Marta wrote the email but decided not to send it.*

prefix (588) A group of letters that attaches to the beginning of a root word to modify its meaning: *act, react.*

prejudice (140, 142) Ascribing qualities to an individual based on generalities about a group, generalities that are often inaccurate. See also *stereotype.*

premise (137–39) A claim or assumption on which the conclusion of an argument is based. See *syllogism.*

preposition (610, 769–86) A word or term that relates nouns or pronouns to other words in a sentence in terms of time, space, cause, and other attributes.

prepositional phrase (620, 633) A preposition followed by its object—a noun or pronoun and its modifiers. Prepositional phrases function as adjectives and adverbs: *the cat with gray fur.*

present participle (757) See *participle.*

present perfect progressive tense (645–47) See *tense.*

present perfect tense (673) See *tense.*

present progressive tense (672–75) See *tense.*

present tense (672–75) See *tense.*

press, or media, releases (503–13) Brief articles that announce events to newspapers, magazines, and online media outlets.

previewing (113) Scanning the title, subtitle, abstract, introduction, conclusion, sidebars, key terms, headings, subheadings, figures, and illustrations of a text to get a sense of its content, organization, and emphases before reading it in full.

primary source (229–32, 260–63, 476) Firsthand information, such as an eyewitness account, a research report, a recorded interview, or a work of literature or art. See also *field research.*

process analysis (65) A pattern of paragraph or essay development that explains a process step by step.

progressive tenses (672–75) See *tense.*

pronoun (65, 605, 652) A word that renames or takes the place of a noun or noun phrase.

pronoun reference (672–96) The relationship between a pronoun and its antecedent (the word it replaces). Pronoun reference is clear when readers can tell effortlessly what a pronoun's antecedent is.

proofreading (99–100) Reading a text to identify and correct spelling and typographical mistakes as well as punctuation and mechanical errors.

proper noun (743–51) See *noun.*

proximity (166) In design, the arrangement of content to show relationships. Material that is related should be placed close together; material that is unrelated should be placed at a distance.

purpose (13, 14–16, 168, 187) Your main reason for writing: to express your feelings or impressions or to entertain, inform, or persuade your audience.

Q

quantifier (748–49) An adjective such as *some, many, much, less,* or *few* that indicates the amount of a noun.

quotation (249–50, 260–63) A restatement of what someone else has said or written, either in a *direct quotation* (word for word) or an *indirect quotation* (a report of what was said or written). See *direct quotation, indirect quotation.*

R

reading journal (122–124) An online or printed record of a reader's reactions to, analysis of, or critique of a text.

reciprocal pronoun (605–06) A pronoun that refers to the individual parts of a plural antecedent: *The candidates debated one another.*

redundancy (522–23) Unnecessary repetition: *It was a cloudy, overcast day.*

reference list (374, 393, 435, 447–48) In APA and CSE style, a section at the end of a writing project in which the writer provides full bibliographic information for all sources cited in the text.

reference work (210–32) Sources, such as dictionaries, encyclopedias, bibliographies, almanacs, and atlases, that provide overview and background information on a word or topic. Specialized reference works may be appropriate sources for college projects, but general reference works are not.

reflection (118–24) The process of thinking about, annotating, and writing about a text in a reading journal; reflection is a necessary step for coming fully to terms with the text. See also *annotation, reading journal.*

reflexive pronoun (605–06) A pronoun that refers back to the subject of a sentence: *She helped herself to the buffet.*

regionalism (563) Nonstandard usage characteristic of people in a particular locality.

regular verbs (666–67) Verbs whose past-tense and past-participle forms end in *-d* or *-ed.*

relative clause (623) An adjective clause introduced by a relative pronoun such as *who, whom,* or *that.* See *adjective clause.*

relative pronouns (622, 685, 691) Pronouns such as *who, whom, whose, that,* and *which* used to introduce a subordinate clause that describes the pronoun's antecedent: *The apartment that I rented is small.*

relevance (52, 54, 233–34) The extent to which supporting evidence not only addresses the general topic of a text but also contributes to the reader's understanding of or belief in the text's main idea (the *thesis*). A relevant source offers information that will enrich understanding, provide background information or evidence to support claims, or suggest alternative perspectives.

reliability (233–39) The extent to which a source is accurate and trustworthy.

research hypothesis (199–200) A tentative assertion of what the writer expects the research to prove.

research log (202–04) A journal in which a researcher records research questions and hypotheses; a working thesis; information gathered from sources; interpretation, analysis, synthesis, and critique of sources; and ideas for next steps.

research questions (199–200) Questions about a topic that research might answer.

response (119, 452–56) Your own reactions to and insights about a text. Response occurs while a reader reads, and it often changes and develops as a result of rereading and studying the text.

restrictive element (787–89) See *essential element.*

résumé (507–11) A brief summary of an applicant's qualifications and experience.

revising (88, 110, 175) The stage of the writing process in which the writer assesses global issues such as whether the text fulfills its purpose, addresses its intended audience, is fully developed, and is organized clearly and logically; also the stage in which the writer assesses local issues such as word choice, sentence variety and emphasis, and wordiness. See also *conciseness, peer revising.*

rhetorical appeal (144) See *appeal.*

rhetorical citation (282) Identifying the source of information, words, or ideas while providing information about the source or your evaluation of it.

rhetorical question (558) A question that is meant to call attention to an issue, not to elicit an answer.

rhetorical situation (13–22) The fluid interplay of purpose, audience, culture, occasion, and topic as a writer devises, develops, and presents a project. See also *writing situation.*

Rogerian model (157–58) A model for organizing an exploratory argument that discusses evidence and counterevidence before drawing a conclusion. Compare *classical* and *Toulmin models.*

roundabout expression (522) A wordy expression that should be more concise.

S

scholarly sources (234–38) Peer-reviewed journal articles and books by experts, often published by university presses.

scratch (informal) outline (40) See *outline*.

search engine (211–23) Computer software that retrieves information from the internet, online databases, and library catalogs.

secondary sources (260–63) Sources that describe, evaluate, or interpret primary sources or other secondary sources. A textbook is a secondary source.

sentence (551–60) A word group with a subject and predicate that does not begin with a subordinating expression. A **declarative sentence** makes a statement: *The phone rang.* An **imperative sentence** gives a command: *Answer the phone.* An **interrogative sentence** asks a question: *Did the phone ring?* An **exclamatory sentence** expresses strong or sudden emotion: *How I hate annoying ring tones!* A **simple sentence** has only one independent clause and no subordinate clauses: *The phone rang.* A **compound sentence** has two or more independent clauses but no subordinate clauses: *The phone rang, and I answered it.* A **complex sentence** consists of a single independent clause with at least one subordinate clause: *My cell phone rang while I was in the elevator.* A **compound-complex sentence** has two or more independent clauses with one or more subordinate clauses: *My cell phone rang, but I didn't answer it because I was in a crowded elevator.*

sentence fragment (623) A word group punctuated like a sentence but lacking one or more of the essential parts of a sentence: an independent clause, a complete verb, and a subject.

sentence outline (41) See *outline*.

separable (753) A transitive phrasal verb is *separable* if its direct object can fall either between the verb and the particle (separating them) or after the particle.

sequence of tenses (676–78) The choice of tenses that best reflect the time relationship among the events described in the clauses of a sentence.

server (180) A computer that links other computers into a network.

setting (455) In works of literature, where and when the action occurs.

signal phrase (277, 305, 307, 364–65, 436, 789) A phrase that identifies, discusses, or describes the author or source being cited: *"How do I know what I think," E. M. Forster asked, "until I see what I say?"*

simile (574–75) An explicit comparison between two unlike things, usually expressed with *like* or *as*: *run like the wind* (see also *figurative language, metaphor*).

simple future tense (673) See *tense*.

simple past tense (673) See *tense*.

simple predicate (615) See *predicate*.

simple present tense (672, 673) See *tense*.

simple sentence (552, 625) See *sentence*.

simple subject (613) See *subject*.

simple tenses (672–73) See *tense*.

singular (648–49) Referring to one thing.

site map (181) A list of a website's contents.

slang (564) The informal, inventive, often colorful (and off-color) vocabulary of a particular group. Slang is usually inappropriate in formal writing.

slash (832–33) Punctuation used to mark the ends of lines in poetry when the poetry is run into a sentence.

spam (504) Unsolicited advertising sent to email or social software accounts such as Twitter.

spatial organization (40) An organizational strategy that structures a description visually, from left to right, from inside to outside, from top to bottom, and so on.

sponsors (304) Corporations, agencies, and organizations that are responsible for creating and making available a website's content.

squinting modifier (716) A modifier that appears confusingly to modify both what precedes it and what follows it.

Standard American English (602) The dialect of English that prevails in academic and business settings in the United States.

stereotype (566) A simplified, uncritical, and often negative generalization about an entire group of people. See also *prejudice*.

styles of documentation (304, 363, 406, 435) A set of specifications for citing and documenting sources. Most of the well-known style sheets, such as MLA, APA, *Chicago*, and CSE, are sponsored and updated by professional organizations or publishers.

subject (613–15, 628) The part of a sentence that identifies what the predicate is making a statement about. The **simple subject** is a noun or pronoun: *The cat hissed at the dog.* The **complete subject** is the simple subject with any modifying words or phrases: *The excitable gray cat chased the dog.* A **compound subject** is a complete subject with two or more simple subjects joined with a conjunction: *The cat and the dog usually get along.*

subject complement (554, 608, 617, 656, 686, 698, 724) An adjective, pronoun, or noun phrase that follows a linking verb and describes or refers to the sentence subject: *This food is delicious.*

subject directory (30, 217) A collection of websites organized into groups by topic and arranged hierarchically from most general to most specific.

subjective case (678–92) See *case*.

subjunctive mood (678–680) See *mood*.

subordinate clause, or dependent clause (535–38, 622, 691, 782) See *clause*.

subordinating conjunction (622) See *conjunction*.

subordination (530, 534–39) The incorporation of secondary or modifying elements into a sentence or clause: *Although he got a late start, he arrived on time.*

suffix (589–90) A group of letters that attaches to the end of a root word to change its meaning and grammatical form: *act, action*.

summary (114–15, 250, 257–58) A passage restating the main idea and major supporting points of a source text in the reader's own words and sentence structures. A summary should be at least 50 percent shorter than the text it restates.

superlative form (702–05)   See *comparison of adjectives and adverbs.*

superstition (140)   A belief with no basis in fact: *A wish made on a falling star will come true.*

s.v. (413)   Abbreviation of the Latin phrase *sub verbo,* "under the word."

symbolism (455)   The use of a character, event, or object to represent something more than its literal meaning.

synchronous media (186)   Communication media such as instant messaging and online chat in which participants discuss topics in real time. Compare *asynchronous media.*

synonyms (61)   Words with similar meanings—for example, *wrong* and *incorrect.* Compare *antonyms.*

synthesis (116, 127–29)   The process of making connections among ideas in a text, ideas in other texts, and the writer's own ideas and experiences. Synthesis is an important component in critical thinking and reading and is central to much successful college writing.

T

table (80)   An information graphic that organizes data into rows and columns.

tense (665, 672)   The form of a verb that indicates the time in which an action or event occurs, when it occurred relative to other events, and whether it is ongoing or completed. The three **simple tenses** are the simple present (*I practice*), the simple past (*I practiced*), and the simple future (*I will practice*). The **perfect tenses** generally indicate the completion of an action before a particular time. They include the present perfect (*I have practiced*), the past perfect (*I had practiced*), and the future perfect (*I will have practiced*). The **progressive tenses** indicate ongoing action. They include the present progressive (*I am practicing*), the past progressive (*I was practicing*), the future progressive (*I will be practicing*), the present perfect progressive (*I have been practicing*), the past perfect progressive (*I had been practicing*), and the future perfect progressive (*I will have been practicing*).

tense sequence (676–78)   See *sequence of tenses.*

theme (452)   The main point of a work of literature.

thesis statement (34–38, 89, 90, 200)   A brief statement (one or two sentences) of a text's main idea.

title page (107)   A cover sheet for a printed portfolio, with identifying information, including the work's title, author's name, course number, and date of submission.

tone (13, 19–20, 119)   The attitude of the writer toward the audience, the topic, and the writer her- or himself as conveyed through word choice, style, and content.

topic (13, 24, 30, 36, 167)   The subject of a text.

topic outline (41)   See *outline.*

topic sentence (53–58)   A sentence (sometimes two) that states a paragraph's main idea.

Toulmin model (158)   A model for organizing an argument based on *claims* (or assertions), *grounds* (or evidence), and *warrants* (or assumptions linking claims to grounds). Compare *classical* and *Rogerian models.*

transitional expressions (60, 554, 783)   Words and phrases, such as *in addition, however,* and *since,* that show the relationship between sentences or paragraphs.

transitive verb (617–19, 671–72)   A verb that takes a direct object.

tree diagram (38)   A way to depict the relationships among topics and subtopics visually by placing the main idea at the top of the page and letting topics and subtopics branch off below it.

U

understatement (574)   The deliberate use of less forceful language than a subject warrants: *An A average is pretty good.* See *figurative language.*

unfamiliar to familiar (40)   An organization pattern that presents surprising ideas, examples, or information first, before moving on to familiar ground.

unified, unity (42, 53)   A quality of a text in which all the examples and evidence support the paragraph's topic sentence and in which each of the supporting paragraphs supports the text's thesis statement.

unmarked infinitive (755)   The base verb alone, without *to.*

URL (239–41)   Universal resource locator, a website's Internet address.

V

verb (605–07, 664–83)   A word that expresses action (*The quarterback throws a pass*), occurrence (*The play happened in the second half*), or state of being (*The fans are happy*). Verbs also carry information about time (tense), as well as person, number, voice, and mood.

verbal (607, 620, 629, 666, 720)   A verb form that functions as a noun, adjective, or adverb. Verbals may have objects and complements, but they lack the information about tense required of a complete verb.

verb phrase (619, 620, 649–50, 667)   A main verb with any helping (or auxiliary) verbs.

verbal phrase (604, 633)   A verbal and any modifiers, objects, or complements.

vested interest (235)   A participant or stakeholder who might personally benefit from the results of a decision, event, or process has a vested (not objective) interest in that decision, event, or process and thus might influence it not for the welfare of others but for personal gain.

voice (524–25, 665, 680–81)   In grammar, the form of a transitive verb that indicates whether the subject is acting or acted upon. In the **active voice,** the subject performs the action of the verb: *The dog chased the cat.* In the **passive voice,** the subject receives the action of the verb: *The cat was chased by the dog.* Also, in writing, the sense of the writer's personality as conveyed through the writer's word, style, and content choices. See also *persona, tone.*

W

warrant (149)   An unstated assumption that underlies an argument's main claim. See *Toulmin model.*

web browser (183)   The software program that interprets HTML code, making it possible for users to view websites and web pages.

weblog (or **blog**) (180, 336)   See *blog*.

web pages (179)   Files on a website in addition to the home page; web pages may include text, audio, video, still images, and database files.

website (179)   A collection of files located at a single address (URL) on the World Wide Web.

well developed (52)   Paragraphs or essays that supply the information readers need to be persuaded of the writer's point.

white space (170)   The portion of a page or screen with no text, graphics, or images.

wiki (180)   A website designed for collaborative writing and editing.

working bibliography (204–09)   A list of sources a researcher compiles before and during the research process.

working thesis (461)   The first version of a thesis that a writer can imagine for the text he or she is writing. Typically the working thesis goes through several revisions as the writer drafts and revises the text.

works-cited list (304, 321, 345)   In MLA style, a section at the end of a research project in which the writer provides full bibliographic information for all sources cited in the text.

writing process (13–110)   The process a writer engages in to produce a writing project. The writing process includes analyzing the assignment, planning the project, generating ideas, drafting, revising, editing, designing, proofreading, and publishing.

writing situation (13–22)   The characteristics of a text, including its purpose, audience, context, and genre, as well as its length, due date, and format.

Z

zero article (744)   See *article*.

Glossary of Usage

This usage glossary includes words that writers often confuse (*infer, imply*) or misuse (*disinterested, uninterested*) and expressions that are nonstandard and sometimes even pretentious. As a responsible writer, strive to avoid words and expressions that will confuse or distract your readers or that will undermine their confidence in you. Of course, not all words and expressions that cause writers problems are listed here; if a word or expression with which you have trouble is *not* included here, check the index, review chapters 30 and 31 ("Choosing Appropriate Language" and "Choosing Effective Words"), review the list of homonyms and near-homonyms on p. 565, consult the usage notes in a dictionary, or consult another usage guide, such as *Fowler's Modern English Usage, The New York Times Manual of Style and Usage, 100 Words Almost Everyone Confuses and Misuses,* or *The American Heritage Book of English Usage.*

A

a, an *A* and *an* are indefinite articles. Use *a* before a word that begins with a consonant sound: *a car, a hill, a one-way street.* Use *an* before a word that begins with a vowel sound: *an appointment, an hour, an X-ray.*

accept, except *Accept* is a verb meaning "agree to receive": *I accept the nomination. Except* is a preposition that means "but": *Everyone voted for me except Paul.*

adapt, adopt *Adapt* means "to adjust": *Instead of migrating, the park's ducks adapt to the changing climate. Adopt* means "to take as one's own": *I adopted a cat from the shelter.*

adverse, averse *Adverse* means "unfavorable" or "hostile"; *averse* means "opposed": *She was averse to buying a ticket to a play that had received such adverse criticism.*

advice, advise The noun *advice* means "guidance"; the verb *advise* means

"to suggest": *I advised her to get some sleep. She took my advice and went to bed early.*

affect, effect As a verb, *affect* means "to influence" or "to cause a change": *Study habits affect one's grades.* As a noun, *affect* means "feeling or emotion": *The defendant responded without affect to the guilty verdict.* As a noun, *effect* means "result": *The decreased financial aid budget is an effect of the recession.* As a verb, *effect* means "to bring about or accomplish": *Submitting the petition effected a change in the school's policy.*

aggravate, irritate *Aggravate* means "to intensify" or "worsen": *Dancing until dawn aggravated Giorgio's bad back. Irritate* means "to annoy": *He was irritated that his chiropractor could not see him until Tuesday.* Colloquially, *aggravate* is often used to mean *annoy,* but this colloquial usage is inappropriate in formal contexts.

agree to, agree with *Agree to* means "to consent to": *Chris agreed to host the party. Agree with* means "be in accord with": *Anne agreed with Chris that a party was just what everyone needed.*

ain't *Ain't* is a nonstandard contraction for *am not, are not,* or *is not* and should not be used in formal writing.

all ready, already *All ready* means "completely prepared"; *already* means "previously": *They were all ready to catch the bus, but it had already left.*

all right, alright *All right* is the standard spelling; *alright* is nonstandard.

all together, altogether *All together* means "as a group": *When Noah's family gathered for his graduation, it was the first time they had been all together in years. Altogether* means "completely": *Noah was altogether overwhelmed by the attention.*

allude, elude, refer to *Allude* means "to refer to indirectly"; *elude* means

"to avoid" or "to escape": *He eluded further questioning by alluding to his troubled past.* Do not use *allude* to mean "refer directly"; use *refer to* instead: *The speaker referred to [not alluded to] slide six of her PowerPoint presentation.*

allusion, illusion An *allusion* is an indirect reference: *I almost missed the author's allusion to Macbeth.* An *illusion* is a false appearance or belief: *The many literary quotations he drops into his speeches give the illusion that he is well read.*

almost, most *Almost* means "nearly"; *most* means "the majority of": *My roommate will tell me almost* [not *most*] *anything, but I talk to my sister about most of my own problems.*

a lot, alot *Alot* is nonstandard; always spell *a lot* as two words.

among, amongst *Amongst* is a British alternative to *among;* in American English, *among* is preferred.

among, between Use *among* with three or more nouns or with words that stand for a group composed of three or more members; use *between* with two or more nouns: *I'm double majoring because I could not decide between biology and English. Italian, art history, and calculus are among my other favorites.*

amoral, immoral *Amoral* means "neither moral nor immoral" or "indifferent to moral standards"; *immoral* means "violating moral standards": *While secularists believe that nature is amoral, religionists often view natural disasters as punishments for immoral behavior.*

amount, number Use *amount* with items that cannot be counted (noncount or mass nouns); use *number* with items that can be counted (count nouns): *The dining hall prepares the right amount of food based on the number of people who eat there.*

an See *a, an.*

G15

and/or   *And/or* is shorthand for "one or the other or both." It is acceptable in technical and business writing, but it should be avoided in most academic writing.

ante-, anti-   The prefix *ante-* means "before," as in *antebellum*, or "before the war"; the prefix *anti-* means "against," as in *antibiotic* ("against bacteria").

anxious, eager   *Anxious* means "uneasy": *Dan was anxious about writing his first twenty-page paper. Eager* indicates strong interest or enthusiasm: *He was eager to finish his first draft before spring break.*

anybody, any body; anyone, any one   *Anybody* and *anyone* are singular indefinite pronouns: *Does anybody [or anyone] have an extra pen? Any body* and *any one* are a noun and pronoun (respectively) modified by the adjective *any*: *She was not fired for making any one mistake but, rather, for making many mistakes over a number of years.*

anymore, any more   *Anymore* means "from now on": *She does not write letters anymore. Any more* means "additional": *I do not need any more stamps.* Both are used only in negative contexts, for example, with *not* or other negative terms such as *hardly* or *scarcely*.

anyplace   *Anyplace* is an informal way of saying *anywhere. Anywhere* is preferable in formal writing.

anyways, anywheres   *Anyways* and *anywheres* are nonstandard; use *anyway* and *anywhere* instead.

as   *As* should not be used in place of *because, since,* or *when* if ambiguity will result: *As people were lining up to use the elliptical machine, the management posted a waiting list.* Does this sentence mean that management posted the sign *while* people were lining up, or does it mean that the management posted the sign *because* there was such demand for the machine?

as, as if, like   Use *as,* or *as if,* not *like,* as a conjunction in formal writing: *The president spoke as if [not like] he were possessed by the spirit of Abraham Lincoln. Like* is acceptable, however, as a preposition that introduces a comparison: *The president spoke like a true leader.*

at   *At* is not necessary to complete *where* questions: *Where is Waldo?* not *Where is Waldo at?*

averse, adverse   See *adverse, averse.*

awful, awfully   In formal writing, use *awful* and *awfully* to suggest the emotion of fear or wonder, not as a synonym for *bad* or to mean *very*. *The high priest gave forth an awful cry before casting the captive from the top of the pyramid toward the crowd below.*

awhile, a while   *Awhile* is an adverb: *They talked awhile before going to dinner. A while* is an article and a noun, and should always follow a preposition: *Rest for a while between eating and exercising.*

B

bad, badly   In formal writing, use the adjective *bad* to modify nouns and pronouns and after linking verbs (as a subject complement): *Because I had a bad day, my husband feels bad.* Use the adverb *badly* to modify verbs, adjectives, and adverbs: *Todd's day went badly from start to finish.*

being as, being that   *Being as* and *being that* are nonstandard substitutes for *because*: *Because [not being as] Marcus did well as a teaching assistant, he was asked to teach a class of his own the next year.* Avoid them.

beside, besides   *Beside* is a preposition that means "next to" or "along side of": *You will always find my glasses beside the bed. Besides* is an adverb meaning "furthermore" or a preposition meaning "in addition to": *Besides, it will soon be finals. Besides chemistry, I have exams in art history and statistics.*

between, among   See *among, between.*

bring, take   Use *bring* when something is coming toward the speaker and *take* when it is moving away: *When the waiter brought our entrees, he took our bread.*

burst, bursted; bust, busted   *Burst* is a verb meaning to break apart violently; the past tense of *burst* is also *burst,* not *bursted. Bust* is slang for *to burst* or *to break* and should be avoided in formal writing: *The boiler burst [not bursted or busted] in a deadly explosion.*

C

can, may   Use *can* when discussing ability: *I know she can quit smoking.* Use *may* when discussing permission: *The server told her that she may not smoke anywhere in the restaurant.*

capital, capitol   *Capital,* a noun, can mean "funds," or it can mean "the city that is the seat of government": *The student council did not have enough capital to travel to Harrisburg, Pennsylvania's capital.* The word *capitol* means "the building where lawmakers meet": *The state's capitol is adorned with a golden dome.* When capitalized, *Capitol* refers to the building in Washington, DC, where the US Congress meets.

censor, censure   *Censor* means both "to delete objectionable material" (a verb) and "one who deletes objectionable material" (a noun): *The bedroom scenes, but not the battle scenes, were heavily censored. Clearly, the censors object more to sex than to violence. Censure* means both "to reprimand officially" (verb) and "an official reprimand" (noun): *The ethics committee censured the governor for lying under oath. Members of his party were relieved that a censure was all he suffered.*

cite, sight, site   *Cite,* a verb, means "to quote" or "mention": *Cite your sources according to MLA format. Sight,* a noun, means "view" or "scene": *The sight of a field of daffodils makes me think of Wordsworth. Site,* a noun, means "location" or "place" (even online): *That site has the best recipes on the Internet.*

climactic, climatic   *Climactic* is an adjective derived from the noun *climax* and means "culminating" or "most intense"; *climatic* is an adjective derived from the noun *climate*: *The climactic moment of a thunderstorm occurs when the center of the storm is overhead. Tornados are violent climatic phenomena associated with thunderstorms.*

complement, compliment   *Complement* is a noun meaning "that which completes or perfects something else"; it can also be used as a verb meaning "the process of completing or making perfect." *Compliment* means either "a flattering comment" or "the act of giving a compliment": *My husband complements me and makes me whole; still, it annoys me that he rarely compliments me on my appearance.*

conscience, conscious *Conscience* is a noun meaning "sense of right and wrong": *Skipping class weighed heavily on Sunil's conscience. Conscious* is an adjective that means "aware" or "awake": *Maria made a conscious decision to skip class.*

continual(ly), continuous(ly) *Continual* means "repeated frequently": *The continual request for contributions undermined her resolve to be more charitable. Continuous* means "uninterrupted": *The continuous stream of bad news forced her to shut off the television.*

could care less *Could care less* is an illogical, and nonstandard, substitute for *could not care less: If one could care less, then one must care, at least a little, and yet this is not the intended meaning.*

could of, must of, should of, would of These are misspellings of *could have, must have, should have,* and *would have.*

criteria, criterion *Criteria* is the plural form of the noun *criterion,* Latin for "standard": *His criteria for grading may be vague, but I know I fulfilled at least one criterion by submitting my paper on time.*

D

data, media, phenomena *Data, media,* and *phenomena* are plural nouns (*datum, medium,* and *phenomenon* are their singular forms): *The data suggest that the economy will rebound by the time you graduate. The news media raise the alarm about public corruption, but it is the voters who must take action. The Aurora Borealis is one of many amazing natural phenomena.* (*Data* is increasingly used as a singular noun, but continuing to use it as a plural is never wrong.)

differ from, differ with *Differ from* means "to lack similarity": *Renaissance art differs greatly from art of the Middle Ages. Differ with* means to disagree: *Martin Luther's forty-nine articles spelled out the ways in which he differed with the Catholic Church.*

discreet, discrete *Discreet,* an adjective, means "tactful" or "judicious": *Please be discreet—don't announce that you saw Ada crying in the bathroom. Discrete* means "distinct" or "separate": *The study revealed two discrete groups, those who can keep a secret and those who cannot.*

disinterested, uninterested *Disinterested* means "impartial": *A judge who cannot be disinterested should recuse him- or herself from the case. Uninterested* means "indifferent": *The book seems well-written, but I am uninterested in the topic.*

don't, doesn't *Don't* is a contraction of *do not;* it is used with *I, you, we, they,* and plural nouns: *I don't want to drive, but the trains don't run very often. Doesn't* is a contraction of *does not;* it is used with *he, she, it,* and singular nouns: *It doesn't matter whether you're a little late; Fred doesn't mind waiting.*

E

each and every *Each and every* is a wordy substitute for *each* or *every;* use one or the other but not both.

eager, anxious See *anxious, eager.*

effect, affect See *affect, effect.*

e.g., i.e. *E.g.* is an abbreviation of a Latin phrase meaning "for example" or "for instance"; *i.e.* is an abbreviation of a Latin phrase meaning "that is." In formal writing, use the English equivalents rather than the Latin abbreviations; the Latin abbreviations are acceptable in tables, footnotes, and other places where space is at a premium.

elicit, illicit *Elicit,* a verb, means "to draw out": *Every week,* American Idol *contestants try to elicit enough support to avoid elimination. Illicit,* an adjective, means "illegal" or "impermissible": *In 2003,* American Idol *contestant Frenchie Davis was disqualified for posing in illicit photos.*

elude, allude, refer to See *allude, elude, refer to.*

emigrate from, immigrate to *Emigrate from* means "to leave one's country and settle in another": *Jake's grandmother emigrated from Poland in 1919. Immigrate to* means "to move to and settle in a new country": *Jake's grandmother immigrated to the United States in 1919.*

eminent, imminent, immanent *Eminent* means "renowned": *The university hosts lectures by many eminent scientists. Imminent* means "about to happen" or "looming": *In the last year of the Bush administration, many felt that a recession was imminent. Immanent* means "inherent" or "pervasive throughout the world": *Many religions teach that God's presence is immanent.*

enthused *Enthused* is a colloquial adjective meaning "enthusiastic." In formal writing, use *enthusiastic: Because of the team's excellent record, Eric was enthusiastic* [not *enthused*] *about joining.*

etc. *Etc.* is an abbreviation of the Latin phrase *et cetera,* meaning "and others." Because *et* means "and," adding the word *and* before *etc.* is redundant. In a series, include a comma before *etc.: A great deal of online media are used in classes today: blogs, wikis, Blackboard, Facebook, etc.* In most formal writing, concluding with a final example or *and so on* (the English equivalet of *etc.*) is preferable.

everybody, everyone; every body, every one *Everybody* and *everyone* are interchangeable singular indefinite pronouns: *Everybody* [or *everyone*] *who went to the concert got a free T-shirt. Every body* and *every one* are a noun and a pronoun (respectively) modified by the adjective *every: Coroners must treat every body they examine with respect.*

except, accept See *accept, except.*

expect, suppose *Expect* means "to anticipate": *I expect to be home when she arrives. Suppose* means "to presume": *I suppose she should have a key just in case.*

explicit, implicit *Explicit,* an adjective, means "overt" or "stated outright": *The rules are explicit : "No running." Implicit* is an adjective that means "implied": *Implicit in the rules is a prohibition against skipping.*

F

farther, further Use *farther* with distances: *I'd like to drive a hundred miles farther before we pull over for dinner.* Use *further* to mean "more" or "in addition": *I have nothing further to add.*

fewer, less   Use *fewer* with items that can be counted (count nouns). Use *less* with items that cannot be counted (noncount or mass nouns): *This semester, I am taking three fewer classes than I took in the fall, but because I have a job now, I have less time to study.*

first, firstly   *Firstly* is used in Britain, but it sounds overly formal in the United States. *First* (and *second* and *third*) is the standard form in the United States.

flaunt, flout   *Flaunt* means "to parade" or "show off": *Ivan flaunted his muscular torso on the quad. Flout* means "to disobey" or "ignore": *He flouted school policy by parading about without his shirt on.*

further, farther   See *farther, further.*

G

get   Many colloquial expressions with *get* should not be used in formal writing. Avoid expressions such as *get with the program, get your act together, get lost,* and so on.

good, well   *Good* is an adjective; *well* is an adverb: *Playing well in the tournament made Lee feel good.* In references to health, however, *well* is an adjective: *She had a cold, but now she is well and back at work.*

H

hanged, hung   Use the past-tense verb *hanged* only to describe a person executed by hanging. Use the past-tense verb *hung* to describe anything else (pictures, clothing) that can be suspended.

hardly   Use *can hardly* instead of *can't hardly,* a double negative: *I can hardly keep my eyes open.*

he, she; he/she; s/he   Historically, the pronoun *he* was used generically to mean *he or she;* in informal contexts, writers avoid bias by writing *he/she* or *s/he.* In formal writing, however, revise your sentence to avoid a gendered pronoun: *Sensible students are careful what they post on social networking sites* [not *The sensible student is careful what he posts about himself on social networking sites*].

hisself   *Hisself* is a nonstandard substitute for *himself.* Avoid it.

I

i.e., e.g.   See *e.g., i.e.*

if, whether   Use *whether* not *if* when alternatives are offered: *If I must go out, I insist that we go to a decent restaurant. I do not care whether we eat Chinese food or Italian, but I refuse to eat at Joe's.*

illicit, elicit   See *elicit, illicit.*

illusion, allusion   See *allusion, illusion.*

immigrate to, emigrate from   See *emigrate from, immigrate to.*

imminent, eminent, immanent   See *eminent, imminent, immanent.*

immoral, amoral   See *amoral, immoral.*

implicit, explicit   See *explicit, implicit.*

imply, infer   *Imply* means "to suggest indirectly": *The circles under Phillip's eyes implied that he had not slept much. Infer* means "to conclude": *From the way he devoured his dinner, I inferred that Raymond was famished.*

incredible, incredulous   *Incredible* means "unbelievable": *Debbie told an incredible story about meeting the Dalai Lama. Incredulous* means "unbelieving": *I am incredulous of everything that the tabloids print.*

infer, imply   See *imply, infer.*

in regards to   *In regards to* is nonstandard. Use *in regard to, as regards,* or *regarding* instead.

irregardless   *Irregardless* is nonstandard; use *regardless* instead.

irritate, aggravate   See *aggravate, irritate.*

is when, is where   Avoid these phrases in definitions: *An oligarchy is a system of government in which the many are ruled by a few,* or *Oligarchy is government of the many by the few* [not *An oligarchy is when the many are ruled by a few*].

it's, its   *It's* is a contraction of "it is" or "it has," and *its* is a possessive pronoun: *It's been a long time since the ailing pigeon flapped its wings in flight.* One trick for distinguishing the two is to recall that contractions such as *it's* are often avoided in formal writing, while possessive pronouns like *its* are perfectly acceptable.

K

kind, kinds   *Kind* is a singular noun: *This kind of weather is bad for asthmatics. Kinds* (a plural noun) is used only to denote more than one kind: *Many kinds of pollen can adversely affect breathing.*

kind of, sort of   *Kind of* and *sort of* are colloquial; in formal writing, use "somewhat" or "a little" instead: *Julia was somewhat* [not *kind of*] *pleased to be going back to school.* Use *kind of* and *sort of* in formal writing only to mean "type of": *E. E. Cummings's poetry creates a new kind of grammar.*

L

lay, lie   *Lay* means "to place"; it requires a direct object. Its main forms are *lay, laid,* and *laid : She laid her paper on the professor's desk. Lie* means "to recline"; it does not take a direct object. Its main forms are *lie, lay,* and *lain: She fell asleep as soon as she lay down.*

leave, let   *Leave* means "to go away"; *let* means "to allow." *If I leave early, will you let me know what happens?*

less, fewer   See *fewer, less.*

like, as, as if   See *as, as if, like.*

loose, lose   The adjective *loose* means "baggy" or "not securely attached": *I have to be careful with my glasses because one of the screws is loose.* The verb *lose* means "to misplace": *I am afraid I will lose the screw and have to attach the earpiece with duct tape.*

lots, lots of   *Lots* and *lots of* are colloquial and should be avoided in academic writing; use terms like *much, many,* and *very* instead.

M

may, can   See *can, may.*

maybe, may be   The adverb *maybe* means "possibly" or "perhaps": *The verb phrase may be means "have the possibility to be": Maybe I'll apply for an internship next semester, but if I wait too long all of the positions may be filled.*

may of, might of   *May of* and *might of* are misspellings of *may have* and *might have.*

media   See *data, media, phenomena.*

moral, morale   *Moral* means "ethical lesson": *Aesop's fables each have a moral, such as "don't judge others by their appearance." Morale* means "attitude" or "spirits": *April's warm weather significantly raised student morale.*

most, almost   See *almost, most.*

must of   See *could of, must of, should of, would of.*

myself, himself, herself, etc.   Use pronouns that end with *-self* to refer to or intensify other words: *Obama himself made an appearance.* Do not use them when you are unsure whether to use a pronoun in the nominative case (*I, she, he, we, they*) or the objective case (*me, her, him, us, them*): *This conversation is between him and me* [not *himself and myself*].

N

nohow, nowheres   *Nohow* and *no-wheres* are nonstandard forms of *anyway, in any way, in any place, in no place,* and *nowhere.* Avoid them.

number, amount   See *amount, number.*

O

off of   Omit *of: Sarah took the pin off* [not *off of*] *her coat.*

OK, O.K., okay   These are all acceptable spellings, but the term is inappropriate in formal writing. Choose a more specific word instead: *Food served in the dining hall is mediocre* [not *okay*].

P

phenomena   See *data, media, phenomena.*

plus   Avoid using *plus* as a substitute for the coordinating conjunction *and* or the transition *moreover.*

precede, proceed   *Precede* means "come before"; *proceed* means "continue": *Despite warnings from those who preceded me, I proceeded to take six classes in one semester.*

principal, principle   *Principal,* a noun, refers to the leader of an organization. *Principal,* used as an adjective, means "main." *Principle,* used as a noun, means "belief" or "standard": *The school principal's principal concern is the well-being of her students. She runs the school on the principle that fairness is essential.*

proceed, precede   See *precede, proceed.*

R

raise, rise   The verb *raise* means "lift up" or "move up" and takes a direct object: *Joseph raised the blinds.* The verb *rise* means "to go upward" and does not take a direct object: *We*

could see the steam *rise* as the solution started to boil.

real, really   Do not use *real* or *really* as a synonym for *very: Spring break went very* [not *real* or *really*] *fast.*

reason is because, reason why   To avoid redundancy and faulty predication, choose either *the reason is that* or *because: The reason Chris fell is that he is uncoordinated. It is not because his shoe was untied.*

refer to, allude, elude   See *allude, elude, refer to.*

relation, relationship   Use *relation* to refer to a connection between things: *There is a relation between the amount one sleeps and one's overall health.* Use *relationship* to refer to a connection between people: *Tony has always had a close relationship with his grandfather.*

respectfully, respectively   *Respectfully* means "with respect": *Ben treats his parents respectfully. Respectively* means "in the given order": *My mother and father are 54 and 56, respectively.*

rise, raise   See *raise, rise.*

S

set, sit   The verb *set* means "to place" or "to establish," and it takes a direct object. *The professor set the book on the desk.* The verb *sit* means "to assume a sitting position," and it does not take a direct object: *You can sit in the waiting room until the doctor is ready.*

shall, will   In the past, *shall* was used as a helping verb with *I* and *we,* and *will* was used with *he, she, it,* and *they: I shall go on dancing, and they will go home.* Now *will* is generally used with all persons: *I will go on singing, and they will all cover their ears. Shall* is used mainly with polite questions (*Shall we invite your mother?*) and in rules and regulations (*No person shall enter these premises after dusk.*).

should of   See *could of, must of, should of, would of.*

since   *Since* can mean "because" or "from that time," so use it only when there is no chance that readers will infer the wrong meaning. In the sentence that follows, either meaning makes sense: *Since I moved to the*

country, *I have had no trouble sleeping.* Revise to make your meaning clear: *Since January, when I moved to the country ...* or *Because I moved to the country, ...*

sit, set   See *set, sit.*

site, sight, cite   See *cite, sight, site.*

somebody, someone   *Somebody* and *someone* are interchangeable singular indefinite pronouns: *Someone* [or *somebody*] *is at the door.*

sometime, sometimes   *Sometime* is an adverb meaning "at an indefinite time"; *sometimes* is an adverb meaning "on occasion," "now and then": *Sometimes I wish my future would come sometime soon.*

somewheres   *Somewheres* is nonstandard; use *somewhere* instead.

stationary, stationery   *Stationary* means "not moving"; *stationery* means "writing paper." (Thinking of the *e* in "stationery" as standing for *envelope* may help.)

supposed to, used to   *Supposed to* means *should; used to* means "did regularly in the past." In speech, the final *-d* is often dropped, but in writing, it is required: *I was supposed* [not *suppose*] *to practice piano daily; instead, I used* [not *use*] *to play hockey.*

sure and, sure to; try and, try to   *Sure to* and *try to* are standard; *sure and* and *try and* are not.

T

take, bring   See *bring, take.*

than, then   *Than* is a conjunction used in comparisons; *then* is an adverb of time. *If Betsy is already taller than I, then I will be impressed.*

that, which   In formal writing, *that* is generally used with essential (or restrictive) clauses and *which* with nonessential (nonrestrictive) clauses: *The project that I am working on now is due on Monday, which is why I really have to finish it this weekend.*

that, who   In formal writing, use *who* or *whom,* not *that,* to refer to people: *I. M. Pei is the architect who* [not *that*] *designed this building.*

their, there, they're   *Their* is a possessive pronoun, *there* is an adverb of place, and *they're* is a contraction of "they are": *They're always leaving their dishes in the sink. Why must they* *leave them there instead of putting them in the dishwasher?*

theirself, theirselves, themself   *Theirself, theirselves,* and *themself* are nonstandard. Use *themselves* instead.

them   In colloquial speech, the pronoun *them* is sometimes used in place of the demonstrative adjective *those;* avoid this nonstandard usage: *Those* [not *them*] *are the books I need for class.*

then, than   See *than, then.*

this here, these here, that there, them there   *This here, these here, that there,* and *them there* are nonstandard for *this, these, that,* and *them.*

to, too, two   *To* is a preposition, *too* is an adverb, and *two* is a number: *To send two dozen roses to your girlfriend for Valentine's Day is too expensive.*

try and, try to   See *sure and, sure to; try and, try to.*

U

uninterested, disinterested   See *disinterested, uninterested.*

unique   *Unique* means "the one and only thing of its kind," so it is illogical to modify it with words like *somewhat* or *very* that suggest degrees: *Your approach to the issue is unique* [not *somewhat unique*].

usage, use   The noun *usage,* which means a "customary manner, approach," should not be used in place of the noun *use: The use* [not *usage*] *of cell phones in this restaurant will not be tolerated.*

use, utilize   The verb *utilize,* which means "to use purposefully," should not be used in place of *use: Students must use* [not *utilize*] *parking lots D, E, and F, not those parking lots reserved for faculty and staff.*

W

wait for, wait on   Although *wait on* is sometimes used colloquially as a substitute for "wait for," it is nonstandard. Use *wait on* to mean "serve" and *wait for* to mean "await": *I am waiting for* [not *waiting on*] *my mother, who is always late.*

ways   *Ways* is sometimes used colloquially as a substitute for "distance." Avoid this usage in formal writing: *We still have quite a distance* [not *ways*] *to go before we get to a rest area.*

weather, whether   *Weather,* a noun, means "the state of the atmosphere"; *whether,* a conjunction, indicates a choice between alternatives: *It does not matter whether you prefer rain*

or snow; the weather will be what it will be.

well, good   See *good, well.*

whether, if   See *if, whether.*

which, that   See *that, which.*

who, that   See *that, who.*

who, whom   Use *who* for the subject of clauses; use *whom* for the object of clauses: *Who will be coming to the party? Whom did you ask to bring the cake?*

who's, whose   *Who's* is a contraction of "who is" or "who has"; *whose* is a possessive pronoun: *Who's at the door? Whose coat is this?*

will, shall   See *shall, will.*

would of   See *could of, must of, should of, would of.*

Y

you   *You* (the second-person singular pronoun) should be used only to refer to the reader, not to refer to people in an indefinite sense (to replace *one*): *In medieval society, subjects* [not *you*] *had to swear an oath of allegiance to the king.*

your, you're   *Your* is a possessive pronoun; *you're* is a contraction of "you are": *You're as stubborn as your brother.*

Index

Non sequitur fallacy, 161
Nonsexist language. *See* Gender bias, avoiding
no one, 653
nor
    choice indicated by, 532
    compounds joined by, 650
    in coordination, 530, 532, 611, 780
    in correcting comma splices and fused sentences, 644
    inverted word order and, 740–41
    in parallelism, 544
    pronoun-antecedent agreement and, 662
no sooner, 741
NOT, as Boolean operator, 222
not, no, 766–67
Note(s). *See also* Endnotes; Footnotes
    APA style for, 391–92
    bibliographic, 251, 344–45, 423–24
    Chicago format for, 423–24, 432–33. *See also Chicago* style
    complete *vs.* abbreviated, 407
    content, 251
    for figures and tables, 320, 348–49, 422–23
    MLA style for, 344–45
    organizing, 251–52, 268
    for speaking, 190
    superscript numbers for, 391, 436
Note making, 252–64
    analyzing, interpreting, synthesizing, and critiquing sources, 263–64
    annotating *vs.*, 252
    by non-native writers of English, 253
    for essay exams, 490–91
    highlighting *vs.*, 252
    paraphrasing in, 114, 253–57
    plagiarism and, 25, 251–57
    quotations in, 260–62
    research notes, 252
    source and page number in notes, 251
    summarizing in, 257–60
    types of notes, 251–52
    in writing about literature, 453, 454
Note taking, 491
nothing, 653
not just . . . but, 532
not only . . . but also
    in contrast, 532
    as correlative conjunctions, 545, 611
    inverted word order with, 740
Noun(s), 743–50
    a, an, the with, 608, 744–47
    abstract *vs.* concrete, 94, 190, 573, 603
    as adjectives, 701
    appositives. *See* Appositives/appositive phrases

collective, 603, 653–54
common *vs.* proper, 603, 743
compound, 593
count *vs.* noncount, 603, 604, 743–46, 748–50
definition of, 804
determiners and, 608
as direct objects, 617
functions of, 604
generic, 659–61, 710, 746
gerund phrases as, 548, 621, 655–56
gerunds, 548, 621, 655–56, 755, 756
as object complements, 700
plurals of, 604–05, 649
possessive, 605, 748, 804–07
present participles as, 666
quantifying words or phrases with, 748–50
singular, that end in *s*, 655
Noun clauses, 624
Noun phrases, 619, 633
Novels, documenting, MLA style for, 313–14, 326. *See also* Literature and humanities, writing in
Number
    definition of, 648, 709
    shifts in, 710
number, no., 851
a number of, 749
Numbers
    apostrophes in, 807
    at the beginning of a sentence, 855
    commas in, 790, 856
    hyphens in, 860–61
    italicizing, 843, 844
    numerals *vs.* spelled-out, 855
    periods in, 856
    prefixes in, 860
    shifts in, 710
    specific formats in, 855–56
    subject-verb agreement in, 654–55
    superscript, 391, 436

O

-o, plurals of words that end in, 592
O (interjection), 839
Object(s)
    complements, 618, 700, 738–39
    compound, 686
    direct, 617, 623, 700, 737–38
    indirect, 618, 737–38
    of prepositions, 620, 738
Object complements
    adjectives or nouns as, 700
    definition of, 618, 700
    sentence structure and, 618, 738–39
Objective case, in pronouns, 685, 686, 688, 689

Objectivity
    in sources, 236
    in writing, 88–89
Object of a preposition, 620
Obligatory words, 726–27
Observational studies, 231
Occupation names, avoiding gender-specific, 568
OED (Oxford English Dictionary), 211, 581
of
    with fractions or portions, 772
    to indicate cause or condition, 772
    to indicate possession, attribute, or origin, 773, 803
    not used with a modal, 670
    to show a reason, 772
offer, 618, 756
often, 764
oh, 839
on, 771–72
once, 631
one, 653, 743
OneNote, 25, 203
one of, 656
Online articles, documenting. *See also* Online sources
    in APA style, 382–85
    in *Chicago* style, 416–18
    in MLA style, 331–32
Online assignment calendars, 198
Online books. *See* e-books
Online chat. *See* Instant messaging
Online communication. *See also* Blogs and blog postings; emails; Instant messaging
    discussion list postings, 217, 241–42
    open *vs.* moderated forums, 241–42
    social networking, 231, 564
    synchronous *vs.* asynchronous media, 186
Online databases. *See* Databases
Online dictionaries, 580–81
Online forums. *See* Discussion list postings
Online journals, documenting
    APA style for, 381–86
    Chicago style for, 414–18
    CSE style for, 441–45
    MLA style for, 330–34
Online magazines, documenting
    APA style for, 383–84
    Chicago style for, 417
    CSE style for, 444
    MLA style for, 332
Online media. *See* Interactive media
Online newspapers, documenting
    APA style for, 384–85
    Chicago style for, 417–18

EFL Index

Notes

Notes

Notes

Notes

Notes

Notes

Quick Reference *A Menu of Resources*

Model Projects

Student Models

Professional Models

Quick Reference *A Menu of Resources*

EFL Notes

Quick Reference *A Menu of Resources*

Tech Tips

Writing Tutorials

Citation Tutorials

Quick Reference *A Menu of Resources*

Quick Reference *A Menu of Resources*

Writing Responsibly Notes

Editing and Proofreading Symbols and Abbreviations

Numbers and letters refer to chapters and sections of *Writing Matters* where these concepts are discussed.

abbr	faulty abbreviation 56	*exam*	example needed 3d	*patch*	patchwriting 15f
add	add missing word, phrase 42c–d	*frag*	sentence fragment 34	*pn agr*	pronoun agreement problem 36l–n
adj	misused adjective 39	*fs*	fused (run-on) sentence 35	*prep*	preposition error 47
adv	misused adverb 39	*gram*	grammar error 33	*proof*	proofreading needed 6h
agr	agreement problem (subject-verb, pronoun) 36	*hyph*	hyphen problem 58	*quote*	quotation problem 15g, 51
appr	inappropriate language 30	*idiom*	faulty idiom 31c	*ref*	pronoun reference problem 38i–n
art	incorrect, missing article (*a, an, the*) 44b	*inc*	incomplete construction 42c–d	*rele*	problem with relevance 5a, 14a
aud	attention to audience needed 1b, 2a	*intro*	stronger introduction needed 4e	*rep*	ineffective repetition 26b, 29f
awk	awkward phrasing	*ital*	italics needed 55	*rev*	revision needed 6a–c
bias	biased language 30b	*jarg*	inappropriate use of jargon 30a	*run-on*	run-on (fused) sentence 35
cap	capitalization problem 54			*sexist*	sexist language 30b
case	problem with pronoun case 38a–h	*lc*	lowercase letter needed 54	*shift*	inappropriate shift (mood, point of view, tense, voice) 40
		mix	mixed construction 42a–b		
cite	source citation needed 17f-j, 18 (MLA), 19 (APA), 20 (*Chicago*), 21 (CSE)	*mm*	misplaced modifier 41a–b	*sl*	slang 30a
		mng?	meaning unclear	*sp*	spelling error 32a–c
		mood	problem with mood 37i–j, 40b	*sub*	subordination problem 27c
cliché	overused expression 31d			*sv agr*	subject-verb agreement problem 36a–k
coh	coherence problem 4c	*num*	problem with number use 57		
concl	stronger conclusion needed 4f			*t*	tense problem 37f–h, 40a
		org	reconsider organization 3b, 16b	*thesis*	thesis needs revision 43a
coord	coordination problem 27b	¶	paragraph 4	*topic*	topic inappropriate 1b, 2a
crit	critical thinking, reading needed 7	P	punctuation problem 48–51	*trans*	transition needed 4c, 4g
		⌄	apostrophe 50	*usage*	usage problem 31a, 32c
cs	comma splice 35	[ ]	brackets 53c	*var*	lack of sentence variety 29
det	problem with noun determiner 44b	⌃⌄	colon 53d	*vb*	verb problem 37
		⌃	comma 48	*w*	wordy 26
dev	development needed 4d	—	dash 53a	*wo*	word-order problem 33
dic	problem with diction 31	. . .	ellipses 53e	*ww*	wrong word 31a
dm	dangling modifier 41c–d	!	exclamation point 52c	⌒	close up
doc	problem with documentation 18 (MLA), 19 (APA), 20 (*Chicago*), 21 (CSE)	( )	parentheses 53b	⌿	delete
		⊙	period 52a	^	insert
		?	question mark 52b	/ /	parallelism problem 28
edit	editing needed 6e	⌄ ⌄	quotation marks 51	#	add a space
emph	problem with emphasis 29	;	semicolon 49	X	obvious error
ethos	writer's credibility needs support 1b	/	slash 53f	??	unclear
exact	inexact language 31a	*para*	problem with paraphrase 15f		
		pass	ineffective use of passive voice 29h, 39		